MONEY,
BANKING,
AND THE
MACROECONOMY

MONEY, BANKING, AND THE MACROECONOMY

DOUGLAS VICKERS

University of Massachusetts

Prentice-Hall, Inc., Englewood Cliffs, N.J. 07632

Library of Congress Cataloging in Publication Data

VICKERS, DOUGLAS, (date)
   Money, banking, and the macroeconomy.

   Includes bibliographical references and index.
   1. Money.   2. Monetary policy.   3. Banks and banking.
I. Title.
HG221.V49   1985   332.1   84-15911
ISBN 0-13-600032-0

Editorial/production supervision and interior design: Rick Laveglia
Cover design: 20/20 Services, Inc.
Manufacturing buyer: Ed O'Dougherty

Printed in the United States of America

10   9   8   7   6   5   4   3   2   1

ISBN 0-13-600032-0   01

Prentice-Hall International, Inc., *London*
Prentice-Hall of Australia Pty. Limited, *Sydney*
Editora Prentice-Hall do Brasil, Ltda., *Rio de Janeiro*
Prentice-Hall Canada Inc., *Toronto*
Prentice-Hall of India Private Limited, *New Delhi*
Prentice-Hall of Japan, Inc., *Tokyo*
Prentice-Hall of Southeast Asia Pte. Ltd., *Singapore*
Whitehall Books Limited, *Wellington, New Zealand*

CONTENTS

PART III   COMMERCIAL BANKING AND FINANCIAL INSTITUTIONS

PART IV   CENTRAL BANKING

PART V   MONEY FLOWS AND THE MACROECONOMY

PART VI   AN ALTERNATIVE MACROANALYTICAL SCHEME

PART VII   MONEY AND ECONOMIC POLICY

PART VIII   THE INTERNATIONAL FLOW AND VALUE OF MONEY

PREFACE

Dramatic changes have occurred in the theory and practice of banking and in the structure, regulation, and functions of the nonbank depository and other financial institutions. These changes have been accompanied by new developments in monetary theory and policy, and the place that money occupies in our lives and in the policies we might adopt for economic stability and growth has been the subject of far-reaching debate.

Money, Banking, and the Macroeconomy presents a clear and up-to-date discussion of the questions that arise on these levels, integrated and interrelated under the threefold headings of monetary analysis, monetary institutions, and monetary policy. The interdependence of analysis, institutions, and policy has determined the structure of the work as a whole. For the perception of the most relevant analytical scheme with which to approach questions of economic policy and well-being depends on an understanding of the institutional framework of the economy, as well as the significance of recent and prospective changes in it. Good and relevant theory needs to be informed by sound institutional awareness. Similarly, the understanding of monetary analysis and institutions leads to recommendations for monetary policy, and to perceptions regarding the possible scope and efficiency of different policy options.

In the important matter of the institutional framework and its regulation, the book takes full account of the legislation of the early 1980s—the Depository Institutions Deregulation and Monetary Control Act of 1980 and the Garn–St. Germain Depository Institutions Act of 1982—and looks forward to the significant changes that undoubtedly lie ahead. Note is taken, for example, that while legislation has not yet been passed, the Study Task Force under the direction of the vice-president has recommended that further significant changes be made in the regulation and supervision of the depository institutions. It has been proposed that many of the functions now performed by the separate regulatory agencies discussed in the following chapters should be combined under a new single regulatory body. *Money, Banking, and the Macroeconomy* endeavors to present an integrated picture of the financial system in such a way that as further changes in these and other directions occur they will be readily understandable by the student who will be prepared to anticipate them and even, perhaps, to participate in the formation of them.

The analytical core of the book is contained in the six chapters in Part V under the general heading "Money Flows and the Macroeconomy." Here the analytical distinctions established in outline in the introductory chapters of Part I are more finely drawn. A new perspective on the historical development of monetary and macroeconomic theory takes note of the threefold divisions of classical, neoclassical, and postclassical thought. Chapters 1 and 2 present a brief introduction to the analytical differences involved, and in Part V a reasonably full development is given of what we have called postclassical analysis. At the same time, the exposition throughout the book develops the relevant perspectives of the neoclassical theory in parallel with the points of postclassical theory under discussion, and a balanced exposition is thereby maintained. In Chapter 1 a fuller indication is given of specific aspects of theory that are emphasized from the respective analytical viewpoints. In general, the book presents in comparative form the main structure of what are termed the *neoclassical–Keynesian synthesis* and the *postclassical theory*. The former, it is argued, combines emphases that have come from the monetarist and the neo–Keynesian wings of that synthesis, and at appropriate points the differences between those wings, in both their theory and their policy recommendations, are clarified.

The summary material in Part I makes an extended indication of contents unnecessary at this stage. In the eight parts of the book a reasonably full discussion is given of the nature, purposes, and functions of money; the commercial banking, financial institutional, and central banking structures and operations; the place of money in economic policy; and the international money flows and policies, in addition to the more-advanced monetary and macroeconomic analysis already mentioned.

Money, Banking, and the Macroeconomy contains numerous innovative features and expository devices that differentiate it from other textbooks in its subject area and make it usable in undergraduate or initial graduate courses, as well as in the relevant parts of business school programs. First, every attempt has been made to provide a text from which students can *learn* and instructors can *teach* the essential descriptive and analytical material that needs to be covered. The writing style has been kept on a level that enables the reader to participate readily and fully in the development of ideas. The literary treatment, while it is leisurely to the extent that seemed necessary, and while it deliberately offers the reader judicious repetitions designed to reinforce learning, nevertheless avoids, it is hoped, the dullness and tedium that all too frequently tarnish the exposition of this subject. Learning is reinforced, for example, by an early development of the money-creating activities of institutions we have referred to as goldsmiths, in anticipation of the full development of modern bank money-creation. The latter, it quickly becomes clear, takes up and develops further the homely principles of multiple money supply creation that were studied earlier. Similarly, the preliminary view of banks and financial institutions given in Chapter 5 lays a sound foundation for the extended discussion of contemporary financial institutions and policies in the four chapters of Part III.

Second, in the course of the development already referred to, the commercial banks are clearly presented as one, albeit a singularly important one, of the range of financial intermediaries in the economy. Changes in financial structure and regulation have diminished the historic uniqueness of the commercial banks. They are presented here as private-enterprise, profit-making institutions that perform a vital financial intermediary function and, in the course of that, are subject to layers of government regulation. The new degrees of competition between the banks and the nonbank depository institutions are clarified, and the activity of the bank as a financial firm supplying a service to the public at a price that provides a realizable rate of return on capital is analyzed. It is explained why the banks realize a return of less than 1 percent of their total assets, measured at the net income level, yet realize a net income return of some 13 percent of the equity capital they employ. The principles of financial leverage in bank financing that give rise to this are explored.

In addition to the foregoing, a number of other features characterize the book:

- At the end of Part II a separate chapter discusses the main "tools of analysis" employed at crucial stages of the work.
- At several points connecting bridges are built to the aggregate analysis from the microeconomic foundations underlying the argument. These include the producing firm's cost-productivity-price relations, as these underlie the development of the economy's aggregate "expected proceeds function" which leads to the aggregate supply curve; the foundation of consumers' commodity demands in budget allocation phenomena, and the relevance of intertemporal consumption-savings preferences, which are foundational to the real consumption expenditure function and the significance for it of the rate of interest; the analytical foundations of the economy's aggregate demand curve and producers' expected demand curves; the microeconomic basis of the wage-cost markup theory of commodity pricing and the phenomena of the distribution of income implicit in it; the foundations of international trade and payments, and the money flows they give rise to, in the comparative production possibilities and trading opportunities that countries enjoy.

- A flexibility of choice as to the sequence in which the twenty-five chapters are assigned and studied is permitted by the arrangement of the material. For example, those instructors who prefer to review the monetary-macroeconomic analysis before proceeding to the banking and other institutional detail may proceed to Parts V and VI after completing Part II. For the preliminary discussions of money, the place and function of money, and the phenomena of financial intermediation and money creation in Part II lay sufficient ground for the macro-monetary studies.
- While discussion of the neoclassical–Keynesian synthesis is carried along in parallel with the postclassical analysis throughout the book, a separate chapter in Part VI presents a summary of that synthesis. Additionally, some highly significant aspects of it are again brought into focus in the discussion in Part VII of economic policy and the place of money in economic policy options. At that point a clear view is given of the different possible constructions of the transmission mechanism, whereby a change in the money supply transmits its effects to the rest of the economic system. The monetarist and Keynesian wings of the neoclassical–Keynesian synthesis hold somewhat different views on this matter. But the book takes full account not only of the transmission of effects from the monetary to the real sector but also of effects in the monetary sector whose causes are found in the real sector. Full consideration is given there to the important questions of the endogeneity or exogeneity of changes in the money supply, and of the relation between the theory of rational expectations, the new classical macroeconomics, and the effectiveness or otherwise of monetary and fiscal stabilization policy.
- Each chapter of the book is introduced by a list of relevant "study objectives" and is followed by (1) a brief summary of the principal issues covered in the chapter, (2) a list of "important concepts," and (3) questions for discussion and review. These pedagogical aids are supplemented by an *Instructor's Manual* where suggested answers to the discussion questions, along with further test questions, are provided.

In writing *Money, Banking, and the Macroeconomy* I have incurred a heavy debt to numerous scholars who have made foundational contributions to this important area of study. I have endeavored to make full acknowledgement in the separate chapters of the work. My heavy indebtedness to those who have argued for new approaches to the work of John Maynard Keynes will be clear, and the new channels of thought carved out by Sidney Weintraub, Paul Davidson, George Shackle, and others I have mentioned will be seen to have exerted a heavy influence on the development of my own thinking. My debt to the architects of what I have called the neoclassical–Keynesian synthesis will be equally clear.

My special thanks are due to Ervin Miller, who read a large part of the book at an early stage of its composition; to Donald Katzner, who discussed several sections of it with me; and to my teaching assistant, Richard McIntyre, whose insightful comments bore fruit at many points and who has prepared the *Instructor's Manual* that accompanies the text. Highly valued editorial contributions were made by Ann Hopkins, who also undertook full responsibility for the word processing and printing of the manuscript. I am deeply grateful for her dedication to the success of the project. All of these colleagues and friends, together with several anonymous readers and critics who greatly enhanced the work, are cheerfully absolved from responsibility for any shortcomings and blemishes that remain.

My sincere thanks are due finally to my wife, Miriam, and to Kimberley and Kristen, who bore even more of the familial pains that authorship so frequently carries with it.

MONEY,
BANKING,
AND THE
MACROECONOMY

1

INTRODUCTION AND OVERVIEW

Money finds its way into every corner of our economic lives. Earning and spending, borrowing and lending, saving, investing, accumulating and bequeathing—all in one way or another find expression in monetary terms. Poverty and wealth, affluence and security, indigence and distress—all have a money dimension. Neither money in itself nor the materialism that the notion of money conjures up is, of course, the whole of life. There are other issues that the gaining of the whole world cannot supplant. But in the wholeness of our lives the economic dimension of things has crucial significance. And within the scope of economic realities the question of money keeps cropping up and clamoring for attention.

John Stuart Mill, the last great systematizer of classical economics in the middle of the nineteenth century, concluded that "there cannot, in short, be intrinsically a more insignificant thing, in the economy of society, than money; . . . It is a machine for doing quickly and commodiously, what would be done, though less quickly and commodiously, without it . . . it only exerts a distinct and independent influence of its own when it gets out of order."[1] This view of things, that money is somehow merely a "veil" over the real aspects of the economy, influenced thought and argument for a long time. There are aspects of truth in it. But the brilliance of Mill's conclusion is not in his view of money as a "veil," or as Pigou early in the twentieth century called it, a "garment or a wrapper," over economic affairs.[2] It is in his recognition that money does "get out of order," and that it is precisely then that its true significance emerges

[1] John Stuart Mill, *Principles of Political Economy,* ed. by Sir W. J. Ashley (London: Longmans, Green, 1909 [1st ed. 1848]), Book III, Chap. 7, p. 488.
[2] A. C. Pigou, *The Veil of Money* (London: Macmillan, 1941); excerpted in R. W. Clower, ed., *Monetary Theory* (London: Penguin, 1970), p. 34.

in full light. Exactly how the monetary and economic system can get out
of order, and what might be done about it to right our affairs, will be
among the principal issues we shall examine in the following chapters.

What money is and what money does, and the expansive significance
of the circulation of money, are the issues we are concerned with. Large
questions of our economic well-being are involved. They concern monetary
analysis, monetary institutions, and monetary policy. They have to do
with the linkages and interconnections between money and the nonmonetary aspects of the economy. They take up the questions of economic
health and economic disorder. They point us to the problem of what can
be done to improve our economic performance and to realize an equitable
distribution of what it is that the economy can produce.

In the following chapter, "What Are the Questions?," the stage for
the ensuing descriptive and analytical discussion will be set more fully.
More-detailed indications will be given there of the range of issues that
our trilogy of (1) monetary analysis, (2) monetary institutions, and (3)
monetary policy will address. Much of the excitement and relevance of
our subject stems from the changing fashions of thought about it, and
from the rapid developments in government regulation and institutional
characteristics that have occurred in recent times. Monetary analysis has
gone through startling, if not always empirically significant, changes of
direction and emphasis. Monetary institutions have evolved at a faster
rate and with larger effects than could have been imagined in the placid
climate of a decade or two ago. Monetary policy has been brought to bear
in various ways on the disruptions and disequilibrium in our affairs. The
changes that have occurred in all these respects make a new approach,
a marshaling of new ideas, and a construction of a new analytical apparatus necessary.

PERSPECTIVES AND ECONOMIC INTERPRETATION

In all intellectual disciplines the development of understanding depends
on the standpoint, the way of looking at things, or the perspectives from
which inquiries are conducted. This is very much the case in the study
of money and monetary economics. We are interested, for example, in
what determines the value of money, the level of commodity prices, or
the extent of the purchasing power command over commodities that money
provides. But our understanding of that question depends on our vision
of how the economic world and the market system function. One prominent school of thought, heavily influenced by the interpretative perspectives of the classical and neoclassical economists, sees price formation, and therefore the value of money, as determined principally by the

amount of money in circulation. Such a perspective gives different weights, in its description of price-forming forces, to the money supply that exists on the one hand and to the rate at which that money supply actually circulates, or its rate of turnover, on the other. From this point of view the price level is essentially a monetary phenomenon. The "real" forces of commodity supplies and demands are the things that determine the relative prices of one commodity in terms of another, and money comes in as an analytical afterthought to translate those relative prices into absolute money terms.

Another school of thought starts its investigation of prices and the value of money with an emphasis on the costs of industrial production. The money prices at which commodities must be sold, in order to provide producers with an acceptable rate of return on their capital, depend on the level of costs of the factors of production employed. Selling prices are set to exceed prime costs, notably the cost of labor, by a margin sufficient to guarantee the desired or necessary rate of return on capital. The theory of prices and the value of money depend in this way on what one thinks is the most appropriate way of looking at and interpreting the larger system of economic affairs.

Perspectives differ also on the way in which money and its circulation are relevant to the determination of the levels of economic activity, employment, and incomes. Some economists have imagined that the amount of money in circulation was not really significant at all for these questions. Prosperity and economic well-being depended primarily on the "real" forces in the economy. There existed, it was thought, an automatic harmony in the aggregative economy and the market system would, if left to itself, automatically produce the maximum benefit and economic welfare for all.

Other economists have taken a very different view of things. They have refused to believe in the presence of automatic harmonies in economic affairs, and they have been much concerned with the dangers of economic disorder and disequilibrium. In that sense they have echoed the concern of John Stuart Mill that money "gets out of order." The amount of money in existence, and possible changes in that amount along with changes in its rate of circulation, are very much relevant to outcomes in the "real" sphere of things. Money matters. It matters because the structure of economic reality and the relationships between income and price-determining forces are such that money cannot be "neutral." Changes in the amount of money in circulation do affect, in vitally important ways, the actual production, the relative commodity prices, and the rate of interest that exist. The entire interpretative journey, therefore, is determined by the underlying vision that inspires the analysis and the investigation. For that vision itself determines the questions that are deemed to be important. It provides the focus on the relations that give the most satisfying explanations of the economic realities under study and investigation.

Similar questions arise when the relations between money and other economic variables, such as the rate of interest, the level of unemployment, and the international exchange rate, are considered. Much of our work will be directed to sorting out the most appropriate ways of looking at these important questions and considering their empirical and policy significance.

CLASSICAL, NEOCLASSICAL, AND POSTCLASSICAL ECONOMIC VISIONS

Early in our work we shall establish a three-point view of the intellectual development of monetary theory and macroeconomics. The strands of analysis that swirl in the economics literature and compete for allegiance will be referred to under the headings of (1) classical, (2) neoclassical, and (3) postclassical theory. It will be important in what follows to keep in view the alternative structures of the competing analytical systems. For they not only emanate from different initial perspectives and visions of reality. They also have very different things to say about the scope and potential of economic and monetary policies. They see the world differently. They see the basic need for policy differently. And they lead to different views of what economic policy should be, and what are likely to be its possible benefits and dangers.

For this reason we shall maintain throughout this book a balanced view of what have become the two main competing systems of thought. Though the first has given rise to a number of important splinters of theoretical development—taking such descriptive names as neoclassical theory, monetarism, Walrasian equilibrium theory, and neo–Keynesianism—it will be referred to in the following chapters as the neoclassical–Keynesian synthesis. Many branches that have stemmed from a classical and neoclassical perspective and emphasis can be brought together and their kinship exhibited under that heading. In fact, it might fairly be said that the term *neoclassical–Keynesian synthesis,* notwithstanding some significant variations on its central themes, represents the mainstream of monetary and macroeconomic thought at the present time.

In the following chapters, however, a large degree of emphasis will be given to what we have termed the *postclassical vision.* It is a vision that centers on the phenomena and the explanatory significance of monetary flows in the macroeconomy. The analytical core of the book is contained in the six chapters of Part V, presented under the general heading "Money Flows and the Macroeconomy." The argument culminates in Chapter 19 where a model of the macroeconomy is presented. This basic model incorporates a new examination of both the demand side and the supply side of the macroeconomy, exhibiting the relevance for both of these of money and money flows. The vision of the supply side that informed the work of John Maynard Keynes is rehabilitated, and an aggregate supply function, of the kind that Keynes referred to as an expected proceeds function, lies at the heart of the analysis. This makes it possible to integrate into the basic macroeconomic analysis the significance of simultaneous changes in activity levels, the price level, interest rates, and the distribution of income. It follows from this that a corresponding perspective is provided on economic and monetary policy.

The focus on monetary flows takes the orientation away from the conventional equilibrium analysis of the usual money and banking textbook literature. It permits the introduction of a new emphasis on uncertainty and expectations. The demand for money, for example, appears in a new form when it is seen to depend on expected or anticipated expenditures, and not simply on currently generated incomes and expenditures in the traditional fashion.

The recurring emphasis on money flows enables the supply side analysis to be integrated with that of the demand side of the economy. There is a double-edged significance in money flows. They generate incomes for the providers of productive services and determine the cost of production and the price level on the supply side, and they determine the level of the demand for goods and services on the demand side. Income earners are also income spenders. Or they may be income savers. Wage incomes, for example, perform an important dual function. They determine costs on the one hand and they determine disposable incomes on the other.

The market for labor in which wage incomes are determined is therefore not analogous to other markets in the system. The money wage rate is not just another price like, say, the price of bananas. The money wage rate will be seen, in fact, as the linchpin of the monetary system. Stability in the efficiency wage rate, meaning by that the money wage rate adjusted for changes in productivity, is essential for stability in the price level. It determines in turn, therefore, the stability or otherwise of the value of money. Wage rate stability determines, in the final analysis, the very moneyness of money itself. This it does because that "moneyness" is dependent on the stability in the value of money, and therefore on its general or universal acceptability in exchange for goods and services.

The place of money is seen, from these perspectives, in clear relation to the needs for money that are thrown up by the functioning of the industrial system. The provision and adequacy of the money supply are related to the activity, production, and employment levels that the system may wish to, or be able to, maintain. A careful perspective on the place and function of monetary circulation also explains the contemporary problems of simultaneous inflation and unemployment. That has been the really worrying problem of the latter half of the 1970s and the early 1980s. Though moderations occur in the severity of both inflation and unemployment, we have unfortunately done very little to tackle the root causes of the disequilibrium and disruption through which we have lived. It is to these big questions that our work in money, banking, and monetary economics needs to be directed.

THE NEOCLASSICAL–KEYNESIAN SYNTHESIS AND THE POSTCLASSICAL VISION COMPARED AND CONTRASTED

While a new conception of a postclassical theory of money will be developed in the following chapters, care will be taken to present the necessary bridges between the neoclassical and the postclassical systems of thought. Only in this way can the maximum benefit result from the institutional, analytical, and policy studies that lie ahead. The parallel discussion of alternative perspectives will enable us to understand the newer viewpoints that arise, and to judge the extent to which deficiencies exist in one or the other of the forms of analysis presented.

The most usual form of analysis encountered in basic macroeconomics courses is the neoclassical or, as we have referred to it, the neoclassical–Keynesian synthesis. Leaving aside at this point any further introductory comment on the postclassical themes, it will be useful to note briefly the manner in which the chapters that follow bring the neoclassical thought forms into recurring focus.

An important question is that of precisely what is responsible for, and what maintains satisfactorily, the moneyness of the monetary economy. What guarantees that money will continue in efficient circulation and that the markets of the economy will, to use a significant term we shall encounter again, *cohere*? By *coherence* is meant the fact or the possibility that all the markets of the economy will clear at levels that are widely accepted as satisfactory, or that, in other terms, the system will generate a high and satisfactory level of employment and a high and stable level of economic well-being and welfare. The alternative views on this fundamental question will be presented in Chapter 14, where notice will also be taken of the significance of uncertainty, time, expectations, the efficiency of market signals, and the special properties of interest and money that bear on these issues.

At the heart of the neoclassical analysis is what has become known as the quantity theory of money. Its main outlines and general usefulness will have been encountered in the basic macroeconomics course. In Chapter 15 an analysis is given of its relevance to the theory of the demand for money, and in Chapter 16 it is looked at again from another perspective, that of the implications that the cash balance form of the quantity theory has for the explanation of changes in the commodity price level.

In Chapter 17, where the postclassical theory of the supply side is developed, a contrasting analysis is also given of the neoclassical supply side theory. It is shown there that the neoclassical aggregate supply curve, a highly significant concept in the neoclassical macroanalysis, differs in many respects from its postclassical counterpart. Those differences are clearly exhibited. The heart of the issue lies in contrasting views of the relevance of the labor market in the economy. Widely different assumptions regarding the structure, conduct, and clearing of that market affect the outcome of the analysis. The labor market, it becomes evident, is the really critical point at which analytical systems diverge in their style, preoccupation, content, and results.

In the discussion of the money expenditure flows in Chapter 18, the general neoclassical microfoundations of the aggregate expenditure or demand functions are emphasized. The microfoundations of interest rates, intertemporal budget allocations, savings, and consumption are discussed. The foundations of investment expenditure flows are similarly examined, as they are also in the course of establishing some tools of analysis in Chapter 6. While the analysis of the money expenditure flows is cast in a form that throws maximum light on the dynamic postclassical argument, full account is taken in Chapter 18 of the more usual analytical forms presented by the neoclassical–Keynesian synthesis.

In Chapter 21 the argument moves to the important question of monetary policy. In that and the following chapters the neoclassical vision of the way in which monetary policy works out its effects is set against the arguments proposed under that heading by the postclassical viewpoint. This highly important question has usually been addressed under the heading of the transmission mechanism, or the transmission channels through which a change in the money supply transmits its effects to the rest of the economic system. In that connection it is most important to take account of the neoclassical and postclassical views of the "exogeneity" or "endogeneity" of changes in the money supply, and the directions of causation between monetary and other changes in the system. For this purpose again, the implications of the neoclassical quantity theory of money are adduced, and a reasonably full discussion is offered of the way in which the respective analyses view the objectives, targets, indicators, and instruments of monetary policy.

In ways such as these the methodological bridges between the alternative thought systems are established and maintained throughout the book. But it is necessary also to bring the strands of analysis together and present a systematic view of the rigor and coherence of the neoclassical–Keynesian scheme. This is done in Chapter 20. At that point the crystallization of this body of analysis in the comparative static, equilibrium scheme commonly referred to as the *ISLM* analysis is presented. The properties of that system, as well as its intellectual parentage, are clarified, and a precise discussion is offered of the logical and methodological difficulties inherent in it. By this means an evaluation can be made of the most useful policy prescriptions that the neoclassical–Keynesian synthesis offers.

PLAN OF THE BOOK

Part V of this book presents the model of the monetary macroeconomy that orients our work. It contains the essence of what has generally been called monetary and macroeconomic theory. But our objective in this book is to exhibit the place, the function, and the importance of money and monetary circulation, and the more rigorously developed macroeconomic theory is subordinated to that end. The theory is developed in such a way as to show the importance of money and monetary flows for the healthy functioning of the economic system. The demand for money, the rate of interest, the determinants of expenditure flows, and their influence on aggregate supplies, demands, and income and employment are presented. This theoretical analysis is preceded by a full discussion of the functions, form, and circulation of money, and the commercial banking, central banking, and financial institutional systems.

Following a somewhat more detailed preview in Chapter 2 of the principal questions that will arise, the four chapters of Part II, under the general heading "The Functions, Form, and Circulation of Money," examine the questions that have arisen historically in the money and banking literature. The reasons for the emergence of a monetary as opposed to a barter system of economic arrangements are examined, and the reasons why money has historically taken specific forms are discussed. Commodity or metallic monetary systems are set against debt or credit money systems, and the "rules of the game" of the gold standard that flourished in the nineteenth century are examined.

Historical perspective is maintained also by the discussion in Chapter 5 of the early forms of banking that were conducted by the eighteenth-century goldsmiths. That early form of fractional reserve banking anticipated many of the features of modern commercial banking systems.

In Part II also an important feature of the book is established. Banks, it is necessary to keep in mind, are only one of a number of important financial institutions or, as they are also referred to, financial intermediaries. The banks are one type of what is known as depository institutions, or institutions that maintain deposits that the holders can transfer to other persons by drawing a check or writing a similar legal document. These depository institutions, which comprise, in addition to the commercial banks, the mutual savings banks, the savings and loan associations, and the credit unions, have all been granted extended powers and prerogatives under the federal government's Depository Institutions Deregulation and Monetary Control Act of 1980. In many respects the historic uniqueness of commercial banks has been broken down as a result. In terms of the 1980 act the nonbank depository institutions are able to offer services and perform functions that were previously the sole province of the commercial banks. They are all now subject to the same reserve requirement regulations of the Federal Reserve Board, and they have the privilege of using the services provided by the Federal Reserve.

Beyond the depository institutions, however, is a range of other financial intermediaries. The functions and activities of the banks must be set in perspective against these also. In fact the banks, in a highly important sense, perform essentially the same function as the other financial institutions (such as the life insurance companies, pension funds, investment companies, money market mutual funds, finance companies, and certain government agencies and retirement funds). For all of these institutions are, in one way or another, intermediaries in the savings-investment process in the economy. That important intermediary function will therefore be clearly explored, and the place of the banks in it will be examined. The relevant issues are summarized briefly, as a means of establishing perspective early in the book, in Chapter 2. This financial institutional framework is further discussed in Chapter 5.

In the final chapter of Part II some tools of analysis are examined. These include those that depend on the time value of money, the determinants of investment decision criteria, the relation between the market values of securities and their yields or the rate of interest, the yield curve or the term structure of interest rates, and the main issues that influence the construction of optimum portfolios of risky assets. Most of these tools of analysis will have been encountered in earlier economic studies, but they are presented in Chapter 6 in the form in which they are used in the chapters that follow.

In Part III the structure, regulation, and functioning of the banking industry are discussed in a way that clarifies the important question of the provision of the nation's money supply. The banks are seen to be the principal creators of money. The principal form of money that serves as the medium of exchange in market transactions is the demand deposits created by the banks in the process of making loans or purchasing investments. Bearing in mind the importance of the nonbank depository institutions and the place of the banks in that larger nexus, the question of the creation and provision of money is discussed in a three-stage process. The analysis and its implications differ significantly, depending on whether the money creation is understood to be made by (1) an individual bank, (2) the banking system as a whole, or (3) the system of depository institutions as a whole. The need for a careful analysis at this point is highlighted again by the provisions of the Depository Institutions Deregulation and Monetary Control Act of 1980.

Part IV examines the structure, purposes, functions, and many of the operating procedures of the Federal Reserve Bank, the nation's central bank. Historical perspective is maintained by the discussion in Chapter 11 of the banking practices, the panics, and the abortive attempts at reform that occurred during the nineteenth century. The Federal Reserve Bank came into existence with the passing of the Federal Reserve Act in 1913, and it established for the first time in the United States a "lender of last resort" whose function it would be to guarantee the ultimate liquidity of the banking and monetary system.

An important aspect of the central bank's operations has to do with the provision of the ultimate reserves, or the so-called monetary base, of the economy. The banks and other depository institutions are constrained in the extent to which they can go in creating deposits, and thereby adding to the money supply, by the amount of the reserves that the regulations of the Federal Reserve require them to keep against those deposits. It is therefore shown in Chapter 13 that the magnitude of the monetary base depends on what is happening from time to time to the size and structure of the assets and liabilities of the Federal Reserve Bank.

The Federal Reserve Board possesses a range of so-called instruments of monetary policy. These have to do with the Federal Reserve Bank's ability to alter the discount rate at which it stands ready to lend to the depository institutions; the extent to which it engages in open market operations, or purchases or sells securities in the open market; and its specification of the reserves that the depository institutions are required to hold against their deposits. A full discussion of these policy instruments is deferred, however, until the larger range of economic and monetary policy possibilities is considered in Part VII.

Bringing together in Part VII the consideration of the instruments and possibilities of monetary policy permits a clear discussion of the policy implications of the theoretical models presented throughout the book. The economic policy discussion in this part follows the construction of the postclassical and the neoclassical–Keynesian models of the macroeconomy in the immediately preceding chapters. In Part VII, therefore, the contrasting policy stances and recommendations of the separate systems of thought are presented.

The concluding Part VIII contains a brief treatment of the nature and significance of international money flows. The material included in Chapters 24 and 25 fulfills the requirements in these respects for the one-semester course for which the book is designed. But questions of international monetary theory and operating arrangements, along with the examination of policy requirements and possibilities, are so important that they deserve a separate course in the economics curriculum.

ORDER OF ARRANGEMENT OF THE BOOK

The subject matter to which this book is devoted is one, on both the analytical and descriptive levels, in which important new developments have occurred and are occurring. New dimensions in monetary policy, and new problems and challenges in the definition and conduct of monetary policy, have come into view. The sequence of the chapters in the book is designed to provide a sound basis for the understanding and interpretation of the structure and functioning of our monetary system, and the still further dramatic changes that undoubtedly lie ahead.

Following the necessary introductory and foundational chapters in Parts I and II, the next seven chapters in Parts III and IV cover the institutional arrangements, functioning, and economic significance of the commercial banking, financial institutional, and central banking systems. The central theoretical vision is then presented. Good theory is always aware of the institutional structures and realities that it sets out to describe and understand. It is in Parts V and VI, therefore, that the most highly developed theoretical analysis is presented. In this context also, taking its proper place in relation to the theoretical development, the question of monetary and other economic policies is confronted in Part VII.

Many readers might wish, however, to proceed immediately to Part V after the completion of the introductory chapters. Indeed, the preliminary discussion of banking, its historical antecedents, the forms of money, and the essential nature of financial intermediation makes such a rearrangement of the chapter sequence possible and appropriate.

Throughout the book the attempt has been made to present a clear view of the essential features of money and banking theory and practice. Developments in both practice and theory make it highly desirable to grasp those essential features of economic arrangements that will make it possible to understand, and even to anticipate, the ongoing developments that occur. For this reason the chapters that follow are deliberately not designed to be encyclopedic in character, or to present all that has been said, or might be said, on the subject. Specialized courses should be offered, and are available in the colleges and universities for which this text is intended, in macroeconomic theory on the one hand, and in the detailed procedures of financial institutions on the other. What we have set out to do in *Money, Banking, and the Macroeconomy* is to present an integration of the important aspects of monetary theory, institutions, and policy that will enable the student to appreciate the unity, importance, and coherence of the subject as a whole. By that means one is best equipped to take a place in, and to understand and anticipate the changes that will occur in, the economic and financial systems.

2

WHAT ARE THE QUESTIONS?

STUDY OBJECTIVES:

• To make an initial survey of the threefold division of our subject: monetary analysis, monetary institutions, and monetary policy
• To gain a preliminary understanding of the six macroeconomic situational variables to which monetary economics is particularly relevant: M^s, y, P, N, r, and e

M^s = the money supply (defined principally as M1 or the "narrow" money supply)

y = real national income

P = the average commodity price level

N = the total level of employment

r = the rate of interest

e = the international rate of exchange

• To examine in an initial manner the relation between money and the "real" aspects of economic activity
• To consider the principal goals or objectives of economic organization and policy and the instruments of economic policy, or areas within which economic policies can be designed
• To note a number of definitions and technical concepts that will be relevant to more-advanced discussion in the following chapters

Money, banking, and monetary economics is a wide-ranging and frequently a difficult subject. It is highly relevant to our understanding of the economy. It enables us to grasp the way in which the economy operates, how resources are allocated in the production of the nation's output, and how the fruits and benefits of that production are distributed in society. Properly understood, monetary economics goes a long way to explaining the swings of our economic fortunes. It throws its light on the alternations of prosperity and depression, boom and slump, and the travails of inflation and unemployment. It enables us to see more clearly the potential for expansion and growth in our well-being and economic activity.

The potential difficulties of the subject need not deter us from a plain understanding of its essential features. In the chapters that follow we shall present a straightforward discussion of the principles of money, banking, and monetary economics, without deceiving ourselves that all of the technicalities can be avoided completely, and without demeaning the subject by emptying it of its true and essential content. Money and banking is, because of its extensive economic interrelations, an important subject. Fortunately, because of the rapid developments that have occurred in monetary theory and in the financial sector, it can also be exciting.

THREEFOLD CONTENT: ANALYSIS, INSTITUTIONS, AND POLICY

We all know what money is and what it does. We use it every day. We earn it. We spend it. We save it. We store a part of our wealth in it, and we call it again to our service at different times and places. But this awareness and behavior conceal more basic issues. For in a sense that has fundamental economic meaning, it is not money that we earn at all. Rather, we earn income. And money happens to be the form in which income is paid to us. If we lived in a society in which money did not exist and circulate, we could still earn income. But in that case our income would be paid to us in real goods and produced commodities. We should in that event be concerned with a barter and not a monetary economy.

Similarly, it is not money we save. We save a part of our income. We save the part we do not consume. Saving is income that has been withheld from consumption and can therefore be made available for other people to borrow and invest. But when it comes to considering the form in which saving or accumulated wealth is stored, then we do in fact keep part of that in the form of money. Money is therefore a wealth asset that has certain properties of liquidity (an important characteristic to be defined more fully in due course), availability, and convenience, which confer a special use value upon it.

But we do have an intuitive, practical grasp of the functions that money performs in our economic society. It functions as a "medium of exchange" in allowing us to make market transactions; and it functions as a "store of value," or as a means of transporting, over both time and space, the purchasing power over goods and services that money provides.

A sound understanding of money requires us to be concerned primarily with such *functions* of money, and not simply with the *form* of money. Money can take a variety of forms. The proliferation of new forms of money and of what, by virtue of their special liquidity properties, are referred to as "near-money" makes the subject both difficult and exciting when its full economic relevance is understood.

The really important question is not what money *is*, but what money *does*. In a final sense still to be explored, money is anything that performs the functions of money. Different forms may have different degrees of functional efficiency. And to the extent that, as the older economists used to say, money "oils the wheels of trade," different forms of money may have widely different effects on the structure and efficiency of the economic system.

This priority of function over form points to the importance of monetary and banking theory as a part of the main body of economic analysis. It leads to the threefold division of the subject we have referred to as monetary analysis, monetary institutions, and monetary policy. Analysis, institutions, and policy are the logical divisions that structure our approach in the following chapters. Let us note briefly how the meaning of the subject radiates from each of these headings.

MONETARY ANALYSIS

Monetary analysis has in view not only the conditions that determine the supply of money. That depends in an important way on the actions of the banking system and of certain nonbank financial institutions. The analytical aspect takes up a number of other important issues also. It examines the relation between the money supply as the banks and other depository institutions actually bring it into existence and, among other things, the rate of interest that is paid on loans of money and on other financial assets. Monetary analysis examines the conditions of the supply of money in such a way as to show its significance for the functioning of the economic system. For the conditions on which money is available, and the rate of interest that has to be paid to obtain it, necessarily affect expenditures and other behavior patterns in the economy.

In another sense, monetary analysis has to do with the transmission effects, or the transmission channels, through which a change in the money supply at any time works out its implications for the rest of the economy. Under this important heading, in fact, wide divergences of view have existed between different segments of the economics profession.

Monetary analysis examines also the determinants of the demand for money. It is concerned with the fact that people need to keep by them a store of money that has some relation to the annual level of their income or expenditure. This might be referred to as the *transactions demand for money*, a demand for money to be used principally as a means of completing transactions in goods and services. On the other hand, money may be demanded because people want to hold it as a store of value. They may do so either because they want to protect themselves against unforeseen circumstances that might raise an unexpected need for money or liquidity or because they want to speculate on the possible gains to be made in asset markets by holding money temporarily rather than other income-earning assets.

The determinants of the supply of money and the demand for money come together in the market for money. In just the same way as the demand and supply in the market for oranges determine the so-called equilibrium or market-clearing price of oranges, so the demand and supply in the market for money determine the market price of money. That market-clearing price is what economists mean by the rate of interest. The rate of interest, in short, is the price of money. That is the definitional concept we shall adhere to. It is what the philosopher John Locke had to say about it in an important work on monetary economics at the end of the seventeenth century. The rate of interest, he said, is "the price of the hire of money."[1] It is the price of money because it measures the rate of return that the holders of money sacrifice by holding their liquid wealth in that form rather than in alternative income-earning assets. On another view the rate of interest is the price paid to receive *loans* of money, or the price of credit that makes money available.

The rate of interest is capable of different interpretations on another level also. When economists speak of the rate of interest as the market-clearing price of money, they have in view the *actual* rate of interest that is paid for money or for loans of money. This actual rate is sometimes referred to as the "nominal" rate. Frequently, however, it is necessary to think in terms of what is referred to as the "real" rate of interest or the actual rate of interest on loans after it has been adjusted to compensate for changes in the value of money, or for the degree of inflation that might have occurred. If, for example, an investment were to return a nominal rate of interest in a certain year of 12 percent, but during that time the general price level rose by 5 percent, then the "real" rate of interest received, after adjustment for the price change, would be not the nominal 12 percent, but only 7 percent. The real rate of interest is then equal to the nominal rate minus the inflation rate. From the opposite point of view, the real rate of interest paid by a borrower would be less than the nominal rate in conditions of an inflationary rise in prices. Unless it is

---

[1] John Locke, *Consequences of the Lowering of Interest, and Raising the Value of Money*, 1691; published with J. R. McCulloch, *Principles of Political Economy* (London: Murray, 1870), p. 221.

indicated to the contrary, however, we shall have in mind the nominal rate of interest, or the rate that clears the market for money.

At this point a further distinction arises. We have just spoken of the *price* of money, and we have indicated the sense in which that term will be used. A closely related concept is that of the *value* of money. This refers to the purchasing power of money, or the extent of its command over goods and services available for exchange in the markets of the economy. It will be important to keep these related, and frequently confused, concepts quite distinct in what follows. The *price* of money refers to the rate of interest. The *value* of money refers to the purchasing power command over commodities and services that money provides.

It follows that at certain times and in certain economic conditions the price of money and the value of money may move in quite opposite directions. In inflationary conditions in the economy the rise in the average level of commodity prices will imply that the value of money, or the purchasing power of money, will fall. But it is in such circumstances that the rate of interest, or the price of money, may be rising. The reasons why this may be so form an important part of the theory of money.

But monetary analysis is in no sense exhausted by an examination of what determines the supply of, the demand for, and the price and value of money. Whatever it is that determines these magnitudes will have deeper effects on other aspects of economic activity. They affect such important variables and economic magnitudes as the level of employment, the level of real output or production, the distribution of income and resource allocation, the international money flows, and the international exchange rate. In each of these cases, important questions need to be asked regarding the significance of the level of monetary circulation in the economy.

Thus the study of money has widening implications for economic analysis in its broadest dimensions. The distinguished Austrian–American economist Joseph Schumpeter said that the study of money must necessarily be the study of the "economic process in its entirety."[2] And in his famous *General Theory of Employment, Interest, and Money*, John Maynard Keynes stated that he saw his task as that of "pushing monetary theory back to becoming a theory of output as a whole."[3] For this reason the study of money and banking takes up the rather large range of questions we have already encountered. It points to the overriding question of the significance of money and its circulation for general economic conditions and health. It welds together the large theoretical and practical questions that make economics the societally relevant study that it is.

[2] Joseph A. Schumpeter, *History of Economic Analysis* (New York: Oxford University Press, 1954), pp. 291–92.
[3] John Maynard Keynes, *General Theory of Employment, Interest, and Money* (London: Macmillan, 1936), p. vi.

MONETARY INSTITUTIONS

Along with monetary analysis we have referred to the study of monetary institutions. It will be useful to look briefly at the identity of the main institutions referred to under this heading and the principal nature of their economic activities.

The term *monetary institutions* refers in particular to those institutions that provide the country's money supply. In our economy the principal form of money is the demand deposits in the commercial banks. These refer to the ordinary checking accounts with which we are familiar. The banks create demand deposits by making loans to commercial, industrial, and personal borrowers and by purchasing government securities and other assets.

In the light of the provisions of the Depository Institutions Deregulation and Monetary Control Act of 1980 a number of other institutions, which were previously not regarded as commercial banks with money-creating power in the full sense, now have the ability to create checkable deposits. Under the heading of monetary institutions it is necessary to consider, therefore, all of those that, according to the wording of the 1980 act, maintain "transaction accounts." These accounts are also referred to as checkable deposits because they can be drawn against by check. These so-called depository institutions include, in addition to commercial banks, the savings and loan associations, mutual savings banks, and credit unions.

In addition to these monetary institutions there exists a range of nonmonetary financial institutions that, together with those already mentioned, play a significant role in the overall monetary economic process. These include such corporations as insurance companies, finance companies, pension funds, mutual funds (in particular a recently invented institution known as a money market mutual fund, which has quickly emerged as a significant force in the money and financial asset markets), and certain other retirement funds.

The principal questions that arise so far as the monetary institutions are concerned have to do with their money-creating ability. On the one hand it is necessary to know precisely how these institutions create money in the form of demand or checkable deposits. On the other hand it will be necessary to investigate the manner in which they are subject to regulation or limitations in expanding those deposits. The amount of such deposits, or the maximum amount of deposits that the institutions can have on their books, is determined by the magnitude of the so-called reserves that the institutions are required to maintain against them. This matter of reserves does, in fact, lie at the heart of the whole question of monetary control. The authority to stipulate reserve requirements rests with the Federal Reserve Board. The Federal Reserve may stipulate that the depository institutions must hold, say, an amount equal to 12 percent of their deposits in the form of reserves. For the main part, such reserves against deposits are required to be held in cash or in the form of deposits at the Federal Reserve Bank. (The 1980 act contains detailed requirements regarding the reserves that must be held by all depository institutions, and the Federal Reserve has authority to vary the requirements as may be thought necessary for monetary policy purposes.)

To summarize their principal economic function and the way in which, as a result, their activities have monetary and economic significance, the monetary and nonmonetary financial institutions are, in one sense or another, what are referred to as financial intermediaries. They act as intermediaries in the savings-investment process in the economy and they perform a number of functions and services in that connection. In short, they are concerned not only with money creation. They also collect, in larger or smaller pools, the savings that are made by individuals and in some cases corporate savers in the economy, and they channel those savings funds to borrowers who wish to use them to finance investment activities. The financial institutions perform a *money-moving* as well as a *money-creating* function.

For the present, two main questions need to be brought into focus. First, what is in fact the structure of the channels of the flow of investable funds as they move from primary savers at one end of the process, through the financial institutions, to the ultimate borrowers at the other end? And second, how can the efficiency with which the financial institutions discharge their intermediary function be evaluated? Different institutions traditionally obtain their funds from certain kinds of sources. Industrial employees channel savings to pension funds, for example, and individuals place savings funds in savings and loan associations. The different institutions also relend their funds in traditionally identifiable ways. Savings and loan associations, for example, traditionally invest the main part of their available funds in housing and construction loans and mortgages.

If, therefore, changes should occur in the total level of the flow of savings to the institutions, or in the structure or distribution of that flow among the institutions, significant implications for the efficient functioning of the money and capital markets may result. Individuals, for example, may begin to place a smaller proportion of their funds in mutual savings banks and a larger proportion in money market mutual funds. This would mean that the borrowers who traditionally obtain their investable funds from the mutual savings banks will now have less funds available to them. This would mean that the cost of those funds, or the rate of interest that is charged for the use of them, will increase. Any number of such examples of changes in the channels of the flow of savings funds could be imagined. But the upshot of the argument would in every case be the same. First, the availability, and second, the cost of funds to specific classes of borrowers, would be affected.

Variations such as these in the structure of the savings-investment flows in the economy will affect the structure of economic activity and production. At certain stages of the business cycle, the housing and construction industry has been seriously affected by such variations in the flow of funds. As a result, employment in that industry has been reduced, and bankruptcies and hardships have abounded. The distribution of investable funds affects the distribution of demands for resources in the economy. It affects the question of who obtains the resources to provide employment and productive output. It affects also the opportunities for the economic system to provide a high and satisfactory level of employment for all of those willing to work. From time to time unacceptable levels of unemployment in the economy as a whole, as well as in specific sections of the economy dependent on certain kinds of activity (automobile manufacture for example), may be generated by developments in the financial institutional sector.

This leads to the second issue that must be noted. Under the heading of institutional efficiency, we refer to *operational efficiency* on the one hand and *allocational efficiency* on the other. Operational efficiency refers to the ability of the institutions to provide economic services at minimum attainable cost, perhaps as a result of healthy competition among them. It refers also to the institutions' ability to provide, at minimum but economically viable rates, services that individuals are not able to provide for themselves as cheaply or as efficiently.

Allocational efficiency, on the other hand, refers to the way in which, as a result of institutional activity, resources are actually channeled to those sections of the economy where the attainable rates of return on investment (or the marginal efficiency of investment) are highest. By achieving such a result, resources will be allocated in a way that generates maximum attainable growth and development. The provisions of the relevant regulatory acts throw fuller light on these important questions of institutional efficiency. The question also arises as to whether the existing arrangements in the monetary and financial sector provide the monetary authorities with an adequate degree of control over the monetary situation. For this also, in turn, has implications for larger questions of economic health and prosperity.

MONETARY POLICY

Monetary analysis, as we have seen, is essentially concerned with the significance of monetary circulation for the health and satisfactory functioning of the economy. Monetary institutions refer to the forms of activity that actually create and provide the nation's money supply, and that help to maintain its circulation by acting in various ways as intermediaries in the money flow processes. The questions that arise under these headings point logically to the third division of our subject, monetary policy. Analysis, institutions, and policy structure our view of the meaning of the money and banking processes in the economy.

Two basic questions arise. First, why is anything that might be called monetary policy necessary? And second, what is to be understood by the term itself, the objectives at which it should be aimed, and the activities of whoever it is that has the authority to design and implement monetary policy?

The first of these questions has frequently occasioned sharp and prolonged debate between individuals of learning and goodwill in the economics profession. On one side is the view that has come down from the earlier classical economists. This says essentially that the economy, if it is left to itself and not cluttered by government interference, will automatically tend to equilibrate at high and satisfactory levels of employment, production, and general well-being. From Adam Smith and the early nineteenth-century classicists down to the fourth decade of the twentieth century, this notion substantially guided economists' thoughts about the overall scheme of things in economic affairs. It was recognized that from time to time a certain amount of unemployment could emerge in the economy. But that, it was maintained, would be substantially of a frictional or temporary nature. The classical economists acknowledged that there might well be pockets of unemployment in particular lines of economic activity. But such a condition would be taken care of as demands for commodities shifted to other areas and generated employment in other parts of the system. It became popular to say at this stage of the development of economic thought that while there might be *particular* overproduction or relative distress in some lines of activity, a *general* overproduction of goods and services could not occur.

This logically tidy theory did not, unfortunately, fit the facts. Large-scale unemployment and economic distress did occur. The underlying assumption of the automatic harmony theorists was that all the incomes earned in producing goods and services would actually be spent in purchasing goods and services. There could not therefore be a deficiency of monetary demand in the system. There could not therefore be prolonged or substantial unemployment. The assumption was sadly fallacious. For while it is true that income receivers are income spenders, they are also, in various ways and in varying degrees, income savers. It became clear in due course that to the extent that incomes are saved rather than passed on to other producers in the form of expenditure, to that extent the total level of the stream of monetary expenditure will fall. The total demand for goods and services will thereby be diminished, and the total level of employment needed to produce goods and services will also be reduced. Deep and disastrous depressions in the economy could and did occur.

Of course it might be rejoined by the automatic harmony theorists that the level of monetary expenditure could not fall permanently because investment outlays would quickly come in to fill the gaps created by any temporary reduction in consumers' expenditures. This was one of the most interesting ideas to come out of the classical period of macroeconomics. It was imagined that incomes saved would automatically be channeled into investment expenditures. This is how Adam Smith saw it. "What is annually saved," he insisted, "is as regularly consumed as what is annually spent, and nearly in the same time too; but it is consumed by a different set of people."[4] Because saving thus automatically flowed into investment, saving, or as Smith referred to it, parsimony, "by increasing the fund which is destined for the maintenance of productive hands . . . puts into motion an additional quantity of industry . . ."[5]

What this classical theorem says is that there exists in the economy an automatic mechanism that transforms savings into investment expenditures. It might appear, from the preceding discussion of the monetary and other financial intermediary institutions, that such a mechanism as the classicists envisaged does in fact exist. Do not the savings funds collected by the intermediary institutions find their way out again into the hands of borrowers who want to use them for various kinds of investment expenditures? That, after all, is the way we described the essential intermediary function of the institutions. Why, then, doesn't the system work with the smooth automaticity the classicists, and now the neoclassicists, envisage? The answer, when we can consider it in greater depth, will explain why savings cannot flow into investment unless potential investment spenders have reason to believe that such expenditures will be economically worthwhile. And there's the rub. Investment will be economically worthwhile only if it can be expected that the rate of return earned on the invested funds will be greater than the cost of obtaining those funds, or the rate of interest on the capital they borrow. It depends also on the level of income or cash flow that can be expected, with more or less confidence or risk, to result from the sale of the goods that will be produced as a result of the investment and capital installations.

The savings-investment process is there to be observed as we have described it. The institutions exist to perform the important economic functions we have noted. But there is no automaticity about the process. There are numerous reasons why savings, rather than being invested in

[4] Adam Smith, *The Wealth of Nations,* ed. by Edwin Cannan (New York: Modern Library, 1937 [1776]), p. 321.
[5] Ibid.

productive and employment-generating activities, may become bogged
down or diverted to investment in liquidity rather than in capital and
income-producing assets.

The answer to the first of our questions under the heading of monetary policy should now be clear in at least a tentative way. Monetary
policy is necessary because there is no reason to believe that if left to
itself the economy will automatically equilibrate at high and favorable
levels of activity, employment, and economic well-being. Although some
economists would argue that the economy would be stable if it were not
dislodged by monetary policies and government intervention, others conclude that economic policies are necessary because the economy is shot
through with tendencies to disequilibrium, disturbance, and disruption,
and not characterized by the tidy solaces of harmonies at all. Uncertainties abound, and money, rather than being at all times directed to productive employment, can frequently become a refuge from uncertainties
and from the rigors of decision making in complex and clouded environments.

The authority for monetary policy rests in the hands of the Federal
Reserve Board, which supervises the nation's central banking system.
The primary responsibilities of the Federal Reserve can be observed in
a brief definition of monetary policy. *Monetary policy,* we can say, refers
to those actions of the monetary authorities designed to influence the cost
and availability of money. Such a definition harks back to our earlier
comments on the supply of money and on the cost or price of it (the rate
of interest). The Federal Reserve can take certain actions to make money
more or less readily available to the economy. It may do this by creating
more reserve funds for the banking system and making it possible for
the banks to increase their loans and the creation of demand deposits.
Or it may change the reserve requirements against deposits and thereby
alter the banks' lending and money-creating ability.

If the Federal Reserve takes action to increase the supply or availability of money, then for given conditions of demand for money this will
tend to reduce the rate of interest or the market-clearing price of money.
On the other hand, if there were reason to think that the money supply
in circulation was increasing too rapidly, as a result, perhaps, of the
banks' willingness to increase the supply in response to the demand for
it, and that the increased demand for money was associated with increased
expenditures that generated inflationary conditions, the Federal Reserve
might take the opposite action and reduce the money supply.

The objectives of monetary policy can now be observed with sufficient
clarity for our present purposes. Monetary policy is one of a number of
economy policy instruments or tools that, taken together and combined
or adjusted in varying ways, aim to preserve stable conditions and favorable levels of prosperity and growth in the economy. The understand-

ing of the larger answers to questions that arise on these levels lies at
the heart of the study of money, banking, and monetary economics.

SIX IMPORTANT MACROECONOMIC
VARIABLES: M^s, y, P, N, r, e

In this introductory chapter we are concerned with the questions that
the study of money and banking needs to ask in order to understand its
place in the larger economic scheme of things. We now look briefly at the
six important macroeconomic variables that will figure prominently in
the central part of our work. It is possible to describe the status of the
macroeconomic system at any time by noticing the actual values or magnitudes of these significant or, as we shall refer to them, situational
variables. The variables have been indicated at the heading of this section
and were defined briefly at the beginning of the chapter.

The money supply

M^s refers to the total money supply in circulation. We have already
hinted at its determination by the banking system. At this stage two
points can usefully be kept in mind. First, the money supply may be
measured by a number of different methods, each implying a somewhat
different definition of money. Each definition has its value for different
analytical purposes, and each corresponding measure of the money supply
can be observed from regularly published data. Two of the most common
definitions and measures are the following.

First, a measure referred to as M1 defines money as being made up
of (a) currency and coin in circulation, plus (b) demand deposits in the
commercial banks, plus (c) other checkable deposits, including certain
interest-bearing savings accounts in the banks, credit union draft balances, and demand deposits in the so-called thrift or nonbank depository
institutions. The latter include savings and loan associations and the
mutual savings banks. Second, a broader measure of the money supply
known as M2 includes all that has just been defined as M1, plus a number
of savings deposits at thrift institutions and money market mutual fund
shares. We shall return to the definitions and their analytical significance
in Chapter 4. For the main part of our study we shall mean by the money
supply the narrower definition of M1.

The second preliminary point to bear in mind is that the willingness
of the banks to create money (principally by creating commercial, industrial, and personal loans and by purchasing government securities)
depends to some degree on the rate of interest available on loans. Given
the banks' reserve situation, their willingness to expand loans and the

money supply may well depend on the pressure of the demand for loans, and thereby on the rate of interest they can command on those loans. In notational terms we shall indicate the dependence of the money supply on the rate of interest by writing $M^s = M^s(r)$. The r inside the parentheses indicates the variable on which, in such a case, the money supply is assumed to depend. It is referred to as the independent variable. The money supply, here described by M^s, is referred to as the dependent variable. The money supply may depend on the market rate of interest, as we have just indicated. Or it may depend on the margin between, say, that market rate of interest and the rate of interest at which the banks can themselves borrow from the Federal Reserve Bank. Taking the latter rate as descibed by r_d, the money supply function might be written as $M^s = M^s(r - r_d)$.

Real national income

The y variable in the set of situational variables refers to real national income. It is a measure of the total level of output of real goods and services in the economy in a given period of time, usually a year. It is a measure of the real gross national product. Its magnitude depends on the total amounts of labor and capital at work in the economy and may be quite different, at any time, from the maximum output the economy is capable of producing. The resources available in the economy may be less than fully employed and the economy may be suffering from any of a number of possible disequilibrium conditions.

The price level

The P variable refers to a measure of the average level of commodity prices. Prices may be measured at the retail level, most frequently by the so-called Consumer Price Index, or by an average of the prices of all goods and services entering into the gross national product or the national output. The latter measure is referred to as the GNP deflator.

Taking y as a measure of the real national product produced during a given year, and multiplying it by P, a measure of the average price level of all goods and services included in that total output, provides a measure of the total money value of national income. We shall refer to this as Y, using the capital letter to distinguish it from the real national income designated by the lower-case letter y. In alternative language, Y will often be referred to as the nominal national income, or the national income in current dollars. It is the same thing as the total market value of all purchases of final goods and services during the year. Furthermore, if we were to observe the nominal national income from current statistics (provided, for example, by the Department of Commerce, the Federal

Reserve Bank, or the Council of Economic Advisers) and were to divide it by the index of the price level, we would again have an estimate of the real national income. This is sometimes referred to as the national income in constant dollars. In this case $y = Y/P$.

Employment

In the set of situational variables N refers to the actual level of employment in the economy. It will generally be less than the size of the total labor force. There will usually be some unemployment, due, if to no other cause, to the fact that some workers will be in transition between jobs as a result of the natural flux and changes that occur in a healthy dynamic economy. Frequently, however, a certain amount of unemployment may exist, in addition to this so-called frictional unemployment, as a result of trade cycle fluctuations or a retardation of the rate of economic growth. In addition there may be a certain amount of what could be called structural unemployment in the economy. This refers to the loss of jobs due to permanent changes in product or materials demands that leave a previously prosperous and active section of the economy in a state of more or less permanent depression and slump. Very different policy measures will need to be directed to the cure of each of these different kinds of unemployment.

The rate of interest

The remaining two situational variables have already been defined. We shall refer to r consistently as the price of money or the nominal interest rate, distinguishing it, as we have said, from the value of money which is now represented in the list of variables by the price level P. Or more particularly, the value of money can be seen to vary inversely with the price level. As P goes up, the value of money goes down.

The international exchange rate

The international exchange rate, e, does not call for further comment at this introductory stage. It refers to the number of units of foreign currency that can be exchanged for one unit of our domestic currency. The value of e is determined on the international foreign exchange markets, such as are operated, for example, by the larger international trading banks in New York and other prominent cities such as London, Tokyo, and Paris.

THE GOALS OF ECONOMIC POLICY

A full discussion of the objectives and instruments of economic policy would take us beyond the scope of our present study of money, banking, and monetary economics. But a brief look at the principal goals or objectives and instruments of policy, or areas within which policy instruments may be designed, will enable us to keep monetary problems and policies in fuller perspective.

High and stable level of employment

In a dynamic and progressive economy, the mobility and changing of jobs among those who are normally employed make it impossible to maintain unemployment at a rate of zero. An attempt to force the unemployment rate to a lower level than the economy can normally sustain will be likely to generate inflationary pressures and a disequilibrium in the economy. We need to develop a sound understanding of the causes of whatever unemployment exists, and to adapt incomes, monetary, and other policies to deal with it.

The employment objective can be expressed as a high and stable level of employment or, in a growing economy, a low and satisfactory level of unemployment.

Maintainable economic growth

The objective of maintainable economic growth is not concerned simply with the maximum realizable rate of growth in any given year or short-term future. The rate of growth in this sense will obviously depend on the level of activity or the degree of capacity utilization from which the economy started the growth that is observed. We are concerned, rather, with the rate of growth that can be maintained over a longer secular trend. That, in turn, must take account of the need to protect the economy from the danger of slipping from a growth path into a condition of inflationary disequilibrium if too rapid a rate of growth is attempted or, on the contrary, from falling below its true potential into a chronic recession and underutilization.

In a comprehensive sense, the achievable rate of growth of the economy depends on such determinants as the rate of growth in the labor force, the annual improvement in technological efficiency per unit of labor input, and the change in the length of the average workweek. In the United States economy there is reason to believe that an annual growth rate of between 3 and 5 percent should be maintainable on these grounds if complementary policies, including monetary, fiscal, and incomes policies, are used to maintain the system on an even keel.

Stable price level

An important part of more technical macroeconomic analysis is concerned with the causes of inflation and the costs that unnecessary inflation imposes on the economy. A stable price level, or stability in the domestic purchasing power of money, is an important objective for an enterprise economic system. We shall observe in due course that it is impossible to hold a monocausal explanation of inflation. A number of forces on both the supply and demand sides of the economy are relevant to any satisfactory explanation. Those economists who see inflation as "always and everywhere a monetary phenomenon"[6] are in danger of ignoring deeper and underlying causes of the malady. If inflation were solely or even primarily a monetary phenomenon, it would be able to be controlled or corrected by primarily monetary means. But that, we have seen, is not the case. A restriction of money supplies, for example, or an upward pressure on interest rates by the monetary authorities, both of which are classic aspects of monetary policies, can never exert an *impact* effect on the price level at all. The *impact* effect of such tight monetary policies, or, that is to say, the point at which they have their initial effects on the economy and the market system, is necessarily on the level of economic activity and employment.

For this reason, although we leave aside the details of the argument at this stage, some economists have concluded that an incomes policy is a necessary adjunct to monetary and fiscal policies. It is not that monetary policy has no part to play in preserving the purchasing power of money by stabilizing the price level. It does have considerable potential and significance in this respect. But its real potentialities and manner of operation will receive careful consideration in a later and larger context of analysis.

Stability in the balance of payments
and the international exchange rate

The determinants of the economy's balance of international trade and payments will be examined in Part VIII. Money and monetary policy are relevant, in a number of ways, to outcomes on those levels. Interconnections exist between domestic economic policies and policies directed to preserving balance in our trade and payments with other nations (and thereby preserving stability in the international purchasing power of our currency). In particular, monetary policy is important when monetary

---

[6] See Milton Friedman, "What Price Guideposts," in George Schultz and Robert Aliber, eds., *Guidelines, Informal Controls and the Market Place* (Chicago: University of Chicago Press, 1966), p. 18; quoted in Sidney Weintraub, *Keynes, Keynesians, and Monetarists* (Philadelphia: University of Pennsylvania Press, 1978), p. 35.

conditions and interest rates in our own money markets are compared with those in international money markets such as London and other European centers. For if interest rates in New York should be higher than they are in, say, London, a tendency will quickly develop for short-term investable capital to flow from London where interest rates are relatively lower to the more favorable rates available in New York. This flow of money funds to New York will increase the demand for dollars in the international currency markets and cause a rise in the value of the dollar in terms of other countries' currencies. Such a movement of exchange rates is known as an appreciation of the U.S. dollar. The same kind of movement could operate in reverse and a devaluation of the dollar against foreign currencies could result. The possibilities that exist have clear implications for the monetary situation and for the management of monetary policy.

Distribution of income

In our analysis of the macroeconomy in Part V we shall give more attention to the question of income distribution than is usually found in macroeconomic and monetary studies. The question of how the national income is shared among those participating in the production of it, and how, in turn, those unable to participate in producing it benefit from the nation's production and welfare, bears heavily on our sense of economic and moral responsibility. From the monetary aspect, the question of distribution is relevant to the structure of monetary demands for goods and services on the one hand, and for the structure of the use of economic resources on the other. Monetary flows are clearly involved.

But not only is that so. Positive action in the area of monetary policy and monetary management, in relation, for example, to interest rates and to the flow of funds through the financial intermediary institutions, also has important effects for the distribution of welfare that is achieved in the economy. Whatever the analytical perspective we command, a reasonable objective of economic policy is an equitable distribution of income and benefits throughout the system.

THE INSTRUMENTS OF ECONOMIC POLICY

We now have before us several goals or economic objectives: (1) high employment, (2) maintainable economic growth, (3) stable domestic prices, (4) balance-of-payments equilibrium and stable international exchange rates, and (5) an equitable distribution of income. Against these goals or objectives it is possible to set the principal instruments of economic policy that will concern us most directly. At this stage, the various policy alternatives call for only a brief summary description.

Monetary policy

Monetary policy, which is the ongoing responsibility of the Federal Reserve Board, can be defined as the actions taken by the monetary authorities for the purpose of influencing the cost and availability of money. This, we have seen, can be expected to influence the rate and direction of monetary expenditure, the generation of incomes and employment opportunities, and thereby the general health and well-being in the economic system. The discussion of monetary policy will occupy us at length in the following chapters.

Fiscal policy

Fiscal policy refers to the actions of the government that have to do with taxing and spending and borrowing and lending. That, of course, is a severely summarized definition. But the economic impact and significance of these government powers and policies can be fairly readily imagined. First, to the extent that the government takes part of the nation's income in the form of taxation, it will diminish the amount of that income that remains in the hands of income earners and is therefore available for spending or saving by them. From the perspectives of either reduced consumption expenditures or lower savings, government taxation will tend to reduce the flow of funds and monetary expenditures in the private sector of the economy. It will correspondingly tend to raise the level of the government's demand for goods and services and will thereby cause a redistribution of resources in the economic system as a whole. This, in turn, will affect the structure of what is produced and the overall distribution of incomes in the production of it.

To the extent that government expenditures in any year exceed the total revenues collected in the form of taxes, the government budget will be in deficit. A large number of interesting and important problems arise for monetary analysis when we confront the question of how such a deficit is financed. Essentially, the only way in which this can be done is by government borrowing. Of course the government could simply print dollar bills to provide the money required. But such a procedure is not adopted in our present complex economy. New money supplies are not simply printed as required, nor do they come tumbling down from the heavens or out of a helicopter. The funds necessary to finance excess government expenditures have to be raised by borrowing.

It is here that the monetary implications emerge. The government may borrow from the central bank, in our case the Federal Reserve Bank.

That would in general tend to be inflationary, an example of increasing the money supply to accommodate demand-induced inflationary pressures. Or it may borrow from the commercial banks. But in that case the Federal Reserve may or may not, depending on its view of monetary policy requirements and alternatives, take action to provide reserves to the commercial banks to facilitate their purchase of the new government securities by which the borrowing is being effected. Or finally, the government may borrow from the public. In that case the borrowing may be mopping up savings funds that, if the government demand for funds were not so high, would find their way into private investment. Depending on the overall economic and monetary situation, such government borrowing may then be said to be "crowding out" private borrowing and investment.

To the extent, of course, that the government engages in lending to specific sections of the productive economy, that will contribute to private sector activity. This may occur, for example, if the government lends to agricultural producers, or to prospective homeowners through construction-financing agencies.

A final impact of government fiscal policy can be noted more briefly. Whenever the government borrows it must issue so-called government securities for the amount of that borrowing. The way in which the government raises funds, or the way in which the actual borrowing is effected, is by the government's selling securities to the banks or to the public in the manner we have described. These securities are all issued with a so-called maturity date on them, meaning that they will "mature" and have to be repaid at some specified date in the future. When that date arrives, the government will generally borrow more funds from the economy in order to provide the money to pay off the securities that are maturing. This operation is referred to as refinancing. Or if, when such securities mature, the government has a budget surplus rather than a deficit, it could use the surplus revenue it has collected from taxation to repay the maturing securities. One way or another, these financing and refinancing operations will have profound implications for monetary policy and the general monetary situation. Thus further linkages occur between monetary policy and what we can summarize for the present as the government's debt management policies.

Incomes policy

Interest in incomes policy stems from an understanding of the forces that generate inflation and the formation of prices in the economy. Inflation, it was imagined in earlier and calmer economic times, was a matter of too much money chasing too few goods. Or to put it a little more precisely, it was a matter of too much money chasing too few goods too quickly. But deeper causes of the chronic inflation malady also need to be examined. Inflation is in a fundamental sense a "real" phenomenon and not simply a "monetary" phenomenon.

Inflation occurs when certain relations in the economy get out of order. Special conditions such as crop failures and dramatic increases in international oil prices may cause inflationary pressures. But the issue that calls for primary emphasis is the relation between the rate at which wage rates and other prime costs are being increased on the one hand, and the rate of increase in the ability of the economy to pay such increased costs on the other. The term *wages* refers here to all forms of wages, salaries, and other kinds of employee compensation. Throughout this book the term *wages* will be used as a shorthand expression in this sense. By the ability of the economy to pay increased wages we refer to the rate of increase in productivity per worker in the economy. With productivity increasing by, say, 1 percent per annum, and labor remuneration increasing by 10 percent, a natural upward pressure on prices of 9 percent, the difference between the two rates of change, must result.

For this reason some economists have suggested that incomes policies that incorporate a system of penalty taxes for excessive wage payments should be introduced. Generally known as TIPs, or tax-based income policies, they would impose a fairly severe tax, designed to operate as a disincentive, on the profits of those firms whose rates of increase in average annual wage payments exceeded a nationally established norm of average annual increase in productivity. It would be hoped, of course, that such a penalty tax would not have to be paid, but that employers and wage earners would remain within the productivity–wage rate guidelines.

Incomes policy, therefore, refers to whatever arrangements might be pursued to ensure a reasonable relation between wages, prices, and changes in productivity. All such policies have implications for the desirable rate of change in the money supply and therefore for monetary policy. Among the trilogy of policies we have mentioned—monetary policy, fiscal policy, and incomes policy—a high degree of complementarity, rather than competition, exists.

Exchange rate policy

Exchange rate policy, a full discussion of which will be deferred to the final part of this book, refers to certain actions that can be taken to change, or maintain, the international rate of exchange between the United States dollar, or whatever domestic currency is under discussion, and other countries' currencies. Implications for the money supply, banking activities, and monetary policy again arise in this connection. For if the rate of exchange between two countries' currencies is changed, this will react on the volume of trade, or exports and imports, between the countries. It will therefore affect the incomes being generated in the two economies and will influence the flow of money between them.

Moreover, variations in these money flows will have impacts on the money supply in circulation in the respective countries, on the interest rates in their respective money markets, and therefore on the rate of flow of capital between them for investment purposes. The ramifications of exchange rate developments and policies go very deeply into our subject of money, banking, and monetary economics. They may be accompanied by other policies directed toward the international trade and payments situation, such as tariffs, subsidies, import quotas, overseas investment controls, and special taxes on interest income earned abroad.

SUMMARY OF ECONOMIC POLICY ALTERNATIVES

Against the several goals or objectives of economic organization we can set the areas or instruments of economic policy. They all, in one way or another, have implications for money and monetary policy and the monetary situation. They fall mainly under the headings of (1) monetary policy, (2) fiscal policy, (3) incomes policy, and (4) exchange rate policy. The policy alternatives will be lurking not very far in the background as we construct our analytical model of the macroeconomic system, and as we examine the policy responsibility for the efficient functioning and the desirable results of it.

AN INTRODUCTION TO SOME TECHNICAL CONCEPTS AND ANALYTICAL IDEAS

The preceding sections of this chapter have provided the minimal background necessary for the study of money, banking, and monetary economics. There are, however, a few more-technical questions which go to the heart of our subject. They have all provided ground for extensive debate among monetary economists. As we shall be referring to them at various points of our subsequent discussions, it will be adequate at this stage to set down only a minimal definition in each case.

Is the money supply exogenous or endogenous?

The question, Is the money supply exogenous or endogenous? has been a source of debate in monetary economics for a long time. Our answer to it will largely determine our understanding of the functioning of the banking system. It is relevant also to some important questions of monetary policy. Let us define the terms we encounter in connection with it in the following way.

A variable is said to be *exogenous* when its magnitude is determined by relations existing *outside* the system of analysis under examination. A variable is *endogenous,* on the other hand, when its magnitude depends on relations *within* the system of analysis. Its value, then, depends on the way in which certain interdependent relations in the system work out their mutual effects. The following example from outside the direct monetary sphere will be useful.

In the neoclassical system of macroeconomic analysis the wage rate, or more particularly the equilibrium wage rate or price of labor, is understood to be determined in the market for labor by the relation between a supply function of labor and a demand function. The supply function is thought to depend on certain attitudes of workers, generally associated with their imagined utility maximization, regarding their so-called supply of effort. The demand function for labor is understood to be defined by the marginal productivity of labor, as that determines the marginal revenue product that business firms are able to generate from different amounts of labor employed. Given, then, supply and demand curves in the market for labor, the equilibrium price of labor will be described by the price level at which the supply and demand curves cross. In such a theory the wage rate, or the price of labor, is an endogenous variable. It is determined by relations, understood to be well defined, existing within the system of analysis.

Other economists, however, among them John Maynard Keynes, do not regard the wage rate as an endogenous variable in this way at all. Rather, the wage rate is thought to be determined by a set of forces—for example, bargaining power and in some cases relevant sociological forces—outside the province of the usual macroeconomic analysis. In that case the wage rate is imported to the macroanalysis as a given datum, or as an exogenous variable, and consideration is given to the ways in which the macrosystem works out the mutually consistent values of other endogenous variables in the light of it.

The question can similarly be raised as to whether the money supply is best understood as an exogenous or an endogenous variable. If it is said to be exogenous, that means that its magnitude is determined at any time principally by, say, the central bank that is primarily responsible for it. Elements of money supply exogeneity may be genuinely contained in the open market purchases of government securities by the Federal Reserve Bank, which thereby places new supplies of money in the hands of the public who sell the securities. On the other hand, it may be thought that to a much more significant degree the creation of the money supply is effected by the banks in response to the demand for it.

In such a case it would to a very large extent be endogenous. The commercial banks find themselves confronted with loan demands by industrial, commercial, and personal borrowers, and to the extent that they respond to such requests by granting loans they thereby create new demand deposits. This creation of demand deposits is actually the creation of money. Much in the area of monetary conditions and monetary policy depends on the extent to which the banks do or can—depending on their possession of reserves—accommodate such demands for money creation.

There might be, of course, under varying economic and monetary conditions, significant degrees of both exogeneity and endogeneity in the money supply, and in the *changes* in the money supply that occur during specified periods of time.

Is money neutral or nonneutral?

The question, Is money neutral or nonneutral? is again a highly analytical question that has significant practical and policy implications. Within a system of macroeconomic analysis money can be said to be neutral if a change in the amount of money in circulation does not lead to any change in the magnitudes of certain important real variables in the economy. For example, if a change in the money supply left unaltered the magnitudes of the level of employment and output, the rate of interest, and relative commodity prices, money would be said to be neutral. The significance of this question and the answer to it lies in the implications for policy that result if money supplies change.

It may be the case, as the classical system of economics tended to argue, that money is nonneutral in the short run, before the economy has had a chance to adjust fully to whatever changes occur, but that it is neutral in the long run. Increases in the money supply may in the long run lead to proportional changes in the general price level. In the system of thought that John Maynard Keynes invented, however, money is taken to be nonneutral in both the short and the long run. Important differences thus emerge in the understanding of the structure and functioning of the macroeconomic system, and in the necessary policies that should be adopted to deal with it.

Is the analysis of the macroeconomy dichotomizable?

Dichotomization of analysis is said to be possible when the analysis of the economic system as a whole can be broken down into separable or independent parts. If, for example, money is to be considered merely a veil over what transpires in the real economy, then conceivably a system of analysis could be constructed in which, for example, the level of national output and the level of commodity prices could be examined independently of each other. There need be no lines of interconnection or interdependent causation between them. At the same time, the rate of interest may also be able to be determined independently of the level of output and the level of employment.

This set of questions has taxed the best minds among monetary economists. Our analysis in the following chapters will discover reasons why dichotomization is not logically possible. We shall see that the analysis of production, prices, interest rates, employment, and the distribution of income are all of a part. They are very much interdependent.

SUMMARY

Five principal areas of thought or perspective have provided a background to our study of money, banking, and monetary economics:

A. The threefold division of our subject into monetary analysis, monetary institutions, and monetary policy. These three divisions are very much dependent on each other. The fuller analysis that follows will take account of the institutions that exist or are in the course of emerging in the economy. New institutions develop as policy needs and action give rise to possible benefits they can confer on the economy. And policy is itself constrained from time to time by the institutional framework that exists.

B. The unavoidable interconnections between the real and the monetary sectors of the economy. This, moreover, is at the heart of the entire study that lies ahead. It is the richness of interconnection and interdependence that exists on these respective levels that gives importance and excitement to our study.

C. The preliminary understanding of the six important situational variables that describe the macroeconomy:
    1. M^s, the money supply
    2. y, the real national income or output
    3. P, the average price level
    4. N, the level of employment
    5. r, the rate of interest
    6. e, the international exchange rate

D. The consideration of the principal goals or objectives of economic policy and organization and the instruments or areas of economic policy.

E. The recognition of a number of more-advanced technical and analytical ideas that will reappear at advanced stages of our work.

IMPORTANT CONCEPTS

Threefold content of monetary analysis, institutions, and policy
Price of money
Value of money
Monetary institutions
Financial intermediaries
Savings-investment process
Neutrality of money
Dichotomization

Operational efficiency
Allocational efficiency
Situational variables
Economic goals or objectives
Instruments of economic policy
Exogeneity and endogeneity of the money supply
The veil of money
Money as cause or effect

wage

QUESTIONS FOR DISCUSSION AND REVIEW

1. Discuss the proposition that monetary analysis, if it is to lead to satisfactory monetary policy, must be fully aware of the realities, the methods of operation, and the constraints imposed by monetary institutions.

2. Why is it important for monetary analysis to distinguish between the functions and the form of money?

3. Why are commercial banks referred to as financial intermediaries?

4. Distinguish between the money-moving and the money-creating functions of financial intermediaries. Can you anticipate some of the economic forces that have diminished the uniqueness of commercial banks, compared with nonbank financial intermediaries?

5. How do the operational efficiency and allocational efficiency of financial institutions contribute to the maximization of economic welfare?

6. What are the principal functions of a central bank?

7. Comment on the proposition that the interrelations between the six situational variables that are important for monetary analysis imply that the theory of the macroeconomy is not dichotomizable.

8. The problem raised by the goals or objectives of economic policy is not their separate reasonableness or legitimacy. It has to do with the inconsistencies and incompatibilities between them. Discuss critically.

9. Identify and explain the forces in an enterprise economic system that make it desirable to supplement monetary and fiscal policy with an incomes policy.

10. Does the "endogeneity" of the money supply affect the likelihood of monetary "neutrality," destroy the possibility that money is a "veil," and by eliminating the "dichotomization" of monetary analysis influence our understanding of the monetary "transmission effect"? On the basis of your previous study of macroeconomics, can you anticipate what arguments would enter a critical discussion of this question?

3

THE FUNCTIONS AND SIGNIFICANCE OF MONEY

STUDY OBJECTIVES:

• To gain an appreciation of the manner in which the existence and circulation of money widens the area of economic activity, production, and exchange
• To observe the distinctions between a barter or nonmonetary system of economic arrangements and a monetary economy
• To understand the functions of money in a developed economic system

The essential characteristic of a monetary economy is that in its exchange arrangements "money buys goods and goods buy money; but goods do not buy goods."[1] Here we have a focus on the function of money as a medium of exchange. It assists us in effecting our market transactions. John Maynard Keynes observed from another perspective that "money, in its significant attributes is, above all, a subtle device for linking the present to the future."[2] Here the focus is on the usefulness of money as a store of value. It provides us with a form in which we can hold our wealth. Keynes concluded that it makes sense to hold money when uncertainty presses upon us so heavily that it is unwise to commit our monetary resources to other economic activities. In that case "our desire to hold money as a store of wealth is a barometer of the degree of our distrust

[1] Robert W. Clower, "A Reconsideration of the Microfoundations of Monetary Theory," *Western Economic Journal*, 1967; reprinted in Clower, ed., *Monetary Theory* (London: Penguin, 1970), pp. 207–8.
[2] John Maynard Keynes, *General Theory of Employment, Interest, and Money* (London: Macmillan, 1936), p. 294.

of our own calculations and conventions concerning the future. . . . The possession of actual money lulls our disquietude."[3]

These perspectives—the use of money in market transactions, and its usefulness as a refuge from uncertainty—go a long way toward exhausting our subject. Together they lie at the heart of monetary economics. They raise the conceptions that give meaning to the study of money, banking, and the financial sector of which banking is an essential part.

NONMONETARY OR BARTER SYSTEMS

The invention and use of money permit a widening of the area of production, trade, exchange, and economic activity. In the absence of money, where goods exchange directly for goods, production, of course, will still occur. But the production and exchange system that would exist in such a case, and the manner in which superior economic arrangements can be realized by the use of money, call for brief examination.

DEFECTS OF A BARTER EXCHANGE SYSTEM

Let us imagine a pure exchange economy. We suppose, for example, that production has taken place and the possessors of commodities come to a marketplace in the village square to exchange their surplus produce for other commodities they desire. We might imagine that there are in all 100 commodities offered in the exchange system. In the trading that ensues we may observe at least four prominent defects or deficiencies of the procedure. These can be identified as (1) the difficulty of establishing the necessary double coincidence of wants; (2) the need to establish a large number of independent price ratios of exchange; (3) the difficulty of establishing mutually consistent cross-rates of exchange; and (4) the absence of a universally acceptable store of value.

Double coincidence of wants

The difficulty of establishing a double coincidence of wants appears in the following example. Suppose a farmer came to the exchange market with pigs and wanted to obtain shoes. He immediately confronts three problems. First, he has to discover another individual in the market at the same time who wishes to obtain pigs. But second, he needs more than

[3] John Maynard Keynes, "The General Theory of Employment," *Quarterly Journal of Economics*, 1937, p. 216.

that. He needs to find another trader who not only wants pigs but also has shoes he wants to give up in exchange for pigs. That considerably intensifies our pig farmer's difficulty. But that still is not the end of the matter. For third, he is then confronted with the difficulty of agreeing on the number of shoes that should be exchanged for a pig. That, perhaps, could be resolved by higgling and bargaining. But two residual difficulties would still exist.

In the first place, neither a pig nor a shoe is divisible. There would not be much sense in bargaining in fractions of shoes or pigs. And further, both the pig farmer and the shoe maker would need to be sure that the rate of exchange they established between pigs and shoes was consistent with what they could establish independently between, say, pigs and bananas on the one hand, and bananas and shoes on the other. This illustrates the need for what was referred to in our summary as consistent cross-rates of exchange.

Large number of independent price ratios

In the potential exchange transaction it might not be possible for the pig farmer to obtain what he wants by direct exchange at all. He may have to exchange his pigs for, say, draft horses, then exchange the horses for cheese, and so on. Only after a long series of exchanges might he end up with the shoes he came to the market to acquire. In all of this a heavy expenditure of time and effort is involved. Valuable resources, which might be put to better use in production, are being absorbed in circuitous trading transactions. At the same time, heavy transactions costs will conceivably be involved.

But even if all transactions were effected to everyone's satisfaction, a large number of price ratios of exchange would have been established in the process. This fact provides us with a view of what is meant by a commodity price. Let us stay with the point for a moment.

A price is essentially a rate of exchange. If, for example, six bananas exchanged for three apples, the rate of exchange between bananas and apples is 6/3. Or in terms that will be useful when the whole system is transformed to one of monetary exchange, the banana price of apples is two bananas. We are able, moreover, to quote the apple price of bananas, as well as the banana price of apples. In short, because the banana price of apples is two, the apple price of bananas is one-half. One price is simply the reciprocal of the other. There are two prices here, but we say also that there is only one *independent* price ratio. When one is established, they are both established.

To anticipate what lies ahead, this same interpretation of price as a ratio of exchange carries over to a monetary exchange system. For suppose it were possible to acquire one dozen apples for six dollars. The dollar price of apples would be one-half. In more familiar language we would say simply that the price of an apple is fifty cents. What we mean by the price of a commodity is, in our developed monetary system, the dollar price. It is a way of stating the established rate of exchange between dollars and the commodity. Furthermore, just as we speak of the dollar price of apples we can also refer to the apple price of dollars. This is no doubt a less-familiar way of speaking of things, but the terminology does have specific application in some branches of our subject. It arises especially in the market for foreign currencies, which we shall refer to again in Chapter 25.

Now consider a system of exchange containing three commodities. We are interested in the number of independent price ratios of exchange that would have to be established. Let us refer to the commodities as A, B, and C. In the outcome A would potentially exchange for B and C; B would exchange for A and C; and C would exchange for A and B. It appears that six price ratios would therefore be established. That is correct. But only three of these would be, in the sense in which the term was used above, independent ratios of exchange. Three of them would be reciprocals of the other three. The A price of B would be the reciprocal of the B price of A, and so on.

In the case of three commodities, we want to know how many combinations of items taken two at a time can be obtained from the set of three commodities. First, A and B are a pair; second, A and C are a pair; and third, B and C are a pair. There are three pairs. There are accordingly three independent ratios of exchange. Assume that there are six commodities in the exchange system. In this case there will be fifteen pairs of commodities and therefore fifteen independent ratios of exchange.

A simple mathematical formula provides us with this result. It is an application of what is known as combinatorial mathematics. To discover, for example, how many such combinations of two items, or how many pairs, there are in the set of six items, we take the value of "six factorial" and divide it by the product of "two factorial" (because we are taking two items at a time) and "six-minus-two factorial." Six factorial is simply the product of six times five times four times three times two times one: $6 \times 5 \times 4 \times 3 \times 2 \times 1$. This is then divided by two factorial, that is by 2×1, multiplied by four factorial (that is six-minus-two factorial), that is $4 \times 3 \times 2 \times 1$. The answer is 15. For memory purposes, six factorial is written in mathematical notation as 6! (six with an exclamation mark beside it). The entire combinatorial formula is written as $C\binom{6}{2}$, and it is described in expanded form as $6!/(2! \times 4!)$.

Let us revert to the example with which we began. We supposed there were 100 commodities in the barter exchange system. In that case there would be the number of pairs, or independent ratios of exchange, given by 100!/(2! × 98!). Computation will show that in this case there would be 4,950 independent ratios of exchange. As the number of commodities being traded in a pure barter system increases, the number of price ratios that have to be established increases at quite an alarming rate. The number of price ratios required in a system of any assumed size, say n commodities, will be $n!/[2! × (n - 2)!]$.

We may imagine, however, that in a system of 100 commodities one of the commodities is assumed to be exchangeable for each of the others. In that case, that one commodity will be performing one of the functions of money. We shall consider later how it might have been chosen. But instead of having to establish 4,950 independent price ratios in the 100-commodity system as before, it would be necessary to establish only 99. The commodity that has now become the "money" commodity will establish a ratio of exchange with each of the 99 others. This gets to the heart of one of the principal issues of the economy and efficiency introduced to exchange arrangements when a monetary system replaces a barter system.

Mutually consistent cross-rates of exchange

This third defect of barter exchange arrangements can be exhibited by taking another simple case. Suppose there is again a three-commodity exchange system. Now the individual holding commodity A can obtain commodity C in either of two ways. First, he can exchange his A directly for C. Or second, he can first exchange A for B, and then exchange the B he thus obtained for the amount he wanted of C. We shall refer to the first possible exchange route as direct exchange, and the latter as indirect exchange. What now determines which of the two exchange routes the holder of A will take? It will depend on the most efficient or economical way of proceeding. But this, in turn, will depend on the rates of exchange involved. The direct route gives a rate of exchange described by A/C. The indirect route will give an effective exchange rate described by the product of the two separate rates, A/B and B/C. The individual holding A will be indifferent between the direct and the indirect routes of exchange when the direct ratio, A/C, is precisely equal to the product of A/B and B/C. When that condition occurs we have mutually consistent cross-rates of exchange. In a pure barter system of exchange it would be difficult to be sure that such mutually consistent rates could be easily and permanently established.

Store of value

A final difficulty of a barter system of exchange arrangements is that no one commodity may be universally acceptable as a store of value. If it were, it would by that reason have become a "money" commodity, and the full barter characteristics of the system would have been modified. On the other hand, when money enters the scheme of things its functioning as a store of value is of paramount importance.

OTHER CONSIDERATIONS OF BARTER ARRANGEMENTS

The foregoing discussion drew attention to the costs as well as the difficulties involved in effecting exchanges in a pure barter system. The economic costs would actually be threefold. First, there is the direct cost of making the actual exchanges when the possibility of achieving them is finally established. Second, there is the cost of search time in ferreting out the exchange possibilities. And third, there is the economic opportunity cost of allocating resources to establishing these roundabout exchange processes, when those resources could conceivably be employed in alternative avenues of direct production.

Let us for the moment suppose that a system of monetary exchange has been established in place of a barter system. Deeper implications emerge, not only for the exchange arrangements but also for the production arrangements in the economy. First, the prospect of being able to exchange surplus production for a money commodity (leaving aside for the moment the question of pure noncommodity money) will make it possible for producers to concentrate their energies and resources on that line of production in which they have superior skills. They will be able, to put it in familiar economic terms, to exploit their comparative advantages in resource availability and production potential. Specialization of production will be encouraged and facilitated by the widened exchange opportunities. This will lead to higher levels of overall production in the economy. The total income of the economy will thereby be increased, with benefits of increased well-being or economic welfare.

In this way the emergence of money accomplishes a widening of the area of exchange, a widening of the potential for economic production, and a general widening of the scope and structure of economic activity.

THE EMERGENCE OF MONEY

As our perspective changes from barter to monetary economic arrangements two questions arise. First, what precisely are the functions that money performs and how do these permit the development of our modern monetary system? Second, what, in the course of that development, are the principal forms that money has taken? One basic proposition can usefully be borne in mind in examining the possible answers to these two questions. Whatever is used, or is proposed to be used, as money must be universally acceptable for that purpose. This has deeper implications than may immediately appear. For individual traders will be prepared to accept and hold the money commodity (or whatever is used as money in a more fully developed noncommodity money system) only so long as they feel confident that they will be able to pass it on to somebody else as money when the need to do so arises. The thing that makes money money, we can say, is its acceptability. There must exist a widespread confidence in the viability and permanence of the monetary system and arrangements.

THE FUNCTIONS OF MONEY

In the preceding chapter it was argued that the *functions* of money are necessarily prior to the possible *forms* of money. Anything will be acceptable as money provided it performs the functions of money efficiently. Much is wrapped up in the notion of efficiency. Certain forms of money may perform one or more functions of money more efficiently and effectively than others. This will influence the shape of the developed monetary system that emerges as the economy and its money-using potential expands.

The deficiencies of barter arrangements point to four essential functions that money can be expected to perform. Money functions as (1) a unit of account, (2) a medium of exchange, (3) a store of value, and (4) a standard for deferred payments.

Money as a unit of account

In the unit-of-account function money acts as a generally recognized measure of value. Suppose, for the want of a name, that the unit of account is called a dollar. Whether, at this stage, the "dollar" is a commodity or a thing is not important. Our sole concern is with the fact that the value of whatever is produced and available for exchange can now be measured in dollars. This concept of a unit-of-account or a measure-of-value function does, however, raise a number of questions.

First, we are not at this point inquiring as to what determines the "value" of commodities produced in an absolute sense. As economics emerged from the earlier classical period of its development, notions of absolute value were almost completely abandoned. At an earlier stage it was thought that progress could be made by interpreting the values of commodities as determined by the amount of labor embodied in the production of them. The labor theory of value had a long history and a reluctant demise. But we are not concerned with values in that sense.

Our focus, rather, is on the values that commodities appear to have or assume in relation to each other in the markets of the economy. Second, then, money as a unit of account enables us to consider *relative* economic values. This is consistent with the earlier notion of a commodity price as a rate of exchange. For purposes of market analysis we are interested in the rates of exchange between commodities. The price of a commodity is its relative value measured in money terms. If, to take our earlier example, a pig has a market price or value of ten dollars, and a pair of shoes has a price of five dollars, then a relative price ratio is immediately established between them. The pig farmer knows that if he sells his pig for its market price he will be able to acquire two pairs of shoes.

Third, the unit-of-account function is significant in that it provides an important source of information. The information content of this money function means that producers are able to know where potential trading opportunities exist in the economy. This will affect their decisions regarding the allocation of resources to the production of commodities. The same significance of the unit of account applies to value measurements wherever they occur—in the measurement of the values of assets and liabilities, the computation of incomes, expenditures, and saving, and the measurement of indebtedness between individuals.

Fourth, the money unit being used in the economy will perform efficiently as a measure of value only so long as its own value is constant. A foot or a yard is a measure of length. But such a measure would not perform its function efficiently if the length of a foot or a yard were to vary. No consistency could be achieved in the comparison of relative lengths at different times and places. Similarly, it is desirable that the unit-of-money measurement should itself be stable in value.

What this important concept refers to can best be described as the general purchasing power of money. The concept itself is admittedly elusive. But ideally, we want to be able to say that at all times and places the unit of money has a constant purchasing power command over commodities in general. Its command over specific commodities may change as the market prices of those commodities vary. But we would like to be able to be sure that on the average, measured over the range of commodities available for exchange in the market system as a whole, the purchasing power of money was constant. If this is not the case, if prices in general are rising and the purchasing power of money is decreasing, the usefulness of the unit of money as a measure of value at different times will be diminished. Let us take a simple example.

We may suppose that the total value of the nation's production measured in money terms during 1984 was $3,000 billion, and in the following year the value in money terms was $4,000 billion. It might seem on the face of it that during 1985 the nation's production increased by one-third. That would be a remarkable achievement. But if, during the same time, the general level of prices or the purchasing power of money had changed significantly, the relative economic performance between 1984 and 1985 would appear in a very different light. Suppose the general price level, measured for example by the gross national product deflator (an index of the prices of all commodities included in the national product), had increased during 1985 by 25 percent.

This information can be used to reduce the money value of the 1985 output to what it would have been, in terms of the unit of measurement, if the price level had not changed. To do this we deflate the 1985 values by dividing them by 125 percent. In that case the 1985 production is said to be measured on the same scale as the one used to measure the 1984 production. In more technical terms, the 1985 production would in that case be measured in "constant dollars." Adopting this measurement-adjustment procedure, the 1985 production will then be registered not as $4,000 billion (its current nominal value) but as $3,200 billion, or its current value of $4,000 billion divided by 125 percent. In that case the national production, measured in 1984 or constant dollars, increased by $200 billion from $3,000 billion to $3,200 billion, or by $6\frac{2}{3}$ percent.

But when the value of money changes, its usefulness as a measuring unit may be further tarnished by confusions lying slightly below the surface. For suppose the composition of the national production, or the relative importance in it of the production of commodities of different kinds, had changed between 1984 and 1985. In that case a price index to measure the change in the value of money could be constructed in more than one way.

First, we could construct what is referred to as a base-weighted index, such as the familiar Consumer Price Index. This would measure the value in 1985 of the same commodity combination as was produced in 1984. The change in those two aggregate values could then be taken as a measure of the change in prices in general. Alternatively, we could take the actual commodity combination produced in 1985 and measure the value it would have had if it had been produced and marketed at 1984 prices, the procedure adopted in computing the GNP deflator. Clearly, the percentage change in values measured in the first case, by using 1984 production volumes as weights, will be different from that obtained from using 1985 production volumes as weights (unless, of course, the weights in the two years were precisely the same).

Money as a medium of exchange

Money functions as a medium of exchange in the sense observed at the beginning of this chapter. When money has been invented, goods no longer exchange directly for goods. Goods now exchange for money, and money exchanges for goods. Considerable economies and conveniences of arrangement are introduced to the exchange system as a result. There will be savings of time, trouble, and transactions costs. There will be a greater readiness on the part of producers to produce in excess of their own requirements and to offer commodities for exchange. The area of economic activity is expanded. The nation's income and well-being are correspondingly increased.

Money, in performing this medium-of-exchange function, has become generalized purchasing power. The possession of money gives the holders a purchasing power command over goods and services which they may exercise at any time or place they choose. The holding of money permits the transference of purchasing power over time and space. Of course the efficiency with which money performs its basic medium-of-exchange function will depend on the form it takes. For this reason, attention was given in the early stages of the development of monetary systems to the desirable properties that the commodity selected for use as money should possess.

The money commodity had to be durable so that it would not be easily destroyed or diminished in value by continued use or natural decay. The money commodity would need to be divisible, and to have a value in relation to its bulk that permitted it to be divided into units or pieces of a size convenient for making transactions. It would need to be portable, or again have a value in relation to size that made it possible to carry an amount adequate for the usual level of transactions contemplated. Finally, it would need to be easily recognizable or identifiable, to guard against counterfeiting and false representation. For these reasons, one of the principal forms of money that appeared at earlier stages of its development was precious metals, principally gold and silver.

Two problems arise, however, in connection with this medium-of-exchange function of money. First, it is subject to difficulties that stem from possible changes in the value of money and, in particular, from the public's expectations regarding possible changes in that value in the future. If, in conditions of extreme economic dislocation, for example, the public should have reason to fear that the value of money would diminish sharply in the period ahead (in conditions, that is, of expectations of rapid inflation), a generally diminished willingness to accept money may develop. This happened during the fantastically rapid German inflation earlier in this century. In such a case money will have lost its acceptability. It can no longer perform its medium-of-exchange function. Individuals cannot have confidence that if they accept it they will be able to pass it on again to another transactor at a value comparable to that at which they had acquired it. For this reason we stated earlier that the thing that makes money money is its acceptability.

Second, particular problems may arise when the material used as money has a dual value. In addition to its value as money it may have a value as a commodity usable for nonmonetary purposes. The question will then continually arise as to whether its value as a commodity, in the ordinary commodity markets of the economy, is greater or less than its value as money. This problem gave rise to considerable disturbances in the early nineteenth-century monetary system in the United States. At that time attempts were made to maintain both gold and silver in circulation as money, though they then simultaneously had obvious commodity values.

Money as a store of value

There are two respects, each with very different implications for monetary analysis, in which money may function as a store of value. The first relates to the fact that money is functioning as a temporary store of value when it is used as a means of transporting generalized purchasing power over time and space. We considered that question in the preceding section. The efficiency with which money functions as a store of value in this sense depends on the prospective stability in the value of money.

More generally, money may function as a store of value when it is used as one of the assets in which individuals decide to hold a part of their wealth. In this sense money competes with other assets as a wealth-holding form. The attractiveness of it for this purpose depends on certain characteristics it possesses in comparison with those other alternative assets. Such wealth assets, or portfolio assets, will possess to greater or lesser degrees the following four properties.

First, they may incur storage costs. Storage costs of money will be minimal, apart, perhaps, from fees paid to banks or other custodians for safekeeping. In the case of real assets, however, storage costs could be significant. If that were the case, such assets need to possess some offsetting characteristics, such as the prospect of an increase in their market value, to make them attractive as a wealth-holding form. Moreover, real assets would not perform efficiently as a store of value unless there was reason to believe that a market existed in which they could readily be sold for money at any time, in order to realize their value and obtain liquidity in the future.

Second, assets may provide the holder with a rate of return, or a rate of interest, earned by holding them. Such assets as shares of stock in industrial corporations or government securities promise the holder a rate of return. That return will be fixed in money terms in the case of government securities and will be variable in the case of corporate common stocks. Money, however, will not provide the holder with a rate of return. (Though this general statement is subject to exceptions at the present time when, as a result of recent government legislation, certain kinds of interest-bearing savings accounts in banks and other depository institutions can effectively be used as money.)

Third, assets have a certain amount of risk associated with holding them. In particular, there are risks associated with the possible income streams to which we have just referred. There is no effective risk that the fixed annual interest on government securities will not be paid when it is due. The government possesses general taxing powers and money-creating powers to ensure that the interest due on its debt obligations will always be met. But this is not the case with the securities of industrial corporations. The income paid on many of them, corporate bonds and common stocks for example, depends on the ability of the firm to generate an income stream large enough to pay the interest or dividends after all necessary production costs have been met.

Moreover, there is a risk of a different kind associated with all marketable and income-earning assets, including government securities. We shall see more clearly in a later chapter that the market value of marketable securities varies inversely with the market rate of interest. Suppose a security promises to pay a perpetual income of $50 per annum in interest, and that the level of the rate of interest available on assets of the same class of risk is 5 percent. Then the market value of that asset will be the amount that individual investors would be prepared to pay for it and be able to expect that they would get a rate of return of 5 percent on their investment. This amount would clearly be $1,000. For by paying $1,000 for the asset the holders would ensure themselves of an annual income of $50, or 5 percent of their investment. Market values of such assets, therefore, are easily obtained by dividing the dollar amount of interest promised to the holder by the rate of return the investor requires. In technical terminology, the market value is the capitalized value of the expected income. This is exactly what is meant by dividing the expected interest by the desired rate of return. This method of determining market values is said to be capitalizing the interest expectation. The required rate of return is referred to as the capitalization rate.

In the case in hand, imagine that the general level of interest rates, and therefore the investors' required rate of return, rose from 5 percent to 6.25 percent. Then the market value of the asset, the capitalized value of the expected income, would be the $50 divided by 6.25 percent. This equals $800. The rise in the interest rate from 5 percent to 6.25 percent has caused the market value of the asset to fall from $1,000 to $800. The risk that this might occur while an asset is being held in an individual's asset portfolio is referred to as the interest rate risk, or market value risk.

Assets in general, then, are subject to a range of risks to which money, to the extent that it is held as an asset, is not subject. Money has a zero or minimal storage cost, a zero or minimal rate of return, but also a minimal risk. That, however, is not the end of the matter. For one generally pervasive risk to which the holding of money is subject still requires consideration. That is the risk that during the period for which money is held the general value or the purchasing power of money may diminish. This refers again to the matter of inflationary changes in the value of money.

Finally, it is necessary to consider, when the choice between different kinds of wealth portfolio assets is being made, the liquidity of the assets. Liquidity is closely related to marketability, or the likelihood that the asset can be sold or turned into money at any time it is necessary or desirable to do so. But liquidity differs from pure marketability. For liquidity refers not simply to the possibility that the asset could be sold for money at any time. It refers also to the possibility that that could be done without realizing a loss on the value of the asset. In this sense, money possesses perfect liquidity. Other assets possess varying degrees of both marketability and liquidity. It would be possible to order assets on a scale describing the extent to which they possess liquidity. Money, by definition, would be at the top of the scale. Those assets that ranked close to money would be given the special name or description of "near-money." In fact, in the complex economy we live in at the present time "near-moneyness" is an important asset characteristic. Such near-money as savings accounts, money market mutual fund shares, short-term government securities, and certain kinds of very short term or overnight loans perform a highly significant function in the money and financial asset markets.

A final point of considerable analytical significance emerges from the discussion of money as a store of value. Consider for this purpose what we referred to in Chapter 2 as the transactions demand for money. This refers to the fact that people keep by them an amount of money that bears some relation to the volume of their incomes or expenditures during a given period, say a year. If, now, the total level of annual expenditures in the economy were divided by the amount of money held in this way, we would have a measure of the rate of turnover of this money stock. It would be a measure of the number of times that, on the average, the stock of money turned over, or passed from one income earner or market transactor to another, in the course of consummating the annual market expenditures. This rate-of-turnover measure has acquired a special name in monetary economics. It is referred to as the velocity of circulation of money.

The significance of this velocity of circulation concept rests in the fact that an increased desire on the part of the public to hold money will be reflected in a decline in the velocity of circulation of money. It is necessary, therefore, to investigate possible causes of variations in this velocity magnitude. The rate of interest, among other things, is very relevant. For the higher the rate of interest that can be earned on lending money rather than holding it, the higher will be the income foregone by holding money for the sake of the liquidity it provides. This income sacrificed describes the opportunity cost of holding money. For our present purposes it is sufficient to observe that anything that causes a change in the velocity of circulation of money also causes a change in the overall rate of money expenditure. It is a short step of analysis, then, to observe that whatever causes a change in the level of monetary expenditure in the economy will have effects on the level of production, incomes, and employment.

Money as a standard for deferred payments

The function of money as a standard for deferred payments is already implicit in the analysis to this point. It means that money provides the measure in which future dated obligations are stated. Indebtedness performs a very important function in our complex economic arrangements, and a method of stating the amounts due for payments between individuals at future dates is vitally necessary. One of the principal features of our enterprise economy is that large numbers of economic relations are conducted on the basis of clearly stated and legally enforceable contracts. Money as a standard for deferred payments enters this nexus of relations by providing the measurement unit in which contractual obligations are defined.

Money as a standard for deferred payments functions with complete efficiency, of course, only to the extent that the value or purchasing power of money is constant. If, during the course of outstanding debt, the value of money should decline, or the general level of prices should rise, this could confer an economic benefit, commonly referred to as a windfall gain, on debtors. This occurs because they would then be able to repay their debts as they become due in dollars that had a lower purchasing power than the dollars they had borrowed at the time of the initial loan contract. Similarly, increases in the purchasing power of money would confer windfall gains on creditors.

Money as a standard for deferred payments has significance for a wide range of such contracts of indebtedness. In our enterprise system many contracts for the payment of current expenses are also extremely significant. Prominent examples are contracts for the payments of wages where trade unions may settle wage arrangements for a period of, say, three years into the future, and contracts for the payment of rents.

WHAT IS MONEY?

Bearing in mind our analysis of the functional approach to the understanding of money, we can summarize its essential characteristic by saying that money is anything that is widely accepted as evidence of the discharge of indebtedness. From another view, money is an abode of purchasing power. It is a medium of exchange and a store of value.

Market transactions, in other words, give rise to forms of indebtedness. When a pair of shoes is purchased, for example, the purchaser immediately incurs an indebtedness to the seller of the shoes. The question then arises, for purposes of economic analysis, as to how that indebtedness can be discharged. It may be discharged by the immediate payment of cash, understanding that in our advanced monetary system cash is a form of money. Or it may be allowed to remain in existence and be discharged by some other form of money payment at a later time. But in one way or another the debt has to be discharged, and the manner in which it will be discharged is by the payment of money. That basic concept, the use of money as a form of discharge of indebtedness, provides a significant linkage between the functional analysis of this chapter and the more extensive banking studies and analysis that lie ahead.

SUMMARY

This chapter has examined the manner in which the invention of money, when an economy emerges from the shackles of a barter system of economic arrangements, expands the area of exchange, production, and economic activity.

The defects of a barter economy include (1) the difficulty of establishing a double coincidence of wants, (2) the need to establish a large number of independent price ratios of exchange, (3) the problem of establishing mutually consistent cross-rates of exchange, and (4) the absence of a generally accepted store of value.

Money performs a number of functions. It is employed as (1) a unit of account, (2) a medium of exchange, (3) a store of value, and (4) a standard for deferred payments.

Money can be anything that efficiently performs the functions of money. In particular, it is anything that is widely acceptable as evidence of the discharge of indebtedness. It is an abode of purchasing power.

The chapter has discussed problems associated with variations in the purchasing power of money, asset risks, liquidity, marketability, near-money, rates of return, and capitalized market values of assets. It has been recognized that in the last analysis the thing that makes money money is its acceptability.

IMPORTANT CONCEPTS

Barter
Price ratios of exchange
Combinations and factorials
Direct exchange
Indirect exchange
Unit of account
Medium of exchange
Store of value

Standard for deferred payments
Information content of prices
Price index
Inflation
Capitalized values
Liquidity
Near-money
Velocity of circulation

QUESTIONS FOR DISCUSSION AND REVIEW

1. Why, and how, does the introduction of money into an exchange system widen the area of exchange and lead to improved specialization of production and economic benefits?

2. It has been said that the store-of-value function of money is logically necessary for the medium-of-exchange function. Comment on and clarify this statement.

3. In what ways would you expect the marginal efficiency of capital to be altered by a change from a barter to a monetary exchange system?

4. In what sense is money essentially an uncertainty phenomenon?

5. What defects of a barter system are overcome by the introduction of money? How is this accomplished?

6. How does the mathematics of combinations find application in the explanation of the deficiencies of a barter exchange system?

7. Describe a modern application of the need for mutually consistent cross-rates of exchange.

8. Describe the construction of the Consumer Price Index and the gross national product deflator.

9. What are the costs, benefits, and risks associated with holding portfolio wealth in (1) monetary and (2) nonmonetary forms? Give several examples of the latter.

10. It has been claimed that the existence of contracts, indebtedness, and institutions to coordinate the relations between them is of the essence of capitalist, free-enterprise systems of economic organization. Comment critically.

4

FORMS OF MONEY

STUDY OBJECTIVES:

• To understand the significance of three forms of money:
   1. Full-bodied or commodity money
   2. Representative full-bodied money
   3. Credit or debt money
• To examine the possible structure of commodity money standards and their inefficiencies
• To observe the historic experiment with bimetallic systems in the early nineteenth century in the United States.
• To consider the meaning and functioning of the international gold standard in the nineteenth and early twentieth centuries, and to exhibit the "rules of the game" of the gold standard
• To gain an understanding of contemporary forms of money and the significance of "near-monies"
• To note some broader issues of monetary significance, including uncertainty and the relevance of money to decision making under uncertainty

The preceding chapter took note of two matters that had special significance for trading arrangements in an exchange economy. First, we observed the costs of making the exchanges that various market participants desired in the light of their production and surplus tradable commodities. These costs included the actual transactions costs incurred in making the exchanges, the search costs involved in ferreting out the possibilities of exchange, and the economic opportunity costs that arose because resources were devoted to roundabout exchange activities instead of being channeled to direct production.

Second, emphasis was placed on the information contained in the market prices of commodities, particularly when those were expressed in money terms. This information, it was seen, guided producers as well as market transactors. It made it possible for producers to allocate their resources to the production of those commodities for which there was reason to believe a market demand existed. They would thereby estimate the economic worthwhileness of allocating resources to various lines of production.

As we consider in this chapter the forms of money that have emerged, or may emerge, in the economy, these two matters of the costs involved in the exchange system and the value of information come back into prominence. They influence the adoption of money as a medium of exchange, as well as the forms that money initially took.

REASONS FOR THE INITIAL FORM OF MONEY

Let us focus on the costs of making transactions in an exchange economy and on the way in which the possession of certain kinds of information can diminish those costs and increase exchange efficiency. If, in a general barter system, a market transactor could know that a particular set of commodities was always in fairly constant demand, it would make good sense for him to exchange his own commodity for one of this rather special set. By doing so he would acquire a commodity that could be exchanged for something else he desired at some time in the future. He might find it convenient to hold such a commodity for a longer or shorter time, depending on his own particular commodity needs and the time at which he desired to fill them. In that case the commodity he held from the set of commodities in fairly constant demand would be acting as a store of value. It would thereby be performing one of the functions of money.

But the extent to which it could do this would depend on three crucial features of it. First, the commodity should possess the characteristics of durability, divisibility, portability, and recognizability referred to in the preceding chapter. Second, the prospective demand for it should be such that it could be exchanged for other commodities at any time in the future without significant loss of value. Third, the holding of it should involve minimal carrying costs.

Within the set of commodities in fairly constant demand, different ones would fill these requirements to varying degrees. The features we have referred to imply ease of use, effectiveness in functioning as media of exchange, and desirable degrees of liquidity. These characteristics take us to the heart of the meaning of the phenomenon of money.

Let us consider the various commodities in this special set of highly tradable commodities. Their intrinsic characteristics under the necessary set of features we mentioned could be assessed and information could be gathered on the following important question: How large, consistent, and dependable is the demand for the commodity likely to be, and how readily will it be able to be exchanged at any time for any other commodity? If a set of commodities satisfied in more or less acceptable ways the requirements of durability, divisibility, portability, and recognizability, it would then be possible to rank those commodities in the order in which, based on the information possessed, they were also generally acceptable in exchange. We could establish, that is to say, a liquidity ranking of them. Gradually, by this means, the list of such commodities could hopefully be narrowed to a smaller set. Ultimately one, or at least a very small number of commodities, may dominate the rest in these respects.

The commodities on the final list of readily exchangeable commodities would be functioning in different ways as money. They would have emerged as "money commodities." If, of course, one such commodity came to dominate all of the rest in this way, it would have become uniquely the desirable form of money in the exchange economy. It would be usable as a means of effecting transactions, or as a medium of exchange, by virtue of the remarkable reduction of exchange costs of all kinds that its use made possible. It would be used as a store of value, as a means of transporting purchasing power over time and distance. Money, in a unique sense, would have emerged.

From time to time throughout the history of exchange systems, a large number of different commodities have been used for these purposes. Many of course have functioned with only a minimal degree of efficiency. Such commodities have included bones, salt, stones, shells, cattle, wool, and tobacco, and even—in some cases—slaves.

CLASSIFICATION OF MONEY

We have spoken of commodity money, or what can now be referred to as full-bodied money. This last phrase has generally been used to mean money that has a value as a commodity fully equal to its value as money. It has also been referred to as dual-valued money.

Even in a full-bodied commodity money system, however, it might not always be necessary for the actual money commodity to circulate. The commodity money may be deposited in a custodial institution such as a goldsmith's office for safekeeping, and the receipt obtained in exchange for it may actually circulate in place of the commodity money to which it conferred ownership. Such a receipt would then be functioning as representative full-bodied money. It attracts this name or description because it represents in every respect a specified amount of the full-bodied money to which it is a claim.

At a later stage of monetary development, at a time when banks had been established, bankers might issue notes against the value of the commodity money deposited with them, and these notes could then circulate as money. These notes may again be regarded as representative full-bodied money, to the extent that they can be exchanged at any time for the value of the commodity, say gold or silver, to which they constitute a claim. An amount of such commodity, equal in value to the notes in circulation, is held as backing against them. In that case such notes may be said to be fully convertible.

On the other hand, forms of money may circulate as media of exchange without any regard to commodity values represented by them. In that case the items of money so employed, such as some kinds of bank notes (or present-day dollar bills), have a money value far in excess of the intrinsic value of the commodity substance of which they are made. They are referred to as credit money. They attract this designation because they circulate, and continue to discharge the functions of money, simply because those who hold them have confidence in the creditworthiness of the issuer. The opinion is very widely held, in other words, that at any time such forms of money may be presented to the issuer in exchange for the full value stamped or written on the face of them and for which they circulate.

At still later stages of monetary development such credit money may be exchangeable only for some other kind of credit money. One form of credit money at the present time, for example, is the notes issued by the Federal Reserve Bank. But these cannot be exchanged for any commodity. They have no right of convertibility into, say, gold or silver. A dollar bill, on presentation to the issuer, could be exchanged only for another dollar bill, perhaps a newer one. Similarly, demand deposits in commercial banks and other depository institutions also represent credit money. They are referred to as credit money because they are liabilities of the bank that created them. They can be confidently used and circulated as money, or transferred from one person to another, so long as public opinion retains confidence in the creditworthiness of the issuer.

In this fact we find one of the most important features of a fully developed monetary system. In its most developed form, money circulates as money because it is an evidence of indebtedness on the part of the issuer of it. Bank demand deposits, understood as liabilities of the bank, represent the bank's indebtedness to the person in whose name the deposits are held. When deposits are transferred from that person to someone else by writing a check, what is really happening is that the indebtedness of the bank is being transferred from one person to another. The bank is still the debtor. The identity of the creditor has changed. The demand deposit is still money. It is still an evidence of indebtedness. It is also therefore known as debt money.

This raises, of course, very acutely in the case of credit or debt money but also in the case of all the forms of money we have mentioned, two important questions. First, who is the issuer of the money form and what is the degree of general confidence held in the issuer? Second, what, if any, are the controls or limitations or regulations to which the issuer of the money is subject? Banks in our highly developed monetary system are subject to important regulations and constraints established by the central bank, in our case the Federal Reserve Board. The understanding of the reserve requirements specified by the Federal Reserve takes us to the heart of the structure and operational characteristics of our monetary and banking system.

But to speak of banks is to get ahead of our story. We now have a method of classifying the types of monetary systems that have attracted the most attention throughout the history of our subject. We summarize them as follows:

1. *Full-bodied or commodity money systems.* These include (a) bimetallism, in which two metals, such as silver and gold, are maintained in circulation as money simultaneously, and (b) a monometallic gold standard.
2. *Representative full-bodied money systems.* In this case warehouse receipts, or bank notes, or the promissory notes of depository institutions circulate as money because they represent full-bodied money and are convertible into that money on demand. The full-bodied money is held by the issuer of the notes as backing for the representative money.
3. *Credit (or debt) money systems.* Examples include (a) token coins and notes issued by the government, (b) notes issued by the central bank or private banks (the latter are no longer permitted in the United States), and (c) demand deposits in banks and other depository institutions.

In the following two sections we shall discuss the United States' experiment with bimetallism in the early nineteenth century and the later functioning of the international gold standard. We do so not only because of historical perspective but also because there continue to arise from time to time nostalgic arguments for a return to some kind of metallic monetary standard. It is the gold standard that has been attracting most discussion in the political and business press in recent times.

BIMETALLISM

The attempt to establish a bimetallic system in the United States dates from the Coinage Act of 1791. The objective of the act was to maintain silver and gold in circulation simultaneously as media of exchange. To achieve this, the government mint announced that it would exchange silver and gold for the established unit of currency, the dollar, at the following rates: Silver was given a mint price of $1.293 per ounce, and gold a mint price of $19.395 per ounce. This meant that the so-called mint ratio of silver to gold was 15/1. Not only could the public buy and sell gold and silver at the mint at those rates, but they were free to melt down and export one or the other of the metals if they so desired.

Unfortunately, the objectives of the act could not be realized and the experiment in bimetallism failed. It quickly became apparent that the value of gold in terms of silver in the commodity markets of the economy (or indeed, as actually occurred, the mint parity in other countries) was different from the mint parity between the metals established by the Coinage Act. Initially, for example, the commodity market value of the metals was such that 15½ ounces of silver exchanged for one ounce of gold. This meant that it was profitable for the public to bring silver to the United States mint and purchase gold, export the gold to the market where its silver value was higher, reimport the silver to the United States, and thereby make a profit on the deal. An ounce of gold would be purchased from the mint in exchange for 15 ounces of silver. That ounce of gold would be sold abroad for 15½ ounces of silver, which could then be imported to the United States. From this amount, ½ ounce could be pocketed as profit, and 15 ounces could be used to acquire another ounce of gold from the mint to repeat the profitable operation.

In this early experiment, therefore, silver remained in circulation in the United States, but the gold was driven out. We have here an example of what became known as Gresham's Law. Simply stated, this said that bad money drives out good. More informatively, it said that undervalued money would be driven out of circulation and overvalued money would remain. Because gold, in the example we have discussed, was valued at the United States mint at 15 ounces of silver it was undervalued there. It was worth more on the external market.

To correct this state of affairs changes were made in 1834 and 1837 in the mint parity between gold and silver, to alter the ratio from 15/1 to 16/1. But at that time the reverse happened. Again the mint parity was not aligned with the external market values of the metals. Now that the mint price of gold was changed from $19.395 to $20.67 per ounce to establish this new parity of 16/1, it was overvalued. Gold and silver could still be exchanged in external markets at the ratio of approximately 15½ to 1. Therefore the relatively undervalued silver was driven out of circulation and the overvalued gold remained. The shortage of silver that resulted meant that the silver coins ordinarily needed to finance business transactions disappeared, and inconveniences in trading arrangements ensued. The country was legally on a bimetallic standard. But de facto it was functioning on a gold standard.

THE GOLD STANDARD

The definition of terms and the operating procedures of a gold standard can vary considerably. It may be a pure gold standard in which gold actually circulates as currency, gold coins may be melted and exported, gold may be sold to a government mint, and certain connections between the country's gold stock and the domestic money supply may be maintained. Or it may be a so-called gold exchange standard in which gold does not circulate, but representative full-bodied money remains exchangeable for gold. Or, as occurred in the United States after World War II, a modified gold bullion standard may be established. In that case the public is not permitted to own monetary gold, and export and import transactions in gold bullion are effected only between the central banks of separate countries and other official government bodies such as the Treasuries. We need not be concerned here with all the possibilities that exist. Suffice it to say that between 1879 and 1933 the United States was on a relatively pure gold standard. The following will indicate the general rules and method of operation of the more or less freely functioning gold standard that characterized international monetary arrangements during the later nineteenth and early twentieth centuries.

Consider first the set of rules that a freely functioning international gold standard system requires. They are summarized as follows:

1. There must be an established mint parity in each country between gold and the country's circulating medium.
2. There must be free convertibility between the country's currency and gold, in the sense that the mint stands ready to exchange currency for gold at any time.
3. There must be free or unimpeded export and import of gold.
4. There must be an established relation, which should be maintained in practice, between the country's stock of gold on the one hand and the total amount of its money supply in existence on the other.

These four rules, taken together, constitute the "rules of the game" of the gold standard.

The country's stock of gold could increase if, as occurred at different times during the nineteenth century, new discoveries of gold were made. But principally, the gold stock would change as a result of normal international trade activities. Suppose a country's exports of goods and services exceeded in value that of its imports. This would imply a balance-of-trade surplus. This would mean that foreign countries owed that country a net amount equal to its excess value of exports. Rather than building up an increasing indebtedness to the country with the excess exports, the other countries would pay the excess amount owed in gold. The manner in which this would normally occur, via transactions in the foreign exchange markets and the operation of gold import and export points, is examined in the following section. In short, then, if the United States maintained a surplus on its balance of trade, gold would flow in. The export trade surplus may, of course, be offset in part by the export of capital from the United States. But after taking account of such an outflow of capital, a balance-of-payments surplus may still exist.

When gold flowed into the United States it would imply, in accordance with rule four of the gold standard, that an increase would occur in the total money supply in circulation. If the rate of increase in the money supply should exceed the rate of increase in the production of goods and services, this would presumably result in an increase in commodity prices. This would generally be accompanied by an increase in the level of money incomes being generated in the country receiving gold. It might also be associated with a tendency for the rate of interest to decline as money became more readily available. On the other hand, the rate of interest might rise somewhat if an increase in the demand for loans, stimulated by increased business activity, temporarily outstripped the increase in the supply of money.

But the increase in prices and incomes that results from the inflow of gold would be likely to set up counteracting effects. For the rise in the domestic price level would make exported goods more expensive for foreigners, and the volume of exports could be expected to decline. At the same time, as foreign goods would have become cheaper relative to domestically produced goods, imports could be expected to rise as individuals switched their purchases to foreign goods. Moreover, the rise in the level of domestic production and economic activity, under the impetus of the increased money supply due to the inflow of gold, might also induce an increase in the import of industrial raw materials. In one way or another, owing to effects of both increasing imports and decreasing exports, the surplus on the balance of trade that gave rise to the inflow of gold in the first place would be reduced. The trade balance might turn into deficit. If, moreover, the rate of interest in the country receiving gold as a result of a balance-of-payments surplus should fall in the manner we suggested, this would tend to open up a differential between interest rates in that and other countries. The resulting outflow of short-term investable capital in search of the higher interest rates would tend to reduce the balance-of-payments surplus that gave rise to the inflow of gold in the first place. The balance of payments might thus turn into deficit, and gold would then flow out. The interest rate effect could, of course, operate in the reverse direction if interest rates rose in the country receiving gold as a result of higher economic activity and increased demand for money.

In this way, international flows of gold can have significantly destabilizing effects on both the economy receiving gold and the countries losing gold. Let us consider the contrary case. In just the same way as the rules of the gold standard require that a country receiving gold should expand its money supply and economic activity in the manner we have analyzed, so too, if the "rules of the gold standard" were followed strictly in actual practice, the country losing gold would have to contract its money supply and economic activity. There might be time lags before such a gold outflow would exert its full depressing effects on prices, economic activity, and employment. A country might have a reserve stock of gold that it could use for international settlement purposes when balance-of-payments troubles first appear. But if the rules of the gold standard were being adhered to, it would be necessary in due course for a country losing gold to react to that loss by engaging in a general economic contraction. Clearly, therefore, one of the prices that may have to be paid for strict compliance with the requirements of the international gold standard is an instability in the domestic economy.

The scheme of events we have envisaged is quite similar to that first described with remarkable clarity by David Hume as early as the middle of the eighteenth century.[1] The overall process became known as the self-balancing international payments mechanism. It is referred to as a self-balancing process because the inflow of gold sets up processes and reactions that tend to correct the imbalances that gave rise to the gold inflow in the first place. This was illustrated in our example by the way in which an initial balance-of-payments surplus could gradually be changed into a balance-of-payments deficit.

A fuller analysis of these processes would require us to distinguish between three sets of forces implicit in what has been said. In the overall reactions to international gold flows the economic repercussions depend on (1) an international relative price level effect; (2) an income effect, meaning by that the change in the level of national income in countries receiving and losing gold; and (3) an interest rate effect, implying international flows of investable capital, as well as effects on domestic investment and economic activity. We shall return to these important questions in a later chapter.

INTERNATIONAL EXCHANGE RATE PARITY, AND GOLD EXPORT AND IMPORT POINTS

The rules of the gold standard have other implications for the functioning of the system. Let us look in slightly more detail at the possible trading and exchange relations between Britain and the United States.

Let it be supposed that the British mint established the value of its unit of currency, the pound, by setting the price of an ounce of gold at 5 pounds. Imagine also that at the same time the United States mint established the value of an ounce of gold at 20 dollars. This implies that 5 British pounds must be equal, at what we can call the international parity rate of exchange, to 20 United States dollars. The parity rate of exchange

[1] David Hume, *Essays, Moral, Political and Literary*, Part II, Essays I to IX (1752, Edinburgh ed., 1817). See also Douglas Vickers, *Studies in the Theory of Money, 1690–1776* (Philadelphia: Chilton, 1959), Chap. 11.

between the two currencies will therefore be 1 pound = 4 dollars. This is indicated as the "par value" magnitude in Figure 4-1.

The typical functioning of the foreign exchange market in which dollars are traded for pounds, and vice versa, can now be observed. United States citizens will need to acquire British pounds in order to pay for commodities they wish to import from Britain, and to acquire pounds if they wish to make investments in Britain. Similarly, British citizens will wish to acquire dollars to pay for United States exports and to make investments in the United States. Thus an active foreign exchange market will develop in which the respective currencies are bought and sold by individual transactors. Our objective now is to understand exactly how and when such transactions may give rise to gold flows between the two countries.

Suppose, for one reason or another, that the United States has a balance-of-trade deficit with Britain. The value of United States imports from Britain exceeds the value of its exports to Britain. An excess demand for British pounds on the foreign exchange market (that is, the market conducted mainly by the large international trading banks in New York and London) will therefore develop. In that case the relatively heavy demand for pounds will tend to increase the market price of pounds, expressed in United States dollars. Over time, the exchange rate will tend to move in the direction indicated by the arrow in Figure 4-1.

At that stage a United States importer will realize that, in accordance with the rules of the international gold standard, he can acquire the British pounds he needs in either of two ways. First, he may buy them, as we have indicated in the figure, in the routine foreign exchange market. But second, as we observed at some length in the preceding section, he may purchase gold from the United States mint, ship the gold

Figure   4-1.

Gold Export and Import Points

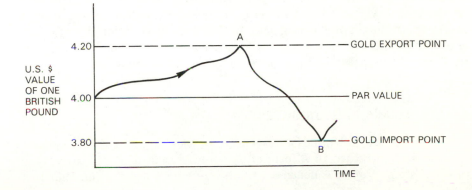

to London, and sell the gold there for British pounds. His choice will depend on which of these is the most advantageous or economically efficient way of proceeding. It depends, that is, on which is the least expensive way of acquiring British pounds.

If gold were purchased in the United States and shipped to London to acquire British pounds, certain costs, including principally shipping and insurance costs, would be incurred. Let us suppose that these costs amounted to about 5 percent of the value of gold shipped. In that event, British pounds would continue to be purchased on the foreign exchange market so long as the market price did not diverge by more than 5 percent from the par value rate of exchange. If, however, the market rate should climb to a level beyond that par-value-plus-5 percent mark, then it would be more advantageous for the importer to cease buying pounds on the foreign exchange market, and to acquire the pounds he needed by purchasing and shipping gold. In that case the level of 5 percent above the par value exchange rate sets the upper limit to which the market exchange rate can fluctuate before the demand for pounds is choked off. This upper limit, which is shown at $4.20 in Figure 4-1, will be the exchange rate at which a gold flow from the United States to Britain will begin. It is therefore referred to as the gold export point.

If, on the contrary, an excess British demand for United States dollars should develop in the foreign exchange market, the exchange rate would move in the opposite direction. In the same way as exchange rate point A in Figure 4-1 marks a gold export point, point B marks a gold import point.

All of this would be possible if, as we have said, the rules of the gold standard were strictly adhered to. This would require free convertibility of domestic currencies into gold at the respective mints, and free export and import of gold. When gold flows actually developed in this way, the economic pressures we noted in the preceding section would also develop. An expansion of the money supply, higher prices, higher national income and economic activity, and variations in interest rates would tend to appear in the country receiving gold. Similarly, tendencies to economic contraction, lower incomes and prices, and general deflation would tend to emerge in the country losing gold. In this way, international protection of exchange rates at or near parity values can cost a rather high price in the form of the instability it induces in domestic economies.

THE GOLD STANDARD
AND CONTEMPORARY DEBATE

From time to time in United States political circles, an interest has emerged in proposals to return to a form of the gold standard. Principally, this interest stems from a concern about the high rate of inflation that has been experienced in recent years. Focusing on what we summarized as the fourth rule of the gold standard, it is assumed that a return to gold would impose a welcome form of monetary discipline. Such an arrangement would, it is said, keep the country's money supply in line with changes in the stock of gold. That, it is then supposed, would make impossible the irresponsible rate of increase in money supplies that, according to this view, is basically responsible for the inflation.

In the light of our analysis a number of brief observations can be made on this set of arguments. First, in any proposal to return to a monetary standard in which the money supply is tied to the gold stock, it would be necessary to understand precisely how that relation was to be established; how, if at all and under what circumstances, it could be altered; and with what rigidity it was proposed the system as a whole should function. Second, we should also bear in mind that one of the principal lessons to be drawn from our analysis of the classical gold standard is that, with any serious kind of automaticity in the functioning of the system, the maintenance of stability in the domestic economy may be all too quickly sacrificed in the interest of international exchange rate stability.

Third, and most important, the argument has been advanced that inflation is not primarily a monetary phenomenon at all, at least if we set aside for the present the so-called hyperinflations, such as Germany experienced in the 1920s when money creation occurred at fantastically rapid rates. There are, it is claimed, deeper underlying causes of inflationary disequilibrium. These have to do not only with escalations of commodity demands or monetary expenditures but also with the relations between rates of wage and other prime cost increases and the rate at which the nation's productivity per worker can be increased. Inflation, according to this view, is to an important degree a problem of arguments about shares in the national output. Because its genesis is deeply embedded in real, or nonmonetary, aspects of the economic system, the remedies for it must be addressed to those real dimensions and must themselves be primarily nonmonetary in form. Our analysis in this chapter should equip us to take a careful view of proposals for a return to gold and should alert us to the profound difficulties and traps in such a move.

CREDIT OR DEBT MONEY

A major advantage of credit money is that the manufacture and use of it do not absorb commodity resources that can be used for other and more directly productive purposes. It is not full-bodied money. It does not have a market value as a commodity comparable with its value as money. It may be made of paper, as in the case of the Federal Reserve notes, or it may be made of alloyed metals, such as the coins issued by the United States Treasury. The metallic value of a dime or a quarter, for example, is considerably less than the value stamped on the face of the coin. For this reason our coins are referred to as token money.

Credit money includes also the demand deposits held in commercial banks and other depository institutions. They are referred to as checkable deposits and are described in the Depository Institutions Deregulation Act of 1980 as transaction accounts. They are so called because they can be activated, or transferred from one person to another, to effect transactions or payments in the markets of the economy. Such deposits are at times described also as accessible deposits. This terminology arises because the holders of them can have access to them, or they can be activated by transfer to another person, on demand at any time.

A number of questions arise in connection with credit money. First, not all forms of credit money may be what is known as legal tender. The term *legal tender* refers to those forms of money that, in accordance with the law, may be offered and are therefore required to be accepted as means of payment that legally evidence discharge of debt. All coin and currency circulating in the United States, for example, is legal tender. On the other hand, by far the largest part of credit money now in existence in our economy is made up of demand deposits or other transferable accounts. But these are not legal tender. No one is legally obliged to accept checks in payment of debts.

Such checks, of course, are not in themselves money. The money is the demand deposit that is capable of being transferred by checks. The checks are simply legal documents, technically bills of exchange, that are used to activate or transfer money. But the money so transferred is not required to be accepted if the person to whom it is offered does not have full confidence in it. To make it acceptable he must actually be confident of two things. First, he must believe that the person offering it actually does have funds in the bank on which the check is drawn. If that is so, then the person who received the check, the payee, can expect that he will actually be paid the money value of it when it is presented to the payer's bank for clearance. Second, the payee must be confident that the bank on which the check is drawn is in fact creditworthy, and that it does possess the ability to honor the check when it is presented. The bank, that is to say, must be solvent.

Thus the thing that makes money money is not whether it is usable as legal tender. The moneyness of whatever is being used as money depends simply on its acceptability. This, in the last analysis, depends on the confident expectation that a holder of it will be able to pass it on to another person in completion of market transactions at any time he should desire to do so.

Table 4-1 provides details of the money supply in the United States, according to the current classifications adopted by the Federal Reserve Board.

Currency refers to the total value of the coins issued by the Treasury and notes issued by the Federal Reserve Bank, which are held in the hands of the nonbank public. It is the total currency issued minus what is held by the banks, the Federal Reserve Bank, and the Treasury. The demand deposits listed in the second data column of the table refer to commercial bank non-interest-bearing deposits which can be transferred on demand. For purposes of the table a small amount of traveler's checks issued by nonbank companies has been included in the figure reported. This procedure is adopted because such traveler's checks are counted as part of the M1 money supply. The traveler's checks issued by commercial banks do not have to be added in separately in this way, because they are already included in the total of demand deposits. When traveler's checks are sold by the commercial banks, the amount involved is transferred to a special deposit liability account to await payment in due course when the checks are presented. The nonbank traveler's checks included in Table 4-1 amounted to only $0.4 billion in 1960, and $4.0 billion in 1982. For purposes of the money supply statistics, the commercial bank demand deposits are shown here after deducting (1) interbank deposits, or deposits held in one bank by another bank; (2) deposits held in the banks by foreign commercial banks; (3) deposits held by the United States

Table   4-1

United States money supply, in billions of dollars, at specified dates

Year	Currency	Commercial bank demand deposits	Other checkable deposits	M1	M2
1960	29.0	112.9	.0	141.9	312.3
1965	36.3	133.1	.1	169.5	459.5
1970	49.1	167.3	.1	216.5	628.8
1975	73.8	216.4	.9	291.0	1026.9
1980	116.2	271.4	26.9	414.5	1656.2
1981	123.1	240.9	77.0	440.9	1822.7
1982	132.6	244.2	101.3	478.5	1999.1

Source: *Economic Report of the President,* February 1982, pp. 303–4, and February 1983, pp. 233–34; and *Federal Reserve Bulletin,* February 1983, p. A14. (Note that the data on nonbank traveler's checks referred to in the text have been obtained from the first and third of these sources.)

* Data refer to average daily figures for the final month of the year indicated, on a seasonally adjusted basis.

Treasury; and (4) checks in course of collection and Federal Reserve Float. The figure reported in the table is often referred to as "adjusted demand deposits," and the detailed adjustments involved in it will be discussed more fully in a later chapter.

The most widely used money supply statistic is referred to in data column four as M1 and includes the amount of so-called other checkable deposits. These refer to a variety of deposit accounts that perform one or more of the functions of money but may, unlike pure demand deposits, pay varying rates of interest. These other checkable deposits include four main items:

1. *NOW accounts* in commercial banks and in the thrift institutions, including savings and loan associations and mutual savings banks. NOW accounts, technically known as Negotiable Order of Withdrawal accounts, are checking accounts that pay interest.
2. *ATS accounts in commercial banks.* These refer to Automatic Transfer Service accounts. They are actually two accounts in one. A depositor's funds are held in an interest-bearing account until the time they are required. When a check drawn by the depositor is presented to the bank for payment, the amount necessary to meet the check is automatically transferred from the interest-bearing account to the depositor's demand deposit account. The check can then clear.
3. *Demand deposits in the thrift institutions.* The ability of these institutions to offer demand deposit or checkable account facilities has been expanded by the Depository Institutions Deregulation Act of 1980.
4. *Share draft accounts in credit unions.* These are in effect NOW accounts maintained by credit unions, but as the word *check* cannot legally be used in connection with them, they are transferable by what are known as share drafts.

Throughout this book, unless specific mention is made to the contrary, we shall use this M1 statistic when the money supply is referred to for descriptive or analytical purposes. In a sense, therefore, we shall speak consistently of a narrow money supply concept, although it is acknowledged that different measures may be valuable for different analytical purposes. One such broader measure of the money supply is shown in the final column of Table 4-1 as M2. This includes, in addition to the M1 total, certain other highly liquid assets, or assets that can readily be converted to money without loss of value. The M2 magnitude includes all that is contained in the M1 figure plus mainly four other categories of funds: first, savings accounts in commercial banks, other than ATS accounts, and time deposits in commercial banks and thrift institutions of amounts less than $100,000; second, overnight repurchase accounts in commercial banks; third, certain kinds of overnight Eurodollar accounts; and fourth, the amounts held in money market mutual funds by noninstitutional holders. A brief comment on each of these additional forms of liquidity, or money stores of value that can function as sources of funds for transactions payments under appropriate circumstances, will be adequate at this stage.

Savings accounts referred to here are pass-book accounts that bear interest. Funds can generally be withdrawn from them on short notice, frequently on demand. They differ from time deposits in that the latter may not be drawn against or repaid by the depository institution to the depositor before the expiration of a time agreed upon when the funds were deposited unless, in the general case, a penalty in the form of a partial loss of interest is paid.

Overnight repurchase accounts are a potentially important source of funds for commercial banks. In effect, a depositor may actually lend to the bank the funds he currently holds in a deposit account, subject to an agreement that the bank will repay them to him on the following day. By this means the depositor will be earning interest on temporarily unutilized funds. The bank will benefit because the funds concerned are, for the duration of the overnight repurchase agreement, transferred out of demand deposit accounts and are not therefore subject to the reserve requirement provisions to which the bank is subject. These latter requirements, as we observed in an earlier chapter, are specified by the Federal Reserve Board, and they play a highly significant part in the procedures of monetary control and the conduct of Federal Reserve monetary policy.

Eurodollars refer to United States dollar balances held in overseas banks. When these balances first became significant in international financial transactions some years ago they were held in European banks—hence the name Eurodollars. At the present time the term refers to overseas dollar balances in general. Some such dollar balances are held in Caribbean branches of United States banks and are placed there on an overnight or day-to-day basis. They are therefore highly liquid funds. Because the Caribbean banks are in the same time zone as the United States, and because the funds can be transferred rapidly to the United States offices of the banks in which they are held, that portion of them held by the public is included in the broader definition of the United States money supply.

Money market mutual funds have rapidly become an important part of our financial institutional structure. Funds deposited in them may earn a high rate of interest. The mutual fund invests those deposits in highly liquid money market securities. In recent years, given the general state of the monetary situation, high rates of return have been available on such funds. Usually the money market funds permit individuals who make deposits with them to transfer amounts to any other person by writing an instruction that is, in effect, a check. In some cases such transfer instructions or checks must be for a minimum of $500. This again means that the amounts held in these funds have a liquidity comparable with that of the other forms of interest-bearing deposit accounts we have mentioned.

The money market mutual funds first became a significant force in the New York market in the early 1970s. At the end of 1974 their total assets amounted to $2.3 billion. Thereafter they experienced rapid growth in periods of high interest rates. Their assets expanded to $10.3 billion by the end of 1978, to $43.7 billion one year later, and to $220.6 billion by December 1982. Of the latter amount, some $43.1 billion was held by institutions and was included in the M3 statistic. The remainder, $177.5 billion, was included also in M2.

Beyond the M1 and M2 definitions of the money supply, statistics are published also on yet a broader money supply definition known as M3. This includes all that is contained in M2, plus large time deposits at all depository institutions, amounts subject to longer-term repurchase agreements, and institutional deposits in money market mutual funds. Beyond this, some economists make use of a still larger or more inclusive measure of liquidity. In official data this is referred to as "L" and includes, in addition to the M3 assets, certain other kinds of highly liquid assets. These include U.S. Treasury bills and U.S. savings bonds, other short-term debts of the federal government, and the short-term commercial paper debts of industrial corporations that enjoy the highest credit ratings. Such items as these are not money in the sense that they can be used as means of payment. But they can generally be changed into money very quickly and without a significant danger of loss. They are therefore a genuine part of the total liquidity of the economy. The possession of them constitutes a repository of potential purchasing power. They may therefore be one of the factors that determine the level of expenditures in the economy. They may accordingly be significant for the overall determinants of business and economic behavior. Because of the properties of liquidity they possess, they are frequently referred to as near-money.

The discussion in Chapter 7 of commercial banking structure and regulation will show that many changes have occurred recently, not only as a result of the landmark legislation of 1980 but following certain decisions of the Depository Institutions Deregulation Committee, made possible by the Garn-St. Germain Depository Institutions Act of 1982. The most important of these for our present purposes are the following.

First, in order to enable them to compete for depositors' accounts with the money market mutual funds, the commercial banks and thrift institutions (mutual savings banks and savings and loan associations) are now permitted to offer accounts that are, in effect, comparable with money market funds. These new accounts, which have been given various names by different banks, were initially required to maintain a minimum deposit of $2,500 (this minimum deposit requirement was amended in December 1983), and the interest that can be paid on them is not subject to any regulatory ceiling. The interest rates currently being paid by the banks compete with the money market mutual funds. The funds in these accounts are now included in the M2 money supply statistics.

Second, the banks are now also permitted to offer a so-called super–NOW account, which also initially required the maintenance of a minimum deposit balance (this requirement was also amended in December 1983), but on which an interest rate not subject to any regulatory ceiling can be paid. These accounts permit more liberal transactions and transfer privileges than the banks' money market accounts. The amounts held in them are included in the M1 money supply statistics.

THE COMPOSITION OF THE CIRCULATING MEDIUM

Focusing on the definition of the money supply most appropriate as a measure of the circulating medium in the economy, Table 4-2 indicates recent changes in its structure.

During the last couple of decades, currency has accounted for about one-quarter of the nation's circulating medium. This proportion does, of course, vary from time to time during a given year. Demands for currency are higher at certain times, such as during the Christmas and other holiday seasons. When the need for currency arises, the public obtains it by drawing against bank demand deposits. The banks in turn acquire currency by purchasing it from the Federal Reserve Bank. The banks pay the Federal Reserve Bank by drawing against their reserve deposits. Such an increase in the amount of currency in circulation does not therefore cause any immediate change in the money supply. One form of money, currency, is increased at the expense of another form, namely demand deposits. But an increase in currency in circulation can have important

Table 4-2

Percentage composition of the M1 money supply at specified dates

Year	Currency	Commercial bank demand deposits	Other checkable deposits	M1
1960	20.4	79.6	0.0	100.0
1965	21.4	78.5	0.1	100.0
1970	22.7	77.3	0.1	100.0
1975	25.4	74.4	0.3	100.0
1980	28.0	65.5	6.5	100.0
1981	27.9	54.6	17.5	100.0
1982	27.7	51.0	21.2	100.0

Source: See Table 4-1.

indirect effects on the monetary and banking situation. For it will decrease the reserves that the banks hold at the Federal Reserve Bank, and this will in turn affect the lending ability of the banks. We shall return to these important points.

As indicated in Table 4-2, the proportion of the money supply represented by currency in circulation has been increasing in recent years. This is no doubt due in part to the increasing importance of the so-called cash, or underground, economy. In times of inflation and high rates of taxation, it is unfortunately true that tax liabilities can be reduced by engaging to a greater extent in cash, and thereby potentially unreported, income transactions.

More significant in Table 4-2 is the recent and rapid increase in the relative importance of the other checkable deposits. Recalling the definition of these accounts, we recognize their important potential significance for the future development of our financial system. Traditionally nonbank institutions are more than ever complementing, or even supplanting, the banks in their money-creating activities. The meaning of this will be examined more fully in Part III of this book.

MONETARY DEVELOPMENT
AND MONEY SUBSTITUTES

Our monetary system has experienced considerable development since the early days of the nation. From pure forms of commodity money in the earliest years, we have developed to a system of complete credit money. Development, moreover, has in no sense ceased. New forms of money, near-money, and money substitutes will undoubtedly emerge in the years ahead. New forms of financial institutions will undoubtedly be invented. The traditional form of pure commercial banks will find their financial hegemony challenged on still further fronts. Credit card usage will undoubtedly increase, thereby lessening the frequency of actual money exchanges. Money-paying terminals in supermarkets will mean that depositors' accounts at banks will be able to be charged directly at the time and place at which market transactions are made. Computer technology will undoubtedly help to diminish the heavy burden of recording payments transactions in our growing and increasingly complex economy. Indeed, some economists are beginning to speculate about the possible appearance of a cashless society. All of our monetary transactions would in that event be recorded automatically, without the need for the actual passing of money at all.

One possible reason why such an extreme development may not occur, however, is that such a large-scale use of automatic recording devices would diminish the degree of confidentiality in commercial and financial transactions. If, moreover, there actually exists a cash or underground economy that has emerged for extralegal reasons, this again will tend to retard the movement to a completely cashless society.

THE DEMAND FOR MONEY AND THE PROBLEM OF UNCERTAINTY

Our studies to this point have anticipated the detailed analysis of the demand for money that will be given in Chapter 15. To establish our initial perspectives, and to permit us to carry in mind a significant issue in the intervening discussion, we look briefly at a question that deserves much more thought than it has generally been accorded in monetary analysis. We refer to the problem of uncertainty. Let us reflect again on the reasons why money is demanded and used in a monetary, as distinct from a barter, economy. Money is required, we have seen, as (1) a means of effecting transactions and (2) a store of value. We shall take the latter point first for slightly more extended analysis.

The reason, essentially, why money is demanded as a store of value is that individuals are uncertain about what the future holds. We saw in the preceding chapter that Keynes, for example, concluded that "our desire to hold money as a store of wealth is a barometer of the degree of our distrust of our calculations and conventions concerning the future. . . ." The holding of money "lulls our disquietude."[2] The possession of money is a means of overcoming, or evading, the pressures of uncertainty. It enables us to take refuge, as it were, in liquidity when the condition we are in makes it too difficult for us to evaluate the possible future events that would warrant our investing in other and more productive lines of activity. Liquidity, or the holding of money, is a refuge from uncertainty. It "lulls our disquietude."

The analytical significance of this is that it will influence the way in which, on an aggregate and economywide basis, we invent certain explanatory functions to describe the demand for money. One of the important variables in the demand-for-money function is undoubtedly the rate of interest. As the rate of interest increases, the opportunity cost of holding money increases, and we are therefore likely to want to hold less of it. But it is not possible to describe the demand for money by a smooth downward-sloping curve in a money-interest rate plane and imagine that we have thereby said the principal thing that needs to be said. For the important thing that waits evaluation in a money-using economy is pre-

[2] John Maynard Keynes, "The General Theory of Employment," *Quarterly Journal of Economics,* 1937, p. 216.

cisely the stability of such a curve or function itself. The interest rate relation is no doubt important and needs to be taken into account. But the stability of that relation is as important as the conception of the relation itself.

Again, the demand for money as a means of consummating exchanges is due also, in the final analysis, to the presence of uncertainty. We need to hold money simply because we are not certain of two important features of our potential market behavior. First, we cannot know with certainty exactly what we shall wish to purchase with our money when the time to dispose of it arrives. And second, we cannot know with certainty just when the need to effect final payment for our purchases will arrive, or when we shall receive inflows of money for whatever it is we sell. This again is a significant form of uncertainty.

George Shackle, a prominent British economist of the mid-twentieth century, has clearly recognized that the *unifying concept* in monetary theory is that of uncertainty. He refers to the medium-of-exchange function as well as the store-of-value function when he observes that money is kept because "we are not yet sure what we want to buy. . . . it is being kept because of uncertainty; a petty rather than a momentous kind of uncertainty, if you wish, but for purposes of theory, of the *unity* of theory, this characterization is important."[3]

If there were no uncertainties in the world, there would be no need for money, which is in effect, as Shackle puts it, "a substitute for knowledge."[4] In the absence of uncertainty there would be no ignorance. We would be able to know at a point in time, once and for all, what transactions would occur, and when they would occur, in the future. There would therefore be other ways of providing for them than holding money. In the absence of uncertainty and ignorance all transactions can be settled at once, and in effect goods exchangd for goods. We are back in a barter economy. Money, to the contrary, is essentially a disequilibrium, not an equilibrium, phenomenon. It is essentially an uncertainty phenomenon. We shall have to take the pressure of these realities into account as the analytical parts of our work unfold.

SUMMARY

This chapter has considered the reasons why, in the initial emergence from a barter system of exchange and economic arrangements, money could be expected to take a specific form. The desirable characteristics of

[3] G.L.S. Shackle, *Keynesian Kaleidics* (Edinburgh: Edinburgh University Press, 1974), p. 62.

[4] G.S.L. Shackle, *Epistemics and Economics* (Cambridge: Cambridge University Press, 1962), p. 216. See also T. W. Hutchison, *The Significance and Basic Postulates of Economic Theory* (New York: Kelley [1938] 1960), pp. 88, 118.

money that made it usable as a circulating medium and a store of value were discussed.

In the context of commodity money systems an examination was made of experiments with bimetallic systems, where attempts were made to maintain both silver and gold in simultaneous circulation as money. The reasons why such attempts failed permit us to characterize such standards as what have been called "limping standards."[5] The monetary system necessarily limps from one metal to the other as the de facto monetary base.

The rules of the game of the international gold standard were also examined. Reasons were explored as to why the rigorous adherence to the rules of the gold standard may preserve the international value of a country's currency at the price of generating serious instability and disequilibrium in the domestic economy.

An outline was given of different forms of money. The discussion proceeded from commodity money forms, through representative full-bodied money, to the description of pure credit or debt money systems. In that context the principal features of our present monetary arrangements were examined. It was seen that certain kinds of money made available by nonbank financial institutions are highly complementary with the traditional commercial bank demand deposits as the principal form of the country's money supply. These developments have important implications for the future possible evolution of our monetary and financial arrangements.

It was observed that money is essentially a disequilibrium phenomenon. It is essentially an uncertainty phenomenon. These parts of our overall vision will forcibly come into play in the analytical parts of our subsequent work.

IMPORTANT CONCEPTS

Full-bodied money
Representative full-bodied money
Credit (or debt) money
Bimetallism
Rules of the gold standard
Self-balancing payments mechanism

Gold export and import points
Checkable deposits
M1, M2, M3, and L
Adjusted demand deposits
Money market mutual funds
Near-money

QUESTIONS FOR DISCUSSION AND REVIEW

1. Discuss the reasons why money should assume specific forms at different stages of economic development.

2. The thing that makes money money is its acceptability. Discuss critically.

[5] D. H. Robertson, *Money* (London: Nisbet, 1948), pp. 67ff.

3. What institutional, legal, and economic arrangements are necessary for the satisfactory functioning of a credit, or debt, money system?

4. In the context of a discussion of Gresham's Law, explain why the early experiments in bimetallism were unsuccessful.

5. Discuss the proposition that adherence to the rules of the gold standard may provide exchange rate stability at the price of destabilizing the domestic economy.

6. Would a return to gold-backed money eliminate the possibility of inflation? Explain clearly why or why not.

7. How do gold export points and gold import points operate?

8. Discuss the price effects, income effects, and interest rate effects associated with international flows of gold. How would your analysis extend to the international flows of money in a pure credit or debt money system?

9. How have recent institutional and regulatory changes affected the definition and provision of the money supply?

10. Examine the proposition that money is a "refuge from uncertainty" and "a substitute for knowledge."

5

A PRELIMINARY VIEW OF BANKS AND FINANCIAL INSTITUTIONS

STUDY OBJECTIVES:

• To understand the significance of the "goldsmith principle" of money creation and the emergence of fractional reserve banking
• To observe the main structure of bank balance sheets, and the relation between bank assets and liabilities
• To gain further insight into the savings-investment process and the functions performed by nonbank financial institutions
• To realize the importance of surplus and deficit sectors in the economy, the meaning of direct and indirect investment, and to note the relevance of primary and secondary securities and security markets
• To look briefly at the main problems of asset portfolio selection, and the need to achieve satisfactory combinations of return, risk, and liquidity

The analysis of the macroeconomy in Part V will place heavy emphasis on the importance of money flows in the economy. The size, stability, and trend of the money inflows that business firms are able to expect from the sale of their output and what we shall call an "expected proceeds function" will be central to the determination of output levels in the economy as a whole. Similarly, we shall be concerned with the money flows generated by individuals' decisions to allocate a part of their incomes to consumption expenditures, and by firms' decisions to make expenditures for investment purposes. A number of other money flows will have to be taken into account also. Some of these will come into clearer focus as we expand our discussion in this chapter of the flow of savings funds through the financial institutions and into the financing of investment outlays.

Two points will enable us to maintain a clear view on the structure of the analysis. First, our understanding of the reasons why, and the manner in which, money emerged to remedy the inhibiting features of a barter system of economic arrangements must now be expanded. We need a clear grasp not only of the phenomenon of money itself but of the forms of the institutions that naturally emerged as the suppliers of money. We have seen that money facilitates trade and exchanges. We have seen it functioning as a store of value. We have seen that in a number of significant ways it links the past (with its inheritance of productive resources and wealth assets), the present (with its stocks of tradable commodities and usable productive facilities), and the future (with its possibilities and hopes for ongoing economic activity). These aspects of our economic affairs, which take up almost completely the functions of money, lie behind the theoretical analysis we shall construct.

Second, we need a sharpened perspective also on an important point referred to at the very beginning of our work. We said there that it was not money we earned. It was income. It is not money we save. It is a part of our income. Similarly, it is not money that we invest. We invest a part of our income or, in another perspective, we invest in various income-earning opportunities the wealth we have accumulated as a result of saving out of successive annual incomes. In all of these important economic activities money serves as the form in which values are expressed and in which the relevant economic transfers and exchanges are made. Our income is actually paid in money form. The money is then passed on and around the income and expenditure circuit as we spend part of it in one way or another. The part of income we save is paid in the form of money to depository institutions or directly to borrowers. The flow of actual money in this way is the surface expression of the more fundamental and underlying flow of funds and economic resources.

For these reasons we shall look in this chapter at the emergence of banks as money-creating and money-lending institutions. Then we shall observe briefly some further aspects of the money flows that represent the savings-investment process, and at the place and functions of the financial institutions in it. Our discussion at this stage will not be exhaustive. It will intentionally leave a number of operational details for discussion in Part III. We begin with the goldsmiths as an early form of banking activity.

THE GOLDSMITH PRINCIPLE

In the preceding chapter we noted the reasons for the early emergence of a form of commodity money. We considered gold as one such form. There were reasons, however, why the use of gold currency, in spite of its many desirable and favorable characteristics, actually prevented trade and exchanges from developing as rapidly as might otherwise have occurred. The high cost and risk of transporting full-bodied gold coin led to the invention and use of a representative full-bodied substitute and to its issuance by a financial institution that became known as the goldsmith.

Initially, the goldsmiths were depository institutions that accepted currency for safekeeping and earned a satisfactory income from the fees they charged for that service. A warehouse receipt would be given to a depositor, and it was understood that on presentation of that receipt at any time the amount of gold it represented could be obtained. The effects of such a depository transaction on the wealth positions of the individuals and the goldsmiths can be represented by the following partial balance sheets. The plus and minus signs indicate the relevant changes in the balance sheet positions.

Balance sheet of the public

Assets		Liabilities
Gold	−$100	
Warehouse receipts	+ 100	

Balance sheet of the goldsmith

Assets		Liabilities	
Gold	+$100	Warehouse receipts	+$100

The deposit with the goldsmith of $100 worth of gold means that the amount of money in actual circulation has been reduced by that amount. To the extent that it is on deposit in this way the money is, in a sense, lying dead. That expression is reminiscent of the language of John Locke, who, in his treatise on money at the end of the seventeenth century, observed that "the money of a nation may lie dead, and thereby prejudice trade."[1] Locke's considerable insight brought into focus the fact that money was beneficial to trade, exchanges, and economic development only so long as it continued to circulate. A large body of important economic literature in the eighteenth century followed up this conceptual lead that Locke had given.[2]

In due course it became apparent to all concerned that there was no need to withdraw gold from the goldsmith deposit in order to make payments. Subject only to holding warehouse receipts in appropriate sizes

---

[1] John Locke, *Consequences of the Lowering of Interest, and Raising the Value of Money,* 1691; published with J. R. McCulloch, *Principles of Political Economy* (London: Murray, 1870), p. 226.

[2] See Douglas Vickers, *Studies in the Theory of Money, 1690–1776* (Philadelphia: Chilton, 1959); and William Letwin, *The Origins of Scientific Economics: English Economic Thought, 1660–1776* (London: Methuen, 1963).

or denominations, the warehouse receipts themselves could be passed
from one person to another in payment of monetary obligations. In this
way the receipts began to circulate as money. They would continue to be
accepted as money so long as the requirements of confidence we have
already discussed continued to be met. Now the problem of the safety of
the possession of money could be solved, without any reduction in the
amount of money in circulation occurring.

The goldsmiths realized at this stage that a part of the gold they
held remained on deposit for a considerable time before it was demanded
in exchange for the warehouse receipts that evidenced ownership of it.
If, moreover, gold was demanded, or if, that is, warehouse receipts were
presented for redemption, it was sufficient only that the goldsmith should
possess at that time enough gold to make the payment demanded of him.
For he had never given any individual depositor a guarantee that the
original ounces of gold he had deposited would be available on demand.
He had simply undertaken to pay, on the presentation of a warehouse
receipt, gold to the value stated on it.

At that point, then, the goldsmith could make a shrewd calculation.
He could estimate that only a proportion, say 20 percent, of the value of
gold deposited with him would be demanded by depositors in the space
of any given period. What was to prevent the goldsmith, therefore, from
retaining just 20 percent of the gold he had on deposit and lending out
to creditworthy borrowers the remaining 80 percent? It would be possible
for him to turn a tidy profit by doing so. He would be receiving gold on
deposit and paying out gold in redemption of warehouse receipts from
day to day. He might judge that he would satisfy all requirements of
safety and prudence if he kept on hand at any time 20 percent of his total
liabilities against warehouse receipts.

This is what happened at an early stage of the development of monetary systems. Consider the advantages that followed from it. First, the
income of the goldsmith could be increased by reason of the interest he
would receive on the new loans he made. It was true that in a sense he
was lending someone else's money. But, as has been indicated, he would
not be defaulting on his fiduciary responsibility so long as he was able
to meet all requests for redemption of warehouse receipts in gold when
they were made. Second, an effective increase in the total amount of
money in circulation in the economy would occur. The balance sheet
entries at the goldsmith level will make this clear.

Goldsmith balance sheet			
Assets		*Liabilities*	
Gold	+ $100	Warehouse receipts	+ $100
Gold	− 80		
Loans	+ 80		

This partial balance sheet represents the loan by the goldsmith of 80 percent of the $100 worth of gold deposited with him. We suppose, moreover, that this loan of $80 is immediately withdrawn by the borrower in the form of gold. It is this that accounts for the change indicated in the goldsmith's assets. The total of his assets still equals the total of his liabilities. But the form of his assets has altered significantly. He still holds, however, as he estimated he needed to do, gold equal to 20 percent of his liabilities.

Consider also the effects on the public and the economy. The principal effects are threefold. First, there has been an increase in the amount of money in circulation. The originally issued warehouse receipts amounting to $100 continue in circulation. But now a further $80 in currency and gold coins has been added to this, making $180 altogether. In fact, the money supply has almost doubled. Second, so far as money in circulation "oils the wheels of trade"[3] in the ways we have considered, the potential area of exchange, production, and economic activity will have been widened. Third, the increased availability of money will mean that loans of money may become more easily available. This will offset to some extent the larger demand for loans that may come from the potentially higher level of trade and productive activity. The overall increased flow of money may well prevent the rate of interest on money loans from rising as high as it might otherwise do.

It might not follow, of course, that loans made by the goldsmith will lead to the immediate outflow of gold in the manner we have just supposed. We can envisage precisely the opposite case. We can imagine that when loans are made the goldsmiths do not pay out gold but simply give the borrower a note or a certificate to the value of the loans agreed upon. Moreover, the amount of the loan may be taken by the borrower in a number of such certificates, or goldsmith notes, each of differing face value but amounting in total to the value of the loan. Each such note would state on the face of it that it was redeemable for a specified amount of gold on presentation to the goldsmith. If, then, such notes remained in permanent circulation, the resulting balance sheet effects could be depicted as follows:

Goldsmith balance sheet

Assets		Liabilities	
Gold	$100	Original deposits	$100
Loans	400	Notes outstanding	400

[3] This phrase gained currency in early monetary discussion. Locke, in *Consequences*, p. 228, had referred to "the current of money, which turns the wheels of trade." David Hume, in his *Essays, Moral, Political, and Literary* (1752, Edinburgh, ed., 1817), p. 279, had said that "money . . . is none of the wheels of trade: It is the oil which renders the motion of the wheels more smooth and easy." Adam Smith was later to refer to money as "the great wheel of circulation . . .," *Wealth of Nations* (New York: Modern Library, 1937), p. 276.

Here we see that the goldsmith now has total liabilities of $500. To the original liability for the $100 gold initially deposited with him has been added $400 in notes he has issued by way of making loans. At the same time, his assets have expanded to $500. He retains the $100 gold deposited with him, by virtue of the assumption in our example that no portion of the new loans would be taken out in gold. In addition he now has new assets of $400 loans. On these he will earn an agreed rate of interest.

We note also that the goldsmith is still operating, even after he has expanded loans to the extent we have suggested, within the limits of safety and prudence he had set. His balance sheet indicates that against his total liabilities of $500 he is still holding gold equal in value to $100, satisfying his required safety margin of 20 percent.

This 20 percent estimate of safety margin can be referred to as the goldsmith's "reserve requirement." Or 20 percent can be referred to as his "required reserve ratio." This same expression will enter our analysis again, with virtually the same significance, when we discuss the reserve requirements imposed on our present-day banks and depository institutions by the Federal Reserve Board.

In his loan operations, assuming as at present that the loans will not give rise to any "leakage" or "drain" of gold into circulation, the goldsmith can use a simple arithmetic device to calculate his maximum permissible lending ability. If he requires his reserves to be at least 20 percent of his liabilities, the maximum permissible amount of those liabilities will be calculated as $100 divided by 20 percent, or $100/.20. The result is $500. Realizing, then, that he already has liabilities of $100 as a result of the initial gold deposit and the warehouse receipts he issued in exchange for it, the goldsmith knows that he has room for a further expansion of liabilities of $400. This is then the amount by which he can, on the basis of his own estimate of necessary prudence and safety, expand his loans.

This kind of operation has led to a significant increase in the total amount of money in circulation. Resulting effects on the potential levels of trade, exchanges, and production will follow. But the goldsmith's loan operations might not work in either of the precise ways we have supposed in our examples. Instead of taking the full amount of their loans in the form of gold on the one hand, or taking it all in notes in the other, borrowers may actually take varying proportions in each of these two ways. Let us suppose that the goldsmith estimated that following the creation of new loans the borrowers would demand gold equal to 30 percent of their holdings of notes. We can now ask again what would be the maximum potential lending ability the goldsmith enjoyed after the initial deposit with him of $100 worth of gold. We approach this question in a slightly different way, as a means of exhibiting its close kinship with modern fractional reserve banking operations.

We define the goldsmith's required reserve ratio by the symbol r. This has been specified, for purpose of the example, as 20 percent. We suppose, moreover, that the borrowers of new loans decide that they wish to hold an amount of gold currency equal to 30 percent of the goldsmith notes in circulation among them. We refer to this "cash requirement ratio" of the public as c.

The basis of new lending ability enjoyed by the goldsmith can be referred to as his "excess reserves." The amount of such excess reserves is calculated as follows. The goldsmith's total reserves, as we may now refer to his total holdings of gold, are $100. But of this total an amount of $20, equal to 20 percent of the original deposits, is held as required reserves in accordance with his estimate of prudence and safety. The remainder of the total reserves, the $80 available as a base for new lending operations, we refer to as his "excess reserves." We want to know now the maximum value of new notes the goldsmith can safely issue and what, as a result, is the maximum amount of new loans he can make. The holders of notes may wish at any time, of course, to redeem their notes for gold, or to increase their demand for gold above the initial 30 percent of their note holdings. We may suppose, therefore, that the goldsmith also decides that prudence and safety require him to hold gold reserves equal to 20 percent of the notes outstanding.

Let us refer to the amount of goldsmith notes that come into existence as a result of the new lending operations by the symbol N. Then we know that when N has been expanded to its maximum permissible limit, the "required reserves" that have to be held against it will be rN, or r percent of N. Similarly, we know from the terms of the example that when the public is holding N in goldsmith notes, they will also want to hold gold currency equal to cN, or c percent of N. At present the goldsmith holds excess reserves of $80. We shall refer to these by the symbol ExR. When the maximum permissible expansion of loans has taken place, what are now excess reserves will have been absorbed, or utilized, in performing one or the other of the following two functions. Either they will have become required reserves against the new notes outstanding, or they will actually have been paid out by the goldsmith in the form of gold. We may refer to these two possible uses of excess reserves as rN in the case of the amount absorbed as required reserves, and as cN in the case of the amount drawn into circulation because of the demands for gold made by the holders of notes at the time they received their loans.

The following important reserve equation can therefore be established:

$$ExR = rN + cN$$

It shows the sum of the ways in which, following the expansion of loans, the initial excess reserves will be absorbed into other uses. By transposition it follows that

$$N = \frac{ExR}{r + c}$$

In our present example this indicates that the value of N, the maximum amount of notes that can come into existence, will be the excess reserves of $80 divided by the sum of (1) the reserve requirement ratio and (2) the public's cash requirement ratio. These ratios are, by assumption for the present example, 20 percent and 30 percent, respectively. They sum to 50 percent. The maximum permissible value of N is therefore $80/.50. This equals $160.

The results for the goldsmith's balance sheet can be illustrated as follows:

Goldsmith balance sheet

Assets		Liabilities	
(a) Gold	$100	Original deposits	$100 (a)
(b) Gold	− 48	Notes outstanding	160 (b)
withdrawn by note holders			
(b) Loans	208		

Here the entries marked (a) illustrate the original gold deposit. Those marked (b) reflect the loan operations. As the public now hold notes to the value of $160, they will demand gold currency to the value of 30 percent of this amount, or $48. The corresponding gold outflow to satisfy this demand is shown on the assets side of the goldsmith's balance sheet. Most significantly, however, in order to achieve this result the goldsmith will expand loans by $208. We could describe the outcome by saying that of the total loans of $208, the public has taken $160 in notes and the remaining $48, or 30 percent of the value of their notes, in gold.

After all these developments have occurred, the goldsmith's balance sheet still balances. He now has total assets of $260 and liabilities of the same amount. What is more, his reserve requirements against his deposit and note liabilities are exactly satisfied. Against his total liabilities of $260 he needs in gold 20 percent, or $52. After the gold outflow we have envisaged, this amount of $52 is the actual level of reserves the goldsmith still holds in the form of gold.

CONTEMPORARY FRACTIONAL
RESERVE BANKING

This example of the goldsmith's operations has actually brought us a very long way and has probed deeply into the functioning of our present-day banking system. The processes exhibited are essentially those that are referred to in modern parlance as fractional reserve banking. Present-day commercial banks operate in the same way as the goldsmiths operated in the preceding example. There are only minor differences. Commercial banks are required to hold reserves against their deposit liabilities in the same way as we imagined in the foregoing example. They hold reserves, however, not in the form of gold, but in the form of cash or deposits with the Federal Reserve Bank. They similarly make loans that are multiples of the reserves they actually hold. Their deposits are also multiples of the reserves they have on hand at any time.

The genesis of bank money can thus be seen by analogy with the goldsmith's operations. We may note, by way of summary, that as the banks create new loans and deposits in response to the public's demand for money, the extent to which they can do so will be constrained by two factors: first, the amount of excess reserves they have at any time; and second, the rate of interest they can obtain on the loans they make.

SUMMARY COMMERCIAL BANK
BALANCE SHEET

Even though we are deferring a full discussion of modern banking operations, it will be useful to look at a composite balance sheet of a large part of our present banking system. This will enable us to see, again by comparison with the lending and money-creating operations we have just examined, the actual posture of this significant part of our contemporary financial system. Table 5-1 shows the principal assets and liabilities of all domestically chartered commercial banks as of December 1982.

The cash assets will be self-explanatory in the light of earlier discussion, with the possible exception of the following. The assets held in the "cash items in course of collection" account refer to the value of checks that have been deposited in banks but have not yet been "cleared." This latter term refers to the process whereby a bank in which a check has been deposited obtains the corresponding amount of funds in payment of the check from the bank on which it has been drawn. This is accomplished through a nationwide check-clearing system conducted by the Federal Reserve, or through various regional or local clearinghouse arrangements.

Table   5-1

Assets and liabilities of domestically chartered commercial banks as of
December 1982, in $billions

Assets		Liabilities and Capital	
Cash assets:		Deposits:	
Currency and coin	20.4	Demand deposits	323.7
Reserves in Federal		Savings deposits	360.8
Reserve Bank	23.7	Time deposits	654.7
		Total deposits	1,339.3
Balances with			
depository			
institutions	67.8		
Cash items in course			
of collection	55.9		
Total cash assets	167.9	Borrowings	221.5
U.S. Government		Other liabilities	106.1
securities	136.1		
		Residual (including	
		Capital)	131.4
Other securities	241.3		
Loans	993.1		
Other assets	259.9		
		Total liabilities	
Total assets	1,798.2	and Capital	1,798.2

Source: *Federal Reserve Bulletin,* February 1983, p. A18. Amounts may not add to totals
because of rounding.

    The distinction between demand, savings, and time deposits as de-
scribed on the liabilities side of the balance sheet has already been mentioned in earlier contexts. The reserves that the banks are required to
hold against demand deposits are somewhat larger than those required
to be held against other forms of deposits.

    A number of points in this summarized balance sheet give it a kin-
ship with the conceptual balance sheets of the goldsmiths. First, the
reserves of the banks, including for this purpose the currency and coin
and the reserves held at the Federal Reserve Bank, together amount to
some $44.1 billion. This represents only about 3.3 percent of the banks'
total deposits. This is a clear example of what was described earlier as
fractional reserve banking. Further, the banks' total cash assets amount
to only 9.3 percent of their total assets. Holdings of government securities
account for 7.6 percent of total assets, and other securities for 13.4 percent.
By far the largest assets item is the composite item here shown as Loans
(including loans to commercial, industrial, and personal borrowers). This
amounts to $993.1 billion and accounts for 55.2 percent of the banks' total
assets.

Present-day banks differ from the goldsmiths in that they are no longer permitted to issue their own notes. During the nineteenth century some very fascinating episodes of financial history occurred as a result of private bank issues of notes. Frequently the banks issued much larger amounts of notes than they could possibly redeem in specie or other legal tender when they were called upon to do so. Liquidity crises and financial panics occurred as a result, and the measures adopted to deal with them make exciting reading.[4] But since the establishment of the Federal Reserve System by the Federal Reserve Act of 1913, and the amendment of its provisions in the 1930s, the nation's note-issuing authority has been located with the Federal Reserve Bank.

AN EXPANDED VIEW OF BANKS AND OTHER FINANCIAL INTERMEDIARIES

The savings-investment process

The banks, the nonbank depository institutions, and certain other financial institutions all perform important intermediary functions in the savings-investment process. The perspective we need on that process, and on the role played within it by the financial institutions, can best be achieved by asking a number of questions. First, what are the sources of savings, the flows of which are reflected in the money flows we are about to consider? Second, what, in addition to such savings generated out of incomes, might also constitute a source of loanable funds and thereby be reflected again in money flows? Third, what are the principal reasons why loanable funds are demanded, or who, in other words, are the principal borrowers into whose hands the money flows are channeled? And finally, how do the operations of the banks and other financial institutions actually facilitate this money flow process?

Individuals who receive incomes face a number of questions relating to the disposal of that income. After the payment of taxes, they can spend all their income immediately on consumption goods, or they can save a part of it in order to be able to make consumption expenditures in excess of income at some future date. Or these individuals' current consumption may actually exceed their present income if they are prepared to finance the increased consumption by borrowing funds for that purpose. Individuals also face the question of how they will dispose of the amount, if any, they have saved. They may invest it directly by lending it to industrial or personal borrowers with whom they may be familiar. Or they may

---

[4] See J. K. Galbraith, *Money: Whence It Came, Where It Went* (Boston: Houghton Mifflin, 1975).

accomplish the same direct investment by purchasing newly issued common stocks or debt securities of industrial corporations. Or they may lend their savings directly to the government by purchasing savings bonds or other government securities.

Apart, however, from such forms of direct investment, the individual savers may prefer to place their savings in the hands of a depository institution, such as a savings and loan association, mutual savings bank, or credit union. Or they may simply leave the money equivalent of their savings on deposit at their local commercial bank. Or they may place their savings in the hands of such other savings institutions as pension funds, life insurance companies, or mutual funds. In such cases the financial institution will be able, if it chooses to do so, to relend the savings funds in any of many different kinds of investment opportunities. What we refer to as indirect investment has then occurred.

In addition to savings generated by individual income earners, savings are also made by corporations, who may appear on both sides of the savings-investment equation. They demand loanable funds in order to finance investment expenditures, and they provide savings in two important ways. First, the amounts they deduct from their income each year as depreciation allowances (which are deductible, according to the income tax law, before taxable income is calculated) are set aside and accumulated to replace capital equipment in the future. While those depreciation funds, or capital replacement reserves, are being accumulated, they are invested in income-earning assets of various kinds, and they thereby provide a source of loanable funds of the kind we are now considering. Second, corporations provide savings and a source of loanable funds to the extent that they retain a part of their net income or profits, rather than distribute it all to the owners of the corporation (the common stock holders) in the form of dividends.

The government may also be looked upon as a source of savings if it has a budget surplus. If its total revenue collections are greater than its expenditures, it will to that extent have surplus funds that may be lent in the capital markets or used to repay previously existing government debt. If, on the other hand, the government budget is in deficit, then the government will appear in the capital market as a net borrower, in order to finance its excess expenditures. Loanable funds, finally, and the money flows reflecting them, may come also from a net inflow of money capital from abroad, and from the creation of new deposits by the banking system.

The total supply of loanable funds, LF^s, is therefore the sum of personal saving, business saving, government saving, foreign capital inflow, and the creation of new money. In equation form it can be written as

(1) $$LF^s = S_p + S_b + S_g + F + \Delta M$$

We shall observe some statistics that illustrate the corresponding money flows later in this section.

Similarly, the demand for loanable funds emanates from individual, business, and government borrowers. Individuals borrow to finance purchase of durable consumer goods, furniture, automobiles, and other heavy items, and to acquire houses or other residential accommodation, or to add to their money balances. Businesses raise investable funds to finance the acquisition of fixed capital equipment, working capital assets such as materials, accounts receivable, and cash accounts, and to add to their investment in land, building, and other fixtures. Expressing investment, I, on this gross aggregate loanable funds basis, we can establish a final savings-investment equation in the form

$$(2) \qquad\qquad\qquad S + \Delta M = I$$

The total demand for loanable funds, this equation says, will be provided for by the saving that takes place in the economy (including in this the foreign capital inflow), plus the amount of new money that has been created by the financial institutions during the time period under examination.

Table 5-2, which concentrates on what we have called the money flow reflection of the savings-investment process, describes the investment aspect of these flows in two recent years.

Table 5-3 looks at the other side of the money flow equation and describes the sources of funds that provided for the total demand of $418.4 billion and $424.2 billion in 1981 and 1982, respectively (as shown in Table 5-2).

Table 5-2 indicates that the government was a heavy borrower in both of these years. Its demand on the credit markets almost doubled in 1982 compared with 1981, rising from $87.4 billion to $161.3 billion as the government's fiscal budget deficit increased and had to be financed from loan sources. By far the largest demand in the money capital markets came, however, from the private nonfinancial sector, whose credit demands fell from $303.7 billion in 1981 to $246.8 billion in 1982, following the lower requirements for funds due to the economic recession that had developed. The data at the end of the table show that while households increased their indebtedness heavily in both years, moderating somewhat in line with the recession of 1982, corporate borrowers also made heavy demands on the credit markets.

Turning to the description of the sources of funds, Table 5-3 shows that by far the largest portion of the total was provided from private sources. While sizable amounts of private funds were placed by direct lending, $101.9 billion in 1981 and $118.1 billion in 1982, the preponderant share of these private funds was what we have already referred

Table   5-2

Funds raised in U.S. credit markets by non-financial sectors in 1981 and 1982, in $billions

	1981	1982
1. By U.S. Government, principally Treasury securities	87.4	161.3
2. By the private domestic non-financial sector		
(a) Debt capital instruments, including residential, commercial and farm mortgages	175.0	168.3
(b) Other debt instruments including consumer credit, bank loans n.e.c.* and open market paper	128.8	78.5
Total private domestic demand	303.7	246.8
3. By foreign borrowers, including bond issues and open market paper	27.3	16.2
TOTAL FUNDS RAISED	418.4	424.2
4. Classification of funds raised by private domestic non-financial sector (Item 2 above)		
(a) State and Local government	22.3	47.2
(b) Households	120.4	85.1
(c) Farm	16.4	9.3
(d) Non-farm, non-corporate	40.5	28.2
(e) Corporate	104.1	77.0
Total private domestic demand	303.7	246.8

Source: *Federal Reserve Bulletin,* April 1983, p. A44. Amounts may not add to totals because of rounding.

* Not elsewhere classified

to as indirect investment. Some $301.3 billion in 1981 and $254.7 billion in 1982 were channeled through the private financial institutions.

In order to focus on the intermediation aspect of this flow of funds through the financial institutions, Table 5-4 analyzes the sources from which those funds were obtained by the institutions. In the light of our preceding analysis three items from Table 5-4 call for specific mention. First, in both years an expansion of checkable deposits occurred. Second, this was accompanied by large increases in time and savings deposits, with small time and savings deposits accounting for almost the entire amount in 1982. Third, a fairly large expansion occurred in money market mutual funds in 1981, followed by a sharp decline in this source of funds in 1982.

We can note also a significant change in the channels of money flows between the two years. In 1982 the share going to time and savings

Table   5-3

Sources of funds supplied in U.S. credit markets to non-financial sectors, in
1981 and 1982, in $billions

		1981		1982
1. Total funds advanced to domestic non-financial sectors, as described in Table 5-2		391.1		408.1
2. Funds advanced to foreign borrowers		27.3		16.2
Total funds advanced in credit markets		418.4		424.3
Funds Provided by				
1. Public agencies and foreign sources				
(a) Total net advances	95.9		115.7	
(b) *Less* credit market funds raised by federally sponsored credit agencies and federally related mortgage pool securities	45.1		60.6	
(c) Net funds advanced		50.8		55.1
2. Private sources				
(a) Private financial institutions				
(i) Commercial banking	103.5		98.8	
(ii) Savings institutions	24.6		24.2	
(iii) Insurance and pension funds	75.8		87.7	
(iv) Other finance	97.4		44.0	
Total private financial institutions	301.3		254.7	
(b) Direct lending by private investors	101.9		118.1	
(c) *Less* borrowings in credit market	35.6		3.7	
(d) Net amount provided		367.6		369.1
TOTAL SOURCES OF FUNDS		418.4		424.3

Source: *Federal Reserve Bulletin,* April 1983, pp. A44–45; and Table 5-2. Amounts may
not add to totals because of rounding.

deposits increased, while that going into money market mutual fund
shares decreased. Here we have a substitution of savings media, induced
by the changes in money market interest rates compared with the rates
that could be paid by the banks on time and savings deposits. This substitutability of the channels of the flow of funds is significant for the
development of financial institutions on the one hand, and for the sectoral
distribution of funds and of economic activity on the other.

What these various developments imply can be summarized under
two headings. First, by far the largest proportion of the overall flow of
money capital funds emanates from private sources. But it finds its way
into indirect, rather than direct, investment. Second, it follows from this

Table   5-4

Analysis of the sources of funds provided to the U.S. credit markets by
private financial institutions in 1981 and 1982, in $billions

	1981		1982
1. Credit funds advanced by private financial institutions (as shown in Table 5-3)	301.3		254.7
2. Sources from which the funds provided by private financial institutions were obtained			
(a) Checkable deposits	18.3	17.8	
(b) Time and savings deposits	82.9	125.6	
(c) Money market mutual fund shares	107.5	24.7	
(d) Security repurchase agreements	2.5	−6.1	
Total private domestic deposits		211.2	161.9
(e) Credit market borrowing		35.6	3.7
(f) Other sources (including insurance and pension fund reserves, Treasury balances, and foreign funds)		54.6	89.1
TOTAL FUNDS AVAILABLE FOR INSTITUTIONAL LENDING		301.3	254.7

Source: *Federal Reserve Bulletin,* April 1983, p. A45. Amounts may not add to totals because of rounding.

that the financial intermediary institutions perform a vitally necessary and important link in the flow of funds and in the continual and satisfactory functioning of the system. The banks, moreover, take an important part, alongside the other financial institutions, in the total picture of financial intermediation and the flow of funds through the savings-investment process. The actual operating behavior and investment practices of the different intermediary institutions will be examined further in Part III.

INVESTMENT AND ASSET
PORTFOLIO CRITERIA

The preceding analysis of the financial intermediaries, and of the function they perform in the savings-investment process, raises the important question of the portfolio selection criteria that guide their investment decisions. We have looked, in effect, at the surplus sectors and deficit sectors in the economy. The former include those parts of the economy in which immediate consumption expenditures are less than current incomes. Those are the saving sectors. Similarly, the deficit sectors are those that make a net demand on the credit markets. Their consumption expenditures may exceed their current incomes, or their consumption and investment expenditures combined may exceed their income plus their previous borrowing.

We have seen, moreover, that a surplus sector may engage in direct or indirect investment. This notion can now be expanded to take account of what are called direct investment securities and indirect securities. Take as an example a debt security or a share of common stock issued by a corporation at the time it raises funds in the money capital market. As the corporation is regarded economically as a final borrower or a final user of funds, the securities it issues are known as direct securities. The investor who holds them is a direct investor. If such direct securities are acquired and held, for example, by a mutual fund, then in order to enable it to purchase those securities the mutual fund would have obtained the money capital from the deposit of money made with it by individual investors. To use the market terminology, individuals will have acquired mutual fund shares. The shares that the individual savers hold in the mutual fund are known as indirect securities. The terminology arises from the fact that the ultimate savers are not investing directly in the corporations that are the ultimate users of money capital. They are indirect investors.

The economic significance of this is that here we have an example of the "layering," or the successive creation, of debt. The mutual fund acquires money capital from individual savers, and in exchange it gives them evidences of the mutual fund's indebtedness (in the form of equity claims on the fund) to them. Then when the mutual fund supplies money capital to corporations, it receives in exchange evidences of the corporation's indebtedness. This layering of claims increases the gross financial wealth of the economy, even though it may not directly affect the total level of net financial wealth or real wealth. By doing so, it adds to the liquidity of the system, so long as the layering of debt does not become excessive to the point of endangering the possibility of repayment on demand. If such an excessive layering of debt were to occur it would increase what has been called the "fragility" of the financial system, leading to possible chain reactions of bankruptcies and defaults in the event of liquidity crises and general economic recession. It is this layering of debt that, in the various ways we have mentioned, contributes to the smooth and efficient functioning of the economic system.

Imagine for a moment that the only line of investment open to a saver was his own direct employment of capital in productive activities. The economic worthwhileness of the joint activity of saving and investment would then depend on what skills, resources, and management abilities the individual possessed. These could all be summarized in the concept of the marginal efficiency of investment that such an individual investor could expect to generate. But clearly, if all savers were thus confined to employing their own funds, a great deal of potential advantages and efficiency would be lost. There would be no opportunity for individuals to exploit their particular comparative advantages in production, and the rates of return they could realize on their investments would be much lower. There would be no possibility of achieving the potential efficiencies that result from economies of scale. Moreover, there would be no opportunity to diminish the risks to which investment is subject by pooling investment projects and taking advantage of the risk-reducing aspects of economic diversification.

When savers place their funds in financial intermediary institutions, they are acquiring indirectly a share in the investment of funds in a potentially wide range of industrial enterprises. Not only do they thereby acquire the benefits of diversification. They also enjoy a reduction of the risks to which they might otherwise be subject. Moreover, by holding an indirect security, or what we have seen as the claims, or the evidences of debt, issued by the intermediary institutions, the investor is acquiring a more liquid as well as a safer security than he might otherwise have available to him. The frequently stated proposition is therefore correct, that the financial intermediaries are manufacturers of liquidity and safety. To a significant degree, of course, and apart from the risk-reducing benefits of diversification that the intermediaries can achieve in their investment portfolios, risk and illiquidity are both shifted from the savers to the financial institutions.

It follows from these several notions relevant to money capital investment that individual savers and financial institutions are continually confronted with the problem of devising optimum investment portfolios. For investment decision makers the threefold criteria of (1) prospective rate of return, (2) risk, and (3) liquidity keep arising for consideration. The task of responsible investment decision making is that of achieving an optimum combination of these three portfolio features. In short, indirect investment can promise an individual a minimization of risk, together with good liquidity, at the same time as it provides an acceptable rate of return. For an institution, the degree of liquidity it needs in its portfolio will depend on the time profile of the maturity of its liabilities, on the regularity of the inflow and outflow of funds it normally experiences, and on the regulations (such as those, in some instances, prescribed by the Federal Reserve Board) to which it is subject. Beyond the question of liquidity, the objective of institutional portfolio composition is that of achieving the maximum rate of return for a given level of risk, or a minimum risk exposure for a desired rate of return. More technical ways of looking at this portfolio selection problem will be introduced in the next chapter.

SECURITY MARKETS

The liquidity of an asset is closely related to its marketability. We distinguished between liquidity and marketability in an earlier chapter by saying that liquidity refers to the ability to sell an asset at any time without loss of capital value. We have already seen that short-term assets are likely to be more liquid than longer-term assets. The latter fluctuate in market price more widely than may the former as the general level of interest rates changes. Different securities can be sold in markets with different degrees of what has been termed depth, breadth, and resiliency. These marketplace terms refer to the volume of transactions that normally take place in a given security during a specified period of time, the size of the market or the number of buyers and sellers that normally operate in it, and the resulting possibility that significantly large amounts of the security could be bought or sold without seriously dislodging the market price.

It is useful to classify security markets in a manner that highlights the characteristics of securities we have discussed in this chapter. First, there is not in general a market for indirect securities, or an open market where they can be bought and sold. But they nevertheless have a high degree of liquidity because they can generally be resold directly to the issuing institution. For example, mutual fund shares can be redeemed at any time by reselling them to the issuing fund. In that case they are repurchased by the mutual fund at a price determined by the market value of the assets in which the fund has invested the money capital available to it. A mutual fund share is actually a proportionate ownership in the assets in which the fund as a whole has been invested. Similarly, credit union shares, shares in savings and loan associations, deposits in mutual savings banks, and the cash surrender values of life insurance policies can be redeemed or turned into cash virtually on demand. They are all highly liquid.

Two separate markets need examination in connection with the direct securities issued by industrial corporations. They can be noted only briefly at this point. First, there exists what is known as a new issue market, in which the newly issued shares of common stock and the debt securities of corporations are sold to the investing public. Textbooks on corporation finance provide considerable detail on the activities of the so-called investment bankers whose function it is to assist the issuing corporation in marketing its new capital securities.

There is also a much larger market for outstanding corporate and government securities. This is frequently referred to as the secondary market, and existing securities are known as secondary or secondhand securities. This market actually exists in two forms. First, many securities are traded on the various stock exchanges, the largest being the well-known New York Stock Exchange and the American Stock Exchange, which is also located in New York. Second, many securities are traded in what is known as the over-the-counter market. This is not actually a marketplace but is a set of arrangements between brokers and dealers who have telephone contact with each other, with clients who desire to buy or sell securities, and with potential customers and sources of financial information. For our purposes it will suffice to note four kinds of securities generally traded on the over-the-counter market.

First, there is a market, which may be more or less resilient, in the common stocks and other securities of corporations whose size, trading record, or willingness or ability to supply the requested financial information has not made it possible for them to list their securities on one of the recognized stock exchanges. Second, all government securities are traded on the over-the-counter market, the major share of the transactions normally being undertaken by a small group of large trading banks and nonbanks that have been recognized as government security dealers by the Federal Reserve authorities. Third, negotiable certificates of deposit are also bought and sold in the market. These are, as the name implies, certificates issued by banks to depositors of funds that remain on deposit at the banks for a specified period of time. Finally, there is an active over-the-counter market also for what are known as federal funds. These refer to funds traded between financial institutions that are frequently ready to make temporarily surplus funds available to each other. Such transactions often involve one-day or overnight loans. The rate of interest at which they are traded, the so-called federal funds rate, is a key indicator of current money market conditions.

Purchases and sales in this market for government securities are made from day to day by the Federal Reserve Bank. Such purchases of securities increase the total amount of reserves available to the banks. This may happen because the Federal Reserve buys securities from the banks and pays for them by crediting the banks' reserve accounts. Or the Federal Reserve Bank may purchase securities from the nonbank public and pay for them by a check, which, when it is deposited in the commercial bank deposit account of the seller and cleared, will again increase the reserves of the banks.

The examination of these and other aspects of financial asset markets are highly relevant to the discussion of banking operations in Part III, and to the later examination of monetary policies and policy possibilities.

SUMMARY

This chapter has examined the "goldsmith principle" of fractional reserve lending and has traced the outlines of present-day commercial banking from that foundation. The dependence of contemporary commercial banking on the fractional reserve principle was evidenced by a brief study of a composite balance sheet of domestically chartered commercial banks in the United States.

The savings-investment process was discussed in order to exhibit the structure of the flows of money through the credit markets. The flow of money reflects the underlying flow of investable funds. The efficiency of the credit markets determines the efficiency of ultimate resource allocation in the economy. Surplus and deficit sectors were identified, and the participation of private investors, intermediary financial institutions, and government borrowers and lenders in the credit markets was noted. The significance for the credit markets of the creation of new money was observed. It was noted that recent changes in some of the channels of the flow of money through the credit markets have implications for the development of differentiated financial institutions on the one hand, and for achievable rates of return and investment efficiency on the other.

Observations were made on the asset portfolio selection criteria of rate of return, risk, and liquidity. The participation of intermediary institutions in the credit markets makes it possible for investors to improve their risk and liquidity exposures at the same time as acceptable rates of return are realized. Distinctions were drawn between direct and indirect investors, direct and indirect securities, and markets for different kinds of securities. Differentiated markets exist for (1) newly issued securities, (2) outstanding securities traded on established Stock Exchanges, and (3) securities traded over-the-counter. The latter include corporate and government securities, federal funds, and negotiable certificates of deposit. The last three of these over-the-counter securities are highly important for the conduct of monetary policy.

The material in this chapter anticipates the detailed banking studies in Part III and the discussion of central banking and policy operations in Part IV, and it provides a background to the macroanalysis contained in Part V.

IMPORTANT CONCEPTS

Goldsmith principle   *Surplus and deficit sectors*
Required reserve ratio   *Direct and indirect securities*
Fractional reserve banking   *Layering of debt*
Savings-investment process   *Direct and indirect investment*
Portfolio selection criteria   *Secondary securities market*

QUESTIONS FOR DISCUSSION AND REVIEW

1. Explain the sense in which the goldsmith principle of fractional reserve banking provides a foundation for modern commercial bank operations.

2. Discuss (1) financial intermediation and (2) disintermediation.

3. What are the respective economic functions performed by (1) surplus sectors and (2) deficit sectors?

4. Discuss the relations between (1) direct securities, (2) indirect securities, (3) the structure of the flow of investable funds, and (4) the liquidity of the financial system.

5. Discuss critically the following two propositions. Economists frequently state that the commercial banks create deposits by making loans. Practical bankers frequently state that banks lend the funds made available to them by depositors.

6. What do you consider are some of the principal factors determining the structure of commercial bank assets—i.e., the relation between the magnitudes of various assets in which they invest?

7. Summarize and explain (1) the principal sources from which funds flow to the loanable funds market and (2) the principal uses for which those funds are borrowed. How would you explain variations in the sources and uses of funds during cyclical fluctuations in economic activity?

8. How do changes in the structure of financial institutions affect the flow of investable funds in the money capital market? Give examples of recent institutional innovations.

9. Describe the principal institutions that participate in the credit market, and indicate the principal sources and uses of their funds. Explain why the commercial banks are to be seen as also performing a financial intermediation function.

10. Discuss the relations between the asset portfolio criteria of (1) rate of return, (2) risk, and (3) liquidity.

6

SOME TOOLS OF ANALYSIS

STUDY OBJECTIVES:

• To understand the time value of money and its significance for economic valuation
• To gain an insight into the formation of investment decision-making criteria, incorporating the time value of money
• To observe the relation between the values of marketable securities, their market yields or rates of return, and supply and demand conditions in asset markets
• To note the meaning and significance of the structure of interest rates, or yields available on marketable assets, in two respects:
    1. The term structure of interest rates on riskless assets
    2. The structure of yields on risky assets
• To consider briefly the criteria for the selection of an optimum portfolio of risky assets

Economic valuation rests on the proposition that a dollar available today is worth more than a dollar available tomorrow or next year or at some other time in the future. This is not simply a matter of saying that a bird in the hand is worth two in the bush. For we may suppose that the expectation of receiving a dollar in the future can be held with absolute certainty. There may be no risk or uncertainty involved at all. In the ordinary course of affairs a dollar available today would still be worth more than a dollar to be received in the future, for it can be invested for the period between the present and the date on which the future expected dollar will become available. The investment will earn income in the form of a rate of interest, and when the date of expectation arrives its accumulated value will be greater than one dollar.

We can therefore envisage what we shall call differently dated money values. We shall speak of present dated money and future dated money. Furthermore, we may speak of the future value of present dated money and the present value of future dated money. We shall pull these concepts together and expand their meaning and significance under the heading of the time value of money. In all of what follows, until a specific indication is given to the contrary, we shall continue to assume that future dated magnitudes can be specified with certainty. For the present, that is to say, we shall set aside the consideration of risk and uncertainty and concentrate on the pure interest rate effects on asset valuation.

THE TIME VALUE OF MONEY

Consider an amount of present-dated money, referred to by the symbol P, which is invested for one year at a rate of interest of r percent per annum. The value of the investment at the end of the year, here designated W_1, can be stated as follows:

$$(1) \qquad\qquad W_1 = P + rP = P(1 + r)$$

This example assumes that the interest on the investment is added only once, at the end of the year. It reflects the most extreme form of what is called discontinuous interest imputation.

If the investment were left to accumulate for another year, the value at the end of the second year could be similarly described. It would be equal to the value that the investment had attained by the end of the first year, plus interest at the assumed rate of r percent per annum on that amount:

$$(2) \qquad W_2 = W_1(1 + r) = P(1 + r)(1 + r) = P(1 + r)^2$$

It follows that if the investment is left to accumulate for any desired number of years, say t years, the value of the investment at the end of that time could be stated as

$$(3) \qquad\qquad W_t = P(1 + r)^t$$

In economics, however, and particularly in connection with the problem of economic valuation, we are frequently interested not in the future value of a present-dated sum, but in the present value of a future-dated monetary magnitude. Present values of future-dated sums can be derived directly from the general expression contained in Equation (3). It follows by transposition that

(4)
$$P = \frac{W_t}{(1 + r)^t}, \quad \text{or} \quad P = W_t(1 + r)^{-t}$$

This procedure of reducing a future-dated sum to its present value equivalent is referred to as "discounting." We can give a more formal definition as follows. The present value of a future expected sum is that amount of money which, if it were invested now at a specified compound rate of interest per annum, would amount to that future sum on the future designated date.

Statistical tables describing the present values of future dated sums are readily available. The data shown in Table 6-1 have been extracted from such a set of tables.

Two points are clear from the table. First, for any specified future sum due on a given date, the higher the discount rate (the applicable rate of interest), the lower the present value. This can also be seen from an inspection of the basic equations with which we are working. Second, for any given discount rate, a future sum will have a lower present value the further into the future it is dated. From the table we can see, for example, that $1,000 due five years from now will have a present value of $783.5 if the rate of interest is 5 percent, and only $497.2 if the interest rate is 15 percent. If the $1,000 were due to be received fifteen years from now, it would have a present value of $239.4 if the discount rate were 10 percent. In the first of these examples, $783.5 is the present value of $1,000 due five years from now, valued at 5 percent, because that amount, $783.5, would have to be invested now in order to amount to $1,000 at the end of five years at the interest rate of 5 percent. The other examples can be similarly explained.

Table   6-1

Present value of $1 due at specified years in the future, discounted (discontinuously) at indicated rates of discount

Years to due date	Discount rate			
	5%	10%	15%	20%
1	.9524	.9091	.8696	.8333
5	.7835	.6209	.4972	.4019
10	.6139	.3855	.2472	.1615
15	.4810	.2394	.1229	.0649
20	.3769	.1486	.0611	.0261

PRESENT VALUES OF FUTURE EXPECTED
SERIES OF MONEY PAYMENTS

We frequently wish to know in economic valuation not simply the present value of a future-dated sum but the present value of a series of such future-dated sums. Let us take the following example from the economics of the valuation of an income-earning asset. Imagine a marketable government security with a face value of $1,000 (the amount, that is to say, written on the face of the security). We may suppose that stated on the face of the bond also are words to the effect that the holders are entitled to receive an interest payment each year equal to 6 percent of the face amount of the bond. In that case this stated rate of interest is referred to as the coupon rate. It implies that the holders will receive $60 per annum interest payment (6 percent of the $1,000 face amount) so long as they hold the bond. We can suppose, to complete the example, that the bond will mature and will be repaid (or redeemed) ten years from the present date. The question now arises as to what value the bond would have in the capital asset market if the current rate of interest were, say, 5 percent. In that case investors in general will be prepared to purchase and hold the bond only if they can acquire it at a price that will make it possible for them to realize a return of 5 percent on their investment.

By purchasing the bond the investors would be assured of receiving in exchange for their outlay the total of (1) $60 interest payment each year for the next ten years, plus (2) the amount of $1,000 as the redemption value of the bond when it matures ten years from the present. We want to discover, then, the total present value of all of these prospective cash receipts. We do this by applying the basic rules we have already derived. Using the notion V_0 to refer to the present value of the bond, and S_t to refer to the interest receipt in year t, we can set up the valuation formula as follows:

$$(5) \quad V_0 = S_1(1 + r)^{-1} + S_2(1 + r)^{-2} + S_3(1 + r)^{-3}$$
$$+ \cdots + S_{10}(1 + r)^{-10} + \$1{,}000(1 + r)^{-10}$$

In general terms, such an expression can be written as

$$V_0 = \sum_{t=1}^{10} S_t(1 + r)^{-t} + \$1{,}000(1 + r)^{-10}$$

The present value of this series of expected future receipts is the sum of the present discounted value of each of the separate elements in the expected cash flow.

This specific valuation problem can be expressed in other terms by saying that here we have the task of valuing essentially two things. First, we have a prospective cash flow stream of $60 per annum for ten years. It is alternatively referred to as a ten-year annuity for the amount of $60. Second, we have the expectation of $1,000 at the end of ten years. In our example the valuation is to be effected at a rate of 5 percent, that being, as has been said, the going market rate of interest.

Statistical tables exist to enable this task to be completed quickly. Table 6-2 has been extracted from such a set of so-called annuity tables.

Table 6-2 indicates that $1 per annum received for ten years and discounted at 5 percent has a present value of $7.7217. The $60 interest annuity for ten years that we have in our bond valuation problem will therefore have a value of sixty times this amount, or $463.302. To this amount we must now add the present value of the $1,000 redemption value of the bond that will also be received ten years from now. Table 6-1 indicates that the present value of $1,000 due ten years from now and discounted at 5 percent equals $613.9. Adding together (1) the present value of the expected ten years' income stream and (2) the present value of the bond's redemption value, we have the actual present value of the bond, or $1,077.2. That amount, then, is what the investors could afford to pay for the bond and expect to get an overall rate of return on their investment of 5 percent.

The reader will have noticed that the first line of Table 6-1 is precisely the same as the first line of Table 6-2. The reason why this is so should be thoroughly understood. More important, we note that the market rate of interest at which the valuation is being effected, namely 5 percent, is less than the coupon rate on the bond. We note also that the computed market value of the bond is greater than its face value. This relationship always necessarily holds. A decline in the rate of interest

Table   6-2

Present value of an annuity of $1 per annum for the number of years specified, discounted (discontinuously) at indicated rates of discount

Number of years	Discount rates			
	5%	10%	15%	20%
1	.9524	.9091	.8696	.8333
5	4.3295	3.7908	3.3522	2.9906
10	7.7217	6.1446	5.0188	4.1925
15	10.3797	7.6061	5.8474	4.6755
20	12.4622	8.5136	6.2593	4.8696

will increase present market values, and a rise in the interest rate will reduce present values.

Market values, that is to say, vary inversely with the rate of interest. A $1,000 security that has a market value in excess of $1,000 is said to be selling at a premium. In the opposite case it would be selling at a discount. The student can prove, by the appropriate use of tables similar to Tables 6-1 and 6-2, that if the market rate of interest (and therefore the investors' required rate of return to be used as their discount factor) were 6 percent, or the same as the coupon rate on the bond, the market value would be exactly $1,000, or the face value of the bond. Tables 6-1 and 6-2 can be used to demonstrate that if the coupon rate were 5 percent and the interest payments $50 per annum, the market value at a 5 percent discount rate would again be the same as the face value of $1,000.

APPLICATION TO BUSINESS INVESTMENT DECISIONS

When business firms invest money capital in plant and equipment, machinery, or other assets, they look on their investment decision problem as one of estimating the economic worthwhileness of the exchange of values involved. *Investment,* that is, can be defined as making a cash outlay now in exchange for the expectation of a future series of periodic cash inflows. The latter, it is hoped, will be generated by the sale of the products that the capital equipment now being installed will make it possible to produce. In much the same way as in our preceding example, investors will want to know the present value of that expected future cash inflow. They can then compare that present value with the money capital outlay it would be necessary to make in order to implement the investment project. If the present value of the cash inflows, also referred to as the present value of the investment, or, more expressively, as the economic value of the investment, is greater than the necessary cash outlay, the investment can be said to be economically worthwhile. This assumes, of course, as we warned at the beginning, that all amounts and expected cash flows are known with certainty. We shall incorporate the problem of uncertainty into our analysis at a later point.

In definitional terms, the economic value of an investment project is the present discounted value (sometimes referred to as the present capitalized value) of the future expected stream of periodic cash inflows that will be generated by the project. Notationally, we refer to the cash inflow as S_t in time period or year t; the discount factor used in the valuation (which will be equal to the business firm's actual cost of money capital) as m; and the number of years for which the cash inflow will be realized (the number of years in the economic life of the investment project) as n. The economic value of the project can then be expressed as

(6)
$$V = \sum_{t=1}^{n} S_t(1 + m)^{-t}$$

In this case we do not include any residual value that might be realized at the end of year n, the final year of the life of the project. We suppose that the assets are at that time worthless. If they did have a residual or, as it is called, a scrap value, then the economic value of the project would also have to include the present discounted value of that residual value. This would in every respect be comparable with the redemption value of the government bond in our earlier example.

On this basis, the business firm's investment decision criterion is put in the form of a question:

(7)
$$V \gtreqless C,$$

where C refers to the necessary cash outlay. If the greater-than inequality sign holds, then on economic grounds the investment should be made.

An alternative procedure may be adopted, using the same economic valuation methodology. In this case we take the same cash inflow stream that is expected to be generated by the project, and we estimate the rate of discount at which it would have to be discounted in order to make its present value equal to the necessary money capital outlay on the project. Referring to this discount factor as k, and employing the same notation as before, the investment decision problem can be set up in the following form:

(8)
$$C = \sum_{t=1}^{n} S_t(1 + k)^{-t}$$

In this case the solution value of k that establishes the desired equality will be what is referred to in the business literature as the true rate of profit on the project. There are actually some possible mathematical difficulties in its computation and interpretation, particularly in those cases where the cash inflow stream might not be positive in every year. If that occurred, then the iterative procedure necessary to establish the solution value of k would give multiple solution values. But these and other problems associated with this rate of return concept need not detain us for our present purposes.

Definitionally, we can say that the rate of profit on an investment project, sometimes referred to as the project's internal rate of return, is that discount factor which will make the present discounted value of the net incremental cash inflows attributable to the project equal to the money capital outlay on the project. The investment decision criterion can again be put in the form of a question:

(9) $k \lesseqqgtr m$

Here it is being asked whether the rate of profit is greater than the firm's cost of money capital. The latter is serving as a measure of the firm's required rate of return. Again, if the greater-than inequality sign holds, the investment should be made.

At this stage of its investment project analysis or its capital-budgeting decision making, the firm can list all of its available investment projects in descending order of their calculated rates of profit. Presumably, other things being equal (and setting aside the computational and conceptual difficulties with the rate-of-profit criterion that we have mentioned but are passing over at this stage), the firm will allocate its money capital first to those projects promising the highest rate of return. The larger the total investment outlay, the lower the rate of return available on the marginal, or the last undertaken, project. An important analytical concept thus emerges. It is what we have referred to previously as the "marginal efficiency of investment."

Definitionally, the marginal efficiency of investment, at a specified level of total investment expenditure, is the expected true rate of profit on that project which is the marginal project at that level of investment expenditure.

In Figure 6-1 the curve shows the marginal rate of profit that can be expected at increasing amounts of total investment outlay, in the sense contained in the definition we have just given. The curve is therefore akin to what has become known in the macroeconomic literature as the marginal efficiency of investment function. Figure 6-1 depicts the marginal efficiency as a function of the total amount of investment undertaken. At investment expenditure of OA the marginal efficiency is k_1. At a total investment outlay of OB the marginal efficiency is k_2.

If the firm's cost of money capital is m, it would not make sense for the firm to cease its investment expenditures at OA. For it would be profitable for the firm to continue to invest from OA toward I^*, as the marginal rates of return on such additional investments would still be greater than the cost of money capital. On the other hand, if investment were continued beyond I^*, say to OB, then the rates of return attainable on marginal investments would have fallen below the cost of capital. It follows that at a cost of capital of m, the optimum level of investment expenditures will be I^*. In that sense, investment expenditure can be said to be functionally dependent on the firm's cost of money capital.

Figure   6-1.

The investment expenditure function

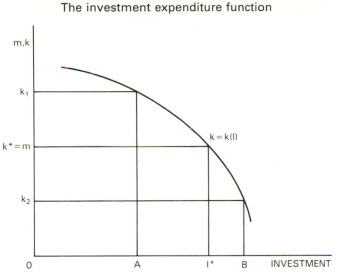

A corresponding proposition holds for the economy as a whole. But some care is needed in specifying the cost of capital. Individual firms, as is again shown more fully in the business and finance literature, measure their cost of capital in various ways, depending on the form in which money capital is raised. In general the cost of money capital will be related in one way or another to the rates of return required by investors, or suppliers of funds, in the money capital market. This, in turn, is related to, or dependent on, the rates of interest that can be obtained on the various kinds of capital asset securities available in the market. It follows, therefore, that the worthwhileness of investment expenditures in the economy as a whole is very much dependent on the going market rates of interest.

It is in this sense that we speak, in macroeconomic analysis, of an investment function in the following form, exhibiting the dependence of investment expenditure on the rate of interest:

(10) $I = I(r)$

We shall see in a later chapter that other important factors influence the level of investment expenditures also. These include the level of output and income, taking account of the manner in which changes in output, and in expectations of changes in output, may increase the need for fixed capital capacity in industry. They include also estimates of the uncertainties surrounding business decisions, the prospects for future price and interest rate changes, possible market and technological developments, and other factors that bear on the developments of markets and market shares realizable by the various producers in the system.

THE FORMATION OF INTEREST RATES

The foregoing analysis implies that the market values of securities (leaving aside for the moment differences of degrees of risk) vary directly with the amount of interest income they pay, and inversely with the market's required rate of return, or the going rate of interest. Imagine, to sharpen our focus on this point, that there existed a government security that promised to pay to the holder of it a perpetual income of $1 per year. (Perpetual securities actually exist in the London capital market. They are known as "consols," an abbreviation for British consolidated debt. They pay a specified annual interest income in perpetuity, without any maturity date at all.) In such a case the market value, making use of the methodology we have already established, can be described as

$$(11) \qquad\qquad V_0 = \sum_{t=1}^{\infty} \$1(1 + r)^{-t}$$

This valuation expression can be recognized as the sum of a geometric series. Let us take the first n terms, employing the convenient transformation: $(1 + r)^{-1} = a$. If, then, these first n terms are summed, the result appears as

$$(12) \qquad\qquad V = a + a^2 + a^3 + \cdots + a^n$$

Multiply Equation (12) by a, to provide

$$(13) \qquad\qquad aV = a^2 + a^3 + a^4 + \cdots + a^{n+1}$$

Subtract Equation (12) from Equation (13):

$$V(a - 1) = a^{n+1} - a$$

Recognizing that $(a - 1)$ equals $-r/(1 + r)$, by making use of the transformation $a = (1 + r)^{-1}$, this last expression simplifies to

$$(14) \qquad\qquad V = \frac{1}{r} - \frac{1}{r(1 + r)^n}$$

In the limit, then, as n goes to infinity (as is the case with a perpetual bond of the kind we are now considering), the final term on the right-hand side of Equation (14) goes to zero. The expression for the value of such a security then becomes simply

(15) $V = 1/r$

In the analysis that follows we shall therefore take this expression, $(1/r)$, as a proxy for the market price of securities, or as a general measure of bond prices. Strictly, $1/r$ is the market price of a dollar of annual income expectation.

We recall now our analysis in the preceding chapter of the money flows through the credit markets, and the issue of various evidences of indebtedness by borrowers on the demand side of the market. There are now two ways of commanding a summary view of the formation of prices in those financial markets. We can consider the supply of loanable funds and the demand for those funds, which we have already discussed at some length. Or on the other hand we can contemplate the supply of bonds and the demand for bonds. Using the notion of a bond to refer to forms of debt or capital market securities in general, the following equivalences can be observed. First, the supply of loanable funds is a precise reflection of the demand for bonds. Second, the supply of bonds that are issued by borrowers is similarly a reflection of the demand for loanable funds.

Making use of these equivalences, we can construct a picture of the working of the bond market on the one hand, and the loanable funds market on the other. For this purpose let us use the following notation: B^d and B^s will refer, respectively, to the demand for, and the supply of, bonds. LF^d and LF^s will similarly refer to the demand for, and the supply of, loanable funds.

The market for bonds is depicted in Figure 6-2. It should be noted that the demand curve is shown as emanating from an intercept on the price axis. This implies that at the interest rate, r^m, at which the intercept occurs, the interest rate is so low, or at a practical minimum, that the public in general are no longer willing to hold bonds. At such a conceivably low interest rate all participants in the market desire to hold money rather than bonds. The demand for money therefore becomes perfectly elastic at that interest rate level, and the demand for bonds becomes zero. This is one of the implications of what Keynes envisaged as the liquidity trap. We shall return to the point in a later chapter in Part V.

Figure 6-2 depicts the fact that the market price of bonds is higher for lower rates of interest. The quantity of bonds demanded becomes larger as the market price becomes lower. In other words, the quantity of bonds demanded increases as the market rate of interest obtainable on bonds rises. Similarly the quantity of bonds supplied varies inversely with the rate of interest. A larger quantity of bonds will be supplied to the bond

Figure 6-2.

The bond market equilibrium

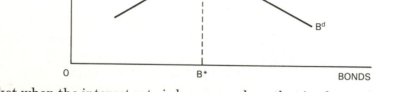

market when the interest rate is lower, or when, that is, the market price of bonds is higher.

Figure 6-3 depicts the alternative way of looking at the same market. Here the supply of loanable funds, referring now to the flow of savings made available out of a given level of income, varies directly with the rate of interest. The demand for loanable funds, on the other hand, varies inversely with the rate of interest. When interest rates are low, the demand for loanable funds is likely to be highest.

Bringing together these two ways of looking at things, we can observe that the rate of interest that clears the loanable funds market, as

Figure 6-3.

The loanable funds market

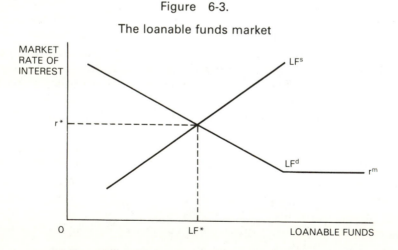

shown in Figure 6-3, must be the same as the rate of interest that clears
the bond market, as shown in Figure 6-2. In both figures this is shown
as r^*. This, in other words, will be the interest rate that just clears the
flow of money capital through the various sections of the credit market.
We examined that at some length in the preceding chapter.

THE STRUCTURE OF INTEREST RATES

The credit markets, of course, and the markets for debt instruments, are
extremely diverse. In the government security market alone a wide range
of securities is available, each having a different maturity date. As conditions vary in the different segments of the market from time to time,
and as the economic and monetary conditions that determine the flows
of money capital change, significant variations occur in the market rates
of interest. Table 6-3 provides a picture of the levels of interest rates in
selected recent periods. By comparing in this way the rates available on
securities of differing maturities, we are focusing on what has become
known as the term structure of interest rates. A curve may be drawn to
depict the way in which interest rates vary for securities of different
maturities at a specific point in time. This is referred to as a yield curve,
and two possible shapes of such a curve are shown in Figure 6-4.

Table   6-3

Interest rates on government securities of varying maturities, during selected
periods (percent per annum). (Percentage rates shown are averages for the
periods indicated.)

Year or month		3 month Treasury Bills (new issues)	6 month Treasury Bills (new issues)	3 year maturities	10 year maturities
	1960	2.928	3.247	3.98	4.12
	1979	10.041	10.017	9.72	9.44
	1980	11.506	11.374	11.55	11.46
	1981	14.077	13.811	14.44	13.91
	1982	10.686	11.084	12.92	13.00
March	1980	15.526	15.100	15.05	12.75
June	1980	6.995	7.218	8.91	9.78
Sept	1980	10.321	10.546	11.57	11.51
Decr	1980	15.661	14.770	13.65	12.84
Decr	1981	10.926	11.471	13.66	13.72
March	1982	12.493	12.621	14.13	13.86
June	1982	12.108	13.310	14.48	14.30
Sept	1982	8.196	9.539	12.03	12.34
Decr	1982	8.013	8.225	9.88	10.54

Source: *Economic Report of the President,* February 1983, pp. 240–41.

Figure   6-4.

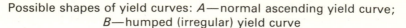

Possible shapes of yield curves: *A*—normal ascending yield curve;
B—humped (irregular) yield curve

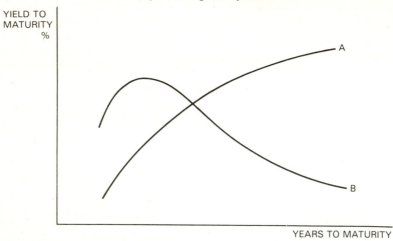

Several points of practical as well as analytical significance may be noted in Table 6-3. First, the data for the early date of 1960 have been given, simply to remind the reader that there were times when interest rates were much lower than they have been in more recent and more troubled times. Second, the short-term rates have in general fluctuated more widely than the long-term rates. This could be put differently by saying that a given percentage point variation in long-term rates will cause a larger fluctuation in the market prices of long-term securities than the same interest rate variation would cause in the prices of short-term securities. Third, when the interest rate structure in general is low, the long-term rates are likely to be higher than the short-term rates. This is exhibited by the data for 1960 and for June 1980, and for the third and fourth quarters of 1982. A possible explanation for this will be noted later in this chapter when we consider the expectations theory of the term structure of interest rates. When this phenomenon is observed, the yield curve is upward sloping, and there is a tendency in practical affairs to regard this as a so-called normal yield curve. Fourth, when interest rates in general are high, a downward-sloping yield curve may appear in the markets. This is illustrated by the data for March 1980 and December 1980. Fifth, for other time periods the interest rate is seen to be higher on intermediate-term securities than on the shortest term, but lower again on the longer-term securities. In that case we observe a humped yield curve.

Such differences in interest rates depend on variations in the rates of money flows to the various segments of the credit markets. They depend also on the expectations held by transactors in the markets as to possible variations in interest rates in the future. This implies that interest rates are affected not only by actual changes in monetary conditions and monetary policy developments but also by general expectations on all of those levels. It can be noted in Table 6-3, finally, that variations in market conditions and interest rates can occur quite quickly as changes occur in the underlying monetary and economic conditions and outlook. The data shown for the different months in 1980 and 1982 illustrate this fact.

THEORETICAL EXPLANATIONS OF THE
TERM STRUCTURE OF INTEREST RATES

The three most common explanations of the phenomena we have just observed have been presented under the headings of (1) the expectations theory, (2) the liquidity preference theory, and (3) the segmented market theory. Cogency attaches to each of these theories, and each has been useful in explaining aspects of credit market developments.

The expectations theory of the term structure of interest rates suggests that the long-term rates are an average of the short-term rates that are expected to exist between the present and the maturity date of the longer-term securities. Consider the following example.

Individuals may wish to invest $1,000 and to have the capital sum available to them two years from now. They will generally have at least two options available to them. First, they could purchase a two-year security that would mature on the date at which they desired to have access to their capital funds. Or second, they could purchase a one-year security, and at the end of one year from now they could reinvest the proceeds of that investment in another one-year security. The latter, then, would mature on the date at which they wished to have their capital available. We can suppose that the rate of interest currently available on one-year securities is 10 percent. It may be expected, moreover, that one year from now the interest rate available on one-year securities will be 12 percent. Let us compute the final capital sum that would be available to these investors if they took the second route and invested in two successive one-year securities.

At the end of the first year their investment would be worth $1,000 (1 + .10), or $1,100. At the end of the second year the total investment would have amounted to $1,100(1 + .12), or $1,232, if the expected change in the one-year interest rate actually occurred. For simplicity of notation we may refer to the current one-year interest rate as r_1, and to the one-year rate that is expected to prevail one year from now as r_2. The terminal value of the initial $1,000 investment is therefore $1,000(1 + r_1) (1 + r_2).

On the other hand, the investors may place their funds immediately in a two-year security. We want to know, then, what two-year rate of interest would enable them to do as well for themselves by that route as we have just seen they could do by purchasing two successive one-year securities. We shall refer to the rate of interest on such a two-year security as R_2. We want to know the solution value of R_2 in the following expression: $\$1,000(1 + R_2)^2 = \$1,232$. This can be shown to be .11, or 11 percent. The two-year rate currently available would have to be an average of the two separate one-year rates, to make investors indifferent between the two separate methods of investing their capital funds for a two-year period. The average, in fact, is a geometric average, the more precise answer in the foregoing case being 10.9955 percent. The general expression for the result can be written as

$$R_2 = \sqrt{(1 + r_1)(1 + r_2)} - 1$$

This follows from the fact that if the two alternative investment routes are to be equally attractive, and the returns available from them both are the same,

$$(1 + R_2)^2 = (1 + r_1)(1 + r_2)$$

It follows that the current market yield or interest rate on an n-year security would be the nth root of the product of the separate n one-year rates expected to intervene between the present and the maturity date of the n-year security. It would once again be the appropriate geometric mean of the n separate one-year rates. The formal expression for the result is as follows:

$$R_n = \sqrt{(1 + r_1)(1 + r_2)(1 + r_3) \cdots (1 + r_n)} - 1$$

In the example we looked at above, the current long-term rate (the two-year rate) was larger than the current short-term rate (the one-year rate) because it was expected that the one-year rate would rise before the expiration of the overall two-year period. In short, long-term rates are higher than short-term rates when short-term rates are expected to rise in the future. In that case the yield curve is upward sloping.

Not all theorists, however, accept this expectations hypothesis as an explanation of the term structure of interest rates. Not all agree that short-term and long-term securities are directly comparable except for their maturity terms. Some would argue that a larger degree of risk attaches to the longer-term securities, and that a higher interest rate is therefore required on such securities as a compensation for bearing that risk. One such risk is that of capital loss or gain resulting from variations in the general level of prices in the economy, or in the purchasing power of money. Another risk is that of the larger effects on the market values of longer-term securities that result from changes in the general level of interest rates. In short, longer-term securities are thought not to have as high a degree of liquidity as short-term securities. They are not such good forms of near-money. For this reason a so-called liquidity premium is required by investors to induce them to hold the longer-term securities. This second way of looking at things is therefore referred to as the liquidity preference theory of the term structure of interest rates.

The third possible approach to this problem we have labeled the segmented market theory. This argues that what happens in one segment of the money capital and securities market does not necessarily affect very closely or quickly what happens in another segment. Different securities, that is, tend to have their own clientele. They are not thought to be highly substitutable for each other. The rates of interest available on securities of different maturities will depend simply on the preferences of investors and the supplies of, and demand for, funds in the separate parts of the overall credit and security markets.

From another perspective, the segmented market theory is relevant to discussions regarding the potential effectiveness of open market sales and purchases of securities by the Federal Reserve Bank in its implementation of monetary policy. If the market is segmented, in a sense that is not given explicit consideration in the expectations theory of the term structure of interest rates, then the Federal Reserve Bank's intervention in the market, in either short-term or long-term securities, may have disproportionate effects on the shorter- or longer-term rates of interest. There may be times, moreover, when, as a matter of monetary policy objectives, it is desired to have such disproportionate effects on the different rates. We shall return to this important point in our later discussion of monetary policy.

THE STRUCTURE OF YIELDS ON RISKY ASSETS

The analysis in the preceding two sections has concentrated on the structure of interest rates on government securities of different maturities. We have been dealing with what the money capital market refers to as riskless assets. There are available, of course, a wide variety of risky assets in different sectors of the market, principally debt instruments issued by industrial corporations and state and local government borrowers. Credit-rating services, such as Moody's Investors Service and Standard and Poor's, rate securities in classifications such as those shown from the Moody's Service in Table 6-4. The table shows percentage yields on

Table   6-4

Yields on risky assets during selected periods (percent per annum).
(Percentage rates shown are averages for the periods indicated.)

Year or month	Corporate bonds of grade			
	Aaa	Aa	A	Baa
1979	9.63	9.94	10.20	10.69
1980	11.94	12.50	12.89	13.67
1981	14.17	14.75	15.29	16.04
1982	13.79	14.41	15.43	16.11
Decr 1981	14.23	15.00	15.75	16.55
March 1982	14.58	15.21	16.12	16.82
Sept 1982	12.94	13.72	15.07	15.63
Decr 1982	11.83	12.44	13.66	14.14

Source: *Federal Reserve Bulletin,* April 1982, p. A27; January 1983, p. A28; and February 1983, p. A28.

classes of risky debt securities in some of the same time periods included in Table 6-3. The more risky securities, those having the lower ratings, consistently offer the higher yields. The calculation of those yields is in every respect similar to the method adopted earlier in this chapter to ascertain the internal rate of return on an investment project.

The rise in risky asset rates of return shown in Table 6-4 is in line with the general upward movement in interest rates already observed in Table 6-3. The comparable decline during the second half of 1982 is also apparent. The yields or rates of interest shown here are directly relevant for the calculation of the cost of money capital to the corporate sector of the economy. It will be clear that rates of the magnitude shown will tend to have an inhibiting effect on corporate investment. Many potential borrowers and investors in the economy find themselves in even higher risk classifications than those included in the table. The maintenance of a high interest rate structure, such as the United States economy has experienced in recent years, has seriously slackened the rate of capital formation and the potential growth rates that the economy might otherwise be able to realize.

ASSET PORTFOLIO SELECTION

Consider the task confronting investors who set out to build a portfolio of risky assets. They will conceivably be interested in two sets of data. First, they will want to know the expected rates of return that each of the available assets offers. These assets might be, for example, the common stocks listed on the New York Stock Exchange or available on the over-the-counter market, and different grades of corporate bonds such as those to which we have just referred. Second, they will make an estimate of the degree of risk to which each of the assets would expose them. They might measure the expected rate of return by taking the average of rates actually realized over some period in the past, say the last forty quarterly periods. But they would be on safe ground in assuming that these historically realized rates of return could be taken as a guide to future possible outcomes only if they had reason to believe that all relevant income-generating forces confronted by firms and industries remained substantially the same as in the past. If such conditions as these were granted, the investors might estimate the degree of risk in the assets by concentrating their attention on the historic variability of rates of return. They would be interested, then, in the likelihood that the rate of return they might earn on an asset in the future would deviate by a greater or lesser degree from its historic average level. This variability might be measured by the variance of the distribution of past rates of return.

At the same time, however, the investors would no doubt be interested in the possible benefit that could be achieved by diversification. This results from distributing investable capital over a set of assets whose prospective income streams are less than perfectly correlated. Investment decision making, therefore, might well be interested in the correlation, or more precisely the covariance, between different asset income streams.

A full description of the techniques frequently used to estimate portfolio risks from these points of view need not detain us at this time. Of more importance than these computational details, which can be passed over for our present purposes, is a grasp of the essential principles of optimum asset portfolio selection. For these principles apply not only to individual investors. They apply also to the institutional investors, and especially the banks, that we shall consider again in more detail in Part III. To summarize, it can be said that after investors have taken account of the amount of their assets they need to hold in liquidity, the remainder of their investment portfolio should be allocated as follows. The portfolio as a whole should be structured in such a way as to promise the highest attainable rate of return consistent with the degree of risk the investors are prepared to bear. Or, alternatively, it should contain the lowest attainable degree of risk consistent with the specified expected rate of return it is desired to achieve.

SUMMARY

In this chapter we have discussed the time value of money and its significance for economic valuation. Analogous with the present value of a future dated sum of money, we have considered the present value of a future expected flow of money, received, in the case we examined in detail, at annual intervals. This present value can be interpreted as the amount of money that would need to be invested, at the specified rate of interest used as the discount factor, in order that as the investment grows at that rate it will generate a cash flow stream similar to that being valued.

Applications of this valuation procedure were made to the determination of both security values and the economic worthwhileness of business investment opportunities. In connection with investment decision criteria, the related concept of the marginal efficiency of investment was clarified.

The supply and demand forces in the security markets were reconsidered, to demonstrate the determination of market-clearing rates of return or security yields. These, it was shown, were directly relevant to the formation of interest rates. The structure of interest rates was discussed, concentrating first on the term structure of interest rates on government or riskless securities. Three different theoretical approaches to the explanation of that term structure were noted. Primary emphasis was placed on the so-called expectations theory, and reference was made also to the liquidity preference theory and the segmented market hypothesis.

A discussion of the structure of yields or rates of return on risky assets led to a consideration of the criteria of optimum asset portfolio selection. Apart from the need to take account of liquidity requirements in asset choice, portfolio criteria have to do with expected rates of return on the one hand and risks on the other. The risk exposure of an asset portfolio, interpreted as the degree of variability in the possible portfolio rate of return, was seen to depend not only on the variances in the rates of return on the assets constituting the portfolio. It depends also on the covariances, or the degree of correlation between the returns on the separate assets. The important concept of correlation between asset returns leads to the notion of economic diversification. This is achievable when investable wealth is distributed over assets whose prospective income streams are less than perfectly correlated.

IMPORTANT CONCEPTS

Time value of money

Present discounted value

Expectations theory of the term structure of interest rates

Security price formation

Segmented market theory

Term structure of riskless interest rates

Investment decision criteria

Marginal efficiency of investment

Liquidity preference theory

Covariances between asset rates of return

QUESTIONS FOR DISCUSSION AND REVIEW

1. Why does money have a "time value"?

2. Explain and distinguish between (1) discontinuous growth and (2) discontinuous discounting.

3. In what ways is the time value of money relevant to the determination of investment decision criteria?

4. Discuss critically the proposition that economic value is always, in some sense, a present discounted value.

5. Examine and compare critically the various theoretical approaches to explaining the term structure of interest rates.

6. Explain the relation between bond prices and the rate of interest.

7. What is the meaning of *economic diversification*?

8. Formulate, explain, and justify a set of optimum portfolio selection criteria.

9. What problems, if any, exist in the use of the probability calculus in the determination of investment decision criteria under conditions of uncertainty?

10. What, if any, is the special significance for monetary policy of the segmented market theory of the term structure of interest rates?

7

COMMERCIAL BANKING STRUCTURE AND REGULATION

STUDY OBJECTIVES:

• To acquire an understanding of the size, structure, and diversity of the commercial banking system
• To recognize the twofold respect in which the commercial banks constitute a dual banking system:

    a. Dual in the sense that some are chartered as national banks, and others are chartered as state banks

    b. Dual in the sense that some are members of the Federal Reserve system, and others are not members

• To note the existence of both unit banks and branch banking corporations, and to observe the relative importance of each form
• To understand the reasons for, and the structure of, bank regulation, and the responsibilities of the various regulatory agencies
• To examine the forces of financial instability and change leading to the Depository Institutions Deregulation and Monetary Control Act of 1980
• To take note of the principal provisions of the 1980 act and the Garn–St. Germain Depository Institutions Act of 1982, the changes they effect in the financial sector, and the prospects for future regulatory developments

In this chapter we begin our detailed description and analysis of commercial banks and other institutions in the financial sector. We have prepared this ground to some extent by our preliminary discussion of the "goldsmith principle" of fractional reserve banking, which led us to the heart of the money-creating activities of the modern commercial banks. But much more detail, regarding both the structure and the functions of the banks, remains to be discussed. Perspective will be maintained by keeping in mind five of the principal characteristics of the banks' position in the financial sector.

First, the banks are private-enterprise, profit-making institutions. Second, they are the principal creators of the nation's money supply. Third, they function also as financial intermediaries, operating beside other institutions in the overall channels through which investable funds flow from the ultimate savers in the economy to borrowers and investors. Fourth, the banks are subject to various kinds and degrees of control in their operations, or constraints or limitations on the extent to which they can engage in their money-creating activities. Finally, the uniqueness of the commercial banks has diminished, as other financial institutions now share in what were previously solely commercial bank functions. A new kind of competitive environment exists. Indeed, competition, efficiency, stability, and safety together sum up a large part of the concerns and characteristics of the banking and financial sector.

We shall concentrate in this chapter mainly on the commercial banks, but some of the nonbank and near-bank institutions will be commented on as that becomes necessary to understand the regulatory environment, and in particular the 1980 Deregulation Act. It will be useful to keep in mind in this and the following two chapters, however, the feature that has traditionally differentiated banks from other institutions.

The difference between the various institutions does relate to some extent to the nature of their assets and the composition of their asset portfolios. More important, however, is the essential difference between their liabilities. For the distinguishing feature of the banks' liabilities is that to a preponderant extent they circulate as money. The demand deposits in the banks are assets from the point of view of the depositors or the holders of them. But from the banks' point of view they are liabilities. A bank is obligated to repay them on demand, or to transfer them to some other individual when it is instructed by a depositor to do so.

The liabilities of what have traditionally been nonbank institutions do not invariably have this economically important characteristic of moneyness. Many of the other institutions' liabilities, such as the funds held in savings accounts for example, or savings and loan association shares, are what we defined in Part II as near-money. They have the property, subject to the financial soundness of the institution concerned, of a high degree of liquidity. They can be changed into money on very short notice, usually without any danger of loss of capital value. Moreover, as a result of recent developments in the financial markets, some of the liabilities of these traditionally nonbank institutions now possess the quality of moneyness to which we have referred. The so-called thrift institutions— the savings banks, savings and loan associations, and credit unions— are now permitted to maintain checkable deposits, in the form of NOW accounts and other interest-bearing accounts, provided such deposits are held by individuals or, as the enabling legislation says, by "an organization . . . which is not operated for profit." Developments such as these are breaking down the barrier of uniqueness between the thrift institutions and the traditional commercial banks.

Moreover, rapid changes are in progress in some states regarding the banking powers permitted to state-chartered savings and loan associations and mutual savings banks. The New England states can be taken as an example. In Connecticut, Maine, Massachusetts, and Vermont, no restrictions exist on the acceptance of personal demand deposits by the mutual savings banks. In the first two of those states mutual savings banks may also accept corporate demand deposits in conjunction with a commercial loan relationship. In Massachusetts and Vermont, no restrictions apply to the acceptance of corporate demand deposits by the savings banks. A mixture of regulations also exists in those states regarding the demand deposit powers available to savings and loan associations, but those institutions do not in general have as liberal powers in accepting demand deposits as do the savings banks. In Massachusetts, however, since July 1983 state-chartered mutual savings banks and cooperative banks have had the same powers as to demand deposits and lending authority as commercial banks. Because those institutions in that state have greater total assets than the commercial banks, the current laws there give them a significant competitive potential.[1]

We saw in Tables 4-1 and 4-2, however, that commercial bank deposits are still at this time by far the most important part of the money supply. At the end of 1982 commercial bank demand deposits accounted for 51.0 percent of the M1 money supply. The "other checkable deposits," which had risen sharply in 1981 and 1982 as a result of the changes brought about by the 1980 act, accounted for 21.2 percent, and the remaining 27.7 percent was accounted for by currency. This reinforces the need to understand clearly the traditional functions and activities of commercial banks. Moreover, the principles of fractional reserve money creation, on which their operations have traditionally been based, are those that will increasingly come into operation in the future in the case of the other depository institutions also.

THE DUAL BANKING SYSTEM

A commercial bank can come into existence only if it obtains a legal charter authorizing it to conduct business. Such a charter may be obtained from the United States Comptroller of the Currency, provided certain

[1] See the full discussion in Joseph Gagnon and Steve Yokas, "Recent Developments in Federal and New England Banking Laws," *New England Economic Review*, Federal Reserve Bank of Boston, January/February, 1983.

conditions are satisfied. In that case the bank is referred to as a national bank. Or a charter may be sought from state banking authorities. In this important matter of the authority to grant a national bank charter, some significant amendments were proposed in January 1984 by a Study Task Force under the chairmanship of the vice-president. The proposals of this Task Force, which will be referred to again below, promise to effect, if they become legislation, a major reorganization of the regulation of the banks and other institutions in the financial sector. The potentially comprehensive nature of the proposals can be judged from the broadly representative membership of the Task Force, which included, in addition to the vice-president, the chairman of the Federal Reserve Board, the secretary of the Treasury, the attorney general, the director of the Office of Management and Budget, the chairman of the Council of Economic Advisers, the assistant to the president for policy development, the Comptroller of the Currency, and the chairmen of the Federal Deposit Insurance Corporation, the Federal Home Loan Bank Board, the Securities and Exchange Commission, the Commodity Futures Trading Commission, and the National Credit Union Administration.

Of immediate importance is the fact that the Task Force proposals would establish a new Federal Banking Agency, to be a part of the Treasury Department and to replace the Office of the Comptroller of the Currency. The authority to charter national banks would then presumably be lodged with that new Federal Banking Agency. In the past the Comptroller of the Currency and the state banking departments have generally applied such criteria as the following when judging whether a charter should be granted:

1. The banking facilities already available to the community in which the bank's proposed business will be principally conducted.
2. The need, in the light of this, for additional banking services in the community.
3. The effects that an entry of a new bank would have on the degree of competition in the community.
4. The adequacy of the proposed capital stock of the bank in relation to its projected deposits (the minimum capital requirement, however, is set quite low by relevant state and federal criteria—rising from a level of only $50,000 for national banks in centers with a population of less than 6,000, to $200,000 for banks in population centers of over 50,000—and being generally of the order of only $25,000 for state banks. We shall note later that the question of the adequacy of bank capital is one to which bank examiners give some attention, and that the Federal Financial Institutions Examination Council, FFIEC, has recommended definitions and guidelines concerning the size of bank capital in relation to deposits and total assets).
5. The qualifications and experience of the proposed managers of the bank.
6. The bank's projection of an earnings level adequate to cover the costs and expenses of operations.

Some indication of the changes that take place in the commercial banking sector from year to year is given in Table 7-1. The considerations

Table   7-1

Changes in the number of banking offices in the United States during 1982

Type of office and change	All commercial banks (including stock savings banks and nondeposit trust companies)					
		Member banks			Nonmember banks	
	Total	Total	National	State	Insured	Non-insured
Banks, Dec. 31 1981	14882	5474	4454	1020	8927	481
Changes during 1982						
New banks	378	240	199	41	77	61
Voluntary liquidations	−4					−4
Suspensions, placed in receivership and ceased banking operation	−8	−1	−1		−5	−3
Banks converted into branches	−246	−116	−87	−29	−130	
Other	−42	−16	−15	−1	−18	−8
Interclass changes						
Nonmember to national		36	36		−36	
Nonmember to state member		11		11	−10	
State member to national			9	−9		
State member to nonmember		−3		−3	3	
National to nonmember		−9	−9		9	
National to state member			−8	8		
Other interclass changes	5	3	1	2	4	−2
Net change	83	145	125	20	−106	44
Banks Dec. 31 1982	14965	5619	4579	1040	8821	525

Source: Board of Governors of the Federal Reserve system, 69th Annual Report, 1982, p. 238.

of profit and loss, economic opportunity, rates of return on investment, and criteria of optimum allocation of investment capital are operative in the private-enterprise commercial banking industry as they are in other parts of the economy. The same dynamic flux occurs here as it does elsewhere in the enterprise system. A fuller interpretation of the data in Table 7-1 will be possible after the economic forces that produce them have been examined. For the present, the following preliminary comments can be made.

Those banks that, as stated above, seek and are granted national charters are required to become members of the Federal Reserve System. Those banks that are members of the system have access to certain services provided by the Federal Reserve Bank. Under the 1980 Deregulation Act the Federal Reserve Bank is now required to make its credit and service facilities available to all depository institutions, and the distinction between member and nonmember banks has become less significant. Those banks that hold charters granted by the state authorities, the so-called state banks, are not required to join the Federal Reserve System, but they may elect to do so. Whether they did so in the past depended largely, as has just been mentioned, on whether they wished to participate in the services the Federal Reserve Bank made available to members. A remaining consideration, now that all depository institutions have access to Federal Reserve Bank services, is that of the principal regulatory agency to which the bank wishes to be subject, and the agency principally responsible for the bank examination (the examination of such things as loan operations, the bank's solvency, and its methods of operation). Table 7-1 shows that at December 31, 1982, only 1,040 state banks had elected to become members of the Federal Reserve. At that date there were 9,346 nonmember banks, all of which were state banks (membership being compulsory for national banks). While the largest proportion of the state banks are nonmembers, the largest of the state banks are members.

The remaining classification in Table 7-1 indicates that some nonmember banks are insured and a small proportion are noninsured. This refers to the fact that banks may insure their deposits with a federal agency, first established by the Banking Act of 1933, known as the Federal Deposit Insurance Corporation. Such insurance is mandatory for all national banks and for state banks that are members of the Federal Reserve System. The details of the FDIC will be referred to again below.

The dynamics of the banking industry can be summarized from Table 7-1 by noting some of the principal results recorded there. During 1982 there was a net increase of 83 in the number of commercial banks. The total number of member banks increased by 145, and nonmember banks declined by 62. Some of the changes internal to the table throw light on our subsequent discussion of the possibilities of change in the banking industry. First, a fairly large number of new banks were established during the year, and only a few ceased trading because of voluntary liquidation. Of the new banks established, some 63 percent were member banks, the remaining 37 percent being nonmember state banks. More interesting is the fairly large number of banks, 246, that were converted to branches. This implies that during the year a number of banks were absorbed by, or merged with, other banks, either because they were encountering financial difficulties or because opportunities for economies of scale of operation, or for improved rates of return for that or other reasons, were thought to be available.

A number of interclass changes can be noted. Some 36 banks that had previously been nonmembers sought membership in the Fed (Federal Reserve System) as national banks. On the other hand, 9 banks moved in the opposite direction and surrendered their national member bank status to become nonmembers. Three state banks made a similar move. During 1982 a net increase of 38 in the number of member banks resulted from interclass changes. In 1981 there had been a corresponding increase of 22, and these movements reversed an earlier pattern of change. In 1980 Federal Reserve membership had declined for these reasons by 32.

This latter statistic points up the arguments we shall make below regarding the reasons why, before the passing of the 1980 act, an increasing number of banks had left or were planning to leave the Federal Reserve System. It was partly for the purpose of preserving a large Federal Reserve membership, in order, as we shall see, to enable the Fed to retain tighter control over the monetary situation, that the 1980 legislation was introduced.

THE COSTS AND BENEFITS OF FEDERAL RESERVE MEMBERSHIP

The benefits of membership of the Federal Reserve System in the past were due to the availability of certain Federal Reserve services. These were provided to members free of charge and included:

1. The provision of currency and coin services (the replacement of worn currency and the delivery of currency as required by member banks who purchased it from the Fed);
2. Participation in the Federal Reserve check-clearing mechanism;
3. The wire transfer of funds;
4. Automated clearinghouse facilities (which allow for the direct deposit, without writing checks, of such items as payroll, social security payments, and a number of private sector transactions such as insurance premiums);
5. The safekeeping of securities;

6. Federal Reserve float (which arises in connection with the delays that occur from time to time in the check-clearing procedure, and which will be explained further below); and, most important
7. The privilege of borrowing at the Federal Reserve Discount window at a rate of interest known as the Federal Reserve Discount Rate.

The 1980 act, however, opened access to all of these Federal Reserve services, including the privilege of borrowing at the discount rate, to all depository institutions. Henceforth any institution that maintains transaction accounts (and is therefore required to maintain a certain percentage of those deposits on reserve in accordance with Federal Reserve regulations) is entitled to the same borrowing privilege as member banks. The act also required the Fed to establish a fee schedule for its services and to make them available to all depository institutions no later than September 1981.

The cost of membership in the Fed, on the other hand, was due to the fact that member banks were required to maintain reserves equal to no less than certain specified proportions of the various kinds of deposits they had outstanding. Those reserve requirements had become complex and quite burdensome at the time of the passing of the 1980 legislation. The required reserve ratios at that time varied on a sliding scale, beginning at 7 percent on the first $2 million of deposits held, and rising to 16¼ percent of deposits in excess of $400 million. The required reserves could be held by the banks either in the form of cash or as deposits at the Federal Reserve Bank. The banks' reserve accounts at the Fed could be used for a number of purposes. Currency could be obtained from the Fed by having the corresponding amount deducted from the reserve accounts. The value of checks drawn against a bank could be cleared, or the amount paid to the banks in which checks had been deposited, by transfer payments that were charged against the reserve account of the bank on which the checks were drawn and credited to the reserve accounts of the banks that had received the checks.

The important point at issue, however, is that the funds thus held in reserve accounts at the Fed did not earn any interest. The cost of Federal Reserve membership could therefore be looked upon as the opportunity cost of holding those reserve deposits, or as the income sacrificed by having to hold funds in this way rather than being able to invest them, or at least a part of them, in other income-earning assets. It was argued by the banks, moreover, that these requirements were inequitable because the funds held in the member banks' reserve accounts could be invested by the Fed in marketable securities, which then earned an income for the Fed. Admittedly, any such income is turned over to the Treasury each year, and it has provided in the past a tidy source of revenue for the Treasury. (Almost all, or some 98 percent, of the Fed's net income is paid to the Treasury as "Interest on Federal Reserve Notes." This payment had risen from about $3 billion in the early 1970s to $15 billion in 1982.)

The reason for the commercial banks' growing discontent with the reserve arrangements was principally twofold. First, the state banks, which, as we have seen, were not compulsorily required to become members of the Fed, generally enjoyed lower reserve requirements specified by the various state banking administrations. State banks, moreover, were generally permitted to hold part of their required reserves in the form of deposits with other banks, so-called correspondent banks, which provided certain services to them in exchange for the deposits. In some cases they could hold reserves in income-earning government securities or in certificates of deposit. Second, in the disturbed financial conditions and in the light of the very high interest rates that prevailed in the months immediately prior to the 1980 legislation, the opportunity cost that the member banks were paying for the privilege of membership had become very high. As a result, the exit of members from the Fed began to accelerate. In testimony before the Senate Banking Committee in February 1980 the Federal Reserve chairman, Paul Volcker, emphasized the seriousness of the declining Federal Reserve membership. He stated that during the fourth quarter of 1979 and the first few weeks of 1980 some sixty-nine banks with aggregate deposits of about $7 billion had given notice of their plans to withdraw from the Fed. This, the Fed stated, would be a loss of deposits greater than that in any full year in the past. The declining Federal Reserve membership, moreover, by diminishing the total amount of deposits in the banking system to which the Fed's reserve requirements were applicable, would seriously diminish the Fed's ability to control the amount of money and thereby the monetary situation.

In the outcome, the 1980 legislation dramatically altered the system of reserve requirements. It stated that henceforth all depository institutions, whether they were members of the Federal Reserve System or not, were to be subject to reserve requirements stipulated by the Fed (we shall return to the details later). But at the same time the level of the required reserve ratio was sharply reduced. It was set at 3 percent of transaction accounts, or demand deposits, up to $25 million, and 12 percent of deposits in excess of $25 million. The 1980 act provided that the $25 million breakpoint on transaction accounts was to be increased or decreased each year by 80 percent of the percentage increase or decrease during the preceding year in the total transaction accounts of all depository institutions. The Federal Reserve Board is permitted to vary the larger reserve reqirement ratio between 8 and 14 percent. (A subsequent amendment made by the Garn–St. Germain Act of 1982 exempts the first $2 million of "any combination of reservable liabilities" from such reserve requirements.) Arrangements have been made to require the depository institutions that were not previously members of the Fed to establish the required level of reserves by stages over a period of years. Nonpersonal time deposits are subject to a reserve requirement of 3 percent, the Federal Reserve Board being permitted to vary this ratio up to 9 percent.

The required reserves of member and nonmember banks must be held in the form of vault cash or on deposit with the Federal Reserve Bank in the district in which the bank is located. However, a nonmember bank may, if it wishes, hold a part of its reserves on deposit with another member bank, provided that other member bank passes such deposits on, dollar for dollar, to a Federal Reserve Bank. The Federal Reserve Board has introduced rules to implement this so-called reserve pass-through provision. Other depository institutions may hold their required reserves in vault cash or deposits at the Fed, or again in an account with a member bank under a pass-through arrangement. Additionally, they may hold reserves on deposit, depending on the kind of institution, with a Federal Home Loan Bank or the National Credit Union Administration, under similar pass-through arrangements.

The upshot of these changes has been to diminish sharply the relative cost of Federal Reserve membership, and to moderate what had become an accelerating tendency for banks to withdraw from the system.

Membership in the Federal Reserve System includes other obligations. Member banks must acquire capital stock in the Federal Reserve Bank equal in amount to 6 percent of the bank's own capital and surplus, though only 3 percent is actually required to be paid in by the banks, with the remaining 3 percent being subject to call. They must be insured by the Federal Deposit Insurance Corporation and, if they are state banks, be subject to periodic examination by the Federal Reserve bank examiners. National banks are examined by the Comptroller of the Currency, though as noted more fully below, changes in these examination regulations have been proposed by the vice-president's Study Task Force. Member banks do, however, receive a dividend from the Fed equal to 6 percent of their holdings of Reserve Bank stock.

Among the reasons why state banks may choose not to become members of the Fed is the fact that they are more typically small banks, and their capital accounts may be too small to meet Federal Reserve requirements; they have in the past benefited from the more liberal reserve requirement provisions that state banking administrations generally specified; and as nonmember banks they are subject to one less supervisory agency. They are not audited by the Federal Reserve Bank.

FURTHER CLASSIFICATION OF
COMMERCIAL BANKS

A further perspective on the structure of the commercial banking industry is provided by Table 7-2.

Of the 14,565 commercial banks operating at the end of 1982, 31.4 percent were national banks, but these accounted for more than half, 57.2 percent, of the total domestic assets of the banks. Only 38.6 percent of the banks were members of the Federal Reserve System, reflecting again the fact that most state banks were not members, but they accounted for 74.8 percent of the banks' total assets. This, from the point of view of the Fed, gave it a firm degree of control over the reserves of the banking system as a whole, and thereby a measure of control over the money supply. Almost all banks, whether they were members of the Fed or not, were insured by the FDIC. Only 0.8 percent had elected not to acquire insurance.

THE FEDERAL DEPOSIT INSURANCE
CORPORATION (FDIC)

The commercial banks, operating as privately owned and managed institutions, can encounter financial difficulties from time to time, in the same way as other corporations in the private sector of the economy.

Table   7-2

Classification of all commercial banks in the United States,
December 31, 1982 (Amounts are in billions of dollars)

Classification	Number of banks	Percent of number of banks	Domestic assets	Percent of domestic assets
By charter				
a. National banks	4,579	31.4	1,070.0	57.2
b. State banks	9,986	68.6	800.8	42.8
By Federal Reserve membership				
a. Member banks	5,619	38.6	1,400.0	74.8
b. Nonmember banks	8,946	61.4	470.8	25.2
By FDIC membership				
a. Insured	14,452	99.2	1,868.8	99.9
b. Non-insured	113	0.8	2.1	0.1
All commercial banks	14,565	100.0	1,870.8	100.0

Source: FDIC, *1982 Statistics on Banking,* p. 19.

Problems of liquidity and solvency can stem from poor loan and investment decisions, from general management deficiencies, and from the pressures of unfavorable, and possibly unforeseen, economic developments. During much of the nineteenth and early twentieth centuries the United States had a high rate of bank failures. To a large extent the failures arose because of the banks' tendency to make excessive note issues and because too many banks had been established during the era of so-called free banking. Adverse economic conditions too easily made loans to local borrowers unrepayable. Bank failures occurred in larger numbers during the periods of liquidity stress and financial panics—for example, in 1873, 1893, and 1907. The small banks, moreover, were frequently unable to realize any of the benefits that larger banks might have enjoyed from economies of scale of operation. Professors Goldfeld and Chandler have reported in their *Economics of Money and Banking* that nearly 3,000 banks failed between 1864 and 1920. Another 5,067 had suspended operations by 1929, and following the onset of the subsequent Depression another 7,763 had closed their doors by the end of 1933.

Against this background, and particularly the accelerating bank failures in the early Depression years, the Federal Deposit Insurance Corporation was established by an act of 1933 and began operations in 1934. Between 1934 and 1981 only 722 banks were closed because of financial difficulties.[2] Of these failures, 490 occurred between 1934 and 1942. Between 1943 and 1970, a period that covered the war years, the immediate postwar reorganization, and the economic growth years of the 1960s, bank failures averaged only 4 or 5 a year. During the rather more turbulent 1970s the rate of failures was somewhat higher. It reached the relatively higher levels of 14 and 17 failures in 1975 and 1976, and stood at 10 failures in each of the three years 1979, 1980, and 1981. During the recession year of 1982, however, the number of failures rose to 42.

Many insured banks, notably those state banks that are not members of the Federal Reserve System, have in the past been subject to examination each year by the FDIC. The Task Force proposals we referred to above recommend that this examining authority over approximately nine thousand state nonmember banks be transferred from the FDIC to the Federal Reserve Board. The examination process consists of a detailed analysis and assessment of all relevant characteristics of the bank's financial structure and operations. The banks are given a rating of their condition and overall operating soundness. The FDIC is, however, apart from possible legislative changes based on the Task Force proposals, only one of the regulatory agencies that periodically examine the banks and other financial institutions under their jurisdiction. The other agencies are the Federal Reserve Board, the Comptroller of the Currency, the

---

[2] FDIC, *Annual Report*, 1982, p. 31.

Federal Home Loan Bank Board (with special responsibilities for savings and loan associations), and the National Credit Union Administration. These five federal regulatory agencies are represented on the Federal Financial Institutions Examinations Council (FFIEC), which in 1980 established a Uniform Financial Institutions Rating System.

The following factors are taken into account in deciding on the rating that the institutions are given:

> The adequacy of the capital base, net worth and reserves for supporting present operations and future growth plans; the quality of loans, investments and other assets; the ability to generate earnings to maintain public confidence, cover losses, and provide adequate security and return to depositors; the ability to manage liquidity and funding; the ability to meet the community's legitimate needs for financial services and cover all maturing deposit obligations; the ability of management to properly administer all aspects of the financial business and plan for future needs and changing circumstances.[3]

These factors suggest that close scrutiny is given to bank operations in the interest, primarily, of economic viability, public confidence, and the need for continuing and safe banking services.

As a result of the examination of the banks, the FDIC maintains a list of so-called problem banks. Banks may be added to that list because of poor loan quality and mismanagement. The number of problem banks declined in 1980, but the highly unstable financial conditions of that year caused many banks to require supervisory attention because of the severe earnings squeeze they encountered. This resulted, as we have indicated in a different context, from the fact that fixed rates of return were being earned on many of the banks' assets while higher rates of interest had to be paid on the banks' liabilities in a period of volatile interest rates. The number of banks on the FDIC problem bank list peaked at 385 in 1976, and after declining steadily it stood at 217 at the end of 1980. During 1982 the number rose slightly to 369. This represented about 2.5 percent of all insured banks.

The Federal Deposit Insurance Act provided that deposit accounts were insured up to a limit of $2,500 when the insurance first became effective in 1934. This insured limit has been increased periodically, and in 1980 was raised to $100,000. Many demand deposit accounts may exceed $100,000, of course, so that not all bank deposits are insured. About 73 percent of total deposits were insured at the end of 1982.[4] But the overall operations of the FDIC do, in fact, provide an element of safety for all deposits, by virtue of its attempt to check on the overall soundness of bank operations. Should a bank fail, even this does not mean that the

---

[3] FDIC, *Annual Report,* 1980, p. 7.
[4] FDIC, *Annual Report,* 1982, p. 42.

depositors lose their uninsured funds. For the FDIC may purchase the assets of a bank in distress, or lend funds to it, or arrange for its merger with another bank. In the case of the First Pennsylvania Bank, the rescue operations mounted by the consortium of twenty banks headed by Citicorp meant that rather than the First Pennsylvania failing, and its depositors losing their uninsured funds, the bank in effect continued its normal operations.

The insurance fund operated by the FDIC is financed by annual premiums paid by the insured banks. The premium has been set for many years at one-twelfth of one percent of the total deposits of the bank. The 1980 Deregulation Act, however, provided that insured banks should receive an "assessment credit," or a refund of the deposit insurance premiums they paid, equal to 60 percent of the amount by which the FDIC gross premium income exceeded its expenses. Many of the banks have complained because the deposit insurance premium is paid as a percentage of the banks' total deposits, not only of their insured deposits. The large banks have maintained that they are thereby paying for an insurance subsidy provided to the smaller banks. For the larger banks have a higher proportion of uninsured deposits, and the small banks have, in general, the higher record of failure. The insurance system has worked well, however, as indicated by the much lower record of failures since the FDIC was established. Moreover, probably about 90 percent of all depositors in failed banks have been paid in full because of FDIC operations.

The proposals of the Study Task Force would effectively remove the FDIC from the sphere of bank examination except for its right to examine banks in financial difficulty. In that case it would cooperate with the bank's principal examining authority. A most radical proposal affecting the FDIC operations, moreover, is that it should have expanded powers to deny insurance, and to set insurance premiums based on its estimate of the riskiness of the bank's activities. We shall return to that highly significant point.

SIZE DISTRIBUTION OF COMMERCIAL BANKS, AND BANK COMPETITION

An important difference between the commercial banking industries in the United States and those in some other countries is that here we have what is substantially a unit banking system. As we shall see, not all states in the union permit banks to maintain branches. Many banks operate out of only one single office. In the United Kingdom, on the other hand, there are only a small number of banks, each of which has branches throughout the nation. Until a movement to bank mergers began recently, it was usual to refer to the famous "Big Five" British banks (Lloyds Bank, the National Provincial Bank, Westminster Bank, Barclay's Bank, and the Midland Bank). These banks between them maintained thousands of branches, and engaged as well in extensive international financial operations. We shall look in a moment at some of the arguments for and against unit banking as opposed to the branch banking system. But the structure of the commercial banking industry in the United States implies that many of the banks are relatively small. Data on their distribution by size are provided in Table 7-3.

Table 7-3 shows the clustering of banks in the smaller-size classes. As many as 85.8 percent of the total number of banks at the end of 1982 had assets of less than $100 million. The largest number of these had assets of between $10 million and $50 million. At the other end of the scale, only 229 banks had assets of more than $1 billion. These accounted for only 1.6 percent of the total number of banks, but they held more than half, 55.9 percent, of the industry's total domestic assets. This suggests that a good deal of concentration exists in the industry, and a high degree of economic and market power is concentrated in a relatively small part of the financial sector. But the banking industry as a whole is, of course, geographically dispersed, and many small banks are serving the needs and interests of local communities with which they are well familiar and which they are able to understand in unique ways.

Geographic or spatial competition is limited by the probibition against interstate banking provided by the McFadden Act of 1927. Full-service

Table   7-3

Size distribution of all commercial banks in the United States,
December 31, 1982

Asset size $ million	Number of banks	Percent of number of banks	Total domestic assets $ billion	Percent of domestic assets
Less than 5	510	3.5	1.69	0.1
5 to 9.9	1,515	10.4	11.62	0.6
10 to 24.9	4,324	29.7	73.17	3.9
25 to 49.9	3,745	25.7	134.15	7.2
50 to 99.9	2,407	16.5	165.34	8.8
100 to 299.9	1,436	9.9	228.26	12.2
300 to 499.9	219	1.5	84.19	4.5
500 to 999.9	180	1.2	125.89	6.7
1,000 to 4,999	188	1.3	392.87	21.0
5,000 or more	41	0.3	653.70	34.9
Total, All banks	14,565	100.0	1,870.87	100.0

Source: FDIC, *1982 Statistics on Banking,* p. 19.
Amounts may not add to totals because of rounding.

interstate banking is still prohibited except in the case of Edge Act Corporations. The latter may be established as subsidiary corporations of banks, specifically for the purpose of engaging in foreign financial activities. They may hold equity interests in other business firms provided the latter are not primarily engaged in United States production for United States consumption. They may, however, finance the production of goods that are primarily for export.

State banking laws and federal regulations, however, have moderated to some degree the prohibition against interstate banking. The Federal Home Loan Bank Board, for example, has recently supervised a number of emergency mergers and acquisitions of failing savings and loan associations across state lines. Similarly, the Federal Reserve Board has approved the acquisition by bank holding companies of some thrift institutions in financial difficulties. The Fidelity Savings and Loan Association of San Francisco, for example, was acquired by Citicorp of New York. But apart from ratifying these emergency mergers and acquisitions, Congress has not acted to allow nonemergency mergers and affiliations across state lines except where they are specifically provided for by state laws.

In New England, the states of Maine and Massachusetts have permitted out-of-state bank holding companies to control in-state banks. The Massachusetts law also permits bank branches to be established across state lines, but this activity is restricted, apart from emergency mergers, to other New England states. The state of New York has also adopted an interstate banking law, and institutions in that state have announced their intention to acquire banks in the New England states.[5]

The prohibition against full service, nationwide, interstate banking has also led to further developments aimed at widening competition in the financial sector. First, early in 1984 the Federal Reserve Board approved a merger between a Connecticut based bank, the CBT Corporation, and the Massachusetts based Bank of New England, and also a merger between the Hartford National Corporation of Connecticut and the Aritru Bancorporation of Massachusetts. A number of other such regional combinations of banks are in progress. Without examining details further, the important implication can be noted that similar regional groupings are now likely to emerge in other parts of the United States also.

Second, it is noteworthy that under the Bank Holding Company Act a bank is defined as an institution that accepts deposits and makes commercial loans. Early in 1984, however, the Federal Reserve Board approved a proposal by the U.S. Trust Corporation of New York that by operating through a subsidiary it should begin accepting consumer deposits and making consumer loans in Florida. As it would be confining

---

[5] See Gagnon and Yokas, "Recent Developments."

its activities to consumer loans, and not making any commercial loans, it would not therefore be contravening the provisions of the Bank Holding Company Act. Again, further developments of this kind can be expected to occur throughout the country.

BANK HOLDING COMPANIES

The prohibition against interstate banking has been overcome to some extent also by the development of group banking, or the establishment of bank holding companies. Such companies have ownership control in two or more banks, which may in turn be either unit or branch banks. The bank holding company may in this way control banks that operate in more than one state. But the expansion of this form of ownership and control was regulated by the Bank Holding Company Act of 1956. This act required holding companies that owned or controlled more than 25 percent of at least two banks to register with the Federal Reserve Board and to be subject to supervision by the board. Their activities were further restricted by the Bank Holding Company Act of 1966. They may hold stock only in banks or in corporations that are engaged in what the law describes as activities "closely related" to banking. Included in this category are finance companies and credit card companies, along with such activities as selling life insurance that extinguishes a borrower's debt to the bank, and activities in which banks have unusual expertise, such as data processing. But holding companies that acquired interstate banks prior to 1956 were permitted to retain their ownership. The holding company device, however, has become increasingly important for banking activities within states. A loophole in the 1956 act was closed by amendment in 1970, and the act now applies to holding companies that own less than 25 percent of a bank's stock but exercise control over such a subsidiary.

The proposals of the vice-president's Study Task Force affect this important matter of bank holding company regulation also. In the past, all of the some 5,200 bank holding companies that exist have been regulated only by the Federal Reserve Board. Under the new proposals, a bank holding company with a national bank (that is, a bank chartered by a Federal Government Agency) as its main subsidiary would be regulated by the proposed new Federal Banking Agency. Those holding companies that own state-chartered banks would continue to operate under the jurisdiction of the Federal Reserve Board. This would have the effect of transferring some 1,400 bank holding companies from the jurisdiction of the Fed to that of the Federal Banking Agency.

The group banking or multibank holding company development has been accompanied by the establishment of one-bank holding companies.

In the latter case a holding company is established for the purpose of holding the ownership shares of a single bank. This is a device for allowing the bank to diversify into nonbank types of activities, or to become, as the language of the market puts it, more nearly a department store of finance. Considerable expansion of one-bank holding companies occurred in the 1960s, and Federal Reserve data suggest that such companies now hold more than one-third of the total deposits in the commercial banks. Many economists have thought that this rapid expansion of the one-bank holding company form might have adverse effects on the industry. Not only might it raise conflicts of interest in bank managements, but it might affect the soundness of banks as diversification into more risky ventures occurred. Moreover, it was thought that this development could lead to undue concentration of market power and to unfair competition. As a result, the one-bank holding companies were brought under the provisions of the 1956 act by an amendment of 1970. Now the multibank and the one-bank holding companies are restricted to the same kinds of activities, which are prescribed by the Federal Reserve Board. We shall observe further implications of the one-bank holding company in our discussion in Chapter 8 of the commercial banks' asset and liability management. Essentially, the holding company can be used as a means of acquiring funds for its commercial bank subsidiary by selling commercial paper (in effect issuing short-term debt) in the short-term money market. In this way it diminishes the commercial bank's liquidity management problem by increasing its command over deposit funds, and by so doing permits it to finance loans and other asset investments more readily.

The degrees and forms of competition in the banking industry can be expected to undergo further rapid change in the 1980s. As the uniqueness of the traditional commercial banks is broken down, and the banks and other financial institutions offer similar kinds of services, the competition between them will increase and new forms of one-stop banking, or one-stop shopping for financial services, will result. We can expect that in spite of continuing opposition, a movement to interstate banking may well develop also, and arguments for the repeal of the McFadden Act will increase. This may even have been anticipated to some extent in the arrangements that such large banks as Chase Manhattan, Morgan Guaranty, and Philadelphia National, members of the Citicorp consortium that rescued the First Pennsylvania Bank, were prepared to accept. The terms of the support operations gave those banks stock warrants representing 20 million common shares of First Pennsylvania stock. The warrants were exercisable at $3 per share. At the time these arrangements were made the stock was selling for more than $5 per share, thereby giving the warrants an immediate real value of more than $2. If the First Pennsylvania should recover and realize good trading results in the future, the warrants, which are exercisable for some years in the future, would become very valuable. But more important, the holding of such shares would give the out-of-state banks a valuable interstate investment if interstate banking activities should become permissible.

CORRESPONDENT BANKING

Table 7-4 indicates that about half the banks in the United States are unit banks, or banks that maintain only a single office. Many of them are small, as suggested by Table 7-3, and serve mainly a local community. Within their own geographical areas, however, such small banks may establish a degree of quasi-monopoly power. The limitation on branch banking in many states, though it was introduced in order to restrict the danger of excessive concentration of power and control over the banking industry's resources, also helps to foster pockets of local banking monopoly. The ability of the smaller localized bank to provide a full range of services is assisted by the existence of correspondent bank relations.

This is an arrangement whereby one bank, known as the *respondent*, maintains deposits with a larger bank or a bank in a different geograph-

Table   7-4

Number of insured commercial banks and banking offices in the United States, December 31, 1982

Type of bank	Unit banks	Banks operating branches	Total number of banks	Unit banks as % of total banks	Number of branches	Total number of offices	Unit banks as % of total offices
Member banks	2755	2863	5618	49.0	25303	30921	8.9
a. National	2244	2334	4578	49.0	20289	24867	9.0
b. State	511	529	1040	49.0	5014	6054	8.4
Nonmember banks	4678	4155	8833	53.0	14481	23314	20.1
Total number of offices	7433	7018	14451	51.4	39784	54235	13.7

Source: FDIC, *1982 Statistics on Banking*, p. 10.

Note: Branches include all offices of a bank other than its head office at which deposits are received, checks paid, or money lent. Banking facilities separate from a banking house, banking facilities at government establishments, offices, agencies, paying or receiving stations, drive-in facilities, and other facilities operated for limited purposes are defined as branches under the Federal Deposit Insurance Act, section 3 (o), regardless of the fact that in certain states, including several that prohibit the operation of branches, such limited facilities are not considered branches within the meaning of state law.

ical center, known as the *correspondent* bank. The larger banks in the important financial centers of New York and Chicago act as correspondents for large numbers of banks throughout the country. The *Annual Report* of the Federal Reserve Board for 1982 indicates that at June 30, 1982, the total interbank deposits held by insured commercial banks amounted to more than $60 billion.[6]

The banks holding these correspondent balances act as agents for the respondent banks in several ways, thus enabling the latter to provide a wider range of services than would otherwise be possible. The correspondent banks may provide check-clearing and collection facilities, supply security analysis advice, assist in making foreign payments, and make loans to the respondent banks. In addition, they may participate in loans to respondent bank customers, in cases where the respondent bank has insufficient resources to handle a large loan demand alone. In earlier times the reserve requirements of some state authorities permitted state banks to count such deposits with correspondent banks as part of their required reserves. Under the provisions of the Monetary Control Act of 1980 all banks, whether members of the Federal Reserve or not, are subject to the same reserve requirements. But required reserves may still be held by nonmember banks in the form of correspondent deposits, provided the correspondent bank passes them on, dollar for dollar, to a Federal Reserve Bank.

UNIT BANKS VERSUS BRANCH BANKING

Table 7-4 indicates that at the end of 1982 the United States had 14,451 insured commercial banks, of which 7,433, or 51.4 percent, were unit banks. The remaining 7,018 banks operated a total of 39,784 branches.

Unit banks accounted for slightly less than 50 percent of both the national and the state member banks, and for somewhat more than 50 percent of the nonmember banks. The member banks tended to maintain a larger number of branches per bank than did the nonmember banks. The unit banks accordingly accounted for just over 8 percent of all banking offices (defined for FDIC purposes as indicated in the footnote to Table 7-4) of member banks, but for over 20 percent of the offices of nonmember banks.

Branch banking laws differ widely among the various states. Some states permit unlimited branching within the state, while others impose various limitations on the establishment of branches. They may permit branches within the same city as the head office, or in contiguous counties. Other states permit no branches to be established at all, and they are

---

[6] Federal Reserve Board, *Annual Report*, 1982, p. 233.

referred to in Table 7-5 as unit banking states. Unit banking is found mainly in the midwestern states. Limited branching occurs principally in the eastern states, with some states there permitting statewide branching. New York is a notable example of the latter. It is in the western states that unlimited or statewide branching is mainly found.

The state banking laws apply, in regard to the establishment of branches, to national banks located in that state, as well as to state banks. The historic emphasis on the unit bank form of banking in the United States was undoubtedly due to the traditions of free enterprise, and to the existence of a "free banking" tradition in which any person could establish a bank subject to his being able to acquire the necessary capital and obtain a charter from the appropriate authorities. Of course the era of free banking virtually came to an end in the reconstruction of the banking industry that was effected by the Federal Reserve Act of 1913, the further banking legislation of the 1930s, such subsequent legislation as the bank holding company acts we have already noted, and the later amendments to them. But banks can be, and are still being, established by adventurous entrepreneurs. It has been widely thought in the United States that an adherence to the unit banking principle would prevent the undue concentration of financial and economic power. Moreover, the tendency to favor historically the establishment of a large number of small, competing, decentralized banking institutions has been consistent with the traditional preference for that same kind of organizational arrangement in industrial and economic affairs in general.

It has been argued on the contrary that small banks may not be able to achieve the economies of scale that would facilitate economically efficient operation, and that the public interest would not be adequately served as a result. It was thought that some protection against the worst kinds of financial panics that hit the economy throughout the latter half of the nineteenth century might be able to be better contained if larger banking entities were permitted. The benefits to be found in diversification exist in banking, as in other industries. These considerations point in the direction of branch banking. They are supported by the fact that a branch bank may have access to larger supplies of investable funds on application to its head office, and via the collaboration of the branch network. Moreover, branch banking makes it easier for a loan officer to say no to a loan applicant when that is necessary on grounds of prudence or economic wisdom. The local manager can always plead the pressure or constraints of head office policy. Branch banking, finally, may make it easier to manage the liquidity problems of local branches, and the overall problem of bank failure would thereby be diminished. A better degree of overall financial stability might occur as a result.

On the other hand, opponents of branch banking have argued that it would draw funds away from local areas, and that if all loan decisions are in local hands a better understanding of the need for loan projects and the economic viability of them would exist. Local people, it is argued, know local needs better. Decisions would be made more quickly, no unnecessary time having to be wasted by reference to the head office. Moreover, it is claimed, the local bank can generally be expected to be able to meet regular demands for funds, by virtue of the availability to it of participation loans in which correspondent banks join with the local unit bank.

Against all of these arguments must be set the fact that in recent years there has been a movement of both industry and population from the cities to the suburban rings, and even to different geographical regions of the country. Banking services must necessarily accompany this relocation. If city banks are prohibited from moving branches to the suburbs, this will mean that the competitive position of local unit banks is considerably enhanced. A quasi-monopoly in one-bank communities may result, to the disadvantage of the emerging population and industrial base that may be developing there. Pointers in the direction of increased branch banking are found in the fact that more intensive degrees of competition are emerging in the financial sector. This can be expected to develop further in the future as the "one-stop banking" and the "department store of finance" concepts are more widely implemented. This is likely to follow also from technological breakthroughs in electronic banking devices, automatic check-cashing facilities, and customer-bank communication terminals (CBCTs) which permit customers to make deposits, withdraw from their accounts, and transfer funds from their own to other individuals' accounts. Such CBCTs may increasingly be located in the future in shopping centers, transportation terminals, and factories and on university campuses.

It seems safe to say that public sentiment is moving toward the extension of branch banking. Public opinion seems to have been impressed by arguments for the benefits of diversification and the economies of scale achievable in branch banking. A picture of the present state laws in relation to branch banking, and of the structure in the commercial banking industry that has resulted, is provided in Table 7-5.

THE BACKGROUND TO BANKING REGULATION

We have already commented on the question of bank regulation in various ways, as that has been necessary to clarify the structure of the banking industry. The basic objective of bank regulation is to maintain a safe, efficient, stable, and competitive commercial banking system. The regulatory responsibilities have in the past been divided, we have seen, between the Comptroller of the Currency, the Federal Reserve Board, the

Table   7-5

Commercial banking structure

Unit banks and total number of offices of banks with branches (including the main office) by State, December 1982
The numbers in parentheses are, respectively, the number of unit banks and the number of offices of banks with branches.

States with statewide branch banking
Alaska (2, 127); Arizona (21, 621); California (157, 4747); Connecticut (6, 666); Delaware (18, 162); Washington, D.C. (6, 176); Hawaii (3, 181); Idaho (5, 283); Maine (2, 349); Maryland (11, 1116); Nevada (6, 171); New Jersey (16, 1780); New York (192, 3424); N. Carolina (13, 1852); Oregon (50, 653); Rhode Island (2, 248); S. Carolina (16, 835); S. Dakota (100, 213); Utah (24, 371); Vermont (3, 205); Virginia (45, 1623); Washington (44, 925).

States with limited branch banking
Alabama (117, 833); Arkansas (97, 576); Florida (154, 1957); Georgia (149, 1196); Indiana (107, 1488); Iowa (363, 800); Kentucky (113, 966); Louisiana (69, 1053); Massachusetts (22, 1115); Michigan (57, 2457); Mississippi (28, 871); New Hampshire (16, 240); New Mexico (24, 332); Ohio (92, 2532); Pennsylvania (98, 2887); Tennessee (78, 1260); Wisconsin (378, 714).

States with unit banking
Colorado (432, 198); Illinois (807, 1111); Kansas (483, 346); Minnesota (526, 552); Missouri (366, 864); Montana (143, 52); Nebraska (381, 219); N. Dakota (100, 202); Oklahoma (386, 266); Texas (1339, 569); W. Virginia (161, 164); Wyoming (108, 8).

Total 50 States and Washington, D.C. (7936, 46556).

Source: FDIC *1982 Statistics on Banking,* pp. 10–18.
Note: See footnote to Table 7-4.

Federal Deposit Insurance Corporation, and the various state banking authorities. These various authorities have cooperated in establishing a Uniform Financial Institutions Rating System, adopted by the five members of the Federal Financial Institutions Examination Council (FFIEC). Collecting together their several responsibilities, these regulatory agencies together supervise the banking industry in the following ways:

1. Regulation of entry into banking by the granting of charters, by the U.S. Comptroller of the Currency or by some other authorized federal agency or the appropriate state banking authorities.
2. Regulation of branch banking, which varies from one state to another, the national banks being subject to the branching regulations of the state in which they operate. Interstate branching is prohibited.
3. Regulation of bank holding companies, and also of mergers that are subject to the Sherman and Clayton Antitrust Acts.
4. Regulation of the kinds of activities in which multibank and one-bank holding companies may engage.

5. Specification of requirements for deposit insurance, and the provision of insurance facilities through the FDIC.
6. Periodic examination of bank asset portfolios and other matters related to bank operations, and the prohibition of certain types of assets from bank investments, such as common stocks or real estate.
7. Regulation of permissible rates of interest on bank savings accounts, and the prohibition of interest payments on demand deposit accounts. (These regulations have recently been amended in important ways by the 1980 legislation summarized below.)

Regulation in the interest of safety stems from the nation's experience with the relatively unstructured banking system of the nineteenth and early twentieth centuries, when recurring panics, liquidity crises, and financial dislocations occurred. The all-too-frequent experience of bank failures during the worst of the Depression years in the 1930s also argued for regulation to meet the objective of safety. In the outcome, this has been met by the establishment of the FDIC and, most important, by the regular procedures for bank examinations.

But the objective of safety can conflict with that of efficiency. In our free-enterprise system economic activities promise reward in relation to the risks undertaken. This risk-return relation, and the need for the adoption of a prudent trade-off between risk and return, apply to the banking industry as they do to other sectors of the economy. The highly significant difference in the case of the banking industry is, of course, that here the public interest is directly and pervasively involved in a unique way. For the banks are the providers of the nation's money supply. In return for the income they make from that socially important activity, they are under obligation to conduct their affairs with an eye to the public interest as well as to their own profit. It is to help them in this direction, and even, perhaps, to save them from themselves in their approach to certain economic opportunities, that bank examination procedures are designed.

Some economists assert that the objective of safety can be overemphasized. Corporate failures, it is argued, perform the useful economic function of weeding out inefficient managements. For that reason we perhaps have too few bank failures. Of course, proponents of such views need to distinguish between the need to protect the public and the depositors, on the one hand, and the need to protect, or the desirability of protecting, the banks themselves. The former, it is said, could be accomplished independently of the latter. If, for example, much of the existing bank regulation were abolished, banks would be free to innovate and take what they considered to be prudent risks in search of profit. Some would doubtlessly fail. But a system of bank insurance, based on the existing FDIC, could be invented to take this into account. Goldfeld and Chandler, in setting out the case for this point of view, have noted that insurance premiums could be related to the nature of the risks being undertaken by the banks, and this, we have seen, is also proposed by the Study Task Force to which we have referred. The more venturesome in assuming risks could be required to pay the higher premiums.

The structure of regulatory responsibilities that has existed in the banking system, apart from the proposals for change made by the vice-president's Study Task Force, can be summarized as shown in Table 7-6.

It is clear from Table 7-6 that a potentially wide range of overlapping regulatory jurisdiction has existed. National banks, for example, have been chartered by the Comptroller of the Currency and have been required to become members of the Federal Reserve System and to be insured by the FDIC, and for purposes of the extent to which they can maintain branches they have been subject to the branching laws of the state in which they are incorporated. State member banks, of course, have not had to apply for their charter to the Comptroller of the Currency, but their membership in the Federal Reserve System has subjected them to supervision by both the Fed and the FDIC as well as to the requirements of their state of incorporation. The intersecting regulatory responsibilities as they relate to the other classes of banks in Table 7-6 can be similarly noted.

Of particular interest is the identity of the regulatory institution that has been primarily responsible for the regular examination of the banks. This important point is summarized in Table 7-7.

The Task Force proposals we have referred to have envisaged, in effect, the reduction of the number of regulatory agencies, apart from the state banking authorities, from three to two. With the creation of the new Federal Banking Agency and the loss of the regulatory powers of the FDIC, the latter body being left to concentrate mainly on the provision of deposit insurance, the regulatory responsibilities and the bank ex-

Table   7-6

Banks under the jurisdiction of regulatory agencies

Class of banks	Agencies responsible for one or more aspects of the banks' regulation
National banks	Comptroller of the Currency (CC) Federal Reserve Board (FRB) Federal Deposit Insurance Corporation (FDIC) State banking authorities (SBA)
State member banks	FRB, FDIC, SBA
State nonmember insured banks	FRB, FDIC, SBA
State nonmember noninsured banks	FRB, SBA

Table   7-7

Agencies having primary responsibility for bank examination

Class of bank	Examining agency
National banks	Comptroller of the Currency
State member banks	Federal Reserve Board
State nonmember insured banks	Federal Deposit Insurance Corporation
State nonmember noninsured banks	State banking authorities

amining functions will be divided between the Fed and the Federal Banking Agency.

It has been recommended that the Federal Reserve Board should retain supervision over about fifty of what the Task Force refers to as "international class" bank holding companies, or some twenty-five having major foreign banking activities and twenty-five other large holding companies. While, as we have seen, the Fed would take over from the FDIC the responsibility for supervising the large number of state banks, regardless of whether they are members of the Federal Reserve System, the Fed would have authority, it is proposed, to surrender to the states the supervision of state-chartered banks and their nonbanking subsidiaries such as brokerage firms and insurance agencies. The proposed Federal Banking Agency would, however, have power to certify which states were competent to accept that authority from the Fed.

If such sweeping changes in bank regulation were effected, a dramatic change in the Federal Reserve Board's regulatory functions and responsibilities would result. The important power to decide what kinds of diversified activities were permissible for banks and bank holding companies would be transferred from the Fed to the new Federal Banking Agency. But it has nevertheless been proposed by the chairman of the Federal Reserve Board, Paul Volcker, that the central bank should retain power to veto any activities that it believed would jeopardize the safety and soundness of the banking system. A two-thirds vote of the Federal Reserve Board of Governors would be necessary for the exercise of that veto power.

Clearly, the highly significant changes in the regulation of banks and the financial sector introduced by the acts of 1980 and 1982 have been only the beginning of still further rounds of deregulation and simplification of the regulatory structure. It is not possible, or necessary, in a book of this kind to examine all the possibilities at length. We can stand back from the regulatory problem and observe that two fundamental questions are at issue. First, in what ways is the ability of the banks and the nonbank monetary institutions to create money and administer the nation's money supply affected, and what changes in insti-

tutional operating procedures occur as a result? And second, what changes
occur in the regulatory supervision of the bank and nonbank institutions,
such as to affect their safety, soundness, and competitive abilities? Variations in the regulatory climate and structure do, of course, affect both
these problem areas. But we can profitably keep separate in our thinking
about the monetary and financial sector (1) the highly significant changes
in (a) the institutions' competitive abilities and (b) the manner of the
central bank's control over those operations as affected, for example, by
the 1980 and 1982 acts we shall comment on more fully below; and (2)
the locus of regulatory decision making and examining responsibility.
The latter, we have seen in this chapter, will conceivably be dramatically
affected by the adoption of legislation based on the vice-president's Study
Task Force.

THE DEPOSITORY INSTITUTIONS
DEREGULATION AND MONETARY
CONTROL ACT OF 1980

Two main influences during the period immediately prior to the passing
of the most important piece of banking legislation since the 1930s—the
Depository Institutions Deregulation and Monetary Control Act of 1980—
should be kept clearly in mind.

First, developments in the financial sector were tending, as we have
seen, to destroy the traditional uniqueness of the commercial banks. Second, in October 1979 the Federal Reserve Board drastically and dramatically changed its policy stance, its policy objectives, and the methods of
achieving them. These two factors combined to produce an urgent need
for something to be done to shore up a faltering financial sector in early
1980.

In 1979 and early 1980 the rate at which banks were departing from
the Federal Reserve System was increasing. This was because the cost
of membership, which we have identified as the opportunity cost of having
to maintain reserves on deposit at the Fed at a time when the rates of
interest available on income-earning opportunities had become very high,
appeared to the banks to outweigh the benefits of membership. The very
high level of interest rates at the time was related to the general conduct
of economic policy. Most notably, a condition of stagflation had set in,
with not only rising unemployment but also persistent price inflation.
The supposed remedy for inflation was a tight money and high interest
rate policy, consistent with what had become known in other economies
and financial centers, notably the British, as the monetarist remedy. The
virtually sole reliance on monetary policy rather than on a mix of policies,

which might have included an incomes policy as well as a different fiscal policy, produced dislocation among the financial institutions.

The thrift institutions, such as the savings and loan associations, were in particular difficulty. They were faced with the need to pay high rates of interest on the savings funds deposited with them in order to prevent the flow of funds they received from drying up completely. But the rates of return they earned on their asset portfolios could not be increased. They held large amounts of investments in mortgages that had been purchased years previously at much lower rates of interest. Their portfolio income could not therefore keep pace with the cost they now had to pay for the money capital they obtained. They were caught in an impossible profit squeeze. They had been given some relief under the administration of the so-called Regulation Q. Technically, the Federal Reserve Board Regulation Q stipulated at that time the maximum rates of interest that the banks were permitted to pay on savings deposits. The maximum rate that the savings and loan associations were permitted to pay on their deposits was actually set by the Federal Home Loan Bank Board, but such regulations, including that imposed by the Federal Deposit Insurance Corporation on the mutual savings banks, are usually referred to collectively in the market as Regulation Q. The savings and loan associations had been given permission to pay interest rates on savings equal to one-quarter of a percentage point higher than the banks could pay on theirs. But this itself, while it might have made it possible for the thrift institutions to compete with the banks for funds to some extent, did nothing to relieve the profit squeeze. For the price being paid for money was still higher than the rate of return being earned.

The banks also experienced the same kind of squeeze. The rate of interest they paid for funds was high and fluctuating, though it was not high enough to prevent the flow of savings to the banks from being diverted to other parts of the money market. Both the banks' savings accounts and the thrift institutions' inflow of funds were diminished as individuals placed their savings funds in such other money market assets as money market mutual fund shares. Some holders of short-term liquid funds placed them directly in the short-term commercial paper market, instead of leaving them on deposit at the banks. This dramatic alteration of the flow of funds in the money market was referred to as *disintermediation*. The flow of funds through the financial intermediaries slackened. Funds were placed, as we have seen, in newer financial institutions, or directly in the investment market. At the same time, some industrial borrowers began offering greatly increased amounts of commercial paper (unsecured short-term debt) in the market, raising funds by this means rather than paying the much higher rates of interest that the banks would have required on traditional working capital loans. The banks' prime rate of interest, or the rate at which they lend to borrowers of the highest credit rating, rose sharply, reaching the region of 20 percent.

The commercial banks fought back. Intense competition for savings accounts ensued. All kinds of gifts and premiums were available to depositors. Some new devices were invented. The banks began to offer ATS accounts, or automatic transfer services. This was a device whereby an individual could place funds in a savings account at a bank, and thereby earn interest, with the understanding that if, at any time, his ordinary demand deposit account at the same bank should not have sufficient funds in it to pay checks drawn against it, the bank would automatically transfer funds from the savings account to cover the checks. These arrangements implied that individuals could in effect maintain zero demand deposit balances and, to all intents and purposes, draw checks against their commercial bank savings accounts. This was, therefore, a way by which, in this period of money shortage, the banks circumvented the regulations of the Federal Reserve which prohibited the payment of interest on demand deposit accounts.

Earlier the banks had begun to offer so-called NOW accounts (Negotiable Order of Withdrawal accounts), which had been made legal in the six New England states, New York, and New Jersey. These were again, in effect, demand deposit accounts on which interest was paid. The banks also in this period began to offer money market certificates, first in denominations of a minimum of $10,000, and then for lesser amounts, paying the depositor a rate of interest closely aligned with that on short-term money market instruments such as Treasury bills. The money market certificates had varying maturities, some extending to thirty months.

The monetary situation reached virtually crisis proportions for many of the depository institutions on October 6, 1979, when the Federal Reserve abruptly announced a change in its monetary policy objectives and procedures. On that date the Fed announced an increase in its discount rate (the rate of interest at which it will lend to commercial banks) to a record 12 percent. It imposed reserve requirements on certain loan funds that the commercial banks had been tapping to bolster their liquidity positions, specifying a reserve requirement of 8 percent on certain so-called managed liabilities. These referred to funds other than demand deposits, such as large time deposits, Eurodollar borrowings, repurchase agreements (an arrangement whereby a bank sold a government security in order to obtain the immediate use of funds, under an agreement to repurchase it at a specified time in the future), and funds borrowed from nonmember institutions. More significantly, the Fed announced at the same time that it would henceforth cease operating in the money market in such a way as to confine fluctuations in interest rates, the federal funds rate for example, within a narrow band. It would instead pay principal attention to the total amount of money in circulation, tightening or loosening its policy stance depending on whether the money supply appeared to be increasing too rapidly or not rapidly enough. The effect was that the rate of increase in the money supply slackened and interest rates rose sharply.

In early 1980 another surge in inflation occurred. The Fed responded by increasing the discount rate again to 13 percent, and by dealing in securities in the open market in such a way as to raise the federal funds rate to nearly 15 percent. The banks' prime rate and the general level of interest rates soared from that point. The monetary situation could hardly be said to be under control.

The Depository Institutions Deregulation and Monetary Control Act, which was passed in March 1980 against this exciting, if somewhat confused and distressing, monetary situation, did not, of course, correct all the forces of financial disequilibrium immediately. The thrift institutions continued to confront serious pressure as the Fed maintained its high interest rate policy. Further dramatic changes undoubtedly lie ahead. But the 1980 act did address the important question of the competitive relations between the banks and the nonbank depository institutions, and it did lay the foundation for a completely new financial climate in the years ahead.

Provisions of the 1980 Act

The principal terms of the 1980 act can be summarized as follows. The main provisions will be referred to again in our subsequent discussions of monetary and economic policies.

1. Reserve requirements To establish a common basis of competition, all depository institutions (those holding demand deposit or so-called transaction accounts), including the commercial banks and the thrift institutions—the mutual savings banks, savings and loan associations, and credit unions—were made subject to reserve requirements specified by the Federal Reserve Board. The requirements were to be the same for all institutions and were set at 3 percent on the first $25 million of deposits, with the provision that they could vary between 8 and 14 percent of deposits in excess of $25 million. The Fed was empowered to set the actual reserve requirement ratio within this range, but it was established initially at 12 percent. The act provided that the $25 million breakpoint on transaction accounts was to be increased or decreased each year by 80 percent of the percentage increase or decrease during the preceding year in the total transaction accounts of all depository institutions.

For nonpersonal time deposits the reserve requirement ratio was set at 3 percent, but the Fed was authorized to vary it between zero and

9 percent. Required reserves against deposits had to be held by member banks either in vault cash or in the form of deposits at the Fed. No interest was payable on such reserve deposit accounts. Nonmember banks could also hold required reserves in these ways, or on deposit with a member bank that had then to pass them on, dollar for dollar, to a Federal Reserve Bank. The nonbank depository institutions could hold their reserves in similar ways, or on deposit with a Federal Home Loan Bank or the National Credit Union Administration, provided they were also passed on by those institutions to the Federal Reserve Bank.

The Fed could from time to time require the depository institutions to deposit additional reserves up to as much as 4 percent of their total transaction account deposits, but the Fed was required to pay interest on such deposits. The act specified that this supplemental reserve requirement could be imposed only upon the affirmative vote of at least five members of the Federal Reserve Board, and if it was deemed to be essential for the conduct of monetary policy. It further provided that such supplemental reserves should be maintained by the Fed in an "Earnings Participation Account," and that interest should be paid on the funds in that account. During each quarter interest was to be paid at a rate that was not more than the rate earned on the securities portfolio of the Federal Reserve System during the previous quarter.

The new reserve requirements were to be phased in over a four-year period for member banks, and over eight years for all nonmember depository institutions.

2. Interest rate ceilings   Interest rate ceilings on savings deposits at all depository institutions were to be phased out over a six-year period. A five-member committee, including the chairman of each of the bank regulatory agencies and the secretary of the Treasury, known as the Depository Institutions Deregulation Committee, was appointed to work out the gradual abolition of the interest rate ceilings. By 1986 the provisions of the previous Regulation Q were to be abolished, and Regulation Q would no longer exist. By that date also the Deregulation Committee should cease to exist.

3. NOW accounts, and other deposit facilities   All depository institutions were authorized to offer NOW accounts to individuals and nonprofit organizations. Share draft accounts in credit unions, ATS (automatic transfer service) accounts in banks, and RSU (Remote Service Unit facilities) were made effective immediately and could be established also by savings and loan associations.

4. Savings and loan association lending powers   Savings and loan associations were authorized to invest up to 20 percent of their assets in consumer loans, commercial paper, and corporate debt securities. This ability to diversify their portfolios was designed to alleviate the profit squeeze from which they suffered when they maintained a portfolio heavily invested in fixed interest rate mortgages.

5. Pricing for Federal Reserve services   The Federal Reserve services referred to earlier were to be made available to all depository institutions, and a fee schedule was to be established by the Fed to cover the cost of providing the services. The act required that, over the long run, fees were to be established on the basis of all direct and indirect costs incurred by the Fed in providing the services. At the same time it was provided that in connection with the Federal Reserve check-clearing services, interest should be charged at the federal funds rate on amounts credited to the banks before they had been collected by the Fed.

6. State usury laws   State usury laws were to be overridden for all federally insured lenders, which include almost all banks and thrift institutions. But those usury provisions were permanent only regarding home mortgages and mobile home loans. However, an individual state legislature could act to override this federal law, provided it adopted an enabling law prior to April 1983, and provided it could certify that such a law was approved by the voters of the state.

7. Federal usury laws   The act established a federal usury limit in terms of percentage points above the Federal Reserve Board's discount rate. The usury ceiling for federal credit unions was raised from 12 to 15 percent, and the National Credit Union Administration was authorized to raise it still further.

8. Investment powers of Federal mutual savings banks   Federal mutual savings banks were permitted to hold 5 percent of their assets in commercial, corporate, and business loans. They were also permitted to maintain demand deposit accounts in connection with a commercial, corporate, or business loan relationship.

9. Other provisions   The Federal Deposit Insurance maximum was raised from $40,000 to $100,000.

The Federal Reserve Board was required to be less restrictive in approving financing arrangements for establishing one-bank holding companies.

Financial regulators were required to conduct a cost-benefit analysis of all new regulatory actions.

10. Discount and borrowing facilities   Of prime importance, finally, was the provision that all depository institutions subject to the reserve requirements of the Federal Reserve Board were to have the privilege of borrowing from the Federal Reserve at the announced discount rate at which it made reserves available to the commercial banks.

In addition, the Fed was to take into account the special longer-term requirements of the thrift institutions, which might be necessary to conform their liabilities more closely to the long-term nature of their assets. It follows that the Fed might in the future be extending longer-term loans at what had previously been an exclusively short-term discount window.

Probable effects of the Act

In the light of the background to the act and the provisions we have sketched, it appears that in the new era of financial institutional competition that lies ahead the distinctions between the banks and the traditional nonbank institutions will be diminished. The savings and loan associations are now able to hold more widely diversified asset portfolios. They can thereby avoid, to some extent, the squeeze on their incomes that they have previously suffered in conditions of high interest rates. They also have new sources of liquidity from the borrowing privileges they have at the Fed. The return on savers' funds can be expected to improve now that the banks and the thrift institutions can compete for them on equal terms

The exodus of banks from Federal Reserve membership has been arrested, and the Fed now imagines itself to have a firmer control over the money supply and the monetary situation. But some economists have argued that the opening of the Fed's discount window to all institutions could mean that it will now have less, rather than more, control over the monetary situation. What degree of "openness" actually comes to exist at the discount window remains to be seen. In any event, the Fed will undoubtedly expect the nonbank depository institutions to exhaust their traditional sources of liquidity before coming to it for funds. For example, the federally chartered savings and loan associations are members of the Federal Home Loan Bank system, which is, in effect, a "lender of last resort" to them, in the same way as the Federal Reserve is to the banks. The Federal Home Loan Bank Board sells securities on behalf of the twelve regional Home Loan Banks to provide them with funds to finance loans to the savings and loan associations. In the ordinary course of business the Home Loan Banks must charge borrowing associations a rate that covers their own borrowing costs. In an emergency the Home Loan Bank Board may borrow from the United States Treasury up to a maximum amount of $5 billion.

THE GARN–ST. GERMAIN DEPOSITORY INSTITUTIONS ACT OF 1982 AND OTHER REGULATORY DEVELOPMENTS

The legislative perspective that gave rise to the 1980 act is reflected in the preamble of the act that states that its purpose is "to facilitate the implementation of monetary policy, to provide for the gradual elimination of limitations on the rates of interest which are payable on deposits and accounts, and to authorize interest-bearing transaction accounts . . ." Much was done, as has been seen, to limit the exposure of the thrift institutions, the savings and loan associations, and the savings banks to the risks of fluctuations in market interest rates and monetary conditions. The new fund-raising privileges and investment opportunities made available by the 1980 act go some way to prevent the heavy disintermediation that too easily occurred in times of high interest rates. And the economic viability of the institutions themselves will to a larger extent be protected. But more, it was thought in many quarters, needed to be done.

Accordingly, the Garn–St. Germain Depository Institutions Act of 1982 was passed with the stated objective, according to its preamble, of "revitaliz[ing] the housing industry by strengthening the financial stability of home mortgage lending institutions and ensuring the availability of home mortgage loans." The act gives the regulatory agencies and insurance funds more latitude in dealing with financially weak institutions, Titles I and II of the act being devoted substantially to that question. It also gives the thrift institutions new capital-raising authority.

Under the terms of the act a savings and loan association, for example, may "raise capital in the form of savings deposits, shares, or other accounts, for fixed, minimum, or indefinite periods of time . . . or in the form of . . . demand accounts of those persons or organizations that have a business, corporate, commercial, or agricultural loan relationship with the association . . ." Further, it may also "accept demand accounts from a commercial, corporate, business, or agricultural entity for the sole purpose of effectuating payments thereto by a nonbusiness customer." Here, in effect, is an inroad into what has traditionally been the demand deposit monopoly of the commercial banks. As is the case with the latter, the thrift institutions are also precluded from paying interest on the demand accounts to which we have just referred.

Of principal importance, however, are the provisions of the act directed to increasing the competition between the banks and the nonbank depository institutions. It provided that no later than January 1, 1984, "interest rate differentials for all categories of deposits or accounts between (i) any bank . . . and (ii) any savings and loan . . . association . . . shall be phased out." The differentials that were in the course of being phased out under regulations prescribed by the Depository Institutions Deregulation Committee, established by the 1980 act, were to be phased out "as soon as practicable."

Additionally, the Deregulation Committee was instructed by the 1982 act to authorize the establishment, within sixty days of the effective date of the act, of a special new deposit account. The banks and the nonbank depository institutions were to be permitted to accept deposits in accounts that were to be "directly equivalent to and competitive with the money market mutual funds . . ." and such accounts were not to be subject to any statutory interest rate ceiling. Moreover, the accounts were not to be subject to any reserve requirements imposed by the Federal Reserve Board on what were described earlier as transaction accounts. In fact, the new money market accounts, which are referred to by different names by the various banks and depository institutions, earn interest comparable with current money market rates. They remain free from reserve requirements so long as no more than a minimum number of transfers from them to third parties are permitted in any one month.

To some extent, the thrift institutions have been successful in attracting money flows away from the money market mutual funds. The latter had grown rapidly since their introduction in the early 1970s. They had reached a peak overall size of $232.6 billion in December 1982, immediately prior to the introduction of the new depository institutions' accounts. By the end of February 1983, after a continuing decline for some sixteen weeks, the total value of the money market funds stood some $48.3 billion below their previous peak level.

At the same time as the Deregulation Committee defined the depository institutions' new money market accounts, it also authorized those institutions to offer a so-called Super–NOW account which also was not to be subject to any statutory interest rate ceiling. The accounts were initially required to maintain a minimum balance of $2,500, the same minimum balance required in the depository institutions' money market accounts, but these minimum deposit requirements were amended in December 1983. They were to be reduced to $1,000, effective in January 1985, and to zero in January 1986. The Super–NOW accounts permit unlimited checking facilities and they are, as a result, subject to the transaction account reserve requirements of the Federal Reserve.

The Garn–St. Germain Act also made a slight change in the reserve requirement regulations we have already noted. It provided that "a reserve ratio of zero percent shall apply to any combination of reservable liabilities which do not exceed $2 million" and that "each depository institution may designate . . . the types and amounts of reservable liabilities to which the reserve ratio of zero percent shall apply," subject to specified limitations. This $2 million amount was to be increased annually by 80 percent of the percentage increase in the total reservable liabilities of all depository institutions.

This new era of depository institutional competitiveness, while it has, as the Depository Institutions Act of 1982 hoped, improved the ability of "all depositors, and particularly those with modest savings . . . to receive a market rate of return on their savings," has increased the cost of operation of the banks. Accordingly, a trade-off in the general scale of bank charges and in their income-earning arrangements has occurred. To illustrate at this point simply the nature of the changes involved, one banking group in Massachusetts has notified its NOW account holders that the required minimum deposit in those accounts has been raised from \$200 to \$750, with the proviso that if that minimum deposit should not be maintained, certain charges would be made against the account. For example, a service charge of \$3 would be made each month, plus 25 cents for each transaction, such as checks paid, other debits, and deposits made or other credits, during the month. The scale of charges on certain other accounts at the same bank has also been increased significantly.

The new money market accounts that the banks and the other depository institutions now offer are available to business corporations as well as individuals and other organizations. Some banks do, however, offer corporations an interest rate on such accounts a fraction of a percentage point lower than that offered to individuals. The Deregulation Committee has restricted the availability of Super–NOW accounts to individuals and organizations "not operated for profit." Clearly, these developments imply a considerable loosening of the previously existing regulations governing the banks' and the thrift institutions' transaction accounts. They instance in a sharp fashion the new degrees of competition in the financial sector. But it should be kept in mind that a virtual monopoly of demand deposits, on which the payment of interest is prohibited, is still retained by the commercial banks.

We recall also, from our discussion of the forms of money in Chapter 4, that the funds held in the Super–NOW accounts are included in the statistics of the M1 money supply, but that the amounts held in the money market accounts are included only in the broader money supply statistic of M2. Both these types of accounts in the depository institutions are subject to the FDIC insurance provisions, a benefit not enjoyed by the money market mutual funds with which these new accounts were intended to compete.

An efficient financial sector makes it possible to realize maximum efficiency in the allocation of capital and other resources in the economy. To employ the categories we raised in Chapter 2, it is likely that the changes the 1980 and 1982 acts have set in motion will result in an improved operational efficiency in the financial sector as institutions compete for savings funds and depositors' other financial transactions. Improved allocational efficiency may also be realized. By the latter term we refer to the improved allocation of money capital to those undertakings that promise the highest marginal rates of return on investment.

Competition in the financial sector can be expected, of course, to weed out inefficient managements as it does in other sectors of the economy. Fair winds never blow for all market participants all of the time. Mergers, realignments, and changes of product emphasis can be expected to occur in different financial institutions. New risks may be undertaken by institutions in search of competitive profits, and a burden will thereby be imposed on the examining agencies we have discussed in this chapter.

It is true that the 1980 and 1982 legislation gives the financial sector the prospect of increased efficiency and competition. But it is also true that it introduces potential uncertainties as to the probable directions of

future developments. Unforeseen, and unforeseeable, changes undoubtedly lie ahead. Not only is a series of further regulatory changes envisaged
by the report of the Study Task Force under the chairmanship of the vice-
president, but pressure for new legislation continues to mount from banks
and other members of the financial industry. A proposed bill (which had
not moved forward to legislation at the time of writing in June 1984)
written in the Senate Banking Committee would drastically extend banking deregulation further and would widen the area of competition between
banks and other financial institutions. It would permit banks to underwrite municipal revenue bonds, offer mutual funds, sell insurance and
invest in the equity securities of real estate ventures. Continuing the
existing trend to the payment of interest on deposit accounts, it would
allow banks and the nonbank depository institutions to pay interest on
regular checking accounts. In addition, it provides that nonbanking companies should be permitted to establish so-called consumer banks without
coming under certain Federal Reserve Bank restrictions. (At the same
time, a bill before the House Banking Committee proposes to prohibit
the entry of banks to many of the traditionally nonbank activities that
advocates of further deregulation recommend.)

While sentiment in the financial industry is by no means uniformly
in favor of such sweeping reforms, and while members of the insurance
industry, for example, oppose the proposal to permit banks to sell insurance, there can be no doubt that further significant changes in the regulatory and competitive climate lie ahead.

SUMMARY

Five characteristics of the commercial banks were noted as a background
to the study of the size, structure, functions, and regulation of the commercial banking industry. The banks are private-enterprise, profit-making institutions. They create money. They act as financial intermediaries.
They compete with other institutions whose activities are progressively
diminishing the uniqueness of the banks. They are subject to various
kinds of federal and state government regulations.

The United States has a dual banking system. Some banks are
national banks, and some are state banks. Further, some are members
of the Federal Reserve System, and others are not. In their organizational
form, some are unit banks, and others are branch banking firms. The
chapter has provided data and analysis relevant to these several characteristics.

The costs and benefits of Federal Reserve membership were examined, and comments were made on the changing trends in membership.
The Federal Deposit Insurance Corporation and its principal functions

were discussed. Various aspects of bank competition were considered, and the arguments for and against unit banking and branch banking were noted.

The reasons for the regulation of commercial banks were discussed against the general objectives of safety, efficiency, stability, and competition. Bank holding companies were seen to be a form of competitive organization that is being more widely adopted. As a background to understanding the important Depository Institutions Deregulation and Monetary Control Act of 1980 and the Garn–St. Germain Depository Institutions Act of 1982, a brief review was made of recent trends in the financial sector that brought the need for new legislation to a head. The principal provisions of the 1980 and 1982 acts were noted, and consideration was given to their effects on the economy and the probable future developments that might follow from them.

In the discussion of bank regulation, consideration was given to the proposals for further change contained in the recommendations of the vice-president's Study Task Force.

IMPORTANT CONCEPTS

Dual banking system

U.S. Comptroller of the Currency

Federal Deposit Insurance Corporation, FDIC

National and state banks

Bank examination

Bank failures

Federal Financial Institutions Examination Council, FFIEC

Unit banks

Criteria for granting bank charters

Member and nonmember banks

Insured and noninsured banks

Costs and benefits of Federal Reserve membership

Reserve pass-through provision

Effects of the 1980 and 1982 banking legislation

Money market accounts

Bank size and competition

Bank holding companies

State branch banking laws

Disintermediation

Federal Reserve services

Depository Institutions Deregulation Committee

Super–NOW accounts

QUESTIONS FOR DISCUSSION AND REVIEW

1. "The commercial banks' principal economic function is that of financial intermediation. But the banks are unique in that their liabilities circulate as money." Comment critically, and explain whether, and why, you agree or disagree with both halves of this statement.

2. Why should the Board of Governors of the Federal Reserve System be concerned whether the commercial banks are members of the system?

Is their attitude likely to be changed by any provisions of the Depository Institutions Deregulation and Monetary Control Act of 1980?

3. Discuss the costs and benefits of Federal Reserve membership.

4. Why has the United States a predominantly unit banking system? Can you adduce any reasons why this could, or should, change in the future?

5. "If the moneyness of money depends on its acceptability, that is enhanced by the existence and operations of the FDIC." Comment critically.

6. How has the historic uniqueness of the commercial banks been diminished by recent institutional and legislative developments? What do you consider the economic costs, if any, and benefits of these developments?

7. The Depository Institutions Deregulation and Monetary Control Act of 1980 stated that "all depositors, and particularly those with modest savings, are entitled to receive a market rate of return on their savings . . ." Do you agree? Why? What achievements have been made in this direction by the legislative and institutional changes of the early 1980s, and what are likely to be their economic effects?

8. Can you adduce any arguments for or against the repeal of the McFadden Act of 1927?

9. Evaluate the costs and benefits of intermediation and disintermediation.

10. Do you consider that recent institutional and legislative changes have improved the likelihood of increased operational efficiency and allocational efficiency in the money capital market? Comment critically and explain as fully as possible.

8

COMMERCIAL BANK OPERATIONS

STUDY OBJECTIVES:

- To examine the operating policies and procedures of the commercial banks as profit-making, competitive, financial intermediaries
- To examine the commercial bank's sources of funds, and the unique characteristics of the liabilities and capital side of its balance sheet
- To relate the asset investment policies of the bank, and the structure of the asset side of its balance sheet, to the portfolio objectives of liquidity, safety, solvency, and profitability
- To consider the commercial banks' competitive procedures, including forms of nonprice competition
- To analyze the bank's income statement, the rate of return it earns on ownership capital, and other measures of operating efficiency
- To note, in connection with the foregoing, new forms of liquidity and liability management
- To indicate possible directions of future innovation and development, including the extension of electronic fund transfer devices

At the beginning of the preceding chapter we drew attention to five summary characteristics of the commercial banks. In short, they are profit-making, competitive, money-creating, financial intermediaries and are subject to unique kinds of federal and state government regulations. In the present chapter we shall examine their operating policies and the asset and liability structures in which those policies are reflected. Focusing on the important economic fact that the banks are private-enterprise, profit-making corporations, we shall look also at their income and expenditures and at the rate of return they earn on the ownership capital entrusted to them.

Once again we must note the special importance of the bank's liabilities. Its liabilities, we observed previously, substantially differentiate it from other financial institutions. For the demand deposit liabilities of the bank constitute a significant part of the country's money supply. But those deposits, along with the time and savings deposits also held by the banks, can now be seen in a new economic light. They constitute also the principal source of funds that the banks put to use in their income-earning investments.

In business firms in general, the accounts appearing on the liabilities side of the balance sheet describe the sources of investable funds that the enterprise uses to finance its investment in assets of various kinds. The firm will choose its asset investments in such a way as to enable it to achieve an optimum economic profit and rate of return on its capital. The same applies in the case of the banking firm. We shall examine the asset selection problem in some detail in this chapter, but it is the structure of the sources of funds employed that makes the bank unique among economic institutions.

Industrial firms and nonfinancial corporations in general finance part of their asset investments from equity or ownership capital, and part from debt capital or, as it is referred to, creditors' funds. The ratio of the debt capital to equity capital funds is a measure of what is called the leverage in the firm's financing structure. The presence of debt allows the rate of return on the equity capital to be levered upward, provided certain hoped-for economic conditions exist. Debt capital may be raised, for example, at an interest cost of 6 percent and put to work in the firm in investment projects that earn 10 percent. Of course a degree of risk may be undertaken by the firm in these financing and investment operations. But the residue of such earnings, or the amount of the earnings above the interest that has to be paid on the debt, accrues to the equity owners. Their overall rate of return is increased as a result.

The commercial banks maintain an extremely highly levered financing structure. By far the most important part of their investable funds is provided by their creditors. Tables 8-2 and 8-3 show that the banks' capital (mostly equity capital, but including a small amount of capital notes and debentures—a form of capital debt) accounts for only about 7.2 percent of their total funds. Approximately 75 percent of their funds is provided by depositors, taking the demand, time, and savings deposits together. Moreover, their remaining fund sources are various kinds of short-term liabilities. The use and exploitation of these have become increasingly important in recent years, as financial conditions have generally become more unstable. In all, more than 90 percent of the banks' funds come from creditor sources. This raises unique problems for bank management policies and gives a unique flavor to bank operating procedures.

Another aspect of the relation between the bank's sources and uses of funds, which has frequently given rise to misunderstanding and confusion, relates to the bankers' own perception of their function as financial intermediaries. We have seen that by making loans and acquiring security investments the bank creates money. This it does by creating demand deposits. For the banking system as a whole, moreover, an increase in the monetary base can potentially lead to a multiple expansion of deposits and the money supply. The relevant money supply multipliers describe what we can refer to as the economist's perception of the asset investment and money-creation relation. The bank's acquisition of assets creates money.

Bankers, on the other hand, frequently have a different perception of things. They tend to see things the other way around. For them it is not so much that the acquisition of assets creates money, though the mechanics, of course, are clearly acknowledged. It is rather that the acquisition of deposits makes possible the acquisition of assets. Bankers are inclined to say that their ability to lend depends on their ability to attract deposits. This is, of course, a perfectly valid perception of things from the viewpoint of the bankers' day-to-day operations. It accounts for the great deal of emphasis that individual bankers place on the competitive techniques that enable them to attract deposits away from other financial institutions.

In the use it makes of its funds, the commercial bank is a multi-product financial firm. Its products are the services and facilities it provides to customers, and for which it earns income in the form of charges and fees. Generally, these direct charges do not cover the direct costs of providing the services, and the bank's net income therefore depends on the earnings on its asset portfolio above its interest and other operating expenses. Details of this income-expense relation are given in Table 8-4. The services provided by the banks include such things, taken from a much longer list, as the provision of a circulating medium, account keeping, financial advice, portfolio management, credit card facilities, safe deposit boxes, wire transfer of funds, foreign exchange, payroll preparation services, credit investigation, and frequently the provision of management advice on customers' routine business problems.

Many of these services have traditionally been provided "free" to depositors. This could be done because the demand deposits in the banking system have not borne interest. In fact, the payment of interest on demand deposits is still prohibited. But in recent times a number of substitutes for the traditional demand deposit accounts have been invented. The commercial banks, as well as the savings and loan associations and mutual savings banks, offer NOW accounts, which bear interest and are activated by a so-called negotiable order of withdrawal. The banks also offer ATS accounts (automatic transfer services), which are in effect interest-bearing deposit accounts. It would appear that competition among the depository institutions in the future will take them closer to providing what is virtually a complete system of interest-bearing demand deposits. This would be the case if the restrictions that limit the Super–NOW accounts and comparable facilities to individuals and nonprofit organizations were withdrawn and these accounts could be made available to corporate customers also.

As interest payments on deposit accounts are extended, the banks will begin to charge for many of the services they provide. In accordance with the requirements of the Depository Institutions Deregulation and Monetary Control Act of 1980, moreover, the depository institutions will have to pay in the future for what were previously free services provided by the Federal Reserve System. In the new competitive environment in the financial sector a new tradition of charges and fees for services will emerge.

TWO TRADITIONAL OPERATING RULES

Contemporary bank operations can be considered against the background of two traditional rules or techniques of management. We refer to (1) the so-called traditional theory of commercial banking and (2) the famous 80–20 rule. The first of these actually became dignified as a widely held economic theory and was imagined for much of the nineteenth and early twentieth centuries to lie at the heart of sound banking theory and policy. The second, or the 80–20 rule, was rather a rule of thumb of banking procedures. It does, however, throw useful light on the techniques and responsibilities of bank management as they are now perceived.

The traditional theory
of commercial banking

The traditional theory of commercial banking is also referred to as the commercial loan theory of banking, or the needs-of-trade or the real bills doctrine. It has historic importance not only because it was espoused for so long during the formative stages of our banking system but also because it provided the viewpoint on which the Federal Reserve System was established when it replaced the National Banking System in 1913. This commercial loan theory would, it was imagined, provide the basis on which the banking system would operate under the supervision of the Federal Reserve Board.

The commercial loan theory said essentially that the banks should lend only against the security of what was called short-term, self-liquidating, commercial paper. This long-sounding term referred to such documents as short-term promissory notes or bills of exchange that were given to the bank in exchange for a loan. The bills of exchange, which were simply legal documents containing a promise or an obligation to pay a specified sum of money to the holder at an agreed date in the future, would be written for the amount of the loan. When the due date for payment arrived, usually between 30 and 180 days in the future, the payment of the amount stated on the bill of exchange would constitute repayment of the loan. The self-liquidating nature of this short-term commercial paper was an important aspect of the transaction. Such promissory notes or bills of exchange would be issued only against the value of industrial materials or marketable commodities. They would thereby be used to finance genuine production and marketing activities. When the maturity date of the loan arrived and the amount of the bill had to be paid, the commodities it was used to finance would have been sold and the sale proceeds would therefore be available to repay the bill. The loan was thereby self-liquidating.

Two advantages, it was thought, followed from this kind of arrangement. First, the bankers had reason to believe that because loans were made only against the security of real commodities, they could be sure of repayment when the due date of the loan arrived. To emphasize the notion on which the arrangements were grounded, the theory was referred to also as the real bills doctrine. Only real commodities were adequate collateral for loans.

Second, it was believed that if banking were conducted consistently in accordance with the theory, the needs of trade for money would always be precisely met. For when trade expanded and an increased need for money arose, it could be issued against the value of the commodities to which the increased level of trade gave rise. Then subsequently, if the level of trade declined and the need for money was reduced, the previously outstanding loans would be repaid and the money supply would again diminish. The money supply would fluctuate in accordance with the requirements of the economy.

A number of problems, however, were associated with the theory. First, the needs-of-trade concept implied that when money was not needed for the purpose for which it was originally issued, an automatic reflux of money to the banking system would occur. But in actual fact such a reflux might not be automatic at all. For in the first place, there was no guarantee that the commodities that were assumed to underpin the system would actually be salable within the time horizon of the loan. Indeed, changes in final demands for goods, or changes in business activity, could quite easily mean that the commodities were not salable at all or were salable for an amount less than the loan for which they were the collateral. Businesses could conceivably be wrong in their projections of market demands. If, then, the funds were not forthcoming to repay the loans or retire the bills of exchange when they matured, the money that had been issued would remain in circulation.

In that event, what started out as a short-term financing arrangement would give rise to a permanent increase in the amount of money in circulation. The same thing could happen for other reasons also. There was no reason why the proceeds of the loan should be used solely for the purpose for which it was granted. Loan proceeds might be used to finance more permanent capital expenditures or to support high-living and consumption expenditures. In such cases there would again be doubt that liquid funds would be available to repay the loan on its maturity. Again, therefore, a permanent increase in the money supply would have occurred.

But a deeper fallacy was contained in the traditional theory. It rested in the fact that as loans were made, the amount of money issued was related to the value of the commodities that served as collateral for the loans. Suppose, then, that when the money supply in circulation had been increased in this way there was not a simultaneous increase in the flow of commodities produced. In that case we might expect that the increased money flow would tend to raise the general commodity price level. The values of commodities that could be used as collateral for loans would tend to rise, along with prices in general. But when this occurred, the higher values of commodities would permit an increased amount of borrowing on the basis of those values. If an increase in the amount of loans outstanding for this reason did occur, this would again increase the money supply. But to follow the argument through one more turn, the resulting increase in the rate of money flow in the economy would, if production did not also increase proportionally, tend again to raise the general price level. Then again the values of commodities would rise, their value as potential collateral for loans would rise, and again further additions to the loans outstanding and the money supply would result. In this way an inflationary spiral would be feeding on itself. The central fallacy of the traditional theory or the real bills doctrine was that the value of the real commodities that assumedly formed the basis of the system was not independent of the money-creating process to which it gave rise.

For these reasons the real bills doctrine potentially gave rise to unstable, rather than stable, monetary conditions. In times of prosperity the spiraling issues of money would reinforce inflationary tendencies in the economy. In times of recession the tendency for prices, production, and incomes to fall would again be reinforced by the induced reductions in the money supply.

The 80—20 rule

The so-called 80—20 rule, which continued to influence the thinking of real-world bankers until very recent times, was related to the provision of banking services. We recall that while rates of interest were payable on savings and time deposits, no interest was payable on demand deposits. Since banks were therefore receiving a large proportion of their funds free of charge, they could afford to provide free services to their customers in return. The idea behind the 80–20 rule was that only about 20 percent of the bank's customers accounted for about 80 percent of the total deposits at the bank. The remaining 80 percent of depositors, each of whom held relatively small accounts, provided only 20 percent of the deposits. The free funds provided by the top 20 percent of depositors gave rise to earnings that made it possible for the banks to supply free services to the remaining 80 percent.

Put another way, the small deposit balances maintained by 80 percent of the bank's depositors might not give rise, when they were invested, to sufficient earnings to cover the cost of providing services to those customers. The earnings of the funds supplied by the top 20 percent of depositors had to fill the gap. This was supposed to be one of the factors that managements had to keep in mind when they were deciding the ways in which the funds available to the bank should be invested.

But this old 80–20 rule is no longer of such clear or undoubted relevance. For increasingly, as we have said, deposits now bear interest, and it will no longer be possible for the depository institutions to provide their wide range of customer services free of charge.

COMMERCIAL BANKS AND THE FINANCIAL INTERMEDIARY FUNCTION

In our preliminary view of banks and financial institutions in Chapter 5 an analysis was made of the structure of the savings-investment process and the functions of the financial institutions in it. The financial intermediaries were seen as "manufacturers of liquidity and safety." The advantages that accrue to individual savers by their being able to make indirect investments and acquire indirect securities, rather than having to make only direct investments, have been explored.

The commercial bank, along with other depository institutions, serves this important intermediary function. The savings accounts offered by the banks, for example, are claims against themselves analogous to the claims against savings and loan associations represented by the shares they issue, or pass-book entries that evidence deposits in mutual savings banks. Much turns, therefore, on the way in which the banks view their obligations and their opportunities for economic investment and profit, in the light of these intermediary features of their positions.

To the extent, moreover, that demand deposits are held in the banks, they are acting as intermediaries in the employment of these funds also. For by holding demand deposits individuals are satisfying their own asset portfolio criteria of liquidity, safety, and convenience. To the extent, of course, that interest-bearing deposit accounts may increasingly be substituted for interest-free demand deposits, the banks are called upon to perform the intermediary function in a more explicit and observable sense. For the individuals holding such interest-bearing deposits will conceivably be doing so after comparing the advantages of this form of wealth-holding with other competing forms.

This means that in formulating its criteria of asset portfolio investment the bank must take account of the relations that exist between its liabilities and its assets. In one sense the bank is in a precarious economic position. For its liabilities are to a preponderant extent short-term or even demand liabilities, while its assets are longer term. The bank, in other words, appears to be contravening a basic rule of investment and financing behavior. If individuals want to be sure of avoiding financial embarrassment, or even insolvency, they should not borrow short and lend long. But that is precisely what the commercial banks are doing.

First, bank assets are long term in the sense that the average maturities of the loans they have made are longer than the average maturities of their liabilities. In the interest of liquidity, as we shall see again below, the bank will keep a reasonable proportion of its assets in fairly short term investments to offset, to whatever extent is thought desirable or necessary, the fact that many of its liabilities mature on demand.

Second, the bank's assets are long term in the sense that the rates of return being earned on them have frequently been set for a specified time that extends into the future. This may apply, for example, to real estate loans, to building and construction mortgages, and to the rates of interest charged on renewable industrial loans and lines of credit, though variable interest rate loans have recently become quite widespread. Fixed interest rate assets can give rise to acute financial discomfort at times when the market rates of interest that have to be paid to attract funds rise above the rates of return the bank is earning on outstanding loans and investments.

These considerations imply that a bank's asset investment criteria will take up the same objectives of liquidity, safety, solvency, and profitability that we have already examined. The bank will confront the same kind of prospective trade-off between risk and return. It will endeavor to benefit from the principles of effective asset diversification. It will formulate a policy on maintaining secondary or liquid reserves as well as the so-called primary reserves that it is required by Federal Reserve regulations to maintain. It is true that under normal economic and operating conditions the apparently extreme liquidity of its liabilities is moderated by the fact that not all of its depositors are going to demand a return of their funds at the same time. A bank can conceivably judge, in the same way as did the goldsmiths in Chapter 5, what liquid assets it needs to maintain in the light of its specific liability structure. But mistakes can be made, and the best-laid plans go awry. This is why we noted in Chapter 7 the need for the bank examination procedures and the Federal Deposit Insurance Corporation.

The way in which the bank confronts and solves these intermediary problems is reflected in the structure of its balance sheet. The typical bank balance sheet is examined in the next section.

COMMERCIAL BANK ASSETS AND LIABILITIES

In the management of its assets a commercial bank typically does not rely on the rules of the traditional theory of commercial banking. Rather, it maintains a highly diversified portfolio of assets, and numerous criteria appear to influence its asset investment decisions. The general problem of liquidity, moreover, is met by more devices than a simple allocation of a part of the bank's total investment to highly liquid assets. Liquidity is met in part also by what has become known as liability management. Liabilities as well as assets are now being handled in highly flexible ways. Variations in the bank's short-term liabilities, including in some cases overnight money market and federal funds loans, figure prominently in the liquidity management problem.

A view of the banking system's asset and liability structure is given in Table 8-1. This presents a composite balance sheet of all commercial banks in the United States as of December 1982. The same data have been presented in percentage form in Table 8-2. Some preliminary comments will enable us to establish perspective before we look in more detail at the separate asset and liability accounts.

First, what we previously observed as the highly levered financing structure of the banks is seen in Table 8-2, which reveals that only 7.2 percent of total funds has been obtained from capital sources. Deposits account for 74.8 percent, and other liabilities, including the fairly volatile federal funds borrowings, account for the remaining 17.9 percent. The proportion of bank funds obtained from capital sources is quite low and has occasioned anxiety regarding the banks' ability to withstand seriously adverse fluctuations in their trading results and asset values. In June 1983 the Federal Reserve Board issued new guidelines requiring banks to maintain their primary capital, defined as common and preferred stock plus certain contingency and capital reserves, equal to at least 5 percent of their total assets.

On the assets side, the cash items, together with marketable securities that make up the banks' secondary reserves, account for about 31 percent of total assets. Table 8-1 reveals that the holdings of what we

Table   8-1

Assets and liabilities of all commercial banks in the United States,
December 31, 1982 (Amounts are in billions of dollars)

Assets		*Liabilities and capital*	
Cash assets		Demand deposits	
Currency and coin	19.6	Individuals, partnerships	
Balances on deposit with		and corporations (IPC)	299.0
Federal Reserve Bank	26.7	U.S. govt.	1.9
Balances with depository		State govts.	15.8
institutions	61.5	Other (incl. foreign)	39.2
Demand balances with		Travelers checks, certified	
U.S. commercial banks	35.1	checks, and letters of	
Cash items in course of		credit	16.3
collection	68.4	*Total demand deposits*	372.2
Total cash items	211.3	Time and savings deposits	
Securities		Individuals, partnerships	
U.S. govt. and govt.		and corporations (IPC):	
agencies	195.1	Savings deposits	299.6
State govts.	154.9	Time deposits	621.4
Other securities	25.4	Total IPC	921.0
Total securities	375.4	U.S. govt.	1.1
Loans (gross)		State govts.	71.6
Commercial & industrial	382.7	Other	40.2
Agricultural	36.2	*Total time & savings*	
Real estate	300.3	*deposits*	1,034.0
Financial institutions	73.8	Federal funds purchased	
For purchasing &		and securities sold under	
carrying securities	13.7	agreements to repur-	
Individuals		chase	179.5
Automobile 58.6		Other liabilities for bor-	
Credit cards 36.8		rowed money	39.1
Mobile homes 9.8		Other liabilities	117.5
Other personal 87.8		Capital accounts	
Total individual	193.0	Capital notes and	
Other loans	33.7	debentures 6.9	
Total loans	1,033.4	Equity capital 129.2	
Less: Allowances for		*Total capital accounts*	136.0
losses and unearned			
income	31.6		
Total loans (net)	1,001.8		
Federal funds sold and se-			
curities purchased under			
agreements to resell	103.6		
Bank premises and miscel-			
laneous assets	186.3	*Total liabilities and*	
Total assets	1,878.3	*capital*	1,878.3

Source: Federal Deposit Insurance Corporation, *1982 Statistics on Banking,* pp. 34–37.
Amounts may not add to totals because of rounding.

Table 8-2

Percentage of assets, liabilities, and equity capital of all commercial banks in the United States, December 31, 1982

Assets			Liabilities and Capital		
		%			%
Cash and amounts due from depository institutions		11.2	Demand deposits		
			Individuals, partnerships and corporations (IPC)	15.9	
Securities			Other demand deposits	3.9	
U.S. govt. and govt. agencies	10.4		*Total demand deposits*		19.8
State govts.	8.2		Time and savings deposits		
Other securities	1.4		Individuals, partnerships and corporations (IPC)	49.0	
Total securities		20.0	Other time and savings deposits	6.0	
Loans (gross)			*Total time and savings deposits*		55.0
Commercial & industrial	20.4				
Agricultural	1.9		Federal funds purchased and securities sold under agreements to repurchase		9.6
Real estate	16.0				
Financial institutions	3.9				
For purchasing and carrying securities	0.7		Other liabilities		8.3
Individuals	10.3		Capital accounts		
Other loans	1.8				
Total gross loans	55.0		Capital notes and debentures	0.4	
Less: Allowances for losses and unearned income	1.7		Equity capital	6.9	
			Total capital accounts		7.2
Total loans (net)		53.3			
Federal funds sold and securities purchased under agreements to resell		5.5			
Other assets		9.9	*Total liabilities and capital*		100.0
Total assets		100.0			

Source: See Table 8-1. Amounts may not add to totals because of rounding.

have referred to as legal reserves actually account for only a small proportion of total assets. The banks may hold their required reserves, it will be recalled, either in the form of vault cash or as deposits with the Federal Reserve Bank. These two accounts in Table 8-1 amount to only $46.3 billion, or 2.5 percent of total assets, and account for 12.4 percent of demand deposits, or 3.3 percent of total deposits, including the time and savings deposits. Not all of the latter, of course, are subject to reserve requirements. We have seen that only nonpersonal time deposits are subject to reserve requirements, and that at the relatively low level of 3 percent. Moreover, only those nonpersonal time deposits whose original maturity was less than two and one-half years are subject to such reserve requirements. The Federal Reserve board has announced that this breakpoint of two and one-half years will gradually be decreased until 1986, at which time the minimum maturity term determining reserve requirements will be the same as what is then specified for any time deposit. Thus the actual balance sheet position of the banks as a whole is within the general reserve requirements of the Federal Reserve. It provides a clear confirmation of the multiple-deposit expansibility, which, we have already observed, characterizes the banking system.

The big investment item, as will be expected from the nature of commercial bank activities, is the total loan account. Table 8-2 indicates that at the end of the 1982 total net loans accounted for 53.3 percent of total assets.

COMMERCIAL BANK LIABILITIES, OR SOURCES OF FUNDS

Demand deposits

The central mission of the commercial banks is highlighted by the fact that the demand deposit accounts of individuals, partnerships, and corporations amounted at the end of 1982 to $299.0 billion and accounted for the large slice of 15.9 percent of the banks' total sources of funds.

The U.S. government maintains only relatively small balances at commercial banks, amounting to $1.9 billion at the end of 1982. These government accounts are frequently referred to as Tax and Loan accounts. The amounts in them come from the purchases of government securities by the commercial banks and, more important, from the payment into them of income tax collections from payroll deductions. These amounts are paid into designated commercial banks in different parts of the country, and the banks then have the choice of retaining the funds as interest-bearing deposits or transmitting the amounts directly to the Federal Reserve Bank for credit to the Treasury's account. The government from time to time transfers these funds from the commercial banks to the Treasury's account at the Federal Reserve Bank. All payments by the government for goods and services, and all other disbursements, are made by drawing checks against that Treasury account. The Tax and Loan accounts in the commercial banks, therefore, constitute a temporary source of funds for the banks. The arrangements we have just described were established by the government as a means of minimizing the Treasury's impact on the availability of funds in local financial markets. When funds are transferred from personal depositors' accounts to government accounts in the same bank, the total liquidity position of the bank is for the time being undisturbed. The authorized banks that hold these government deposits are also required to hold government securities equal to the amount of such government funds, and they are further required to be insured banks under the Federal Deposit Insurance program. The amounts held in these Tax and Loan accounts are not included in the statistics of the money supply, and the banks are not required to hold reserves against them.

The amount standing under traveler's checks and related items in the demand deposit section of the balance sheet represents liabilities undertaken by the banks for the eventual payment of traveler's checks or other checks they have already guaranteed. When traveler's checks are sold by the banks to individuals, an amount equal to their value is credited to a special deposit account to await presentation and payment of the checks.

Time and savings deposits

Included in the IPC time and savings deposits are the nonpersonal time deposits, which, according to the reserve requirements of the 1980 act, are the only part of the time accounts that are subject to reserve requirements. In this total of time deposits also is the very important item of Certificates of Deposit (CDs). Time deposits are deposits that have been placed with a bank on the understanding that they will not be withdrawn before a specified date in the future unless a penalty in the form of loss of interest is paid by the depositor to the bank. The interest rate ceiling on such deposits was removed in October 1983.

In some instances, however, corporations may place funds with a bank in exchange for an interest-bearing Certificate of Deposit that can be sold and purchased in the short-term money market. At some times the volume of these negotiable CDs outstanding has become very large, and the banks have encountered difficulty when they have matured and had to be repaid. In earlier times, when the rates of interest payable on these negotiable CDs were subject to ceilings imposed by Regulation Q, it was necessary for the Federal Reserve Board to temporarily remove the ceiling when holders threatened to allow them to mature without renewing them. Such a large-scale runoff of CD maturities would have caused the banks embarrassment in conditions of tight money, when interest rates available on alternative assets were higher. Such episodes occurred in June 1970, following the shock to the financial markets of the bankruptcy of the Penn Central Railroad, and in May 1973 when market rates again threatened a large runoff of the outstanding CDs.

Nondeposit funds

Apart from the capital accounts, the two most significant items for bank liquidity and liability management are the $179.5 billion shown in Table 8-1 under "federal funds purchased and securities sold under agreements to repurchase," and the $39.1 billion described as "other liabilities for borrowed money." A variety of short-term financing devices are included in these classifications.

We have seen that corporate deposits in the form of negotiable CDs became an important source of funds during the 1960s. By the middle of that decade, in August 1966, they stood at a total of some $18.6 billion. We have also seen that at certain times the Fed raised the Regulation Q interest ceiling on these CDs in order to prevent a large runoff. But this did not always happen. In a high interest rate situation in 1966, for example, the Fed refused to raise the ceiling and the banks were unable to replace their CDs as they matured. In the second half of 1966, as a result, the CDs outstanding declined sharply to $15.5 billion.

Experiences of this kind led the banks to begin tapping nondeposit sources of funds more actively. The federal funds market had come into existence earlier as a means of buying and selling, or borrowing and lending, deposits at the Federal Reserve banks. Banks with temporarily excess reserves would lend them to banks in need of reserves, frequently on a one-day basis or subject to renewal. The market has broadened over the years and now includes other depository institutions as well as the banks, securities dealers, and agencies of the federal government. Funds obtained in this way are not subject to reserve requirements. Nor were they subject to interest rate ceilings when those were in effect. The rate of interest on loans of federal funds is frequently taken as an indicator of current money market conditions, as the funds borrowed and lent in this market are made available immediately, or on the same day as the transaction. The rate of interest fluctuates sharply at times. Because the depository institutions subject to reserve requirements end their reporting week on Wednesday, and because they must be in their required reserve positions by the close of business on that day, perceived surpluses in the system can diminish the federal funds rate sharply on Wednesdays, just as a shortage of reserve funds can cause it to increase rapidly.

Highly important also are the borrowings under repurchase agreements (RPs, or sometimes referred to as Repos). An RP agreement is one in which a bank sells an asset, generally a U.S. government security, under an agreement to repurchase it on a specified date at a specified price. The effective rate of interest paid by the bank is determined by the differential between the price at which the security is sold and the price at which it is repurchased. The rates of interest on RPs tend to move with the federal funds rate. The latter rate moves also with the Federal

Reserve discount rate, because borrowing in the federal funds market is, for the banks, an alternative to borrowing from the Fed. The RP market now enters the picture as another alternative. But the RP rate is likely to be slightly lower than the federal funds rate, because in the latter case no collateral is exchanged in connection with the loan. The RP transaction, being an actual exchange of securities, is, of course, completely collateralized, and it therefore attracts a slightly lower rate of interest.

As an example of a repurchase agreement that can become significant for both the borrower and the lender, a bank may borrow temporarily idle funds from a large depositor by selling the depositor a security it agrees to repurchase on the following day. The depositor benefits because he is receiving a rate of interest on what is in effect an overnight loan, at a time when he has no alternative use for his funds. In effect, he is thereby receiving interest on his demand deposit. The borrowing bank benefits on two counts. First, it is able to put the funds to use in whatever income-earning asset it has in view; and second, the amount is for that night transferred out of the bank's demand deposit accounts and is not therefore subject to reserve requirements. As the bank's weekly reserve requirement is calculated on a two-weekly average of the end-of-day deposit balances, the reduction of the demand deposits on any day by such RP transactions works in the bank's favor from this point of view. (Actually, the method of computing a bank's reserve requirement liability against demand deposits was altered in February 1984 to what is referred to as a system of "contemporaneous accounting." Prior to that date, reserve requirements were calculated on a "lagged basis," being based in any week on the average daily balances of deposits that were held for a seven-day period two weeks previously. The vault cash that could be counted as legal reserves was taken as the vault cash held two weeks previously, so that the adjustment in the reserve position at any time was made entirely in the portion that is represented by deposits at the Fed. The contemporaneous accounting procedure shortened to two days the lag between the end of the reserve calculation period and the beginning of the period for which reserve requirements must be held. The required reserves, however, are calculated on the average daily deposits held over a two-week period. Reserve requirements against nonpersonal time deposits continue to be maintained on the previous lagged basis.)

A final source of short-term borrowed funds is referred to as Eurodollars. These are dollar-denominated funds available in European and other overseas money markets, including some in Asia and the Caribbean. At times in the past the banks have borrowed heavily in the European markets, but this has been somewhat restricted by the imposition of reserve requirements on such borrowings. In late 1969, for example, a marginal reserve requirement of 20 percent was imposed on such borrowings. Though those reserve requirements were subsequently reduced, a lower marginal reserve requirement was imposed in October 1979 as part of a dramatic change in monetary policy and procedures by the Fed. In that month the Fed imposed a reserve requirement of 8 percent on certain so-called managed liabilities above a base amount. The liability accounts subject to the reserve requirement included Eurodollar borrowings, repurchase agreements, federal funds borrowings from nonmember institutions, and large time deposits.

Under the Monetary Control Act of 1980 the reserve requirement on all Eurodollar borrowings is set at 3 percent. For purposes of overnight borrowing of the kind we have considered above, the source of Eurodollar funds tapped by the banks consists of those balances held in the Caribbean. We noted in Chapter 4 that because these funds are readily available to U.S. banks, as they are held in the same time zone as the U.S. banks, the overnight Eurodollars held by the public in the Caribbean branches of United States banks are included in the M2 definition of the money supply.

A further means of obtaining funds is by use of the one-bank holding company device. A bank may establish a holding company that issues short-term promissory notes, referred to as commercial paper, in the money market. With the funds so obtained, the holding company may purchase some of the loans of the bank, thereby releasing bank funds for reinvestment in other, and conceivably more profitable, income-earning opportunities.

SUMMARY OF COMMERCIAL BANK
SOURCES OF FUNDS

The summary of commercial bank sources of funds shown in Table 8-3 indicates the pattern that has prevailed over the past eight years. In 1960, demand deposits accounted for approximately 60 percent of total bank funds, with time deposits accounting for some 7 percent. In recent years, as shown in Table 8-3, the picture has changed dramatically. Demand deposits accounted for only 19.8 percent in 1982, while time deposits had increased their share to 38.8 percent. In 1960 short-term borrowed funds of the kind we have just discussed were virtually zero. At the end of 1982 the borrowed funds accounted for 2.2 percent, quite apart from the amounts raised in the federal funds and the RP markets, which, as Table 8-3 indicates, accounted for a further 9.6 percent. The trends in bank financing that we have discussed in this chapter are confirmed in Table 8-3. During 1975–82 the percentage share of the federal funds and RP markets increased by almost three-quarters and the share of other borrowed funds more than tripled.

Table   8-3

Percentage distribution of sources of funds of insured commercial banks in the United States at December, 1975–1982

Source of funds	1975 %	1976 %	1977 %	1978 %	1979 %	1980 %	1981 %	1982 %
Demand deposits	34.2	33.0	33.3	31.4	30.7	28.1	22.8	19.8
Savings deposits	17.1	20.2	19.3	17.4	14.7	13.0	13.2	16.2
Time deposits	31.8	29.0	29.0	31.0	32.4	36.3	39.5	38.8
Borrowed funds	0.6	0.6	0.6	1.9	2.1	1.9	1.7	2.2
Federal funds purchased and securities sold under agreements to repurchase	5.6	7.0	7.3	7.3	8.0	8.6	9.7	9.6
Other liabilities	3.2	2.6	2.9	3.7	4.7	4.6	5.6	6.1
Capital	7.5	7.6	7.5	7.3	7.3	7.4	7.4	7.2
Total sources of funds	100.0	100.0	100.0	100.0	100.0	100.0	100.0	100.0

Source: FDIC, *1982 Statistics on Banking,* p. 42; *1981 Statistics on Banking,* p. 42; and FDIC *Annual Report,* 1980. Percentages may not add to totals because of rounding.

COMMERCIAL BANK ASSETS, OR USES OF FUNDS

In considering the distribution of bank funds over various kinds of asset investments, three points should be kept in mind. First, this brings us directly to the considerations of liquidity, safety, solvency, and profitability, which, as we have said, are primary objectives of bank management. Second, the management of assets and the management of liabilities are very much interdependent. Third, it is here that we can observe the policies determining the rate of return earned for the shareholders of the bank, remembering that the bank is a private-enterprise, profit-making institution.

Banks invest in assets in order to earn income. But in doing so, they necessarily undertake risks. In the investment and financial markets in general, a higher rate of return can be expected if greater risks are accepted. A trade-off between risk and return generally has to be made. Diversification of investments can frequently help in maintaining an acceptable or desired rate of return while the overall risk of the asset portfolio is diminished. Given the absence of geographical diversification, however, recalling that interstate banking is prohibited in the United States, many smaller banks are locked into a set of local or regional loan opportunities that do not permit significant diversification. Yet diversi-

fication comes from the law of large numbers even in those cases, provided
the bank sensibly distributes its funds over the different kinds of loans
we shall consider—loans for commercial and industrial working capital,
agriculture, real estate, automobile, and credit card purchases. Regional
industrial areas may, however, become dependent on specific industrial
activities, such as Detroit's dependence on the automobile industry. When
the local industry experiences a cyclical downturn or a declining trend,
the support services in the region, including the banks, can quickly encounter difficulties.

The interdependence between liability and asset management occurs on more than one level. The bank's liabilities are short-term and
highly liquid. We have noted that problems may arise in financial management if precaution is not taken against excessive reliance on borrowing short and lending long. But that, unfortunately, is substantially what
the commercial banks have to do. For that reason we must pay attention
again to the liquidity problem, as it comes to focus now on the assets side
of the balance sheet. Second, the bank must continually be conscious of
the relation between the costs of funds with which to finance its asset
investments and the rates of return that investments are expected to
provide. As in all portfolio management responsibilities, a threefold problem enters at this point.

First, the rates of return that different assets provide, suitably adjusted for risks, should be compared in order to maximize the overall
profitability of the portfolio. This, in the language of economic analysis,
implies a balancing of prospective rates of return at the margin of investment. Asset portfolios should be constructed in such a way as to place
funds in earning opportunities whose marginal rates of return, given
comparable risks, are highest.

The extent, however, to which this principle could be, or should be,
implemented literally and to the last dollar of investable funds may depend on other operating factors that the bank must also consider. It may
be necessary for the bank to conduct and invest in activities that, while
they may at the time be only marginal income earners, nevertheless make
it possible for the bank to provide a wider range of services that may
attract and retain customers and depositors. Investment portfolio decisions, in other words, cannot afford to be shortsighted and focus only on
the immediate returns available. The long run is important. Diversification in the short run into activities that are not immediately profitable
may be necessary in order to establish a reputation for providing reliable
and comprehensive customer facilities.

Second, portfolio management needs to make a comparison of the
marginal costs of funds obtained from competing sources. As prospective
rates of return need to be carefully compared on the assets side, so the
costs of the different sources of funds need to be compared on the liabilities

side. In the important matter of using nondeposit funds, for example, three sources are likely to be highly substitutable for each other: borrowing from the Federal Reserve Bank, borrowing in the federal funds markets, and the use of RP funds. The costs of funds from these sources, given their substitutability, will tend to be fairly comparable. The bank will pay careful attention to the marginal differences that exist, however, particularly as large amounts of money may be involved in raising funds from any one of these sources at a given time.

But the costs of other funds need to be compared also. This will be particularly relevant in the future as the banks compete not only with each other but with the other depository institutions also. The latter, we have seen, are breaking down the barriers of uniqueness behind which the banks previously operated. The depository institutions in general, including the banks, can be expected to move increasingly toward the provision of what are, in effect, interest-earning demand deposits. We have seen this happening as such devices as NOW accounts and ATS accounts are introduced. The costs of raising funds from such interest-earning liability sources will therefore have to be considered in new ways.

Third, the cost of raising funds at the margin must be compared with the prospective rate of return that can be earned from investing them at the margin. In portfolio management, therefore, the overall task is not simply that of choosing the optimum portfolio of a given asset size. It is that of deciding on the optimum size of the portfolio as well as its optimum structure, or its asset composition. The size of the asset portfolio can be changed, as we have suggested, by raising additional finance in order to use it to acquire additional asset investments.

This last point is very important in the case of the banks. They will be competing for funds in the ways we have already suggested. They will want to see the size of their assets grow as the economy in general grows. But they will each, in their various ways and in their different situations, wish to attract resources away from competitors, and to provide more-integrated banking services and facilities. They will wish to participate, where that can be shown to be profitable in response to public demand, in the technological changes or revolutions in banking that we shall refer to again later in this chapter.

Cash items and the banks' liquidity

The banks' cash assets, as shown in Table 8-1, include four main items. They are currency and coin held in the banks' vaults, deposits with the Federal Reserve Bank, deposits with other banks and depository institutions, and cash items in course of collection. The first two of these are legal reserves that may be used to satisfy the banks' reserve requirements. In the case of nonmember banks, deposits with a member bank may also be used to satisfy reserve requirements, provided they are passed on, dollar for dollar, to a Federal Reserve Bank. These cash items are seen in Table 8-2 to have accounted for 11.2 percent of the banks' assets at the end of 1982. In 1960 the comparable percentage was approximately 20 percent, but this has declined as the banks have diversified, as we shall see, into more extensive loan operations.

A bank's need for liquidity stems from the nature of its inflow and outflow of cash in the course of normal operations. Cash flows in from (a) the receipt of income from assets, (b) the repayment of loans, and (c) the receipt of new deposits. Cash flows out to meet (a) depositors' demand for increased currency, especially at certain seasons of the year, (b) the drain of reserves to other banks as a result of adverse check-clearing balances, and (c) the expenses of current operations. Bank failure results if, at any time, the bank is unable to meet those demands for cash.

It would appear on the face of it that the cash items in the balance sheet are the first line of defense against liquidity demands. In a sense that is so; though we have seen that the astute management of short-term liabilities can be as important for liquidity management as the control of short-term assets. The cash accounts in the balance sheet, moreover, cannot be looked upon as being perfectly liquid. This is because by far the largest part of the cash items are actually held as required reserves. And it is only the excess reserves, not the total legal reserves, that can be thought of as being available at any time to meet liquidity drains.

One reason why the ratio of the cash accounts to total assets has declined so far in the last twenty years is that the Federal Reserve has lowered the reserve requirements. This naturally pleased the banks, who were thereby enabled to divert a larger proportion of their assets to income-earning forms. But it has exposed more seriously the actual liquidity management problem. Moreover, we have seen that in order to meet their reserve requirements at the close of business each Wednesday, the banks may be heavy operators on that day in the federal funds market. This attests that the cash items, taken as a whole, are generally directed more to the reserve requirement obligations than they are to the operating liquidity problem.

Banks, of course, are not allowed to be, or at least to continue, in reserve deficiency situations. They must cover their reserve requirements each Wednesday, based on their average deposit funds over a two-week period that ended two days previously in the case of demand deposits and two weeks previously for non-personal time deposits. A bank is, however, permitted to be deficient in required reserves at the end of a given week provided the deficiency is not greater than 2 percent of required reserves, and provided it is made up in the following week. But a bank is not permitted to be deficient two weeks in a row. The reserve balances at the

Fed do not carry any interest, though the chairman of the Federal Reserve Board recommended to the Senate Banking Committee in September 1983 that interest should be paid on these balances. They are in a sense interest-free loans from the depository institutions to the Fed. The Fed can and does earn an income on the investment of those funds in government securities, which it does, in turn, pass on to the Treasury.

The Monetary Control Act of 1980 contains provisions that permit the Federal Reserve Board to impose supplemental reserve requirements on the transaction accounts held in the depository institutions if that should be thought necessary for purposes of controlling the monetary situation. Such supplemental reserve requirements must be terminated after ninety days, however, and in the meantime the amounts are to be held by the Fed in an earnings participation account. Interest is to be paid to the depository institution on these funds at a rate no greater than the average rate of earnings for the previous quarter on the securities portfolio of the Fed. Conceivably, this provision could be the first step toward the payment of interest on reserve funds in general. If the required reserves were to begin to pay interest, this would of course change the complexion of the banks' asset and liquidity management procedures.

The demand balances with other commercial banks, shown as part of the cash items in Table 8-1, include the correspondent balances we discussed previously. The cash items in course of collection refer to the amounts of checks that have been deposited in the banks and drawn on other banks but have not yet been collected. The details of the check-clearing procedures will be looked at again when we discuss the services provided by the Federal Reserve System.

Securities investments

The banks' holdings of U.S. government securities accounted for 10.4 percent of total assets at the end of 1982. In 1960 the comparable percentage had been 23.7 percent. The relative decline in these security holdings, together with that in the cash items we noted above, has been due to the asset portfolio redistribution that has taken the banks more largely into loans and, in the case of the securities section of their portfolios, into state and local government securities. This latter asset form has risen to 8.2 percent of total assets in Table 8-2 against approximately 6.8 percent in 1960.

The government security investments, of course, provide liquidity and safety, and with 20 percent of total assets in securities at the end of 1982, this, or particularly the shorter-term U.S. government securities portion of it, could be looked upon as the banks' secondary reserves. The cash items, as we have seen, serve principally the reserve requirement obligations. The reserve requirements imposed by the Fed are in fact not designed primarily to guarantee the liquidity of the banks. They are prescribed primarily as a means of facilitating the Federal Reserve Board's control of the monetary situation, as an arm of monetary policy. The banks' secondary reserves, then, become an important second line of defense against liquidity failures.

Loans

The loan portfolio of the banks is the largest part of their total assets, and it accounts for the greatest part of their earnings. Commercial and industrial loans, which in Table 8-2 account for 20.4 percent of total assets at the end of 1982, have always figured prominently in bank operations. The diversity of loan operations can be judged from the detail given in Tables 8-1 and 8-2. Twenty years ago real estate loans equaled about 60 percent of the amount invested in commercial and industrial loans. By 1982, as indicated by the Tables, real estate loans expanded to approximately 80 percent of the commercial and industrial loans. Table 8-1 also gives some indication of the diversity of loans within the "Individuals" section. In Table 8-2 this accounts for 10.3 percent of total assets. These individual loans include loans for automobile purchases, credit card purchases, mobile homes, and a range of other purposes.

Several features of bank operations closely associated with the loan portfolio deserve brief mention. First, loans are made at varying rates of interest. The banks in general announce a rate of interest, known as the prime rate, at which they will make funds available to their most creditworthy customers. Smaller customers and more-risky borrowers will generally be required to pay a number of percentage points above the prime rate. The rate of interest on real estate mortgage loans may also be tied to the prime rate, and at certain times, as in the disturbed monetary conditions that existed in 1981 and 1982, the mortgage rate can go so high that it virtually brings the housing market and the construction industry to a halt. The rate of interest on automobile loans also rises with the prime rate and with the costs that the banks have to pay for funds. In 1981 and 1982, also, this caused a serious slump in the automobile industry.

Second, in the important commercial and industrial section of the loan portfolio the banks do not confine themselves to short-term working capital loans of the kind previously advocated by the traditional theory of commercial banking. The banks now make longer loans, the so-called term loans. These may be for durations of from three to five years and may be subject to gradual repayment or amortization. The availability of these loans and the rate of interest charged on them depend again on the general credit standing of the customer. They may be secured or unsecured, or they may be granted under a line of credit established by the bank, whereby the customer is permitted to draw loan amounts up to a previously agreed total at any time. The advantage of these arrangements to the industrial customers is that they can mix these funds with their other fund sources and use them for any purpose, including, if they wish, capital investment.

In conditions where the demand for finance is heavy and loanable funds are in relatively short supply, the banks may impose on borrowers what are referred to as compensating balance requirements. This is an arrangement whereby the borrower is required to maintain on deposit at the bank an amount no less than a certain proportion of the loan. A loan for $100,000 at a rate of interest of 12 percent, which is subject to a compensating balance requirement of $10,000, means that the borrower is actually obtaining the use of only $90,000 but is paying interest of $12,000 per annum, or 12 percent of the full amount of $100,000. The effective rate of interest is therefore approximately 13.3 percent. The advantage to the bank is not only that its effective rate of return is higher but that it has retained some of the loan funds. This means that the entire amount does not give rise to a possible adverse drain on the bank's reserves, such as would happen if the bank had loaned its funds in the open market.

In connection with routine working capital advances, the banks will frequently require that the borrower be completely free of debt to the bank at some point each year. But a bank will realize that its ability to lend funds profitably is to some extent dependent on the treatment it accords its customers and potential borrowers. The bank would generally wish to be known as an institution that meets all reasonable loan demands from its customers who have traditional and longstanding connections with it. In some cases, however, banks may engage in, or be thought to engage in, what is known as redlining. This is a practice whereby a bank will discriminate against borrowers from a certain geographical area or district by refusing to lend to them at all or by charging discriminatory rates of interest.

In general, banks can be expected to engage in a certain amount of discrimination in their loan operations. This is because the potential borrowers are far from homogeneous in their economic situations and characteristics, and they do not all have the same creditworthiness or risk profile. The rate of interest on loans is set by the banks in a manner that takes account of the risks they are assuming in granting the loans. The local banks, as we have indicated previously, frequently enjoy a quasi-monopoly position, and in the interest of providing a full range of banking services to their local customers they will engage in forms of price discrimination in the setting of loan rates, as well as forms of nonprice competition to attract customers.

While real estate loans have become an important component of bank investment portfolios, not all such loans are carried by the banks to their maturity. The banks may arrange real estate loans in parcels for resale to the Federal National Mortgage Association. At times when funds are required for reinvestment in other opportunities, the banks may take advantage of the secondary mortgage market established by such institutions as the FNMA to sell their mortgages and rearrange their loan portfolios.

The rearrangement of asset portfolios can become very important in times of heavy demand for funds. In periods of intense business activity, for example, the banks may switch out of government securities into commercial and industrial loans. If, at such times, the rates of interest are relatively high, it will mean that the banks may have to take a capital loss on their security portfolios if they decide to sell. It will be recalled from the discussion in Chapter 6 that the market values of income-earning securities will decline as the rate of interest rises. But the banks do in fact have an inducement to make such a portfolio switch in the interest of accommodating industrial borrowers. A special provision of the income tax law works in their favor. Unlike other businesses and individuals, the commercial banks are permitted to deduct all losses on security sales from normal operating income for tax purposes. Thus for a bank that normally pays 50 percent tax on its income, the Treasury would absorb one-half of whatever loss might be sustained by the bank if it were to sell securities in order to be able to meet an increased industrial loan demand.

Finally, it is important to bear in mind the conditions under which a general increase in loan demands might occur. First, there might be a general revival of industrial activity following recessionary conditions in the economy. Or the economy may be continuing through a more or less stable growth phase, such as developed during the middle 1960s.

Second, there might be a general rise in prices, making it necessary for industrial borrowers to increase their loan demands on the banks in order to enable them to finance existing levels of output and sales at new higher price levels. This kind of situation might well arise, and did in fact arise in the 1970s, because of the upward pressure on prices resulting from a heavy wage cost increase. In such situations, the new higher price level may be caused by the fact that money wage rates are increasing more rapidly than average productivity. If, then, the new higher price level is to be sustained or ratified, the banks will have to increase their loans and the money supply.

But the banks will be able to do this only to the extent that they have reserves available or are able to engage in the kind of asset portfolio switching we have referred to. If the banks should in general attempt to meet the increased loan demand by liquidating security investments, this will tend to depress security prices and raise the rate of interest. Such a rise in the interest rate could, in turn, be expected to dampen the economy's ability to maintain the level of production and employment at which it was operating before the wage increase, and the induced price increase, that started the process. In one way or another, therefore, such a development will put pressure on the Federal Reserve Board to take action to ease the monetary situation, by creating bank reserves, to enable the banks to make the loans that the increased wages and prices have made necessary. If the Federal Reserve chooses not to accommodate the increased demand for money, the result will be a reduction in the level of activity and employment that the economy can maintain.

COMMERCIAL BANK INCOME AND RATE OF RETURN ON CAPITAL

Table 8-4 sets out a percentage distribution of the commercial banks' income and expense items for 1981 and 1982. The general structure of the income and expense statement follows from our preceding discussion of asset management. In those years almost two-thirds of the banks' income was derived from interest and fees on loans. This is understandable, as Table 8-2 indicates that loans accounted for 53.3 percent of the banks' total assets in 1982, almost the same as in the preceding year. Interest on the security portfolio was another main source of income, accounting in 1982 for about 12 percent of total income. Balances maintained with other depository institutions, and operations in the federal funds and the RP markets, accounted for about 14 percent of the total income.

It is noteworthy that the income from service charges and associated fees on deposit accounts did not provide a very large source of income. If, however, as we have suggested might occur in the future, the banks begin to charge fees for the maintenance of deposit accounts as interest is paid on more of those accounts, the profile of the banks' income statement will change accordingly.

This matter of the banks' liability for interest on deposit accounts refers, of course, to the movement toward the payment of interest on demand deposits. The magnitude of the issue is seen to some extent from the fact that, as things stand at present, interest on deposit accounts is the bank's largest expense item. Table 8-4 indicates that taking domestic and foreign offices together, the interest on deposit accounts represented more than 50 percent of the banks' total expenses in 1981 and 1982. The table also indicates that the expense of operations in the federal funds and the RP markets accounted for 9.60 percent of the banks' expenses in 1981 and 8.02 percent in 1982. This again underlines the importance that these sources of short-term funds have assumed in the banks' routine operations.

Table   8-4

Operating income and expense items as percentages of operating income of all insured commercial banks operating throughout 1981 and 1982 in the United States

	1981	*1982*
Operating Income:	%	%
Interest and fees on loans	65.72	64.69
Interest on balances with depository institutions	9.78	9.39
Income on Federal funds sold and securities purchased under agreements to resell	4.93	4.39
Interest on securities of U.S. government and government agencies	7.28	8.17
Interest on securities of State governments	3.90	4.13
Income from other securities	0.66	0.67
Income from fiduciary activities	1.28	1.40
Service charges on deposit accounts, commissions and fees	3.69	4.19
Other operating income	2.76	2.97
Total operating income	100.00	100.00
Operating expenses:		
Salaries and employee benefits	11.27	12.15
Interest on deposits in domestic offices	37.26	38.69
Interest on deposits in foreign offices	18.82	16.17
Expenses of Federal funds purchased and securities sold under agreement to repurchase	9.60	8.02
Other interest payments	2.63	2.66
Occupancy expenses of premises, and furniture and equipment expense	3.45	3.87
Provisions for possible loan losses	2.03	3.22
Other operating expenses	6.81	7.76
Total operating expenses	91.86	92.54
Income before taxes and security gains and losses	8.14	7.46
Total operating income	100.00	100.00

Source: FDIC, *1981 Statistics on Banking,* p. 79; and *1982 Statistics on Banking,* p. 80. Percentages may not add to totals because of rounding.

Data on rates of return on capital employed and other performance measures are given in Table 8-5. Net income in each of the two years shown was less than eight-tenths of one percent of total assets. This might seem to be an extremely low figure. But we must bear in mind the importance of the point with which we began our discussion of bank operations in this chapter. We indicated that the banks are highly levered institutions. The great bulk of their funds has in the past been interest-free, though interest has been payable on time and savings deposits. The actual equity capital employed in the banks, as we have seen, amounts

Table   8-5

Rates of return earned and other performance measures of all insured
commercial banks operating throughout 1981 and 1982 in the United States

	1981	1982
1. *As percent of total assets*	%	%
Operating income	12.87	12.37
Operating expenses	11.82	11.45
Income before taxes and security gains and losses	1.05	.92
Net income	.77	.72
2. *As percent of equity capital*		
Net income	13.08	12.17
Cash dividends on common stock	5.15	5.29
3. *Special ratios*		
Rate of return earned on loans	15.59	14.43
Rate of return earned on U.S. government securities, and securities of government agencies	10.76	11.72
Rate of return earned on State government securities	6.56	7.01
Service charges on domestic deposits	.99	1.30
Interest paid on time and savings deposits	11.29	10.45

Source: FDIC, *1981 Statistics on Banking,* p. 80; and *1982 Statistics on Banking,* p. 81.

to only 7 percent of the total assets. Because of that fact, the apparently
very low net income of only .72 percent of assets in 1982 translates into
a healthy rate of return on equity capital of more than 12 percent.

It is this last figure that bank managements are interested in maintaining. For as we pointed out at the beginning, the banks are charged,
in our system and tradition of private enterprise, with the responsibility
of earning an acceptable and competitive rate of return on their owners'
investment. If they do not do so, then capital funds can be expected to
migrate to other lines of economic employment.

ELECTRONIC BANKING

Significant developments in bank operations in the future will undoubtedly lie in the direction of electronic banking. Highly interesting experiments have already been made. The range of procedures under this
heading are usually referred to as Electronic Funds Transfer systems. In
1980 the Federal Reserve Board began an extensive educational program
to make the public and the banking industry aware of the many possibilities that exist.

Under the terms of the Electronic Funds Transfer Act of 1978, a
principal concern of which is to protect the rights of customers in con-

nection with electronic funds transfers, the Federal Reserve has written a set of rules, referred to as Regulation E, to cover operations of this kind. The new regulations establish ground rules for consumers and financial institutions that use this new technology. Moreover, the Federal Reserve has made available to educational institutions, especially high schools, written and filmed materials explaining the electronic transfer of funds, the possible risks in its use, and the rights and responsibilities of consumers and financial institutions in connection with it. The Federal Reserve Board has produced a sixteen-page pamphlet, *Alice in Debitland,* describing EFT services. The Federal Reserve Bank of Philadelphia has produced a fourteen-minute color film, *EFT at Your Service,* showing how the electronic movement of funds can change the ways in which financial transactions are conducted. The Federal Reserve had printed 3 million copies of *Alice in Debitland* by the end of 1980, and it had received hundreds of demands for prints of the EFT film.

Electronic funds transfers are not new. For some time the Fed has made available to member banks a so-called wire transfer service by which funds could be transferred to any point in the country without delay. Now, under the terms of the Depository Institutions Deregulation and Monetary Control Act of 1980, this service is made available to all depository institutions.

We have noted other electronic banking facilities in previous chapters, such as the use of CBCTs, or customer-bank communication terminals, which permit customers to make deposits and withdrawals at remote terminals, and RSUs, or remote service units. In some parts of the country, stores such as supermarkets have experimented with so-called POS, or point-of-sale, terminals. In this kind of arrangement the customer makes settlement for her purchases by having her bank account debited immediately by electronic funds transfer. The advantage to the store, of course, is that it comes into possession of the cash value of the transaction immediately, and the problem of financing its inventories is thereby reduced. The disadvantage to the customer, as in every case where immediate payment is made, is that she cannot take advantage of the delay, or "float," provided by the existing ability to purchase on credit. By surrendering her funds immediately, moreover, the purchaser is sacrificing the interest she could otherwise be earning on her deposit account.

Other EFT systems include ATMs, automatic teller machines, which can be located in shopping centers, airports, and factories and on university campuses, and arrangements for the preauthorization of credits and debits to deposit accounts. For example, arrangements can be made for the automatic credit of payroll payments and social security payments to individuals' accounts. These are at the present time distributed through an ACH system, or automatic clearinghouse system, operated by the Federal Reserve Bank in conjunction with the commercial banks in certain regions. Preauthorized debits would include the automatic payment of regularly recurring bills, such as insurance premiums.

There are some difficulties in the way of the expansion of such EFT arrangements. We have seen that under the McFadden Act interstate banking is forbidden and it would be difficult to extend such facilities across state lines. Moreover, the state banking administrations are not agreed as to whether CBCTs and ATMs are to be considered branches for purposes of the law. There are also some reasons for customer resistance to the EFT systems. First, there is a fear that confidentiality of transactions will be jeopardized, and that the absence of the traditional check as evidence of the transaction might be prejudicial. Under the EFT payment systems the customer would simply get a printout record of the transactions passing through his account. Further, as was suggested above in connection with the POS payment systems, the EFT prevents the individual from arranging the timing of payments in the manner most convenient to him.

Should the banks begin to pay interest on virtually all of their transaction deposits accounts, however, it will become increasingly necessary to find ways of achieving economies of operation. Though the initial capital costs of EFT system installations can be high, the marginal operating costs are extremely low, and collaboration between banks in a given region may well mean that many of the systems we have mentioned could be used more extensively in the future. It has been suggested that the advent of EFT might mean the demise of the smaller banks that are not capitalized strongly enough to permit them to establish and operate the systems. But the opposing view is also held. The EFT systems may enable the smaller banks to link into terminals throughout the country and to offer their customers services that permit business to be transacted with hometown banks from any place in the country.

One of the main purposes for which EFT might increasingly be used in the future is the replacement of the check-clearing procedures at present operated by the Federal Reserve. The details of that procedure will be explained in Part IV. But the actual processing and the physical transfer of checks have reached burdensome proportions. In 1982 the number of checks handled by the Federal Reserve totaled 14.7 billion, and the number of food stamps redeemed amounted to 2.6 billion. This is clearly an avalanche of paper. In the same year the check-clearing operations of the Fed cost $304 million and accounted for 29.7 percent of the Federal Reserve Board's total current expenses of operation.

REGULATORY DEVELOPMENTS AND BANK OPERATIONS

In the early 1980s pressures for deregulation in the financial sector were widespread, as they were also in other industrial sectors of the economy. We have already discussed at some length the relevant provisons of the 1980 and 1982 acts which moved a long way in this direction, and we have indicated the nature of the further changes proposed by the vice-president's Study Task Force in January 1984. Indeed, the operations of commercial banks and nonbank institutions were becoming mixed and blurred to such an extent that officials at the Federal Reserve Board and the Treasury were calling for a moratorium on change.

Early in 1983, for example, the chairman of the Federal Reserve Board, Paul Volcker, argued before the Senate Banking Committee that an amendment of the Bank Holding Company Act was necessary to correct what was thought to be an abuse of its intention. Under that act a *bank* was defined as an institution that accepts deposits and makes commercial loans. While the act prohibited the common ownership of banking and commercial enterprises, it was possible for a bank to divest itself of its business loans and technically become a nonbank under the act. It could then be acquired, quite legally, by another commercial organization. But at the same time it could remain a bank for other purposes, such as obtaining insurance from the FDIC. A number of securities firms and other companies had begun to use this loophole more extensively. The Dreyfus Corporation, a major mutual fund, purchased a small New Jersey bank in 1983 by agreeing to end the bank's lending activities and relinquish its commercial loan portfolio. At the same time Merrill Lynch, a foremost brokerage and financial firm, announced its intention to purchase a small New Jersey savings and loan association. Numerous other similar arrangements came into existence. In December 1983 the Federal Reserve Board issued regulations requiring companies that acquired banking subsidiaries in this way to register under the Bank Holding Company Act or divest themselves of those subsidiaries that the Fed considers to be engaged in banking.

The widening tendency to a crisscrossing of lines and a blurring of traditional functions among the financial institutions stemmed also from certain state legislative actions. Several states in the early 1980s gave state-regulated banks and thrift institutions permission to engage in a range of financial activities that were denied to federally supervised banks. We saw in the preceding chapter that deregulation bills in some of the New England states, for example, gave state-chartered banks and bank holding companies greatly extended powers. They were in some cases permitted to underwrite, sell, and distribute all forms of securities and commercial debt instruments.

The same trends were developing on a national scale. In 1981, for example, the Bank of America purchased a brokerage house, claiming that it did not violate federal regulations if it confined its activities to brokerage business and did not give customers investment advice or underwrite corporate security offerings. The Federal Reserve approved this Bank of America deal, and the acquired brokerage house, Charles Schwab and Company, which operated as the largest discount brokerage firm in the country, continued to generate a tidy income for the Bank of America. Numerous other banks have followed suit, and the discount brokerage business was, at that time, being quite widely absorbed into the banking industry. This is part of a tendency for one-stop financial service centers, or so-called supermarkets of finance, to develop.

These trends, however, were moderated to some extent by the preference of many financial institutions to concentrate on those activities that, it was thought, gave them a comparative advantage by virtue of the skills and experience they had accumulated in them. It was not likely that a large number of financial supermarkets would emerge from the institutional turmoil that existed. The federal laws, moreover, stood in the way. The National Banking Act of 1933, also known as the Glass-Steagall Act, prohibits banks from underwriting and dealing in corporate securities or engaging in general investment banking activities, thus accounting for the somewhat special arrangements in the Bank of America's entry into the discount brokerage business. But arguments for the repeal of the Glass-Steagall Act were increasingly being made.

It was claimed that the Glass-Steagall Act was essentially concerned with issues that were no longer relevant in the 1980s. Out of the extensive banking and financial institutional regulation of the 1930s came strict laws regarding the disclosure of information in connection with security issues and transactions, and the establishment of the FDIC. These and other regulatory arrangements made it clear, it was argued, that the earlier conflicts of interest and the financial distresses associated with the collapse of the 1930s would not be tolerated again.

A number of state legislatures, which, as we have seen, made it possible for banks under their jurisdiction to circumvent the intentions of the Glass-Steagall Act, also extended the lending powers of banks and other financial institutions. In Massachusetts, for example, savings banks and cooperative banks were granted the same lending powers as commercial banks in July 1983. Mutual savings banks were permitted to make commercial and industrial loans up to a maximum of 10 percent of their assets. They could make loans to individuals, including credit card loans, up to 20 percent of their deposits, and under a so-called Leeway Provision, they could invest 3 percent of their deposits in unrestricted investments. The Massachusetts law extended the same facilities to cooperative banks.

The lending powers of commercial banks in general had also been extended by the Garn–St. Germain Depository Institutions Act of 1982. The act extended by 50 percent the legal lending limit of nationally chartered commercial banks. They were now permitted to lend to any one borrower a maximum of 15 percent, in place of the previous 10 percent of their capital and surplus. The limits for the state-chartered banks generally equal or exceed those of the national banks. This provision could theoretically change the banks' lending patterns considerably. At the time of the change the Bank of America, for example, would have been able to lend nearly $700 million to a single borrower. But banks will not necessarily take full advantage of this provision and hold the highly concentrated loan portfolios that it might involve. They might well judge it wiser to maintain a more broadly based diversification of their loan operations.

Given the short-term nature of the banks' traditional lending, it was probably more significant that the Export Trading Company Act of 1982 extended the volume of acceptances that the banks may hold. The act specified that such trade-financing instruments may be held up to an amount equal to 150 percent of the bank's capital and surplus. This level was increased from the previous 100 percent of capital and surplus. With the approval of the Federal Reserve, moreover, the ratio may be increased to 200 percent.

A number of further changes of this kind, each directed to liberalizing the lending ability of the banks, were effected by the Garn–St. Germain Depository Institutions Act of 1982. They complemented and extended the provisions of the Depository Institutions Deregulation Act of 1980, which had liberalized the lending powers of the thrift institutions also. Many of the provisions were directed, as the preamble to the 1982 act stated, to improving the availability of mortgage financing. These various changes, along with the developments in financial institutional structures that we have also observed, imply that new possibilities exist for responses by the depository institutions to the demands for money in the economy. In the following chapter, therefore, we shall look directly at the money-creation process and consider the ways in which the nation's money requirements, or, as the older economists used to say, the "needs of trade," can be met.

SUMMARY

This chapter has examined the operations of the commercial banks as profit-making, competitive, money-creating, financial intermediaries. The high degree of leverage in the banks' financing structure was explained, and the historic significance of interest-free deposit funds was observed. It was suggested that the advent of interest-paying deposit accounts on a wider scale will lead to the introduction of service charges for many of the facilities provided by the banks.

Two historically significant rules or techniques of bank operations were noted. First, the traditional theory of commercial banking, which argued that banks should lend only against short-term, self-liquidating commercial paper, was examined, and its inherent defects were discussed.

The old 80–20 rule with which bank managements approached their day-to-day responsibilities was also reviewed.

It was noted that commercial banks function as financial interme-diaries and perform a traditional intermediary function as "manufactur-ers of liquidity and safety." But their money-creating function was seen to be paramount. This led to a detailed examination of the banks' liabil-ities and assets, treating the former as sources of investable funds and the latter as uses of funds. Note was taken of the very high liquidity of the banks' liabilities, which are principally depositors' funds. The banks' own capital amounted to only about 7 percent of their total assets. The discussion of fund sources was related to the banks' liquidity management problem, and it was seen that short-term liability management has be-come an important aspect of the overall provision for liquidity. A number of so-called managed liabilities became increasingly important in the disturbed financial conditions of the late 1970s and early 1980s.

The problems of the banks' asset portfolio construction and diver-sification were examined, and the significance and relative importance of different kinds of assets were discussed. The diversification of the loan portfolio was noted, and questions were raised concerning the rates of interest charged on loans, the banks' prime rate, the practice of discrim-ination in lending, and some forms of nonprice competition such as the provision of services. The need for the banks to integrate as wide a range of banking services as possible with their loan operations was noted.

A summary of the banks' income and expense statement indicated that loan interest was the principal source of income. Interest payments on time and savings deposits were the principal expense item. The highly levered financial structure of the banks resulted in the fact that while their net income amounted to only eight-tenths of one percent of their total assets, the rate of return on equity capital was a healthy 12 percent.

A comment was given on the progressive implementation of forms of electronic banking, and it was noted that the Federal Reserve Board has undertaken an extensive educational program in this connection. The chapter concluded with a brief discussion of the impact on bank operations of recent regulatory developments and some proposals for further amend-ments in existing legislation.

IMPORTANT CONCEPTS

Traditional theory of commercial bank-
    ing
The financial intermediary function
Asset portfolio criteria: liquidity, safety,
    solvency, and profitability
Tax and Loan accounts
Federal funds market

Repurchase agreements (RPs)
One-bank holding company
Compensating balances
Electronic banking
Liability management
Discount brokerage
Glass-Steagall Act

QUESTIONS FOR DISCUSSION AND REVIEW

1. Examine the proposition that liability management is as important as asset management in meeting a bank's liquidity requirements.

2. What potential conflicts of interest or objectives arise from the fact that the banks, while they are the principal providers of the nation's money supply, are private-enterprise institutions?

3. How does financial leverage, and the benefits and costs of it, come to expression in the banking and financial institutional sector?

4. Examine the central weakness of the commercial loan theory of banking, and explain how, if at all, it might contribute to cyclical instability in the economy.

5. "While commercial banks are the foremost monetary institutions, their economic function is properly understood only in terms of their financial intermediary significance." Comment critically.

6. In the light of the overall structure of their sources of funds, do you think that the commercial banks are undercapitalized? Explain why or why not.

7. How have financial and economic developments during the past two decades changed the methods and problems of the banks' management of their sources of funds?

8. Why can the banking industry attract ownership capital when the banks' net income is, in general, less than one percent of their total assets?

9. How does disintermediation affect the commercial banks?

10. How would the banks be affected by further developments toward a "cashless" society?

9

THE SUPPLY OF MONEY

STUDY OBJECTIVES:

• To gain an understanding of the money-creating function of the commercial bank, based on its acquisition of assets
• To illustrate the relevance and impact of the reserve requirements specified by the Federal Reserve Board
• To observe the effects of (1) internal drain and (2) external drain on the potential expansibility of bank deposits and the money supply
• To extend the money-creation analysis to the banking system as a whole
• To take account of the public's decisions regarding their portfolios of money and near-money assets
• To expand the examination of the total supply of money to incorporate the effects and activities of the nonbank depository institutions
• To summarize the money supply multipliers that describe the potential functioning of the monetary system under alternative assumptions

The commercial banks, together with the nonbank depository institutions, determine the nation's money supply. We shall examine in this chapter how this is accomplished in the course of their day-to-day operations. For this purpose we shall assume in the first part of this chapter that commercial bank demand deposits are, apart from currency, the sole form of the money supply. Initially, that is, we shall ignore the nonbank depository institutions completely. Then at a later point, when the mechanics and the logic of the money-creating process are well in hand, we shall expand our analysis to incorporate all the depository institutions. This procedure is justified and rendered necessary for two reasons. First, the commercial banks are still by far the principal source of changes in the money supply. But second, the principles of fractional reserve lending that the banks have traditionally followed are also the principles on which any other institution that holds transaction accounts must depend.

In the following analysis frequent use will be made of specimen or partial bank balance sheets, of the kind included in Chapter 5. These are sometimes referred to as T-accounts because of their obvious appearance. A balance sheet, of course, must always balance. It follows that whenever a change in a bank's position is being considered, such as a change following an expansion of loans or investments or the creation of new money, it will be necessary to make sure that we have reflected the effects of the change in at least two places in the balance sheet. These changes will be indicated in the following analysis by the use of plus and minus signs as appropriate. If a change in a bank's position is reflected initially, for example, in an increase in its assets, it will be necessary to keep in mind that this will have to be offset in the balance sheet by either (1) a decrease in some other asset or (2) a corresponding increase in liabilities. Numerous examples will follow in due course.

Our development of the money-creation processes can now take account of the three stages that reflect the real-world financial sector: (1) the individual commercial bank, (2) the commercial banks as a whole, and (3) the sum of all the depository institutions.

DEMAND DEPOSIT CREATION
BY AN INDIVIDUAL BANK

Let it be supposed that an individual received a cash payment of $100, in the form, for example, of a wage payment from his employer the Federal Reserve Bank, so that the $100 represented "new money" entering the monetary circulation process for the first time. We shall assume that the $100 is deposited at a commercial bank for credit to the individual's account. The balance sheet of the bank, so far as it reflects the deposit of the $100, will appear as follows:

Commercial bank balance sheet

Assets		Liabilities	
Cash	+ $100	Demand deposits	+ $100

The bank has thereby acquired what we refer to as primary deposits. They are so called because they did not, unlike cases we shall observe below, result from any direct action taken by the bank itself. The commercial banks, as we have seen, are required to hold reserves against their deposit liabilities. These reserves may be held in the form of cash or as deposits at a Federal Reserve Bank. Let us, then, for the sake of uniformity of procedure in what follows, refer to the bank's acquisition of $100 in the foregoing case simply as an acquisition of $100 in reserves that it did not previously possess. The bank's balance sheet can be re-stated:

Commercial bank balance sheet

Assets		Liabilities	
Reserves	+$100	Demand deposits	+$100

The individual who owns this $100 demand deposit may now use it to make payments. Suppose he draws a check against it for $30 to pay for clothing or some other purchases. If the person to whom the check is paid deposits it again in the same bank, the bank's overall balance sheet position would not change. There would be a transfer from the demand deposit account of individual A to that of individual B, the payer and payee, respectively:

Changes in bank's balance sheet

Assets		Liabilities	
		Demand deposits of individual A	−$30
		Demand deposits of individual B	+ 30

If, however, the payee were to deposit the check in another bank, say bank #2, there would be a more complex set of balance sheet changes to be worked out. Bank #1 would in that case have to pay bank #2 the amount of $30 to "clear" the check when it was presented to it for payment. This would be effected by a transfer of reserves between the banks. In more complex cases the transfer would actually take place via a check-clearing mechanism, such as that operated by the Federal Reserve System. The reserve account at the Fed in the name of bank #1 would be debited (or reduced) by the amount of $30, and the reserve account of bank #2, the receiving bank, would be credited (or increased) by the same amount. We then have three sets of balance sheet changes:

Changes in bank #1 balance sheet

Assets		Liabilities	
Reserves	−$30	Demand deposits	−$30

Changes in bank #2 balance sheet

Assets		Liabilities	
Reserves	+ $30	Demand deposits	+ $30

Changes in Federal Reserve balance sheet

Assets	Liabilities	
	Reserve account bank #1	− $30
	Reserve account bank #2	+ 30

In this case the new demand deposits of $30 acquired by bank #2 would be regarded by that bank as primary deposits. Both its deposit liabilities and its reserves have increased. Bank #1, on the other hand, has had to deduct the amount of the check from the account of the individual who, by this means, instructed the bank to pay the amount to someone else. This reduction in demand deposits is then offset in the books of the bank (to make sure the balance sheet still balances) by the reduction in reserves by which the amount was transferred to the receiving bank.

The bank that received the original deposit in this example, bank #1, will conceivably feel that it does not need to retain the entire $100 addition to its reserves. It may lend out some of the funds it has received. Suppose it makes a loan for $45. The borrower will actually receive the proceeds of the loan by having a demand deposit account in his name credited with that amount in the books of the bank. The balance sheet effects are as follows:

Changes in the bank's balance sheet

Assets		Liabilities	
(a) Reserves	+ $100	Demand deposits	+ $100 (a)
(b) Loans	+ 45	Demand deposits	+ 45 (b)

The making of the loan has actually and immediately, we should note, caused an increase in the money supply. Anything that changes the total amount of demand deposits in existence thereby changes the money supply. In this case the money supply has increased from $100 to $145. The implication of this is that the banks, in the very act of making loans, and by the very stroke of the pen by which that is effected, actually create money. This is money creation at work in the simplest case.

We might suppose that this lending bank decided it would be quite satisfied with its balance sheet and liquidity position if, at any time, its reserves-to-deposits ratio did not fall below 50 percent. The bank would then compute what we shall call its money position. To do so, the bank will ask three questions: First, what are its total reserves? These are usually referred to as *legal reserves* because they describe the total amounts that may legally (legally, that is, in accordance with Federal Reserve regulations) be used to satisfy reserve requirements. Second, what are its *required reserves*? And third, what, if any, are its *excess reserves*? In the case of the bank before it undertook its loan operation, the money position would be computed as follows:

Legal reserves (LR)	$100
Less:	
Required reserves (RR) (50% of deposit liabilities)	50
Excess reserves (ExR)	50

The required reserves are stated as $50 because the bank, we supposed, had imposed on itself a 50 percent reserve or liquidity requirement.

Granted that the bank had an excess reserve position of $50, it could proceed to lend out that amount. In the case we examined above, the bank's loan amounted to $45, so that after it recomputed its money position it would still have excess reserves that it could still proceed to lend:

Money position after loan operation

Legal reserves (LR)	$100
Less:	
Required reserves (RR) (50% of total deposits)*	72.5
Excess reserves (ExR)	27.5

*Note: Total deposits of $145 are made up of (1) the initial primary deposits of $100 plus (2) the deposits of $45 created by the bank loan. The latter are frequently referred to as secondary or derivative deposits.

It is then on the basis of its possession of this $27.5 excess reserves that the bank could continue to lend further.

It should be noted, however, that the bank is in this excess reserve position because we have not yet confronted the possibility that the person to whom the initial loan of $45 was made might actually pay away some of the $45 to persons who deposit it in another bank. So long as the checks drawn by the borrower against the initial $45 loan were deposited in the same bank, then that bank would not have to pay any reserves away to any other bank, as we saw could happen in an earlier case. But suppose now that $35 of the $45 loan was paid to someone who deposited it in bank #2. The (a) and (b) entries shown in the following balance sheet of the bank that made the initial loan are intended to refer to (a) the original receipt of $100 primary deposits that made it possible for the bank to consider lending in the first place, and (b) the making of the loan. The new demand deposits created at stage (b) are referred to as derivative or secondary deposits because they result from direct action taken on the initiative of the bank.

Now, however, the $35 payment by the borrower will be reflected in the following set of balance sheet entries:

Changes in bank #1 balance sheet

Assets		Liabilities	
(a) Reserves	+ $100	Demand deposits	+ $100 (a)
(b) Loans	+ 45	Demand deposits	+ 45 (b)
(c) Reserves	− 35	Demand deposits	− 35 (c)

Changes in bank #2 balance sheet

Assets		Liabilities	
(c) Reserves	+ $ 35	Demand deposits	+ $ 35 (c)

Changes in Federal Reserve balance sheet

Assets		Liabilities	
		Reserve account bank #1 − $ 35	
		Reserve account bank #2 + 35	

If we recompute the money position of bank #1, we see that its potential lending ability is now very different:

Legal reserves (LR)	$65
Less:	
Required reserves (RR) (50% of total deposits)	55
Excess reserves (ExR)	10

The bank's required reserves now amount to $55, or 50 percent of the deposits that remain on its books [$110 (i.e., $100 + 45 − 35)]. The legal reserves have fallen to $65, following the transfer of $35 to pay for (or to clear) the check drawn on it, and the bank's further lending can then be based only on the remaining excess reserves of $10.

Suppose, alternatively, that immediately after receiving the initial primary deposit of $100 the bank, while it adhered to a policy of maintaining a 50 percent reserves-to-deposits ratio, had actually lent all of what would then have been its excess reserves of $50. If, further, the entire $50 of the new loan had been paid away to persons who deposited the checks in another bank, the final money position of the lending bank would have been computed as follows. The details can be filled in as an exercise by the reader.

Legal reserves (LR)	$50
Less:	
Required reserves (RR) (50% of total deposits of $100)	50
Excess reserves (ExR)	Nil

In that case the bank would no longer have any excess reserves at all. It would be, to use the market terminology, fully lent.

These elementary exercises exhibit a number of important practical points. First, an individual bank in the real world must be careful at any time not to lend more than the excess reserves it possesses, as shown by its daily money position computation, or the reserves it can obtain as a result of the borrowing or "liability management" we considered in the preceding chapter. Second, bank lending can always be expected to be accompanied by a loss of reserves as reserves are transferred to other banks to clear checks drawn on the accounts of the borrowers. Such a loss of reserves is referred to as internal drain because it describes a drain of reserves away from one bank while they are being simultaneously received by another bank somewhere in the system. Third, this internal drain is frequently referred to as resulting from what is called adverse clearing balances. Banks are receiving and paying large numbers of checks drawn on each other every day. At the end of the day a net balance of the amount due from one bank to another is computed. A net outflow of reserves on this amount is then referred to as an adverse clearing balance.

We summarize, then, by saying that by confining new loans to the amount of its excess reserves a bank can feel comfortably sure that it will not in general fall below a fully lent position even if, as a result of that lending, a maximum possible internal drain or adverse clearing balance is experienced. The latter would result if the entire amount of such new loans was paid to individuals who deposited the funds in other banks.

THE COMMERCIAL BANKING SYSTEM AS A WHOLE

Let us introduce a little more realism into our example. For ease of computation we shall assume a required reserve ratio of 10 percent against all demand deposits. Let us assume also that an initial primary cash deposit of $100 is received, as before, by a bank somewhere in the system.

We can then envisage the balance sheet changes of the bank that received the primary deposit, imagining that it proceeded to lend its excess reserves. It lent, that is, as much as it could, consistent with the rule we derived from the previous example. Finally, we shall assume that following the expansion of loans in this fashion, the entire amount of the loan is actually paid away to persons who deposit it in another bank.

In this situation the bank's balance sheet changes are as follows:

Changes in bank #1 balance sheet

Assets		Liabilities	
(a) Reserves	+$100	Demand deposits	+$100 (a)
(b) Loans	+ 90	Demand deposits	+ 90 (b)
(c) Reserves	− 90	Demand deposits	− 90 (c)

The bank initially expanded its loans by only $90 and retained $10 reserves because it desired to satisfy the official reserve requirement of 10 percent. In the outcome, after the adverse internal drain, the bank is in a fully lent position.

Consider now a comparable reaction on the part of bank #2, the bank that received the $90 reserves drained away from bank #1 following the latter's loan expansion and check-clearing experience:

Changes in bank #2 balance sheet

Assets		Liabilities	
(c) Reserves	+$90	Demand deposits	+$90 (c)
(d) Loans	+ 81	Demand deposits	+ 81 (d)
(e) Reserves	− 81	Demand deposits	− 81 (e)

The second bank thus retains 10 percent of its primary deposits to satisfy the reserve requirement, lends out 90 percent, or $81, experiences the maximum possible adverse internal drain, and similarly ends up in a fully lent position.

Imagine that this happens a third time, in the bank that receives the $81 reserves from bank #2. We may call it bank #3:

Changes in bank #3 balance sheet

Assets		Liabilities	
(e) Reserves	+$81	Demand deposits	+$81 (e)
(f) Loans	+ 72.9	Demand deposits	+ 72.9 (f)
(g) Reserves	− 72.9	Demand deposits	− 72.9 (g)

Again bank #3 will be in a fully lent position.

If we consider the banking system as a whole, each stage of this lending process is adding a further amount to the total level of demand deposits in existence. The money supply is thereby being increased. Focusing on the final net positions of the three banks in the example so far, the net increases in deposits are $100 in bank #1, followed by $90 in bank #2, followed by $81 in bank #3. In fact, we have here a chain of deposit expansion in which each link has a magnitude that is 90 percent of the preceding link. Consider the sum of all the magnitudes of all the links in the chain, assuming that the chain of expansion will continue in this fashion so long as a bank anywhere in the system possesses excess reserves to form the basis of increased lending. The ultimate total increase in demand deposits that results from the multiple expansion is clearly the sum of a geometric series. It can be written as

$$\$100 + 90 + 81 + 72.9 + 65.61 + \ldots$$

Taking D_{max} as the maximum permissible expansion of demand deposits, the outcome can be expressed alternatively as

$$D_{max} = \$100(1 + .9 + .9^2 + .9^3 + .9^4 + .9^5 + \ldots$$

It is known that the sum of such a series can be written as

$$D_{max} = \$100\frac{1}{(1 - .9)}$$

The maximum permissible expansion of deposits for the banking system as a whole, therefore, is simply $100/.10, or $1,000.

It is best, however, to look at this possible outcome in two clearly different ways. First, the maximum amount of deposits that can be supported by the reserves of the banking system will always be equal to the total reserves held by the system multiplied by the reciprocal of the required reserve ratio. The total reserves of the banking system in the case supposed are $100, and the required reserve ratio is .10. Using the notation R for total reserves, and r for the required reserve ratio, it follows that

$$D_{max} = R/r$$

This is a general rule that applies in all cases of the strict simplicity we have so far considered.

Second, this total permissible demand deposit level of $1,000 is made up of (1) an increase in primary deposits of $100, plus (2) an increase in derivative, or secondary, deposits of $900. This secondary increase in derivative deposits could have been determined in a slightly different way.

For this purpose we revert to the balance sheet changes of bank #1 and consider the computation of what we previously called its money position. The reader can set this out in the same fashion as before to demonstrate that the bank's excess reserves amount to $90. Then it is with this initial loan expansion of $90 that the chain of derivative deposit expansion actually begins. This expansion of derivative deposits can be seen in the same way as before to proceed in a geometric series of the form

$$\$90(1 + .9 + .9^2 + .9^3 + .9^4 + \ldots$$

Using the symbol ΔD_{max} to indicate the maximum permissible expansion of derivative deposits, the sum of the series can be shown to be

$$\Delta D_{max} = \$90/.10$$

We can put this result in a form in which it will reappear in more complex cases. We use the term ExR to indicate excess reserves, in this case the excess reserves of the banking system as a whole. It follows that

$$\Delta D_{max} = ExR/r$$

In words, the maximum permissible expansion of the derivative deposits equals the excess reserves multiplied by the reciprocal of the required reserve ratio.

SUMMARY PROPOSITIONS
ON DEMAND DEPOSIT EXPANSION
BY THE BANKING SYSTEM AS A WHOLE

We have now reached a conclusion that differentiates our analysis of the banking system as a whole from that of a single commercial bank. Making use of the twofold way of looking at the deposit expansion potential we have just referred to, we can state the following results. First, for an individual bank the maximum permissible expansion of deposits that it can engage in at any time is equal to the amount of its excess reserves. Second, for the banking system as a whole we focus not on the expansion in deposits that can occur *at a point in time* as in the case of an individual bank, but on the maximum permissible expansion that can take place *over a period of time*. The period of time we have in view in the case of the banking system as a whole is the length of time it would take for the multiple expansion we have discussed to work itself out completely. In that case we can say that the maximum permissible expansion of deposits for the system as a whole is equal to its possession of excess reserves multiplied by the reciprocal of the required reserve ratio.

Third, looking again at the banking system as a whole, we can state that the maximum total deposits the banks can have outstanding at any time will be equal to their total legal reserves multiplied by the reciprocal of the required reserve ratio. These conclusions, of course, follow strictly only under the kinds of assumptions we have made so far. In actual fact there will be reasons why the results have to be modified to take account of variations in the total level of reserves the banking system holds and, as we shall see, variations in the public's demand for cash and time deposits, rather than demand deposits. But analysis in all such cases is grounded in the kinds of results we have reached so far.

The reasons for the difference between the way in which we have to look at an individual bank's deposit expansibility (recognizing it can lend only its excess reserves at any time) and the expansibility of the banking system as a whole (recognizing it can expand up to a multiple of its excess reserves) is that in the case of the individual bank we must take account of the possibility of internal drain. But such a phenomenon does not, of course, affect the banking system as a whole. On the contrary, the drain of reserves away from one bank to another permits the successive rounds of deposit expansion by different banks. Internal drain simply causes a redistribution of the existing total reserves throughout the banking system. The total level of reserves remains unchanged.

The system as a whole can, however, suffer from what is called external drain. In that case something happens to cause the total reserves in the banking system as a whole to diminish. When that occurs, the maximum level of deposits that the banks can have outstanding will, of course, be reduced. There are two main causes of external drain. First, a decision on the part of the public to increase their demand for currency will reduce bank reserves. The public obtain currency from the banks and pay for it by reducing their demand deposits. But we recall that the banks' holdings of cash constituted part of their total reserves. An increase in currency in circulation, therefore, reduces both demand deposits and bank reserves by the same amount. The reader can confirm that if deposits and reserves decrease by the same amount, there will actually be a decline in excess reserves. This decline that is due to the external drain would set in motion a multiple contraction, not a multiple expansion of deposits as in the preceding case.

Second, an external drain can result from a deficit in the international balance of payments. For to the extent that funds are flowing out of the monetary sector to meet financial obligations to foreigners, this will diminish the demand deposits of domestic depositors and increase the United States dollar funds owned by foreigners. Ultimately, when those foreign holders of dollar balances use them to purchase foreign currencies, the reserves of the banking system will be reduced.

The phenomenon of external drain is actually the opposite of what we assumed at the beginning of our examples in this chapter. We assumed there that the chain of deposit expansion was caused by an initial flow of cash to the banking system. This, it was seen, gave rise to an increase in the total reserves of the system. Now, in contemplating an outflow of cash, we are assuming precisely the opposite case. It follows, then, that in the same way as an inflow of cash to the system gave rise to a potential multiple expansion of deposits, an outflow of cash would give rise to a potential multiple contraction of deposits. The possibility that this may occur should be kept well in mind. For at different seasons of the year, at Christmas and other holiday seasons for example, the public's demand for cash increases. At such times, therefore, multiple contraction of deposits would tend to occur if some action were not taken by the Federal Reserve Bank to increase the reserves of the banking system to offset the drain. We shall consider at a later point how such offsetting monetary policy action may be taken.

We may take the following as a single example of the need for a multiple contraction of deposits by the banking system as a whole, following an increase in currency in circulation. We imagine that the following partial balance sheet represents the position of the banks as a whole:

Changes in the balance sheet of the banking system

Assets		Liabilities	
(a) Reserves	$200	Demand deposits	$2,000 (a)
(b) Cash	− 50	Demand deposits	− 50 (b)
(c) Loans	− 450	Demand deposits	− 450 (c)

We suppose here that at situation (a) the banking system is fully lent, with a required reserve ratio of 10 percent. We imagine that the balance sheet items (b) reflect the public's increase in demand for cash. In that case the banks' reserves decline to $150. If no further changes occurred, the banks would be in a reserve deficiency position. Against their deposits of $1,950 they would hold reserves of only $150. This would not satisfy the required reserve ratio of 10 percent. To retrieve the situation we must calculate the maximum deposits the banks could support on a reserve base of $150. Using our previous formula, this would be given by

$$D_{max} = R/.10 = \$150/.10 = \$1,500$$

In order, then, to get back to a total deposit level of $1,500 and reestablish a fully lent position, the banks would have to contract loans by $450, thereby reducing demand deposits by the same amount. There are, as we have said, other developments that may occur. We shall return to them. But the main issue for the present is that of the possibilities of both demand deposit expansion following an addition to reserves and deposit contraction following a reduction of reserves.

DEPOSIT EXPANSION
IN THE BANKING SYSTEM AS A WHOLE
UNDER VARYING ASSUMPTIONS

In our discussion in the preceding chapter of commercial bank operations and the problems of bank asset and liability management, we saw that there are many ways in which a bank may gain reserves. The inflow of cash we have supposed in our examples so far is not the only, or even the most important, source of reserves. Bank management is very much concerned with the sources and uses of funds as a whole.

 An individual bank could at any time bolster its reserve position by selling securities to individuals or, to use the usual market description, to the nonbank public, which includes the nonbank financial institutions as well as individuals. We may suppose that a bank sold $100 securities in this way to an insurance company that paid for them by drawing a check on its demand deposit account at the bank. The scope that thereby arises for the bank's further loan operations is also illustrated in the following partial balance sheet:

Changes in the bank's balance sheet

Assets		Liabilities	
(a) Reserves	$200	Demand deposits	$2,000 (a)
(b) Securities	− 100	Demand deposits	− 100 (b)
(c) Loans	+ 100	Demand deposits	+ 100 (c)

We continue to suppose a required reserve ratio of 10 percent. The sale of securities has enabled the bank to switch its asset investments to loans, a portfolio management decision that would have depended on the rate of return available on loans compared with the rate previously being earned on securities.

 If, on the other hand, the bank had sold the securities to the Federal Reserve Bank, a net addition to its reserves would have resulted. In that case there would have been a net increase in the reserves of the banking system as a whole, and a multiple expansion of loans and deposits could again have been made in the manner we have previously examined:

Changes in the balance sheet of the banking system

Assets			Liabilities	
(a) Reserves	+	$100	Demand deposits	+$1,000 (b)
(a) Securities	−	100		
(b) Loans	+	1,000		

THE PUBLIC'S DEMAND FOR CURRENCY

Our previous examples of deposit expansion supposed that it was not accompanied by any external drain of cash to the public. The maximum permissible expansion of demand deposits, therefore, was simply the excess reserves multiplied by the reciprocal of the required reserve ratio. Let us suppose now that the public wishes to maintain currency holdings equal to 10 percent of their demand deposits. We shall refer to that ratio in what follows as c. The public is, in other words, making a judgment that they will be maintaining an optimum structure of their liquidity and asset portfolios when the cash-to-deposits ratio is at that level. Entering our analysis at this point is the important proposition that the level of bank reserves, and therefore the expansibility of bank loans and the money supply, are dependent on the liquid wealth portfolio decisions of the public.

On a slightly different level we can say that when the supply of money is increased in the form of demand deposits and more active economic conditions occur, with possibly higher incomes, employment, production, and price levels, the public will require larger holdings of currency to effect the purchases of those things for which currency, rather than bank deposits, is the most convenient means of payment. These may include, for example, many retail purchases, some payroll payments, expenditures in restaurants, gasoline purchases, and transit fares. In general, we are supposing in the present example that these considerations lead the public to maintain a specifiable desired ratio of currency holdings to their demand deposits.

We can now ask what would be the maximum permissible expansion of demand deposits in the banking system as a whole if the banks were to increase their borrowing from the Federal Reserve Bank by $100. Before we illustrate the possible outcomes, let us establish a rule of procedure, or a consistent method of analysis.

We focus first on the addition to excess reserves that results from the borrowing operation, supposing the banks are fully lent prior to the borrowing. We shall again use the symbol ExR to refer to the addition to excess reserves. We know that when the banks have undertaken the maximum permissible expansion of loans and deposits that can be based on those excess reserves, they will again be fully lent. There will then no longer be any excess reserves. In other words, all the existing excess reserves that were available to start the multiple lending process will have been absorbed into required reserves as a result of that multiple expansion, or they will have been used by the banks to provide the public's desired increase in currency holdings. We can focus, therefore, on the ways in which, during the loan and deposit expansion, the initially existing excess reserves are absorbed or transformed. In the present case they are absorbed by (1) increased required reserves or (2) the cash outflow from the banks.

We know that when the maximum permissible increase in demand deposits has occurred, which we again refer to as ΔD_{max}, the required reserves will have increased by r percent of that amount, where r is again the required reserve ratio. At the same time, an amount of reserves equal to c percent of the increase in demand deposits will have been absorbed to provide the public with their desired increase in currency holdings. We can therefore establish a simple excess reserves absorption equation, showing the disposition of excess reserves due to the deposit expansion:

$$ExR = r\Delta D + c\Delta D = \Delta D(r + c)$$

It follows by simple transposition of this excess reserves absorption equation that the result we seek is

$$\Delta D_{max} = ExR \frac{1}{(r + c)}$$

The expression $1/(r + c)$ is referred to as the incremental demand deposit multiplier in this case. In the example we have in view the results would be as follows:

Changes in the balance sheet of the banking system

Assets		Liabilities	
Reserves	+ $100	Borrowings from Fed	+ $100
Loans	+ 550	Demand deposits	+ 500
Reserves	− 50		

These balance sheet changes come about for the following reasons. First, the initial borrowing at the Fed provided the banks witn new excess reserves of $100. In our ΔD_{max} formula the value of r is by assumption

10 percent, and the value of c is also 10 percent. We accordingly calculate ΔD_{max} as

$$\Delta D_{max} = \$100/(.10 + .10) = 100/.20 = \$500$$

Demand deposits can expand by $500.

But second, we know that as a result of this expansion the public's demand for currency will increase by 10 percent of the amount of new demand deposits, or by $50. The balance sheet therefore shows a decline in reserves by this amount. To make this end result possible, the banks will actually expand their loans (or, as we have also seen, their purchases of securities) by $550. We can then say that of the total new loans of $550, the public will hold $500 in new demand deposits and will take the remaining $50 in cash.

When this expansion process has worked itself out, the banks are once again back to a fully lent position. This final result is exhibited as follows:

Final money position computation:

Legal reserves	$50
Less: Required reserves (10 percent of $500 deposits)	50
Excess reserves	Nil

The total money supply in this case will have increased by the sum of the new demand deposits and the increased currency in circulation. We can accordingly establish an incremental money supply multiplier as well as the incremental deposit multiplier. Using ΔC to refer to the increase in currency in circulation, and ΔM to refer to the increase in the money supply, it follows that

$$\Delta M = \Delta D + \Delta C = \Delta D + c\Delta D = (1 + c)\Delta D$$

Reverting to our ΔD_{max} formula, it follows that the incremental money supply multiplier can be expressed as

$$\Delta M = ExR \frac{1 + c}{r + c}$$

In the case we have considered, the results may be summarized as follows:

1. Increase in demand deposits	$500
2. Increase in currency in circulation	50
3. Increase in the money supply	550
4. Increase in bank loans	550

THE PUBLIC'S HOLDINGS OF
NONPERSONAL TIME DEPOSITS

In addition to requiring the banks to maintain reserves against demand deposits, the Federal Reserve also requires them to hold reserves against nonpersonal time deposits, or against time deposits held by business corporations or profit-making organizations. For ease of calculation in what follows, we shall assume that this required reserve ratio against nonpersonal time deposits is 4 percent. We shall designate the ratio as r_t. Additionally, we may suppose that the portfolio-holding habits and wishes of the public are such that they will in general hold such time deposits equal to 1.25 times their demand deposits. We shall refer to the ratio of these time deposits to demand deposits as t. Again, in other words, we shall observe that the reserve position and the money-creating potential of the banks is affected by the wealth portfolio-holding habits of the public.

We can extend the preceding example by supposing that following their borrowing from the Fed, the banks expand their loans and deposits to the maximum extent possible under these new assumed conditions. In that case the excess reserves absorption equation will appear as follows:

$$ExR = r\Delta D + c\Delta D + r_t t\Delta D = \Delta D(r + r_t t + c)$$

The increase in the required reserves against the nonpersonal time deposits is described as $r_t t\Delta D$ in this equation. This follows from the need to multiply the increase in demand deposits by t to calculate the increase in time deposits, ΔT, and then to multiply this resulting total by r_t to find the increased required reserves to which they give rise. It follows from the new form of the excess reserves absorption equation that

$$\Delta D_{max} = ExR \frac{1}{r + r_t t + c} = ExR \frac{1}{.10 + (.04)1.25 + .10} = ExR \frac{1}{.25}$$

If we add the increased currency in circulation to the increase in demand deposits, we can again describe the overall increase in the money supply. This will be equal, as in the preceding case, to ΔD plus $c\Delta D$. The increase in the money supply will therefore be described by

$$\Delta M = ExR \frac{1 + c}{r + r_t t + c}$$

The balance sheet changes reflecting these developments, and the resulting changes in the monetary magnitudes, can be summarized as follows:

Changes in the balance sheet of the banking system

Assets		Liabilities	
Reserves	+$100	Borrowings from Fed	+$100
Loans	+ 940	Demand deposits	+ 400
Reserves	− 40	Nonpersonal time deposits	+ 500

1. Increase in demand deposits, ΔD	$400
2. Increase in nonpersonal time deposits, ΔT	500
3. Increase in currency in circulation, ΔC	40
4. Increase in total deposits, $\Delta D + \Delta T$	900
5. Increase in bank loans, ΔL	940
6. Increase in the money supply, $\Delta D + \Delta C$	440

It can readily be seen that when this final outcome has been reached, the banking system is again fully lent:

Legal reserves		$60
Less: Required reserves		
1. Against demand deposits .10 × 400 =	40	
2. Against nonpersonal time deposits .04 × 500 =	20	60
Excess reserves		Nil

The foregoing examples show that the introduction into the incremental deposit multiplier and the incremental money supply multiplier of (1) the public's demand for currency and (2) the public's holdings of nonpersonal time deposits reduces the magnitude of the demand deposit and M1 multipliers that potentially come into play following an increase in the banking system's excess reserves. In the latter case, however, there has been an increase in the economy's financial wealth, or its total liquid assets, taking account of the increase in both demand and nonpersonal time deposits. In the most elementary case, on the other hand, where neither an outflow of currency nor an increase in nonpersonal time deposits reduced the demand deposit multiplier, the potential increase in demand deposits, and therefore in the money supply, was even greater, namely $1,000.

THE BANKING SYSTEM'S DESIRED
EXCESS RESERVES

The preceding examples have all assumed that the banking system consistently conducts its lending and other asset expansion policies in such a way as to remain in a fully lent position. This may not always be true. The banks may in fact desire to hold excess reserves, or to vary the intensity of their borrowing from the Fed (so far as the Fed permits them to exercise that privilege) in order to increase the availability of excess reserves as new lending and investment opportunities arise. The banks may be more ready to reduce the amount of excess reserves they are holding when the rates of return they can earn on loans and investments increase. The banks are, as we noted at the beginning, profit-making institutions, and we can expect them to be more ready to lend, and even, perhaps, to undertake higher degrees of risk in their loan operations, when interest rates and the rates of return they can earn on their loans are higher. Such a policy on the part of the banks will be reflected in a willingness to maintain a lower excess reserve position.

We can visualize the banks' desired excess reserves as a ratio of their demand deposits. We shall refer to this ratio as e. As we have just suggested, e is a behavior variable whose magnitude depends on the rate of interest, i. We may write $e = e(i)$. Or we may consider the possible relation between the rate of return, i, that the banks can obtain on loans and the rate of interest they have to pay on borrowings from the Fed, or the discount rate which we shall refer to as r_d. We can then focus, not on the banks' excess reserves, but on another variable that has been widely discussed among monetary economists. If we take the banks' actual excess reserves at any time and deduct from them the total amount of the banks' borrowings from the Fed, or their so-called borrowed reserves, we can refer to the difference as their net free reserves. If, then, the differential between i and r_d should increase, this may tend to increase the banks' borrowings from the Fed and thereby decrease their net free reserves. This would also provide a larger reserve base for use in expanding deposits and the money supply. In that case the money supply would depend, indirectly, on the differential between the going market rate of interest on loans and the Federal Reserve discount rate. We could write this functional dependence as $M^s = M^s(i - r_d)$.

For our present purposes, however, we assume simply that the banks' desired holdings of excess reserves depend in some way on the rate of return available on loans, or the general economic conditions that exist and the strength of the demand for loans. We may incorporate the banks' desired excess reserve ratio, e, into our incremental deposit and money supply multipliers by concentrating on the manner in which it affects the excess reserves absorption equation. In this case we can write that equation as

$$ExR = r\Delta D + r_t t\Delta D + c\Delta D + e\Delta D$$

By reasoning similar to that employed in the preceding examples, the incremental demand deposit multiplier then takes the form

$$\Delta D = ExR \frac{1}{r + r_t t + c + e}$$

and the relevant money supply multiplier will be

$$\Delta M = ExR \frac{1 + c}{r + r_t t + c + e}$$

THE TOTAL DEPOSIT AND TOTAL
MONEY SUPPLY MULTIPLIERS

The preceding analysis has concentrated on the derivation of incremental demand deposit and incremental money supply multipliers under different assumed conditions. It has focused on the public's liquid portfolio requirements and the banks' own desired reserve positions. We sometimes wish to know for analytical and policy purposes, however, the answer to a slightly different question. We may ask what, at any given time, is the maximum amount of demand deposits, and accordingly the money supply, that can be supported by the existing total reserve position of the banking system. We are then interested in total deposit and total money supply multipliers, rather than the incremental multipliers we have considered so far. Let us approach this question by focusing in a slightly different way on the allocation to different uses of the banks' total reserves.

Making use of the same notation as previously, we can state that the amount of reserves absorbed to satisfy reserve requirements against demand deposits will be rD. Similarly, an amount equal to $r_t tD$ will be held against nonpersonal time deposits calculated in the same manner as previously. Finally, eD will be desired by the banks as excess reserves. Defining total reserves as R, it follows that a total reserves absorption equation can be written as

$$R = (r + r_t t + e)D$$

The total demand deposits supportable by the total reserves is therefore

$$D = \frac{R}{r + r_t t + e}$$

Given that the currency holdings of the public can be stated as cD, the total money supply can be written in the same way as before as M, or as $D + C$, or $D + cD$, and it can then be described by the equation

$$M = \frac{R(1 + c)}{r + r_t t + e}$$

We have in these last two expressions what can be called the total demand deposit multiplier and the total money supply multiplier. They can be compared in summary with the previous incremental multipliers:

1. Incremental demand deposit multiplier:

$$\Delta D = ExR\frac{1}{r + r_t t + c + e}$$

2. Incremental money supply multiplier:

$$\Delta M = ExR\frac{1 + c}{r + r_t t + c + e}$$

3. Total demand deposit multiplier:

$$D = R\frac{1}{r + r_t t + e}$$

4. Total money supply multiplier:

$$M = R\frac{1 + c}{r + r_t t + e}$$

The public's currency-to-deposits ratio, c, does not appear in the denominator of the total demand deposit and total money supply multipliers. The reason for this will be apparent on a moment's reflection and should be kept clearly in mind. It follows from the fact that in establishing the total deposit multiplier, as distinct from the incremental multiplier, we are assuming a given situation as to both the banks' actual reserve position and the public's currency holdings. We are not in this case considering a change in deposits or currency in circulation. We are simply asking what, if the banks are fully lent at a given point in time, is the maximum amount of demand deposits they can support on the basis of their actual reserve position. If, of course, we change the assumptions and the argument, and consider a change in deposits and in the money supply that may result from a change in reserves, then as the level of deposits increases, the public's currency requirements will also increase. In that case, therefore, the public's currency-to-deposits ratio, c, must be taken into account. It will then appear as before in the denominator of the incremental deposit and money supply multipliers.

EXTENSION OF THE MONEY SUPPLY ANALYSIS TO INCLUDE ALL DEPOSITORY INSTITUTIONS

It is now possible to extend our analysis from the preceding assumption that the commercial banks are the sole creators of the money supply other than currency. It is necessary to do so in view of the fact that the Depository Institutions Deregulation and Monetary Control Act of 1980 has extended to all depository institutions the right to maintain transaction accounts, including NOW accounts and other checkable deposits.

In making this transition it is important for the reader to bear in mind that we shall make extensive use, from this point on, of a new concept we shall refer to as the *monetary base*. This is also defined as the total amount of high-powered money in the system. It is the sum of (1) the total reserves in the depository institutions, which we shall designate by the symbol R (expanding the meaning of this term now to refer to the depository institutions' total reserves and not simply the reserves of the banks as in the preceding discussion), and (2) the amount of currency in circulation in the hands of the public, which we shall continue to refer to as C. Describing the monetary base as B, we write

$$B = R + C$$

A clear understanding of the concept of the monetary base is vital at this point. It is the statistic that the Federal Reserve Board is very much concerned with in its attempt to keep track of the total money supply and general monetary conditions, and to influence these by monetary policy measures. The two variables of R and C are taken together to form the monetary base for the following reasons: (1) They indicate the total amount of reserves that the system could possess if all the currency in circulation were paid into the depository institutions and converted into reserves; and (2) they similarly describe the total amount of currency that could circulate if all the reserves were used to provide currency in exchange for deposits. The monetary base will be seen in the following discussion to support deposits in the depository institutions on the one hand and currency in circulation on the other. We shall be very much concerned to observe the ways in which the influence of the total monetary base is divided between these various important functions.

In the following analysis we shall employ notation analogous to that used in the preceding discussion of the commercial banks. The following definitions will apply:

D_b = demand deposits in commercial banks
D_o = other checkable deposits in commercial banks, including NOW and ATS accounts
D_n = checkable deposits in nonbank depository institutions
D_t = total checkable deposits
$D_t = D_b + D_o + D_n$

We shall also employ some previous notation with appropriately different definitions, in order to put analogous concepts to work in our new expanded depository institutional system. We therefore define the following:

c = the public's desired holdings of currency as a ratio of the total transaction accounts in all depository institutions
t = the ratio of nonpersonal time deposits to all transaction accounts
r = the required reserve ratio against transaction deposits
r_t = the required reserve ratio against nonpersonal time deposits
e = the depository institutions' desired excess reserves as a ratio of transaction deposits

Given the definition of the monetary base, it follows that this will
be divided or absorbed in the following way:

$$B = rD_t + r_t tD_t + cD_t + eD_t$$

It follows by rearrangement that

$$B = D_t(r + r_t t + c + e),$$

and the total transaction deposit multiplier follows as

$$D_t = B\frac{1}{r + r_t t + c + e}$$

Moreover, if it could be supposed that in the presence of monetary
changes all the parameters and behavior variables in this multiplier were
to remain fixed, then an incremental deposit multiplier could be defined
as follows:

$$\Delta D_t = \Delta B\frac{1}{r + r_t t + c + e}$$

In this expression ΔB describes any net change in the monetary base,
such as an increase in the total reserves of the depository institutions or
in the currency in the hands of the public. In the course of our studies of
the Federal Reserve and its policy operations in Part IV, we shall observe
various reasons why either or both of these magnitudes may vary.

THE M1 AND M2 MULTIPLIERS

We recall now the definitions we have given of the two important measurements of the money supply. The M1 measure includes currency in
circulation in the hands of the public and the checkable deposits in the
depository institutions. The M2 measure includes M1 plus certain other
savings accounts and, in particular, deposits in money market mutual

funds held by noninstitutional depositors. In the notation we adopted in the preceding section, the following equivalence can be defined:

$$M1 = D_t + C$$

We may assume further, for purposes of the present analysis, that the funds held in the near-money accounts that are also included in the M2 measure of the money supply will in general bear a ratio to transaction deposits defined as k. Then describing these other accounts, or, as we may refer to them, other short-term financial assets, as OSFA, we can define

$$OSFA = kD_t$$

It follows then that

$$M2 = D_t + C + OSFA = D_t(1 + c + k)$$

We note now that $M1 = D_t + C$, and writing this as $(1 + c)D_t$ we may incorporate it into the total transaction deposit multipliers already derived. The M1 multipliers can then be described as follows:

$$M1 = B\frac{1 + c}{r + r_t t + c + e}$$

If, then, it could be supposed that all parameters and behavior variables remained constant in the presence of monetary change, the incremental M1 multiplier would appear as

$$\Delta M1 = \Delta B\frac{1 + c}{r + r_t t + c + e}$$

The derivation of the M2 multipliers makes use of the definition of M2 as $(1 + c + k)D_t$. It follows, under the same kind of assumptions as previously, that

$$M2 = B\frac{1 + c + k}{r + r_t t + c + e}$$

The incremental M2 multiplier follows similarly as

$$\Delta M2 = \Delta B\frac{1 + c + k}{r + r_t t + c + e}$$

WHY DOES THE MONEY SUPPLY CHANGE?

The preceding sections may appear to have been rather mechanical in their exposition of the creation of checkable deposits, and therefore of the money supply. In a sense this has been the case. But it was necessary and important to have before us an understanding of the money-creation process in order that, at a later stage of our work, it can be incorporated into the larger consideration of the forces that determine the conditions of economic activity and prosperity or recession. We shall consider in due course the deeper reasons why money is demanded by the economy and is created by the depository institutions in response to that demand. We shall bring into focus again the question we asked at the beginning as to whether the money supply is to be considered as primarily exogenous or endogenous, and whether, in particular, changes in it are exogenous or endogenous.

Although it has not yet been possible to examine the operations of the Federal Reserve at length, we have seen that the Fed may, by the use of its so-called open market operations, purchase government securities from the nonbank public. If it does so, demand deposits will be created as the sellers of the securities deposit the proceeds of the sale in their checking accounts. This can be looked upon as exogenous money creation. But a significant part of the money creation is what we have called *endogenous*. By this term we have consistently meant that money is created by the banks in response to the demand for it. When business firms request additional bank loans to finance the purchase of inventories of materials and finished goods, or to finance the acquisition of capital equipment, the loans granted by the banks will, in ways we have seen, automatically create demand deposits. It is this creation of demand deposits that we refer to as endogenous money creation.

It will be an important part of our theoretical argument in Parts V and VI that this endogenous money creation may occur when certain developments, such as an increase in industrial costs or an expansion of expenditures, push up the level of commodity prices. Such cost increases may be due to the fact that industrial wage payments increase at a more rapid rate than does the average productivity in the economy. But whatever might be the cause of the price increases, it follows clearly that if, when the increases occur, the economy is going to be able to maintain the same level of real production and output as before at the new higher level of prices, the money supply will have to be increased to make that possible. Thus we shall observe reasons for the need for higher money supplies, as well as the ways in which the banks and other depository institutions may respond to that need and bring higher money supplies into existence.

Holding, then, to the high degree of endogeneity in the changes in the money supply, and understanding from the preceding sections how the need for money may be met, we may leave aside at this time any further consideration of both the analytical significance of these relationships and the practical policy issues to which they give rise.

WHO CONTROLS THE MONEY SUPPLY?

This chapter's examination of the determinants of the economy's money supply may appear complex. But the various possibilities that exist, and the combinations of explanatory forces that have to be taken into account under different assumed conditions, are all grounded in a small number of fairly straightforward ideas. Everything depends, essentially, on the total reserves that the banking system and the nonbank depository institutions possess, the reserve requirements imposed by the Federal Reserve Board, the public's currency-holding habits, and their liquid asset portfolio decisions. Relevant also are the depository institutions' decisions regarding the holding of excess reserves.

Let us recall the variables on which, at various stages of the foregoing discussion, the money supply has been seen to depend. These have been designated as r, r_t, c, t, e, and k. In addition, we have referred by implication to the ratio of "other checkable deposits" in all depository institutions to transactions deposits. This can be taken as the sum of what we referred to as D_o and D_n, expressed as a ratio of D_t, and for purposes of the following summary can be designated as v.

To answer the question of who controls the money supply, we need to know who controls the magnitudes of these variables. It is the asking and answering of this question that takes our analysis beyond the mere exposition of mechanical formulas and relationships to a genuine theory of the supply of money. We need to be interested also in the relative stability of these variables and the likelihood that they can change, more or less quickly and by greater or lesser degrees, in differing economic and monetary conditions. For the present we can summarize by saying that the level of the depository institutions' reserves, R, is more or less under the control of the Federal Reserve Board, which does, of course, also control the reserve requirement ratios. The Fed's monetary policy actions, as we shall see in subsequent chapters, can influence the total level of reserves in the monetary system and the size of the monetary base to some extent.

Of the remaining variables, however, c, t, k, and v are determined by the public, largely as a result of their short-term financial asset and liquidity portfolio decisions. Their holdings of currency, interest-bearing checkable deposits, and liquid forms of near-money, such as are included in M2, depend on the set of factors having to do with convenience, desired rates of return, attitudes to risk and uncertainty, and their expectations of future monetary and economic developments that determine in their minds the optimum distribution of liquid wealth portfolios over these different kinds of assets. The extent to which the Federal Reserve Board has control of the money supply depends also, then, on the extent to which they can track, and predict, the movements in these four variables that are substantially under the public's control.

The last of the variables, e, is a decision variable of the depository institutions. Again, the Federal Reserve, in its attempts to control the monetary situation, can only react to, and endeavor to predict, the changes that occur in this variable.

It would appear, then, that the control of the money supply is in no sense a simple or straightforward matter. There are numerous reasons why slippages occur in the determining processes we have examined in this chapter. Moreover, a large number of estimations have to be made of the likely or possible values of behavior variables. The central bank does not have an easy task in shaping policy for monetary control. But that is another way of saying that monetary analysis cannot be as simple as some schools of thought would have us believe. The transmission channels between policy changes and ultimate results are complex and, unfortunately, likely to be highly unstable.

But the analysis in this chapter has presented the essential nature of the relevant determinants. The reader can now study the various multipliers and behavior reactions under different possible conditions and can observe the ways in which changes in the different variables will work through to effect changes in overall monetary conditions.

SUMMARY

The money supply processes, taking full account of the ways in which they have been amended and refined by the recent Depository Institutions Deregulation and Monetary Control Act, and further affected by the Garn–St. Germain Depository Institutions Act and subsequent regulatory changes, are grounded in the notions of fractional reserve banking and multiple deposit expansion. This chapter has therefore explored systematically the lending ability and the demand deposit expansibility of the commercial banks. The significance of the phenomena of internal drain and external drain was noted. The analysis, still retaining certain basic assumptions, was extended to the consideration of the banking system as a whole.

The deposit expansibility of the commercial banking system under a number of different assumptions was examined. Notice was taken of the way in which certain decisions of the public, regarding the forms in which they wish to hold their portfolios of short-term financial assets, can affect the money-creation potential in the economy. It was shown that the slippages that occur within the money-creating processes for reasons of this kind make it extremely difficult to be confident that the Federal Reserve Board actually does, at any time, have a firm degree of control over the money supply and the monetary situation.

The analysis was broadened from its foundation in the commercial banking system to embrace all depository institutions. This was done in order to acknowledge the implications of the recent banking legislation. It was seen that considerable importance attaches to what is referred to as the monetary base, or the total amount of high-powered money in existence.

The analysis was highlighted and summarized by the derivation of a number of transaction deposit and money supply multipliers. Different degrees of significance can be attached, under different monetary and economic assumptions, to incremental deposit and money supply multipliers on the one hand, and total deposit and money supply multipliers on the other.

Depository institutions create money. The manner in which they do so is subject to various kinds and degrees of federal and state government regulation. The extent to which they do so is subject to further regulation and monetary policy actions of the Federal Reserve Bank. Changes in the money supply occur, to a very large extent, in response to the demand for it by business firms and other decision makers in the economy. In that sense there is, to return to a concept that will become important again in our analytical model of the macroeconomy, a high degree of endogeneity in the money supply.

IMPORTANT CONCEPTS

Primary deposits
Derivative, or secondary, deposits
Money position computation
Legal reserves
Excess reserves
Internal and external drain
Adverse clearing balances
Multiple deposit expansion

Excess reserves absorption equation
Incremental demand deposit multiplier
Incremental money supply multiplier
Monetary base
M1 and M2 multipliers
The r, r_t, c, t, v, k, and e ratios
The locus of control of the money supply

QUESTIONS FOR DISCUSSION AND REVIEW

1. "Although the money-creation process is well understood, the really difficult problem for policy makers is that of defining the money supply in order to address policies to the regulation of it." Discuss critically.

2. "Internal drain introduces problems of bank management; but external drain introduces problems of official monetary policy." Comment critically.

3. Examine the ways in which the historic uniqueness of the banks has been broken down, not only in relation to their assets but also in relation to their liabilities.

4. Who controls the money supply?

5. Comment on the ways in which the magnitude of the money supply, and the difficulties of defining and regulating it, depend on the wealth portfolio-holding habits of the economy.

6. Recalling previous studies in macroeconomic theory, can you anticipate the reasons why an understanding of macroeconomic equilibrium, following an exogenous change in expenditure, requires a consideration of both the real income multiplier (depending on the marginal propensity to consume) and the money supply multiplier?

7. Why does the M2 money supply multiplier differ from that for M1? Is there any potential policy significance in this difference?

8. What possible differences arise, on the levels of both analysis and policy, if the money supply or changes in the money supply are regarded as primarily endogenous rather than exogenous?

9. What relations exist between the supply of money and the velocity of circulation of money? Is the rate of interest relevant?

10. "Banks create deposits by making loans." "Banks must attract deposits in order to make loans." Are these statements consistent or contradictory? Explain fully.

10

NONBANK FINANCIAL INTERMEDIARIES

STUDY OBJECTIVES:

• To review the essential economic feature of financial intermediation: the structure of the channels of the flow of funds in the savings-investment process
• To note the economic effects of changing degrees of intermediation and disintermediation in the financial sector
• To consider the implications of financial intermediation for the money supply, expenditure flows, financial wealth, and money market conditions
• To summarize the asset and liability structures of the principal financial intermediaries
• To observe the sectoral impact in the economy of the principal institutions' sources and uses of funds, and the implications of asset portfolio specialization

The principal characteristics of the financial intermediaries have surfaced at several points in the preceding chapters. We assumed the existence of financial intermediation as we examined the functions and the competitive position of the banks. In Chapter 2 we took an initial look at the financial institutions' identity and economic function, and a fuller analysis of the savings-investment process and the place of the financial intermediaries in it was made in Chapter 5. We examined there the structure of the flow of funds through the credit markets in two successive years, 1981 and 1982. In Chapter 6, in the course of reviewing some tools of analysis, we observed the way in which interest rates and security prices are formed in the markets in which the financial institutions operate.

In this chapter we shall present a brief but systematic view of the principal nonbank financial intermediaries, focusing in particular on their asset and liability structures or their sources and uses of funds. In the course of doing so, we shall look at some further aspects of disinterme- diation, as well as intermediation, in the financial sector. The sectoral impact in the economy of some financial institutional developments, and the spillover implications for expenditure flows, financial wealth, and money market conditions, will also be noted.

CLASSIFICATION OF FINANCIAL INTERMEDIARIES

Table 10-1 summarizes the principal institutions in the financial sector. The first section of the table brings together the depository institutions. These have assumed a new importance in the economy as new relations and new forms of competition between them have been brought about by the Depository Institutions Deregulation and Monetary Control Act of 1980, the Garn–St. Germain Depository Institutions Act of 1982, and developments in state government legislation such as we noted in Chap- ters 7 and 8.

In many respects the uniqueness of the commercial banks has been broken down. The four depository institutions are referred to in the table in order to retain perspective and to note a relative specialization of function among them, in spite of their growing similarities. It is reason- able to expect that in the future this specialization of function, implying as it does a specialization of asset investment portfolios, will continue in the case of many of the nonbank intermediaries. They enjoy benefits that result from the exploitation of the comparative advantages and skills they have developed.

The second section of Table 10-1 lists the contractual savings insti- tutions that are heavy suppliers of funds to the corporate securities seg- ment of the money capital market. They are referred to as contractual savings institutions because the flow of funds to them occurs in a regular and more or less predictable fashion, by virtue of certain established and contractual arrangements. Insurance premiums are paid regularly, for example, and pension fund contributions from both employers and em- ployees occur at regular intervals.

Another heavy influence in the corporate securities market, affect- ing the flow of funds for both corporate stock and bond purchases, comes from the investment companies in the fourth section of Table 10-1. A special form of open-end mutual fund, which is referred to separately in the final section of the table, has recently come into existence. This so- called money market mutual fund concentrates its investments in short- term money market assets. In the period of inordinately high interest rates in the late 1970s and early 1980s these funds were high-income

Table   10-1

Classification of financial intermediaries

Type of institution	Principal sources of funds	Principal uses of funds
1. *Depository institutions*		
Commercial Banks	Demand deposits Time and savings deposits	Commercial and industrial loans Various other loans Government securities
Savings and Loan Associations	Savings accounts	Mortgages
Mutual Savings Banks	Deposits	Mortgages Securities
Credit Unions	Savings capital	Loans to members
2. *Contractual savings institutions*		
Life Insurance Companies	Life insurance reserves (from premiums)	Corporate bonds Mortgages
Property and Casualty Insurance Companies	Insurance reserves (from premiums)	State and local government securities Corporate bonds Corporate stock
Private Pension Funds	Employer and employee contributions	Corporate stock Corporate bonds
State and Local Government Retirement Funds	Payroll deductions	Corporate bonds Corporate stock
3. *Finance Companies*		
Sales Finance Companies	Borrowing	Consumer credit
Personal Finance Companies	Borrowing	Consumer credit
Factors	Borrowing	Accounts receivable
4. *Investment Companies*		
Open-end Investment Companies (Mutual Funds)	Capital accounts	Corporate stock Corporate bonds
Closed-end Investment Companies	Capital accounts	Corporate stock Corporate bonds
5. *Other financial institutions*		
Money Market Mutual Funds	Capital accounts	Short-term liquid assets
Federal National Mortgage Association (Fanny Mae)	Borrowing	Mortgages

Table   10-1

Classification of financial intermediaries (continued)

Type of institution	Principal sources of funds	Principal uses of funds
Government Agencies: Banks for Cooperatives Federal Intermediate Credit Banks Federal Land Banks Federal Home Loan Banks Federal Home Loan Mortgage Corporation (Freddy Mac) Government National Mortgage Association (Ginny Mae)	Borrowing	Loans

earners. In our discussion of the "Forms of Money" in Chapter 4 it was noted that the money market mutual funds have grown rapidly, and because of the high degree of liquidity enjoyed by the shares they issue, the claims against them held by noninstitutional investors are included in the broader measure of the money supply. Some details of the other institutions mentioned in Table 10-1 will be referred to as we proceed.

In viewing these financial institutions as a whole, we should keep in mind the essential economic feature of financial intermediation. We have referred to this already as the structure of the channels of the flow of funds in the savings-investment process. A number of questions need to be sorted out in this connection, having to do with the effects of changes in the level and the composition of these flows of funds, with changes in the degree of financial intermediation, and with the resulting impacts on the cost and availability of money capital.

THE LEVEL OF THE FLOW OF INTERMEDIATED FUNDS

There are two reasons why the flow of funds to the financial intermediaries may increase. They have potentially quite dissimilar effects on the economy. First, an increase may occur in the economy's propensity to save, reflected in an attempt to raise the flow of savings funds to the institutions referred to in Table 10-1. In the classical economists' view of things a mechanism existed in such a case to guarantee that savings would automatically flow into investment. But a different view can be taken of the analytical relations involved.

While income earners may be looked upon as income savers, they are also income spenders. Saving represents income that has not been consumed. An increase in the propensity to save, therefore, will be reflected in a reduction in the propensity to spend, and this will imply a lowering of the general level of the consumption expenditure streams in the economy. The critical question, then, is whether the investment expenditure streams will rise sufficiently to offset the decline in immediate consumption expenditure, thereby maintaining the total level of income-generating expenditure and the level of national production and income. But whether this happens does not depend simply or only on the increased availability of investable funds that comes from the attempt to save. The demand side of the money capital market is also important. The demand for investable funds will not hold up or expand sufficiently to absorb the savings unless the marginal efficiency of investment is high enough. This, in turn, depends on the income-generating potential that new investment outlays are thought to possess; and this will depend on the expected strength of the market demand for the output made possible by the new investment outlays.

For these reasons, the attempt to increase the rate of savings may abort, and the attempt to maintain a higher level of the flow of funds through the financial intermediaries may not be permanently realized.

THE STRUCTURE AND DEGREE OF INTERMEDIATION

The second reason for a possible increase in the level of the flow of funds through the financial institutions is quite different. It comes from a change in the degree of intermediation that the economy wishes to maintain at a given level of activity and income.

Increase in the degree of financial intermediation

Depository institutions, we recall, are required to hold reserves against their transaction accounts or demand deposits. No reserves are required, however, against savings deposits that are not also checkable accounts. Similarly, the savings and loan associations are required to hold reserves against their checkable deposits, but not against the funds they hold in the form of capital accounts. The latter represent the savings funds deposited with the savings and loan associations in exchange for what are technically known as shares of capital. If, then, the public were to change their wealth-holding habits in such a way that their demand for transaction accounts diminished, and their demand for noncheckable savings accounts or savings and loan association shares increased, this could have significant effects on the monetary situation. It would change what we are now calling the degree of financial intermediation.

Let us take as an example the transfer of $100 from commercial bank demand deposits to savings and loan association shares, understanding, as suggested above, that the funds are not placed in checkable or transaction accounts in the savings and loan association. When this happens, the savings and loan association has issued more capital shares on which, of course, it will have to pay a rate of return in the future. It will therefore not keep the new $100 of bank deposits idle but will invest it in some income-earning asset. We may suppose that it is used to purchase mortgages or, in other words, to make loans for the purchase or building of new homes.

Consider now the overall effects of these developments. First, there has not been any change in the M1 money supply. There was first a redistribution of the money supply away from the public to the savings and loan association. Then as mortgage lending was increased as a result, a reverse movement of the money supply occurred, away from the savings and loan association to the public. But the total level of demand deposits, and therefore of the money supply, remained unchanged.

An increase has occurred, however, in the total level of financial wealth in the economy. For while, as we have seen, the M1 money supply is unchanged, the public now holds savings and loan association shares that did not previously exist. Total financial wealth is therefore higher by that amount. Two implications follow. First, the total volume of liquid assets in the economy has increased, introducing a potential for increased expenditure at some time in the future. Second, to the extent that the level of consumption expenditure in the economy depends on the level of perceived wealth as well as on currently generated or expected income, there might be some induced effect on consumption expenditure as a result of the change in the ratio of financial wealth to income. To the extent, of course, that the mortgage lending of the savings and loan association created more employment, income, and real wealth, that would also raise consumption expenditure. That would be, to anticipate a concept we shall examine more fully in Part V, a movement up along the economywide consumption function. The possible financial wealth effect that we noted above would be not a movement *along* the consumption function, but a wholesale movement *upward* of that function. We shall return to these important points.

Apart from these questions of the money supply effect and the financial wealth effect of a change in the degree of intermediation, there exists also a money capital market or interest rate effect. In the case examined, the increased supply of investable funds has increased the level of operations in the building industry. But we remember that this occurred without any change in the money supply. If, then, the previously existing money supply is now supporting a higher level of activity and national income, an increase has occurred in the rate of turnover of the money supply or in the income velocity of circulation of money. This makes possible the higher level of economic activity, the beneficial effect in the loanable funds market, and the lower rate of interest.

These effects, taken together, follow from a rise in the degree of financial intermediation. They imply that the amount of money an economy needs in order to conduct its desired transactions level depends very much on the degree or extent of financial intermediation that exists. This was one of the principal conclusions of the important study *Money in a Theory of Finance* made some time ago by Gurley and Shaw.[1] The same point has other implications that we might summarize as follows.

We may imagine an economic situation in which a tendency to inflation persists and in which, as an anti-inflation policy move, the Federal Reserve Board tightens the monetary situation. It endeavors to reduce the growth in the money supply and to raise the rate of interest. In these conditions the monetary tightness might very well be defeated to some extent by the kind of increase in the degree of financial intermediation we have just discussed. That did occur in the 1970s and the early 1980s. Holders of idle funds learned how to protect themselves to some extent against inflation by moving their wealth from money into near-money liquid assets. New financial institutions were created in the process, such as the money market mutual funds. Existing institutions invented new ways of tapping savings funds. All of this can be put in the same way as before by saying that monetary tightness can be offset to some extent by the induced rise in the velocity of circulation of money. Alternatively, we could put it in the terms we employed in discussing the formation of interest rates or the market-clearing price of money. In the conditions of monetary tightness we have just referred to, the rise in the opportunity cost of holding money reduces the amount of money the public desires to hold. Additionally, the invention of the new forms of money substitutes and near-money moves the public's demand for money schedule to the left. Both of these effects tend to alleviate the monetary tightness.

We emphasize, finally, the important point at issue in this discussion of intermediation. The demand for, or the need for, money in the economy at any time is not unique, and cannot be defined unambiguously, until first of all some specification is made, or some assumption is introduced, regarding the degree of financial intermediation in the system.

Disintermediation

Against the significant fact of intermediation, an important opposing effect also has to be analyzed. The depository institutions, as we have seen, have encountered acute financial difficulty in periods of high in-

[1] J. G. Gurley and E. S. Shaw, *Money in a Theory of Finance* (Washington, D.C.: Brookings Institution, 1960). See also the same authors' "Financial Aspects of Economic Development," *American Economic Review*, September 1955; and "Financial Intermediaries in the Saving-Investment Process," *Journal of Finance*, May 1956.

terest rates as a result of what we referred to as disintermediation. So long as the depository institutions were allowed to pay no more than a specified maximum rate of interest on their deposits, they were unable to prevent savers from diverting their funds to more direct forms of asset investment. The flow of funds through the traditional financial inter- mediaries slackened. The degree of intermediation was reduced. But more important, a further reason existed for the difficulties that the institutions experienced.

In the high interest rate climate at that time, it was necessary for the financial institutions to offer high rates of interest on savings funds in order to attract a cash flow, but the rate of return being earned on their asset portfolios could not be raised simultaneously. Generally, this was because the institutions were locked into longer-term assets that had been acquired some years previously at lower rates of return. The price of the sources of funds was higher than the rate of return being earned on the uses of funds. A severe profit squeeze resulted. This has to some extent been alleviated by the deregulation legislation of 1980 and 1982. Under the 1980 act the ceilings on the rates of interest that the depository institutions can pay on deposits are being abolished. In addition, changes have been made in the permissible composition of asset portfolios. Savings and loan associations may henceforth invest 20 percent of their assets in consumer loans, commercial paper, and corporate debt. Federally char- tered mutual savings banks may hold 5 percent of their assets in com- mercial, corporate, and business loans. This move toward portfolio di- versification will do something to moderate the profit squeeze those institutions have experienced.

This disintermediation process, however, or the movement of in- vestable funds away from the traditional intermediaries to more direct investments such as government securities and corporate stocks and bonds, has important implications for certain specific sectors of the economy. We saw in Table 10-1 that the mutual savings banks and the savings and loan associations are the traditional suppliers of the main part of the mortgage funds in the financial markets. If, for the kind of reason we have dicussed, the flow of funds to those institutions should slacken, then the availability of mortgage funds will in general be correspondingly lower. This will mean, in turn, that the cost of mortgage funds will be higher. In periods of very high interest rates the housing and construction industry may be affected adversely in just this way. As mortgage interest rates rise and the supply of mortgage funds diminishes, housing con- struction and the sales of existing houses may fall dramatically.

Disintermediation in the case of nonbank institutions diminishes their reserve assets. In the case of banks, disintermediation takes the form of a movement away from time and savings deposits to demand deposits. For as the holders of savings deposits convert them into more direct forms of asset investments, such as government securities, the demand deposits of the banks will be increased as the funds so transferred find their way into active circulation. But we recall that savings accounts at the banks, provided they are not checkable accounts, are not subject to reserve requirements. As the funds are moved, therefore, from savings to demand deposits in the banking system, the level of required reserves will increase. Unless action is taken by the monetary authorities to increase the availability of reserves, this will mean that the banks will have to reduce their loans and deposits in order to avoid an excess reserve deficiency. In this roundabout manner the problem of disintermediation comes to expression for the commercial banks, as well as for the nonbank institutions.

SECTORAL IMPLICATIONS OF INTERMEDIARY INSTITUTIONS' PORTFOLIOS

The understanding of the functions that the intermediaries perform in the savings-investment process turns on a view of their asset and liability structures. The following summary of their balance sheet positions at the end of 1982 exhibits the characteristic structure of the uses of funds, in such a way as to contemplate the significance for different sectors of the economy of possible changes in the structure of the flow of funds through the financial intermediary system.

In each of the following cases the fundamental feature of financial intermediation may be observed. Individual savers and wealth holders acquire so-called indirect securities in the form of claims against the financial institutions. The institutions, in turn, invest these funds in direct securities. This transformation of what would otherwise be direct investment into forms of indirect investment constitutes the essence of financial intermediation in the savings-investment process. We discussed the characteristic features of it more fully in Chapter 5. We have seen that individuals, by holding indirect securities or assets that the institutions have issued as claims against themselves, are able to achieve combinations of portfolio liquidity, safety, and profitability superior to what they would otherwise be able to realize.

SAVINGS AND LOAN ASSOCIATIONS

Table 10-2 indicates that the principal source of funds for the savings and loan associations is savings capital. This accounted for 78.8 percent of total funds employed at the end of 1982. The savings and loan associations do have borrowing privileges at the Federal Home Loan Banks,

Table   10-2

Assets and liabilities of Savings and Loan Associations, December 31, 1982

Assets (uses of funds)

	$billion	% of total assets
Mortgages	482.2	68.3
Cash and government securities	84.8	12.0
Other assets	139.0	19.7
Total assets	706.0	100.0

Liabilities and net worth (Sources of funds)

	$billion	% of total liabilities
Savings capital	556.2	78.8
Borrowed money:		
Federal Home Loan Bank Board	63.9	9.1
Other borrowing	34.1	4.8
Loans in process	9.9	1.4
Other liabilities	15.7	2.2
Net worth	26.2	3.7
Total liabilities and net worth	706.0	100.0

Source: *Federal Reserve Bulletin,* April 1983, p. A30, based on data supplied by the Federal Home Loan Bank Board.

and some 9.1 percent of total funds had been obtained from that source. The Federal Home Loan Bank Board also operates the Federal Savings and Loan Insurance Corporation and the Federal Home Loan Mortgage Corporation (referred to as Freddy Mac—see Table 10-1). The Federal Home Loan Bank System has divided the country into twelve regional districts. Each regional bank can extend credit to its members in emergencies, to enable them to extend mortgage lending when they otherwise hold insufficient funds. All federally chartered savings and loan associations and most of those chartered by the states are members of the Federal Home Loan Bank System. The Federal Home Loan Bank acquires funds by selling its own bonds in the money capital market. Those bonds are guaranteed by the federal government.

Under the banking legislation of the early 1980s the savings and loan associations that maintain transaction accounts also have borrowing privileges at the Fed. The same applies to the mutual savings banks and credit unions. We have discussed these aspects of the depository institutions, however, and shall not refer to them again in the following summary. Likewise, we recall that the institutions' sources of funds will change in the future to the extent that they move aggressively into checking accounts, as they are now permitted to do. We have also considered the Federal Reserve Board's reserve requirement provisions to which these intermediaries are now subject, and it will not be necessary to comment further on the corresponding cash items in their balance sheets.

Table 10-2 confirms that mortgages represent the principal asset held by the savings and loan associations. They accounted for 68.3 percent of total assets at the end of 1982. The borrowing and loan facilities we referred to above enable the savings and loan associations to maintain their investments in mortgages to a better extent than would otherwise be possible when the flow of funds to them slackens for any reason. But the Federal Home Loan Banks do not encourage the use of their facilities for permanent financing purposes. The savings and loan associations, therefore, do remain subject to the stresses of disintermediation we considered earlier in this chapter. In some instances they may acquire funds by selling their existing mortgages in the secondary mortgage market. For example, they may sell off low-yield mortgages to the Federal Home Loan Mortgage Corporation (Freddy Mac), which was established in 1970 to provide such a secondary market for mortgages insured by the Federal Housing Administration or guaranteed by the Veterans' Administration. By selling their older and low-yielding mortgages in the secondary market, the savings and loan associations are enabled to reinvest in higher-yielding mortgages.

A private corporation, the Federal National Mortgage Association (Fanny Mae) provides liquidity to the mortgage market in a similar way. Originally established as a government institution, it became a private corporation in 1968 and is now very active in the market. The Government National Mortgage Association (Ginny Mae), which was established by the federal government when Fanny Mae became a private corporation, performs a similar function.

MUTUAL SAVINGS BANKS

The sources and uses of funds statement for the mutual savings banks, provided in Table 10-3, indicates that some 89.1 percent of funds is obtained from savings and other deposits. A large part of these are time deposits, though ordinary savings accounts are, of course, also prominent. Once again, the mutual savings banks have traditionally been heavy investors in mortgages. Table 10-3 indicates also that securities account for a good proportion of total assets, most of the securities being corporate issues.

Table   10-3

Assets and liabilities of Mutual Savings Banks, December 31, 1982

Assets (uses of funds)		
	$billion	% of total assets
Mortgage loans	94.5	54.2
Other loans	16.9	9.7
Securities:		
U.S. government	9.7	5.6
State and local government	2.5	1.4
Corporate and other	36.3	20.8
Total securities	48.5	27.8
Cash	6.9	4.0
Other assets	7.5	4.3
Total assets	174.2	100.0

Liabilities (sources of funds)		
	$billion	% of total liabilities
Deposits:		
Ordinary saving	56.5	32.4
Time	96.2	55.2
Other (including checking deposits)	2.5	1.4
Total deposits	155.2	89.1
Other liabilities	9.7	5.6
General reserve accounts	9.2	5.3
Total liabilities	174.2	100.0

Source: *Federal Reserve Bulletin,* April 1983, p. A30, based on data supplied by the National Association of Mutual Savings Banks.
Amounts may not add to totals because of rounding.

LIFE INSURANCE COMPANIES

Life insurance funds are derived principally from the so-called policy reserves that are built up from the annual receipt of premiums. While term insurance policies, along with accident and health policies, offer the insured individuals only protection against hazards, the nonterm life policies and annuities also provide a form of saving to the individual who is insured. They therefore acquire a cash surrender value after they have been in force for some time. For this reason they are a form of asset holding for individuals that adds to the total near-money or liquidity in the financial system. Moreover, individuals may generally borrow from insurance companies against the surrender values of their policies. Such so-called policy loans can usually be obtained at rates of interest specified in the original policies.

This practice has been a source of some difficulty to the life insurance companies in recent times, giving rise to a particular kind of disinter-mediation as interest rates in general have risen. Policyholders have found it to their advantage to take out policy loans at the lower rates of interest specified in their policies and to employ the funds to advantage in higher-yielding investments.

Table 10-4 describes the asset portfolios of the life insurance companies at the end of 1982. It indicates that these institutions traditionally provide funds to a different segment of the money capital market than do the depository institutions. Once again a good share of the insurance companies' assets are placed in mortgages, mainly large mortgages such as those on industrial buildings, offices, and apartment complexes, these assets accounting for 24.3 percent of the total. But an economically significant part of the asset portfolios is in corporate stocks and bonds, particularly the latter. At the end of 1982 these accounted for 39.1 percent of total assets. The companies' liquidity requirements are provided for by government security holdings, which amounted to 5.9 percent of total assets.

Table   10-4

Assets of Life Insurance Companies, December 31, 1982

	$billion		% of total assets	
Government securities				
U.S. government	16.1		2.8	
State and local				
government	8.1		1.4	
Foreign	10.4		1.8	
Total government				
securities		34.6		5.9
Business securities				
Bonds	228.2		39.1	
Stocks	55.6		9.5	
Total business securities		283.3		48.6
Mortgages		141.9		24.3
Real estate		21.0		3.6
Policy loans		53.1		9.1
Other assets		49.9		8.5
Total assets		584.3		100.0

Source: *Federal Reserve Bulletin,* April 1983, p. A30, based on data supplied by the American Council of Life Insurance.
Amounts may not add to totals because of rounding.

The liabilities of the insurance companies are, unlike those of the depository institutions, long-term liabilities. Their maturity dates can be actuarially calculated. The insurance companies are therefore able to lend long, as they are in effect borrowing long. This is the principal reason why they can give such strong support to the long-term capital market, in particular the corporate borrowers. The insurance companies invest in a diversified portfolio of corporate bonds, with, however, a fairly heavy concentration in utility corporations, and such industrials as chemicals, petroleum, and machinery.

We have seen that the flow of funds to the depository institutions may fluctuate to some extent with the business cycle, quite apart from the pressures of the changing degrees of intermediation and disintermediation. The insurance companies, on the other hand, do not generally experience such pronounced cyclical fluctuations. As their operations are largely contractual, their cash flow tends to be much more stable over time.

CREDIT UNIONS

Credit unions, which may be federally chartered by the National Credit Union Administration or by the states, obtain their funds from the savings deposited with them by their members. Credit union membership is restricted to individuals having a common socioeconomic bond, such as a common place of employment or a common religious affiliation.

The assets of credit unions consist mainly of loans to their members. They are therefore a principal source of supply of consumer installment credit. Table 10-7 indicates that at the end of 1982 credit unions held 13.7 percent of the total consumer installment debt outstanding. Only the commercial banks and the finance companies held larger amounts. These loans are made for a wide variety of purposes, including automobile purchases, home improvement, vacations, and debt consolidation.

At the end of 1982 the National Credit Union Administration estimated that the total assets held by a sample group of credit unions, which, it was further estimated, accounted for about 30 percent of the assets of all credit unions, amounted to $88.8 billion. Five years previously the corresponding figure had stood at $53.8 billion. The total assets had expanded between 1977 and 1982—a period, as we have seen, of particularly unstable financial conditions and markets—by some 65 percent.

FINANCE COMPANIES

The term *finance companies* refers to a group of companies that includes commercial and business finance companies, sales finance companies, personal finance companies, and mortgage finance companies. A summary balance sheet position of these companies is provided in Table 10-5. Apart from bank loans, their principal sources of funds are long-term debt, accounting for 35.4 percent of total funds at the end of 1982, and short-term commercial paper which amounted to 25.5 percent of the total. Some of these companies enjoy high credit ratings, such as the General Motors Acceptance Corporation, which specializes, of course, in making automobile loans, and they are able to borrow in the unsecured commercial paper market. Their assets are mainly various forms of consumer and business accounts receivable.

Table   10-5

Assets and liabilities of domestic finance companies, December 31, 1982

Assets (uses of funds)

	$billion	% of total assets
Accounts receivable		
Consumer	89.5	49.9
Business	81.0	45.1
Total accounts receivable	170.4	94.9
Less:		
Reserve for losses and unearned income	30.5	17.0
Accounts receivable (net)	139.8	77.9
Securities and other assets	39.7	22.1
Total assets	179.5	100.0

Liabilities and capital (sources of funds)

	$billion	% of total liabilities
Bank loans	18.6	10.4
Commercial paper	45.8	25.5
Debt:		
Short term	8.7	4.8
Long term	63.5	35.4
Other debt	18.7	10.4
Capital and surplus	24.2	13.5
Total liabilities and capital	179.5	100.0

Source: Federal Reserve Bulletin, April 1983, p. A39.
Amounts may not add to totals because of rounding.

The business and commercial finance companies, which operate by purchasing the accounts receivables of business corporations, are referred to as factors (see Table 10-1). Some of the large industrial finance companies also make sizable loans to businesses for general financing purposes. Mortgage finance companies specialize in servicing and temporarily financing mortgages that they then sell to other institutions in the secondary mortgage market, such as the Federal National Mortgage Association (Fanny Mae), which we referred to above. Personal finance companies tend to be high-cost sources of finance for individual borrowers, as they concentrate on small and frequently high risk personal loans. Their generally higher interest rates on loans (which in many states are exempt from usury laws) are due in part to the high cost of investigating the creditworthiness of the large numbers of small borrowers they serve. The sales finance companies specialize in financing heavier consumer purchases such as automobiles and household items. Such purchases are generally made on an installment plan.

SUMMARY OF PRINCIPAL SOURCES OF MORTGAGE DEBT AND CONSUMER INSTALLMENT DEBT

Tables 10-6 and 10-7 illustrate the distribution of two important kinds of financial accommodation among the principal institutions we have discussed. In view of its social as well as economic significance, and in the light of its tendency to pronounced cyclicality, the sources of mortgage finance are described in Table 10-6. Four major financial institutions— commercial banks, mutual savings banks, savings and loan associations, and life insurance companies—between them account for just over 60 percent of the total real estate mortgage debt outstanding at the end of 1982. We have already emphasized the problems that arise for the real estate sector when, as a result of high interest rates, disintermediation occurs among these principal lenders. The remaining sources of mortgage funds are spread over a number of institutions indicated in the table, with government agencies accounting for 8.4 percent of the total. This share held by the government agencies was only slightly less than that held by the life insurance companies, and somewhat larger than the share of the mutual savings banks. As we implied in our preceding analysis, by far the largest holders of mortgage debt outstanding are the savings and loan associations.

Table 10-7 focuses on consumer installment credit. We commented above that the credit unions were one of the principal holders of consumer debt. Their share, as indicated by Table 10-7, was roughly half that of

Table   10-6

Real estate mortgage debt outstanding, December 31, 1982

Type of holder	$billion	% of total
Major financial institutions		
Commercial banks	301.7	18.2
Mutual Savings Banks	93.9	5.7
Savings and Loan Associations	484.3	29.3
Life Insurance Companies	141.3	8.5
Total, major financial institutions	1,021.2	61.7
Federal and related agencies		
Government National Mortgage Association (GNMA)	4.6	0.3
Federal National Mortgage Association (FNMA)	71.8	4.3
Farmers Home Administration	1.8	0.1
Federal Housing & Veterans Administration	5.9	0.4
Federal Land Banks	50.4	3.0
Federal Home Loan Mortgage Corporation	4.8	0.3
Total, Federal and related agencies	139.3	8.4
Mortgage pools or trusts	214.4	13.0
Individuals and others (including Mortgage companies, Real Estate Investment Trusts, State & local retirement funds, non-insured pension funds, credit unions)	279.5	16.9
Total mortgage debt	1,654.4	100.0

Source: *Federal Reserve Bulletin*, April 1983, p. A41.

the finance companies, and about 31 percent of the share held by the commercial banks. The gasoline companies hold 1.2 percent of consumer debt, though some of the gasoline companies have recently announced that they are planning to abolish their credit card operations.

Table   10-7

Consumer installment debt outstanding, December 31, 1982

Holder	$billion	% of total
Commercial banks	152.1	44.1
Finance companies	94.3	27.3
Credit Unions	47.3	13.7
Retailers	30.2	8.8
Savings and Loan Associations	13.9	4.0
Gasoline companies	4.0	1.2
Mutual Savings Banks	3.0	0.9
Total consumer installment credit	344.8	100.0

Type of credit	$billion	% of total
Automobile	130.2	37.8
Revolving	67.2	19.5
Mobile homes	19.0	5.5
Other (including mainly sundry credit advances by commercial banks, finance companies and credit unions)	128.4	37.2
Total consumer installment credit	344.8	100.0

Source: *Federal Reserve Bulletin*, April 1983, p. A42.
Amounts may not add to totals because of rounding.

Note: The Federal Reserve Board series reported in the table covers most short and intermediate term credit extended to individuals through regular business channels, usually to finance consumer goods or refinance consumer debt, and scheduled to be repaid in two or more installments.

OTHER FINANCIAL INSTITUTIONS

Only brief comments need be made on the other financial intermediaries mentioned in Table 10-1, as their principal sources and uses of funds are indicated there. Prominent among them are the open-end investment companies, or the so-called mutual funds. These companies sell shares to the investing public at a price equal to the asset value of their existing shares outstanding, plus in most cases a loading fee or service charge. The asset value of the shares is calculated by dividing the number of shares outstanding into the total market value of the assets in which the funds held by the company have been invested. Some mutual funds are so-called common stock funds, meaning that apart from a minimal cash balance the assets held are entirely the common stocks of a diversified list of industrial corporations. Other mutual funds are referred to as balanced funds, meaning that their assets are a judicious mixture of industrial stocks and bonds. The mutual funds as a whole are heavy purchasers of common stocks. They have enjoyed a rapid growth during the last quarter of a century. During the more stable growth years of the 1960s, the total amount of funds held by these investment companies expanded not only as a result of a steady net cash inflow each year but also as a result of the unrealized capital gains on their common stock portfolios.

In the much more unsettled stock market conditions of the 1970s and early 1980s, however, the mutual funds have not fared so well. In 1958, as indicated in the first definitive study of the mutual fund industry by Professors Friend, Brown, Herman, and Vickers,[2] the open-end investment companies held assets amounting to some $12 billion. At that time the investment companies were experiencing a net annual cash inflow (sales of new shares less redemptions) equal to between 13 and 16 percent of their total assets. By the end of 1982 the total assets of the industry had risen to $77 billion, though the net cash inflow experience was much less stable. In 1981, for example, the net inflow of cash was only $4.7 billion, or about 8 percent of the assets at the end of the preceding year, but in 1982 the corresponding net inflow of $15.6 billion represented 28.3 percent of the previous year-end assets.

The open-end investment companies place their funds in the secondary securities market. They do not participate in the new issues market, as do the pension funds and the life insurance companies. But the impact of the flow of funds from the investment companies to the corporate securities markets does, of course, influence the market prices and yields of corporate securities and therefore the cost of capital to corporations. The displacement of funds by such secondary purchases, moreover, causes ripples throughout the capital market in general, increasing the overall availability of funds in which the new issues market can participate.

As indicated above, the holders of investment company shares can resell them to the company at any time. They receive in return the net asset value of the shares at the time of resale. Given the minimum cash balances held by these companies, and given the dependence of their asset values on the general level of the common stock market, this form of indirect investment does not enjoy a high degree of liquidity.

The closed-end investment companies are much less important in actual size. They do not continue to sell shares on an open-ended basis as do the investment companies we have just described. Shares in closed-end investment companies are traded in the secondary securities markets just like the shares of any other corporation. Closed-end investment com-

[2] Irwin Friend, F. E. Brown, E. S. Herman, and Douglas Vickers, *A Study of Mutual Funds*, for the House of Representatives Committee on Interstate and Foreign Commerce Washington, D.C.: Goverment Printing Office, 1962).

panies do not perform a strictly intermediary function of the kind we are concerned with in this chapter, except in the extremely infrequent instance in which they make a new issue of capital. In that case they, like the open-end investment companies, channel the funds they acquire into the corporate securities available in the secondary market.

The remaining important intermediary institution referred to in Table 10-1 has already been commented on from a number of different perspectives. It is the money market mutual fund. Its place in the short-term securities market should be kept in mind. The inclusion of its asset totals in the M2 measure of the money supply follows from the high degree of liquidity that the shares in such funds enjoy.

SUMMARY

After a summary description of the principal financial intermediary institutions, this chapter examined a number of questions related to the flow of funds from the ultimate savers in the economy to the ultimate users of money capital. The chapter is an extension of the material on financial institutions introduced in Chapters 2, 5, and 6.

A number of reasons may exist for changes in the level of the flow of intermediated funds. Examples were given of changes in the savings habits of the economy, and changes in the degree of intermediation in the financial system. The latter possibility points to the important phenomenon of disintermediation that has caused difficulties in some areas of the financial markets in recent years. Emphasis was placed on the significance of intermediation for the effective velocity of circulation of money, and for the actual level of expenditures, the level of financial wealth, and the rate of interest or general money market conditions.

An examination of the typical asset and liability structures of the various financial intermediaries highlighted the fact that different institutions are traditionally suppliers of money capital funds to different sections of the capital market. Savings and loan associations and mutual savings banks are heavy purchasers of mortgages. Credit unions, along with the commercial banks and the finance companies, are among the principal holders of consumer installment debt. Life insurance companies also participate in the mortgage market but are among the principal purchasers of corporate bonds. Private pension funds and open-end investment companies purchase principally industrial common stocks. Money market mutual funds concentrate their assets in short-term, highly liquid securities.

This relative specialization of the intermediaries' investment activities and portfolios has important implications for the economy. When changes occur in the structure of the channels of the flow of investable funds, noticeable impacts can be felt on the relative costs and availabilities of funds to different sectors of the economy. In times of heavy disintermediation the housing and construction sector of the economy, for example, is likely to suffer quite quickly and seriously.

Summarized analyses were given of the sources and uses of funds of the principal kinds of financial intermediaries. It was noted that while some of the intermediaries, notably those that are referred to as depository institutions, are now able to compete more closely with the traditional commercial banks, a fairly high degree of specialization of function and the exploitation of comparative advantages and skills may well persist into the future. But the richness of the complex institutional nexus in the financial sector of the economy cannot be easily conveyed in a short chapter such as we are confined to in this book. The subject deserves a study to itself, particularly in the light of the dynamic changes that have recently occurred and the changes that will undoubtedly continue in the years ahead.

IMPORTANT CONCEPTS

Degree of intermediation

Disintermediation

Financial wealth

Sectoral impacts of institutional asset portfolios

QUESTIONS FOR DISCUSSION AND REVIEW

1. Discuss the extent to which a national money capital market exists, as opposed to a series of segmented regional capital markets, and explain the contribution that the various financial intermediaries make to such a national market.

2. What do you consider the principal economic, legislative, and institutional forces that have affected the level of competition and the mobility of funds in the money capital market?

3. Discuss the proposition that the level of the economy's required money supply cannot be specified independently of the degree of financial intermediation.

4. What connections exist between the demand for money, the rate of interest, the velocity of circulation of money, and the degree of financial intermediation?

5. Will an increase in the economy's savings propensity increase the level of the flow of funds to the money capital market? Explain clearly why or why not.

6. Why is the housing and construction industry highly sensitive to cyclical fluctuations in the economy?

7. "Disintermediation is as important for the commercial banks as for the insurance companies and other financial institutions, but its impact and significance are very different." Explain and evaluate this statement carefully.

8. What relations, if any, exist between the efficiencies of financial institutions in the monetary sector and the marginal efficiency of capital in the real sector of the economy?

9. Why might the degree and structure of financial intermediation change in an economy, and what might be the principal implications of such a development?

10. Recalling previous macroeconomic studies, can you anticipate the implications of financial intermediation for the level and significance of the consumption function? How, if at all, might such a set of relationships affect the prospect of stability in the aggregate economy?

11

THE CENTRAL BANKING QUESTION BEFORE 1913

STUDY OBJECTIVES:

• To develop an outline history of banking in the United States during the nineteenth and early twentieth centuries, noting the principal features of the five periods:

 1791–1811 The First Bank of the United States
 1811–16 State banking
 1816–36 The Second Bank of the United States
 1836–63 State banking, or "free banking" under widely varying state legislations
 1863–1913 The National Banking System

• To gain an understanding of the main recurring problems in early banking arrangements, such as excessive bank note issues, inconvertibility of notes, and illiquidity in the financial sector

• To observe the respects in which the defects of the final attempt to establish centralized banking in this period led to the establishment of the Federal Reserve System

The first bank to be established in colonial America with anything like modern characteristics was the Bank of North America, founded in Philadelphia in 1782. The First Pennsylvania Bank, which maintains its head office in Philadelphia at the present time, traces its ancestry to that bank. In 1784 the Bank of New York and the Bank of Massachusetts were established and remained the only ones in existence when the First Bank of the United States was established in 1791. A few unincorporated banks were in operation, as any person was permitted under the common law to engage in banking. It was only after 1800 that the states began to limit banking by requiring that charters must be obtained by special acts of the state legislatures.

The century and a quarter between these early years and the Federal Reserve Act of 1913 contains a fascinating history of banking development, overexpansions, failures, and new beginnings. In this chapter we shall give a brief view of the highlights of that period. The full history provides many case studies of financial adventurers, banking irregularities, and the economic impact of the changes that emerged in the provision of the country's money supply. The complete history deserves a volume to itself.

Three problems that recurred at different times and for different reasons throughout this period provide historical perspective. First, the overissue of bank notes contributed to financial and economic instability and to bank failures at certain times. Second, as a result of the overissue of notes some banks were not able to maintain convertibility of their notes into gold or silver specie. Disruption of trade and the circulation of bank notes at varying discounts from their face values resulted. Third, problems of insufficient liquidity in the financial sector led to panics and the temporary suspension of cash payments by the banks in a number of years. Following disruptions of this kind in 1873, 1884, and 1893, the serious panic of 1907 finally gave rise to more concerted attempts at financial reform and to the introduction of genuine central banking arrangements. But the threefold problems continued to appear throughout the nineteenth century—overissue of notes, inconvertibility, and illiquidity—and a virtually complete history could be written in terms of their significance.

The public's attitude regarding the formation of banks in the earliest years was related to political and social controversies. The nation at that time was composed mainly of small, relatively self-sufficient farmers, and neither manufacturing nor trade had as yet become very important. There were some individuals, such as Alexander Hamilton, who was the first secretary of the Treasury and was largely responsible for the establishment of the First Bank of the United States, who wanted to see a developing commercial and industrial economy. For them the establishment of banks was important, and they argued for a degree of centralization of banking and financial power. The political federalists favored a centralization of political power, and they argued that banks should be chartered by a federal authority.

Others, such as Thomas Jefferson, preferred that the country remain largely agricultural and were opposed to any large-scale expansion of banking. The political antifederalists were much concerned with states' rights, and they thought that if banks were established they should be chartered by the states. Thomas Jefferson argued, in fact, that the First Bank of the United States was unconstitutional because the constitution did not confer on the federal government any right to establish a bank. In the clashes of personalities, power, and economic history, the controversy between Alexander Hamilton and Thomas Jefferson at the time of the First Bank of the United States, and that between President Andrew Jackson and Nicholas Biddle, who was president of the Second Bank of the United States, are worthy of closer study than we can give them.

THE FIRST BANK OF THE UNITED STATES, 1791–1811

Initially, the forces of public suspicion that looked askance at the concentration of financial power were overcome in the interests of introducing some regularity and order to early banking affairs. In 1791 the First Bank of the United States was established with a charter that was to run for twenty years. It was the first, and at that time remained the only, federally chartered bank. The bank had a capital stock of $10 million, of which $2 million was provided by the federal government with funds borrowed from the bank. The remaining capital was subscribed by private individuals, a number of whom were foreigners. The bank's head office was in Philadelphia and branches were established in a number of principal cities.

The First Bank of the United States had two features that were unique in the context of the times. First, it was jointly owned by the government and private investors. Second, it functioned both as the fiscal agent of the government and as a commercial bank. It possessed note-issuing authority, made commercial loans, purchased securities, transferred funds throughout the country (and in this respect provided an early clearing mechanism for interbank payments), and exercised significant influence over the activities of the state banks that came into existence. It was permitted to issue notes up to an amount of $10 million, and these notes were to be legal tender. In these various ways it competed with the state banks, over whose activities, in effect, it had considerable influence. For by expanding its loans it indirectly supplied the state banks with funds. But equally, when it contracted its loans it drained reserves away from the other banks. Moreover, in an attempt to maintain the convertibility and soundness of state banks' notes, the First Bank of the United States would collect the notes of certain banks and present them for redemption in specie, thereby causing a specie drain from the issuing banks and placing severe constraints on their note-issuing ability.

Complaints of unfair competition against the state banks emerged, and in the outcome this and other complaints led to the failure to renew the bank's charter when it expired in 1811. It was objected that a part ownership of the bank by foreign investors was not in the best interests of the country. Dividend payments would cause funds to flow abroad, and foreigners should not, it was thought, have a voice in the control of the country's economic affairs.

At that early time, it will be recalled, a preference existed for hard or commodity money, and a general and widespread acceptability of paper currency had not yet emerged. It was this sentiment that continued to give rise to difficulty. For as we have seen, part of the problem of the times was that banks were expected to be able to convert their notes into specie whenever they were called upon to do so. The young economy was still a very long way from the credit money systems that we have today. The First Bank in effect discouraged the growth of state banks, and this, together with the anticentralist or antifederalist opinions that existed in some political circles, led to the demise of the bank in 1811.

STATE BANKING, 1811–16

The number of state banks in existence grew rapidly in the relative free-for-all that followed. In the context of the inflationary conditions associated with the financing of the War of 1812 and after, the number of state banks expanded from 88 in 1811 to 246 in 1816. The total value of bank notes outstanding rose from about $45 million in 1812 to more than $100 million five years later.

Speculative excesses punctuated the times. Many banks issued more notes than they could possibly redeem, and many notes began to circulate at a discount. This meant that the prices charged for commodities in normal trade transactions depended on which bank's notes were being offered in exchange. Dislocation in an inflationary environment ensued. Uncertainty abounded as to the actual value to be attached to the medium of exchange. During this period also bank demand deposit money became a significant part of the circulating medium in the larger cities. But the more widespread expansion of demand deposits was to come later. During the latter decades of the nineteenth century demand deposits gradually became more important than bank notes as a circulating medium throughout the country. This, in fact, provides one reason for the actual operating experience of the National Banking System that was established in 1863.

THE SECOND BANK OF THE UNITED STATES, 1816–36

The second major attempt to introduce some order into the financial system was made with the establishment of the Second Bank of the United States in 1816. Again the bank was given a twenty-year charter. It was established on a somewhat larger scale, having an authorized capital of $35 million. One-fifth of this was subscribed by the federal government and the remaining four-fifths was provided by private individuals, corporations, and the states. Again there was a diversified ownership. The bank was to be managed by a Board of Directors of whom five were appointed by the president of the United States and twenty were elected by the other shareholders. The bank, which maintained twenty-five branches throughout the country, possessed authority to issue up to $35 million in paper currency. These notes were again to be legal tender. The other provisions and responsibilities of the bank were similar to those of the First Bank of the United States.

Like the First Bank, the Second Bank competed with the state banks for loans and deposits. Once again a discipline was imposed on the state banks by the device of collecting state banks' notes and presenting them for redemption in specie. This directly affected the specie holdings and the reserves of the banks, and it again operated as a constraint on their lending ability and the extent to which they could create credit. Evidently the Second Bank was not consistently well managed. Among the unsound practices it adopted was that of making loans to shareholders against the collateral of the bank's own stock. In due course its operations ran into strong political opposition.

Prior to his election to the presidency in 1828, Andrew Jackson had been opposed by those in control of the Second Bank. It seems that the bank had even used its lending power to influence votes in the election. Open opposition between Jackson and the bank worsened during the next four years, and Nicholas Biddle, who was president of the bank, opposed Jackson's reelection in 1832. After his election Jackson withdrew the federal deposits from the Second Bank and placed them in state banks. In response, Biddle contracted the loans and demand deposits of the bank, and a general recession and contraction of credit followed. In 1836 the bank's charter was allowed to expire as a result of a presidential veto, and this action gave rise to a quarter of a century of serious monetary disorder and financial disarray.

STATE BANKING, 1836–63

With the demise of the Second Bank of the United States, the disarray endemic to the period of unstable state banking ensued. Prior to 1837 a bank could be chartered by the states only by a special act of the legislature. This was now thought to be unsatisfactory, as it could too easily give rise to political favors and lead to a corruption of powers. From this time on, a movement to so-called free banking set in. This term meant that any person could now establish a bank, provided only that he was able to comply with certain state requirements regarding the capitalization of the bank and other registration conditions.

Michigan passed its Free Banking Act in 1837, and the New York Free Banking Act was passed in the following year. The New York act contained some features that set an example in this area of legislation, and which were incorporated to some extent into the National Banking Act of 1863. The New York Banking Act required an applicant for a charter to deposit with the state comptroller securities of the United States government, or certain securities of the states, equal to the value of the notes that the bank proposed to issue. In the event of the failure of the bank the comptroller would be able to pay the holders of the bank's notes out of the proceeds from the sale of the securities deposited with him.

Provisions of this kind, however, differed widely from state to state. It cannot be said that in the country as a whole a very significant degree of control over the banks existed. In some cases the state authorities required the banks to lend to designated companies, such as those in canal building, railroads, and other industries that were particularly beneficial to the state. As a result of the relative laxity in the regulatory provisions, a large number of banks came into existence during this period. Again, as had occurred before, not all of them were well managed, and the overall effect was that the money supply they created tended to vary during business fluctuations in a decidedly procyclical fashion. When times were good and the demand for loans was high, the banks generally responded by accommodating potential borrowers. But when times were bad the banks contracted, or they were forced to do so by the failures that resulted from their earlier speculative expansion. Many of the banks did not possess adequate capital to support their operations, and it seems that they often paid excessive dividends on the capital they held. Moreover, the banks again tended to make excessive note issues, and they did not possess adequate reserves to guarantee the convertibility of notes into specie on demand. Many banks' notes, therefore, again began to circulate at discounts.

THE INDEPENDENT TREASURY SYSTEM

While not all banks during this "free banking" era were guilty of the worst of the inefficient or scandalous practices with which some could be charged, the general monetary conditions were nevertheless quite unstable. The federal government observed that in some cases the banks with which government funds were deposited engaged in unsound expansionary policies on the basis of those funds. As bank failures became more numerous, the federal government withdrew its funds from the banks and in 1846 set up a system of subtreasuries throughout the country. This became known as the Independent Treasury System. In doing this, the government may well have improved the general safety of its deposits, but the action had unfortunate consequences.

The Independent Treasury System meant that the federal government in effect withdrew entirely from the arena of bank regulation. It relinquished whatever powers of monetary regulation it might have possessed. The banking system was left, as a result, totally unregulated. Fluctuations in the flow of funds to the subtreasuries meant that the government either built up money balances there, which directly depleted the specie reserves of the banks, or gave rise to a new outflow of funds into circulation. The monetary and banking conditions in the country were too easily destabilized as a result.

THE NATIONAL BANKING SYSTEM, 1863–1913

The National Banking Act of 1863, which ushered in a fifty-year experiment in a form of centralized banking, had two main objectives. First, it reacted to the unsettled conditions that preceded it by setting out to establish a safe and generally acceptable banking and currency system. Second, it was designed to assist the Treasury to finance the Civil War. The national banks did not, however, become a principal source of Treasury finance, and the operation of the banking system under the act was directed principally to the first objective.

The National Banking Act provided for a continuation of free banking, but it set up the office of the Comptroller of the Currency in the Treasury Department and made that office responsible for chartering national banks subject to the requirements of the act. Definite capital requirements were established. Banks that planned to operate in population centers of less than 6,000 were required to have a minimum capital of $50,000. In population centers of between 6,000 and 50,000 the capital requirement was $100,000, and for larger population centers it was $200,000. The act further provided that at least 50 percent of the capital must be paid into the bank before it could begin operations. The shareholders had what was called double liability. In the event of the failure of the bank they could be required to pay to the bank a further capital sum equal to the amount of their original investment. As we shall see below, the national banks were restricted as to the amount of notes they could issue; they were subject to very rigid reserve requirements; they were subject to lending restrictions (for example, they could not make loans against real estate, and they could not lend to any one borrower an amount greater than 10 percent of the bank's own capital); and they were subject to examination by the Comptroller of the Currency, who was authorized to receive reports on their financial condition.

Provisions of the National Banking Act

Apart from the capital requirements and the loan restrictions we have already referred to, and leaving aside some operating regulations (such as the requirement that all national banks must redeem each other's notes at par value), the important provisions of the National Banking Act had to do with reserve requirements and with note-issuing authority.

National banks were permitted to issue notes only up to an amount no greater than 90 percent of the face value of the bank's holdings of government securities. In 1900 this provision was changed to permit the banks to issue notes up to 100 percent of their holdings of such securities. Initially it was provided that the total note issue of all national banks combined could not be greater than $300 million, and that a bank's share in that total would depend on its location and size. Those limitations, however, and the initial provision that a bank could not issue notes for an amount greater than its own capital were removed in 1875.

The principal objective of the act was to establish a safe and uniformly acceptable currency. To the extent that the national banks competed successfully with the state banks and banking operations were thereby brought under the provisions of the act, this could be accomplished. But state banks initially continued to flourish. This was because under state regulations they enjoyed lower capital requirements, less onerous reserve requirements, less supervision, and more liberal lending powers. To remedy the situation the Congress passed a further act in 1865, which went into effect in 1866 and placed an annual tax of 10 percent on all state bank note issues. This effectively forced the state banks to seek reincorporation under the federal legislation if they wished to continue issuing notes. The decline in the number of state banks and the rise in national banks following the inception of the National Banking System is illustrated in Table 11-1.

The interesting feature of Table 11-1 is the decline in the number of state banks following the passing of the 1865 legislation, and the sharp increase in the number from about 1890 onwards, though the increase had begun by about 1870. This is accounted for by an important change in the trading and payments habits of the economy. During the final decades of the nineteenth century the use of bank demand deposits as a circulating medium had become widespread and had largely displaced bank notes from that function. As demand deposits became relatively more important, the state banks could revert to operating as they had done previously, under the more liberal state requirements. They could concentrate principally on maintaining reserves as a percentage of their demand deposits, rather than having to sustain also the tax liability on the issue of notes. Table 11-1 indicates also the rapid expansion in the number of state banks in the first two decades of the twentieth century.

Table   11-1

State and national banks in the United States, 1864–1914

	Number of banks	
Year	State banks	National banks
1864	1,089	467
1868	247	1,640
1870	325	1,612
1880	650	2,076
1890	2,250	3,484
1900	5,007	3,731
1910	14,348	7,138
1914	17,498	7,518

Source: Board of Governors of the Federal Reserve System, *Banking Studies* (Washington, D.C., 1941), p. 418; reproduced in Stephen M. Goldfeld and Lester V. Chandler, *The Economics of Money and Banking*, 8th ed. (New York: Harper & Row, 1981), p. 192.

The other main provision of the National Banking Act related to reserve requirements. This provides an understanding of the ultimate effectiveness of the system and its eventual demise. The reserve requirements gave rise to what became known in practice as the pyramiding of reserves. It was this that led to the system's inability to perform the vital central banking function of guaranteeing the liquidity of the financial system.

The reserve requirements denominated the national banks as central reserve city banks, reserve city banks, or country banks. The first-mentioned class were required to maintain reserves equal to at least 25 percent of their note and deposit liabilities. Those reserves were required to be held in the form of vault cash. Reserve city banks, those operating in financial centers of lesser size and importance, were also to hold reserves equal to at least 25 percent of their note and deposit liabilities, but only one-half of those reserves need to be held in vault cash. The remaining half could be held in the form of deposits with central reserve city banks. The country banks, finally, were required to hold a reserve of 15 percent against their notes and deposits. But they were permitted to hold as much as 60 percent of their reserves in the form of deposits with the reserve city banks or the central reserve city banks. Only the remaining 40 percent need be held in vault cash.

The practical implications of these regulations were important. The structure of the national banking system in effect formed a pyramid, with the banks in the central reserve cities (initially only New York, but by 1887 including also Chicago and St. Louis) at the top. In the center were a larger number of reserve city banks, with the much more numerous country banks forming the base of the pyramid. It would obviously be profitable for the country banks to keep their reserves in the form of deposits with the banks in the tiers of the pyramid above them, rather than keep them in non-income-earning vault cash. The same applied to the banks in the middle tier, which would similarly be motivated to pass on their reserves to the small number of banks in New York, Chicago, and St. Louis. Moreover, one further complication ensued. The banks in the higher tiers of the system would naturally regard the deposits made by the banks below them as adding to their own reserves, and as contributing to the basis of their lending ability. Thus the banks expanded loans on the basis of funds that other banks in the system regarded as their legitimate reserves.

The upshot of this can be seen if we consider the possible effects that might follow from a liquidity problem in the banks at the base of the system. If, for example, the farmers experienced a poor harvest and realized lower incomes and cash flows, their demand for liquidity at the country banks would rise. In order to satisfy this demand, the country banks would call in their deposits from the reserve city and the central reserve city banks. But the banks in the middle tier of the system would, of course, have to do likewise. The result would be that a liquidity crisis appearing anywhere in the system could quickly be passed along and concentrated at the central reserve city banks.

In a sense it was the small number of central reserve city banks that were called upon to discharge the essential central banking function of guaranteeing the liquidity of the entire financial system. In the nature of the case, the central reserve city banks were unable to do this. All too quickly, a liquidity stress could focus in what became known as a panic at the heart of the financial system. It was this kind of event that precipitated the notorious panic of 1907, which finally gave rise to recommendations for a radical change in the system. At that point it was finally acknowledged that a more traditional type of central bank needed to be established. This had to be one that could act in a reliable way as a lender of last resort.

These implications of the pyramiding of reserves do not, however, fully describe the difficulties that inhered in the system. For we have supposed, in the foregoing example of the effects of a liquidity crisis, that the country banks and the reserve city banks might simply withdraw their deposits, or attempt to withdraw their deposits, from the central reserve city banks. It must be remembered, however, that if all the banks were fully lent at the time the liquidity crisis appeared, they could not withdraw their interbank deposits in this way and use them to satisfy liquidity demands without reducing their overall reserves below their legally required reserve positions. In that case the interbank deposits were not in effect liquid at all. They were in a sense frozen by the reserve requirement regulations. It is in this further sense that a lender of last resort was required.

A lender was needed who could take action to increase the overall supply of liquid funds when an acute demand for them arose. We shall see in the following chapter how the design of the Federal Reserve System addressed this problem.

Other defects of the National Banking System

Apart from the problem of the pyramiding of reserves and the resulting illiquidity, the principal defect of the National Banking System was related to the inelasticity of the money supply. This came to expression in several ways.

First, the reserve requirements were quite rigid. No provision was made for any variation in the reserve requirements to permit an expansion of the money supply in conditions of expanding economic activity or of seasonal variations in the needs of trade. The same problem arose also in another way. The total amount of bank notes in circulation was strictly tied to the amount of securities that the banks held as backing for the notes, and there was no way in which seasonal variations in the need for currency could be met.

Bank notes, it will be recalled, could be issued only if government securities were held by the banks equal in value to the amount of notes issued. Let it be supposed, then, that in a period of high business activity an increased demand for currency occurred. The banks would be able to meet that demand only if they first acquired additional government securities and then issued notes against the value of them. But in the conditions in which the demand for currency was likely to be high, the level of business activity and the consequent higher demand for funds would be likely to have raised the market rates of interest also. It was therefore quite likely that the rates of return available on investments in loans to businesses and other assets would be higher than the rate of interest that could be earned on government securities. In that case the banks would have no incentive to acquire government securities. Whatever excess reserves they possessed could be more profitably invested in direct loans. There actually existed, therefore, an incentive to avoid government security investments. But that being the case, the lack of motivation to increase their government security holdings implied a corresponding lack of motivation to increase the supply of notes, as the latter could be issued only against the government securities held as backing for them.

In these ways the most serious complaint against the National Banking System was related to the several kinds of inflexibility or inelasticities inherent in it. Illiquidity and inelasticity were the twofold origins of difficulty that ultimately spelled the end of the system

Finally, the National Banking System was unable to accommodate in one significant respect to the widespread emergence of demand deposit checking accounts as the principal form of the money supply. The system contained no provision for an adequate and efficient check-clearing mechanism. This also, as we shall see, was a deficiency remedied by the initial construction of the Federal Reserve System.

THE CENTRAL BANKING QUESTION

We have titled this chapter "The Central Banking Question before 1913." We can now observe that prior to 1913 no genuine central bank, in the modern sense of that term, had functioned in the United States. There had been no central *bank*. But there had been from time to time a concern with the central banking *question*. This, in short, reduced to three principal issues. First, how could a safe, flexible, money supply be assured and how could it be managed in such a way as to avoid the inflationary and speculative excesses that frequently jarred the financial system during the century and a quarter we have surveyed? Second, how could an adequate and efficient set of arrangements be established to bring the private enterprise commercial banks that were the source of the money supply under appropriate supervision? And third, how could provision be made to ensure that a responsible and residual source of liquidity would prevent the financial crises that had also plagued the developing industrial, commercial, and financial economy? The history of the attempts made in practice to address these questions is complex, and the findings of scholars who have evaluated them are controversial. Our discussion in this chapter has indicated only the main features of this important period of monetary and banking history.

An effective money supply, a safe, stable, and appropriately supervised banking system, and a residual source of liquidity—these were the real requirements of the United States economy at the point at which it stood in its development in the second decade of the twentieth century. Unfortunately, not all of these problems were solved by the original Federal Reserve Act. The system introduced in 1913 has continued to evolve, and we shall look at its beginnings and some of its current activities and responsibilities in the next chapter.

SUMMARY

This chapter began by characterizing the financial problems of the years between 1791 and 1913 as threefold. They had to do repeatedly, in different ways at different times, with (1) an excessive issue of bank notes,

(2) a resulting inconvertibility of bank notes, and the consequent lack of a uniform and widely acceptable medium of exchange, and (3) the lack of a reliable and ultimate guarantor of the liquidity of the financial system. A summary view of the financial history of the period was set against the background of early political and social divergences of view. Arguments for and against centralization, coming from the federalists and the antifederalists, were noted. The controversies between Alexander Hamilton and Thomas Jefferson at the time of the First Bank of the United States, and between Nicholas Biddle and Andrew Jackson at the time of the Second Bank of the United States, were noted as examples of the cleavages of view that existed.

The financial history of the century and a quarter preceding the establishment of the Federal Reserve System includes, in addition to the abortive attempts to operate the First and Second Banks of the United States, periods of "free banking" under widely diverse state legislations, and the rather more ambitious National Banking System. The principal provisions and the operational defects of that system were examined, and the basis was laid for an investigation in the chapters ahead of our contemporary central banking arrangements.

The provision of a safe and uniformly acceptable money supply, the appropriate supervision of the money-creating institutions, and the existence of a reliable and ultimate guarantor of liquidity were the issues of principal concern that emerged from the period we have reviewed.

IMPORTANT CONCEPTS

Inconvertibility   *Comptroller of the Currency*
Illiquidity   *Pyramiding of reserves*
National Banking System, 1863–1913   *Inelasticity of the money supply*

QUESTIONS FOR DISCUSSION AND REVIEW

1. "The difficulties that characterized the financial system in the earliest period of banking development were focused in the problems of excessive note issue, inconvertibility, and illiquidity." Comment on the appropriateness of this summary statement and explain how and why such problems might arise.

2. What connections exist between the early financial difficulties referred to in question 1 and the early nineteenth-century experiments in bimetallism referred to in Chapter 4?

3. Can you throw more light than this chapter contains on the Hamilton-Jefferson controversy at the time of the First Bank of the United States and that between Jackson and Biddle at the time of the Second Bank of the United States?

4. What relation can you discover between the banking and financial history of the nineteenth century, the sociopolitical structure of the country, and the principle of states rights?

5. What is the relevance to the issues raised in question 4 of the federalist–antifederalist debates?

6. Why did "free banking" lead to recurring financial panics?

7. "The essential problem in nineteenth-century banking history was the absence of an effective and reliable custodian of the country's liquidity, or a 'lender of last resort.' " Discuss critically.

8. How did changes in transactions and payments habits in the later nineteenth century lead to changes in the banking structure, and what implications did this have for the safety and solvency of the system?

9. What is "pyramiding of reserves"?

10. How would you summarize and explain the principal defects of the National Banking System that ultimately led to the introduction of the Federal Reserve System?

12

THE FEDERAL
RESERVE SYSTEM

STUDY OBJECTIVES:

• To observe the form in which the Federal Reserve System was established following the panic of 1907 and the dissatisfaction with the functioning of the National Banking System
• To note the initial inadequacies of the Federal Reserve, its failure to provide full central bank facilities, and its subsequent evolution
• To form a systematic view of the contemporary organization and functions of the Federal Reserve System
• To examine two important aspects of the operations of the Federal Reserve:
  1. The management of the member banks' reserve accounts
  2. The operation of the check-clearing mechanism
• To take note of the manner in which the organizational structure of the Federal Reserve facilitates the conduct of monetary policy

The liquidity crisis and the notorious panic of 1907 led to several suggestions for the reform of the commercial banking system. The banks had met the crisis, as they had done in 1893, by the simple device of suspending cash payments. The public continued to use checks for making payments, but the banks temporarily refused to pay cash on demand. In 1908 the government passed the Aldrich-Vreeland Act, which provided a partial remedy. The act provided for the establishment of National Currency Associations, in which ten or more banks would cooperate in setting up pools of reserves in the event of a banking emergency. These National Currency Associations were authorized to issue currency to their members up to amounts equal to 75 percent of certain private credit instruments and 90 percent of certain state and local government bonds. National banks were similarly authorized to issue currency against credit instruments deposited with the Treasury.

The Aldrich-Vreeland Act also established a National Monetary Commission to study the banking system and make recommendations for its improvement. In 1912 Aldrich presented to Congress his *Suggested Plan for Monetary Legislation*. This plan, which was backed by the Republican party, met opposition in the Democratically controlled House of Representatives and did not come out of committee. Instead, the Congress finally passed, two days before Christmas 1913, the Federal Reserve Act.

But the earlier Aldrich-Vreeland Act did have some success. The emergency currency arrangements made possible under the provisions for National Currency Associations were put to a test when banking panic emerged again in 1914. At the outbreak of the war in that year, Europeans began heavy selling of securities on the New York Stock Exchange. The Exchange closed on April 13, 1914. In the financial uncertainties surrounding these events, a number of country banks began to withdraw their balances from the New York banks. Depositors began to demand cash from the banks, and the emergency provisions of the Aldrich-Vreeland Act came into effect. The currency issues made by the National Currency Associations, as reported by Robert Auerbach in his *Money, Banking, and Financial Markets*, amounted to probably one-quarter of the total amount of currency the public had held at the outbreak of the war. The Aldrich-Vreeland remedy was successful. A large-scale banking panic was averted.

The more thoroughgoing remedy and reconstruction of the banking system that was necessary, however, could not easily be achieved. Sentiment against the excessive concentration of economic and financial power still existed. The banking industry at that time was a heterogeneous mixture of state and national banks. Table 11-1 in the preceding chapter shows that in 1914 there were 17,498 state banks and 7,518 national banks in operation. These were subject to a diversity of state banking regulations and requirements. Into this mixed situation it would have been impossible, without more thoroughgoing reforms, to introduce a central bank charged with the responsibilities for the range of monetary management that we know today.

The Federal Reserve as it was originally established was not designed to control the money supply. That was assumed to be taken care of by the functioning of the international gold standard. The monetary base was determined by the balance of international payments, the inflow and outflow of gold, and the nonmonetary uses of gold. The financial community continued to be satisfied with the gold standard arrangements, given the old and deeply embedded feeling for real money. Paper money was acceptable, as we have seen, and the need for it was obvious as the routine medium of exchange. But it was required to be what we described in Chapter 4 as representative full-bodied money. At the time of the establishment of the Federal Reserve a distinction continued to be drawn between the control of the money supply as such, or the conception of full-scale monetary management that was not looked upon with widespread favor, and the requirements of an elastic currency.

The inelasticity of the currency supply was, as we have seen, one of the principal defects of the National Banking System. The other main defect related to the basic problem of illiquidity. It was these that the architects of the Federal Reserve Act addressed. In the preamble to the act reference was made to the need "to furnish an elastic currency" and to establish a "lender of last resort." This, we can say with the benefit of hindsight, did not meet the full needs of the times. But a start had been made on the road to a more comprehensive central banking organization. The full history of those early times cannot detain us at present. Indeed, almost immediately after the establishment of the Federal Reserve, the international gold standard was suspended in the light of the existing wartime conditions, and monetary affairs suddenly took on a different shape. After the return to the gold standard in the 1920s, and through the history of the boom of that decade and the slump that followed the 1929 crash, the Federal Reserve gradually developed banking powers and authority that it did not originally possess. The troubled times of the 1930s led to further extensions of the Federal Reserve's responsibilities.

INITIAL ACHIEVEMENTS OF THE FEDERAL RESERVE SYSTEM

The early organization of the Federal Reserve was intended to provide a remedy for the defects of the previous national banking system. It did so by essentially two basic provisions. First, a new note-issuing authority was established that in due course effectively concentrated the supply of notes in the hands of the Federal Reserve Bank. And second, the commercial banks that were members of the Federal Reserve System were required to maintain reserve accounts at the Federal Reserve Bank. These reserve accounts were to be used for a number of purposes and to perform a number of highly important functions.

The concentration of a new note-issuing authority in the hands of the Federal Reserve was designed to correct the previous inelasticity of the currency supply. The Federal Reserve Bank was authorized to issue a new form of currency to be known as Federal Reserve Notes. Private bank notes continued to be issued until 1935, but the currency supply, apart from the coins that continued to be minted by the Treasury, was mainly Federal Reserve notes. Member banks could acquire the notes they needed from the Federal Reserve Bank by making withdrawals from their reserve accounts. If the banks held insufficient funds in their reserve accounts, they could borrow from the Federal Reserve Bank at a rate of interest referred to as the Federal Reserve discount rate. By this means the needs of trade for currency could be satisfied. Commercial bank customers had no reason to fear that currency would not be available on demand. The currency supply was now elastic.

The old problem of the pyramiding of reserves was also corrected. Interbank deposits could no longer be counted as satisfying reserve requirements for member banks. All national banks were required to become members of the Federal Reserve System, and state banks could elect to become members. Previously the central reserve city banks had been the *de facto* custodians of the economy's supply of liquidity. But they, along with banks in general throughout the National Banking System, had expanded their assets and therefore their demand deposits on the basis of the reserves that other banks had deposited with them. The Federal Reserve Bank, on the contrary, or the twelve regional Federal Reserve Banks that were established to provide the reserve bank facilities, were not to act as commercial banks. They were solely bankers' banks, apart from the provision of checking account facilities to the federal government and certain international agencies and central banks. All the reserves of the commercial banks were, so far as the banks were members of the Federal Reserve System, concentrated in the Federal Reserve Bank, and they could be drawn against in times of emergency in the manner we have described. These borrowing privileges at what became known as the Federal Reserve discount window became increasingly important in the disturbed financial conditions that lay ahead.

Finally, the Federal Reserve Banks also established a check-clearing mechanism that we shall discuss in more detail later in this chapter. This meant that the money supply and money capital had now become highly mobile.

EARLY DEFECTS OF THE FEDERAL RESERVE SYSTEM

In spite of the considerable advance toward financial stability made by the Federal Reserve Act, the central banking system that emerged was still a far cry from what we know at the present time. In fact, in the Great Depression that hit the country in the 1930s there were more bank failures than had occurred at any previous time in the nation's history. The Federal Reserve System was sadly unsuccessful if the ultimate test of effectiveness was the prevention of bank failures. In 1933 some four thousand banks closed their doors to the public. It was after this experience that the Federal Deposit Insurance Corporation was established.

Second, the Federal Reserve did not initially possess the contra-cyclical monetary policy powers with which we are now familiar. It was only in the 1930s that the Federal Reserve was given the power to vary reserve requirements in a flexible manner if that was thought necessary in the interest of monetary stability and the needs of the economy. The Federal Reserve Bank's open market operations, or its purchases and sales of government securities, were also not initially used for contra-cyclical purposes, or as a deliberate policy means of controlling the money supply. The monetary base was more dependent in those early years on the inflow and outflow of gold. There does not seem to have been a very clear understanding in the 1920s of the way in which the monetary base could be affected by the relation between the Federal Reserve discount rate and other open market rates of interest.

Initially, under the *de facto* leadership of the Federal Reserve Bank of New York, the discount rate was kept below the market rate of interest, thereby encouraging the commercial banks to increase their borrowing and raise the money supply. The spread between the rate at which the banks could borrow from the Federal Reserve and the rates they could earn on money market assets provided a tidy source of income. In 1920, however, the discount rate was raised, causing a reversal of the situation, and a sharp decline in the money supply occurred. This, unfortunately, coincided with a mild recession, which was thereby worsened and became a fairly rapid decline in the mid-1920s. An inflow of gold in 1920 prevented the larger decline in the money supply that might have resulted from the reduction of commercial bank borrowing in that year.

In the initial years a high degree of coordination did not exist be-tween the operations and policies of the twelve district Federal Reserve Banks. The Federal Reserve Bank of New York tended to dominate the system because of its close association with the most important money and capital market in the country. In the 1930s a firmer degree of co-ordination was established by the creation of the present Board of Gov-ernors of the system, and by the mandatory centralization of open market operations.

In the matter of operating policy, the most prominent defect of the early Federal Reserve System was the apparent concurrence with the traditional theory of commercial banking or the real bills doctrine, which, as we saw in Chapter 8, underpinned the practice of commercial banking at the time. We have already examined the fallacies in the theory. An all too clear danger existed that the money supply could fluctuate in a procyclical manner and aggravate the instability of the business cycle.

It appears from the history of the times that the Federal Reserve Bank did recognize the dangers in this scheme of things during the 1920s, and it did to some extent begin to vary its discount rate in a contracyclical manner. Appropriate lessons had apparently been learned from the unfortunate experience that, as we mentioned above, was associated with the recession of the early years of the Federal Reserve's history.

STRUCTURE OF THE FEDERAL RESERVE SYSTEM

At the present time the structure of the Federal Reserve System consists of seven main elements (1) the Board of Governors, (2) the Federal Advisory Council, (3) the Thrift Institutions Advisory Council (which was added to the system when, after the passing of the Depository Institutions Deregulation and Monetary Control Act of 1980, the nonbank depository institutions were brought under the reserve requirement regulations of the Fed), (4) the Consumer Advisory Council, (5) the twelve regional Federal Reserve Banks and their branches, (6) the member banks, and finally (7) the important Federal Open Market Committee that is primarily responsible for the Fed's policy of purchasing and selling open market securities.

THE REGIONAL FEDERAL RESERVE BANKS

The establishment of the Federal Reserve System was the outcome of a compromise between the contrasting political viewpoints that argued for and against a strong, centrally administered institution to control the banking affairs of the nation. The matter was settled by the provision for twelve regional Federal Reserve Banks, each operating within a defined geographical area. These twelve banks were at first somewhat loosely connected under the administration of a Federal Reserve Board. It was only in 1935 that the Banking Act of that year recognized the need for a strong central controlling body and established the present Board of Governors.

Figure 12-1 indicates the geographical structure of the regional bank system. Federal Reserve Banks are located in Boston, New York, Philadelphia, Cleveland, Richmond, Atlanta, Chicago, St. Louis, Minneapolis, Kansas City, Dallas, and San Francisco. The largest of the twelve banks is the Federal Reserve Bank of New York, which had assets totaling $61.2 billion at the end of 1982. The Federal Reserve Banks of Chicago and San Francisco were next in size, holding assets of $24.8 billion and $22.7 billion, respectively. The dominance of the Federal Reserve Bank of New York comes largely, of course, from the fact that it is located in the principal money market center of the nation. The New York Fed acts as the open market agent of the Federal Reserve System, and at the end of

Figure   12-1.

The federal reserve system:
boundaries of federal reserve districts and their branch territories

Source: Board of Governors of the Federal Reserve System.

1982 it held outright ownership of more than $42 billion of government securities.

Each regional Federal Reserve Bank supervises the operations of the member banks in its district, and it holds the reserve accounts of the depository institutions in that district. In addition, each district bank performs a number of services for the depository institutions in its district, such as the clearing of checks, the provision of borrowing facilities, the supply of currency, and the provision of other services to which we have already referred.

Each Federal Reserve Bank is administered by a Board of nine directors, comprising three members of each of three Classes, A, B, and C. The six directors from Classes A and B are elected by the member banks of the Federal Reserve district. The Class A directors are elected to represent banking interests, and Class B directors, who must not be bankers, are required to be actively engaged in commerce, agriculture, or industry in the district. The Class C directors are chosen by the Board of Governors, and one of them is appointed chairman and another is appointed deputy chairman of the Board of Directors. The Class C directors must also not be engaged in the banking business. The directors of each Federal Reserve Bank appoint the president and the first vice-president and other officers of the bank, but these appointments are subject to approval by the Board of Governors.

In a number of ways a good degree of control from the central Board of Governors is exercised. This should be borne in mind as we consider later in this chapter the real locus of control of the Federal Reserve, as distinguished from its technical ownership. The powers of the Board of Governors need to be seen, in turn, in the light of the fact that the members of that Board are appointed by the president of the United States, subject to confirmation by the Senate.

Each Federal Reserve Bank is owned by the member banks in its district. Member banks are required to purchase stock in the Federal Reserve Bank equal to 6 percent of the member bank's own paid-up capital and surplus. They are, however, required to pay in only one-half of this total subscription. The member banks receive an annual dividend equal to 6 percent of the Federal Reserve Bank's stock. The balance of the Federal Reserve Bank's earnings are used to build up the surplus accounts of the Reserve banks, or to provide revenue for the Treasury. The Federal Reserve Banks have channeled large amounts to the Treasury in recent years, such payments amounting to $15.2 billion in 1982. This payment is referred to as "Interest on Federal Reserve Notes." We have seen that a large part of these earnings accrues from the Fed's holdings of government securities, a portfolio position that is made possible, to some extent, by the fact that the Fed is holding the reserve accounts of the depository institutions but is not paying any interest on those accounts.

It should be kept in mind that the primary purpose of each of the Federal Reserve Banks is to regulate the operations of the member banks and other depository institutions in its district, and to provide services to them. The regional Federal Reserve Banks discharge those responsibilities within guidelines laid down by the Board of Governors. The Reserve Banks are not profit-making institutions in the ordinarily accepted sense of that term, and they do not engage in commercial banking business.

THE BOARD OF GOVERNORS OF THE FEDERAL RESERVE SYSTEM

The relation of the Board of Governors to the rest of the Federal Reserve System can be seen in Figure 12-2. The seven members of the Board are appointed by the president of the United States and serve a fourteen-year term. No more than one member of the Board can come from any one Federal Reserve District. The chairman and the vice-chairman of the board are selected by the president from among the Board members. The

Figure 12-2.

The federal reserve system: organization.

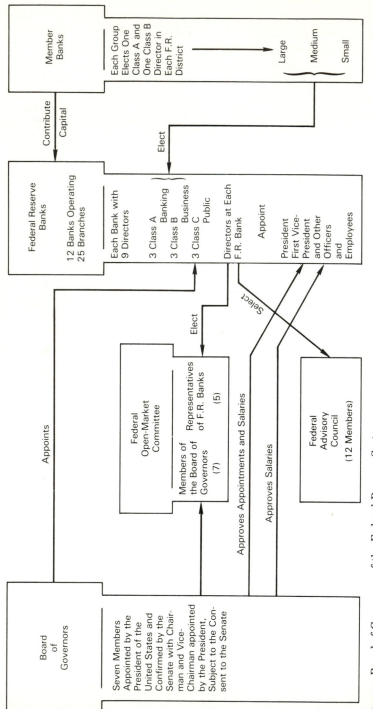
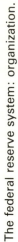

Source: Board of Governors of the Federal Reserve System.

Board is ultimately responsible for the operation of the Federal Reserve System, for the formulation of monetary policy, and for decisions as to whether its policy stance at any time should be expansionary or contractionary. The instruments of policy by which the Board attempts to realize its objectives will be discussed in this and the following chapters. Among those policy instruments are possible changes in the discount rate, or the rate of interest at which reserves are made available to the depository institutions, variations in the reserve requirements those institutions are called upon to meet, and changes in the bank's purchases and sales of open market securities. By virtue of its responsibility in relation to this last-mentioned matter of open market operations, the real seat of ultimate monetary policy power is the Federal Open Market Committee we shall refer to below.

In addition, the Board is responsible for conducting regular examinations of the member banks, for implementing the provisions of the Depository Institutions Deregulation and Monetary Control Act and participating in the Depository Institutions Deregulation Committee, for conducting such public educational services as it deems advisable, and for other services and publications of general benefit to the public. The members of the Board, particularly its chairman, appear regularly before Congress to advise on matters of economic and financial policy and legislation. The entire seven members of the Board of Governors serve on the Federal Open Market Committee.

Summarizing to this point, it is clear that the Board of Governors occupies the dominant position in the control and functioning of the system. The powers of the Board include (1) the decision on critical matters of monetary policy, including the setting of the discount rate, the determination of reserve requirements, and open market operations; (2) the majority membership of the Federal Open Market Committee; (3) the appointment of three members of the Board of Directors of each Federal Reserve Bank, one of its appointees at each bank being chairman of that bank's Board of Directors; and (4) the approval of the appointment of each Federal Reserve Bank's president and first vice-president.

THE FEDERAL OPEN MARKET COMMITTEE

The Federal Open Market Committee (FOMC) consists of twelve members, the seven members of the Board of Governors of the system being permanent members of the committee. In addition, a further five members join the FOMC in rotation, chosen from among the presidents of the twelve Federal Reserve Banks. The president of the Federal Reserve Bank of New York, however, serves permanently on the FOMC and acts as its vice-chairman. This permanent membership comes from the fact that the

New York Fed acts as the market agent of the Open Market Committee. The chairman of the Board of Governors serves as the chairman of the FOMC. In practice, all presidents of the Federal Reserve district banks attend the meetings of the FOMC, even though they do not, apart from the year for which they are elected members of the FOMC, have a right to vote.

At the regular meetings of the FOMC the members review recent trends and developments in the economy, considering both the financial and nonfinancial sectors, and conduct a wide-ranging discussion as to what their monetary policy stance should be.[1] Reports of the meetings of the FOMC are published from time to time in the monthly *Federal Reserve Bulletin*. The following policy directive issued by the FOMC at the conclusion of its meeting in February 1983 appeared in the *Federal Reserve Bulletin* for April 1983. It was preceded by a fairly detailed report of the proceedings of the meeting, from which it is clear that not all members of the FOMC adopted the same view of detailed developments in the economy. It was indicated that the following directive was approved by a majority vote (8 to 4) of the committee:

> The information reviewed at this meeting indicates that real GNP declined in the fourth quarter because of a sharp reduction in business inventories. Final sales increased appreciably, and the rise in prices remained much less rapid than in 1981. Retail sales and housing activity have strengthened in recent months, but business fixed investment has weakened further. Nonfarm payroll employment rose in January, after an extended period of declines, and the civilian unemployment rate fell 0.4 percentage point to 10.4 percent. In recent months the advance in the index of average hourly earnings has slowed further.
>
> The weighted average value of the dollar against major foreign currencies depreciated moderately further from mid-December to mid-January, but a subsequent appreciation has more than offset that decline. In the fourth quarter the U.S. merchandise trade deficit was close to the relatively high third-quarter rate.
>
> Growth of M2 surged to an extraordinary pace in January, apparently reflecting shifts of funds into recently authorized money market deposit accounts. Growth of M3 accelerated, following very slow expansion in December. Growth of M1 remained rapid in January, although it was down appreciably from the average pace in recent months. Market interest rates on U.S. Treasury obligations have risen somewhat since the latter part of December, while rates on most private market instruments are about unchanged to slightly higher. Mortgage rates have declined further.
>
> The Federal Open Market Committee seeks to foster monetary and financial conditions that will help to reduce inflation further, promote a resumption of growth in output on a sustainable basis, and contribute to a sustainable pattern of international transactions. In establishing growth

---

[1] See the informative and valuable discussion of the operations of the FOMC in Paul Meek, *U.S. Monetary Policy and Financial Markets* (New York: Federal Reserve Bank of New York, 1982).

ranges for monetary and credit aggregates for 1983 in furtherance of these objectives, the Committee recognized that the relationships between such ranges and ultimate economic goals have been less predictable over the past year; that the current impact of new deposit accounts on growth rates of monetary aggregates cannot be determined with a high degree of confidence; and that the availability of interest on large portions of transaction accounts, declining inflation, and lower market rates of interest may be reflected in some changes in the historical trends in velocity. A substantial shift of funds into M2 from market instruments, including large certificates of deposit not included in M2, in association with the extraordinarily rapid build-up of money market deposit accounts has distorted growth in that aggregate during the current quarter.

In establishing growth ranges for the aggregates for 1983 against this background, the Committee felt that growth in M2 might be more appropriately measured after the period of highly aggressive marketing of money market deposit accounts has subsided. The Committee also felt that a somewhat wider range was appropriate for monitoring M1. Those growth ranges will be reviewed in the spring and altered, if appropriate, in the light of evidence at that time.

With these understandings, the Committee established the following growth ranges: for the period from February-March of 1983 to the fourth quarter of 1983, 7 to 10 percent at an annual rate for M2, taking into account the probability of some residual shifting into that aggregate from non–M2 sources; and for the period from the fourth quarter of 1982 to the fourth quarter of 1983, 6 ½ to 9 ½ percent for M3, which appears to be less distorted by the new accounts. For the same period a tentative range of 4 to 8 percent has been established for M1, assuming that Super NOW accounts draw only modest amounts of funds from sources outside M1 and assuming that the authority to pay interest on transaction balances is not extended beyond presently eligible accounts. An associated range of growth for total domestic nonfinancial debt has been estimated at 8 ½ to 11 ½ percent.

In implementing monetary policy, the Committee agreed that substantial weight would be placed on behavior of the broader monetary aggregates, expecting that the current distortions in M2 from the initial adjustment of the new deposit accounts will abate. The behavior of M1 will be monitored, with the degree of weight placed on that aggregate over time dependent on evidence that velocity characteristics are resuming more predictable patterns. Debt expansion, while not directly targeted, will be evaluated in judging responses to the monetary aggregates. The Committee understood that policy implementation would involve continuing appraisal of the relationships between the various measures of money and credit and nominal GNP, including evaluation of conditions in domestic credit and foreign exchange markets.

This is obviously a very broad directive. It implies that the manager of the open market account should add moderately to the Fed's holdings of government securities in order to achieve the expansion in the monetary base and the money supply that is envisaged. But the account manager, the Federal Reserve Bank of New York, is in touch with monetary conditions from day to day, and it may sell securities from time to time to offset other forces bearing on the monetary base and the reserve positions of the depository institutions. The dramatic change in the Federal Reserve Bank's overall policy stance in October 1979 implied that henceforth primary attention would be given in the formulation and conduct of monetary policy to the level and growth of the money supply, rather than to money market conditions as represented by the prevailing rates of interest. In particular, the Fed has adopted a policy since 1979 of "targeting," or varying its intervention in the money market in order to influence, the level of the depository institutions' "nonborrowed reserves."[2]

Of course, things are never precise and clear-cut in the difficult art of monetary management. Too many forces are continually coming to bear on the situation. It is therefore of interest to note that the foregoing directive does give some recognition to the importance of keeping an eye on other targets also. It is highly significant that while the statement says that the "total domestic nonfinancial debt" will not be "directly targeted," it "will be evaluated in judging responses to the monetary aggregates." This important matter of the appropriate targets and objectives of monetary policy has attracted a good deal of discussion in professional debates and will be referred to in later chapters dealing with alternative monetary policies. In particular, the possible wisdom and usefulness of targeting change in total debt has been considered by a number of economists.[3]

THE FEDERAL ADVISORY COUNCIL

The Federal Advisory Council consists of twelve members, one of whom is selected from each Federal Reserve district by the Federal Reserve Bank. The council is strictly an advisory group that meets four times a year to survey general business conditions and make policy recommendations to the Board of Governors. The members of the council are generally bankers from the various Federal Reserve districts, and its prin-

---

[2] See the extensive discussion in Meek, *U.S. Monetary Policy.*

[3] See the symposium on this subject by James Fackler and Andrew Silver, Marcelle Arak, and John Weinninger in the Federal Reserve Bank of New York's *Quarterly Review,* 7, No. 4 (Winter 1982–83). See also Frank E. Morris, "Monetarism without Money," Federal Reserve Bank of Boston, *New England Economic Review,* March/April 1983; Edward J. Kane, "Selecting Monetary Targets in a Changing Financial Environment"; and Benjamin M. Friedman, "Using a Credit Aggregate Target to Implement Monetary Policy in the Financial Environment of the Future". Both of the last-mentioned papers appeared in *Monetary Policy Issues in the 1980s,* a symposium sponsored by the Federal Reserve Bank of Kansas City, August 1982.

cipal objective is to endeavor to make sure that the Federal Reserve Board is responsive to their needs and interests. The Board, however, is under no obligation to accept any recommendations of the council.

THE MEMBER BANKS

The final element of the Federal Reserve System comprises the member banks themselves. They have ongoing relations with the Federal Reserve Board in a number of ways: (1) the member banks own the shares of stock of the Federal Reserve Banks; (2) they are subject to reserve requirements, along with all other depository institutions; (3) they have borrowing privileges at the Federal Reserve discount window; (4) they benefit from Federal Reserve services such as ACH (automatic clearinghouse) and other check-clearing services, wire transfer and other EFT facilities; (5) they are subject to examination by the Federal Reserve examiners; and (6) they participate in the election of the directors of the Federal Reserve Banks.

Two of the most important day-to-day operations that bring the commercial banks and the Fed into close relation have to do with (1) the administration of the member banks' reserve accounts and (2) the operation of the check-clearing mechanism.

MEMBER BANKS' RESERVE ACCOUNTS

The reserve accounts of the banks and other depository institutions, along with the amount of currency held by the institutions and the amount in circulation in the hands of the public, make up the monetary base. We have seen that the banks can increase the funds in their reserve accounts by borrowing from the Fed, and that this borrowing privilege has been extended by the 1980 banking legislation to all depository institutions subject to reserve requirements specified by the Fed. Additionally, the banks may obtain currency from the Fed by drawing on their reserve accounts. The following brief examples of reserve account operations will illustrate some of the principal transactions that occur for these several reasons.

Increases in currency in circulation

When the banks experience an increased demand for currency from the public they acquire it from the Fed, and the resulting transactions will be reflected as follows in the balance sheets of both institutions:

Commercial bank balance sheet

Assets		Liabilities	
(a) Cash	− $100	Demand deposits	− $100 (a)
(b) Cash	+ 100		
(b) Reserve account at Fed	− 100		

Federal Reserve Bank balance sheet

Assets	Liabilities	
	Member bank reserve accounts	− $100 (b)
	Federal Reserve notes outstanding	+ 100 (b)

We have supposed that the public increases its demand for currency by $100. The entries in the commercial bank balance sheet against the indicator (a) describe the effects on the bank's deposits and cash account of the withdrawal of the $100. The bank, then, will wish to replenish its cash account in order to maintain a cash balance adequate for its day-to-day operations. Consequently, the acquisition of $100 cash from the Federal Reserve Bank will be reflected in the entries indicated by (b) in the bank's balance sheet. At the same time the corresponding entries at the Federal Reserve Bank level are indicated by (b) in the Federal Reserve Bank balance sheet.

A number of possible implications of these developments will occur to the reader, in the light of our previous discussions of bank operations. First, the commercial bank has experienced a net reduction of $100 in its total legal reserves, offsetting the similar reduction in its deposit liabilities. This loss of reserves was referred to in an earlier context as an external drain because, as a result of it, reserves were completely drained away from the banking system. An increase in the amount of currency in circulation in the hands of the public therefore reduces, or absorbs a part of, the monetary base.

Second, if the banks were not holding any excess reserves at the time this drain occurred, they would be pushed into a reserve deficiency position. Two possible consequences would ensue. First, the banks may retrieve their required reserve position by selling other assets, government securities for example, or by contracting loans, or by engaging in what we described in Chapter 8 as liability management. They may borrow in the federal funds market, or borrow in the Eurodollar market, or adopt any of the other means we examined of increasing their short-term liabilities.

On the other hand, the Fed may respond to the increased demand for cash by taking action to increase the total amount of reserves available to the banks. It could do this, for example, by engaging in open market purchases of government securities, such as we shall illustrate below. But if, when the banks are in a fully lent position, the Federal Reserve does not take action to accommodate the public's increased demand for currency, the induced restrictive action on the part of the commercial banks, or possibly their own sales of securities among themselves or to the nonbank public, will have a depressing effect on the asset markets and will tend to raise the general level of interest rates.

Open market operations

Let us suppose that for the kind of reason we encountered in the foregoing example, or perhaps for the reason that the Fed desired to adopt a somewhat looser monetary stance, the Fed increased its purchases of government securities. We may consider two possible lines of action. First, the Fed may purchase securities from the commercial banks. Second, it may purchase them from the nonbank public. The monetary effects are slightly different in the two cases.

If the Fed were to purchase $100 securities from the banks, the balance sheet reflection of the transaction would be as follows:

Commercial bank balance sheet

Assets		Liabilities
Reserve accounts	+$100	
Securities	− 100	

Federal Reserve Bank balance sheet

Assets		Liabilities	
Securities	+$100	Member bank reserve accounts	+$100

In this straightforward case the reserves of the banks, and therefore their excess reserves and their maximum potential lending ability, have increased. The potential expansionary effects will now be familiar. Money market conditions will be easier, and interest rates will tend to edge downward. Depending on the actual magnitude of the security purchases the Fed desires to make, it may have to bid up the price it is offering for securities above the existing market level and thereby depress the rate of interest.

Alternatively, the Fed may purchase securities from the nonbank public. The nonbank public includes the nonbank financial institutions, and we might assume that the Fed in this case purchases $100 securities from an insurance company. The Fed will now pay for the securities by a check drawn on itself. When the insurance company deposits the check in its commercial bank demand deposit account, both the deposit liabilities of the bank and its reserves will increase by a corresponding amount:

Commercial bank balance sheet

Assets		Liabilities	
(a) Cash items in course of collection	+$100	Demand deposits	+$100 (a)
(b) Cash items in course of collection	− 100		
(b) Reserve accounts	+ 100		

Federal Reserve Bank balance sheet

Assets		Liabilities	
(b) Securities	+$100	Member bank reserve accounts	+$100 (b)

In the books of the commercial bank, we have shown the two stages in which the overall effects occur. At the first stage, as shown by indicator (a), the demand deposits of the bank have increased, and at the second stage (b), when the check has been cleared through the local Federal Reserve Bank the bank's reserve account will have increased in the manner indicated. Again the bank will hold new excess reserves, which will have implications for its lending ability and the maximum potential expansion in the money supply that may result.

Reverse transactions could, of course, occur in connection with (1) an inflow of currency from the public to the banks, instead of the outflow we imagined in the foregoing example, or (2) the sale of securities by the Fed rather than the purchases we have just examined. The opposite balance sheet effects and the possible induced effects on the monetary situation, the money supply, and interest rates can be worked out as a straightforward exercise by the reader.

Member bank borrowing from the Federal Reserve

The Federal Reserve discount rate is the rate of interest at which the Fed is prepared to sell or lend reserves to the depository institutions. This somewhat unusual language, "sell or lend," is current in the marketplace because when the Fed purchases securities it is said to sell reserves, and when the Fed lends to the member banks it is said to lend reserves.

If the Fed purchases securities, as a means of making reserves available to the banks at the announced discount rate, it will pay the price for the securities that will imply (taking account of the discounting procedures we explained in Chapter 6) that the banks will in effect be paying a rate of interest for the funds (or, in other words, sacrificing a rate of return on the securities they have just sold) equal to the Federal Reserve discount rate. In the case of a sale of reserves to the banks, the balance sheet effects are precisely the same as we indicated above in the case of the Fed's purchase of securities from the banks.

A difference appears, however, when the Fed lends reserves to the banks. In this case the banks will lodge securities with the Fed as collateral for the loan, but the title to the securities remains with the banks. The securities will be retrieved from the Fed when the loan is repaid. The balance sheet entries will be as follows:

Commercial bank balance sheet

Assets		Liabilities	
Reserve accounts	+$100	Borrowings (notes payable)	+$100

Federal Reserve Bank balance sheet

Assets		Liabilities	
Loans to member banks (notes receivable)	+$100	Member bank reserve accounts	+$100

Again the possible secondary-induced effects of the change in the monetary situation can be left for description as an exercise for the reader.

THE CHECK-CLEARING MECHANISM

The existence of an efficient check-clearing mechanism facilitates the mobility of funds throughout the economy and raises the efficiency level of economic transactions in general. The introduction of its check-clearing facilities was one of the ways in which the establishment of the Federal Reserve System represented a considerable advance over the National Banking System. At the present time the clearing of checks is an enormously large and expensive operation for the Fed. The number of checks being cleared annually is now approximately 15 billion. In 1982 the Fed incurred an expense on its check-clearing operations of approximately

$304 million, representing approximately 30 percent of the Fed's total operating expenses.

Not all of this expense, however, is a net cost of operation to the Federal Reserve. For in terms of the Monetary Control Act of 1980, not only were all Federal Reserve services made available to all depository institutions but the Fed was required to establish a schedule of fees to be charged for the provision of the services. The revenue collected by the Fed in connection with the check-clearing procedure in 1982 amounted to $283 million, or some 80 percent of the expenses incurred. Further details of comparable revenues and expenses are provided in Table 12-1.

The scale of fees charged by the Fed for the provision of services is in the course of evolution, and Table 12-1 indicates that in 1982 a net loss was recorded in connection with all the services after incorporating the Private Sector Adjustment Factor (PSAF). This last-mentioned term is an imputed cost intended to reflect the taxes that would have been paid and the return on capital that would have been provided if the service had been furnished by a private sector firm. In 1982 a PSAF of 16 percent was applied to Federal Reserve expenses for priced services. This same

Table   12-1

Revenue and expense of priced services at Federal Reserve Banks, 1982, in $million

Service	Revenue	Expense	Net revenue	Private sector adjust- ment	Net revenue after PSA
Wire transfer	49.3	47.9	1.3	7.7	−6.3
Commercial ACH	1.3	9.6	−8.3	1.5	−9.8
Commercial check clearing	283.0	304.0	−21.0	40.6	−61.6
Book entry securities	13.3	16.1	−2.8	2.6	−5.4
Definitive safekeeping and noncash collection	14.5	20.3	−5.8	2.9	−8.8
Cash transportation	24.1	29.5	−5.3	.2	−5.5
Coin wrapping	1.2	1.1	.1	.1	−.0
Total Federal Reserve System	421.6	456.8	−35.3	55.7	−90.9

Source: Board of Governors of the Federal Reserve System, *69th Annual Report*, 1982, p. 226. Amounts may not add to totals because of rounding, and because revenue and expense data shown do not reflect the income and expense related to clearing balances established by depository institutions.

Note: The total Federal Reserve System revenue comprises $386.7 million of income from fees for services and $34.8 million of income related to clearing balances, providing the total revenue shown in the table. Total expense includes $28.3 million of earnings credits granted to depository institutions on clearing balances.

PSAF of 16 percent has been incorporated also into the service expenses for 1983.

To observe the procedures involved in the check-clearing process, let us imagine that a check drawn on a bank in Minneapolis is deposited in a bank in Boston. Five institutional entities will enter the check-clearing process: (1) the receiving bank in Boston, (2) the paying bank in Minneapolis, (3) the Federal Reserve Bank of Boston, (4) the Federal Reserve Bank of Minneapolis, and (5) the Federal Reserve Interdistrict Settlement Fund. We can trace the check through the clearing mechanism in the following manner.

The individual who receives the check in Boston will deposit it in his demand deposit account in Bank R (where R stands for the receiving bank). The following balance sheet effects result:

Balance sheet of Bank R

Assets		*Liabilities*		
(a) Cash items in process of collection	+	Demand deposits	+	(a)
(b) Cash items in process of collection	−			
(b) Reserve account	+			

At the initial stage the effects are those described by the indicator (a). On receipt of the check the bank will send it to the Federal Reserve Bank of Boston for collection. The clearing process is then commenced by the Boston Fed in the following way:

Balance sheet of the Federal Reserve Bank of Boston

Assets		*Liabilities*		
(a) Cash items in process of collection	+	Deferred availability cash items	+	(a)
(c) Cash items in process of collection	−	Deferred availability cash items	−	(b)
(c) Interdistrict settlement fund account	+	Member bank reserve account (of the receiving bank)	+	(b)

We concentrate initially on the entries against the indicator (a) in the balance sheet of the Federal Reserve Bank of Boston. These are critically important to the understanding of the process and, what is even more important, to the understanding of certain significant monetary effects that may, and frequently do, follow from the check-clearing process. On receipt of the check, the Federal Reserve Bank of Boston will record the amount in the asset account labeled "cash items in process of collection," and simultaneously in the liability account described as "deferred availability cash items."

As an integral part of the check-clearing arrangements there exists what we may call a check payment time schedule, or a clearing funds availability schedule. This states the maximum time that is permitted to elapse after a Federal Reserve Bank receives a check for collection before the amount involved is actually paid to the receiving bank. Let us suppose that this time schedule stipulates that a check received in Boston and drawn on a bank in Minneapolis must be credited to the member bank reserve account of the receiving bank no later than two days after it is received. Of course, the check cannot actually be cleared and the amount received by the Boston Fed until it is physically presented to the paying bank in Minneapolis. It may take longer than two days for the check to reach Minneapolis. But that is not the point at issue immediately. Quite apart from how long it may or may not actually take for the check to be presented in Minneapolis, the Boston Fed is obligated by the check payment time schedule to credit the amount of the check to the reserve account of the receiving bank two days after it has been received.

At the time specified in the check payment time schedule, then, the Federal Reserve Bank of Boston will make the entries described in its balance sheet against the indicator (b). It will transfer the amount out of the liability account "deferred availability cash items" and place it in the liability account "member bank reserve account." In doing so, it has actually made the amount available to the receiving bank. The transaction is therefore also reflected in the balance sheet of the receiving bank at the same time. The receiving bank will transfer the amount out of the asset account "cash items in process of collection" and place it in its reserve account. So far as the receiving bank is concerned, the check has been cleared and it has received the funds due to it.

An important point arises in connection with the initial stages of the clearing process we have considered so far. After the two days contemplated in the example, the "deferred availability cash items" on the liabilities side of the Federal Reserve Bank of Boston's balance sheet has been reduced. But we recall that the entry initially appeared in that account at the same time as the corresponding amount was entered in the "cash items in process of collection" account on the assets side of the Federal Reserve Bank of Boston's balance sheet. We have so far said nothing about clearing the item from this last-mentioned asset account. That will not happen until the check has actually been cleared through the paying bank in Minneapolis. At that time also the funds will be deducted from the reserve account of the paying bank at the Federal Reserve Bank of Minneapolis. If it takes more than two days for the check to be presented in Minneapolis, that final step will not happen until some time after the "deferred availability cash items" liability account was cleared from the balance sheet of the Boston Fed.

We can observe, then, that the "cash items in process of collection" account (on the assets side of the Federal Reserve balance sheet) may well exceed for a time the amount in the "deferred availability cash items" (on the liabilities side). Or we can put this in another way. Recalling that when the amount was cleared from the "deferred availability cash items" it was credited to a member bank reserve account, we can say that, as part of the check-clearing process, the reserve account of the receiving bank may be increased (or credited with the amount of the check) before the reserve account of a paying bank somewhere else in the country has been reduced (or debited with the amount of the check).

Let us concentrate now on the amount by which, as a result, the total value of the "cash items in process of collection" account in the Federal Reserve balance sheet may exceed the total amount in the "deferred availability cash items" account. This amount has a special designation. It is referred to as Federal Reserve float and is the measure of the extent to which certain banks' reserve accounts have been increased in the course of the check-clearing process before other banks' reserve accounts have been reduced by corresponding amounts.

Federal Reserve float, therefore, represents a net addition to the total reserves in the banking system at any time. It represents, to use our previous language, a net addition to the monetary base. As such, it may potentially have very significant effects on the monetary situation.

As the clearing process continues, the Federal Reserve Bank of Boston will have forwarded the check to the Federal Reserve Bank of Minneapolis for collection. When the Minneapolis Fed receives the check and presents it to the paying bank, the Federal Reserve Bank of Minneapolis will reduce the member bank reserve account of the paying bank and make the amount available to the Federal Reserve Bank of Boston.

At this stage also the check, having been presented by the Federal Reserve Bank of Minneapolis to the bank on which it was drawn, Bank P (P standing for paying bank), that bank will record the situation as follows:

Balance sheet of Bank P

Assets		Liabilities		
(c) Reserve account	–	Demand deposits	–	(c)

The paying bank has deducted the amount of the check from the demand deposit of the individual who drew the check. At the same time it has lost reserves.

The Federal Reserve Bank of Boston will not, however, physically receive the amount of the check from the Federal Reserve Bank of Minneapolis that collected it. Rather, the Federal Reserve Bank of Minneapolis will pay the amount to an agency operated by the Federal Reserve System for precisely this purpose. It is known as the Interdistrict Settlement Fund and comes into operation when, as in the case we examined, checks drawn on banks in one Federal Reserve district are deposited at banks in a different Federal Reserve district. In such a case the Interdistrict Settlement Fund account of the Federal Reserve Bank presenting the check (in this case Boston) will be credited, and the Interdistrict Settlement Fund account of the bank collecting the check (in this case Minneapolis) will be debited. The Interdistrict Settlement Fund balance sheet will reflect the entries that have been made in their own balance sheets by the respective Federal Reserve Banks:

Balance sheet of the Interdistrict Settlement Fund

Assets	Liabilities
	Federal Reserve Bank of Boston + Federal Reserve Bank of Minneapolis −

The balance sheet of the Federal Reserve Bank of Boston at the beginning of this section indicates that in the final outcome the Federal Reserve Bank of Boston will close out the check-clearing process by making the balance sheet entries referred to by the indicator (c), or transferring the amount out of the "cash items in process of collection" account into its account with the Interdistrict Settlement Fund.

Meantime, the corresponding entries in the balance sheet of the Federal Reserve Bank of Minneapolis appear as follows:

Balance sheet of the Federal Reserve Bank of Minneapolis

Assets		Liabilities	
(c) Interdistrict Settlement Fund account	−	Member bank reserve accounts (of the paying bank)	− (c)

As a result of the check-clearing operation, therefore, reserves have been lost by the paying bank in Minneapolis and gained by the receiving bank in Boston. When the clearing process has been completed, there has not been any permanent increase in the total reserves in the banking system. There has simply been a redistribution of reserves among the banks within the system. This is an example of what we have referred to as internal drain. In the course of the process, however, there may have been a temporary increase in the level of reserves in the banking system, due to the emergence of float in the manner we described.

FEDERAL RESERVE FLOAT

It will be useful to return briefly to the phenomenon of Federal Reserve float, mainly because of its possible monetary policy implications. Float arises, it will be recalled, because of delays in the actual check-clearing process. If, for example, bad weather prevented a check from being presented to the paying bank as quickly as would normally occur, the delay involved would give rise to an increase in the amount of Federal Reserve float outstanding. It will, at the same time, cause an increase in the total amount of commercial bank reserves, and an increase, therefore, in the monetary base.

Such an increase in the monetary base will potentially lead to an increase in the loan and deposit expansion of the banking system as a whole. Or it may give rise to increased purchases of income-earning assets, government securities for example, by the commercial banks. If, however, the Federal Reserve Board, as a part of its management of the monetary situation, did not wish to see such a loosening of monetary conditions as this would imply, it might take action to counteract it. The Federal Reserve Board, for example, operating through the open market agent of the Federal Open Market Committee, could sell securities with a view to mopping up the excess reserve funds that had appeared as a result of the float.

Such an action on the part of the Open Market Committee agent would be referred to as defensive monetary policy because it is, in effect, simply defending the previously existing situation against a disruption that is tending to result from the emergence of float. This, in fact, has in the past been an issue to which the Federal Reserve has had to give attention in its day-to-day management of the overall monetary situation.

The foregoing analysis has described the phenomenon of float as it has traditionally occurred in the banking system. As a result of changes introduced by the Federal Reserve Board following the implementation of the Depository Institutions Deregulation and Monetary Control Act of 1980, however, the Federal Reserve Board has announced that improvements in operations are expected to eliminate a large proportion of the float that has hitherto tended to emerge.[4] Continuing the trend that began in 1980, the float declined to a daily average of $2.3 billion in 1982, mainly as a result of operating improvements. The 1982 level was slightly more than half that in 1980. Some float may well remain, of course, however efficient the clearing process may become. The Board has announced that in that event it will levy a charge on the commercial banks that are the beneficiaries of the float. This is in accordance with the intention under the terms of the 1980 act to charge a fee for each of the services the Federal Reserve supplies to the depository institutions.

OTHER ASPECTS OF CHECK CLEARING AND THE MOBILITY OF FUNDS

The example of the check-clearing process would have been simpler if we had considered the case in which the receiving bank was located in the same Federal Reserve district as the paying bank. In that instance the Interdistrict Settlement Fund would not have come into the picture at all. If, in the case examined, the paying bank had also been in the Federal Reserve Bank of Boston's district, the Boston Fed, at step (c) of the process, would have cleared the amount of the check from the "cash items in process of collection" account, not by adding it to its own Interdistrict Settlement Fund account as in the example, but by deducting it from the member bank reserve account of the paying bank. No other Federal Reserve Bank would have been involved.

Two other possibilities arise in connection with the clearing of checks. First, checks may be deposited in banks in the same cities as the banks on which they are drawn. They may then be cleared, not through the facilities of the Federal Reserve check-clearing mechanism we have described, but through local clearing houses. At the end of each day the banks may calculate the amounts due to and from each other as a result of checks deposited during the day. Then the net balance due from one bank to another will be settled simply by the banks' drawing checks on their Federal Reserve accounts.

Finally, the Federal Reserve Board, in cooperation with the commercial banks, has established in some regions of the country what are known as ACH (automatic clearinghouse) facilities, the use of which has increased sharply, with the volume of checks cleared increasing by some 16 percent in 1982. These regional clearing arrangements operate through Electronic Funds Transfer arrangements. They are cost saving, expeditious, and efficient, and they no doubt point the way in which the mam-

---

[4] See the announcements regarding improvements in the Check-Clearing Service that appear from time to time in the monthly *Federal Reserve Bulletin,* such as the issue for January 1983.

moth task of clearing checks and transferring funds throughout the nation will increasingly and more economically and efficiently be handled in the future.

THE FEDERAL RESERVE AS FISCAL AGENT
FOR THE GOVERNMENT

The Federal Reserve Bank acts as the fiscal agent for the federal government in a number of ways. First, it maintains the checking account of the Treasury Department, and almost all Treasury payments are made by drawing against that account. We have noted the process whereby tax revenues and the proceeds of the sale of government securities are deposited in the first instance in tax and loan accounts in the commercial banks. As funds are transferred from those accounts to the Treasury's account at the Fed, the reserves of the commercial banks are diminished. Then as the Treasury spends the funds by drawing on its account at the Fed, the reserves of the banking system are increased again. Of course, Treasury receipts and payments do not necessarily coincide, and fluctuations in the reserve base of the banking system can therefore result from such Treasury operations. It may then be necessary for the Federal Reserve Bank to engage in defensive monetary policy operations in order to iron out what would otherwise be instabilities in the financial markets and in the depository institutions' ability to maintain the money supply. Again in this case, the defensive operations of the Fed are likely to take the form of variations in the open market purchases and sales mandated by the FOMC.

The Federal Reserve Bank also acts as the government's agent in issuing and redeeming government securities. The interest on the federal debt is paid by the Federal Reserve Bank on the government's behalf.

The government's international financial relations are also conducted largely through the Federal Reserve Bank. The bank buys and sells foreign currency on behalf of the U.S. government, not only to provide the government with the supply of foreign currencies it needs for its operations abroad but also as a means of offsetting exchange rate fluctuations that tend to occur as a result of deficits or surpluses on the international balance of trade and payments. Most of the actual foreign exchange operations of the Fed are conducted by the Federal Reserve Bank of New York. Additionally, the Federal Reserve Bank maintains the deposits in the United States of such international agencies as the International Monetary Funds and the World Bank.

It should not be overlooked, finally, that the Federal Reserve Bank is a major source of economic advice and information for the federal government. The government does, of course, have its own regularly established economic analysis and advisory mechanism. Important in this connection are such bodies as the President's Council of Economic Advisers, the Treasury Department and the Department of Commerce, the Office of Management and Budget, and the specialized information sources within other departments, such as the Departments of State, Interior, and Agriculture. But the Federal Reserve Bank is in close touch with current financial and economic developments on a day-to-day basis, by virtue of its market operations and its responsibilities for the control of the monetary situation, as well as its supervision of the activities of the depository institutions. The federal government is under no obligation to adopt any recommendations offered to it by the Federal Reserve Bank. But in spite of the nominal independence of the Fed, on which we shall comment again in a later chapter in connection with the formulation and implementation of monetary policy, the government does in fact seek and heed its advice.

SUMMARY

Recurring financial panics in the latter part of the nineteenth century, and especially that of 1907, gave rise to a number of suggestions for the reform of the banking system. The Aldrich-Vreeland Act of 1908, the Aldrich proposals for banking reform, and the deliberations and report of the National Monetary Commission culminated in the Federal Reserve Act of 1913. The Federal Reserve Bank was established to "furnish an elastic currency" and to act as a "lender of last resort." Initially, it was not envisaged that the Federal Reserve Bank would hold the more comprehensive powers of monetary management that we associate with it today. Broader powers to make use of contracyclical monetary policy instruments were introduced only during the Great Depression years of the 1930s. This chapter has traced the emergence of the existing structure of the Federal Reserve System from its early beginnings.

Note was taken of the manner in which the Federal Reserve System was initially designed to overcome the principal defects of the National Banking System that preceded it. At the same time, some of the initial defects of the Federal Reserve System were noted, such as the absence of a high degree of central coordination in the system, its lack of contracyclical policy instruments, and its early embrace of the traditional theory of commercial banking or the real bills doctrine.

The present structure of the Federal Reserve System was examined, noting the functions of (1) the Board of Governors, (2) the twelve Federal Reserve Banks, (3) the Federal Open Market Committee, (4) the member banks, and (5) the various advisory committees—the Federal Advisory Committee, the Thrift Institutions Advisory Council, and the Consumer

Advisory Council. The Board of Governors' high degree of control over the constituent parts of the system was discussed. Particular attention was paid to the policy responsibilities and the operating procedures of the Federal Open Market Committee.

An analysis was made of the ways in which the operations of the Federal Reserve bank, particularly its open market operations, affect the reserve positions of the commercial banks. The latter are directly affected also by changes in the amount of currency in circulation in the hands of the public. The management of the reserve accounts of the depository institutions is one of the principal activities of the Federal Reserve Bank. The second important function that has day-to-day operating significance for the banks and other depository institutions is the Federal Reserve check-clearing mechanism. A detailed example of that function of the system was given. The importance in this connection of Federal Reserve float was highlighted. The phenomenon of float raised the importance of Federal Reserve defensive monetary policy action. Account was taken of the improved efficiencies in the operation of the check-clearing mechanism resulting from the introduction of fees for services provided by the Fed. The relevance of the PSAF (Private Sector Adjustment Factor) in connection with service fees was noted.

The chapter concluded by noting the activities of the Federal Reserve Bank as the fiscal agent of the federal government.

IMPORTANT CONCEPTS

Aldrich-Vreeland Act of 1908
Federal Reserve Act of 1913
Regional Federal Reserve Banks
Board of Governors of the Federal Reserve System
Federal Open Market Committee
Internal and external drain
PSAF (Private Sector Adjustment Factor)

The discount window
Check-clearing mechanism
Federal Reserve float
Interdistrict Settlement Fund
ACH (automatic clearinghouse) facilities
Open market operations

QUESTIONS FOR DISCUSSION AND REVIEW

1. What historical or causal relations can be established between (1) the panic of 1907, (2) the Aldrich-Vreeland Act of 1908, and (3) the Federal Reserve Act of 1913?

2. "The Federal Reserve System set out to improve on the National Banking System that preceded it, but its early history was not marked by signal success." Evaluate critically.

3. "The effective control of the Fed is an important question quite independent from that of the ownership of the Federal Reserve Bank. The federal government does not own the Fed, but it controls it." Evaluate critically.

4. How are the Fed's holdings of the depository institutions' reserve accounts relevant for meeting the economy's needs for an elastic currency supply?

5. Discuss the various ways in which Federal Reserve operations affect the reserve balances of the depository institutions and thereby the monetary base.

6. Why is the PSAF (Private Sector Adjustment Factor) relevant to the pricing of Federal Reserve services?

7. What connections exist between Federal Reserve float and defensive monetary policy operations? Why?

8. Why has an increased use of ACH (automatic clearinghouse) facilities affected the functioning of the Federal Reserve check-clearing mechanism?

9. Is internal drain relevant for monetary policy? Why or why not?

10. Do you think the Fed should be brought under (a) public ownership and/or (b) stricter control by Congress? Discuss as fully as possible.

13

FEDERAL RESERVE ASSETS AND LIABILITIES AND THE MONETARY BASE

STUDY OBJECTIVES:

• To review the determinants of the money supply, the M1 money supply multiplier, and the central bank's influence over the supply of money created by the depository institutions
• To trace the causes of change in the reserves of the depository institutions as reflected in the assets and liabilities of the Federal Reserve
• To clarify the relation between the depository institutions' reserve position and the monetary base
• To develop the depository institutions' reserve equation
• To consider the degree of control over the money supply and the monetary situation actually possessed by the Federal Reserve

The question of who controls the money supply cannot be answered simply and unambiguously. The Federal Reserve operations influence the reserves of the depository institutions, which, together with the amount of currency in circulation, constitute the monetary base. It may appear from our construction of the money supply multipliers in Chapter 9 that by controlling the monetary base the Federal Reserve can control the money supply. But matters are not that simple. Two operational problems inhibit such a direct relation.

First, the Federal Reserve's control over the monetary base is itself not precise. Actions of the Treasury, for example, in the transfer of funds through the commercial banks' Tax and Loan accounts to the Treasury account at the Federal Reserve Bank, the creation of Treasury currency, delays in the clearing of checks that give rise to Federal Reserve float, and central bank participation in foreign exchange markets all affect the monetary base. Second, even if a fair degree of control over the monetary base could be achieved, a good deal of room would still exist for slippage between the monetary base and the actual amount of money in existence. A number of factors responsible for that slippage have to do with the asset-holding portfolio decisions of the public, and with the financial institutions' own decisions regarding the holding of excess reserves.

To control the money supply, therefore, the Federal Reserve would have to be able to offset a number of factors that are not directly under its control. This may be due to changes in the public's desire to hold cash, leading to an external drain of reserves from the depository institutions. Or it may result from a change in the level of float outstanding. In such instances defensive monetary policy action by the Federal Reserve would most frequently be centered in open market operations.

These difficulties do not destroy the fact that the overriding responsibility of the Federal Reserve is that of influencing the money supply and the monetary situation, thereby contributing to economic stability and growth. In this chapter we shall look more closely at the impact of the Federal Reserve's operations. We shall do this by studying the ways in which changes in the Federal Reserve's assets and liabilities influence the reserve positions of the depository institutions and how, as a result, the monetary base is affected. The discussion can be abbreviated at a number of points by incorporating the results of the preceding chapters.

Our discussion has frequently referred to the commercial banks as prime examples of the depository institutions in general. In this chapter we shall speak of the determinants of the reserve position of the depository institutions as a whole. For it is this that is described in the reserve deposit accounts on the liabilities side of the Federal Reserve balance sheet. Moreover, the nonbank institutions are affected in the same way as were the commercial banks in the preceding chapter by changes in the public's demand for currency, by the Federal Reserve open market operations, and by the other forces that impact on reserve positions.

THE MONEY SUPPLY MULTIPLIER

Our concern now is with the size of the monetary base at any given time, and with the explanation of changes in it. This follows from the fact that the monetary base, as we saw in Chapter 9, underlies the determination of the money supply. The most directly relevant expression from Chapter 9 is that for the M1 multiplier described as follows:

$$M1 = B\frac{1 + c}{(r + r_t t + c + e)}$$

The M1 measure of the money supply, it will be recalled, includes currency in circulation in the hands of the public and all transaction accounts or checkable deposits in the depository institutions.

In the multiplier expression the variable B refers to the total monetary base, which includes (1) the total reserve deposit accounts held by the depository institutions in accordance with Federal Reserve requirements, (2) the cash held by the depository institutions as part of their required reserves, and (3) currency in circulation in the hands of the public. The remaining variables in the multiplier expression were defined as follows:

r = the required reserve ratio against transaction deposits
r_t = the required reserve ratio against nonpersonal time deposits
t = the public's desired ratio of nonpersonal time deposits to transaction deposits
c = the public's desired currency-to-deposits ratio
e = the depository institutions' desired excess reserves ratio

Not all of the determinants of the money supply summarized in this multiplier are under the control of the Federal Reserve. It has direct control over the reserve requirement variables r and r_t, which it is empowered to set within ranges prescribed by the Depository Institutions Deregulation and Monetary Control Act. The t and the c variables, however, depend on the asset portfolio decisions of the public. The magnitude of e is decided by the depository institutions as a result of their decisions regarding their optimum asset portfolios. If the Federal Reserve is to maintain a close control over the money supply, it will need to conduct its defensive monetary policy actions in such a way as to offset changes in the variables we have just described. Optimally, it would need to be able to predict such changes and to react as required in an optimal method and with optimal timing.

FEDERAL RESERVE ASSETS
AND LIABILITIES

The basis of our analysis is described in Table 13-1, which lists the assets and liabilities of all the Federal Reserve Banks combined as of March 31, 1983. Some of these asset and liability accounts, as well as their analytical significance, will be recognized on the basis of previous discussions. It will be useful for our subsequent analysis if we begin by describing the accounts briefly and indicating the ways in which changes in them set in motion forces that affect the depository institutions' reserve positions.

Table   13-1

Consolidated assets and liabilities of the Federal Reserve Banks,
March 31, 1983 (amounts are in millions of dollars)

Assets		Liabilities and capital	
Gold certificate account	11,138	Federal Reserve Notes out-	
SDR certificate account	4,618	standing	141,497
Coin	477	Deposits	
Loans to depository		Depository institutions	23,419
institutions	2,808	U.S. Treasury	3,572
Acceptances under		Foreign	425
repurchase agreements	0	Other	533
Federal agency obligations	8,915	Deferred availability cash	
U.S. government securities		items	6,098
Bills	55,469	Other liabilities (including	
Notes	62,187	accrued dividends)	1,752
Bonds	18,995	Total liabilities	177,296
Total U.S. government securities bought outright	136,651		
U.S. government securities held under repurchase agreements	0		
Total U.S. government securities	136,651		
Cash items in process of collection	6,584		
Other assets (including bank premises and foreign currencies)	9,187	Capital (including surplus)	3,082
Total assets	180,378	Total liabilities and capital	180,378

Source: *Federal Reserve Bulletin,* April 1983, p. A12.

FEDERAL RESERVE BANK ASSETS

Gold certificate account

In earlier times, under the functioning of the international gold standard described in Chapter 4, the country's supply of gold constituted the basis for the money supply. One of the rules of the gold standard was that each country should preserve a defined relation between its gold stock and the amount of money in circulation. Any paper currency that circulated would be representative full-bodied money, in the sense that it was freely convertible into gold.

Since the 1930s the United States has not been on a full gold standard, and in 1968 the requirement that the Federal Reserve should hold a reserve of gold, or gold certificates, against its note and deposit liabilities was abolished. At the present time gold affects the monetary base only to the extent that the gold acquired by the Treasury is monetized. Not all of the Treasury's gold stock may be monetized. But when it is, the Treasury issues gold certificates to the value of the gold it desires to use for this purpose and deposits those certificates with the Federal Reserve Bank. The corresponding amount is credited by the Federal Reserve Bank to the Treasury's account, shown in Table 13-1 on the liabilities side of its balance sheet. The legal price of gold, which is considerably lower than the international open market price, is $42.22 per troy ounce. This price was set in 1973. Because it is lower than the world market price, which is currently somewhat more than $400, no gold is at present sold to the United States Treasury.

When the legal price of gold was increased from $38 to its present level in 1973, the Treasury was able to increase the value of the gold certificates it had issued against its monetary gold stock. This meant that additional amounts of gold certificates were deposited at the Federal Reserve Bank, and the Treasury's account was increased accordingly. When the Treasury monetizes gold in this way and spends the funds that are thereby placed in its account at the Federal Reserve Bank, the expenditure will lead to an increase in the depository institutions' reserves. This will result from the deposit in those institutions of the checks paid to the public by the Treasury and cleared by the Federal Reserve Bank, a process that adds to the institutions' reserve deposits. A demonetization of gold would have the opposite effects.

If the Treasury were to sell gold in the open market at, say, $350 per ounce, this would have induced effects on the depository institutions' reserves. Initially, the sale of gold, one ounce for example, would cause funds to move from the depository institutions' reserve accounts to the Treasury's account, as shown in the following Federal Reserve partial balance sheet:

Federal Reserve balance sheet

Assets	Liabilities	
	Depository institutions'	
	reserve accounts	−$350 (a)
	Treasury account	+ 350 (a)

The indicator (a) describes the initial effect of the transaction. At this stage the Treasury will have to retire the gold certificates that had previously been issued against the gold, assuming that the gold had been monetized. In that case further entries in the Federal Reserve balance sheet will appear, as described by the indicator (b) in the following:

Federal Reserve balance sheet

Assets		Liabilities	
(b) Gold certificate account	− $42.22	Treasury account	− $ 42.22 (b)
		Treasury account	− 307.78 (c)
		Depository institutions' reserve accounts	+ 307.78 (c)

We have supposed, in constructing this partial balance sheet, that the Treasury spends the net proceeds of the sale of gold. After deducting the $42.22 that resulted from the retirement of the gold certificates, the Treasury can spend the balance of $307.78. In the same way as before, this expenditure will increase the reserves of the depository institutions in the manner shown against the indicator (c). The net effect of the sale of gold, therefore, is to reduce the monetary base by $42.22. The balance sheet of the depository institutions will reflect these transactions:

Depository institutions' balance sheet

Assets		Liabilities	
(a) Reserve accounts	− $350	Demand deposits	− $350 (a)
(c) Reserve accounts	+ 307.78	Demand deposits	+ 307.78 (c)

The (a) and the (c) indicators in the depository institutions' balance sheet correspond to the preceding Federal Reserve balance sheets. Once again, the monetary base is seen to fall by a net amount of $42.22.

Special Drawing Rights certificate account

Special Drawing Rights (SDRs) are issued by the International Monetary Fund to its members as a means of increasing their international liquidity. The SDRs issued to the United States are held in the Exchange Stabilization Fund. The Treasury may from time to time monetize these SDRs in precisely the same way as it can monetize its gold stock. If the Treasury desires to make payments to foreigners, it may monetize a part of its holdings of SDRs. The Federal Reserve Bank is obligated to accept the SDRs and credit the corresponding amount to the Treasury's account. The Federal Reserve's asset "SDR certificate account" will be increased at the same time as the Treasury's account on the liabilities side of the Federal Reserve balance sheet is also increased. Then when the Treasury uses the funds to pay amounts to foreigners as planned, its account at the Federal Reserve Bank will be decreased again, and the foreign deposit accounts at the commercial banks will increase. The latter will in turn cause the banks' reserve accounts at the Federal Reserve Bank to increase also.

Coin

The coin account is an asset account that consists of the Federal Reserve Bank's holding of Treasury currency. The account increases when the Federal Reserve Bank receives newly issued currency from the Treasury, or when Treasury currency is returned to the Federal Reserve Bank by the depository institutions. Conversely, the coin account will decrease when the banks or other depository institutions increase their demand for coin, or when the Treasury withdraws the coin from circulation.

When the Treasury issues new coin, the reserves of the depository institutions are not immediately affected. The value of the coin the Treasury issues to the Federal Reserve Bank is credited to the Treasury's account. If the Treasury should increase its expenditure as a result, then the depository institutions' reserve accounts will be increased in the now familiar way.

When the depository institutions obtain coin from the Federal Reserve Bank, they pay for it by drawing against their reserve accounts. In such a case there is no immediate effect on the institutions' total reserve position. There has simply been a change in the form in which reserves are being held at that time. There is therefore no immediate effect on the monetary base. For the amount of currency that, as we have seen, is included in the computation of the monetary base refers to the currency in the hands of the public, or the existing currency that is not held by the Treasury or the Federal Reserve Bank. We shall present a fuller analysis of the currency position later in this chapter.

Loans

The loan account on the assets side of the Federal Reserve balance sheet refers mainly to loans granted to the depository institutions as a result of their borrowing at the discount window. The balance sheet effects of these borrowings were examined in the preceding chapter.

Acceptances

From time to time amounts may be held in the acceptances account, which refers to the bankers' acceptances (or commercial bills of exchange that have been accepted by bankers, thereby indicating the bankers' liability to pay the amount of the bills when they mature) that have been purchased by the Federal Reserve Bank as part of its open market operations. The bills are generally short-term assets. The asset classification under this heading in Table 13-1 indicates that such acceptances may be acquired by the Federal Reserve Bank under agreements that they will be repurchased from the bank. The bills would in such a case have been acquired from the depository institutions. An increase in either the Federal Reserve Bank's loan account or its acceptances account will cause an increase in the level of the depository institutions' reserves.

U.S. government and federal agency securities

Open market operations of the Federal Reserve Bank, as reflected in Table 13-1, are conducted mainly in U.S. government securities. These, together with the securities of federal agencies, accounted for some 80 percent of the total assets of the Federal Reserve Banks at March 31, 1983. Open market purchases of these securities will increase the reserves of the depository institutions, whether the purchases are made from the banks or from the nonbank public.

Cash items in process of collection, and deferred availability cash items

Two accounts, "cash items in process of collection" and "deferred availability cash items," shown in Table 13-1 on the assets side and the liabilities side of the Federal Reserve Bank's balance sheet, respectively, were explained in Chapter 12 in the context of the check-clearing process. It will be recalled that the difference between them, with the amount outstanding in the "cash items in process of collection" account exceeding that in the "deferred availability cash items" account, represents the amount of Federal Reserve float. An increase in float will cause a temporary increase in the depository institutions' reserves, and therefore in the total monetary base. The Federal Reserve Bank might or might not, depending on the overall needs of the situation, offset this increased float by defensive monetary policy action. It may, for example, sell government securities or the securities of federal agencies in the open market.

Other assets

Other assets are included below in the factors that create depository institutions' reserves and thereby the monetary base. For when the Federal Reserve Bank pays to acquire such assets as bank buildings and operating equipment or foreign currencies, it will increase the commercial banks' or other depository institutions' reserves when the checks it draws on itself to pay for the assets are cleared.

FEDERAL RESERVE BANK LIABILITIES

Federal Reserve Notes outstanding

The first item on the liabilities side of the Federal Reserve Bank balance sheet, "Federal Reserve Notes outstanding," refers to the currency supply created by the Federal Reserve under its note-issuing authority. The notes will be issued when they are demanded by the depository institutions, and the amounts will be deducted from their reserve accounts. Such an issue of notes does not immediately affect the reserve positions of the depository institutions. It is reflected simply in a change in the form in which their reserves are being held. But if the increased issue of currency has followed from an increased demand for currency by the public, then the effect will be a net external drain of reserves from the depository institutions in the manner we have already described.

Deposits

The deposit accounts at the Federal Reserve Bank will be familiar from previous discussion. The deposits of the depository institutions represent the portion of their required reserves that are being held in that form, and the manner in which their total can vary has been examined in Chapter 12. The Treasury deposit account has also been referred to in several contexts. In the detailed analysis later in this chapter of the depository institutions' reserve equation and the monetary base, it will be seen that the deposit accounts at the Federal Reserve Bank, other than those of the depository institutions, represent an absorption of the monetary base.

Capital account and surplus

The capital account in the balance sheet of the Federal Reserve Bank represents (1) the paid-in capital received from the member banks and (2) the surplus paid by the bank into its capital account as a partial allocation of its annual income. Only a relatively small amount is derived from the last-mentioned source, however. In 1982 the Federal Reserve Bank's net earnings amounted to $15,362.3 million. Of this amount, $79.4 million was paid to the member banks as dividends on their holdings of Federal Reserve Bank stock, $78.3 million was transferred to surplus, and $15,204.6 million was paid to the Treasury, a payment referred to as interest on Federal Reserve notes.

Federal Reserve float

Among the balance sheet items over which the Federal Reserve Bank does not have direct control are the accounts that determine the amount of float in existence. The Federal Reserve Bank expects that in the near future, as a result of increased efficiencies in operations, the float will be considerably diminished. In the past, however, the amount of float outstanding has been a very variable item. We have commented on the need for defensive policy action to which it might give rise.

Table 13-2 summarizes the variations in float during the early months of 1983. The data for the nine weekly reporting dates in February and March 1983 indicate that the highest week-end total on March 2 was considerably greater than the lowest week-end total reported two weeks later. The significance of these figures will be seen again from another perspective in the following analysis of the depository institutions' reserve equation and the monetary base.

FACTORS AFFECTING THE DEPOSITORY INSTITUTIONS' RESERVES

The foregoing description of the Federal Reserve Bank's balance sheet leads to an analysis of the factors determining the overall reserve position of the depository institutions. In Table 13-3 an analysis of the factors

Table   13-2

Federal Reserve Float, on selected dates (amounts are in millions of dollars)

Date in 1983	Cash items in process of collection	Deferred availability cash items	Float
February 2	9,989	7,350	2,639
February 9	8,125	6,229	1,896
February 16	9,921	7,231	2,690
February 23	12,413	9,755	2,658
March 2	12,479	8,731	3,748
March 9	8,834	6,292	2,542
March 16	7,844	7,667	177
March 23	8,164	6,574	1,590
March 30	8,818	7,075	1,743

Source: *Federal Reserve Bulletin,* April 1983, p. A12.

Table   13-3

Factors affecting the reserves of the depository institutions, March 31, 1983
(amounts are in millions of dollars)

Factors supplying reserve funds		
Federal Reserve Credit		
U.S. government securities		136,651
Federal agency securities		8,915
Acceptances		0
Loans to depository institutions		2,808
Float		486
Other Federal Reserve assets		9,187
Total Federal Reserve Credit		158,047
Gold stock		11,138
SDR certificate account		4,618
Treasury currency outstanding		13,786
Total factors supplying reserve funds		187,589
Factors absorbing reserve funds		
Currency in circulation (outside of the Federal Reserve and the U.S. Treasury)		154,307
Treasury cash holdings		498
Deposits at the Federal Reserve Bank, other than depository institutions' reserves:		
Treasury	3,572	
Foreign	425	
Other	534	4,531
Other Federal Reserve liabilities and capital		4,834
Total of factors absorbing reserve funds, other than Depository Institutions' reserves		164,170
Reserve accounts of depository institutions, as shown in Table 13-1		23,419
Total factors absorbing reserve funds		187,589

Source: *Federal Reserve Bulletin,* April 1983, pp. A4, A12.

supplying reserve funds, and the factors absorbing reserve funds, has been made in such a way as to enable the reader to compare the data with the Federal Reserve balance sheet that has just been discussed. In the following analysis repeated reference to the Federal Reserve balance sheet will not be made, but the correspondence should be traced. The end result, or the statement that the reserves of the depository institutions at the end of Table 13-3 amounted to $23,419 million, corresponds to the same figure stated on the liabilities side of the Federal Reserve Bank balance sheet in Table 13-1. The objective of Table 13-3 is to show how the activities of the Federal Reserve Bank, as reflected in its balance sheet accounts, do in fact supply or absorb depository institutions' reserves. For this reason the following analysis will culminate in the specification of the depository institutions' reserve equation.

The largest source of supply of reserve funds, as summarized in Table 13-3, is what is referred to as Federal Reserve credit. This term refers in a comprehensive way to the accounts of the Federal Reserve Bank that, taken together, reflect the actions of the Federal Reserve that create depository institutions' reserves. The largest part of Federal Reserve credit is the bank's holdings of government securities. Taking the six items included in Federal Reserve credit in Table 13-3—government securities, federal agency securities, acceptances, loans, float, and other assets—it will be clear by now that the actions of the Federal Reserve Bank that cause these items to increase also cause the depository institutions' reserves to rise. Each of them has been discussed in preceding contexts.

The gold stock and the SDR certificate accounts also cause additions to reserves whenever they are increased. On first appearance, some difficulty may be caused by the amount shown in the top half of Table 13-3, as a factor supplying reserve funds, under the heading "Treasury currency outstanding." This refers to the actual amount of currency that has been issued by the Treasury. In actual fact, some of it will be held by the Treasury itself, some by the depository institutions, some by the Federal Reserve Bank, and some by the public. The actual issue of the currency is a source of reserve funds. For when it is issued to the Federal Reserve Bank, its value is added to the Treasury's account. Then when the Treasury spends the funds, they find their way into the banking system as additions to the depository institutions' reserves. To the extent, however, that such Treasury issues of currency are held by the public, indicating that the public has chosen to surrender its demand deposits for increased currency holdings, to that extent the reserves of the depository institutions will not be as high as they would otherwise be.

Because of the need for a thorough understanding of the actual distribution of currency, we have summarized the issue and disposition of it in Table 13-5. We shall refer to further details in connection with it a little later. In the meantime we can focus on the $13,786 million item in the upper portion of Table 13-3 as furnishing a source of potential increase in reserves. In that sense it is included in this analysis as one of the factors supplying reserve funds.

In the lower portion of Table 13-3 we note the way in which the factors supplying reserve funds actually gave rise to reserves or, on the other hand, were absorbed in different ways. To enable us to grasp the analysis more readily, let us take note of an important point. Consider the factors supplying reserves as we have just discussed them. Take, for example, the Federal Reserve Bank's purchases of government securities. In effect, the Federal Reserve Bank could pay for these securities either by crediting amounts to the depository institutions' reserve accounts or by paying out cash or Federal Reserve notes. Of course the Federal Reserve Bank will, at the point of immediate purchase, pay for these purchases of securities by check, which implies that initially the reserve accounts we are analyzing will be increased. But hypothetically, the persons who have thus received payment could demand currency from the depository institutions, and the net effect would be, not that reserve accounts have been increased, but that currency in circulation in the hands of the public has increased. Once this principle is grasped, it can be seen that any part of the activities anywhere in the system that initially create reserve funds could in due course give rise to increased holdings of currency.

When we look, therefore, as we do in the lower portion of Table 13-3, at the factors absorbing the reserve funds that have been created, we must begin with the total extent to which these funds have found their way, by one route or another, into currency in circulation rather than permanently into reserves. In Table 13-3 the currency in circulation, standing at $154,307 million at the end of March 1983, has in fact absorbed the greatest part of the total of $187,589 million of reserve funds created. This currency in circulation refers to currency held by the public and in the vaults of the depository institutions, and not by the Federal Reserve Banks or the Treasury.

It follows from what has just been said that the second item among the factors absorbing reserve funds, the Treasury cash holdings, also operates to diminish what would otherwise be larger amounts of reserves held by the depository institutions. The $498 million cash held by the Treasury will reappear in our summary of the disposition of currency shown in Table 13-5.

The third factor absorbing reserve funds is shown in Table 13-3 as the $3,572 million held in the Treasury's deposit account. This has already been analyzed from various perspectives. To the extent that the Treasury has amassed funds, perhaps by tax collections through the commercial banks' Tax and Loan accounts or from the sale of securities or the monetization of gold or SDRs, the reserves in the depository institutions will again be lower than they would otherwise be. The foreign deposits shown with the Treasury deposits in Table 13-3 refer to deposits held by other central banks. They are usually small balances that are used principally for the finance of international payments. The other deposits are principally deposits held by international organizations.

The other Federal Reserve liabilities and capital must also be looked upon as factors absorbing reserve funds. For the payment of funds to the Federal Reserve Bank to purchase its capital stock will again imply a diminution of reserves below the level at which they would otherwise have stood. Other liabilities function in this respect in the same way.

If, then, we take the total of the factors supplying reserve funds and deduct the total of the factors we have so far discussed as absorbing reserve funds, the residue must describe the actual amount of reserve deposits held with the Federal Reserve Bank by the depository institutions. This exercise has been illustrated in Table 13-3 where the final item preceding the total at the bottom of the table reconciles this analysis with the Federal Reserve balance sheet data shown in Table 13-1.

DEPOSITORY INSTITUTIONS' RESERVE EQUATION

The foregoing analysis can be summarized in a depository institutions' reserve equation written in the following form:

$$
\begin{Bmatrix}
\text{Depository} \\
\text{institutions' total} \\
\text{reserve deposits} \\
\text{with the Federal} \\
\text{Reserve Bank}
\end{Bmatrix}
=
\begin{Bmatrix}
\text{Federal Reserve} \\
\text{credit} \\
+ \\
\text{Gold stock and} \\
\text{SDR certificate} \\
\text{accounts} \\
+ \\
\text{Treasury currency} \\
\text{outstanding}
\end{Bmatrix}
\text{ minus }
\begin{Bmatrix}
\text{Currency in} \\
\text{circulation} \\
+ \\
\text{Treasury cash} \\
\text{holdings} \\
+ \\
\text{Treasury,} \\
\text{foreign, and} \\
\text{other deposits} \\
\text{with the} \\
\text{Federal} \\
\text{Reserve Bank} \\
+ \\
\text{Other Federal} \\
\text{Reserve} \\
\text{liabilities} \\
\text{and capital}
\end{Bmatrix}
$$

THE MONETARY BASE

The objective of our analysis, however, is not simply the specification of the depository institutions' reserve position. The analysis to this point has explained only that portion of the institutions' reserves that is held on deposit at the Federal Reserve Bank, amounting to $23,419 million at the end of March 1983. The actual reserve position of the depository institutions would be the sum of these amounts and the currency they held in their vaults. In the absence of precise data for the date in question, it can be estimated from relevant sources that on March 31, 1983, the depository institutions held about $18,000 million in currency. This estimate is presented only as an order of magnitude. But the point of our statement will be clear. It is twofold.

First, the total legal reserves of the depository institutions at the date we are examining, March 31, 1983, consisted of the $23,419 million deposits at the Federal Reserve Bank plus some $18,000 million currency. Total reserves therefore amounted to some $40 billion. Second, this implies that the balance of the total amount of currency in circulation, or the total of $154,307 million as shown in Table 13-3, was divided between the depository institutions and the public, with $18,000 million held by the institutions and $136,307 million held by the public.

With our principal objective of the monetary base in view, the information contained in the analysis to this point, particularly that relating to the depository institutions' reserve deposits in Table 13-3, has been recast in Table 13-4 to focus precisely on the determination of the monetary base. We have consistently defined the monetary base as being the sum of (1) the total reserves of the depository institutions and (2) the currency held by the public. This reconciliation is demonstrated in Table 13-4. The details have already been commented on from different perspectives and will be clear to the reader.

The reasons why this analysis is significant hark back to the point with which we began this chapter. For purposes of monetary analysis and

Table   13-4

Summary statement of the monetary base, March 31, 1983
(amounts are in millions of dollars)

Sources of the monetary base		
Factors supplying reserve funds, as in Table 13-3		187,589
Less:		
Treasury cash holdings	498	
Deposits at the Federal Reserve Banks, other than depository institutions	4,531	
Other Federal Reserve liabilities and capital	4,834	
Total deductions, as in Table 13-3		9,863
Total monetary base		177,726
Distribution of the monetary base		
Deposits at Federal Reserve Bank by depository institutions, as in Tables 13-1 and 13-3		23,419
Currency in circulation		
Held by the public	136,307	
Held in the vaults of depository institutions (estimated)	18,000	
Total currency in circulation, as in Table 13-3		154,307
Total monetary base		177,726

Source: Tables 13-1 and 13-3.

policy we need to have a clear understanding of what it is that determines the monetary base at any time. For it may be thought that if an adequate degree of control over the monetary base can be achieved, then the money supply can be kept under more or less firm control also. This, in turn, may be thought to have significant implications for general financial market conditions and for the performance and trend of the economy in general. We shall return to some differences of view as to the importance of these questions for monetary policy in Part VII, where we shall discuss the place of money in economic policy.

In analytical terms, we need to have some means of envisaging the determinants of the monetary base in order that it may be incorporated into such money supply multipliers as that shown for M1 at the beginning of this chapter. But our analysis to this point has confirmed the warning with which we also began. The Federal Reserve Bank does not have a tight control over all the elements of the monetary base. The three most volatile elements are (1) currency in circulation, (2) float, and (3) Treasury deposits. The first results from the public's asset portfolio decisions and can vary at different times of the year. The Federal Reserve Bank can at best endeavor to predict it and to take whatever action is necessary, and thought to be potentially effective, to offset it. The float again depends on forces outside the direct control of the Federal Reserve Bank. For reasons we have noted, however, its fluctuations are expected to be moderated in the future. The third important element of instability, the Treasury deposits, again is not under the control of the Federal Reserve Bank.

The Treasury cannot always match its inflows and outflows of cash in such a way as to prevent fluctuations in them from having an impact on depository institutions' reserve and on general monetary conditions. If, however, the amount in the Treasury's Federal Reserve Bank deposit account is kept fairly stable, and the fluctuations are in the Treasury tax and loan accounts at the commercial banks, the destabilizing effects on the monetary base will not be as great. For the funds held in tax and loan accounts do not in themselves diminish the commercial banks' reserves. Payments to the government that are retained in tax and loan accounts simply transfer the ownership of deposits from the public to the government while they leave the total of the banks' reserves undisturbed. When funds are transferred from the banks to the Federal Reserve Treasury account, however, the reserves of the banking system are diminished.

The Treasury's deposit account at the Federal Reserve was in fact held fairly steady until 1974. At that time the tax and loan accounts in the commercial banks did not bear interest, and the Treasury subsequently began to transfer larger amounts to its Federal Reserve account to minimize the implicit subsidy being paid to the commercial banks. Moreover, it appears to be in the Treasury's interest to hold funds in its Federal Reserve account for two reasons. First, by having access in this way to larger deposit funds, the Federal Reserve would invest more heavily in government securities, the interest earnings on which, we recall, are substantially transferred by the Federal Reserve to the Treasury as its annual payment of "Interest on Federal Reserve Notes." Second, the Federal Reserve would conceivably find itself in the position of having to extend larger Federal Reserve credit in order to offset the effects on the commercial banks' reserve positions of the Treasury's transfer of funds to the Federal Reserve Bank, once again tending to increase the Federal Reserve's government security portfolio. Since 1977, however, the Treasury earns income on most of its tax and loan account funds, and this has tended to moderate the transfer of funds to its Federal Reserve deposit account. By this means the volatility of Treasury cash receipts and payments does not now feed through in as serious a fashion to an induced instability in the monetary base.

THE SOURCES AND DISPOSITION OF CURRENCY

The various references to currency in the foregoing discussion, particularly those in Tables 13-1, 13-3, and 13-4, can give rise to confusion if a clear picture of the issue and disposition of currency is not kept in mind. For this reason the question is analyzed more fully in Table 13-5. The

Table   13-5

Currency issued and in circulation, March 31, 1983 (amounts are in millions of dollars)

Sources of currency	
Federal Reserve Notes issued to Federal Reserve Banks	159,568
Less:	
Notes held by Federal Reserve Banks	18,130
Plus: Statistical discrepancy	59
Federal Reserve Notes outstanding, as per Federal Reserve Consolidated Balance Sheet shown in Table 13-1	141,497
Treasury currency outstanding, as shown in Table 13-3	13,786
Total currency issued	155,283
Disposition of currency	
Coin held by Federal Reserve Banks, as shown in Table 13-1	477
Treasury cash holdings, as shown in Tables 13-3 and 13-4	498
Currency in circulation, as shown in Tables 13-3 and 13-4	154,307
Total currency issued	155,282

Source: Tables 13-1, 13-3, and 13-4; *Federal Reserve Bulletin,* April 1983, p. A12. Amounts may not add to totals because of rounding.

entries will be largely self-explanatory at this stage. They are designed to effect a reconciliation with the data contained in the preceding tables. Table 13-5 adds to the net issue of Federal Reserve notes outstanding the amount of Treasury currency issued, to obtain the total amount of currency in circulation. This total, it is shown in the lower portion of Table 13-5, is held partly by the Federal Reserve Banks and by the Treasury (in both of those cases only very small amounts being involved), with the remainder being in circulation. This residual amount, it was shown in table 13-4, is held partly by the public and, to a much smaller extent, in the vaults of the depository institutions.

THE IMPACT OF GOVERNMENT FINANCE

Government expenditure can be financed by any one or more of three means: (1) the issue of new currency, (2) taxation, and (3) borrowing, or the issue of new debt. In the United States the first means is not generally employed. We have seen in this chapter that when the Treasury deposits new currency in the Federal Reserve Bank, its deposit account will be increased. This does not immediately add to the monetary base. But when the Treasury spends the funds obtained in this way, the reserves of the depository institutions will be increased. In due course the currency in circulation in the hands of the public may also increase, thus tending to moderate what might otherwise be the potential expansionary effects of the addition to the monetary base. But this method of government financing is not adopted as a general revenue-raising device. The United States government does not resort to what we might call such printing press or mint financing.

More important are the tax revenue-raising policies and the issue of new debt. The impact of tax revenue financing has already been traced through the effects on the tax and loan accounts at the commercial banks, and it need not be discussed at length at this point. Only a few remaining points need be mentioned.

First, even though the transfer of funds from the public to the government's tax and loan accounts does not change the banks' reserve positions or therefore the monetary base, it will nevertheless have an impact on the money supply. This is because the tax and loan account balances are not counted as part of the bank deposits for purposes of defining the M1 or M2 money supply. Moreover, the banks are not required to hold reserves against the amount of deposits in tax and loan accounts. Funds will therefore be released from the required reserves of the depository institutions, and an expansion of lending could occur as a result.

When the government finances by issuing new debt—that is, by selling new securities—the monetary effects depend on the manner in which the government borrowing is conducted. At the end of 1982 the total gross public debt outstanding, including the amounts held by U.S. government agencies and trust funds, amounted to $1,197.1 billion. This was some $168.4 billion higher than it had been one year previously. Over the year the amount held by U.S. government agencies and trust funds increased by $6.1 billion, the amount held by the Federal Reserve Bank increased by $8.3 billion, and private investors increased their holdings by $143.7 billion.

At the time of new issue, government securities may be sold to (1) the Federal Reserve Bank (though in 1981 the legal authority that the Federal Reserve possessed, permitting it to buy up to $5 billion of securities directly from the Treasury after authorization by five members of the Board of Governors, was canceled); (2) the financial institutions; or (3) the nonbank public. Only the first-mentioned method of financing, or sale of securities to the Federal Reserve Bank, would increase the monetary base. For in that case the Federal Reserve Bank's holdings of securities would increase at the same time as the Treasury account increases. This increase in security holdings can be interpreted as an increase in Federal Reserve credit, which, it was seen earlier in this chapter, is a source of reserve funds or of an increase in the monetary base. In effect, the Treasury would in this case come into possession of new spendable funds, its account at the Federal Reserve Bank having been increased, without there being any offsetting reduction in any deposit account anywhere else in the system. When the Treasury spent the funds, there would be a new addition to the deposits and reserves of the depository institutions. This method of financing, however, is not usually adopted. The Treasury generally makes use of this financing method only to provide funds temporarily to enable it to pay tax refunds.

Generally, the Treasury will sell new issues of securities (using the Federal Reserve Bank as its fiscal agent to arrange and effect the sales) to the public, including the financial institutions. The proceeds of the sale are transferred to the government's tax and loan accounts at the commercial banks in ways with which we are now familiar. In the impact the monetary base is not affected, though, as we have seen above, the money supply is temporarily reduced because the tax and loan accounts are not included in the money supply definitions. When the funds are transferred to the Treasury's account at the Federal Reserve Bank, the monetary base is reduced. But when the Treasury spends the funds, the deposits and reserves of the banks and other depository institutions are increased again. The net effect on the monetary base is therefore to leave it unchanged.

A slightly different effect is involved if the purchaser of a newly issued security is a depository institution. If the institution made use of excess reserves to purchase the securities, there would be an increase in the money supply. But the same effect could have been produced, of course, if the institution had used those excess reserves to acquire any other income-earning asset. The money-creating effects will be permanent, therefore, only if the depository institution has made a policy decision to reduce permanently its holdings of excess reserves. This might well follow if the larger supply of securities now in the market causes the market price of securities to fall and their yields to rise. This would imply an upward pressure on the general level of interest rates. This, in turn, might well induce the depository institutions to reduce their excess reserves in order to benefit from the higher-income-earning prospects that are now available. This implies that the lending institutions would be induced to effect a permanent change in the size and structure of their asset port-folios.

It should be borne in mind in this analysis that if the increased government borrowing is imposed on a money capital market where the competition for funds from private borrowers is already strong, there will be a heavier pressure on the interest rates. As rates in general rise, the Federal Reserve might well decide to intervene in the market and supply funds via open market purchases of securities. Such an action would, of course, directly increase the monetary base and would lead to the pos-sibility of multiple deposit expansion. As a result of this, in turn, the increased supply of government securities will be able to be accommo-dated.

SUMMARY

Preparatory to examining the forces determining the monetary base, this chapter reviewed the basic M1 money supply multiplier and discussed the extent to which the Federal Reserve Bank is able to control the money supply. Two problems arise. First, the extent to which the Federal Reserve Bank is able to control the monetary base is uncertain. Second, a number of the variables that together determine the magnitude of the money supply multiplier are beyond the control of the Federal Reserve Bank. The Federal Reserve Bank is left to predict, where that is thought to be possible, the changes that may occur from time to time in such variables and to adapt its policy operations to them.

A description and analysis of the asset and liability accounts in the Federal Reserve Bank's balance sheet led to the derivation of the depos-itory institutions' reserve equation. Attention was given to the ways in which changes in the values of Federal Reserve assets and liabilities affected the reserves of the depository institutions and contributed to changes in the monetary base.

Our analytical interest in the monetary base stems from the potential policy significance of the Federal Reserve Bank's defensive operations to offset changes in it. A fuller discussion of the instruments of monetary policy will be given in Part VII. Particular attention was given in this chapter to the sources and disposition of the currency supply, clarifying the manner in which the Treasury, along with the Federal Reserve Bank, is responsible for currency issues.

A concluding comment was made on the effect on the monetary base and the money supply of the various methods by which the government may finance its expenditure. The effects of taxation revenue were traced through the commercial banks' tax and loan accounts. The impact of new government security issues was examined, noting that in the general case such securities are sold to the financial institutions, including the depository institutions, and the public. The effects on the money capital market and on security prices and interest rates were considered. The possibility of Federal Reserve intervention in the market was recognized. This may be necessary in order to support the market and to provide the depository institutions with the reserve funds to enable them to accommodate the demand for funds inherent in the new government security financing.

IMPORTANT CONCEPTS

Monetary base

Treasury currency outstanding

Float

Factors supplying and absorbing reserve funds

Depository institutions' reserve equation

Federal Reserve credit

Sources and disposition of currency

Currency in circulation

QUESTIONS FOR DISCUSSION AND REVIEW

1. Does the Fed control the money supply? Does it control the monetary base? Discuss critically.

2. Using the latest available data published in the monthly *Federal Reserve Bulletin*, calculate the changes that have occurred in the monetary base during the last six months.

3. Is government deficit financing inflationary? Answer this question by tracing the possible implications of government financing for financial institutions' balance sheets.

4. What connections exist between the determinants of the depository institutions' reserve position and the determinants of the monetary base?

5. Making use of current Federal Reserve data, analyze the sources and disposition of the currency in circulation.

6. Establish and quantify the depository institutions' reserve equation as it currently exists.

7. Discuss critically the proposition that the existence of an extensive and resilient government securities market is essential to the efficient conduct of monetary policy.

8. Making use of the latest available *Annual Report* of the Federal Reserve Board, explain why the Fed is able to make payments to the Treasury (in excess of $15 billion per annum), and consider how the general level of the government's financing costs is relevant to this question.

9. Trace the manner in which the Federal Reserve Board's defensive and dynamic monetary policy actions are reflected in the aggregate Federal Reserve balance sheet.

10. What, if any, is the relevance of changes in the velocity of circulation of money for the Federal Reserve Board's reaction to changes in the monetary base?

14

INTRODUCTION TO MACROECONOMIC SYSTEMS

STUDY OBJECTIVES:

• To gain further light on the "moneyness" of a monetary economy and the reasons for the possible lack of "coherence" or mutually consistent market-clearing outcomes within it

• To note the principal features of the three main approaches to macroeconomic analysis:
  1. classical
  2. neoclassical
  3. postclassical

• To obtain a preview of the structure of a postclassical analysis of the macro-economy

• To observe the relevance of a number of analytical issues that will subsequently be employed, such as uncertainty, time, expectations, equilibrium, market signals, and the special properties of interest and money

This chapter is designed as an introduction to the analysis of the macroeconomy and the distinctions between the neoclassical and post-classical views examined in Chapters 15 through 19. None of the issues raised is developed fully at this stage. Our main concern is to probe somewhat further than has yet been possible into what we have called the "moneyness" of the monetary economy. The existence and use of money introduce some worrying sources of disequilibrium and disruption, as well as facilitating the advantages we have already observed. The principal feature of the system in its money form is the possibility that money may serve as a store of value. This, of course, is nothing new. But in serving this important function, frequently in the face of unsurmountable uncertainty, the holding of money can cause damaging interruptions to the money expenditure flows. This, in turn, can lead to interruptions in the rate of flow of economic goods and services and in the level of production and employment.

The introduction of money into an otherwise barter system, as we saw in Chapter 3, had numerous advantages in widening the area of economic activity, production, and exchange. It enabled a considerable reduction in costs of all kinds to be achieved. It facilitated the specialization of production and the exploitation of comparative advantages in resource endowments and skills. It led to higher potential levels of general economic well-being. There was a significant information content in the prices established in money terms. Commodity price levels served as signals to producers and holders of exchangeable goods, indicating to them what lines of investment and production could be expected to be economically worthwhile.

But in all this we cautioned that money was not to be understood as merely a veil. Production levels and relative prices are not determined independently of the presence and circulation of money. Money cannot come in only as an afterthought to translate relative commodity prices into absolute money prices. John Stuart Mill was not on good ground when he said that money was "a machine for doing quickly and commodiously what would be done, though less quickly and commodiously, without it . . ."[1] John Locke's dictum at the end of the seventeenth century was nearer the mark: "The money of the nation may lie dead, and thereby prejudice trade."[2] Money, as we have seen, might not be "neutral" in the sense in which the classical economists understood it. The circulation of money, and particularly changes in the amount of it in existence, may have important implications for the structure and functioning of the real sectors and aspects of the economy. Locke's notion was taken up and given extensive development in the eighteenth century, but the classical economists in the nineteenth century proceeded in substantial disregard of it.

To the extent that income is saved rather than spent on consumption goods, the volume of market signals being transmitted to the producers of consumption goods is diminished. When income earners decide not to consume, they are deciding to retain in money form part of the income that has been paid to them. They are saving. But the act of saving does

---

[1] John Stuart Mill, *Principles of Political Economy* ed. by Sir. W.J. Ashley (London: Longmans, Green, 1909), Book III, Chap. 7, p. 488.
[2] John Locke, *Consequences of the Lowering of Interest, and Raising the Value of Money*, 1691; published with J.R. McCulloch, *Principles of Political Economy* (London: Murray, 1870), p. 226.

not in itself transmit any market signal to the potential producers of commodities. Those individuals who have saved have no idea at that point in time as to what they might use their money to acquire in the future. There is therefore no way of transmitting any signal to producers to prepare a particular commodity output for those individuals' subsequent purchase.

It may be thought, however, that the savings will find their way into the hands of borrowers who wish to use the funds to finance investment expenditures. In that case an increase in the demand for capital goods would offset the reduced demand for consumption goods, and the overall level of production and employment need not fall. This was, in fact, a line of argument advanced by Adam Smith, and it has become enshrined in economics as the Turgot-Smith doctrine of saving.[3] But such a proposition is not as simple as it may sound, and it is not as cogent as it may appear in the context of a money-using economy. For the question arises as to precisely what kinds of investment in capital goods should be made. Or what capital goods should the savings funds be used to acquire. Basically, there is no way of knowing, at the point in time at which the saving is made, what consumer goods will be in demand at a later time, and what capital goods should therefore now be acquired to make them.

Moreover, it is not a significant alleviation of this problem to say that the rate of interest will equilibrate the flows of savings and investment, and that the flow of savings will be absorbed and transformed into investment outlays at some positive rate of interest. This only begs the question. For who or what is to say that there must necessarily be a positive rate of interest that will perform this nicely equilibrating function? The flow of saving, on the other hand, may very well be too large for the potential investment and capital goods requirements to absorb it at any rate of interest. In that case the savings funds will have been permanently withdrawn from the sphere of circulation. They will not flow into investment. The supply and demand for loanable funds curves in Figure 6-3 might not cross in the positive quadrant at all.

The problem we have to confront is that when saving is made, no immediate signal is thereby transmitted to the production and employment-creating side of the economy. Producers, and therefore potential investors, are at that time quite uncertain of what future demands and income-earning opportunities might exist. At this fundamental point the most basic uncertainty enters the picture. Investment in capital goods is always and necessarily made under conditions of uncertainty. What pro-

---

[3] See the discussion of this doctrine in Douglas Vickers, "Adam Smith and the Status of the Theory of Money," in Andrew S. Skinner and Thomas Wilson, eds., *Essays on Adam Smith* (Oxford: Clarendon Press, 1975), pp. 482ff.

ducers need, in order to induce them to make expenditures on capital equipment in the presence of uncertainty, is some way of forming more or less reliable expectations of the future.

That, essentially, is the critical problem of a money-using economy that has to be brought into focus. A critical stage of decision making exists at which no market signals at all are available to guide producers. They have no true knowledge of future outcomes. Ignorance abounds. And in the face of ignorance the best that can be done is to form expectations of future outcomes and have the courage to act upon them. That is why Keynes spoke so much of animal spirits underlying investment decisions in the money-using economy. But what is it, we can ask, that guides the formation of expectations?

To this there is no one answer. Perhaps economic behavior is predominantly conventional behavior, or based on the extrapolation to the future of recently developed trends in relevant economic data.[4] But when we face the future we face only ignorance. As Keynes said about it, "We simply do not know."[5] A money-using economy is therefore burdened by the fact that some of the most critical decisions in it have no clearly logical basis for resolution and for action.[6]

In a money-using economy, therefore, there may not be a harmonious reconciliation among all individuals' decisions at all. There might not be, to use the concept we introduced above, a coherence between all market outcomes in the system. Moreover, there does not exist any necessary mechanism that would ensure that the market signals a producer received from current market developments would guide him safely to future resource commitments and outputs. Even the current consumption expenditure patterns do not necessarily provide a reliable guide to future expenditures. Tastes may change. The commitment of resources to future

---

[4] See the discussion of the significance of conventional behavior in Douglas Vickers, *Financial Markets in the Capitalist Process* (Philadelphia: University of Pennsylvania Press, 1978), Chap. 2.

[5] John Maynard Keynes, "The General Theory of Employment," *Quarterly Journal of Economics*, February 1937, p. 214.

[6] This should not be taken to imply that decision makers in the presence of genuine uncertainty are paralyzed into inaction, or that no rules of procedure or criteria for action can be constructed. See the highly relevant discussion in G.L.S. Shackle, *Decision, Order, and Time in Human Affairs*, 2nd ed. (Cambridge: Cambridge University Press, 1969); and Vickers, *Financial Markets in the Capitalist Process*. The proposition in the text has in view the essential exogeneity and volatility of expectations. Theories of endogenous expectations have, of course, been invented and enjoyed some vogue in macroeconomic analysis. The theory of rational expectations, for example, which consciously purports to advance beyond the earlier hypothesis of adaptive expectations, has become an integral part of the so-called new classical macroeconomics. See Michael Parkin, *Macroeconomics* (Englewood Cliffs, N.J.: Prentice-Hall, 1984). This will be commented on further in the discussion in Chapter 23 of the place of money in economic policy. A further discussion is contained in Douglas Vickers, "On Relational Structures and Non-Equilibrium in Economic Theory", *Eastern Economic Journal*, forthcoming 1985.

production depends on what we can now call, following Keynes, long-term expectations.[7] Current market developments will not necessarily give rise to long-term expectations that would establish coherence in the system. We mean by *coherence* in this sense mutually consistent outcomes in all markets, such that the resources of the economy will be fully employed and the level of economic well-being thereby maximized.

THE CLASSICAL, NEOCLASSICAL, AND POSTCLASSICAL PERSPECTIVES

The classical system of macroeconomic thought solved the problem we have just encountered by essentially assuming it away. We have noted Adam Smith's conclusion that savings would automatically flow into investment. This doctrine became enshrined, in another aspect, in what became known as Say's law. This proposition stated, in simplest form, that supply created its own demand. More fully, it claimed that all the incomes earned in producing the national output would be spent and respent in purchasing that output. There could not therefore be a deficiency of aggregate demand for the total supply of goods and services produced. There could not therefore be any reduction in the overall flow of monetary demand for goods and services. There could not therefore be any reduction in the demand for employment to produce those goods and services.

But if Say's law said that there could not be a deficiency of demand for goods and services at a *specified* level of employment and output, it followed logically that the same could be said of *all conceivable* levels of output. There was no reason, then, why full employment in the economy could not be automatically realized and maintained. The central problem of a money-using economy as we characterized it above simply did not exist. Of course the demand for specific goods may be reduced from time to time. Employment in the production of them may decline. To use the language of the times, partial overproduction may occur. But this did not mean there could be, or would be, a general overproduction. Resources released from one line of productive activity would be freed to move into another line of production for which the demand was now correspondingly higher. A high degree of flexibility of resource movement and use in the economy was assumed to exist. As a result, automatic full employment

---

[7] Keynes, *General Theory*, Chap. 12. On the important question of uncertainty and expectations in macroeconomic analysis, see also J. A. Kregel, "Economic Methodology in the Face of Uncertainty: The Modeling Methods of Keynes and Post-Keynesians," *Economic Journal*, 1976; Paul Davidson and J. A. Kregel, "Keynes' Paradigm: A Theoretical Framework for Monetary Analysis," in E. J. Nell, ed., *Growth, Profits and Property* (Cambridge: Cambridge University Press, 1980); and Paul Davidson, *Money and the Real World*, 2nd ed. (New York: John Wiley, 1978), Chap. 16.

of all those willing and desiring to work would be achieved. All the incomes earned would be spent. There would not be any permanent interruptions to the aggregate production and money payments flows. Wage rates would be set to clear the labor markets. The total achievable national output would thereby be determined. There could be no general overproduction. The system, to use our now familiar concept, cohered.

John Maynard Keynes, in his *General Theory* published in 1936, argued forcibly against this core proposition of the classical economics. He saw that the history of the times perversely refused to reflect the tidy logic of the theory. The solaces of automatic harmony and coherence did not exist. Men were involuntarily unemployed. The facts too clearly belied the claims of the theory. Distress abounded. What was needed was a system of thought that overthrew the inner core of logic contained in Say's Law. Supply, it had to be seen, did not necessarily produce its own demand.

But all too quickly Keynes' achievement was sidetracked. One of his foremost concerns, that the formation of long-run expectations underlying investment in an uncertain economy might not be such as to ensure coherence, was submerged. A rediscovered general equilibrium form of theorizing that had been invented earlier by Walras was used to interpret what Keynes was thought to have said.[8]

This form of analysis was in effect an end run by the refurbished classical economics around the essential propositions that Keynes had made. At this stage, classicism had become a very healthy neoclassicism. It was healthy in the sense that it was to enjoy a long and still continuing life, quite apart from what might be thought to be the logical difficulties within it. The outlines of the refurbished classical theory can be summarized very briefly as follows.

THE BEQUEST OF THE CLASSICAL MACROECONOMIC SCHEME

We mention first the essential core proposition of the theory. This has to do with what subsequently became an important part of the neoclassical vision of the market for labor. Here it was imagined that a supply curve of labor could be defined, describing the offer of different amounts of labor as a positive function of the real wage rate. The higher the real wage rate (the money wage rate divided by the price level), the greater the

[8] See John Hicks, *Value and Capital*, 2nd ed. (Oxford: Clarendon Press, 1946); and the same author's "Mr. Keynes and the 'Classics': A Suggested Interpretation," *Econometrica*, 1937, reprinted in *Readings in the Theory of Income Distribution* (Philadelphia: Blakiston, 1946)

amount of labor supplied to the market. Similarly, a demand curve for labor could be traced out by the marginal product of labor as determined by the production functions of the employing firms. The demand curve was downward sloping, indicating that a larger quantity of labor would be demanded at a lower real wage rate. The upshot of this theory was that the equilibrium or market-clearing price of labor was determined uniquely by the coordinates at which the demand curve and the supply curve in the labor market crossed. Thus we can say, to use a notion we introduced earlier, the real wage was determined endogenously. This was determined at the same time as the equilibrium amount of labor supplied and demanded was specified. The labor market therefore cleared. It cleared at the supply and demand cross point. It solved the full-employment problem. It gave full employment by definition. It solved the unemployment problem by defining it away.

The classical theory having solved the employment problem in the market for labor, the corresponding full-employment level of output was determined by substituting that amount of employment into the so-called aggregate production function. This was a functional relation that showed the dependence of output, or real income, on the amount of labor employed, given the existence of the amount of capital equipment with which the labor force cooperated in production. The relationships so far envisaged are depicted in Figure 14-1.

Summarizing our comments on the classical system to this point, and observing a little more deeply the analytical bequest it made to the neoclassical theory, we note that three of its core propositions have now been introduced. First, it embraced the notion that savings, or the portion of incomes diverted from consumption expenditures, would automatically flow into investment outlays. Say's law would automatically hold and guarantee coherence in the aggregate system. The variable that brought the level of savings and the level of investment expenditure into equality with each other was the rate of interest.

Second, the level of employment was determined as a result of the interaction of supply and demand conditions in the market for labor. The equilibrium level of employment determined in that market was automatically a full-employment level because it described the level of employment of those willing and desiring to work at the equilibrium real wage rates. This important market-clearing phenomenon is shown in Figure 14-1.

Third, the level of employment in turn determined the equilibrium level of real output or production in the economy, by substitution into the economy's aggregate production function. This relation, as shown in Figure 14-1, was generally thought to be positively inclined and concave. This indicated that larger labor inputs to the production process would

Figure   14-1.

Neoclassical labor market and production function

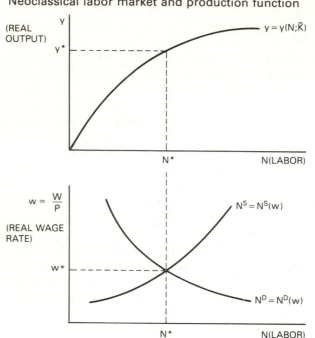

bring forth larger outputs, but that the marginal product of labor (employed with a given amount of capital equipment and other cooperating factors) would diminish.

We can usefully summarize the general flavor of the classical theory at this point by noting its fourth main element of analysis. This had to do with the so-called quantity theory of money, or the determinants of the general level of prices. This said that if the average stock of money that existed during a specified time period, M, was multiplied by its velocity of circulation, V, the product, MV, could be taken to describe the level or rate of monetary expenditure or the demand for goods and services in the economy. Another way of conceiving of the level of money flows, of course, was to take the measure of the level of real output, y, and multiply it by the average commodity price level, P. Thus the classical theory had, in effect, two different ways of visualizing the level of total money expenditures. They were measured by both MV and Py.

The quantity equation of exchange brought these two magnitudes together and established the definitional equation

(1) $$MV = Py$$

Under certain behavioral assumptions regarding the constancy or givenness of V and y (the velocity of circulation, V, being determined by the
structure of payments habits in the economy, and the level of real income,
y, being determined by the equilibrium employment level in the labor
market), it was argued that changes in the supply of money on the left-
hand side of Equation (1) would give rise to corresponding changes in the
price level, P, on the right-hand side.

Here we have the essential function of the money supply in the
classical system. It determined the absolute price level after the overall
level of output (and the structure of output as dependent on relative factor
costs and price levels) was determined in the real sector of the economy.
In this thought system money functioned simply as a medium of exchange.
The demand for it depended simply on the level of income or transactions
it was desired to finance.

These four important relations or assumptions of the classical system will be seen in sharply different light in the following macroanalysis.
They should be kept in mind clearly as (1) the automatic flow of savings
into investment and the importance of Say's law for this result; (2) the
automatic realization of the full employment of labor as a result of endogenous market-clearing forces in the market for labor; (3) the existence
of an aggregate production function, exhibiting generally diminishing
marginal productivity of the variable input labor; and (4) the presence
of the quantity theory of money to determine the general level of commodity prices. The scheme of thought is summarized in the set of diagrams
shown in Figure 14-2.

On the left-hand side of Figure 14-2 we have incorporated the labor
market and the production function relations shown in Figure 14-1. On
the right-hand side the determination of the price level is shown, along
with the resulting determination of the endogenous money wage rate.

In Figure 14-2 the market-clearing employment level, N^*, determines the equilibrium level of real output, y^*, in the top left-hand section.
This level of output, when transferred to the top right-hand diagram,
determines the equilibrium general price level, P^*. This follows from the
operational significance of the quantity theory of money. The money
supply and the velocity of circulation are assumed to be given and are
referred to as M and V in the figure. These magnitudes being given, the
total level of monetary circulation, or the monetary demand for commodities, is given as MV as shown. But this magnitude also equals, as
previously argued, Py. The curve shown in the top right-hand diagram
of the figure is therefore a rectangular hyperbola, such that all points on
the curve represent P and y magnitudes which, when multiplied together,
equal a given or constant amount.

Introducing the y^* magnitude from the left-hand side of the figure,
therefore, throws out the P magnitude, P^*, consistent with it under the

Figure   14-2.

The classical macroeconomic system

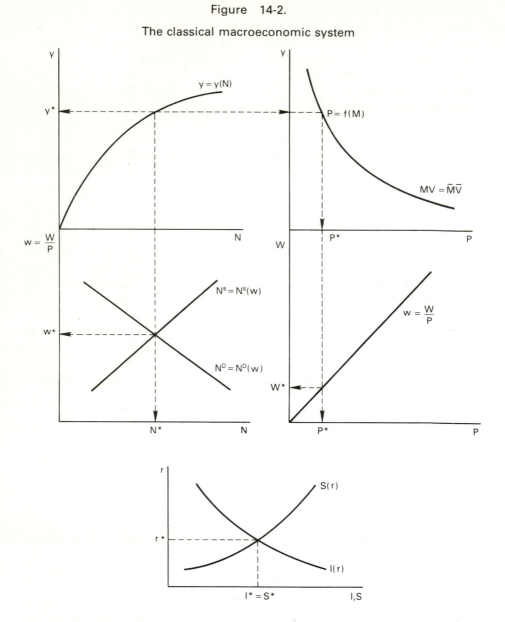

assumed money supply conditions. Below this diagram we have shown the relation between the price level and the money wage rate, W, implicit in the real wage rate, which, as shown to the immediate left, is determined as the market-clearing variable in the labor market. The real wage rate, or the purchasing power of the money wage rate, is there defined as $w = W/P$. This determines the slope of the ray in the price-money wage relation. Importing the equilibrium price level, P^*, from the top right-hand corner of Figure 14-2, then, provides, as shown, the equilibrium money wage rate.

Up to this point we have said nothing about the rate of interest except that it is the variable that brings the flows of savings and investment expenditures into equality. In other words, the rate of interest is the equilibrating variable that equilibrates the savings and investment flows. The relation is shown in the bottom diagram of Figure 14-2. In this classical system the rate of interest performs simply an allocative function. It determines how much saving will be made out of the incomes generated in the production process, and it thereby allocates the economy's total output between consumption and saving. But, as we have seen from the first of the classical postulates, by thus allocating the economy's output between consumption and saving it automatically allocates it between consumption and investment. The theoretical system reflects perfectly Adam Smith's dictum that "what is annually saved is as regularly consumed as what is annually spent, and nearly in the same time too; but it is consumed by a different set of people . . . That portion which [a rich man] annually saves . . . for the sake of profit it is immediately employed as capital. . . ."[9]

There is thus a beautiful logic and harmony in the classical economic system. It is shot through with the assumption that automatic harmonies exist in the aggregate scheme of things. The aggregate economy is, happily, inherently stable. This, moreover, is the essential bequest that the classical scheme made to the neoclassical thought system that has enjoyed a vigorous life in later times.[10]

THE FOUNDATIONS OF POSTCLASSICAL THEORY

Keynes, we shall see, understood all of these macroeconomic relationships rather differently. To focus at this preliminary stage on only two central points, it can be noted, first, that for Keynes and for the postclassical

[9] Adam Smith, *The Wealth of Nations* (New York: Modern Library, 1937), p. 321.

[10] There had been some ambivalence and ambiguity in the classical economics, notwithstanding its substantial commitment to the theorem regarding the impossibility of general overproduction. While John Stuart Mill clearly embraced the theorem, he argued significantly in his *Essays on Some Unsettled Questions of Political Economy* (first edition, 1844; London School of Economics reprint, 1948, pp. 69–70): "If, however, we suppose that money is used, these propositions cease to be exactly true . . . The buying and selling being now separated, it may very well occur, that there may be, at some given time, a very general inclination to sell with as little delay as possible, accompanied with an equally general inclination to defer all purchases as long as possible. This is always the case, in those periods which are described as periods of general excess." Similarly, Alfred Marshall, the principal architect of the later neoclassical economics, embraced the classical savings-investment assumptions, and observes that "it is a familiar economic axiom that a man purchases labor and commodities with that portion of his income which he saves just as much as he does with that he is said to spend." See Marshall's *Pure Theory of Domestic Values* (London School of Economics reprint, 1949), p. 34, quoted in Wallace C. Peterson, *Income, Employment, and Economic Growth* 4th ed. (New York: Norton, 1978), p. 110. But Marshall also observes in his *Principles of Economics*, 8th ed. (London: Macmillan, 1920), p. 710: "But though men have the power to purchase they may not choose to use it."

theory the rate of interest is not the equilibrating variable that brings savings and investment into equality. That important function is performed by the level of income. Income is the equilibrating variable in the savings-investment flows. It is this conclusion that stands at the heart of the so-called Keynesian revolution. Releasing the rate of interest from its endogenous slot in the savings-investment sector, therefore, Keynes was confronted with the need to develop an alternative theory of interest. He argued that the interest rate should be looked upon as the equilibrating price of money, or the market-clearing price of money, in the market for money. The theory became known as the liquidity preference theory of interest.

Second, Keynes and postclassical theory do not conceive of the wage rate as being endogenously determined in the labor market as does the classical system in Figure 14-2. Workers, moreover, are understood to bargain, not for real wages as the classical system supposed, but for money wages. And the money wage rate is introduced into the economics of Keynes as an exogenous variable. The real wage rate, as we shall see, results from the relation between the exogenous money wage and the endogenously determined price level. The relations envisaged at this point open the way to the essential difference between the classical and the postclassical systems of macroeconomic thought.

The assumption of the exogeneity of the wage rate is accompanied by a different view of the demand for labor also. In Figure 14-1 the demand-for-labor curve is essentially a derived demand curve, stating that the demand for labor is derived from the marginal productivity of labor in relation to the selling price of output that the market demand makes possible. Postclassical theory sees things at this point from a very different perspective. For instead of arguing in the neoclassical manner from the labor supply (recall that the equilibrium amount of labor is determined in the labor market) to the level of output as in Figure 14-1, it argues from the level of output that the economy can produce and sell to the amount of labor that will be demanded to produce that output. The argument is summarized in Figure 14-3.

In Figure 14-3(a) we have shown what will later be described as the aggregate supply curve, $Z(N)$. This will be embedded in an expected proceeds function. It shows the total sales proceeds that producers must expect to receive from the output of a given number of workers in order to make their employment economically worthwhile. The aggregate demand curve, $D(N)$, shows the expenditure on output that would be made out of the incomes received at different levels of employment.[11] The in-

---

[11] This aggregate demand curve, following some ambiguity in Keynes' *General Theory*, has been subject to varying interpretations in the literature and will be discussed in depth in Chapters 18 and 19.

Figure   14-3.

Postclassical aggregate supply and demand and the demand for labor

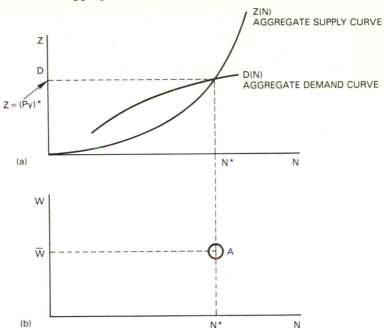

tersection of the aggregate supply and demand curves provides the level of so-called effective demand. It reveals the actual level of employment that can be sustained in the system under the conditions specified.

The operative level of employment is therefore determined only after aggregate demand and supply conditions have been taken into account. At each point of the aggregate supply curve, it will be shown, there is embedded an exogenous money wage rate and an implied commodity price level (as well as an implied distribution of income). Figure 14-3(b), therefore, specifies the amount of labor that will be utilized, or demanded by the producers in the economy, at the specified exogenous money wage rate. This is shown by point A in Figure 14-3(b) with reference to an assumed exogenous money wage rate $\overline{W}$. Point A accordingly lies on the economy's implicit demand curve for labor. But we shall see that the direction of causation is not from the real wage rate to the level of employment, as the neoclassical theory supposes, but from the level of employment, as determined by aggregate supply and demand conditions, to the real wage implicit in the money wage and price level consistent with that output and employment.

Anticipating our subsequent analysis, a higher money wage rate (given the level of productivity) would have associated with it a $Z(N)$

function lying to the left of that shown in Figure 14-3. In such a case, realizing also that the higher money wage rate will generate a higher price level, higher money incomes, and a higher demand function, $D(N)$, the aggregate supply and demand cross, such as that shown in Figure 14-3, will generate a different equilibrium employment level. Thus, in a very importantly indirect way, different money wage rates will have associated with them different employment levels, and an implicit labor demand curve can be traced.

THE ESSENTIAL PROPERTIES OF MONEY

In a money-using economy there is no guarantee that all the incomes earned in the course of producing the national product will be spent. Part will conceivably be saved. The classical doctrine of Say's Law has been irreparably punctured. Let us suppose for the present, therefore, as a means of exhibiting the significance of the flow of unspent incomes into money stocks, that savings are held in money form. We want to inquire, then, what it is about money that has such profound significance for the subsequent health of the system. We need to understand, also, what it is that makes money serviceable as money in this respect.

We take the last point first. An entity, in our case a form of credit money, will serve as money so long as two fundamental characteristics are present in it.[12] First, it must have what Keynes referred to as a minimal or zero elasticity of production. If, for example, when the demand for money increases, expenditures fall, and the price level declines or the value of money increases, it must not be possible to increase the supply of money by putting labor to work to produce it. In a commodity money economy such as we looked at in Chapter 4, the elasticity of production of gold would be related to the cost of mining it. In the case of credit money, its elasticity of production in that sense is zero, though, of course, its supply can be altered by actions of the banking system and the central bank.

Second, the money entity must have what has been called a minimal or zero elasticity of substitution. This means that when the demand for money increases, it should not generally be possible for that demand to spill over onto other commodities that are substitutable for money, for the purposes for which it is being demanded. If the demand did spill over to other substitutable commodities, then the supply of those commodities might be increased to meet the demand, and new quantities of labor might be employed as a result.

---

[12] Keynes, *General Theory*, Chap. 17. See also the very valuable and insightful discussion in Paul Davidson, *Money and the Real World*, 2nd ed. (New York: John Wiley, 1978), p. 145 and passim, on which our present argument is heavily dependent.

If, then, money has a low elasticity of production, the demand for it will not give rise to increased employment to provide it. Similarly, if it has a low elasticity of substitution for other commodities, an increased demand for labor will not arise to provide those substitutable commodities. The implications of this for our present problems of saving and hoarding of money can be seen immediately.

Income is allocated to either the demand for commodities or the demand for money. That part which is directed to the demand for commodities will continue to provide employment for those members of the work force engaged in producing the commodities demanded. But that part which is directed to the demand for money will not provide any such employment. An increase in the demand for money will therefore, by its very nature, cause a rupture of the circular flow of income-generating expenditure. Some part of the incomes received are not then being passed on to other producers in the system. To that extent the volume of market signals being transmitted to potential producers has diminished. It is not that the level of production and employment falls because of some defect in the signal transmission mechanism in the economy. It is rather that holding money instead of spending it implies that no market signals actually exist. The transmission mechanism is not necessarily faulty. The signals are just not there to be transmitted.

THE *SINE QUA NON* OF A MONETARY SYSTEM

Our analysis to this point has focused to a significant extent on the different visions of the labor market held by the classical (and neoclassical) and postclassical theories. As a first byproduct of this emphasis the postclassical theory refuses to solve the full-employment problem by defining it away. But a second reason for this emphasis now emerges. It relates to the degree of price flexibility that might be thought to exist in the system.

For the neoclassical system the market for labor is just like any other market in one important respect. Its equilibrium price is endogenously determined. The market-clearing price of labor serves the same analytical function as the market-clearing price of bananas. Indeed, the neoclassical theory claims that flexibility in all prices is desirable, in that it imparts a maximum flexibility to the solution of resource allocation problems in the economy as a whole. But consider more closely the question of flexibility in the money wage rate.

We shall show at some length in Chapter 16 that the price level of produced commodities is dependent on the relation between (1) the money wage rate and (2) the average product of labor. The details need not detain us at this stage. We can refer to the ratio of the money wage rate to the average product of labor as W/A. In order to provide a margin for profit and the payment of a return to the creditors who have supplied money capital to the firm, a producer will mark up this so-called efficiency wage by a multiple to determine his economically viable unit selling price of output. We may refer to the markup factor as k, and the selling price of output may then be represented as $P = kW/A$.

If, then, we envisage flexible money wage rates in the market for labor, we are forced to contemplate flexibility in the price level or the value of money. But it is a short step to realize that such instability in the value of money is precisely what we do not wish to contemplate if money is going to serve efficiently the functions we have already spelled out at some length. Money will continue to function as money, we have said, only so long as confidence in its acceptability is preserved. This requires that the value of money be constant in an ideal sense. Extreme instability in the value of money destroys the moneyness of it.

Let us turn the argument around. If money is to continue to serve as money, or if, in other words, a money economy is to remain viable in an optimal sense, then the value of money must be stable. The public must have reason to be confident that if they accept money in discharge of indebtedness, they will be able to pass it on again to someone else at the value at which they received it. But if the value of money is to be stable, then the money wage rate must also be stable. If the productivity phenomena in the economy are not subject to change in the short run, and if the efficiency wage markup factor is constant, the wage rate must also be stable in order for prices to be stable. The money wage rate, therefore, turns out to be the crucial variable in the system. It is the linchpin of the monetary economy.

But the notion of price flexibility has for a long time occupied an important place in economic analysis. It has been deeply connected with the dynamics of a market economy. It has played a significant part in the economics of optimum resource allocation. In all these respects market fluidity, price flexibility, and resource mobility are highly desirable in fact and in theory. But what is being suggested at this point is something different. It is being acknowledged that there is one particular market, the market for labor, in which the market-clearing price is not simply like any other price at all. The price of labor, because it enters into the determination of incomes and spending power in a way in which this does not occur anywhere else in the economy, has a very different function and significance. We may argue, therefore, that stability in the price of labor underlies, in ways we shall explore further, the stability of the monetary system itself.

This in no sense implies that controls should be imposed on the price of labor in order to guarantee its desired stability. That would completely violate the freedom of functioning of the market system that needs to be preserved. What the propositions before us argue for is simply that a sustainable relation should be preserved between the rate of increase of the money wage rate on the one hand and the rate of increase in the economy's ability to pay increased wages on the other. The latter depends on the rate of change in the average productivity per worker in the economy. If, as has been suggested, the money wage rate is an exogenous variable, then to preserve the monetary and market system a set of guidelines or bargaining constraints must be established in the determination of that wage rate by whatever exogenous forces are relevant to it. The intention would not be to circumvent or destroy the market system. The hope would be to preserve it.

EQUILIBRIUM AND UNCERTAINTY

The notion of price flexibility and market fluidity lies at the heart of the Walrasian theory of general equilibrium, which has had a heavy influence on macroeconomic theory in recent decades. The Walrasian view of a market economy conceives of supply and demand curves or functions in each of the markets in the system. In the goods markets, for example, the supply curve is generated by producer decisions based on the criteria of profit maximization. The demand curve emanates from comparable processes of consumers' utility maximization. Excess demand curves can be specified by subtracting quantities supplied from quantities demanded at each of a specified set of prices. When the entire market system is in mutually determined equilibrium, all excess demands will be equal to zero. All markets clear at the so-called solution vector of prices.

In the Walrasian scheme of things market-clearing prices are defined as equilibrium prices. In a deeper sense there are really no decision makers in the system. Rather, the analysis envisages endowments or supplies of goods and factors of production, and concentrates on specifying the relations that can be shown to exist between them when, as the theory specifies it, full general equilibrium conditions exist. Fictions exist in the theory about bids and offers for commodities and factors of production and the so-called tâtonnement process by which the equilibrium price vector is established. This process, which is a fictional conception without any real time dimension, imagines that an auctioneer continually shuffles bids and offers until a consistent set of market-clearing prices and quantities is defined.

In the rigorous theoretical specification of the Walrasian system, no transactions are allowed to occur until that full set of equilibrium prices has been decided upon. All trading takes place at equilibrium prices. There is no false trading, to use the term that would describe the settlement of transactions at other than equilibrium prices. The Walrasian process does not take place in real time. It is thoroughly timeless. It is static. It is concerned with equilibrium conditions, not with real-world processes that might lead to a conceived equilibrium. Notional prices may change. But they are not real or actual prices that change. They are notional bid-and-offer prices. For no transactions occur until the equilibrium price set is established. There is no actual or real-world trading process in the Walrasian scheme of things.

Difficulties arise, therefore, when attempts are made, as they have been seriously made in macroeconomic theory, to wed the Walrasian equilibrium scheme to the problem of optimum outcomes in the macroeconomy. For in the first place, macroeconomics is concerned with the problems that arise when the large number of separate plans of individual decision makers in the system do not mesh or equilibrate at all. We have seen an example of precisely that problem in this chapter. We have drawn attention to the fact that at the heart of the macroeconomic problem is the possibility that the spending plans of income earners might not mesh with the production plans of the suppliers of commodities. The market signals emanating from today's economy will not necessarily generate those long-term expectations in the minds of investors and producers that would guarantee coherence in the economy.

Second, the absence of real-world, or real-time, trading processes in the Walrasian scheme makes it impossible to argue whether, in a conceived disequilibrium situation, prices would adjust more rapidly than quantities to bring the markets back to equilibrium. For some time there was argument in the macroeconomic literature that a great deal of significance attached to the fact that price adjustment velocities might be less than quantity adjustment velocities. But the argument was rather pointless. For the heart of the conceptual system is not speaking about adjustment processes. It is speaking about the conditions that can be demonstrated to exist when full general equilibrium conditions are satisfied.[13]

In its macroeconomic expression the Walrasian theory has usually conceived of four markets, which, taken together, provide an overall view of the macroeconomy. These are the goods market, the money market, the bond market, and the labor market. Frequently, the labor market is dropped from the system by making the assumption that that market will always be in a position of equilibrium at full employment. In other terms, the nature of the supply and demand conditions in the market for labor are deemed to be such that we continually have full employment by definition, or market clearing at full employment with infinite ad-

---

[13] On the question of price and quantity adjustment velocities, see Axel Leijonhufvud, *On Keynesian Economics and the Economics of Keynes* (New York: Oxford University Press, 1968), p. 37 and passim, and the same author's retraction in his argument on this point in "Keynes' Employment Function," *History of Political Economy*, Summer 1974, p. 169.

justment velocity. We have looked at a neoclassical expression of precisely that condition or assumption earlier in this chapter.

Dropping the labor market in this way leaves the analysis with a three-market system. It follows, then, that when equilibrium or market-clearing conditions have been established in any two of these markets, in the sense that zero excess demand exists, equilibrium in the same sense must exist also in the remaining market. On these grounds one market can be eliminated from the three-market system. If, say, the bond market is dropped, the analysis can concentrate on equilibration in the remaining goods and money markets. This procedure has frequently been adopted. In this theoretical construction, however, the real problem of the macroeconomy, that of the effective level of employment, has been defined away.[14]

The real problems with equilibrium analysis in macroeconomics have to do with the absence of real processes in real time, the absence of any recognition of the uncertainty that abounds in the real world and influences the formation of expectations and decisions, and the absence of any logical place or role for money. For we have already seen that if everything happens at once, if all markets have been brought to their equilibrium postures before any transactions occur, if goods then effectively exchange for goods, then there is no real function for money to perform. All is certain in this scheme of things. All that is to be known is known. There is no future. Everything is reduced to the present. There is no ignorance. There is therefore no need for money.[15]

A good deal of discussion has ensued as to whether macroeconomics should properly be understood as equilibrium or as disequilibrium theorizing. Argument on this level has taken up the notion of market clearing, as distinct from what we have been calling equilibrium conditions. Frequently, however, these separate conceptions have been confused. Universal market clearing, for example, has frequently been claimed as a sufficient, though not a necessary, condition for equilibrium. This means that an overall market situation could be described as one of generalized equilibrium, even though one market, principally the labor market, does not clear. There may be a surplus supply of labor in the labor market, even though all markets are in equilibrium in the sense that no decision maker is under any motivation to change his behavior or plans for further action. This has led to the notion, frequently encountered in macroeco-

---

[14] The seminal work in the reconstruction of neoclassical macroeconomic theory can be found in D. Patinkin, *Money, Interest, and Prices,* 2nd ed. (New York: Harper & Row, 1965). See also Paul Davidson's analysis in "A Keynesian View of Patinkin's Theory of Employment," *Economic Journal,* September 1967.

[15] Joan Robinson, in an incisive review, has made a similar point in "What Has Become of the Keynesian Revolution?" in Joan Robinson, ed., *After Keynes* (Oxford: Blackwell, 1973), p. 6: "For a world that is always in equilibrium there is no difference between the future and the past, there is no history and there is no need for Keynes."

omic theory, of the possibility of an underemployment equilibrium in the system. From that point argument has ensued as to how theoretical systems should be specified in order to exhibit just that possibility of underemployment equilibrium, rather than the automatic full-employment equilibrium inherent in the neoclassical scheme of things.

Advantages would seem to exist, however, in defining terms and concepts somewhat differently. Market-clearing conditions and equilibrium conditions can usefully be kept distinct. With this in view, our analysis will incorporate a genuine recognition of the realities of time, uncertainty, expectations, and implied economic behavior. We shall wish to say, therefore, that even if markets clear today, those outcomes may generate longer-term expectations, in the context of the uncertainties and ignorance that exist, that point to very different market conditions in the future. Markets may clear at the same time as the economy is in process of movement to vastly different situations and postures. This is precisely why money has real significance and usefulness.

Of course, in all the kaleidic changes that continually occur in the macroeconomy, the ignorance and uncertainties that abound do not paralyze action and events. Rather, conventions and institutions exist to alleviate the burdens of uncertainty. In a fundamental sense money itself is one such institution. Money functions in one of its aspects as a refuge from uncertainty.[16] Other institutions come into existence to share uncertainties. One is the pervasiveness in the market economy of contracts.[17] Contracts for the provision of labor at an agreed price for some years into the future enable producers to have some degree of control over their production costs, and this imparts an element of stability to price levels. Contracts similarly exist for the provision of commodity outputs for some time into the future. Contracts exist for the provision of money capital funds, including the important example of commercial bank lines of credit that we encountered in our studies in commercial banking. Financial intermediary institutions come into existence as devices or vehicles for sharing uncertainties and providing liquidity, and

---

[16] Keynes made the point well in his "General Theory of Employment," pp. 215–16: "Why should anyone outside a lunatic asylum wish to use money as a store of wealth [as holding it does not yield an income]? Because . . . our desire to hold money is a barometer of the degree of distrust of our own calculations and conventions regarding the future . . . . The possession of actual money lulls our disquietude; and the premium which we require to make us part with money is the measure of our disquietude." See also T. W. Hutchison, *The Significance and Basic Postulates of Economic Theory* (New York: Kelley, 1960), p. 88.

[17] Paul Davidson has emphasized this important point in his *Money and the Real World*, passim.

these institutions change and develop as conditions in the economy make it necessary.

SUMMARY

This chapter has provided a minimal summary of some of the principal characteristics of the classical, neoclassical, and postclassical systems of macroeconomic thought. At this introductory stage no exhaustive or systematic exposition of the competing systems was intended. The classical way of looking at things was heavily dependent on Say's law and the implicit theorem regarding the impossibility of general overproduction. In post-classical theory this basic proposition is rejected, and the possibility that a general deficiency of demand for goods and services may develop is related to the fact that money may be demanded as a store of value and a refuge from uncertainty. The reasons why such a demand may lead to a deficient demand for commodities are related to what were termed the essential properties of money. The processes by which such variations in demand may lead to a less than perfect coherence in the macroeconomy have to do with the absence of market signals for transmission to potential producers.

The neoclassical theory emphasized the endogeneity of the real wage rate and thereby assumed the unemployment problem away by definition. Postclassical theory, on the other hand, focuses attention on the money wage rate and envisages this as an exogenous variable. The money wage rate, in turn, is directly relevant to the formation of commodity prices. It was seen that stability in the money wage rate (or the efficiency wage rate if the average level of productivity is changing) is necessary for the stability of the price level. This, in turn, is necessary for the continuing ability of money to discharge efficiently the functions of money. The money wage rate emerged as the linchpin of the monetary system.

The postclassical theory introduces the concepts of the economy's aggregate supply curve and aggregate demand curve. These are both related to the level of employment, and the conjunction between them determines the employment level at any time.

Introductory comments were made on the relation between Walrasian general equilibrium theory and macroeconomic analysis. Real-time processes, uncertainty, and the formation of expectations were brought into the picture. The development of the themes sketched in this chapter will begin immediately in the chapters that follow.

IMPORTANT CONCEPTS

Classical, neoclassical, and postclassi-
cal systems of macroeconomic analy-
sis
Market signals
Coherence
Long-term expectations
Turgot-Smith doctrine of saving
Say's law
Essential properties of money
Wage-cost markup factor

Aggregate supply curve, Z(N)
Aggregate demand curve, D(N)
Expected proceeds function
Effective demand
Elasticity of production
Elasticity of substitution
Sine qua non *of a monetary system*
Efficiency wage
Market-clearing conditions

QUESTIONS FOR DISCUSSION AND REVIEW

1. Examine and evaluate the assumptions of the classical macroeconomics that guaranteed the "coherence" of the aggregate market system.

2. What postclassical dimensions of the demand for money raise problems associated with a lack of "coherence" in the aggregate economy?

3. Following the references quoted in footnote 10 of this chapter, how did the classical and neoclassical economists encounter difficulties in their analysis when the realities of time were taken into account?

4. "The problem with the classical macroeconomic system is not in the cogency of its arguments but in the realism of its premises." Discuss critically.

5. What differences are introduced into macroanalytical systems if the wage rate is understood to be exogenous rather than endogenous? Explain fully.

6. Evaluate the proposition that for the classical economists money functioned only as a medium of exchange.

7. On the basis of previous studies in macroeconomics, can you explain how a revolution in the theory of interest was effected by incorporating the interest rate as a determinant variable in the demand for money?

8. Examine the logical validity and the empirical relevance of assuming either (1) that causation runs from the wage rate to the level of employment or (2) that the reverse causation is operative.

9. "The essential properties of money, in real-world conditions of uncertainty, while they guarantee the satisfactory performance of its functions in general, also give rise to potential dislocation and disequilibrium." Discuss critically.

10. Evaluate the proposition that the weakness of general equilibrium theory is that while it focuses on the conditions that exist when full general equilibrium conditions are satisfied, it has no theory of actual trading behavior.

15

THE DEMAND FOR MONEY AND THE PRICE OF MONEY

STUDY OBJECTIVES:

• To observe the essence of the quantity theory of money approach to the demand for money
• To distinguish the reasons for the demand for money:
   1. Transactions demand, M_t^d
   2. Asset demand, M_a^d
   3. Finance demand, M_f^d
   Total demand for money, $M^d = M_t^d + M_a^d + M_f^d$
• To understand the principal determinants of the demand for money: real output, the price level, and the rate of interest:

$$M^d = M^d(y, P, r)$$

• To note the relevance of price, income, and expenditure expectations
• To understand the theory of the market rate of interest

Money functions as a medium of exchange and as a store of value. It is a store of value in more than one sense. Money may be held with the intention of using it in the normal process of consummating commodity transactions. It will then in due course function as a medium of exchange. But between the exchanges in which it participates, the money is held as a temporary store of purchasing power. The medium-of-exchange function and the store-of-value function are necessarily interrelated.

Money is a store of value in the sense also that it is one among a number of assets in which liquidity may be held. In this sense the decision to hold money is the outcome of an individual's wealth portfolio decision.

Individuals will need to decide from time to time what proportion of their total wealth they should hold in liquid asset form, and what proportion of that liquidity they should hold in the form of money. Ideally, a wealth portfolio will be distributed over various assets in such a way that the marginal net benefit from each asset form is equal. Some monetary economists, in fact, have elevated this notion of portfolio optimization to a place of primary importance. They have expanded the concept of the temporary abode of purchasing power to include in this category not only money in the narrow sense in which we are considering it at this stage but also various forms of near-money, corporate securities, and even certain kinds of durable goods. The notion is held that all of these asset forms may be, in one way or another, money substitutes in the sense that they compete for the individual's portfolio dollar.

The difficulty with this way of looking at things, however, is that there may be a serious break in the chain of liquidity between money proper at one end and real assets at the other. Money and money substitutes may be considered competing forms of liquidity, provided there is reason to believe that all such asset forms may be turned into money at any time without a significant possibility of loss of value. But this requirement does not necessarily hold in the case of corporate equity securities and real capital assets. In the case of the latter, for example, they could not be said to enjoy significant liquidity unless there existed a ready spot market in which they could be sold at any time. But ready and viable spot markets for secondhand physical assets do not generally exist.[1]

It is well to focus, therefore, on the significant relations between money proper and the various forms of what we have called near-money, understanding that they each possess high degrees of liquidity. The development of new forms of depository institutions, in which money funds can be held in interest-bearing accounts, has complicated the decisions regarding the form in which liquidity should be held. New forms of nonmonetary financial institutions have also emerged, offering their own indirect securities to the public in exchange for money. Those indirect securities, or the evidences of debt in the form of the claims these institutions issue against themselves, also serve as highly liquid substitutes for money. The money-holding decision, therefore, is the outcome of a complex process of weighing considerations of rates of return, transactions

---

[1] Paul Davidson has examined these aspects of liquidity extensively, and in emphasizing the importance of viable spot markets for portfolio assets he has thrown serious doubt on the cogency of the portfolio theory's reliance on assumptions of substitutability between assets. See his *Money and the Real World,* 2nd ed. (New York: John Wiley, 1978); and his "Keynesian View of Friedman's Theoretical Framework for Monetary Analysis" in Robert J. Gordon, ed., *Milton Friedman's Monetary Framework: A Debate with His Critics* (Chicago: University of Chicago Press, 1974).

and possibly storage costs, risks, and liquidity. These apply to each of the assets considered as candidates for a place in the wealth or asset portfolio.

MOTIVES FOR DEMANDING MONEY

Progress is best made in the theory of the demand for money by considering the motives for demanding money, or the reasons or use for which it is required. These may be summarized as (1) the transactions motive, (2) the asset motive, and (3) the finance motive.

   An individual or a corporation will not, of course, consciously decide to set aside so much money to satisfy the transactions motive, so much for the asset motive, and a certain amount to satisfy the finance motive. Rather, the amount of money held at any time will be simply a homogeneous, undifferentiated sum. What we are concerned with here is the set of logical reasons why money is demanded, and the set of explanations that, taken together, explain why an individual's demand for money at any given time is what it is.

THE TRANSACTIONS DEMAND FOR MONEY

The transactions demand for money is closely related to the fact that money functions as the medium of exchange. It is reasonable to expect that people in general will hold an amount of money for this purpose that is proportional to the value of the transactions they plan to make during a specified period of time. We might consider an individual's total monthly income or expenditure and relate to this the average amount of money that individual holds during the month. Or we could observe the total level of national income during a year and could relate to this the amount of money in circulation, understanding that during the year all the money is being held by some person or other in the economic system. Under headings such as these a number of so-called quantity theories of money have been developed. We begin our examination of the transactions demand for money by looking briefly at the more usual forms of these theories.

THE QUANTITY THEORY OF MONEY

Employing notation with which we are already familiar, we can refer to the total level of national income or expenditure, measured in current dollar values, as Y, and to the average price level of the goods and services included in that national income as P. A measure of real national income is then given as $y = Y/P$.

Alternatively, this is expressed in the now familiar way as $Y = Py$. We can also conceive of the total level of monetary expenditure on goods and services by taking the value of the total stock of money in existence during the year (or an average value of the money stock if it has been fluctuating during the year) and multiplying this by an estimate of its velocity of circulation. This then provides a measure of actual monetary expenditure.

Thus we have two different ways of looking at the total national income or expenditure, measured in current or nominal dollar magnitudes. It is described as

$$(1) \qquad\qquad Y = Py = MV$$

This is an expression of what became known, together with certain appropriate behavioral assumptions, as the transactions approach to the quantity theory of money. It was associated principally with the famous American economist Irving Fisher.[2]

It might appear that it would be a simple matter to extract from this definitional identity a theory of the price level. For by transposition of Equation (1) it may appear that

$$(2) \qquad\qquad P = MV/y$$

Arguments in this direction have frequently been made. But we are not yet ready to take such a step. For in the first place, Equation (1) is at this stage simply a definitional identity. It is not possible to extract a theory from such a definition until certain behavioral assumptions about what determines the values of the variables involved have been introduced. We shall illustrate such possible steps in the next chapter, where the value of money is discussed at length. For the present we are interested in the nature and the possible determinations of the velocity variable, V, as this, it will appear, is directly related to the determinants of the demand for money.

Understanding the velocity variable, V, as a measure of the rate of turnover of money, we could imagine that its magnitude will principally be determined by the structure of payments habits in the economy. Or we can say that it will be determined by the structure of the institutional network through which payments in general are effected, and by the degree of integration of industrial firms (thereby determining the extent to which firms need to pay money for their purchases of material inputs

[2] Irving Fisher, *The Purchasing Power of Money* (New York: Macmillan, 1911).

or, alternatively, provide their own inputs and value them simply by bookkeeping entries without the actual payment of money). The rate of turnover of money will also be affected by the frequency with which wages and salaries are paid or the frequency with which outstanding accounts and liabilities are settled by money payments.

This last-mentioned point conveniently focuses our attention on a totally different way of constructing the quantity theory of money itself. We have envisaged so far the fact that the total level of money payments, Py, divided by the total money stock, M, provides a measure of the rate of turnover of the money supply. Suppose, however, we invert the idea. Instead of asking how many times during a year the average stock of money turns over, let us ask what, on the average, is the proportion of the total money payments that is actually held in money at any time. The answer to this question provides a measure that is the inverse of the velocity of circulation. We shall refer to this factor of proportionality by the symbol k. The total demand for money, and therefore the existing money stock when, as we shall see in the next chapter, P and y are adjusted to it, will be describable as a certain proportion of the total annual money payments. We refer to this relation as

$$(3) \qquad\qquad\qquad M = kPy$$

This way of looking at things also has a distinguished history and has been known as the Cambridge cash balance approach to the quantity theory of money. It has been associated mainly with a tradition emanating from Cambridge University (England) and has been taken up again in recent times by the monetarist economists in the United States under the leadership of Milton Friedman.[3]

The transactions approach to the quantity theory is concerned with "money on the wing," as Dennis Robertson used to refer to it. The cash balance approach, to use again Robertson's expressive phrase, is concerned with "money sitting."[4] What this difference implies is highly important for the theory of money. For the "money sitting" approach potentially provides us with a theory or an explanation of the demand for money. It is asking what, on the average during any period of time, will be the amount of money demanded. It is this aspect of the approach that has been emphasized by the latter-day monetarists, who have seen in the so-called new quantity theory of money an explanation of the demand for money.

[3] See Alfred Marshall, *Money, Credit and Commerce* (London: Macmillan, 1923); A. C. Pigou, "The Value of Money," *Quarterly Journal of Economics,* November 1917; John Maynard Keynes, *A Tract on Monetary Reform* (London: Nisbet, 1922); Milton Friedman, "The Quantity Theory of Money: A Restatement," in Milton Friedman, ed., *Studies in the Quantity Theory of Money* (Chicago: University of Chicago Press, 1956).
[4] D. H. Robertson, *Money* (London: Nisbet, 1948), p. 37.

Whatever it is that determines V, then, will also determine k. Let us return to our proposition regarding the frequency of money payments in the transactions sphere in the economy. We take as an example the periodic payment of wages and salaries. Let it be supposed that an individual worker is paid wages at a rate of $250 per week and that payment is made weekly. If he were to spend that income completely, at an even rate, during the week, his average cash balance on hand during the week would be $125. He would have $250 on hand at the beginning of the week, immediately after the receipt of his wage payment, and zero dollars on hand at the end of the week. His average cash balance is therefore half of his weekly wage receipt.

Suppose now that without any change in the rate of wage payment to which the worker is entitled, his employer decided to make payments monthly, or at four-week intervals. The wage paid at each such payment date would then be $1,000. If we assume again that the worker spends his income at an even rate during the wage interval, his average cash balance, following the same calculation as before, would now be $500. We can imagine this kind of change in payments arrangements to be adopted on an economywide basis.

This implies that the average cash balance held by income recipients will be four times as large after the change as it was before. We can say that the change in payments habits has caused the value of k, or the demand-for-money proportionality factor, to become four times as large as before. Alternatively, the velocity of circulation has been reduced to one-quarter of the magnitude it had before.

Again, we leave aside until the next chapter the manner in which economists have extracted a theory of the price level from this alternative expression of the quantity theory of money. For the present we concentrate on the demand for money. Figure 15-1 depicts the relation we have summarized from the cash balance approach to the quantity theory of money in Equation (3).

Expressing this relation as a demand-for-money function, it can be written as

(4) $$M^d = kPy$$

Consider now the slope of the demand curve shown in Figure 15-1. If the relation is strictly linear, as shown in the heavy line in the figure, this implies that as the level of national income increases, the demand for money increases in a constant proportion. If, however, the relation were as depicted by the nonlinear broken curve in Figure 15-1, this would imply that as the level of income and expenditure increased, the demand for money would not increase proportionally. This would imply, in turn, that as income and expenditure increased, the velocity of circulation of

Figure   15-1.

The quantity theory demand-for-money function

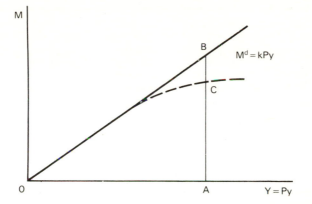

money would also increase. Under the linearity assumption, an income level of OA, for example, would call for a demand for money of AB. But if, as the income level rose, the velocity of circulation also increased, the income level of OA would be able to be supported by a demand for money of only AC. Individuals and business firms would then be managing their cash balances more efficiently. They would be economizing on the holding of idle cash. There might be a good reason why this could happen. As the level of national income rises, there may be a tendency for the rate of interest to rise also. In that case the opportunity cost of holding idle money balances will rise. This, in turn, may induce greater efficiency of cash management, thereby inducing an increase in the velocity of cir- culation. This improved efficiency of cash management and the increase in the velocity of circulation may be one of the ways by which the in- dustrial payments sphere overcomes what would otherwise be the costs and burden of rising interest rates. We shall return to the point.

An indication of the empirical behavior of the velocity of circulation in the United States economy in recent years is provided by Table 15-1.

The third and fourth data columns of Table 15-1 describe what we have referred to respectively as the velocity of circulation, V, of the M1 money supply and the demand-for-money proportionality factor, k. During the two decades there has been almost a doubling of the velocity measure, and a corresponding decline in its reciprocal. This points to difficulties in interpreting the analytical significance of the quantity theory of money, or using it for purposes of guiding monetary policy. First, the amount of money demanded by the economy at any time in relation to its income and expenditure cannot be determined or judged independently of the structure of the financial institutions by which the money flows are ac- tivated. An important reason for the strong upward trend in the velocity

Table   15-1

The income velocity of circulation of money, and the ratio of the money
supply to Gross National Product for selected periods.

Year	GNP	M1 (Money supply as shown in Table 4-1)	Income velocity (GNP/M1)	Ratio of money supply to GNP	Alternative measure of velocity (GNP/M2)
1960	506.5	141.9	3.56	.281	1.62
1965	691.1	169.5	4.08	.245	1.50
1970	992.7	216.5	4.59	.218	1.58
1975	1,549.2	291.0	5.32	.188	1.51
1980	2,633.1	414.5	6.35	.157	1.59
1981	2,937.7	440.9	6.66	.150	1.61
1982	3,057.5	478.5	6.39	.157	1.53

Source: *Economic Report of the President,* February 1983, pp. 163, 233; and Table 4-1.

GNP and money supply values are in $billions. Data refer to (1) average daily values of
the money supply for the final month of the year indicated and (2) annual GNP in current
dollars.

of circulation is the emergence in recent years of new forms of money
substitutes, new ways of making payments for transactions such as the
use of credit cards, and an increase in the relative level of consumer
credit. These developments have made it less desirable or necessary to
hold as much money as previously in relation to actual transactions volumes.

Most important, however, has been the emergence of new forms of
financial institutions and new ways in which the public has been able to
hold liquidity. A larger proportion of liquidity is now being held in interest-bearing accounts in depository institutions. This implies that the
transaction accounts we have used in our money supply data of M1 have
not increased as rapidly as the alternative and broader definition of the
money supply we previously described as M2. Thus the rate of turnover
of the narrower money supply, or its velocity of circulation, has increased
sharply, while the M2 velocity has been lower and more stable. This is
shown in the final column of Table 15-1. Considerable care must therefore
be exercised in the monetary policy use of such velocity-of-circulation
measures, as it is entirely possible that still further and dramatic changes
in institutional arrangements lie ahead.

Second, it follows that the demand for money cannot always and
confidently be interpreted as a cause of the changes that occur in the
total level of monetary expenditures. Nor can a change in the amount of
money in existence always be understood to have direct and proportional
effects on such expenditures. For the money requirements of the economy

now appear as an effect of developments on other levels, such as the structure of payments habits and financial institutions, and, as we shall see in the next chapter, changes in other markets, such as the labor market, in the system. Money is not always and simply a cause. It is frequently an effect.[5]

FURTHER DIFFICULTIES IN THE QUANTITY THEORY APPROACH TO THE DEMAND FOR MONEY

The quantity theory of money, despite its distinguished history and reluctant demise, is defective on two other grounds. First, the demand for money we have envisaged so far has been dependent only on the level of income and money expenditures. In the development of the cash balance approach, for example, no reference was made to the possible influence on the demand for money of the rate of interest. Pigou, the Cambridge economist who earlier in this century did much to popularize this way of looking at things, did speak of the rate of interest and the level of wealth as being possibly relevant to money demand. But in his formal presentation of the theory the relevance of the interest rate factor was ignored and suppressed, in order to bring the exposition into line with the transactions approach being developed simultaneously by Irving Fisher in the United States.

Second, the income and expenditure level contemplated in the quantity theory analysis is the currently generated income in the economy. But it would be entirely reasonable to suppose that people demanded money not only in relation to their current levels of expenditure but also in relation to the levels of expenditure they planned or expected to make in the future.

AN ALTERNATIVE VIEW OF THE DEMAND FOR MONEY

As a means of taking account of both the expectations effect and the interest rate effect, let us revert to the more-detailed analysis of the motives for demanding money.[6] We shall refer to the transactions demand as M_t^d and relate this magnitude to the expenditure and interest rate variables. Consider first the income or expenditure level.

---

[5] See Paul Davidson and Sidney Weintraub, "Money as Cause and Effect," *Economic Journal*, December 1973.

[6] The following argument is indebted to Davidson, *Money and the Real World*, Chap. 7.

If the transactions demand for money depended only on the currently generated level of income, we could write the simple demand function as

(5) $$M_t^d = M_t^d(Y),$$

and it could be represented adequately by the curves contained in Figure 15-1. The only difference would be the change in the money variable from M^d (total demand for money) to M_t^d (transactions demand). We could still conceive the relation to be linear, under the assumption of a constant velocity of circulation, or nonlinear, under the assumption of a variable velocity. In this case the velocity measure would, of course, be describing Y/M_t^d.

But the scheme of things changes significantly if we envisage a demand for money based on the formation of expectations and the anticipation of money payments. Let us divide total monetary expenditure for this purpose into (1) consumption expenditures and (2) investment expenditures. Of course other expenditures take place in a fully developed economy, government outlays for example, but the point now in view can be made concisely by imagining a purely private sector economy.

We can suppose, as we shall see at length in Chapter 18, that the level of consumption expenditure is related principally to the level of income in the economy. A simple description of the relationship might appear as in Figure 15-2. The so-called consumption function in Figure 15-2 is described by the equation

(6) $$C = a_1 + b_1 Y$$

In this equation, and in the figure depicting it, it is supposed that even

Figure   15-2.

Consumption expenditure function

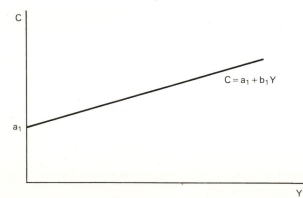

if income were zero there would still be a positive level of consumption expenditure represented by the magnitude a_1. Consumption expenditure out of zero income need not be regarded as the conundrum it might seem. For at low-income levels consumption expenditure will be supported by dissaving, or the using up of previously accumulated wealth, and by the receipt of income support payments such as unemployment benefits. The slope of the consumption function in Figure 15-2 is described by b_1. This measures the rate at which consumption expenditure will increase as income increases. It has acquired an important name in macroeconomic analysis and will be referred to later as the marginal propensity to consume.

The determinants of investment expenditure were discussed in Chapter 6, and the possible form of the investment expenditure function was described in Figure 6-1. We can assume, for purposes of exhibiting the relations we are now considering, that investment expenditures are a linear function of the rate of interest. The relationship may be described as

$$(7) \qquad I = a_2 - b_2 r$$

Equation (7) implies that investment expenditure can be expected to be lower at higher rates of interest.

Let us now conceive of the consumption expenditure level described in Equation (6) and the investment expenditure described in Equation (7) as the expenditures the public expects to make during the period immediately ahead. Then the demand for money for transactions purposes can be assumed to depend on those planned expenditures. For, conceivably, individuals will want to make sure they have access to sufficient money funds to enable them to meet the payments obligations that are expected to fall due during the period ahead. We might say, then, that the transactions demand for money could be described by the following relation:

$$(8) \qquad M_t^d = \alpha C + \beta I$$

Equations (6) and (7) describing the C and I variables can then be substituted into Equation (8) to provide another view of the transactions demand for money:

$$(9) \qquad M_t^d = \alpha(a_1 + b_1 Y) + \beta(a_2 - b_2 r)$$

or

$$(10) \qquad M_t^d = \alpha a_1 + \beta a_2 + \alpha b_1 Y - \beta b_2 r$$

If we were now to envisage the transactions demand for money in the same kind of money-income plane as depicted in Figure 15-1, Equation (10) could be described as shown in Figure 15-3. Here, as attention is being focused on the significance of the income variable for the demand for money, it is assumed that the rate of interest is given. In that case the final term on the right-hand side of Equation (10) will be constant. We now write the transactions demand for money function as

(11) $M_t^d = M_t^d(Y; \bar{r})$

indicating that we are considering the demand at different possible levels of income, on the assumption that the interest rate is given.

The major difference between Figure 15-1 and Figure 15-3 is that now the transactions demand for money function does not emanate from the origin as in the pure quantity theory argument. In other words, the demand for money does not now depend simply on what we referred to previously as the structure of payments habits. It depends also on expenditure plans and expectations. For the magnitude of the intercept term in Figure 15-3 is dependent on the α, β, a_1, and a_2 parameters contained in Equation (10).

This means that a shift in consumption or investment expenditure plans or expectations in the economy, such as a movement upward in either of these functions reflected in an increase in the a_1 or a_2 parameters in Equations (6) and (7), will imply a movement upward of the transactions demand-for-money function. Interesting developments can thus occur in the monetary sector as activity and expenditure levels change. An improvement in the marginal efficiency of investment, for example, in-

Figure   15-3.

Transactions demand for money

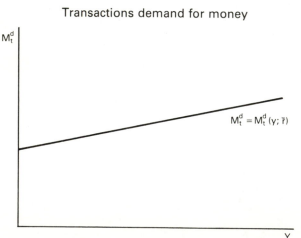

duced by changes in prospects in product markets or a change in technology, would now have a twofold effect on monetary conditions. First, the increase in investment expenditure would cause the demand-for-money function shown in Figure 15-3 to rise also. Second, the increase in income caused by the higher investment expenditure would cause the economy to move up along its new higher money demand function. The implications of both these reasons for increases in the demand for money are that unless there are offsetting increases in the supply of money as the economy expands, there will be added pressure on the rate of interest to rise. For the rate of interest, as we have said, is simply the price of money.

THE INTEREST RATE EFFECT ON THE TRANSACTIONS DEMAND FOR MONEY

Figure 15-3 depicted the demand for money on the assumption that the interest rate was given. We could envisage, in the money-income plane shown there, a family of such demand-for-money curves, each of which would relate to a different assumed rate of interest. Let us now focus on the influence of the rate of interest itself. We can visualize a demand-for-money function that depends on the rate of interest, under the assumption that the level of income is given. We could then speak of a demand-for-money curve in a money-interest rate plane. The corresponding functional relationship would be described by

(12) $$M_t^d = M_t^d(r; \overline{Y})$$

The difference between this equation and Equation (11) is that now the interest rate is the determinant variable, and it is the level of income that is taken as given. The relationship is depicted in Figure 15-4.

If it were assumed that the rate of interest had no effect at all on the demand for money for transactions purposes, the demand curve in the money-interest rate plane would be vertical. Its location would be determined simply by the level of income. The interest elasticity of the demand for money would be zero. We have seen earlier in this chapter, however, that there may be good reasons why, when the rate of interest and therefore the opportunity cost of holding idle money rises, individuals and business firms may manage their cash balances more efficiently or economize on their money holdings. We traced this effect through at that stage to a possible increase in the velocity of circulation of money. If, then, a rise in the interest rate has this kind of effect, the demand curve shown in Figure 15-4 will turn toward the money axis at high interest rates. This means that at interest rate r_1, for example, the amount of

Figure   15-4.

Transactions demand for money

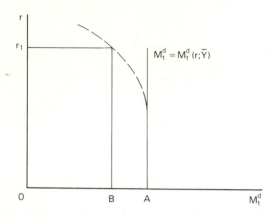

money demanded would no longer be OA, as it would be if no such interest rate effect existed, but OB instead.

Bringing these considerations together, we can conclude that the transactions demand for money is likely to be dependent on the level of income and expenditure, modified in the way we have seen by expectations of expenditures, and the rate of interest.[7] Realizing that the income level can be written as $Y = Py$, and realizing also that expectations of the price variable may be important in the sense that expectations of expenditures were seen to be significant, we can write our transactions demand-for-money function as

(13) $M_t^d = M_t^d(y, P, r, P^e, y^e)$

The variables superscripted by e now refer to expectations of the price level and the real output or income level, respectively.

THE FINANCE DEMAND FOR MONEY

At the beginning of this chapter we referred to what we termed a finance demand for money,[8] described as M_f^d. This is closely related to the transactions demand when that is interpreted in the expectational sense we

---

[7] The dependence of the transactions demand for money on the rate of interest is treated from another perspective in W. Baumol's important paper, "The Transactions Demand for Cash: An Inventory Theoretic Approach," *Quarterly Journal of Economics,* November 1952; and in James Tobin, "The Interest-Elasticity of the Transactions Demand for Cash," *Review of Economics and Statistics,* September 1956.

[8] See Paul Davidson, "Keynes' Finance Motive," *Oxford Economic Papers,* 1965; and "The Importance of the Demand for Finance," *Oxford Economic Papers,* 1966.

have just considered. It is also related to the fact that in real-world business firms production takes time, and money funds are required in order to make payments to factors of production before the firm's output can be produced and sold. A contemplated increase in output, then, can give rise to an immediate increase in the demand for money. Anticipations of capital expenditures also exert an impact on the demand for money in unique ways.

Imagine a contemplated increase in investment expenditure, such as a $10 million investment project to increase production capacity in some respect. The actual expenditure of this $10 million will not all take place at once. In fact, the capital expenditure may occur gradually in the form of so-called progress payments as the fixed asset facilities are in course of construction. Such progress payments, moreover, may be financed by the temporary acquisition of bank loans, and an increased demand for money may therefore occur as the business firm gets into a position to make the progress payments as they fall due. At a subsequent time, when the investment project has been completed or at a later stage of its construction, the firm may issue $10 million of long-term debt or equity securities in the money capital market and use the proceeds to repay the short-term bank loans it has accumulated. This operation is referred to in the money capital market as refinancing. But in the meantime the demand for bank loans, by increasing the demand for money, will have contributed to an upward pressure on the rate of interest in the way we have noted previously.

Another example of the same kind of upward pressure on the demand for money when investment increases is found in the larger need for working capital that accompanies fixed capital investment. For if a firm is building larger production facilities, it will also have to acquire larger inventories of materials in order to keep the larger plant operative and in income-generating condition.

If, however, the level of investment expenditures depend on the rate of interest, and if the demand for money depends on investment expenditures in this way, then the demand for money is again, indirectly, dependent on the rate of interest. We can therefore write

$$(14) \qquad M_f^d = M_f^d(r), \quad \text{or} \quad M_f^d = M_f^d[I(r)]$$

THE ASSET DEMAND FOR MONEY

The asset demand for money, it was suggested earlier, is related to an individual's wealth portfolio optimization decision. We now want to know how changes in the rates of return available on nonmonetary assets, in particular liquid assets, will affect the proportion of asset portfolios that people desire to hold in the form of money. We have seen that those alternative rates of return are reflected in security prices and are dependent on the going market rate of interest. We may therefore posit an asset demand-for-money function in the form

(15) $$M_a^d = M_a^d(r)$$

and depict it as in Figure 15-5.

We have drawn the asset demand-for-money function negatively inclined in the money-interest rate plane. This implies that individuals will hold a larger proportion of their liquid portfolio in the form of money when interest rates are low. Two reasons might account for this. They relate to the opportunity cost of holding idle money balances on the one hand, and to the possibility of speculative capital gains on the other.

The question of opportunity cost has already entered our discussion in other contexts. We recall that when the rate of interest is low, the opportunity cost of holding money is low. For what we mean by opportunity cost is the rate of return that could be earned by placing wealth in nonmonetary income-earning assets, rather than keeping it idle in money. Much more important for our present argument is the question of capital gains or losses on alternative income-earning assets.

We recall from Chapters 5 and 6 that when the rate of interest is high, the market prices of securities are low. Let us now focus on a government bond as the asset in which wealth may be held as an alternative to money. If, then, the going market rate of interest were at the relatively high level of r_1 in Figure 15-5, a reduction in that market rate for any reason would imply a rise in the price of bonds. Any individuals who held bonds at the interest rate level r_1 would therefore enjoy an increase in their total portfolio wealth when the interest rate fell. This increase in wealth is referred to as a capital gain. On the other hand, if

Figure   15-5.

Asset demand for money

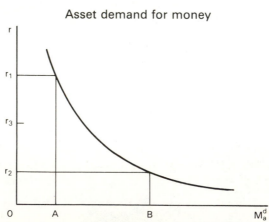

interest rates were low, at r_2 in Figure 15-5, an increase in the rate from that level would cause a portfolio capital loss.

We can make use of these basic relationships in the context of an individual's expectations of changes in interest rates from the levels that exist at different times. In the light of those expectations the individual may speculate in asset prices and in the holding of money. When the rate of interest is as high as r_1 in Figure 15-5, a fairly large number of individuals are likely to expect that the rate will decline rather than rise still further. Those individuals, therefore, might well back their judgment by deciding to acquire and hold bonds, in the expectation, as we have seen, that when the hoped-for decline in the rate of interest occurs they will realize a capital gain on their bond holdings. They will therefore devote a relatively large share of their liquid asset portfolio to bonds and a relatively small proportion to money.

Similarly, at a lower rate of interest such as r_3, a rather smaller number of individuals would expect the rate to continue to fall. Not so many people, therefore, would be inclined to hold a large proportion of their asset portfolio in the form of bonds. For at that interest rate, not so many would expect to realize a capital gain from holding bonds. The lower the interest rate fell, moreover, the smaller might become the number of people who expected it to decline still further. The larger would become the number of people who had begun to expect that at any level of interest rates the next move in the rate could well be upward rather than downward. If, of course, the rate of interest were, at a given level, to rise again rather than fall further, then the holders of bonds would experience a capital loss rather than a capital gain. At lower interest rates, therefore, a relatively larger number of people would be inclined to hold the largest proportion of their portfolios in the form of money. By holding money when interest rates are low and are expected to rise, the money can be used, when the expected rise in the interest rate occurs, to acquire bonds at a cheaper price than would have been possible when interest rates were low.

Managers of liquid portfolios, therefore, might well speculate on possible interest rate movements and determine the extent of their bond holdings and their holdings of idle money balances accordingly. Bringing these possible liquid asset market forces together, we can explain the proposition in Equation (15) that the asset demand for money is uniquely dependent on the rate of interest.[9]

[9] The question confronted in the text is that of explaining the downward slope of the demand-for-money function. We shall see below that the question of the stability of the function is as important as that of its form or slope. Concentrating on the negative inclination of the curve describing the function, however, much interest has been shown in the literature in the use of probability analysis in a portfolio-theoretic approach to explaining it. The seminal work in this direction appeared in James Tobin, "Liquidity Preference as Behavior towards Risk," *Review of Economic Studies*, February 1958. See also, for a critique of portfolio theoretic analysis, Douglas Vickers, *Financial Markers in the Capitalist Process* (Philadelphia: University of Pennsylvania Press, 1978).

THE DEMAND FOR MONEY

We are now in a position to combine the several reasons why money is demanded and to construct a total demand-for-money function from the separate transactions, finance, and asset demands we have considered. A composite demand-for-money function, M^d, may be written in the following form:

(16) $M^d = M_t^d(y,P,r,P^e,y^e) + M_f^d(r) + M_a^d(r)$

This total demand function may be depicted in a money-interest rate plane as shown in Figure 15-6.

For clarity of presentation we have illustrated in Figure 15-6 the sum of the transactions demand for money and the asset demand for money. We have for the present suppressed the finance demand for money, with the objective of not cluttering the figure unnecessarily. If the finance demand were also included we could visualize a negatively inclined curve, reflecting the likelihood that at lower rates of interest a larger investment demand would occur, and therefore a larger finance demand for money would result. Incorporating these possibilities into the diagram would mean that the total demand for money, labeled M^d in the figure, would be that much farther to the right.

The total demand for money in Figure 15-6 will be the lateral summation of the separate transactions and asset demands. But as we are considering here only the money-interest rate plane, the curves in the figure are drawn on the assumption that the level of income is given. As we saw previously, a family of curves would exist in the plane we are

Figure   15-6.

The demand for money

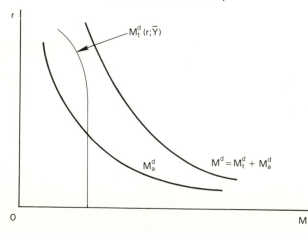

working with, one for each different possible level of income. Moreover, as a reference to Equation (16) will confirm, the single relationship we are able to capture in Figure 15-6 also assumes that the level of prices, as well as price and income expectations, is also given.

In many parts of monetary and macroeconomic analysis a relation is understood to exist between the demand for real money balances (that is, the demand for nominal money that we are showing here, divided by an index of the price level, or M^d/P) and the rate of interest. If, in Figure 15-6, the price level is assumed to be given, then movements along the horizontal axis reflect changes in the amount of real money demanded, as well as changes in the demand for nominal money.

THE MARKET FOR MONEY AND THE RATE OF INTEREST

Now that we have a view of the total demand for money, we can bring this into relation with the supply of money and consider the determination of the market-clearing price of money or the rate of interest. Consider the money supply and demand curves in Figure 15-7. Here we have inscribed a supply-of-money curve that indicates that the money supply is likely to increase at higher rates of interest. The banks might well be expected to expand their loans and create more money as the demand for loans, and therefore the interest rate, rises. We can now marry our total demand for money to such a supply curve, as shown in Figure 15-7.

In the money-interest rate plane we can expect to find a family of total money demand curves. The higher the assumed level of income, the

Figure   15-7.

The market for money

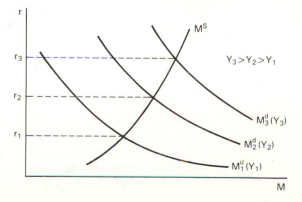

farther from the origin of the diagram will the total demand curve be located, because of the higher transactions demand that the higher income level is assumed to generate. We have drawn three such possible total demand functions in Figure 15-7. It is possible, then, to envisage the rate of interest that will clear the money market for each assumed level of income. Three such market-clearing prices of money, or rates of interest, are shown in the figure.

Neoclassical economics, or the neoclassical–Keynesian synthesis we referred to in Chapter 14, has made much of this implied relation between the level of income and the so-called equilibrium rate of interest. We shall return to some analytical developments in these directions in Part VI. For the present we leave our development of the money market relations at the point we have reached, subject only to the following clarifying observation.

UNCERTAINTY AND THE MARKET FOR MONEY

We have implicitly introduced the highly important questions of uncertainty at several points of the preceding discussion. The asset demand for money, as we have seen, is deeply embedded in uncertainty. Individual decision makers have to make what estimates and form what expectations they consider reasonable in the light of the uncertainties that abound. We have also seen that the transactions demand for money is embedded in similar expectations as individuals and business firms require money to finance not only current expenditures but also their expected expenditures on consumption and investment goods.

Uncertainty, together with expectations in the presence of uncertainty, lies at the heart of the discussion of money, banking, and monetary economics. For this reason it is important to realize that the demand-for-money function we have derived in this chapter should not be looked upon, in any sense, as describing a uniquely definable functional relation. The final points to be made on this money market analysis, therefore, are twofold. First, what we have now derived can be taken as highly suggestive of the most significant underlying relations that together determine, at any time, the rate of interest and the demand for money in the economy. But second, the functions thereby derived should not be regarded as necessarily stable, but as unstable, relations. Indeed, they may at different times and in differing economic circumstances experience quite serious instability. It was to the inherent instability of the relations we have discussed that Keynes, for example, endeavored to draw principal attention. Shackle also, in numerous books and articles throughout the past thirty years, has endeavored to insist on the same point, and to

develop the significance for macroeconomic analysis of what he felici-
tously termed the possibility of kaleidic changes in the state of affairs.[10]

SUMMARY

This chapter has presented an analysis of the demand for money, broken
down into the transactions, finance, and asset demands. A description
was given of the classic quantity theory of money and its attempts to
explain the demand for money. Its analytical shortcomings were discussed.

The fuller understanding of the transactions demand for money required an examination of the relevance of interest rates and of both
consumers' and investors' expenditure expectations. Consideration was
given to the manner in which the structure of monetary and financial
institutions partly determines the relation between the level of national
income and expenditure and the need for money to sustain it.

The principal determinants of the demand for money were seen to
be the level of real output, the general commodity price level, and the
rate of interest. Expectations of changes in these variables in the presence
of uncertainty were also seen to be relevant.

The rate of interest was interpreted as being the market-clearing
price of money. Emphasis was placed, however, not principally on the
precise shapes or elasticities of the determinant functions in the market
for money, but on their general form and inherent instability. Assumptions of givenness or stability in functional relations point in the direction
of equilibrium analysis and the neoclassical synthesis. Uncertainty, expectations, and instabilities point to an alternative postclassical analysis.

IMPORTANT CONCEPTS

Quantity theory of money   *Transactions, asset, and finance de-*
Velocity of circulation   *mands for money*
Payments habits   *Opportunity cost of holding money*
Expectations and interest rate effects on   *Capital gains and losses*
*   the demand for money*   *Instabilities in functional relations*

QUESTIONS FOR DISCUSSION AND REVIEW

1. It has been claimed that excessive reliance on a "general substitution
theorem" invalidates the demand-for-money analysis. Explain and comment critically on this observation.

---

[10] See G.L.S. Shackle, *Decision, Order and Time in Human Affairs*, 2nd ed. (Cambridge: Cambridge University Press, 1969); *Epistemics and Economics* (Cambridge: Cambridge University Press, 1972); and *Keynesian Kaleidics* (Edinburgh: Edinburgh University
Press, 1974).

2. Explain the elasticity properties of a linear transactions demand-for-money function.

3. What do you consider would be the significance for the aggregate economic system of a declining elasticity of demand-for-money function as the level of national income increased? If money is, in some sense, a "luxury" good, the income-elasticity of demand for it may well be greater than unity. Do you think this likely in actual fact? What would be the significance of such a condition?

4. Do you perceive any potential relations between the demand for money and the problem of inflation? If so, in what direction does the relation point? Explain fully.

5. Is it possible to hold a reconstructed quantity theory of money if the rate of interest is admitted as a determinant variable in the demand-for-money function?

6. "Both expectations and uncertainty must be fully taken into account to explain the demand for money because money, essentially, is an uncertainty phenomenon." Explain and discuss critically.

7. Is the M2 velocity of circulation of money more stable or less stable than the M1 velocity? Why?

8. How is the analysis of the demand for money in this chapter likely to be affected by further developments in depository and nondepository financial institutions, and in the consequent changes in the definition of money?

9. Following the work of Baumol referred to in footnote 7 of this chapter, discuss the meaning and significance of the inventory-theoretic approach to the explanation of the demand for money.

10. Why should a business firm hold money when it does not provide any income? Does your answer apply to an individual who has larger opportunities to hold money in interest-bearing deposit accounts? Explain fully.

16

THE VALUE OF MONEY

STUDY OBJECTIVES:

- To develop a general definitional equation of the commodity price level, or the value of money
- To understand the relevance for the value of money of the money wage rate in a market economy
- To see the importance of the wage-price-productivity nexus
- To observe the foundations of the theory of inflation, stagflation, and anti-inflation policy
- To consider the linkage between the theory of the price level, the demand for money, and changes in the amount of money in circulation
- To distinguish between monetary exogeneity and endogeneity, and money as a cause and an effect
- To note the implications for the theory of the price level of the cash balance approach to the quantity theory of money

The commodity price level has frequently been considered principally a monetary phenomenon. Money has often been regarded as a veil over what transpired in the real sectors of the economy where relative commodity prices were formed. The task of money as a measure of value was that of transforming relative prices into an absolute general price level. The quantity theory of money, as it was integrated with the classical macroeconomics, came into vogue at precisely that point. At times, and principally again in the classical tradition, money was thought to be neutral. Variations in the amount of money in existence, it was imagined, could not have any permanent or long-run effects on the real income and output of the economy, the relative prices of commodities, or the rate of interest.

The theory of the general price level, however, and therefore the theory of the value of money, are deeply embedded in what transpires in certain real markets of the economy. In this chapter we shall trace the price-forming forces to the part that is played by the supply functions of business firms in the commodity markets, and to the way in which things operate in the market for labor. In the latter, we shall see, the money wage rate emerges as what we have termed the linchpin of the monetary system.

We have already argued that the continued viability of a monetary economy depends on the projected stability in the value of money. People will be prepared to accept and use money as money only so long as they can have confidence that they will be able to pass it on again to some other transactor when they wish to do so, at a value comparable with that at which they acquired it. The thing that makes money money, and the thing, therefore, that sustains the viability of the monetary system, is the acceptability of the money medium.

This stability and acceptability turn, to an important degree, on what is happening to the money wage rate, or, more precisely, on changes in the money wage rate in relation to the productivity of labor. The money wage rate is not just another price in a multimarket system that is in every respect comparable with, say, the price of bananas. The wage rate is unique. It is on the one side the determinant of production costs and money incomes. On the other side it determines the ability of income receivers to spend. Wage and salary incomes constitute both the principal element of industrial costs of production on the one hand and the principal source of the demand for commodities on the other. In short, a money economy is fundamentally a wage-price economy.

The basic propositions central to the analysis have a distinguished parentage and a long history. The prices at which firms sell their products are clearly related to the level of costs and the desired profit margins at which they operate. From Joan Robinson's *Economics of Imperfect Competition*[1] and Edward Chamberlin's *Theory of Monopolistic Competition*,[2] which restructured the analysis of the firm in the early 1930s, through Sidney Weintraub's *Price Theory*[3] two decades later and the deluge of modern presentations, the argument has been clear that firms do, in one way or another, enjoy varying degrees of market and price-making power. Their selling prices, accordingly, are set at a level that will not only cover their current or variable operating costs but also provide for the amortization of the capital equipment and resources they employ, as well as realize an acceptable or target rate of return on the

[1] Joan Robinson, *The Economics of Imperfect Competition* (London: Macmillan, 1933).
[2] Edward H. Chamberlin, *The Theory of Monopolistic Competition: A Re-orientation of the Theory of Value* (Cambridge: Harvard University Press, 1933).
[3] Sidney Weintraub, *Price Theory* (New York: Pitman, 1949).

money capital they have invested. In a highly important sense, the selling price is interpretable as equaling a relevant measure of production costs plus a markup, or, in other words, the cost level multiplied by a suitably defined markup factor.

Paul Davidson, for example, in his *Money and the Real World,* has observed that "this standard volume-target return pricing approach has been found to be the predominant method used by management in such major industries as aluminum, automobiles, chemicals, and steel,"[4] and he refers to the very valuable work in this direction by W. Adams, *The Structure of American Industry.*[5] Donald J. Harris has surveyed the same set of questions relating to industrial pricing in his "Price Policy of Firms, the Level of Employment and the Distribution of Income in the Short Run,"[6] and further contributions, notably from a post-Keynesian perspective, have been made by Alfred Eichner and J. A. Kregel.[7] The issue has been broadened to the consideration of "Cost Inflation and the State of Economic Theory" by P. Wiles,[8] and the exchange of comments on Wiles' article by G. C. Means, A. Nove, Sidney Weintraub, and Wiles himself bring many relevant issues into clear focus.

But a survey of the relevant literature is not necessary or possible at this point. We shall see in what follows that the microfoundations in the theory of price have been broadened to form the basis of the macroeconomic theory of the price level, and of changes in the price level, that we are seeking. On this broader dimension the argument turns on the analysis of the aggregate supply side effects in the economy. We have already seen that well-established, even though significantly diverging, views of the aggregate supply function are held by neoclassical and postclassical economists. The supply side is important in both systems of thought.

It has long been acknowledged, as the distinguished American economist and Nobel Laureate Lawrence Klein observed in his presidential address to the American Economic Association, that "Keynes included the aggregate supply function in the *General Theory,* but . . . that part of his analysis dealing with supply has been largely played down by the

[4] Paul Davidson, *Money and the Real World,* 2nd ed. (New York: John Wiley, 1978), p. 39.
[5] W. Adams, *The Structure of American Industry,* 3rd ed. (New York: Macmillan, 1961).
[6] Donald J. Harris, *Australian Economic Papers,* June 1974.
[7] Alfred S. Eichner and J. A. Kregel, "An Essay on Post–Keynesian Theory: A New Paradigm in Economics," *Journal of Economic Literature,* December 1975; and A. S. Eichner, "A Theory of the Determination of the Mark-up under Oligopoly," *Economic Journal,* December 1973. See also Peter Kenyon's chapter on "Pricing" in Alfred S. Eichner, ed., *A Guide to Post–Keynesian Economics* (New York: M. E. Sharpe, 1978).
[8] P. Wiles, "Cost Inflation and the State of Economic Theory," *Economic Journal,* 1973. See also the discussion of Wiles' article in the *Economic Journal,* June 1974.

profession at large—not by all students of macroeconomics."[9] And Klein here refers to the work of Sidney Weintraub, which will influence our own analysis prominently at later points.[10] Joan Robinson also, one of the most prominent and articulate interpreters of Keynes, has referred to Keynes' seminal exposition of "the concept of effective demand governed by volatile expectations,"[11] a line of analysis that, apart from its expectations element, early found its way into the reconstructed neoclassical economics. But then, taking up the point we have just examined, Robinson observes that "the other half of the Keynesian revolution was to recognize that, in an industrial economy, the level of prices is governed primarily by the level of money wage rates."[12] It is precisely this, the relation between the money wage rate and associated income payments on the one hand and industrial prices on the other, that provides the linkage between microeconomic analysis and the explanation of macroeconomic outcomes and stability.

Keynes himself made these points quite clearly. The theory of aggregate supply appears at the very beginning of his *General Theory*, where he establishes that what he calls the "aggregate supply price," or the proceeds that entrepreneurs expect to get from the sale of their output, will determine the amount of employment it will be economically worthwhile for them to offer.[13] Having begun his revolutionary work on that note, Keynes carried the perspective through the following chapters until, in the final sentence of the substantive part of his book, he drew out the implication that the behavior of the price level depended directly on the behavior of wage costs, or, to use his terminology, the wage-unit. He states that "the long-run stability or instability of prices will depend on the strength of the upward trend of the wage-unit (or, more precisely, of the cost-unit) compared with the rate of increase in the efficiency of the productive system."[14]

In this Keynes opened to scrutiny the highly significant wage-price-productivity nexus that lies at the heart of the general theory of the price

[9] Lawrence R. Klein, "The Supply Side," *American Economic Review*, March 1978.

[10] Sidney Weintraub, "A Macroeconomic Approach to the Theory of Wages," *American Economic Review*, December 1956; and "The Micro-Foundations of Aggregate Demand and Supply," *Economic Journal*, September 1957. The latter article, which has had a seminal influence on later work, is substantially reproduced in Chapter 2 of Weintraub's *Approach to the Theory of Income Distribution* (Philadelphia: Chilton, 1958). See also Sidney Weintraub, *Classical Keynesianism, Monetary Theory, and the Price Level* (Philadelphia: Chilton, 1961); *Some Aspects of Wage Theory and Policy* (Philadelphia: Chilton, 1963); and *Capitalism's Inflation and Unemployment Crisis: Beyond Monetarism and Keynesianism* (Reading, Mass.: Addison-Wesley, 1978).

[11] Joan Robinson, "What Has Become of the Keynesian Revolution?" in *After Keynes* (Oxford: Blackwell, 1973), p. 7.

[12] Ibid., p. 6.

[13] John Maynard Keynes, *General Theory of Employment, Interest, and Money* (London: Macmillan, 1936), pp. 24–25.

[14] Ibid., p. 309.

level. But it is correct to say, as Lawrence Klein has acknowledged, that Keynes' supply side analysis and his wage-productivity-price relationship were substantially submerged in the high tide of neoclassicism in the decades that followed. The analysis of Keynes, between his opening definitions of the aggregate supply function and his closing explanation of price level behavior, was generally interpreted as though his contribution to economic thought was concentrated in what became known as demand side analysis.

Happily, a more expansive vision of macroeconomic and monetary analysis is now current in the economics profession. And though, as we have seen, divergent views of the ways to corral it and deal with it have been presented, a broadened and substantive consensus exists that the economics of the supply side must be taken into account and given full weight in handling the questions of aggregate stability and progress. Our intention in the following chapters is to draw out the implications of the competing viewpoints on this important set of ideas. Principally, as we shall see, it is here that the postclassical vision of the macroeconomic system enters and throws its most significant light. We begin in the following section with a consideration of some of the microeconomic foundations. Our comments on that level will necessarily be minimal and designed only to provide a motivation for coming to grips with the macroeconomic analogies that are our primary concern.

INDUSTRIAL PRODUCTION
AND INCOME PAYMENTS

A business firm will produce its optimum level of output when the marginal revenue from the sale of that output just equals its marginal cost of production. If the firm is producing and selling under conditions of perfect competition in both its variable factor input market and its output market, the marginal revenue of output is precisely indicated by its unit selling price. Similarly, the marginal cost of a unit of factor input will be the going market unit price of the factor. But the firm is concerned principally with the so-called marginal cost of output, so that that magnitude can be compared with its marginal revenue from the sale of output. The relevant geometrical exposition can be inspected in any text on microeconomics.

The firm's total revenue will be described as PQ, where the symbols refer, respectively, to the unit selling price and the quantity of output sold. The firm's so-called demand curve, or its average revenue curve or unit selling price function, is in that case described by a horizontal line. The firm is assumed to be able to sell as much as it wishes at the going competitive market price. The additional revenue obtained from the sale of a marginal unit of output will be precisely equal to P, the going market price.

On the production side, the firm is interested in the marginal product of the variable input factor, or the addition to total output that results from the employment of a marginal unit of the factor. Notationally, the marginal product of labor, taking labor as the variable factor, may be referred to as MP_L. If, then, the marginal product of the last unit of labor input is multiplied by the marginal revenue from the sale of that output, in our present competitive case measured by P, the resulting product can be described as the marginal revenue product of the factor input. In the competitive case this is describable as

(1) $$MRP_L = P{\cdot}MP_L$$

Optimization conditions require the firm to continue to employ additional units of labor up to the point at which the marginal revenue product is no less than the unit price that has to be paid for the factor. Using the notation already introduced, the marginal optimization condition can be stated as

(2) $$P{\cdot}MP_L = W,$$

where W refers to the unit cost of labor, or the money wage rate.

When optimization conditions are satisfied, the selling price is related to the money wage rate in the following way:

(3) $$P = W/MP_L$$

In other words, the price level equals the money wage rate multiplied by a markup factor, where the markup factor is the reciprocal of the marginal product of labor.

More interest attaches, however, to the general case where the firm is selling its output in an imperfectly competitive market. In that case an important relation exists between the firm's unit selling price and its marginal revenue. The firm's total revenue in that case is described as

(4) $$R = P(Q)Q,$$

where $P(Q)$ indicates that the selling price is functionally dependent on the quantity of output being sold. The marginal revenue is then given by

(5) $$MR = P + Q\frac{\Delta P}{\Delta Q}$$

In this expression the term $\Delta P/\Delta Q$ describes the amount by which the unit selling price will change (in this case be reduced) by the sale of a marginal unit of output. The marginal revenue of output, then, will be the unit selling price received, minus the product of this selling price adjustment term and the number of units being sold. The minus sign occurs because the value of $\Delta P/\Delta Q$ is negative. The unit selling price will fall in order to make a larger volume of sales possible.

Taking the right-hand side expression for marginal revenue in Equation (5), the following equivalence can be stated:

$$(6) \qquad MR = P\left(1 + \frac{Q\Delta P}{P\Delta Q}\right)$$

The final term inside the parenthesis on the right-hand side of Equation (6) will be recognized as the reciprocal of the price-elasticity of demand for output. The marginal revenue for an imperfectly competitive firm, therefore, can be written as

$$(7) \qquad MR = P(1 + 1/E)$$

where E refers to the elasticity of demand.

Again the firm will be interested in the MRP_L in the same way as in the competitive case. This is described as

$$(8) \qquad MRP_L = P(1 + 1/E)(MP_L)$$

The firm will then be employing the optimum amount of labor input (continuing to assume that labor is purchased in a competitive labor market) when this MRP is just equal to the money wage rate W.

It follows from this factor employment optimization condition,

$$(9) \qquad W = P(1 + 1/E)(MP_L),$$

that the unit selling price will bear the following relation to the wage rate:

$$(10) \qquad P = \frac{W}{(1 + 1/E)(MP_L)}$$

Once again the unit selling price is equal to the money wage rate multiplied by a markup factor. But in this case the markup factor is not simply the reciprocal of the marginal product of labor as in the previous case. It is equal to that magnitude multiplied by the reciprocal of $(1 + 1/E)$. In short, the selling price must now be marked up by a factor that is dependent on the nature of the competitive conditions, or the elasticity of demand, in the market in which the firm sells its output. For larger values of the elasticity of demand, the markup factor approaches more closely the previously given reciprocal of the marginal product of labor. When the firm is selling in a perfectly competitive market and the elasticity of demand is infinitely large, the value of $(1 + 1/E)$ approaches unity, and the previous markup value is established. The value of the additional multiple in the markup factor, $1/(1 + 1/E)$, will be larger for lower absolute values of elasticity. In other words, the less elastic the demand for output, the larger the extent to which the unit cost of the variable factor, in this case labor, will be marked up to determine the unit selling price.

THE GENERALIZED WAGE-COST MARKUP FACTOR

We focus now on the general case of the firm selling in an imperfectly competitive market.[15] Its schematic income statement will read as follows:

Income Statement

	Total sales revenue
minus	Cost of raw materials
equals	*Net value added in production*

The net value added, NVA, will be divided between the rewards paid to the variable factor, labor, on the one hand, and the residue available to the providers of the fixed factors, here subsumed under the designation of capital, on the other. This residual profit element will include both the annual amortization necessary to provide for the replacement of the firm's real capital assets (to maintain capital intact) and the true residual rate of return on the money capital employed in the firm. The firm's total wage bill may be indicated as WN, where W and N refer, respectively, to the money wage rate and the number of workers employed. The latter is assumed to be appropriately defined as the number of man-hours of labor at work in the firm during whatever time period is under review.[16]

[15] See the discussion of the pricing and output optimization model for the imperfectly competitive firm in Davidson, *Money and the Real World,* Chap. 3; and Douglas Vickers, *Financial Markets in the Capitalist Process,* (Philadelphia: University of Pennsylvania Press, 1978), Chap. 2.

[16] Comparative data are available from the Bureau of Labor Statistics of the Department of Labor and may be inspected in the source referred to in Table 16-2.

Referring to the gross profit element of the NVA as R, it follows that

(11) $$NVA = WN + R$$

Given, then, that NVA necessarily exceeds WN by the amount that is necessary to reward the providers of money capital and maintain the real capital intact, the simple markup condition can be stated as follows:

(12) $$NVA = kWN,$$

where k now serves as the general wage-cost markup factor.

We may leave the microeconomic theory at that point, understanding that the firm's revenue, and thus its NVA, will have incorporated into them a unit selling price determined by marking up factor costs by an appropriately specified markup factor. It is this latter procedure in which we are now interested, and we can immediately contemplate the aggregative or macroeconomic analogue of the same relationship.

For the economy as a whole, the sum of the NVA of all the producing firms will be equal to the gross national product. The computation of the GNP from this so-called value-added approach provides an estimate equal to that reached by the alternative computational routes of the incomes approach or the expenditure approach. The details may be inspected in most economics principles texts and are usually given fuller treatment in texts on macroeconomic theory.

With this relation in hand we can revert to notation employed in the preceding chapter and refer to the total national income as $Y = Py$, where, once again, Y is equal to the total NVA in the economy. Generalizing to the economy, it follows that for the system as a whole

(13) $$Py = kWN$$

This expression corresponds to the sum of the NVA of all the individual producing firms in the economy. The value of k contained in it is the economywide average wage-cost markup factor, and WN now refers to the aggregate economy's wage bill.

The general definitional equation of the commodity price level for which we are searching is already implicit in Equation (13). Before we comment on its possible short-term and longer-run or secular characteristics, we note that by transposition of Equation (13)

(14) $$P = kWN/y$$

The expression N/y contained in the right-hand side of Equation (14) is readily recognizable as the reciprocal of the average product of labor. We refer to this average product as A, and we can then rewrite the expression for the price level as

(15) $P = kW/A$

Equation (15) now emerges as the general definitional equation of the commodity price level. The price level is directly related to the money wage rate and the wage-cost markup factor, and inversely related to the average product of labor. Alternatively, we can refer to the ratio of the wage rate to the average product of labor, or W/A in the formula, as the efficiency wage, and we can state that the price level is determined by the efficiency wage rate multiplied by the previously defined wage-cost markup factor.

This, of course, makes intuitive sense. Understanding the business firm's production and revenue-producing possibilities and its income payment obligations in the way we have summarized them, it is natural to expect that if money wage costs, or efficiency wage costs, are higher, then the firm's selling prices will have to be higher. If they were not, then the necessary rate of return on money capital employed would not be realized. In that event money capital could be expected to migrate to other lines of productive and economic activity. The economywide markup factor and the price level we have derived are simply generalizations of those homely propositions from the level of the individual firm.

FURTHER CHARACTERISTICS OF THE
WAGE-COST MARKUP FACTOR

Our discussion earlier in this chapter of the microeconomic foundations established that the markup factor depended on basically two forces. First, the productivity relations within firms determine the marginal product of labor at any given level of output or of labor use. As additional quantities of labor are employed, the marginal product of labor may generally be expected to diminish. In that case, as output increases, the diminished marginal product of labor will put an upward pressure on the markup factor. Later it will be seen that this accounts for what has been called diminishing returns inflation. The rise in the markup factor resulting from labor's diminished productivity will feed through to an increase in the general level of prices.

Second, the size of the markup factor was related, in our microeconomic foundations, to the elasticity of demand for the firm's output. We can redefine this second influence and refer to it as the degree of monopoly in the product markets. In a general microeconomic sense, the elasticity of firms' revenue functions can be taken as an indication of the degree of monopoly that exists. If, then, firms in general enjoy a higher degree of monopoly power, or if, that is to say, they enjoy a high degree of pricing power as a result of their monopoly shields, then the extent to which they can mark up their basic efficiency wage costs will be higher. In the short run, therefore, the markup factor, k, may change if a change occurs in the degree of market power that firms enjoy. If, for example, monopoly power were greater during a recession, the markup factor might tend to decline when the recovery gets under way. Alternatively, buyers might not be so price conscious during the bright days of prosperity, and firms might then be able to raise their markup margins. In all these cases the different possible influences feed through to partially determine the shape of the economy's aggregate supply function and its general price level.

Another way of stating the last point is to recognize that the markup factor is dependent on what profit margin the producing firms imagine they can wring out of the markets they face. This, however, is simply stating that it depends on what rate of return firms imagine they can generate on the money capital they employ. Those desired rates of return will depend also on what degree of pricing or monopoly power firms imagine they possess. Variations in markup factors may occur at different phases of the business cycle simply because firms think that at those times they can increase the rate of return on capital they extract from the economy. The desired rate of return, moreover, may depend also on the business firm's need for money capital to finance projected investment, and to enable it to share in the ongoing growth of the economy.

For all of these reasons there might well be some short-term instability in the wage-cost markup factor in our basic price formula. But it is important to note that the trend value of the economywide markup factor is remarkably stable. We shall observe the reasons for that in a moment. Before doing so, we can observe that if the markup factor is virtually stable over medium-term and secular trends, then price formation in the economy as a whole is very much dependent on the relation between the money wage rate and the productivity of labor. It was on precisely that note that Keynes, as we have seen, concluded the substantive part of his *General Theory*. Sir John Hicks has recently referred to this proposition as Keynes' "wage theorem"[17] that needs to be imported

---

[17] Sir John Hicks, *The Crisis in Keynesian Economics* (New York: Basic Books, 1973), pp. 58ff. See the review by Sidney Weintraub, "Revision and Recantation in Hicksian Economics," *Journal of Economic Issues,* September 1976, reprinted in Sidney Weintraub, *Keynes, Keynesians, and Monetarists* (Philadelphia: University of Pennsylvania Press, 1978), Chap. 6.

back into macroeconomic analysis, particularly when that claims to derive any inspiration from Keynes' reconstruction.

Turning, then, to the trend or secular magnitude of the wage-cost
markup factor, we can put our propositions regarding it in a form that
will subsequently throw light on the possibilities of price level stability
and inflation control. Let us return to our general definitional equation

(15) $P = kW/A$

The value of the k factor in this expression can be written as

(16) $k = Py/WN$

This follows from Equation (13) and expresses the fact that WN is marked
up by the indicated amount to derive the national income, Py. Equation
(16) indicates, alternatively, that the value of k is simply the reciprocal
of the ratio of the total wage bill to the national income. Or k is the
reciprocal of the wage share in the national income.

It is a remarkable fact that historically this wage share has been
virtually stable. That being so, it is true by implication that the economywide k is also virtually stable. Recent data bearing on this important
point are shown in Table 16-1.

Table 16-1 focuses on the relation between the national income and
total employee compensation. Comparable data may be derived from an
analysis of the Gross Business Product statistics, which are also regularly
available. On the comprehensive national income basis shown in Table
16-1, the wage share has been stable for the last couple of decades. After
a downward move during the post–World War II reconstruction period,
the markup factor shown in the table has stabilized at approximately one
and one-third. This means that total employee compensation has stabilized at approximately three-quarters of the national income. This relative magnitude and its stability imply that the price formation forces
summarized in Equation (15) focus attention on significant issues in the
theory of aggregate prices. We shall comment further below on the precise
causation involved.

THE EXOGENEITY OF THE MONEY WAGE RATE

The money wage rate, as we have suggested, may be regarded as an
exogenous variable. It is in general determined by collective bargaining,
frequently in terms of contractual arrangements which may run for three
years at a time. Of course it may happen from time to time, as occurred
in the United States economy in the early 1980s, that in conditions of

Table   16-1

The economywide wage-cost markup factor in selected periods

Year or Quarter	National Income	Total Employee Compensation	k
1940	79.7	52.1	1.53
1950	237.6	154.8	1.53
1960	415.7	294.9	1.41
1970	810.7	612.0	1.32
1980	2,117.1	1,598.6	1.32
1981	2,352.5	1,767.6	1.33
1982	2,436.5	1,855.9	1.31
1982 Qr. 1	2,396.9	1,830.8	1.31
2	2,425.2	1,850.7	1.31
3	2,455.6	1,868.3	1.31
4	2,471.7	1,876.1	1.32

Source: *Economic Report of the President,* February 1983, p. 186; and *Federal Reserve Bulletin,* April 1983, p. A52.

Data on National Income and Total Employee Compensation are in $ billions. Employee compensation includes wages, salaries, and supplements, including employer contributions for social insurance.

recession some workers and some trade unions may agree to accept wage and salary reductions or modifications of existing wage contracts. This may appear to imply an element of endogeneity, or the working of market-clearing forces in the market for labor, in the formation of the money wage rate. But in such a case the wage rate is still being set by bargaining processes that establish it at a level that is fixed for a term of years or a defined period into the future. For that reason it can be taken, for purposes of the short-run analysis we are now engaged in, as given from outside the system of relations being examined and as therefore an exogenous variable.

We leave unexamined the actual process of the formation of the money wage rate, noting that forces other than purely economic, such as those having to do with the concentration and possible exploitation of power, are involved in it. In his *General Theory* Keynes, for example, did not present a theory of the money wage rate. His Chapter 19 was judiciously titled "Changes in Money-Wages," and the focus of analysis was the transmission mechanism through which wage changes work out their effects. Joan Robinson has observed that "the level of money wages in any country at any time is more or less an historical accident going back to a remote past and influenced by recent events affecting the balance of power between employers and trade unions . . ."[18] Patterns of wage pay-

[18] Robinson, *After Keynes,* p. 7.

ments set by collective bargaining in some sectors of the economy flow through to the determination of wage payments and money income standards in general.

CHANGES IN THE PRICE LEVEL
AND IN THE VALUE OF MONEY

From our basic price level formula in Equation (15) we can focus on the explanation of price variations. Using the familiar delta sign to refer to incremental changes, we can write

(17) $$\Delta P = \Delta(kW/A)$$

This implies that

(18) $$\Delta P = \frac{W \cdot \Delta k}{A} + \frac{k \cdot \Delta W}{A} - \frac{kW \cdot \Delta A}{A^2}$$

Dividing throughout by P, using $P = kW/A$ on the right-hand side, yields

(19) $$\Delta P/P = \Delta k/k + \Delta W/W - \Delta A/A$$

It follows that the rate of change in the price level is explained, as shown in Equation (19), by the algebraic sum of the three rates of change shown on the right-hand side of the equation. If, however, the value of k can be taken to be constant, then its change is of course zero, and the first term on the right-hand side of Equation (19) drops out of the picture. The rate of change in prices will then be directly determined by the rate of change in the money wage rate minus the rate of change in the average productivity of labor.

For those interested in the application of the differential calculus, Equation (15) can be put in logarithmic form:

(20) $$lnP = lnk + lnW - lnA$$

and by taking the derivative with respect to time, the proportional time rates of change of the terms in the equation may be derived. The result follows:

(21) $$(1/P)(dP/dt) = (1/k)(dk/dt) + (1/W)(dW/dt) - (1/A)(dA/dt)$$

Using familiar dot notation to represent proportional time rates of change, the expression for the rate of change of prices can be written as

(22)
$$\dot{P} = \dot{W} - \dot{A}$$

assuming once again that the rate of change of k is zero, for the reasons previously examined. It is in the form of Equation (22) that results of this kind are usually shown.

The level of commodity prices in the economy can be expected to change at a rate equal to the difference between the rates of change of money wages and average productivity. If, for example, the money wage rate increases by 10 percent per annum, but average productivity increases during the same time period at a rate of only 1 percent, Equation (22) or Equation (19) indicates that the price level will increase by the difference, or by nine percentage points. This, unfortunately, is not too far removed from the rates of change experienced in the United States economy during recent years.

Table 16-2 focuses on the relevant data for the United States business sector during 1970–82 and shows, in the first two data columns, the simultaneous percentage rates of change per annum in output per hour and compensation per hour of all persons employed in the Business Sector. The data are aggregative and do not focus directly on the production workers as the price level equation envisages. They include, among all persons employed, those engaged in other than direct production activities. A further analysis of the compensation-output-price relationship will be made in Chapter 21.

Focusing on the pattern of trends inherent in Table 16-2, we observe that in the first five years of the 1970s the annual rate of increase in compensation per hour rose from 6.6 to 9.6 percent. At the same time the increase in output per hour declined from 3.6 to 2.2 percent. As might be expected from the conjunction of these data, the rate of price increase more than doubled between 1971 and 1975, rising from 4.4 to 9.8 percent. In the second half of the 1970s the rate of increase in output per hour declined from 3.3 percent to less than zero, while the rate of increase in compensation actually rose to 10.4 percent. The result was that the rate of price increase doubled from 4.7 percent to 9.4 percent.

Other forces have come to bear on the price inflation problem in the years covered by the table, of course, with international harvest failures in some years and heavy oil price increases in international markets in other years. It is not intended to suggest that there is a monocausal explanation of inflation. But it can clearly be concluded at this point that in highlighting, as we have done, the significant wage-price-productivity nexus, we have isolated an important and fundamental influence around which the influence of other factors swirl.

Table   16-2

Changes in output per hour, compensation per hour, and the implicit price
deflator in the U.S. Business Sector, 1970–1982

	Percentage change from preceding period (Quarterly data at seasonally adjusted annual rates)		
Year or Quarter	Output per hour of all persons	Compensation per hour	Implicit Price Deflator
1970	0.8	7.3	4.5
1971	3.6	6.6	4.4
1972	3.5	6.5	3.4
1973	2.6	8.0	5.5
1974	−2.4	9.4	9.5
1975	2.2	9.6	9.8
1976	3.3	8.6	4.7
1977	2.4	7.7	5.6
1978	0.6	8.6	7.5
1979	−0.9	9.7	9.0
1980	−0.7	10.4	9.4
1981	1.8	9.6	9.5
1982	0.4	7.3	5.5
1982 Qr. 1	−1.0	7.3	3.8
2	1.4	6.9	4.3
3	3.6	6.1	4.4
4	4.1	6.0	3.5

Source: *Economic Report of the President*, February 1983, p. 209.

In 1980 and 1982, both years in which real gross national product
declined, the change in output per hour shown in Table 16-2 was negative
or only marginally positive. But in those years the rate of increase in
compensation maintained the momentum it had built up during the preceding decade. As a result, price increases continued at a high rate, with
a tapering off in the recession year of 1982. Wage rate changes were
slightly moderated during the latter part of that year, though, as the
table indicates, a structural imbalance between the rates of change referred to there continued to exist.

If it were possible to maintain the economy at a reasonably full
employment level of operation and enjoy its potential growth rate of 3 to
5 percent per annum, money wage rates would be able to increase by a
corresponding amount without danger of price instability. The possibility
of stability would be enhanced, it would seem, if arrangements could be
made to keep these money wage rate and productivity changes in line
with each other.

THE CAUSES OF INFLATION

We do not digress at this point to discuss the causes of inflation in a systematic way. But we can summarize the possible causes of inflation implicit in the theory of prices we have developed so far. We shall be able to discuss these issues more completely after we have developed the full supply and demand model of the macroeconomy and can then integrate the demand side pressures with those we have just observed on the supply side.

For the present, a partial explanation of the inflation phenomenon can be summarized under the headings of (1) money wage inflation, resulting from too rapid a rate of increase in money wage rates, or, alternatively, an inflation in the efficiency wage rate, W/A, if money wage rates are increasing more rapidly than average productivity; (2) diminishing returns inflation, resulting from the reduction in the marginal productivity of labor as additional quantities of labor are employed during an upswing in business activity, though in the early stages of recovery from a recession productivity may increase for a time as a more effective utilization of installed capacity and capital equipment is achieved; and (3) administered pricing or profit rate inflation, resulting from an upward pressure on industrial markup factors.

THE PLACE OF THE MONEY SUPPLY

We have not yet spoken, in our discussion of price formation and the problem of inflation, of the supply of money. We have found some principal determinants of the price level to be embedded in the real sector, and changes in the price level to emanate from disturbances in that sector. But money, of course, is important, and it is necessary now to fit the supply of it, and changes in its supply, into the picture.

In our detailed discussion of the banking system in Part III we examined the ways in which the banks actually create and supply the circulating medium. We placed heavy reliance on the fact that to a very large degree the banks create money in response to the demand for it. It is this, which is in many respects a resurrection of the banking principle that enjoyed considerable discussion in the earlier part of the nineteenth century, that we mean when we refer to the endogeneity of the money supply.

For the present, an important linkage needs to be established between the changes in the general commodity price level that our preceding discussion has seen to be possible and the supply of money. Imagine, then, that the money wage rate increases during any given time period by 10 percent, but that during the same period the average productivity of labor increases by 2 percent. Invoking previous analysis, we can expect that the result will be an upward pressure on prices of some eight percentage points.

Suppose that it is desired, following the increase in prices, to maintain the same level of real production, activity, employment, and market exchanges as existed before the increase in prices occurred. We may suppose a previously existing level of real income, referred to as y_1. If this level is to be maintained at the new higher level of prices, $P_2 > P_1$, the total level of monetary expenditures will have to rise to $P_2 y_1 > P_1 y_1$. Part of this increased level of monetary expenditure may be accommodated by a rise in the velocity of circulation of money. In the preceding chapter we observed that during the last couple of decades there has been a sharp rise in the velocity of circulation of the M1 money supply. At this point the possibility of changes in the institutional structure of the economy become very important. We have noted ways in which financial institutions have provided new facilities in recent years to accommodate to the increased demand for finance, and to make it possible for the public to economize on the use and holding of money.

Such changes in velocity, however, might not be very large in the short term in which the increased financial accommodation is required, and there will conceivably be a need for an increase in the basic money supply. We can expect to see, then, an increased demand by business firms and others for bank loans to provide that needed finance. Much will depend on the banking system's response to those demands. Indeed, to put the question on another level that will engage us at length in due course, much will depend on the action that the Federal Reserve Board is prepared to take to provide the commercial banks with the additional reserves they need to permit them to expand the money supply in response to the industrial sector's request.

The increase in the money supply may not come only in the manner we have supposed, by the banks responding to the demand for loans and thereby endogenously creating money. The Federal Reserve may take the initiative in purchasing government securities (an example of what we have referred to as open market operations) from the nonbank public. This could be referred to as an exogenous increase in the money supply. For the purchase of the securities would add to the holdings of money by the public as they deposited in their demand deposit accounts the checks they received from the Federal Reserve Bank in payment for the securities.

We can conceive that in one way or another an increase in the money supply will occur. The important question, however, is whether the extent of the increase in the money supply will be sufficient to meet the increased requirements of money. If it is precisely equal to the increased requirements, the previously existing level of real economic activity will be able to be maintained. If, however, the increase in the money supply were positive but less than the amount by which the money requirements had increased, then it would not be possible to maintain the same real income and output as before. The net increase in the demand for money could be expected to put pressure on the market for money, and the general level of interest rates could be expected to rise. This would tend to induce reductions in employment and production, in the manner in which that happened in the early 1980s.

Changes in the money supply, then, cannot always be understood to be causal in what is happening in the economy. In the kinds of situations we have just discussed, the change in the money supply is accommodative rather than causal. With this perspective we can now observe that if, in the presence of an upward pressure on prices because of unfavorable wage-price-productivity relations, the monetary authorities maintain an unduly restrictive monetary policy, the level of employment and activity will decline. We would then experience a recession in the economy at the same time as inflationary price increases are occurring. This conjunction of recession and inflation, with which we have become all too familiar in recent times, has been referred to by the grotesque neologism of stagflation.[19]

CAUSATION AND RESPONSE IN PRICING
AND POLICY DEVELOPMENTS

The perspective we have established implies a direction of causation from (1) money wage rate variations, to (2) induced increases in prices, to (3) increased demands for money to accommodate existing trade levels or, in other words, to validate the price change, and to (4) increased supplies of money, which may or may not be sufficient to maintain existing activity levels. Monetary thought, however, has frequently seen things the other way around. It has been claimed, in the long history of the quantity theory of money in particular, that the direction of causation runs as follows: from (1) autonomous or exogenous increases in the money supply, to (2) increased prices, or, if there should for any reason be unutilized capacity in the economy, to (3) increased levels of output, and to (4) increased money wage rates. But no clear analysis has been offered, in this traditional way of looking at things, of the extent to which changes in the money supply will affect either the commodity price level or the level of activity or both. The analysis we have foreshadowed, however, does get

[19] See Paul Davidson and Sidney Weintraub, "Money as Cause and Effect," *Economic Journal*, December 1973.

at precisely that important analytical distinction. For it takes account of the need for money in response to what has been termed the needs of trade, and it traces out the possible effects on the economy of the different changes that may occur. We shall be able to develop the argument more fully after we have completed our analysis in the next two chapters of the aggregate supply and demand functions in the economy.

THE QUANTITY THEORY AND THE PRICE LEVEL

The long history of the quantity theory of money and its incorporation into some expressions of the neoclassical theory, particularly in what has become known as monetarism,[20] make it necessary to look also at the price level implications of it. We have already encountered the quantity equation of exchange in our introductory comments in Chapter 14 on the classical macroeconomics, and in our discussion of the transactions demand for money in Chapter 15. We saw at the last-mentioned point that the equation of exchange, given the association with it of appropriate behavioral assumptions, pointed to an explanation of changes in the general level of prices. But we set that aspect aside at that earlier point in order to concentrate on the implications of the quantity theory for the demand for money. It is because of its significance for the demand for money, in fact, that the quantity theory has been resurrected and made the basis of the present-day monetarist explanation of monetary and macroeconomic affairs.

But the theory has served for a long time, throughout the history of the neoclassical analysis, as a vehicle for the explanation of price level changes also. The dynamic processes that give rise to an increase in the price level following a change in the supply of money have frequently been referred to as the transmission mechanism of monetary policy. We shall address this question directly and in more detail in a later chapter. Our comments here will be confined to the implications of the cash balance approach to the quantity theory of money, as that is the form of the theory in which it has enjoyed its recent redevelopment.

We recall the basic equation of the quantity theory as

$$(23) \qquad\qquad M^d = kPy,$$

where the variables are interpreted as in Chapter 15. Let it be supposed now that the monetary authorities cause an exogenous increase in the money supply. We refer to the new level of the money supply as M_1^s. On

---

[20] See Milton Friedman, "The Quantity Theory of Money: A Restatement," in Milton Friedman, ed., *Studies in the Quantity Theory of Money* (Chicago: University of Chicago Press, 1956).

the assumption that in the immediate impact there has been no reason for any change in the terms on the right-hand side of Equation (23), the new money supply will be greater than the demand for money that exists at the current level of output and prices. In other words, $M_1^s > M^d$.

The question then arises as to what the public can be expected to do with the excess supply of money it now finds itself holding. In modern terminology, the public is now presented with a wealth portfolio optimization problem. For now that its holdings of money have increased, even though that is in the immediate situation involuntary, the proportion of total wealth portfolios now occupied by money will be too large relative to the other assets in which wealth is held. Money holdings will be too large in the sense that the increase in money stocks will have caused the marginal utility of money as an asset to fall relative to the marginal utilities of the competing nonmonetary asset forms. The reaction of the public, then, it is supposed, will be to spend some of the additional money supplies until a preferred portfolio balance has been attained. The money may be spent on acquiring real commodities, that is, on consumption expenditures, or on acquiring other wealth assets.

If, however, the economy was already operating at a full-employment level, the expenditure of the new money on goods and services would not elicit any increase in commodity supplies. The level of real output would remain the same as before. As a result, the expenditures would lead to an increase in commodity prices. The price increases would mean that the new total expenditure level, $P_1 y$, would be greater than the previously existing level of Py. In fact, prices could be expected to increase until they reached a level at which the total monetary expenditure in the economy was high enough to cause the public's demand for money to equal the new higher amount of money now in existence.

We could say that as a result of this dynamic transmission process, new so-called equilibrium levels of (1) commodity prices, (2) asset values, (3) rates of return on assets or rates of interest, and (4) the demand for money will have been reached. In this sense the change in the money supply is imagined to have caused an increase in the price level. We could write

$$(24) \qquad\qquad \Delta P = f(\Delta M)$$

Allegiance to this way of looking at possible developments has led monetary economists to hold to the primary causality of changes in the money supply. It has led to the proposition, on which the monetary authorities in the United States depended heavily following the Federal Reserve Board's change of policy in October 1979, that instruments of monetary control are sufficient, and should be used, to wring inflation out of the system. A reduction of the money supply would, it was imagined, lead to a reduction of prices. But unfortunately, as we shall see, even in terms of the quantity equation itself the reduction of the money supply may lead to a reduction of real output also.

It follows from the analysis of price and monetary behavior we have given in this chapter, however, that money has a subsidiary, accommodative, and reactive role to play. If a restrictive monetary policy is employed with the intention of correcting inflationary pressures, the result can only be to worsen the situation. For monetary policy does not in general have a *direct* or *impact* effect on the price level. The *impact* effect, or the *direct* effect, of monetary policy is on the level of economic activity and employment, with, in turn, indirect implications for the level of prices.

This in no sense implies that monetary policy has no role to play in the total scheme of economic policies. It has an important and significant role. Its function and potentialities, along with those of fiscal policies and incomes policies, will be brought into a fuller perspective after we have completed our examination of the alternative macroanalytic systems.

SUMMARY

This chapter has examined the foundations of the theory of the price level and the value of money in the real sectors of the economy. In particular, the significance of the money wage rate was explored, and the causes of price level changes were traced to developments in the wage-price-productivity nexus. Considerable significance was attached to variations in the money wage levels compared with those in the average productivity of labor. The microeconomic foundations of the relations in view were also discussed.

The importance of the wage-cost markup factor was emphasized, and comments were made on its short-run and longer-term trend and stability. Data were given on the share of employee compensation in the national income, noting the relevance of this to the stability of the wage-cost markup factor.

A discussion of possible changes in the price level and in price-forming forces led to a comment on the meaning and causes of inflation. The money supply was found to be to a large degree endogenous, and changes in the money supply were recognized as being frequently accommodative rather than causal in the monetary system. The chapter concluded with a discussion of the theory of the price level inherent in the cash balance approach to the quantity theory of money. It drew attention to some aspects of the monetary transmission mechanism as that is viewed by the quantity theory of money.

IMPORTANT CONCEPTS

Wage-cost markup factor   *Causes of inflation*
Efficiency wage, W/A   *Endogeneity of the money supply*
Wage-price-productivity nexus   *Marginal utility of money holdings*
Exogeneity of the money wage rate

QUESTIONS FOR DISCUSSION AND REVIEW

1. What would you expect to be the implications for the money supply of an increase in average wage rates of 10 percent in a given year, accompanied by an increase of 2 percent in the average productivity of labor? Why? Explain fully.

2. What light does the wage-cost markup theory of industrial pricing throw on the endogeneity of the money supply?

3. What empirical evidence can you gather of recent changes in wage rates, unit labor costs, and prices in the United States major oligopolistic industries?

4. How would you expect the wage-cost markup factor to be affected by changes in the elasticity of demand for commodities? Why?

5. Distinguish between the causes of cyclical and secular variability or stability in the wage-cost markup factor.

6. Using official data, trace the trends or variations during recent years in the distribution of incomes, and consider their significance for changes in industrial prices.

7. On the basis of previous studies in macroeconomics and the relevant discussion in this book to the present stage, examine the part played by the money supply in the explanation of inflation.

8. Discuss the relations, from the perspective of the quantity theory of money, between (1) the level of monetary expenditure, (2) the rates of interest on income-earning assets, (3) the price level, and (4) the level of real output, following a change in the money supply.

9. On the basis of studies to this point, how would you begin to establish a theory of inflation?

10. What is "stagflation"? How can it be controlled or corrected?

17

THE SUPPLY SIDE

STUDY OBJECTIVES:

• To gain an understanding of the aggregate supply function in a monetary economy
• To observe some of the principal analytical features of aggregate supply, for example:
  a. Its microfoundations
  b. The relevance of the wage-price-productivity nexus
  c. The significance of the state of expectations
  d. Its linkage to the demand side and the concept of effective demand
• To note the basic relation between employment levels and producers' "expected proceeds functions"
• To distinguish the postclassical aggregate supply analysis from the neoclassical theory and its derived supply curve

The main propositions of the preceding chapter have made it clear that cost and supply conditions in producing firms play an important part in the determination of industrial prices. They are relevant also to the achievable levels of real output, incomes, and employment. A consensus exists in macroeconomic analysis that supply conditions need to be carefully taken into account. The classical economics placed heavy reliance on the supply side and on the explanatory significance of supply conditions. The labor market cleared at equilibrium wage rate and employment levels, and the substitution of the effective employment into the aggregate production function determined the equilibrium level of output. The same scheme was taken over into the neoclassical system.

The supply side perspective actually provides a turning point in the history of analytical development from more than one point of view. Much has been made, for example, of the fact that during the early decades following the publication of Keynes' *General Theory* it was thought that an adequate presentation of his ideas could be made by concentrating on the determinants and significance of aggregate demand. It was true that in the Depression years in which the *General Theory* was produced conditions of demand deficiency prevailed. But Keynes' achievement was in no sense simply a demand side analysis. We saw in the previous chapter that he actually began his book with a definition of the concept of the aggregate supply function and ended it with a statement of the implications of wage and other costs for the theory of prices.

The demand side analysis of early Keynesianism was consolidated in the Hicksian *ISLM* apparatus we shall examine more fully in Chapter 20.[1] J. R. Hicks in England, and Alvin Hansen[2] and Paul Samuelson[3] in the United States, built substantial systems of analysis upon it. But the supply side came back into prominence in the 1970s, and the neoclassical emphasis on it was integrated with the earlier Keynesianism to produce the neoclassical–Keynesian synthesis. In a highly articulate version of that synthesis, Rudiger Dornbusch and Stanley Fischer included a full exposition of neoclassical aggregate supply in the first edition of their *Macroeconomics* in 1978.[4]

One of the most valuable and moderately mathematized versions of that synthesis appears in William Branson's *Macroeconomic Theory and Policy*.[5] We shall have occasion to return to its emphasis and format of analysis at a later point. In all of this work, the neoclassical incorporation of the earlier classical supply analysis is seen. Again, the labor market clears at equilibrium wage rate and employment levels, and the substitution of the market-clearing employment level into an aggregate production function provides the effective level of real output.

In this neoclassical development a genuine synthesis, or an integration of demand and supply, was thought to have been achieved. For the supply conditions in the real sectors of the economy were no longer separable, as in the earlier classical scheme, from the market for money

---

[1] J. R. Hicks, "Mr. Keynes and the 'Classics,'" *Econometrica*, 1937.

[2] Alvin H. Hansen, *Monetary Theory and Fiscal Policy* (New York: McGraw-Hill, 1949); and *A Guide to Keynes* (New York: McGraw-Hill, 1953). See also Sidney Weintraub, "Hicksian Keynesianism: Dominance and Decline," in Sidney Weintraub, ed., *Modern Economic Thought* (Philadelphia: University of Pennsylvania Press, 1977).

[3] Paul A. Samuelson, *Economics* (New York: McGraw-Hill, 1st ed., 1948, 11th ed., 1980).

[4] Rudiger Dornbusch and Stanley Fischer, *Macroeconomics*, 1st ed. (New York: McGraw-Hill, 1978), Chap. 11.

[5] William H. Branson, *Macroeconomic Theory and Policy*, 2nd ed. (New York: Harper & Row, 1979).

and monetary conditions. Money was no longer always and everywhere neutral in the classical sense. Money was not merely a veil over real economic affairs. The determination of real output was interdependent with demand and monetary conditions. The theory achieved an elegance and a high plausibilty, provided only that confidence could be placed in the assumed realism of its premises and in its abstraction from the realities of time, history, and uncertainty.

This, however, was not regarded as adequate by those economists who kept alive Keynes' original aggregate supply function and wage cost analysis.[6] For this reason the following sections will set out the essence of both the neoclassical and the postclassical supply side analyses. In the same way as these alternative perspectives were brought to bear on the demand-for-money argument in Chapter 15 and on the theory of prices in Chapter 16, it will be useful at this point to observe them both constructing their distinctive supply side analyses. Following the emphasis on wage, cost, and supply concepts in the preceding chapter, it will be convenient to present the postclassical view of things first. This will be followed later in the chapter by the neoclassical theory.

SOME POSTCLASSICAL DISTINCTIVES

The postclassical aggregate supply curve describes a linkage between a specified level of employment and the proceeds from the sale of output that producers must expect in order to make that level of employment economically worthwhile. It is embedded in what will be called an "expected proceeds function." Employing the notation we introduced in an earlier chapter, this relationship will be described by $Z = Z(N)$, where N refers to the level of employment. This important Z function will be referred to as the aggregate supply function. It should be carefully noted that the determinant variable in the function is the level of employment.

The neoclassical theory also develops an aggregate supply function. It purports to describe the manner in which the level of real national output, y, depends on the aggregate commodity price level, P. Using

[6] See the seminal article by Sidney Weintraub, "The Micro-Foundations of Aggregate Demand and Supply," *Economic Journal,* September 1957, reprinted with minor changes in the same author's *Approach to the Theory of Income Distribution* (Philadelphia: Chilton, 1958); Paul Davidson and Eugene Smolensky, *Aggregate Supply and Demand Analysis* (New York: Harper & Row, 1964); Paul Wells, "Keynes' Aggregate Supply Function: A Suggested Interpretation," *Economic Journal,* 1960; and the same author's "Keynes' Employment Function," *History of Political Economy,* Summer 1974, together with comments by E. Roy Weintraub and Axel Leijonhufvud. From a very long list of later discussions, see the expository papers by Carlo Casarosa, "The Microfoundations of Keynes's Aggregate Supply and Expected Demand Analysis," *Economic Journal,* March 1981; and A. Asimakopulos, "Keynes' Theory of Effective Demand Revisited," *Australian Economic Papers,* June 1982.

previous notation, this neoclassical relationship is described by $y = y(P)$. But an important difference in viewpoint and analytical procedure exists between the neoclassical and the postclassical arguments. The neoclassical aggregate supply curve describes a relation, as we have seen, between the price level and real output. It is described by $y = y(P)$. The postclassical aggregate supply curve, on the other hand, emanating as it does from very different analytical assumptions and procedures, describes a relation between a very different set of variables. It relates the level of employment and the "expected proceeds" that producers envisage. It is described by $Z = Z(N)$. The concept of "the aggregate supply curve" therefore means very different things in the neoclassical and postclassical bodies of analysis. The distinctions should be borne clearly in mind as the argument proceeds.

Our derivation of the aggregate supply curve from the relationship $Z = Z(N)$ will lead to its marriage with an aggregate demand curve. Demand, or the level of monetary expenditure on goods and services, will also be shown to depend on the level of employment in the economy. Again using previous notation, the aggregate demand relation will be described by $D = D(N)$. The essential integrative notion in the analysis is that wage incomes (recalling that we are using "wages" to refer consistently to all forms of employee remuneration, including wages, salaries, and other compensation) perform an important dual function in the monetary economy. On the one hand wages are a principal element of industrial costs of production, and they thereby influence the determination of the market-selling prices of goods and services. On the other hand they constitute the principal source of purchasing power that determines the level of consumption expenditures. The level and structure of wage payments, moreover, determine the distribution of total incomes between wages on the one hand and profits on the other. The phenomena of income distribution influence the levels of commodity demands and market outcomes.

The important point to be noted for future reference is that aggregate supply and aggregate demand are therefore very much interdependent. The aggregate supply and demand curves are very much like the "two blades of the scissors," to use the analogy that Alfred Marshall applied to the individual market phenomena that underlie the aggregate relations.[7] With this in view, we shall marry the aggregate supply, or $Z = Z(N)$, function and the aggregate demand, or $D = D(N)$, function to generate a supply and demand cross. The point at which the aggregate supply and demand curves intersect will indicate what we shall call the level of "effective demand." That level of demand will be "effective" in the sense

[7] Alfred Marshall, *Principles of Economics*, 8th ed. (London: Macmillan, 1920), p. 348.

that it is the level at which producers' hopes and expectations, as embedded in the supply curve, are precisely satisfied by purchasers' intentions, as embedded in the demand curve.

It follows that both supplies and demands are related, in various ways, to decision makers' expectations. Concentrating here on the supply side analysis, we shall assume that producers are making their decisions within the context of a given state of short-term and longer-term expectations. Short-term expectations refer to perceptions regarding immediate and near-term market outcomes. Long-term expectations refer to the manner in which producers judge that future market demands will make it worthwhile to purchase and install capital equipment and expand productive facilities. Short-term expectations influence producers' decisions regarding the amount of employment they should offer in order to produce the output that, it is estimated, the market can absorb in the immediate future. Long-term expectations, on the other hand, influence their decisions regarding capital investment expenditures.[8]

The model we are constructing is a short-run model. We shall assume at the outset that the capital stock and productive facilities in the economy are given, and that the decision confronting producers relates to the amount of labor that can be, or should be, optimally employed in cooperation with that capital stock. Such a procedure is consistent with the preoccupation of general macroeconomic analysis since Keynes effectively revolutionized our way of looking at it. We shall not in the first instance be concerned with the important questions of economic growth and development. A number of considerations relevant to such questions will be inherent in our analysis. But they will be deferred for later examination. We shall be concerned almost exclusively in the next three chapters with the questions of what determines at any time, given the level of capital stock and productive equipment in place at that time, the effective levels of employment, commodity demands, aggregate incomes, and the price level. Insofar as a part of total monetary demand during our short period is devoted to the acquisition of capital stock, or, in other words, to net investment expenditure, we shall make the usual short-run assumption that any such additions to capital stock do not affect the attainable level of output in the time period we have under consideration. Of course, such net additions to capital stock will determine the attainable levels of output in future time periods. At that point and in that connection

---

[8] On the place and significance of expectations in aggregate analysis, see John Maynard Keynes, *General Theory of Employment, Interest, and Money* (New York: Harcourt, Brace and World, [1936] 1964), Chap. 12; J. A. Kregel, "Economic Methodology in the Face of Uncertainty," *Economic Journal,* 1976; Paul Davidson, *Money and the Real World,* 2nd ed. (New York: John Wiley, 1978), pp. 372ff.; and Paul Davidson and J. A. Kregel, "Keynes' Paradigm: A Theoretical Framework for Monetary Analysis," in E. J. Nell, ed., *Growth, Profits, and Property* (Cambridge: Cambridge University Press, 1980).

the important questions of stable economic growth and development arise. But the latter questions will be set aside for the present.

In constructing this short-run analysis it will be necessary to introduce and observe the relevance of some key analytical propositions we have already discussed. We shall continue to acknowledge, for example, that the money wage rate should be introduced into the analysis as an exogenous variable. Its significance for the determination of commodity prices will be recalled. The connections we examined in the preceding chapter between the wage rate and per capita productivity underlie the supply function we now have in view. It will be useful, therefore, to look briefly at some of the microanalytical foundations of aggregate supply. For our present purposes it will suffice to obtain a clear grasp of the microanalytic analogues that come into view, rather than give an extended examination of the micro-theory and the ways in which aggregation from it might best proceed.

One final preliminary comment will assist in establishing perspective. We observed in Chapter 14 that the classical system was grounded in the assumptions underlying what was referred to as Say's Law. This was the law or proposition that "supply creates its own demand." By this it was meant that the incomes earned in producing the national output would all be spent in purchasing that output. What was not spent directly on consumption goods would, it was imagined, be channeled to expenditure on investment goods as savings automatically flowed into investment. There was a natural harmony in the system. There was no reason why there should be a general overproduction of goods. There was no reason, in the theoretical scheme of things, why full employment should not be continuously and automatically realized. All incomes earned would be spent and respent. Supply would create its own demand.

It has been said that the essence of Keynes' reconstruction of macroeconomics implied, not that supply, in the manner of the classicists, created its own demand, but that demand created its own supply. It was thought, in other words, that the essence of the Keynesian scheme was that the aggregate supply and demand apparatus he invented was applicable simply to the economics of an underemployed economy. Because the economy was underemployed, it was imagined that any increase in monetary demand would call forth a corresponding increase in the supply of goods and services. This could result because, in line with the supposition, the existing unemployed resources in the economy could be put to work to produce the incremental output necessary to meet the incremental demand. It was thought, that is, that Keynes simply turned the classical economics on its head. But this was hardly the essence of the matter. A number of comments might be made upon it.

First, the proposition we have just noted, that Keynesian economics is simply the economics of underemployment, was usually taken to imply that supply functions in the economy could be assumed to be perfectly elastic. This is the rather more technical way of saying that output could readily be increased to meet an increase in monetary demand. But this, in turn, implied that if production could readily be increased to meet demand, then there was no reason why commodity prices would need to rise in response to the larger demand and higher output. In the interest of analytical convenience, therefore, the price level could be assumed to be given and fixed. The argument could devolve into one of what determined the attainable level of output and employment at a given price level.

In many formulations of the theory it was imagined that money wage rates could vary, being endogenously determined in the labor market, without any thought being given to a consequent dislodgment of commodity prices. But this was hardly in the spirit of Keynes' *General Theory*. For Keynes had explicitly envisaged that even though the economy was underemployed, and while the production levels moved up toward full employment, any increase in demand and output would be likely to carry along with it increases in commodity prices. This would result from the presence of diminishing productivity as labor inputs were increased in existing production systems.

Second, Keynes' analytical system consistently acknowledged the possibility that the macroeconomy might become bogged down at an employment level less than full employment. There was no inherent or automatic reason at all why the system would tend to full employment. In what follows we shall have to take good account of precisely that possibility. We must endeavor to present a system of thought that sees output, employment, and prices, as well as the level of interest rates and the money supply, as being mutually and simultaneously determined.

SOME MICROECONOMIC FOUNDATIONS

Consider a perfectly competitive firm.[9] It will be recalled that a competitive firm can sell as much output as it wishes at the going market price. Its unit selling price curve, or its average revenue curve, therefore also defines its marginal revenue curve. The firm will produce its optimum output and maximize its profit when it produces that volume at which its marginal cost equals its marginal revenue. For the competitive firm, its marginal cost curve will then define its supply curve as it traces out

---

[9] The following analysis is heavily indebted to Paul Davidson and Eugene Smolensky, *Aggregate Supply and Demand Analysis* (New York: Harper & Row, 1964), which is in turn based on Weintraub, "Micro-Foundations of Aggregate Demand and Supply." Highly relevant also is the article by Casarosa, "Microfoundations of Keynes's Aggregate Supply and Expected Demand Analysis."

the successively higher marginal revenues or selling prices that will be required to induce the firm to increase the quantity of output produced and offered on the market. The familiar propositions on this level are summarized in Figure 17-1.

At market price P_1 in Figure 17-1, marginal revenue will equal marginal cost at output volume Q_1. At price P_2 the corresponding equality will be established at output volume Q_2. The points (P_1, Q_1) and (P_2, Q_2) therefore lie on the firm's supply curve.

The marginal cost curve, it will be recalled, is in general nonlinear, or convex, because of the diminishing marginal productivity of the variable factor input, assuming for the present a single variable factor. Diminishing marginal productivity is reflected in increasing marginal cost. If we assume that the variable factor is labor and that it is purchased by the firm at an exogenously determined wage rate W, the familiar optimization condition can be established:

(1) $$P \cdot MP_L = MRP_L = W$$

The marginal revenue product of labor will equal the unit cost of labor when the optimum amount of labor input is employed. It follows from Equation (1), as we saw in the preceding chapter, that

(2) $$P = W/MP_L$$

At the firm's profit maximization point the price available in the market must equal the unit factor cost, here the money wage rate, multiplied by

Figure   17-1.

The competitive firm's supply curve

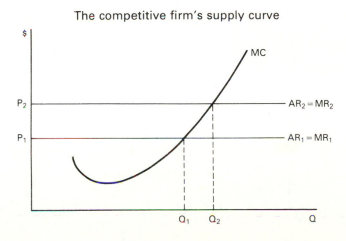

a markup factor equal to the reciprocal of the marginal product of labor. The amount of employment the firm offers to workers at any specified output price and exogenously given wage rate will depend on the productivity of labor, specifically its marginal productivity, in the firm.

We can imagine that in order to produce an output volume of Q_1 the firm would have to employ an amount of labor equal to N_1. Similarly a labor force of N_2 would be necessary to produce the output Q_2. The total revenue from the sale of output Q_1 will be given by the product P_1Q_1, and the revenue from the sale of Q_2 will be P_2Q_2. It follows that the firm can relate the revenue necessary from each production volume (necessary in the sense that it would just make the production of that volume economically worthwhile) to the amount of labor it would have to employ to produce that volume. Such a relation is depicted in Figure 17-2. The resulting curve ZZ in the figure then defines the firm's expected proceeds function. It defines the total proceeds that the firm must be able to expect to receive from the sale of the output produced by a designated number of workers, in order to make the employment of those workers worthwhile in the sense that the firm's profits are maximized.

The firm's expected proceeds, therefore, underlie its supply function and the amount of employment it can offer at different possible price levels. Along the supply function that we shall define as $Z(N)$ in what follows, the firm's maximization conditions are satisfied. We can say, moreover, that each point on the supply curve has implicit in it a definite and calculable price level. We shall see in what follows that it has implicit in it also a definable distribution of income, or distribution of the firm's net value added. Let us approach this latter question in the following way.

Figure   17-2.

The firm's expected proceeds function

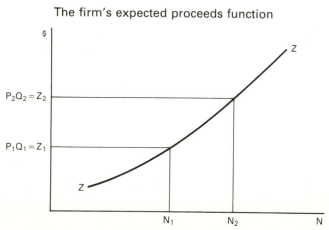

THE DISTRIBUTION OF THE FIRM'S
NET VALUE ADDED

A number of interesting questions turn on the different possible shapes of the firm's ZZ curve, or its expected proceeds function. Consider for this purpose the relationships shown in Figure 17-3.

The ray OW_1 in Figure 17-3 defines the wage bill that would be incurred by the firm as the amount of labor employed increased if the wage rate were given and fixed at W_1. This wage bill curve is obviously linear on the assumption that the wage rate does not change as the amount of labor employed increases. The question now arises as to whether the expected proceeds function as defined above would also be linear, as in OZ_1, or nonlinear convex, as in OZ_2. The answer will depend, we shall see, on the production possibilities within the firm and on the incidence of diminishing marginal productivity. To perceive the issues involved, let us take Equation (2) and put it in the form

$$(3) \qquad \frac{W}{P} = MP_L$$

This is saying that the real wage (the money wage rate divided by the price level) is equal to the marginal product of labor at the firm's optimum production point and employment level. If we now multiply both sides of Equation (3) by N/Q, we obtain

$$(4) \qquad \frac{WN}{PQ} = \frac{MP_L \cdot N}{Q}$$

Recognizing that N/Q is simply the reciprocal of the average product of

Figure   17-3.

Expected proceeds functions

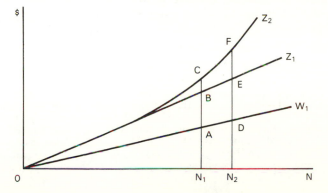

labor, and writing the marginal product of labor as M, the right-hand side of Equation (4) can be reduced to M/A, or the ratio of the marginal to the average product.

The left-hand side of Equation (4) is recognizable as the ratio of the firm's wage bill (the product of the wage rate and the amount of employment) to the total sales proceeds (or selling price times output). We have in Equation (4), therefore, the proposition that when the firm is producing at the optimum output level, or employing the optimum amount of labor, the wage share of the total proceeds will equal the ratio of the marginal and average products of labor.

The significance of this can be seen by reference again to Figure 17-3. At employment level N_1, for example (and therefore at the output and price levels implicit in that employment level), the ratio of the wage bill to the total proceeds may, under certain conditions, be described by N_1A/N_1B. At this employment level N_1A describes the wage bill at the given wage rate, and the distance AB describes the residual profit share, or the share of the fixed factors that we here subsume under the designation of capital, of the total proceeds. At the higher employment level of N_2, the corresponding share-of-proceeds ratio is given by N_2D/N_2E.

We have seen that given the money wage rate, the wage bill curve OW_1 will be linear. If, then, the wage share in total proceeds is to be constant as the amount of labor employed increases, or if N_1A/N_1B is to equal N_2D/N_2E, the total proceeds function must also be linear. But we have seen from Equation (4) that this share-of-proceeds ratio is precisely defined by the ratio of the marginal to the average product of labor. It follows, then, that for the wage share to be constant, or, that is, for the total proceeds function also to be linear, the ratio of the marginal to the average product must be constant.

If, however, the ratio of the marginal to the average product remains constant as the level of employment increases, this implies that the relative importance of diminishing marginal returns remains constant as the quantity of labor employed relative to the stock of capital increases (recall that we here assume a short period analysis in which the stock of capital is given).[10] If, on the other hand, the ratio of marginal to average product were to rise as employment increased, this would imply an increasing wage share and the OZ curve in Figure 17-3 would then turn downward, or be nonlinear concave (not shown in the figure). But such

[10] The interested reader can show that some industrial production functions may, in fact, exhibit this property. Assume, for example, a Cobb-Douglas production function where $y = N^\alpha K^{1-\alpha}$, where y, N, and K refer to output and labor and capital input, respectively. The ratio of the marginal product, $\alpha N^{\alpha-1}K^{1-\alpha}$, to the average product of labor, $N^{\alpha-1}K^{1-\alpha}$, is constant at α, even though the marginal product is continuously diminishing, as can be shown by the negativity of the second partial derivative of the production function, d^2y/dN^2, given $0 < \alpha < 1$.

a case can be dismissed because it would imply that in spite of the assumption of diminishing marginal productivity and its implication of increasing marginal cost, smaller increments of total revenue would suffice to induce entrepreneurs to employ additional increments of labor. This would mean that as the MP_L continued to fall in Equation (1), given the wage rate, W, it would not in fact be necessary to offset this by higher selling prices, P. To argue this, however, is to contradict the established conditions of profit-maximizing output and employment under conditions of diminishing marginal productivity.

If, however, diminishing marginal returns were to become relatively more important as employment increased, or, that is to say, the ratio of the marginal to the average product of labor were to diminish, then, by reference again to Equation (4) and Figure 17-3, the wage share in output would decrease. The profit share would therefore increase, and this would imply that the total proceeds function would be nonlinear convex. In that case the total proceeds function would be as shown in OZ_2. The wage share of the total proceeds will then be N_2D/N_2F at employment level N_2, instead of the larger wage share depicted by the linear proceeds curve OZ_1.

The behavior of the ratio of marginal to average product, and therefore of the wage share of total proceeds, depends on the productivity characteristics within the firm. Thus the supply function also has implicit in every point on it a determinable income distribution as well as a calculable price level.

It may be the case in actual cyclical fluctuations, of course, that the wage share in total output will increase as employment increases, and the profit share will diminish. This would appear to contradict the proposition regarding the wage income and profit shares that we have just seen to be implicit in the convex expected proceeds function in Figure 17-3. But the reasons for such possible changes in income shares in actual cyclical fluctuations may have to do, first, with changes in the firm's markup factor, based conceivably on changing perceptions of the degree of market power it possessed, as we suggested in Chapter 16 may be the case. Second, such changes in income distribution may follow also from variations in money wage rates which, in the present analysis, we have assumed to be given and fixed.

RELAXING SOME INITIAL ASSUMPTIONS

The preceding argument has concentrated on the basic relations involved in the total proceeds function of a perfectly competitive firm. Firms in general, however, produce and sell in imperfectly competitive markets, even though they may be purchasing their variable factor inputs, in the present case labor, in markets where the input price has been exogenously determined. We know, moreover, from the discussion at the beginning of the preceding chapter, that for an imperfectly competitive firm the market-selling price of its output will not be describable simply as the unit wage cost times a markup factor defined as the reciprocal of the marginal product of labor. In the imperfect competition case the markup factor incorporates the elasticity of demand for the firm's output. The details can be inspected in Chapter 16.

More important, it will be recalled from studies in microeconomics that a supply curve (see Figure 17-1) is logically definable only for a perfectly competitive firm. Given that a supply curve describes the price at which a firm will be prepared to supply different amounts of output, that price is uniquely defined in the case of the perfectly competitive firm by the going market price (equal to the firm's marginal revenue). At that price, of course, the firm's elasticity of demand is infinite. For an imperfect competitor, however, it is impossible to relate each possible level of output in this way to a uniquely defined price level. For the price level appropriate for each different output volume will depend on the elasticity of demand at that level of production and sales. These relations were explored in the preceding chapter.

It would be possible, in familiar ways, to aggregate the supply curves of perfectly competitive firms to derive the supply curve of the competitive industry. But again there can logically be no such industry counterpart under conditions of imperfect competition. Simply put, the supply curve of an imperfectly competitive industry is undefined. Everything depends on the degrees of price-elasticity of demand enjoyed by the different constituent firms in the so-called industry.

Aggregation to an economywide basis would be possible, therefore, only if all firms were perfect competitors, and if certain other conditions which need not detain us at this point were satisfied. As we proceed, then, to the concept of an aggregate total proceeds function, we must rely, not on the notion of aggregation over all producing firms in the economy, but on a proposition we brought into prominence at the heart of the preceding argument. That states that the form of the total proceeds function will depend on what is happening, by and large over the entire economy, to the ratio of the marginal and the average product of labor. The analogous aggregate or economywide relationship can now be considered against this perspective.

THE AGGREGATE SUPPLY CURVE

From this point on, we can conceive of the aggregate economy's expected proceeds function and define this as our aggregate supply function. Such a function is described by the expected proceeds curve in Figure 17-4. It

Figure   17-4.

Aggregate supply curve, or expected proceeds function

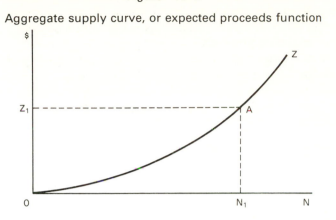

is drawn nonlinear convex on the assumption that in the economy as a whole, the relative importance of diminishing marginal productivity is likely to increase as the amount of labor employed increases. Here again we assume that as we are dealing with a short-run analysis, the increasing amounts of labor are being put to work with a given and fixed amount of capital equipment. The labor-to-capital ratio, or the labor intensity of production processes, is increasing in the short run as employment increases. This, it is supposed, tends to increase the relative importance of diminishing returns in the economy. It would be difficult to assume as an empirical matter that all producing firms enjoyed a constant marginal-to-average-product ratio as employment increased.

This, then, is the aggregate supply curve for which we have been searching. It is a nonlinear convex curve in the expected proceeds–labor input space. It defines the total proceeds from the sale of output that must be expected in the economy in order to make the employment of specified amounts of labor economically worthwhile. This aggregate supply curve will be brought into juxtaposition with aggregate demand relationships at subsequent points of our analysis. It will be useful at this stage to comment briefly on some of the more important properties or implications of it.

PROPERTIES OF THE AGGREGATE SUPPLY CURVE

Every point on the aggregate supply curve has embedded in it, as we have seen from the preceding analysis, a specific price level. This follows from the general propositions we have made regarding the productivity of labor at the employment level relevant to the given point on the supply curve, and the generalized wage-cost markup factor. Thus a direct relation exists between (1) the employment level specified, (2) the level of real output consistent with that employment level, (3) the expected or required selling price, given the generalized formula $P = kW/A$, and (4) the total expected or required proceeds.

Given the expected selling price, we can multiply by the relevant output volume to obtain the total expected proceeds:

(5) $$PQ = (kW/A)Q$$

Substituting $Q = NA$, or the employment level times the average product of labor, it follows that

(6) $$PQ = (kW/A)NA = kWN = Z$$

In other words again, the total expected proceeds are a multiple, k, of the total wage bill, WN.

The supply curve in Figure 17-4, or the total expected proceeds function, is based on the assumption of a given money wage, and if the wage rate were assumed to change it would be necessary to redraw the aggregate supply curve to account for that change.

If the money wage rate is assumed to be given, however, then by reason of the wage-cost markup definition of price formation that we have just recalled, the price level is also specifiable. We have seen that the trend value of the wage-cost markup factor is remarkably steady, though we acknowledged reasons why it may vary over different phases of the business cycle and in the short run. We can recognize also that if, during the prosperity phase of the business cycle the market power of producers increases, they may endeavor to increase their profit margins and thereby increase the markup factor. That would, in turn, tend to increase the convexity of the aggregate supply function, as firms increased the total proceeds they required for any specified level of employment.

This important notion that every point on the aggregate supply curve has associated with it, or implicit in it, a specific price level can be considered in a different and more direct manner. The argument is summarized in Figure 17-5, where it is observed, first, that any point on the supply curve will have associated with it a specifiable level of employment. Point A in Figure 17-5, indicating total expected proceeds of OZ_1, is referable to employment level ON_1. This employment level of ON_1 will in turn have associated with it a calculable level of total real output, which is specifiable by reference to the short-run production possibilities for the economy. Any designated total level of employment will therefore have associated with it an observable level of total real output. Let us refer to the level of real output associated with employment level ON_1

Figure   17-5.

The aggregate supply curve and the implicit price level

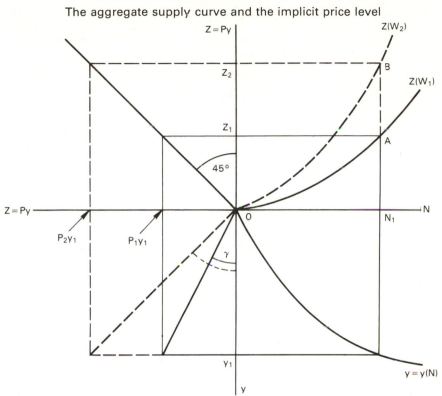

as y_1. It follows that an implied association exists between expected proceeds OZ_1 and real output y_1.

Suppose now that point A on the supply curve is observed to be an operative point, or that, in other words, the economy is actually observed to be at that employment and proceeds level. We shall see in the following chapters that this is tantamount to saying that point A is an observed point of actual "effective demand." Then the expected proceeds of Z_1 will also measure the actual total monetary demand for goods and services. In other terms, this will be also an alternative expression for the nominal national income, or, to express the relation in the same manner as in Chapter 16, at all such points $Z = Py$. The expected proceeds will be equal to the real output times the average price level at which that output is sold in the markets of the economy. In alternative language that we have also employed previously, the price level implicit in this relation, P, will be a measure of the implicit gross national product deflator. It follows immediately, then, that if the value of Z referable to the effective demand point is divided by the level of real output associated with that point, the result will provide an indication of the implicit price level. In other words, $P = Z/y$, or $P = Py/y$.

We can consider this implicit price level further with the aid of Figure 17-5, into which we have incorporated also the implications of changes, an increase for example, in the money wage rate.

INCREASES IN THE MONEY WAGE RATE

Consider first the heavy curves in Figure 17-5. If point A on the aggregate supply curve in Figure 17-5 is an effective demand point, it will have associated with it an employment level of ON_1 and a total proceeds, or nominal national income, of OZ_1. In the fourth, or southeast, quadrant of the figure the short-run production possibility relation for the economy describes the real output level, y_1, associated with the operative employment level of N_1. In the second, or northwest, quadrant a 45-degree line construction transfers the proceeds level of Z_1 to the horizontal axis. We then have the nominal national income (or Z) measured westward on the horizontal axis, and the real output, y_1, measured southward on the vertical axis. To determine the implicit price level it is necessary to divide the nominal national income by the real output. To accomplish this we complete the rectangle in the southwest quadrant subtended from these proceeds and real output points. We then inscribe the diagonal of that rectangle, making an angle at the origin described in the figure as γ.

We wish to observe now the value of Z_1/y_1, or in other terms, P_1y_1/y_1, to determine the implicit value of the price level P_1. This is given by the trigonometrical tangent of the angle γ.

Let us consider now the significance of an increase in the money wage rate. We establish first that such a wage rate increase will cause the aggregate supply function to turn to the left and assume, possibly, the position designated in Figure 17-5 as $OZ(W_2)$. The assumption is that wage rate W_2 is greater than wage rate W_1. Reflection on the preceding analysis will confirm that a rise in the money wage rate will raise the producing firms' marginal cost curves, and that this, in turn, will raise producers' supply curves in general. On an economywide basis this will cause producers to require a larger total proceeds for any specified level of employment. This, in other words, implies that the total expected proceeds function, or in our present terms the aggregate supply curve, will turn to the left in the manner indicated in the figure.

As we are not yet in possession of the method of determining the effective demand point on the new supply curve, we shall merely suppose for sake of argument that point B indicates such a point. If we now proceed through the same construction as previously, we can arrive at a new rectangle in the southwest quadrant of Figure 17-5, subtended from the y_1

output point and the new higher-proceeds point. We shall refer to the latter as Z_2, which will alternatively be described as P_2y_1. As before, the diagonal of the subtended rectangle will describe an angle at the origin of the figure. This will in the present case be higher than previously. It implies that the rise in the money wage rate will tend to cause an increase in the implicit price level in the economy. We shall incorporate analysis of this kind into the model of the macroeconomy in Chapter 19, after we have also considered the effect of an increase in the money wage rate on demand conditions and the aggregate demand curve.

THE QUESTION OF INCOME DISTRIBUTION

In our development of the aggregate supply curve it was observed that every employment level will have associated with it a definable distribution of the total expected proceeds. The argument has been adequately explored in earlier sections of this chapter, and it was seen that this very distribution of proceeds contributed to determining the form or shape of the aggregate supply curve itself.

This fact will be highly relevant again when the importance of that distribution of income, or of the net value added by producers, is considered in connection with the demand side of the model. To summarize at this stage, we observe that every point on the supply curve thus has associated with it both (1) an implicit price level and (2) an implicit distribution of the national income.

THE NEOCLASSICAL AGGREGATE SUPPLY CURVE

Our construction of the aggregate supply curve has highlighted a specific direction of causation in the determination of employment, output, and the price level. We refer again to Figure 17-5. From an effective demand point on the supply curve, we observe the effective level of employment associated with it. This, in turn, implies the level of real output at which the economy is operating. The relation between this real output and the level of monetary demand, or $Z = Py$, describes the price level, which is determined by the underlying productivity relations in the system.

Neoclassical economics, however, particularly as expressed in the neoclassical–Keynesian synthesis, sees things somewhat differently. A summary of the relationships on which it is based will highlight the distinctives of the postclassical analysis and will anticipate the fuller description of neoclassical equilibrium that we shall give in Part VI.

Again we observe a crucial difference of viewpoint with regard to the understanding of the market for labor. Throughout our analysis the money wage rate has been regarded as exogenously determined. It is imported into the analysis of the market system in such a way that other endogenous variables are determined by means of reaction or accommodation to it. For the neoclassical system, on the other hand, the wage rate is endogenous. For this purpose a demand-for-labor curve and a supply-of-labor curve are incorporated into the analysis. They can be summarized as follows.

The demand for labor is understood to be a derived demand described by the marginal product curve of the labor input. We recall the basic optimization condition for the firm, as reproduced in Equation (3):

(3) $$\frac{W}{P} = MP_L$$

This states that the firm will employ the optimum amount of labor when the real wage, shown on the left-hand side of Equation (3), is equal to the marginal product of labor. The implied demand curve for labor is shown as the downward-sloping N^d curve in Figure 17-6. Diminishing marginal productivity of labor implies that a lower real wage will be necessary to induce a larger employment of labor.

The supply of labor is understood in the neoclassical scheme to be determined by utility optimization decisions on the part of the suppliers of labor. Workers are assumed to decide on the amount of effort they will supply at various money wage rates by comparing the marginal utility of the money wage with that of the leisure they would sacrifice by working an extra hour. A so-called supply-of-effort curve can be derived showing, it is supposed, the supply of labor as a function once again of the real

Figure   17-6.

The neoclassical labor market

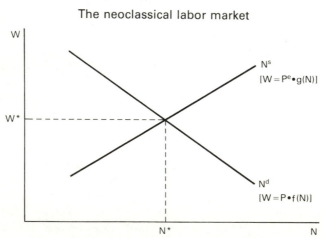

wage. Such a relationship implies the supply-of-labor curve shown in Figure 17-6 as N^s.

In the neoclassical analysis, however, there is a difference between the real wage to which the demanders of labor respond and that to which the suppliers of labor respond. The point is of considerable importance to the development of the neoclassical aggregate supply curve.

The demanders of labor respond to the real wage rate as determined by the actual price level that is currently observed. Making use of Equation (3) the labor demand function can be written as

$$(7) \qquad\qquad N^d = N^d(W/P)$$

where P is the current price level. The suppliers of labor, on the other hand, respond to the real wage as determined by what they expect will be the price level during the period for which they have contracted to supply labor. We may refer to that price level as P^e, where the superscript indicates an expected price level. The supply-of-labor function can then be written as

$$(8) \qquad\qquad N^s = N^s(W/P^e)$$

These demand and supply functions are translated into functions of the money wage rate in Figure 17-6. We refer now to Equation (3) and write the marginal product of labor on the right-hand side as $f(N)$, showing its dependence on the amount of labor employed. It follows that from the point of view of the demand for labor the relation can be written:

$$(7a) \qquad\qquad W/P = f(N)$$

Equivalently, this implies that the demand for labor can be written as a function of the money wage rate, and that by the transposition of Equation (3) the labor demand function can be written as

$$(9) \qquad\qquad W = P \cdot f(N)$$

Similarly, the supply of labor can be written as

$$(10) \qquad\qquad W = P^e \cdot g(N)$$

This follows from the fact that the real wage on which the supply of labor depends is, as the suppliers of labor see it, described by W/P^e, or the money wage rate divided by the expected price level. Expressing the willingness of labor to supply effort as dependent on this expected real wage, or $W/P^e = g(N)$, the effective supply-of-labor function in Equation

(10) follows by transposition. The equilibrium amount of labor employed, together with the endogenously determined money wage rate, is then described by the intersection of these supply and demand curves as shown in Figure 17-6.

At this stage of the neoclassical argument everything depends on the way in which the suppliers of labor react, in forming their price expectations, to changes in the existing price level. If P^e (the relevant price variable as seen by the suppliers of labor) always equaled P (the current price level as seen by the demanders of labor), price expectations would always be changing proportionally with changes in current prices. In rather more technical language we could say that the elasticity of price expectations was in that case unity. If, at the other extreme, the expected price level did not change when current prices changed, we could say that the elasticity of price expectations was zero. In such a case another important term could be used to describe the behavior and reaction of the suppliers of labor. They could be said to exhibit complete money illusion. This important notion of money illusion, which will occur again at later points of our analysis, can be defined as follows.

Decision makers in the economy are said to exhibit money illusion when their demands for real commodities or services, or their supplies of real valued goods or services (in our present case the supply of effort), are dependent only on the level of nominal or monetary variables. Complete money illusion will exist on the supply side of the labor market if the supply curve depends only on the nominal or money wage rate. If, to take an intermediate case, there is some money illusion on the supply side of the labor market but not complete money illusion, then a change in the existing price level would cause some, but not a completely proportional, change in the expected price level. These relations and their implications are illustrated in Figure 17-7.

In Figure 17-7 it is supposed that the current price level increases from P_0 to P_1. The microeconomic foundations behind the labor demand curve imply that such an increase in the price level will shift the demand-for-labor curve to the right, as shown by N_1^d in the figure. Similarly, an increase in the expected price level, P^e, representing as it does a prospective reduction in the real wage for any given money wage level, will shift the supply-of-labor curve to the left. This is shown in the figure as N_1^s. We might add that for the case of complete money illusion, the labor supply curve would not move in this fashion at all. It would remain in the position described by N_0^s. For the opposite extreme, where price expectations adjust fully to changes in current prices, the labor supply curve would move to the left by the same degree as the labor demand curve moves to the right. It would then follow that the intersection of the new curves, N_1^d and N_1^s, would be vertically above the intersection of the pre-

Figure   17-7.

The neoclassical labor market

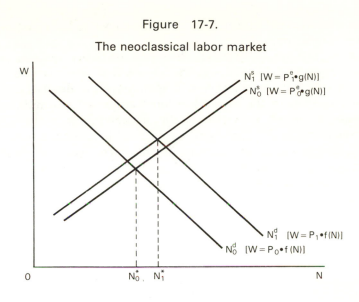

vious curves. In that case there would be no change in the equilibrium amount of labor supplied.

Alternatively, we may envisage that following an increase in the price level from P_0 to P_1, the wage rate could remain temporarily fixed because of previously established wage contracts that will not expire, and thereby permit a change in wage rates, until some date in the future. In that case the supply-of-labor curve becomes temporarily horizontal at the previously established equilibrium wage in Figure 17-7. A larger increase in employment and output may then be temporarily realized before the suppliers of labor adjust their price expectations and new wage contracts are established.

In Figure 17-7, however, we have described the intermediate case, or the so-called general case, of the neoclassical–Keynesian synthesis. An increase in the price level is understood to cause some increase in the amount of labor supplied. It does this because the expected price level, P^e, does not rise as much as the actual current price level, P, and the suppliers of labor are said to exhibit some degree of money illusion. They do not move their supply curve to the left as far as the demand curve has moved to the right. We can conclude that the extent of the increase in the labor supply in response to an increase in the current price level will depend on the reactions of this kind made by the suppliers of labor. This is the important conclusion of the theory we are now considering. Its linkage with the concept of the aggregate supply curve can now be observed.

The aggregate supply curve in the neoclassical view describes a relation between a postulated price level on the one hand and the level of real national output on the other. Such a curve is described in Figure 17-8.

This aggregate supply curve, shown as positively inclined in the $P-y$ space in Figure 17-8, follows from the fact that the increase in prices causes an increase in the amount of labor employed, as described in Figure 17-7. This increase in the amount of labor employed will make possible an increase in output, by virtue of the assumed form of the aggregate production possibilities. The chain of relationships is summarized in Figure 17-9. Here the assumed increase in the price level of P_0 to P_1 raises the level of employment from N_0 to N_1. This, in turn, raises the level of output, as shown in the lower section of the figure, from y_0 to y_1. It is then this increase in the output level in response to the increase in the price level that enables us to posit the positively inclined aggregate supply curve in Figure 17-8.

It follows that a given increase in the price level will induce a greater increase in employment and output, and thereby reduce the slope or increase the elasticity of the aggregate supply curve, the less rapidly the suppliers of labor adjust their price expectations. Complete, immediate, and proportional adjustments will prevent any change in employment and output and will imply a vertical aggregate supply curve. A complete absence of adjustment, or complete money illusion, will produce a supply curve such as that shown in Figure 17-8. Temporary money wage rigidity will imply an even shallower supply curve and a temporarily higher elasticity of supply.

In Part VI, where a fuller exposition will be given of the neoclassical–Keynesian synthesis, it will be possible to introduce also the neoclassical aggregate demand function. This, as might be anticipated, will be a downward-sloping curve in the same $P-y$ space as shown in Figure 17-8. In the neoclassical analysis, the intersection of such aggregate sup-

Figure   17-8.

The neoclassical aggregate supply curve

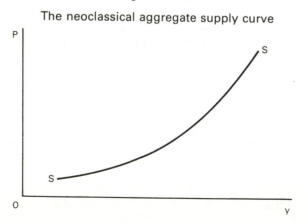

Figure   17-9.

Neoclassical price and output variations

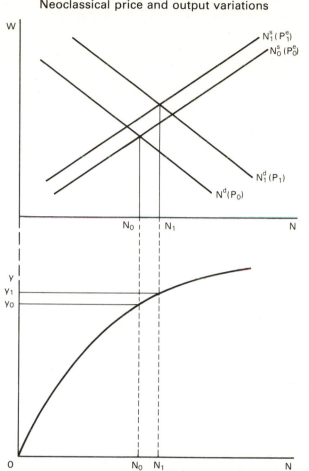

ply and demand curves determines the equilibrium output and price level in the economy.

The analysis need not be taken further at this time, however. The foregoing summary suffices to highlight the very different way of looking at things that leads to what we have called a postclassical analysis. We have seen that different directions of causation are envisaged. Different views of the supply and demand forces in the labor market are involved. A different significance attaches to the money wage rate. In summary, a very different conception of the aggregate supply curve is implied. The neoclassical aggregate supply curve describes a relation between P and y, as shown in Figure 17-8. The postclassical aggregate supply curve, on the other hand, describes a relation between total expected proceeds and the level of employment, as shown in Figure 17-4. It follows, by way of anticipation, that the aggregate demand curves in the respective analyses are similarly differentiated. We have hinted at that in our preceding comments on the postclassical concept of effective demand. We shall return to the important questions that arise on the demand side of the model in the next chapter.

SUMMARY

In the development of the postclassical aggregate supply curve, this chapter has emphasized a number of postclassical distinctives. The analysis was differentiated from that of the neoclassical theory or the neoclassical–Keynesian synthesis. The differences in the fundamental concept of the aggregate supply curve were established. The present analysis was shown to be essentially a short-run analysis, and the interdependence between aggregate supply and demand was emphasized. This follows from the fact that wage incomes are an important element of costs on the production side, and the most important source of consumption expenditures on the demand side.

A summary was given of the microeconomic foundations of the aggregate supply curve. The form of the aggregate supply curve was seen to depend on the characteristics of diminishing marginal productivity in the economy in the short run. It was related also to the significance that this phenomenon has for the distribution of income. This distribution was reflected in the division of the proceeds of the sale of output between the wage bill on the one hand and the residual profit on the other.

From the properties of the aggregate supply curve the level of employment and the implied level of real output were exhibited. It was argued that every point on the supply curve had implicit in it both (1) a calculable price level and (2) a calculable distribution of income. The properties of the supply curve incorporated the notion that the money wage rate in the economy is an exogenous variable.

An examination was made of the neoclassical supply curve, and the importance of possible degrees of money illusion on the supply side of the labor market was discussed.

IMPORTANT CONCEPTS

Aggregate supply curve   *Microfoundations of aggregate supply*
Expected proceeds function   *Wage and profit shares*
Dual function of wage incomes   *Implicit price level*
State of expectations   *Elasticity of price expectations*
Exogenous money wage rate   *Money illusion*

QUESTIONS FOR DISCUSSION AND REVIEW

1. Do you consider Keynes' *General Theory* to be the economics of depression? Why? Explain as fully as possible.

2. "The concept of *aggregate supply* is congenial to the classical system of thought, but the modern concept described by the same term envisages a very different structure of causation." Evaluate critically.

3. How do you consider the existence of money relevant to the refutation of the following propositions: "Supply creates its own demand" and "Demand creates its own supply"? Discuss as fully as possible.

4. "The microfoundations of the aggregate supply function depend on commodity market conditions and the elasticities of market demands." Comment critically.

5. Explain the connections between the determinants of the form of the aggregate supply function and the distribution of income.

6. From a postclassical perspective, how would you explain the implications of an increase in money wage rates for the levels of output and employment?

7. How is money illusion relevant to the neoclassical aggregate supply function?

8. Evaluate the proposition that the crucial difference between the neoclassical and the postclassical macroeconomic systems depends on contrasting views of the market for labor.

9. "An increase in money wage rates will lead to an increase in employment in both the neoclassical and postclassical analyses, but the lines of causation are very different." Is this statement correct? Could a wage increase lead to a reduction of employment in the postclassical system of thought? Why?

10. What is "effective demand"? How is it relevant to the equilibrium level of employment?

18

MONEY EXPENDITURE FLOWS

STUDY OBJECTIVES:

• To trace the consumption and investment expenditure flows and the government demand for goods and services, and to develop the aggregate demand curve in a monetary economy

• To observe the foundations of money expenditure flows in real demands for goods and services

• To note briefly some microfoundations of consumption and investment expenditures

• To understand the simple real income multiplier, and its adjustment for a proportional tax rate

• To obtain a clear grasp of the significance for consumption expenditures of the distribution of income and the propensities to consume out of wage and profit incomes

• To note the relevance to consumption expenditures of other determinants— for example, wealth, the rate of interest, price levels and price expectations, the population size and its age distribution, and the availability of consumer credit

• To anticipate the relation between the aggregate supply curve and the aggregate demand curve in determining trends in real national output and employment

The model of the macroeconomy we are constructing is based, in both its demand and supply side aspects, on the significance of monetary expenditure flows. In the preceding chapter we examined the relation between money flows on the cost or input side and the level of real output and employment. Similarly, we focus in this chapter on money flows on the demand side of the model. We shall examine the determinants of consumption and investment expenditure flows and the manner in which they generate an aggregate demand curve. In the following chapter this aggregate demand curve will be brought into relation with the aggregate supply curve to exhibit the determinants of real output, employment, and the price level in the economy.

Our focus on money expenditure flows will take account of the simultaneous determination of the general commodity price level. We have seen in the preceding two chapters that the aggregate supply curve has an implicit price level (along with an implicit income distribution) embedded in every point on it. It is desirable, therefore, to incorporate these significant characteristics directly into the scheme of things. We can do this by focusing attention on the ways in which the expenditure flows in the economy, such as consumption, investment, and government expenditures, react to changes in price levels as well as to changes in real income or output and the distribution of income.

In addition, it will still be necessary to show that the money expenditure flows are embedded in underlying real economic relations. Our work will therefore begin with the real consumption and investment functions. It will be useful to clarify at the beginning the way in which some traditional microeconomic foundations underlie the argument. We take the consumption expenditures and the traditional consumption function first.

SOME MICROECONOMIC FOUNDATIONS

An individual's demand for a commodity can be assumed to depend principally on (1) the price of that commodity; (2) the level of his income, or the so-called expenditure budget against which he is making his consumption decisions; and (3) the prices of all other commodities that may be substitutes for, or complements with, the commodity whose demand is being examined. This assumes that the structure of the individual's tastes and commodity preferences, along with other relevant socioeconomic factors, such as his intertemporal preferences and savings desires, his sociocultural status, and his price and income expectations, are taken as given. In that case an individual's demand for a commodity can be described as

(1) $$Q_i = Q_i(P_i, \ldots, P_n, Y) \qquad (i = 1, \ldots, n)$$

This states that the demand for the ith commodity depends on the price of that commodity, the prices of all other commodities in the n-item commodity set, and money income. The division of the expenditure

budget, here taken as Y for convenience of exposition, can be depicted in
the usual manner in Figure 18-1.

Here we are envisaging the division of an income Y (taken as equal
to the expenditure budget, thus abstracting for the moment from the
decision to save) between commodities x and y. The linear curve AB in
Figure 18-1 describes the budget constraint. It is, in more technical language, the boundary of the consumption opportunity set. The individual
can consume any commodity combination in the interior of that opportunity set, or in the triangle OAB. But the choice of a commodity combination interior to the set would not exhaust the expenditure budget.
The budget will actually be exhausted by those commodity combinations
that lie on the boundary AB. If all of the budget were allocated to commodity x the maximum amount that could be purchased would be OB,
given by dividing the income by the price of x, that is, Y/P_x. Similarly,
the maximum amount of commodity y that could be purchased would be
Y/P_y. As the prices of x and y are assumed to be given for the argument
in hand, any point on AB, which would indicate the extent to which x
had been substituted for y, would also exactly exhaust the budget.

Given the individual's tastes and preferences, as described by the
traditional indifference curves in the figure, the optimum budget allocation will be the one that provides a commodity combination lying on
both the expenditures constraint and the highest attainable indifference
curve. This is shown as point M in the figure. At that point the subjectively
acceptable marginal rate of substitution between x and y (described by
the slope of the indifference curve) equals the objectively attainable marginal rate of transformation between x and y (described by the slope of
the budget constraint or the expenditure opportunity line). If the price

Figure   18-1.

Consumer's optimum budget allocation

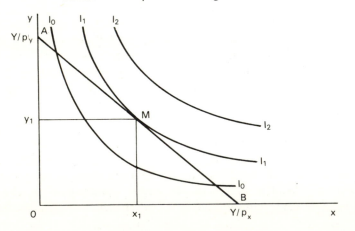

ratio were different, the slope of the budget line would be different. And if the individual's income were higher, the budget line would lie farther from the origin but (for a given price ratio) would be parallel to AB. The details can be inspected in any microeconomics text.

Imagine, however, that while the commodity price ratio remained as given, all prices and the individual's income were to double. A moment's reflection will confirm that the budget constraint line would remain exactly where it is in Figure 18-1. It would continue to be described by AB. There is no reason, therefore, why there should be any change in the individual's budget allocation. He would continue to consume the same relative combination of commodities x and y as before. There is an important, if somewhat technical, way of stating this conclusion. The individual's demand for commodities is said to be homogeneous of degree zero in prices and income.

A demand function is said to be homogeneous of degree zero if an equiproportional increase in all the variables in it (in our present case income and prices) does not cause any change in the quantity of the commodity demanded.

The significance of this lies in the analogy it projects onto the aggregate or macroeconomic scale of things. Let us conceive of the total volume of consumers' demand for commodities in general. We can make the following intuitive statements. If all demand functions for all commodities are homogeneous of degree zero in the manner we have indicated, then there is reason to believe that the aggregate demands for commodities in general will be homogenous of degree zero in the price level and income. Proportional changes in prices and money incomes will leave the actual volume of commodity demand unchanged, assuming that such price and income changes are not accompanied by a change in the distribution of income.

This argument implies that real commodity demand depends essentially on the level of real income. Taking Q to refer to a measure of aggregate real demand for commodities, and Y and P to describe total money income and the price level, respectively, we can say that the consumption demand relation is described by

$$(2) \qquad\qquad\qquad Q = f(Y/P)$$

We may work, therefore, with what we can refer to as a real consumption expenditure function of this general form.

In what follows we shall employ the capital letter C to refer to total money expenditure on consumption, and the lower-case c to refer to real consumption. Similarly, in the same way as in previous chapters, we shall refer to real income, or Y/P, by the lower-case y. The real consumption function can then be written as

(3) $c = f(y)$

But our argument to this point has warned us that in actual fact more than this simple relation may be involved in determining real consumption expenditures. At the least it is necessary to be alert to the possible significance of changes in the distribution of incomes, and we might accordingly write our consumption function in the form

(3a) $c = f(y, \theta)$,

where the new variable θ is introduced to refer to the distribution of income. We shall make an important use of this income distribution factor in more rigorous ways below. Moreover, certain other factors that we have already mentioned, such as wealth levels (which may affect individuals' preferences) and the rate of interest, will also have to be taken into account. But we may leave our commodity demand or consumption function in the form of Equation (3) for the time being and treat this as a useful and significant initial approximation to the aggregate consumption relation.

INTERTEMPORAL CONSUMPTION CHOICE

One further aspect of the microfoundations deserves slightly fuller mention, as a means of introducing the relevance of the saving decision (at any given income level) and taking note of the possible significance of the rate of interest. The analysis is summarized in Figure 18-2.

The relations in Figure 18-2 take up the conclusions we reached in Chapter 6 regarding the time value of money. They are central to the saving and consumption decision at any given level of income. Given the intertemporal nature of the analysis, we measure on the horizontal axis present dated incomes and consumption demands, Y_0 and C_0, and on the vertical axis we measure future dated values, such as those referable to one time period into the future, Y_1 and C_1.

Refer to point E in the figure. This is the so-called endowment point and indicates that an individual has reason to believe that his income in the current period, Y_0, will be OA, and his income next period, Y_1, will be OM. The analysis begins with the assumption that such an income "endowment" is specified. The allocation of that intertemporal endowment between consumption now and consumption in the next period is subject to an intertemporal income constraint. This is where the inter-

Figure   18-2.

The intertemporal consumption allocation decision

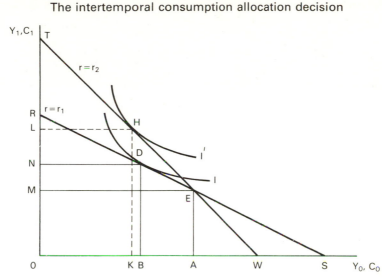

temporal valuation problem, or the intertemporal value of money, comes in.

We know from Chapter 6 that the present value of future income can be stated as $Y_1/(1 + r)$, where r refers to the rate of interest or discount factor at which the present value is being computed. Similarly, the present value of future consumption will be $C_1/(1 + r)$. The income-consumption constraint says that over the two time periods taken as a whole, the total value of consumption can be no greater than the total value of income available for expenditure. Expressing all values in present-dated terms, the constraint, when it is operative, appears in the form

(4) $$C_0 + C_1/(1 + r) = Y_0 + Y_1/(1 + r)$$

The right-hand side of this equation describes the present-dated value of the two-period income stream. If the endowment is indicated by point E in the figure and the rate of interest is assumed to be r_1, the present value of the income stream will be OS. This equals the present period's income of OA plus the present value of the next period's income OM, which, when discounted at r_1, equals AS. It can similarly be shown that any endowment described by any other point on the line RS will have the same present value of OS. This line RS is referred to as the present value line at interest rate r_1.

Take an endowment point that, while it is slightly different from point E, lies on the line RS and has the same present value. Let the endowment at that new point (not shown in the figure) be $Y_0 + \Delta Y_0$,

$Y_1 + \Delta Y_1$. The endowment at E is described as Y_0, Y_1. By assumption the difference between the present values of the respective endowments is zero. That difference is defined as

(5) $\qquad Y_0 + \Delta Y_0 + (Y_1 + \Delta Y_1)/(1 + r_1) - Y_0 - Y_1/(1 + r_1) = 0$

It follows that

(6) $\qquad\qquad\qquad \Delta Y_0 + \Delta Y_1/(1 + r_1) = 0$

Therefore

(7) $\qquad\qquad\qquad \Delta Y_1 = -\Delta Y_0(1 + r_1)$

and

(8) $\qquad\qquad\qquad \Delta Y_1/\Delta Y_0 = -(1 + r_1)$

In other words, the slope of the present value line is $-(1 + r_1)$.

The indifference curves in Figure 18-2, I and I', describe the individual's intertemporal indifference, or, alternatively, his intertemporal utility function, describing the utility he imagines he would receive from a combination of consumption amounts in the respective time periods. Without considering the intertemporal preference map more fully, we can observe that the individual will have made an optimum intertemporal allocation of his consumable income when he has so arranged his consumption pattern that he lands himself on the highest attainable indifference curve. If the interest rate is still assumed to be r_1 and the present value of his income stream is OS, consistent with the right-hand side of Equation (4), then the individual can move to his highest attainable indifference curve, I, by moving along RS to D. Everything depends now on our understanding of how this can be done.

Suppose we are at point D. In that case a two-period endowment of OA and OM in periods 1 and 2, respectively, has been transformed into a two-period consumption sequence of OB and ON. To accomplish this, or to move from E to D, the individual must sacrifice consumption in the present period of BA in order to increase consumption in the next period by MN. In other words, out of his present period endowment only OB is consumed and BA is saved. Then the BA that is saved is invested at the assumed rate of interest r_1, in order that when the next period arrives that investment will have a value of $BA(1 + r_1)$, or MN. The total consumption that can be enjoyed next period will be the next period's income, OM, plus the accumulated value of the previous period's saving, MN.

Suppose now that the rate of interest had been larger, at a level of r_2 instead of r_1. Then the slope of the present value line through the endowment point of E would have been $-(1 + r_2)$, and the present value of the same income endowment would have been OW instead of OS as previously. Following the same argument as before, the individual would now arrive on his highest attainable indifference curve at point H. He would achieve this by sacrificing consumption of KA in the present period in order to increase consumption by ML in the next period. In other words, his saving in the present would increase from BA to KA. The assumed rise in the interest rate would have led to a rise in saving, or to a decline in present consumption.

A rise in the rate of interest may not, of course, always have this kind of effect on consumption and saving out of a given level of income. The outcome would depend on the location of point H in Figure 18-2 or, in other words, on the form of the individual's indifference curves and therefore his intertemporal utility function. Individuals' intertemporal indifference relations may be such that a rise in the interest rate would decrease rather than increase saving. If individuals are saving with a specific monetary target in view, for example, then they will be able to achieve it with a lower level of present saving if the interest rate is higher. The direction of the relationship cannot be specified uniquely.

It is important at this stage to note, however, that the rate of interest does conceivably have a significant role to play in the consumption decision, and it is for that reason that its basic analytical significance has been exhibited. In fact, it enters in more ways than the simple manner we have just indicated. For it is conceivable that an individual's consumption expenditures may depend to some extent on his total wealth, as well as on his income and the price level as we have assumed so far. We can recall the conclusion in previous chapters that a person's wealth, or, in other words, the market value or the capitalized value of his income-earning assets, will be inversely related to the rate of interest. If the rate of interest declines, the market value of wealth will increase. A decline in the interest rate, therefore, tending to make asset-holding individuals feel more wealthy, may tend to increase consumption. A rise in the interest rate may have the opposite effect. In that case the rise in the interest rate would induce a lower level of consumption out of a given level of income, or increase the rate of saving.

A fuller specification of the real consumption function, expanding on the relation envisaged in Equation (3), would introduce the rate of interest as a determinant variable also, and we might write our consumption function in the form

(9) $$c = f(y, \theta, r)$$

THE REAL CONSUMPTION FUNCTION

Bearing in mind the modifications that the foregoing analysis may subsequently require us to incorporate, we return for the present to Equation
(3) and what we have called the real consumption function. For the present we set aside both the potential interest rate and the income distribution effects and concentrate on the simple relation between real income
and real consumption expenditure. This implies a simple consumption
function of the form, derived from Equation (3),

(10) $c = f(y)$

Relevant data from the United States economy over recent years
are given in Table 18-1. The data in the table are given in 1972 dollars.
This means that the gross national product for the years indicated is
stated in dollars of constant purchasing power. In order to express the

Table   18-1

Real national income (gross national product) and real consumption
expenditure for selected years (Data are in billions of 1972 dollars)

Year	Gross national product	Personal consumption expenditure	Consumption as percent of income
1950	534.8	337.3	63.1
1953	623.6	363.4	58.3
1954*	616.1	370.0	60.1*
1955	657.5	394.1	59.9
1957	683.8	413.8	60.5
1958*	680.9	418.0	61.4*
1959	721.7	440.4	61.0
1960	737.2	452.0	61.3
1965	929.3	557.5	60.0
1970	1,085.6	672.1	61.9
1973	1,254.3	767.9	61.2
1974*	1,246.3	762.8	61.2*
1975*	1,231.6	779.4	63.3*
1976	1,298.2	823.1	63.4
1977	1,369.7	864.3	63.1
1978	1,438.6	903.2	62.8
1979	1,479.4	927.6	62.7
1980*	1,474.0	930.5	63.1*
1981	1,502.6	947.6	63.1
1982*	1,475.5	957.1	64.9*

Source: *Economic Report of the President,* February 1983, p. 164.

1980 GNP in 1972 dollars, or in so-called constant dollars, it is necessary to divide the 1980 GNP in nominal dollars by the GNP deflator for 1980. By way of example, the GNP deflator for selected years is given in Table 18-2, and the real GNP is derived by dividing the deflator into the nominal GNP for the year indicated. The real GNP shown in the final column of Table 18-2 corresponds to the GNP data in the first column of Table 18-1.

The data in Table 18-1 indicate that during 1950–82 real consumption expenditure accounted for a fairly constant proportion of real GNP, at about 60 percent. The percentage has nudged upward in the last decade, as less stable economic conditions and slower growth rates have been experienced. But the data go some way to support the proposition, frequently encountered in the macroeconomic literature, that the long-run trend ratio of consumption to income in real terms is constant.

On the other hand, some short-run fluctuations in the real consumption ratio are discernible in the table. Each of the years against which an asterisk has been placed was a year in which the real GNP was lower than it had been in the preceding year. In each of those years the proportion of income consumed rose above what it had been previously. Generally, when the income level returned to its normal upward trend the consumption ratio declined again. To indicate this, the years 1953 through 1955 have been grouped in the table, as have the years 1957 through 1959. In the mid-1970s a similar decline in real GNP raised the consumption ratio. The relatively smooth growth trend the economy experienced in the 1960s was not repeated in the following decade, however, and a higher degree of instability in the data can be observed. In the 1980 and 1982 recessions also, the edging upward of the consumption ratio is apparent.

Table   18-2

Nominal and real gross national product for selected years (Data are in billions of dollars)

Year	Nominal GNP	GNP Deflator (1972 = 100)	Real GNP in 1972 dollars
1955	400.0	60.84	657.5
1960	506.5	68.70	737.2
1972	1,185.9	100.00	1,185.9
1975	1,549.2	125.79	1,231.6
1980	2,633.1	178.64	1,474.0
1981	2,937.7	195.51	1,502.6
1982	3,057.5	207.23	1,475.5

Source: *Economic Report of the President,* February 1983, pp. 163, 166.

This suggests that the real consumption relation takes on a somewhat different picture during short-run business fluctuations from what it does over the longer-run trend, and discussions on precisely these levels have occupied a large part of the relevant professional literature. Suggested forms of the short-run and the long-run consumption functions are depicted in Figure 18-3.

If the long-run ratio of real consumption to real income is constant, the long-run consumption function is described by a ray from the origin of Figure 18-3. If, when income declines temporarily, the consumption ratio rises, the short-run function may be described by the rather shallower slopes in the figure. In either case the slopes of the curves depicting both the long-run and the short-run functions will be less than unity, as not all of income is allocated to consumption expenditure. A number of ingenious theories have been developed to explain this difference between the short-run and the long-run consumption relations. They need not detain us at this time but may be inspected in the advanced literature of macroeconomics under the descriptive titles of (1) the Ando-Modigliani life cycle hypothesis, (2) the Friedman permanent income hypothesis, and (3) the Duesenberry relative income hypothesis.[1]

For our present purpose of constructing a short-run model of the macroeconomy, we shall concentrate on the short-run consumption re-

Figure   18-3.

Short-run and long-run consumption functions

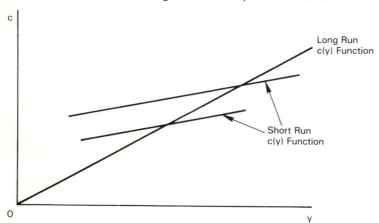

[1] See Albert Ando and Franco Modigliani, "The 'Life Cycle' Hypothesis of Saving: Aggregate Implications and Tests," *American Economic Review*, March 1963; Milton Friedman, *A Theory of the Consumption Function* (Princeton: Princeton University Press, 1957); and James S. Duesenberry, *Income, Saving, and the Theory of Consumer Behavior* (Cambridge: Harvard University Press, 1949). See also Duesenberry's "Income-Consumption Relations and Their Implications," in *Income, Employment, and Public Policy: Essays in Honor of Alvin H. Hansen* (New York: Norton, 1948).

lation. The consumption function we shall work with is shown in Figure 18-4. The consumption function, which shows the level of consumption expenditure that will be made at specified levels of income, is here assumed to be a linear function of real income. At income OA, for example, the consumption expenditure would be AB. The consumption ratio AB/OA is referred to as the average propensity to consume. As the income level rises, the average propensity to consume decreases.

If we focus on marginal changes in income and consumption we can relate the increment in income, AD for example, to the increment in consumption expenditure to which it gives rise. This is shown in the figure as FG. The ratio of incremental consumption expenditure to the increment in income that gave rise to it is referred to as the marginal propensity to consume. In the figure it is the ratio of FG to BF. The average propensity to consume, described by the trigonometrical tangent of the angle AOB, declines as income rises. But the marginal propensity to consume, described by the tangent of the angle FBG, will remain constant if the consumption function is linear. If there were reason to believe that the marginal propensity to consume out of income declined as income rose, then the consumption function would be nonlinear concave. This would imply that as income rose, the marginal propensity to save increased.

The relations between the propensity to consume and the propensity to save are shown in Figure 18-5. Leaving aside for the present the fact that a part of income will be absorbed in the payment of taxes, we can imagine a purely private sector economy in which income will be either consumed or saved. In short,

(11) $y = c + s$

where y, c, and s refer, respectively, to real income, real consumption,

Figure   18-4.

The short-run real consumption function

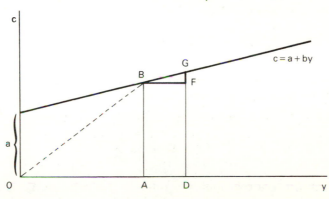

Figure   18-5.

The consumption and savings functions

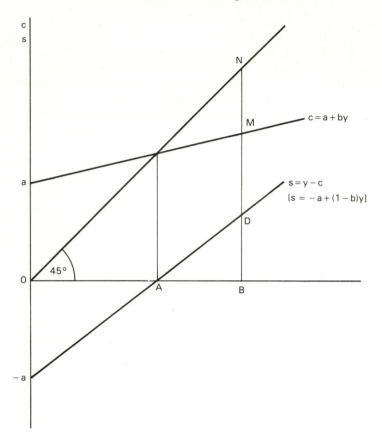

and real saving. The form of the saving function follows from the relation $s = y - c$, and in the case of the linear consumption function we are working with the saving function takes the form

(12) $$s = y - c = y - a - by = -a + (1 - b)y$$

Focusing again on incremental changes, we note that an increase in income will be allocated to either increased consumption or increased saving. We can write

(13) $$\Delta y = \Delta c + \Delta s$$

Combining these relations, we refer to the ratio $\Delta c/\Delta y$ as the marginal propensity to consume, described in Figure 18-5 as b, the slope of the consumption function. The ratio $\Delta s/\Delta y$ is referred to as the marginal propensity to save. It follows that these marginal propensities must sum to unity:

(14) $\Delta c/\Delta y + \Delta s/\Delta y = b + (1 - b) = 1$

The form of the saving function described in Equation (12) implies that when the income is zero the consumption expenditure, a, must equal the dissaving, $-a$, that is taking place in the economy. When income is equal to OA in Figure 18-5 the whole of income is being consumed, as indicated by the 45-degree guideline from the origin of the figure. In that case the level of saving is zero, and the saving function therefore crosses the horizontal axis at that point. At higher income levels saving is positive. At income OB, for example, the saving out of income can be represented in two ways in Figure 18-5. Saving is equal to the difference between income and consumption, or the distance MN. This must be equal, by derivation and construction, to the distance of BD, as read directly from the saving function.

THE TOTAL EXPENDITURE OR
TOTAL ABSORPTION FUNCTION

In a private sector economy the total level of expenditure will equal the consumption plus investment expenditures. We can refer to this total spending stream in alternative ways. We can describe it as the total level of income-generating expenditure, focusing on the notion that expenditure generates income. Or we can refer to the sum of the consumption and investment functions as the total absorption function, focusing on the idea that income-generating expenditures absorb, or put to use, economic resources. The determinants of investment expenditure and the form of the investment function were discussed in Chapter 6, as an illustration of intertemporal valuation and the time value of money. Taking as adequate for present purposes the proposition that investment expenditures depend on the rate of interest (as a proxy for the business firm's cost of money capital), we can write the real investment function as

(15) $i = i(r)$

or, in specific form,

(16) $i = \alpha - \beta r$

The investment function as defined in Equation (16) implies that the level of real investment expenditure does not depend on the level of income or on changes in that level. In actual fact, such a dependence may exist. For it may be necessary to increase investment outlays in order to expand industrial productive capacity if the level of income and output is increasing. The level of real investment may depend also on the size and age of the existing capital stock in the economy, and on the rate of technological progress that is occurring. The investment function could be expanded to take account of all of these possible factors, and also of the flow of profits that conceivably facilitate investment outlays. But for the present we concentrate on the principal determinant, the rate of interest. This implies that, for our national income analysis, we can introduce the investment expenditure function in the manner shown in Figure 18-6.

The relation shown in Figure 18-6 states that the level of investment expenditure does not depend on the level of income. The investment outlay function is therefore depicted as a horizontal line in the real income space. Investment is referred to, as far as the income-generating forces are concerned, as an exogenous or autonomous variable. In the income analysis here in view, investment expenditure is exogenous, but consumption expenditure is, as the preceding analysis has implied, endogenous.

If we now add together the amount of consumption expenditure and the amount of investment expenditure that can be expected to occur at various income levels, we can derive the total absorption function. This is depicted in Figure 18-7. The total expenditure at any income level is the vertical summation of its components, as shown in the figure.

THE EQUILIBRIUM LEVEL OF REAL INCOME

The macroeconomic literature since Keynes' *General Theory* has usually examined the so-called equilibrium level of real national income, or the level of income at which, in the short run, the economy will tend to settle

Figure   18-6.

The real investment function

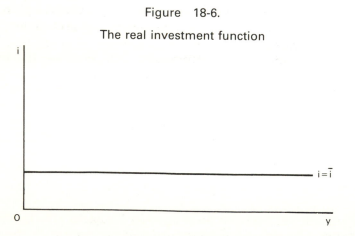

Figure   18-7.

The total expenditure function

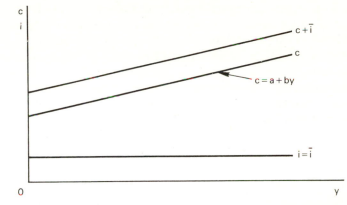

in the light of the forces that bear upon it. This will depend, assuming all other things and factors bearing on the economic situation remain unchanged, on the economy's willingness or plans to spend on consumption and investment. We can summarize the argument in the following way.

An observed level of income will be permanently maintainable only if the level of income-generating expenditure that gives rise to it is maintained. But we know from what has been said that not all of the income generated will actually be passed on directly in the form of consumption expenditure. Part of the income received will be saved. The part that is saved will not, at the moment it is saved, generate income in anybody else's hands, but it is withdrawn from the circular flow of income-generating expenditure. Alternatively, we can say that saving is a leakage from that circular flow of income-generating expenditure.

If, then, the level of the flow of income-generating expenditure is to be maintained (and thereby the level of income and production is to be maintained), the leakage we have just envisaged must be offset by what we can call an injection to the spending stream. The possible injection we have in view is, of course, the investment expenditure we have just discussed. We can say intuitively that the level of spending, and therefore of income, will be maintained only if the injections exactly equal and offset the leakages. In even more sophisticated and highly developed forms of income analysis, this is the basic so-called equilibrium condition. Leakages must equal injections.

But some care is necessary in stating the condition. For we are interested in the level of injections, as well as the level of consumption expenditures, that the economy is actually willing to make (or plans to make, or intends to make) at different specified levels of income. In the macroeconomic literature this is often referred to as the *ex ante* level of spending. We speak of *ex ante* consumption and investment and say that an existing income level will be maintainable as an equilibrium level only if *ex ante* injections exactly equal and offset *ex ante* leakages.

Consider this condition and relationship in the light of the total expenditure function in Figure 18-8. The so-called equilibrium level of income will be that level at which the total of $c + i$ just equals the level of income currently being generated. Reading the current level of income from the horizontal axis of Figure 18-8, and the sum of $c + i$ from the vertical axis, the two will be equal when the total expenditure function crosses a guideline drawn at an angle of 45 degrees from the origin. In the figure this is shown as y^*. At this income level the consumption expenditure of y^*M plus the investment expenditure of y^*A (which equals MN) provides a total expenditure of y^*N. But by the construction of the 45-degree guideline this precisely equals the currently generated income level of Oy^*. Income level Oy^* will therefore, on the elementary conditions we have so far laid down, be a permanently maintainable equilibrium level of income.

If the currently generated income level were Oy_1, the expenditure the economy would wish to make at that income level, or the *ex ante* expenditures, would be y_1W. This would be made up of the planned consumption expenditure of y_1R plus planned investment of RW. But assuming such expenditure plans are implemented, the total demand for goods and services would exceed the currently generated income, or the value of current production, by the amount TW. This amount could be regarded as an excess demand for goods and services, and it would be able to be met in the markets of the economy only if sales were made from previously

Figure   18-8.

Equilibrium real income

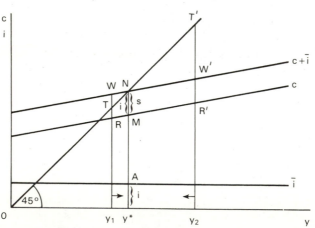

existing stocks of commodities. The amount TW, therefore, can be re-garded as inventory disinvestment. Producers will react to this unplanned inventory disinvestment by increasing production and causing an in-crease in incomes. The national income will then increase from Oy_1 in the direction of the arrow.

Conversely, if the currently generated level of income is Oy_2, it can be shown by similar argument that the total demand for goods and serv-ices of y_2W' is now less than the current production level of y_2T'. As a result, involuntary inventory accumulation will occur. Unsold goods will pile up in producers' warehouses, equal in magnitude to the distance $W'T'$. The situation is the opposite of that analyzed in the case of income level y_1. It implies that income level Oy_2 is also not a permanently main-tainable income level. Producers will react to the unplanned increase in inventories of unsold goods by cutting production. Incomes will therefore fall, and the national income level will in this case decline from Oy_2 in the direction of the arrow. It follows again that the unique income level at which the equilibrium condition will be satisfied is Oy^*. At that income and production level there is neither involuntary inventory disinvestment nor involuntary inventory accumulation. There are neither excess leak-ages, as in the case of income level Oy_2, nor excess injections, as in the case of income Oy_1.

This national income equilibrium condition can be exhibited in a different manner, again by reference to Figure 18-8. At income level y_1, for example, the level of planned or *ex ante* injections (in this case in-vestment expenditure) is equal to RW. But the level of leakages (in this case saving) is equal to RT, measured by income, y_1T, minus consumption expenditure, y_1R. Injections thus exceed leakages and the expenditure stream will rise. But these leakages and injections, we recall, are those the economy plans or intends to make at the level of income specified. They are *ex ante* leakages and injections. We have already seen that it is when the leakages and injections are brought into equality, in this important *ex ante* sense, that equilibrium can be said to have been es-tablished.

Consider, however, the investment and saving that actually take place in the economy. These actual or realized magnitudes are referred to as *ex post* saving and investment. In the realized or *ex post* sense saving and investment can always be shown to be equal. In Figure 18-8 the actual saving at income level y_1 is equal to RT, as we have seen, or actual income minus actual consumption expenditure. Similarly, actual invest-ment expenditure is equal to RW, the same distance as can be read from the investment function in the lower section of the figure. But we must recall also that at the income level y_1, the total of actual expenditures will give rise to an involuntary inventory disinvestment of TW. If, then, we take account of (1) the actual investment expenditure of RW and (2) the inventory disinvestment of TW, it follows that an actual realized net investment of RT (or $RW - TW$) has occurred. It is this actual net investment that is equal to the actual saving as previously defined.

At income level y_2 in Figure 18-8, on the other hand, actual saving would be $R'T'$, or again equal to income minus actual consumption expenditure. Actual investment expenditure is equal to $R'W'$. But when we add to this the amount of involuntary inventory investment, $W'T'$, we have an aggregate net investment of $R'T'$. This actual or realized investment then equals the actual or realized saving. Saving and investment are again equal in the *ex post* sense.

The essential property of the equilibrium income level, however, is that at that point saving and investment, or, more generally, the leakages and injections, are equal not only in this *ex post* sense but also in the *ex ante* sense we previously explored.

THE SIMPLE REAL INCOME MULTIPLIER

The short-run real income equilibrium condition can be alternatively stated by saying that it will be satisfied when the total demand for goods and services equals the total value of goods and services being produced at existing price levels. Referring to this as the product market equilibrium condition, it can be written as

(17) $$y = c + i = a + by + i$$

When the condition in Equation (17) is satisfied, the following relation obtains:

(18) $$y(1 - b) = a + i$$

It follows that equilibrium income will then be describable as

(19) $$y^* = (a + i)\frac{1}{(1 - b)}$$

This proposition says that the equilibrium level of income will be equal to the sum of the autonomous components of the income-generating expenditure stream (here observed to be the sum of the autonomous element of the consumption expenditure, a, plus the autonomous investment expenditure) multiplied by the reciprocal of one minus the marginal propensity to consume. The latter term is referred to as the simple real income multiplier. Alternatively, the multiplier can be expressed as the reciprocal of the marginal propensity to save. It is the reciprocal of the slope of the saving function, as shown previously in Equation (12).

We refer to this as the multiplier derived in total expenditure form. The same expression follows, so long as the consumption and saving propensities are stable and the consumption function is linear in the fashion we have so far supposed, from a consideration of incremental changes in spending and incomes. Equation (19) implies that following an increment in autonomous investment expenditure, the new equilibrium income level could be expressed as

$$(20) \qquad y^* + \Delta y = (a + i + \Delta i)\,\frac{1}{(1 - b)}$$

Subtracting Equation (19) from Equation (20) yields

$$(21) \qquad \Delta y = \Delta i\,\frac{1}{(1 - b)}$$

In this expression the autonomous increase in investment expenditure is referred to as the multiplicand, and the multiplier appears in the same form as previously.

The argument may be inspected also in Figure 18-9.

We suppose in Figure 18-9 that at an existing equilibrium income level of Oy_1^* an increment of autonomous investment expenditure equal to MN is introduced to the spending stream. The total expenditure function thereby rises to the new higher level indicated, and by the previously

Figure   18-9.

The incremental real income multiplier

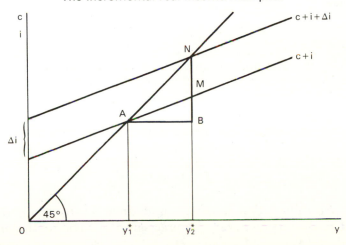

stated equilibrium condition the equilibrium income level is raised to Oy_2^*. During the expansionary process that raises the income level from y_1^* to y_2^*, consumption expenditure will have increased as the economy moves up along its consumption function. We can invoke Equation (13) and say that when the multiplier process has worked itself out, the overall increment in income will have been divided between an increase in saving and an increase in consumption. But because saving equals investment (leakages equals injections) at the new equilibrium income level, just as saving equaled investment at the old equilibrium level, the increment in saving must be precisely offset by the increment in investment that started the multiplier process.

Now the increment in investment, the incremental multiplicand in the present exercise, is equal to MN in Figure 18-9. This therefore also equals the final resultant increment in saving. But as the overall increment in income equals the distance $y_1^*y_2^*$, or, by construction, AB, it also equals (by the 45-degree guideline construction) BN. The difference between the increment in income, BN, and the increment in investment, MN, must equal the induced increase in consumption expenditure, or the distance BM. We can therefore derive the incremental multiplier as follows:

$$\Delta y = k\Delta i,$$

or, in Figure 18-9,

$$BN = k(MN)$$

where k describes the multiple by which the increment in autonomous expenditure is multiplied up to the new equilibrium income level. It follows that

$$k = \Delta y/\Delta i = BN/MN$$

Substituting the marginal equilibrium condition that $\Delta i = \Delta s$,

$$k = \Delta y/\Delta s$$

Dividing the numerator and denominator of the last expression by Δy yields

(22) $$k = 1/(\Delta s/\Delta y)$$

The multiplier, that is to say, is defined as the reciprocal of the marginal propensity to save. It is precisely the same as the multiplier expressed in Equations (20) and (21). Alternatively, we can say that in every case the multiplier will be shown to be equal to the reciprocal of the marginal propensity for leakages to occur from the income-generating expenditure stream. In the present simple case the only leakage is the saving that is taking place. But the same proposition holds in more complex cases. These occur when, for example, tax payments give rise to leakages, when expenditures on imports divert expenditure from home-produced goods, and when reductions in investment expenditures occur as a result of induced increases in the rate of interest. But we are not yet ready to take these complications into account.

THE PROPORTIONAL TAX MULTIPLIER

We do not need to enter questions of fiscal policy fully at this stage. But we can extend our basic model to incorporate government expenditure in a simple manner and indicate a number of issues that continue to apply in more complex cases. For this purpose we shall amend our basic product market equilibrium condition by incorporating government expenditure on goods and services, denominated by g, and a tax revenue function denominated by ty. In this expression t is understood as the rate of proportional taxation applied to all incomes earned. The product market equilibrium condition then appears as

$$(23) \qquad y^* = c + i + g = a + b(y - ty) + i + g$$

In this equation the level of consumption expenditure is now understood to be a function of what will be called disposable income. The latter is equal to total income minus tax revenue collections. It follows from Equation (23) that

$$(24) \qquad y^*[(1 - b(1 - t)] = a + i + g$$

Again, as before, treating the a and the i components on the right-hand side of Equation (24) as autonomous components of the spending stream, and now introducing the government expenditure as similarly autonomous, it follows that

$$(25) \qquad y^* = (a + i + g)\frac{1}{1 - b(1 - t)}$$

Again the multiplier is the reciprocal of the propensity for leakages to occur from the spending stream. Writing the denominator of the multiplier as $(1 - b + bt)$ it is clear that $(1 - b)$ is the savings leakage, specifying as previously the marginal propensity to save, and bt is the amount by which consumption is reduced in order to pay taxes. This last term can be explained more completely as follows. For every dollar of income received, an amount equal to t percent of it is absorbed in the payment of taxes, and disposable income is therefore reduced by that amount. The extent to which consumption expenditure is reduced as a result is, in turn, equal to b percent of this reduction in disposable income. To that extent the overall spending stream is reduced. The effective leakage is thereby increased, and the multiplier is accordingly lower than it would have been without the tax liability.

PROBLEMS WITH THE SIMPLE REAL
INCOME EQUILIBRIUM ANALYSIS

The foregoing, of course, does not exhaust the theory of the consumption function or consumption expenditure. Among the other factors that determine consumption expenditures we have noted the possible significance of individual wealth and changes in wealth, as one of the channels through which changes in the rate of interest might have an effect. We should bear in mind also the possible significance of individuals' expectations regarding future price and income levels, and of changes in those expectations. But for the present we can assume the state of expectations to be given, in the same manner as in our consideration of the supply side.

Further factors that affect the level of consumption expenditure, or, more precisely, affect the manner in which it is related to income levels, include the size and age distribution of the population, the changes in fashion and consumer tastes, and the availability of consumer credit. In the short run with which we are concerned in the present analysis, all of these factors might be taken to be reasonably stable, with the possible exception of consumer credit. We know from earlier discussions that at different times during the swings of the business cycle, or during, perhaps, a more or less prolonged inflationary trend, the financial institutional structure of the economy may change in such a way as to alter the availability of credit facilities and credit terms. Purchases on credit may alter the relation between consumption and incomes. But in the short run, the significance of credit purchasing would depend not on its actual level at any time, but on the changes in that level that were taking place. In other words, the important variable that should be inspected in order to judge the impact on the spending streams in the economy is not the level of consumer debt outstanding, but the changes in that debt during any given period of time.

The reference in the heading of this section to problems with the simple real income equilibrium analysis is to three more fundamental questions. First, how should the full effects of the rate of interest, and possible changes in that rate, be taken into account? Second, how should the price level and changes in the price level be incorporated into the analysis? And third, what, if anything, is the significance of the distribution of income?

For the present we shall concentrate on the second and third of these problems. Our derivation in Chapter 17 of the aggregate supply curve provides us with an entry to this analysis. For we have seen there that every point on the supply curve has associated with it (1) an implicit price level and (2) an implicit distribution of income.

MONEY FLOWS ON CONSUMPTION EXPENDITURES

The relation between real income and real consumption expenditure remains fundamental to our analysis. But we now need a method of transforming the relation from one in the real flows of commodity demands to one in the flows of money outlays. Let us begin by referring again to the aggregate supply curve, as reproduced in Figure 18-10. Here, in the now familiar fashion, we have drawn the supply curve nonlinear convex, to reflect the phenomenon of diminishing marginal productivity as the level of employment and output increases. It is this diminishing marginal productivity that induces a rise in the price level as employment increases. We cannot, that is to say, stay with the initial assumption of the preceding real analysis that the price level and changes in it can be ignored. For by reason of the very structure of industrial processes we are likely to experience rising price levels as employment increases from N_1 to N_2 in Figure 18-10.

This rise in prices needs to be taken into account in considering the implications for consumption expenditures. Of course there may be a number of producing firms, possibly a fairly large number, that endeavor

Figure   18-10.

The aggregate supply curve

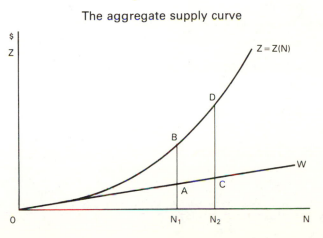

to maintain existing price levels as long as they can when their activity level and output increase. This may result from possible excess capacity in their production arrangements as the upward trend begins. But experience, as well as *a priori* reasoning, tells us that in an economy made up of producing firms in a wide range of imperfectly competitive markets, enjoying different degrees of integration and having to acquire material inputs in widely differing market environments, there is a tendency for prices to rise as employment and production increase. If, also, the money wage rate should rise as employment increases, then the upward pressure on prices is reinforced. We have seen in Chapter 17 that a rise in money wage rates will cause the aggregate supply curve to turn upward to the left. We have traced out the implications for price changes that result.

In Figure 18-10 we have again assumed that the money wage rate is given. As employment increases, therefore, the wage bill will increase along the linear ray OW. At employment level N_1 the wage share of total proceeds is N_1A and the residual profit share AB. At employment level N_2 the shares are N_2C and CD. The convexity of the supply curve indicates that, under the assumptions that generate it, the profit share is increasing.

We focus, then, on the basic question of how the money incomes generated for wage earners and profit earners, respectively, at different levels of employment, will be reflected in consumption expenditures in actual money terms. We want to build up a new specification of the consumption function. It will not be a function that, as previously, related consumption to real income in the manner of $c = c(y)$. Our consumption function will relate the money expenditure on consumption to the level of employment. The form of the relation will therefore be $C = C(N)$. We are here using the capital letter C to refer to consumption expenditure in money terms, retaining the lower-case c to refer to consumption in real terms. For the remainder of this chapter we shall ignore the question of taxation payments out of wage and profit incomes. The propensities to consume will be adjusted for the impact of taxation in the following chapter.

Wage income and consumption expenditure

Progress at this point is best made by concentrating on the income distribution phenomena implicit in the aggregate supply curve.[2] Let us take the wage incomes first. So long as the money wage rate is unchanged,

[2] As in the case of the supply side analysis in the preceding chapters, the following analysis of the demand functions is heavily indebted to the seminal work of Sidney Weintraub in his chapter "Aggregate Supply and Demand" in his *Approach to the Theory of Income Distribution* (Philadelphia: Chilton, 1958), and to the subsequent work based on that by Paul Davidson and Eugene Smolensky in their *Aggregate Supply and Demand Analysis* (New York: Harper & Row, 1964).

the money incomes of labor will increase proportionally with the employment level, as shown in Figure 18-11. The parameter C_w in the figure refers to the wage earners' propensity to consume out of money income. The value of WN, or the money wage rate times the amount of employment, describes the level of wage earners' money income. The line $C_w \cdot WN$ therefore describes the level of consumption expenditure out of that money income. We need to know what determines the form of this money income-consumption relation.

We know from the preceding sections of this chapter that the underlying determinant of consumption expenditure is the level of real income. As the level of employment rises, say from N_1 to N_2 in Figure 18-10, the price level will rise, and all of those workers previously employed will experience a reduction in their real incomes. Their wage rate is, by assumption, unchanged, and the rise in prices therefore diminishes the purchasing power of their wage. Their real wage has therefore declined, and we can expect that either of two things may happen as a result. First, those workers may be forced to reduce their real consumption, even though they maintain their actual money expenditure at the same level as before. In conjunction with this, they may make substitutions in their consumption budgets onto commodities not previously consumed, or change the composition of their consumption budgets in such a way as to approximate their real standard of living with the same total consumption money outlay. Second, they may increase their money consumption outlays when prices rise and diminish their saving rate. In either case we can expect that in the light of the price rise associated with the new higher employment level, the previously employed workers will tend to maintain or somewhat increase their money expenditures.

Figure   18-11.

Wage earners' income and consumption expenditure

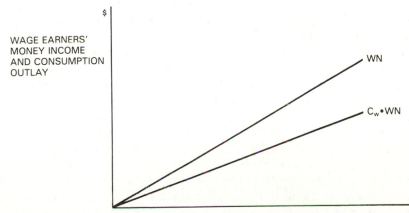

We have to consider also the new money incomes received by the newly employed workers as the employment level rises. Their real income as well as their money income has obviously increased, and we can expect a rise in their money consumption outlay as a result. Taking this increased money consumption expenditure in conjunction with the stable or increasing expenditure of the previously employed workers, we can conclude that there will be a rising consumption expenditure outlay for the work force as a whole. In Figure 18-11 we have depicted such a positive consumption expenditure relation in the rising consumption function $C_w \cdot WN$. We have drawn this consumption outlay curve below the money income curve to reflect the assumption that the propensity to consume out of wage income is less than unity.

Profit income and consumption expenditure

We turn now to the profit share of total proceeds, the amounts of AB or CD in Figure 18-10. Here an additional caution is necessary. The money capital provided to industrial producers (as reflected in our earlier discussion of the money capital market) is supplied partly in the form of debt capital and partly in the form of equity capital. The providers of debt capital are entitled to receive a fixed interest income each year. They have frequently been referred to in the economic literature as rentiers. The providers of equity capital, on the other hand, receive the residual income after all costs of production and the interest due to the rentiers have been paid. This residual income that accrues to the equity holders may be paid to them in the form of dividends, or it may be retained in the firm. In the latter case the equity holders' total investment in the firm will have increased.

As employment increases from N_1 to N_2 in Figure 18-10, the rentier income in money terms will not have changed. The debt holders will continue to receive simply the contractual interest on their capital. But the rise in prices implicit in the convexity of the supply curve will mean that while the rentiers' money income is unchanged, their real income will have fallen. Their position in this respect is precisely the same as that of the previously employed workers we discussed above. We can expect, therefore, that the rentiers may make either or both of the same kinds of reactions. They may maintain their money consumption expenditures while they reduce their real consumption. Or they may maintain real consumption and reduce saving. In any event, we can expect again that rentier consumption in money terms will be likely to remain fairly constant or increase somewhat. Again, that is to say, we have a nondecreasing money consumption relation in the rentier section of the income earners. In Figure 18-12 the curve RR refers to rentier money

Figure   18-12.

Rentier income and consumption expenditure

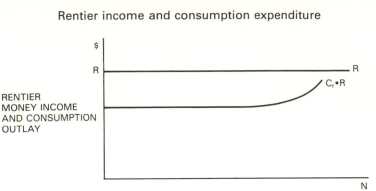

income. The parameter C_r refers to the propensity of the rentiers to consume out of money income. The curve $C_r \cdot R$ describes the rentier money consumption relation.

The remainder of the profit share, after the payment of rentier incomes, accrues to the residual owners of business firms. For low levels of employment this final income share may well be negative. In those cases the total proceeds of the sale of output may not be sufficient to cover all production costs and pay the interest on debt capital. If the latter is not paid as it becomes due, insolvency and bankruptcy may result for the delinquent firms. The firm may remain in existence, however, by drawing down its previously accumulated reserves, and paying the debt interest out of those funds. In that case the equity owners are in effect using a part of their capital investment in the firm to satisfy their legal obligations to the debt holders and to keep the firm afloat. It may be thought worthwhile to do this because of favorable prospects for market sales and incomes that lie ahead.

This means that the residual income earners' money income function (we shall refer in what follows simply to profit incomes) may be of the form shown in Figure 18-13. The curve PP in Figure 18-13 describes the profit incomes, depicting the possibility that profits will not become positive until a certain minimum employment level has been reached. After that point the profit income function is drawn nonlinear convex, to reflect the nonlinearity and convexity of the total proceeds function. As employment increases, the price level rises and confers a direct benefit on the profit earners. Both their real and money incomes increase as their share of total proceeds rises for the reasons we have already explored. In that case it can be expected that their money consumption outlays will also rise. This is depicted in the curve $C_p \cdot P$ in Figure 18-13 where the parameter C_p refers to the propensity to consume out of profit income.

Figure   18-13.

Profit income and consumption expenditures

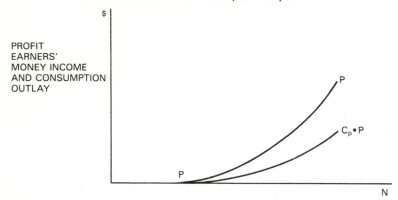

THE AGGREGATE MONEY CONSUMPTION FUNCTION

We can now bring together the money consumption expenditure relations
we have examined. We add together the wage earners', rentiers', and
profit earners' money consumption expenditures out of the money incomes
that will accrue to them at different employment levels. In so doing, we
are taking account of the income distribution that is implicit in differing
employment levels or points on the aggregate supply curve. This aggregate consumption function is depicted in Figure 18-14. The consumption
function is labeled $C = C(N)$ to describe the fundamental relation we
have now established. The level of money consumption expenditure in
the economy can be understood as functionally related to the level of
employment, via, as we shall see more fully, the distribution of income.

Figure   18-14.

The aggregate money consumption function

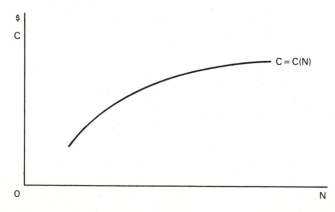

The consumption function, moreover, is drawn as a nonlinear concave relation to exhibit the possibility that as employment and incomes increase, the rate of increase in consumption may diminish. This possibility is inherent in the analysis we have established to this point. For the aggregate consumption expenditure will be the sum of the expenditures made by the different income recipients, and it will therefore depend on the relative importance of the consumption propensities of the different income classes. The actual total consumption expenditure will depend on what is happening to the distribution of income as the income and employment levels increase. Writing the wage share of income as WN, the rentier share as R, and the profit share as P, it follows that total consumption is defined as

$$(26) \qquad\qquad C = C_w WN + C_r R + C_p P$$

We know from the logic behind the construction of the aggregate supply curve that as employment increases, the share of wage income in the total income payments will diminish. This implies that the weight given to the wage earners' propensity to consume will become less important in the aggregate relative to the other consumption propensities. Furthermore, the rentier share will also diminish, given the fixed nature of their money income payments, and the residual profit share will increase.

As these developments occur, greater relative weight will be given in the overall consumption pattern to the consumption propensity of the profit earners. But the consumption propensity of these income earners is likely to be lower than that of the wage earners, as the profit recipients are likely to be larger suppliers of savings. For these reasons, the overall proportion of income allocated to consumption expenditure is likely to decline as income and employment increase, thus imparting a concavity to the consumption relation as drawn in Figure 18-14.

It is also possible, moreover, that as income increases, some of the incremental profit incomes will be retained in business firms instead of being paid to the owners in the form of dividends. In that case the disposable incomes of the profit recipients will not increase proportionately with the rise in employment or incomes, thus tending again to prevent consumption expenditures from rising proportionately, and thereby imparting a concavity to the aggregate consumption relation.

As incomes increase, the consumption propensity of the wage earners may well diminish, or the C_w parameter in the consumption function may decrease, as wage earners begin to save a larger proportion of their disposable incomes. Further additions to the determinants in the aggregate consumption relation may be made. If, for example, we were to envisage the influence of total assets on consumption expenditures, some interesting and possibly conflicting forces might develop. First, higher asset values associated with the higher incomes and improved industrial prospects may improve investors' asset portfolio values to such an extent that their willingness to spend on consumption is increased. But on the other hand, if the increase in employment and economic activity is accompanied, as we have already seen may be the case, by a rise in the interest rate, this will tend to decrease the market value of income-earning assets. We would then have a negative wealth effect working to offset the previous positive wealth effect, with a consequent possible tendency to reduce consumption expenditures.

THE AGGREGATE DEMAND CURVE

Our analysis leading to the construction of the aggregate demand curve is now almost complete. By analogy with the real expenditure analysis in the preceding sections, we can add the consumption expenditure and the investment expenditure at given levels of employment to obtain the total demand or total monetary outlay function. A brief comment is necessary on the investment expenditure function.

We supposed earlier in this chapter that investment expenditure could be introduced into the income analysis as an autonomous or exogenous variable. We assumed that the level of investment expenditure was dependent on the rate of interest and not, for purposes of the present analysis, on the level of income. We can now bring the same assumptions over to our monetary expenditure analysis and assume that in the short run the level of investment outlays is similarly not affected by the level of employment. But there remains the consideration of the relation between real investment outlays and money expenditures, analogous to the same kind of relation we have just considered in the case of consumption.

We acknowledge again that as employment increases, the price level will rise. This will conceivably imply that the price of capital goods will be increasing. To the extent that that is so, a given capital expenditure budget in money terms will correspond to a lower real outlay than was previously intended. In the face of this, business firms may react in either of two ways.

First, they may simply maintain, in the short period, the actual money capital outlay budget they have already established, and they may accordingly decrease their real investment by deferring or canceling some real asset installations. Or second, they may endeavor to maintain real outlays and real additions to their capital stock by increasing their total money capital outlays. The extent to which the latter could be done in the short run would depend, of course, on a number of possible developments in the money capital markets. It may depend on the extent to

which the commercial banks and other financial institutions are willing
or able to increase their lending to accommodate the additional demand
for finance. Such a maintenance of real investment in the face of rising
prices may depend also on the availability and mobility of investable
funds in the money capital market. The outcome will depend also on the
policy adopted by the Federal Reserve Board in making reserves available
to the banking system to enable it to expand loans to industrial borrowers
and thereby expand the money supply.

    If, for the present, we make the assumption that as employment
increases and the price level rises the level of money capital outlay on
investment remains as initially given in business firms' capital budgets,
the money investment expenditure function can be represented by the *II*
curve in Figure 18-15.

    At the same time, we might imagine that the level of government
money outlays is given by the government budget, and the government
expenditure function may then be represented by the *GG* curve in Figure
18-15. There may be reasons, of course, why the actual level of government money outlays will increase as employment increases. Recalling
again that the price level will be rising as employment increases, government expenditures may well increase as the real commitments made
by the government are met. Some government expenditures, social security payments for example, are indexed to the price level, and they will
automatically increase as prices rise. Certain other expenditures, such
as those on defense contracts, may rise as the price increase causes cost
overruns. On the other hand, the increase in employment may be accompanied by a reduction in the level of government expenditure on unem-

Figure   18-15.

The aggregate demand curve

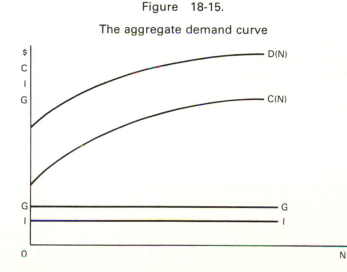

ployment compensation and other welfare benefits. But for the present short-run analysis we shall continue to assume, in line with general macroeconomic theory, that government expenditure, concentrating as we must for national income theory on expenditures on goods and services rather than on transfer expenditures, can be introduced into the analysis as an exogenous variable. But the precise form of the government money expenditure function is not material to our present analysis. Forms other than that shown in Figure 18-15 may be assumed.

In Figure 18-15 we have aggregated the consumption, investment, and government expenditure functions to give us the aggregate demand curve. This is labeled $D(N)$ in the figure. It describes the level of expenditure the economy is willing to make or, in some expressions of the theory, the level of expenditure the economy is expected to make, at different possible levels of employment. It is the aggregate demand curve we have been searching for, in order to bring it into relation with the aggregate supply curve we developed in Chapter 17.

SUMMARY

This chapter has focused on the fact that an implicit price level and an implicit distribution of income are associated with every point on the aggregate supply curve developed in Chapter 17. These features have been employed to develop the aggregate demand curve. As a background to this, the chapter has explored some of the microeconomic foundations of consumption expenditure decisions. This led to the clarification of the dependence of real consumption expenditure on the level of real income. A digression on the problem of optimum intertemporal consumption expenditure allocation brought into prominence the significance of the rate of interest.

The real income-consumption relation was exhibited from recent data for the United States economy. On the basis of the short-run consumption function deduced from that relation, as distinct from the long-run function which was also discussed, the simple real income multiplier was derived. The magnitude of the multiplier was seen to depend on the magnitude of the marginal propensity to consume, or on its complement, the marginal propensity to save. The introduction of a proportional income tax enabled the relevant multiplier to be described in an analogous fashion, depicting the general conclusion that in the real income model the multiplier is describable as the reciprocal of the marginal propensity for leakages to occur from the income-generating expenditure streams.

Three principal problems with the short-run real income analysis were noted: (1) the effect of interest rate changes as income and employment levels increase, (2) the tendency for price levels to rise with increasing employment, and (3) the need to take account of the distribution of income, and changes in that distribution, as employment increases. Taking account of both these implicit price level and income-distribution phenomena, the earlier real consumption function was transformed into a money outlay consumption function. Separate treatment was given to wage earners', rentiers', and profit earners' consumption expenditure behavior. On the basis of this development, taking account also of the money expenditure flows inherent in investment and government expenditure decisions, the aggregate demand curve was defined.

Most of the necessary analysis is now in place for the juxtaposition of the aggregate supply and demand curves. The implications that follow will be explored in the next chapter.

IMPORTANT CONCEPTS

Optimum budget allocation

Homogeneous demand functions

Intertemporal consumption allocation

Income-consumption constraint

Present value line

GNP deflator

Short-run and long-run consumption functions

Marginal propensity to consume

Marginal propensity to save

Aggregate demand curve

Equilibrium real income

Leakages and injections

Involuntary inventory investment

The simple real income multiplier

Multiplicand

Proportional tax multiplier

Distribution of income

Wage, rentier, and profit incomes

Propensities to consume out of wage, rentier, and profit incomes

Income-generating expenditure

QUESTIONS FOR DISCUSSION AND REVIEW

1. Discuss the effects of an increase in interest rates on the level of consumption expenditures (1) if the level of income is assumed to be given and (2) if the level of income and employment increases.

2. What factors other than the level of income and interest rates may affect the economy's aggregate propensity to consume? Discuss as fully as possible.

3. "The most important task of consumption analysis is to take full account of simultaneous changes in (1) income and employment levels, (2) the price level, and (3) the distribution of income." Explain and discuss critically.

4. Explain what differences you would expect to find between the short-run and the long-run consumption functions, and consider the effects on the consumption propensity of fluctuations in economic activity and incomes.

5. Explain why wage earners', rentiers', and profit earners' consumption expenditure patterns may change differently when the level of employment changes.

6. Can you anticipate how the form of the simple income multiplier may change when income distribution effects are taken into account?

7. Explain clearly why savings and investment are necessarily equal *ex post*, even though there may be significant divergences between them *ex ante*. In the light of your argument, examine the relevance of such divergences for the determination of equilibrium income and employment.

8. "The problem with the simple equilibrium income analysis is that it fails to take account of the underlying microeconomic phenomenon of diminishing marginal productivity." Discuss critically.

9. What determines the expenditure flows in investment and government expenditure as employment, prices, and income levels change?

10. In what ways, if at all, are monetary policy and the conditions of the supply of money relevant to the working of the multiplier and income equilibrium effects as employment and expenditures change? Explain fully.

19

A MODEL OF THE MACROECONOMY

STUDY OBJECTIVES:

• To construct a postclassical short-run model of the macroeconomy, based on the elements contained in the preceding chapters
• To review the principal characteristics of the aggregate supply function and the relevance of the cost, productivity, and price phenomena implicit in it
• To develop the demand side of the model further, and to exhibit the distinction between the aggregate demand function and the "producers' expected demand function"
• To trace the dynamic expectations formation and the employment and output adjustments implicit in the model of the macroeconomy
• To observe the significance of variations in the money wage rate and in efficiency wages
• To develop the relevant short-run income and employment multipliers
• To note the implications of the model for the determination of the situational variables M^s, y, P, N, and r
• To consider briefly the relevance of the model to recent trends in the United States economy

The preceding four chapters have provided us with substantially all the material we need to construct a postclassical short-run model of the macroeconomy. In this chapter the building blocks will be assembled to provide an explanation of the levels of income, employment, prices, and the rate of interest.

The analysis is embedded in the notion of the nonlinear aggregate supply curve developed in Chapter 17. This explains the level of employment that it is economically worthwhile for producers in the system to provide at different money wage rates and price levels. The money expenditure flows generated at different levels of employment and output are captured in the aggregate demand curve of Chapter 18. The aggregate supply and demand cross in the expenditure-employment space provides an indication of the effective demand. This is generated by the decisions of consumers and investors, along with government expenditures, in re-action to the implicit price level and the distribution of income associated with employment levels specified by the aggregate supply curve. The determination of the rate of interest is influenced by the demand for money generated by the need to finance the levels of expenditures and production implicit in the effective demand points that emerge from the analysis.[1]

THE AGGREGATE SUPPLY FUNCTION

The aggregate supply function is embedded in producers' expected pro-ceeds functions and depends on the nature of the production possibilities, particularly the likelihood of diminishing marginal productivity, as the level of employment increases. It is reproduced in Figure 19-1 and again labeled $Z(N)$. It defines the total level of sales proceeds that the producers in the economy must be able to expect from the sale of output in order to make the employment of a designated number of workers economically worthwhile. The criterion of economic worthwhileness is that of the profit maximization, or more particularly the expected profit maximization, of the producing firms.

A problem exists, however, in connection with the aggregation from the supply functions and profit optimization criteria of individual firms to a uniquely specified aggregate supply function for the economy. If, of course, we were to envisage an economy in which perfect competition prevailed in all markets, and in which, unrealistically, a single product was being produced by the economy, aggregation would be straightfor-ward. The relevant techniques involve a summation in the price-output space of all the separate firms' supply functions, and the procedures may be inspected in any text in microeconomic theory.

---

[1] In addition to the references in the preceding chapters to the aggregate supply and demand analysis, particularly in relation to the microfoundations, contained in the works of Sidney Weintraub, Paul Davidson, Paul Wells, Carlo Casarosa, and A. Asimakopulos, see also the earlier papers by H. Vandenborre, "An Integration of Employment Economics within the Keynesian Theory of Money Flows," *Oxford Economic Papers*, June 1958; and F. J. de Jong, "Supply Functions in Keynesian Economics," *Economic Journal*, March 1954. A more extensive bibliography of the relevant discussion and controversies is included in A. Asimakopulos, "Keynes' Theory of Effective Demand Revisited." See also John Maynard Keynes, *General Theory of Employment, Interest, and Money* (London: Macmillan, 1936), Chaps. 3 and 5.

Figure   19-1.

The aggregate supply curve

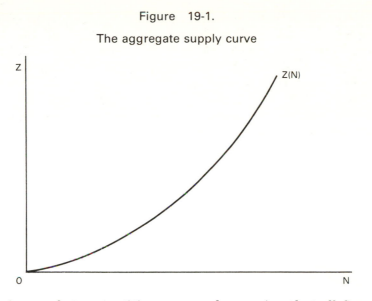

In that perfect competition case, and assuming that all firms are operating under the profit maximization conditions we specified previously, the individual firm's profit function can be written as

$$(1) \qquad \pi_i = p_i y_i(n_i) - w n_i - F_i$$

where π_i refers to the residual profit after the deduction from sales proceeds of variable and fixed costs of operation. In the first term on the right-hand side of Equation (1) the firm's selling price, which under conditions of perfect competition is uniform for all firms, is multiplied by the level of output, y_i, which depends on the level of employment, n_i. The money wage rate is assumed to be given for all firms at w, and the final term, F_i, refers to the firm's fixed factor operating costs.

Aggregating across all firms provides the total profit relation for the economy:

$$(2) \qquad \Sigma\pi_i = \Sigma p_i y_i(n_i) - w\Sigma n_i - \Sigma F_i$$

This implies that

$$(3) \qquad \Sigma p_i y_i(n_i) = wN + F + \Pi$$

where the capital letters on the right-hand side refer, respectively, to total employment, fixed factor costs, and profit.

This aggregate relation describes, on the left-hand side, the total expected proceeds that would provide profit maximization for all firms in the economy. If that expected proceeds should actually be realized, or if, that is, it should actually become what we shall call the "effective demand," then it represents also the actual total of the monetary expenditures in the system. We shall refer to that total expenditure later in this chapter as D, in accordance with the aggregate demand function $D(N)$. In that case, then, while the left-hand side of Equation (3) refers to total demand, the right-hand side describes the manner in which the total proceeds are divided among the providers of the factors of production. The three terms on the right-hand side refer, respectively, to the total wage bill or the wage share in total proceeds, the operating costs of maintaining fixed capital factors in the firm and other fixed costs of operation, and the residual profit share. The last will provide that rate of return on the money capital employed that is just sufficient to maintain capital intact in its given line of employment, even though, as the microeconomic literature makes clear, the true residual economic profit, after deducting that normal rate of return, is, in full equilibrium, zero.

In fact, of course, the stringent conditions of generalized perfect competition that are necessary to effect such an aggregation do not exist. The different firms in the economy are producing heterogeneous, not homogeneous, outputs, and direct aggregation to the total economy's supply curve is accordingly inhibited on the two grounds of (1) imperfectly competitive market conditions and (2) heterogeneous products. Equations (2) and (3), therefore, must be regarded, not as a summation of perfectly competitive firms' optimization outcomes, but as a summation of the definitional identities describing profit outcomes that fully reflect market imperfections and product heterogeneity.

Significantly, therefore, the aggregate supply function described in Figure 19-1 is to be regarded as the aggregative analogue of the microeconomic relations underlying the analysis.

The aggregate supply function emphasizes the relation between employment on the one hand and the expected, or required, total proceeds on the other. Of course, at the level of generality at which we are working, the total level of employment referred to in the figure conceals within it a wide range of different skills, capacities, and types of employment. We may, if we wish, regard the labor supply as homogeneous, or alternatively we may, in the manner of Keynes, assume that "the quantity of employment can be sufficiently defined for our purpose by taking an hour's employment of ordinary labour as our unit and weighting an hour's employment of special labour in proportion to its remuneration; i.e. an hour of special labour remunerated at double ordinary rates will count as two units."[2] Keynes goes on to say that "we shall call the unit in which the

[2] Keynes, *General Theory*, p. 41.

quantity of employment is measured the labour-unit; and the money-wage of a labour-unit we shall call the wage-unit."[3]

For our present purposes we understand the aggregate supply function to contain and reflect three significant macroeconomic properties we shall make use of in the following discussion.

First, the total proceeds referable to each designated employment level on the aggregate supply curve indicates the total proceeds at which all producers in the economy expect to maximize their profit, or, in other words, to optimize their employment and production levels. We emphasize that along the supply curve this profit maximization objective is satisfied in an expectational sense. The total proceeds describes in every instance the proceeds the producers expect to receive, or need to receive for purposes of profit maximization, at any specified level of employment.

Second, each point on the aggregate supply curve has implicit in it an average commodity price level. This was seen in Chapters 16 and 17 to depend on the underlying productivity relations in the economy, and on the pressure to diminishing marginal and average product as the level of employment increased. From these directions the form of the supply function, its nonlinearity and convexity, were seen to be derived.

Third, each point on the aggregate supply function similarly has embedded in it an implicit distribution of income. The wage share and the profit share, dividing the latter for purposes of some aspects of the analysis into a rentier and residual profit share, again come into play in the determination of the demand side of the model.

THE AGGREGATE DEMAND FUNCTION

The aggregate demand side of the model calls for a more extensive examination than we have yet given it. In Chapter 18 we derived an aggregate demand curve, which is reproduced in Figure 19-2 and again labeled $D(N)$. This was built up from underlying consumption, investment, and government expenditure functions. It describes the total level of monetary expenditure, or the demand for goods and services, that can be expected to be forthcoming out of the incomes generated by a specified level of employment. In the course of the analysis behind the aggregate demand curve, note was taken of the influence of the distribution of income on consumption expenditures, and of the ways in which changes in the price level as employment increased would, by varying real incomes, cause variations in consumer demands. Similarly, business firms may react in different possible ways to the decreased real value of budgeted money investment expenditure as prices increased. Account was

[3] Ibid.

Figure   19-2.

The aggregate demand curve

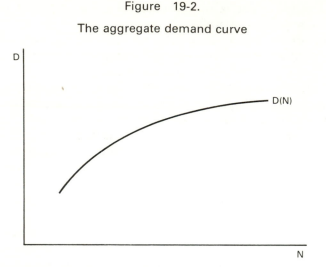

taken of possible reactions on that level, as well as in the government budget outlays. But an important clarification of this aggregate demand curve, which has not yet entered our analysis, is now called for.

The aggregate demand curve so far derived describes the expenditure outlays that will be made at different employment levels as those outlays are seen by, and planned and anticipated by, the consumers, investors, and government expenditure decision makers. In other words, the aggregate demand curve is a monetary outlay function as seen by the demand side of the markets for goods and services. It can be regarded, in an *ex post* sense, as an actual market demand function or an actual outlay or expenditure function. It is not, it is important to note, an expected demand curve as seen by the producers or as underlying the latters' production and marketing decisions. This very important point, which has not been clearly understood and unambiguously interpreted in the macroeconomic literature, can be clarified as follows.

We shall continue to refer to the aggregate demand curve as reflecting the actual behavior of expenditure decision makers. But we shall now introduce another function descriptive of certain expected or anticipated conditions on the demand side, and refer to it as the "producers' expected demand function." It is illustrated in Figure 19-3 as $E(N)$ and is shown in the figure in relation to what we have already discussed as the expected proceeds function, or the aggregate supply curve.

THE PRODUCERS' EXPECTED DEMAND FUNCTION

The producers' expected demand function indicates what, on the basis of the expectations they have formed, the producers expect or anticipate would be the demand in the markets for output if different specified

Figure   19-3.

The producers' expected demand curve

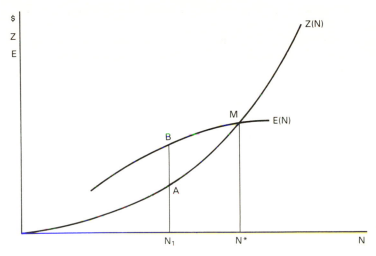

employment levels were to exist. We note that if, for example, employment equal to N_1 in Figure 19-3 were offered, then the incomes generated at the relevant money wage rate (not shown in the figure), along with the investment and government expenditure in the economy, would be expected, in the minds of the producers, to provide a total monetary demand of N_1B. It should be emphasized that N_1 would not, therefore, be likely to be an operative employment point. For in the light of what we have already adduced regarding producers' optimization decision criteria, N_1 would not provide a profit maximization production volume. The sensible production and employment decision would be for the producers to proceed immediately to employment level N^*. At that level the demand that is expected to be forthcoming is equal to N^*M, and that, it is seen, lies on the aggregate supply curve also. In other words, what we are now calling the producers' expected demand function is very much a notional demand function from which, at any time, the only operative point on the curve depicting it is that at which it coincides with the expected proceeds or aggregate supply curve.

It can now be seen why the language "expected proceeds function" was chosen to describe what underlies the specification of the aggregate supply curve. For the supply curve, it is recalled, indicates the proceeds that must be expected in order to make the employment of a designated number of workers economically worthwhile. That is precisely determined at the point at which the producers' expected demand function assumes a value equal to what is necessary to support a designatable level of employment in an economically optimum sense. It follows that the aggregate supply curve traces out a locus of points on a series or family of successively higher producers' expected demand curves. We shall examine this more fully in a moment. But first, a final question of some importance warrants our attention in connection with the producers' expected demand curve itself.

Recall, for this purpose, the manner in which the aggregate supply curve was constructed and, in particular, the fact that the productivity and cost characteristics underlying it meant that each point on the curve had implicit in it a calculable price level. Now the question can be asked, What general commodity price level do the producers assume is implicit in the expected demand curve we have just examined? Clearly, given the manner in which that expected demand depends on the money incomes that producers are distributing to the factors of production, any specified point on the expected demand curve must have implicit in it the same price level as is implicit in the supply curve at the same level of employment. In Figure 19-3 the price level implicit in the expected demand curve, $E(N)$, at point B is the same price level as is implicit in the supply curve, $Z(N)$, at point A. They both, in other words, are the same price level as is implicit in the productivity and cost conditions consistent with the employment level corresponding to points A and B, namely N_1.

These arguments and definitions imply that in order to present a full model of the macroeconomy that incorporates both the aggregate supply and demand conditions, it is necessary to bring into juxtaposition with the aggregate supply curve both (1) the aggregate demand curve we examined previously, or the actual market expenditure curve, and (2) what we have now brought into focus as the producers' expected demand curve. We may do this most directly in the following way.

THE ESSENTIAL MODEL OF THE MACROECONOMY

Consider the relations shown in Figure 19-4.

The aggregate supply curve in Figure 19-4, $Z(N)$, has the properties attributed to it in Chapter 17. Let it be supposed, then, that producers, in the light of their knowledge of cost and productivity conditions and therefore of price levels and income payments, expect that at different possible employment levels the demand forthcoming in the markets of the economy would be described by the curve labeled $E_1(N)$. On the basis of their implicit set of short-term expectations, the producers will provide employment N_1 in order that expected sales proceeds out of the income generated at that employment level, indicated by the point Z_1, would precisely satisfy profit maximization and output optimization conditions.

But this initial employment level and expected proceeds, N_1 and Z_1, will not be an optimally maintainable situation. For as Figure 19-4 also

Figure   19-4.

The aggregate supply and demand model

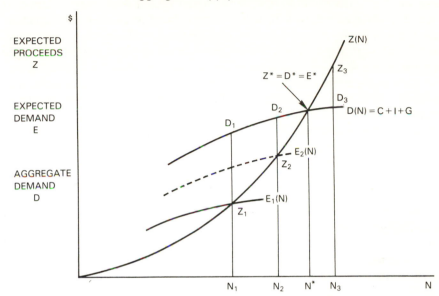

indicates, the actual monetary expenditure out of incomes generated by employment level N_1 (and at the price level set at that employment level) will be D_1. The latter point, in other words, lies on the actual market expenditure curve, or aggregate demand curve, as generated by the consumers', investors', and government expenditure decisions.

At employment level N_1, therefore, the actual market demand for goods and services, D_1, exceeds the level that the producers expected or planned for, Z_1. An excess demand in the goods markets therefore exists, and this can be expected to set in motion a number of reactions.

First, the impact effect will be a reduction in the economy's inventories of commodities as stocks are run down in an attempt to meet the excess demand. Or perhaps, depending on the inventory/sales ratio the economy is at that time maintaining, delivery dates for commodities may be extended and demands may temporarily be unsatisfied. But such situations can be expected to induce industrialists to increase the supply of output, first to replace the unintended inventory disinvestment, and second in response to the observed level of monetary expenditures.

This condition can be expected to give rise to a change in producers' short-term expectations. The excess market demand might cause the producers to revise their expectations and consider whether the higher demand level of D_1 is likely to be permanent. It may, of course, be thought to be a temporary deviation from underlying demand conditions that promise a somewhat lower permanent level of monetary expenditure.

Given the formation of revised expectations, however, producers might raise their market forecasts and expectations from the previous level given by the curve $E_1(N)$ to the rather more robust expectations implicit in the higher curve $E_2(N)$. In other words, producers may modify their expectations in the direction of the higher present demand, without necessarily revising them to levels as high as those implicit in the aggregate demand curve $D(N)$.

Any adjustment of expectations that occurs is likely to be partial in the sense we have just indicated because the entire basis of expectations formation, and the set of optimization decisions based on it, are vastly different in respect to the $E(N)$ and the $D(N)$ curves. The $E(N)$ curve, it should be borne in mind, is determined by whatever gives rise to expectations and decisions in the minds of producers. The $D(N)$ function, on the other hand, is the outcome of expectations and decisions formed in the minds of actual spenders in the markets of the economy.

Given, then, the revision of producers' expectations in the light of the initial excess demand at employment level N_1, producers will raise their production and employment levels to that indicated by N_2. This will be done in accordance with the new assumed expected demand curve of $E_2(N)$, and its crossing, at Z_2, the aggregate supply curve. But it is clear from Figure 19-4 that when employment is raised to N_2, the actual demand does not emerge as Z_2, but at the somewhat higher level of D_2. Again, in other words, the producers have underestimated the strength of total market demand and monetary expenditure. An excess demand again exists, and the adjustment process we have been examining can be expected to continue.

If the actual market demand is maintained in accordance with the relation $D(N)$ in Figure 19-4, recognizing that this is, as shown in Chapter 18, a summation of the C, I, and G expenditure data, producers will continue to revise their expectations and increase employment and production. In due course the revision of expectations, and the adjustment of employment and output decisions in the light of them, will raise employment to N^*. At that point the expected demand consistent with the income and price levels implicit in the employment level, E^*, will be equal to actual demand, D^*. At the same time, of course, it is equal to the profit optimization expected proceeds point, Z^*, as implicit in the aggregate supply curve. At that point, then, the three-way equality between Z^*, D^*, and E^* is established. The system is then at a point of short-run equilibrium, and no further change in the employment level can be envisaged.

Two significant points in connection with this adjustment process warrant further comment. First, the fact that at employment level N^* the magnitudes of D^* and E^* are equal should not be taken to suggest that the $D(N)$ and the $E(N)$ curves then coincide. That in no sense necessarily follows. The magnitudes of the producers' expected demand and the market's actual demand are equal, as we have shown. The $E(N)$ and the $D(N)$ curves intersect at that point. But the intersection of the curves tells us nothing about the form of the respective relations at points other than that intersection point. Indeed, there is every reason to believe that even though they now intersect, the forms of the curves are quite different because, as we noticed above, they are determined by, and are derived from, very different sets of underlying relations. The $D(N)$ curve derives from actual decisions of expenditure decision makers, while the $E(N)$ curve is a construction in the minds of producers.

Second, it should be borne in mind that as employment rises along the aggregate supply curve, the price level will rise because of the properties of the supply curve itself. It is precisely this induced increase in prices that, along with the rising incomes, determines not only the willingness of producers to supply but also the levels of monetary demand that are forthcoming from income earners.

We see, then, that a process of interaction between supply and demand conditions is set up, and the economy is propelled upward under the initial conditions stated. From the initial position we observe (1) excess demands, (2) involuntary inventory disinvestment, (3) induced increases in output and employment, (4) induced increases in prices, and (5) a step-process reaction leading to a short-term or temporary equilibrium position.

If, on the other hand, producers were initially to offer employment of N_3 in Figure 19-4, in the expectation of proceeds of Z_3, their expectation would not be fulfilled. In that case there would be a deficiency of demand and a consequent involuntary buildup of unsold goods, which would motivate producers to reduce employment and production. A step-process in a direction opposite to what we have just examined would be established.

Arguing from either side of the implicit dynamic processes, it is clear that, *ceteris paribus*, the chain of reactions we have envisaged will tend to a temporary equilibrium point at $Z^* = D^*$. At that point the actual money expenditures exactly equal the expected proceeds that producers envisaged when they offered employment to a labor force of N^*. At that point also both the plans and expectations of suppliers on the one hand, and the actual expenditure intentions of consumers, investors, and the government on the other, are fulfilled. Because, moreover, the outcomes in the system are then consistent with plans and expectations, there is no reason why the employment and production levels should be dislodged from N^*.

We have at that position what we have called a temporary equilibrium. We have deliberately used the word *temporary* in connection with it because it is, as we have emphasized before, based on a definite and describable state of expectations. It is very much a short-run result. It is the outcome of a short-run analysis. There still remains the question of whether the long-range expectations that industrialists and others formulate on the basis of the short-run outcomes will be consistent with the maintenance of stable conditions in the system. In an earlier chapter we argued at some length that the capital expenditure plans formulated in reaction to this short-run outcome may dislodge the aggregate demand curve in the next ensuing short period and destroy the supposed equilibrium that has been established. We have spoken of what might be termed a short-run dynamics in the system. It has to be seen logically as what might be termed a *ceteris paribus* dynamics. The expectational basis of it may change, and change drastically and disruptively, at any time. It is this process and this set of determinant relations that caused Keynes to observe that "a monetary economy . . . is essentially one in which *changing* views about the future" must be taken fully into account.[4] He expressively referred to a "*shifting* equilibrium" which was "liable to change without much warning, and sometimes substantially."[5]

At this point also the significance of possible reactions in the monetary sector must be taken into account. As the employment level increases in the manner indicated in Figure 19-4 from N_1 toward N^*, the higher level of industrial costs and income payments will generate a higher demand for money. Recalling the analysis in Chapter 15 of the transactions demand for money, the increase in incomes and expenditures will raise the demand for money for at least two reasons. First, higher cash balances will be needed to finance the higher market value of transactions. This follows not only from the higher production and trade volumes associated with the higher level of employment but also from the higher price level that accompanies the higher employment. Second, an increased demand for money and financial accommodation will be generated by the producers' need to invest in larger inventories of materials and other working capital assets, in order to maintain production processes in operation at the new higher levels. We shall return to these monetary implications in the next section.

CHANGES IN MONEY WAGE RATES

The supply side analysis in Chapter 17 indicates that an increase in the money wage rate will, *ceteris paribus,* cause the aggregate supply curve to turn to the left. This results from the fact that the rise in the wage rate automatically raises marginal costs of production. It thereby increases the price level and the expectations of sale proceeds that producers

---

[4] Ibid., p. vii, italics added.
[5] Ibid., pp. 293 and 249, italics added. See also the significant analysis in J. A. Kregel, "Economic Methodology in the Face of Uncertainty," *Economic Journal,* June 1976.

require in order to make any specified level of employment economically worthwhile. We need to trace now the ways in which such a wage increase can be expected to affect the aggregate demand curve also.

Focusing first on the wage earners' incomes, it is clear that the wage increase will raise the incomes of the workers currently employed. Their higher disposable incomes can be expected to give rise to higher consumption expenditures, given their propensity to consume as previously discussed. Of course, the rise in the wage rate may lead to a lower level of employment, as we shall see in the following analysis. In that event the overall change in the wage earners' consumption expenditures may not be as large as it would be if the previous employment and production levels were maintained. But we are concerned at this point with the description of the consumption demand curve, as that would appear at differing levels of employment, under the assumption of a higher money wage rate. In that case both the money income function, WN, in Figure 18-11 in the preceding chapter, and the consumption outlay function, $C_w \cdot WN$ in the same figure, will rise, or turn to the left.

As the wage rate rises there will not, however, be any change in the rentier incomes discussed in Figure 18-12. Given the contractual nature of the annual interest payments that have to be made on the debt capital supplied by the rentiers, their money income will remain unchanged. The residual profit earners, whose money income and money consumption outlay functions were described in Figure 18-13, can also be expected to receive higher money incomes. For if the wage-cost markup factor is unchanged, the supply curve will rise proportionally with the increase in the money wage rate. If, as has just been noted, the rentier share of the increased flow of sales proceeds decreases (because the rentier incomes remain fixed in money terms), the residual profit share of total proceeds will increase in the short run. Again, therefore, the rise in profit earners' disposable incomes can be expected to lift their consumption outlays also. This supposes, of course, that business firms increase their dividend payments as the available cash flows and profits increase. If the marginal cash flows accruing to producers, following the rise in prices induced by the increase in the money wage rate, were retained in the business firms rather than distributed to the shareholders, then the effects on the profit earners' money incomes and consumption expenditures would be moderated.

Assuming for the present that following the increase in the money wage rate and the price level the actual investment expenditure and government expenditure outlays remain constant, the aggregate demand curve can be expected to rise. The possible impacts on both supply and demand conditions have been brought together in Figure 19-5.

The aggregate supply and demand curves consistent with wage rate W_1 are labeled in the figure as $Z(W_1)$ and $D(W_1)$, respectively. The cor-

Figure   19-5.

An increase in the money wage rate

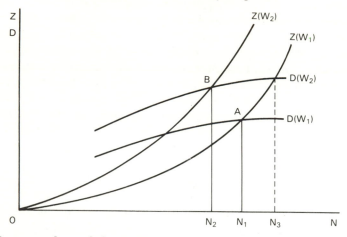

responding supply and demand curves $Z(W_2)$ and $D(W_2)$ refer to an assumedly higher money wage rate W_2.

The conditions summarized in Figure 19-5 might suggest that the increased wage payments will imply an increase in wage earners' disposable incomes. This might be expected to raise the consumption expenditure function and thus the aggregate demand curve in the manner we previously examined. This would lead to excess market demands, which might be expected to lead to higher employment and production levels. In Figure 19-5, however, the economy will tend to move up along its new aggregate supply curve to an employment level N_2, lower than could have been realized, N_3, if an increased demand could have occurred at the same wage rate as previously. In Figure 19-5 the possibility exists that the simultaneous movements of both the supply and demand curves will result in both higher prices and lower employment. The rise in the wage rate causes the employment level to change from N_1 to N_2. This is the phenomenon that existed in the United States economy during the 1970s, as shown in Table 16-2 in Chapter 16. This conjunction of supply and demand determinants explains what has been referred to as stagflation, involving the simultaneous occurrence of inflation and unemployment.

This decline in the employment level as the money wage rate rises does, in fact, imply that the demand for labor curve implicit in the analysis is negatively inclined in the classical manner. The higher wage rate has associated with it a lower level of employment. This effect is to be expected for a number of reasons. If, for example, the wage rate rises by 5 percent and the markup factor remains constant, total expected proceeds will rise by 5 percent, and the wage share will remain unchanged. But a redistribution of the profit share may occur, with the relative share of fixed income earners (rentiers) diminishing relative to that of residual profit earners. Moreover, the disposable income of the latter will not increase proportionately if, as we noted previously may be the case, a large part of the increased profits is retained in the producing firms. If, as we have suggested, the propensity to consume out of residual profits were lower relative to the consumption propensities of other income earners, this redistribution of income will prevent consumption expenditures from rising as far as might otherwise be the case. This, together with the general impact of saving out of the increased money incomes, implies that, as suggested in Figure 19-5, the aggregate demand curve will not rise sufficiently to intersect the supply curve at as high a level of employment as before.

The price level impact can be further illustrated in Figure 19-6, which is similar in construction to Figure 17-5 in Chapter 17. The figure assumes that the short-run nature of the analysis, or the fixity of the capital stock, permits us to think in terms of a short-run production possibility relation. In the short run, the level of real output, y, is dependent on the amount of labor employed, in accordance with the relation $y = y(N; \overline{K})$, where the $\overline{K}$ is an indication that the existing capital struc-

Figure   19-6.

Wage rate, employment, and price level changes

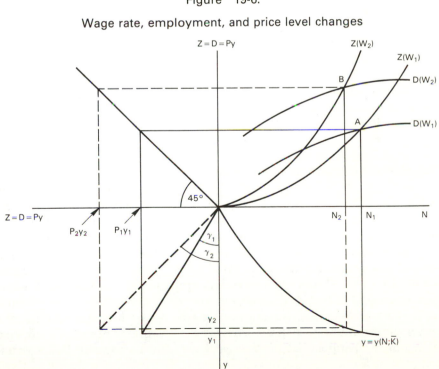

ture is given. This production possibility relation is described in the fourth (southeast) quadrant of Figure 19-6.

Figure 19-6 is based on the same kind of analysis that accompanied Figure 17-5 except that in the present case both the supply and the demand curves are assumed to shift. As in the previous case, the effective price level implicit in the change in the effective demand point from A to B (which is also reflected in the move from A to B in Figure 19-5) is explained by the magnitude of the angle γ in the third (southwest) quadrant. The relations we have in view in Figure 19-6 exhibit an increase in that angle from γ_1 to γ_2, indicating that the price level has increased.

At this stage we can look again at the same kind of monetary sector implications that we noted previously. For when the wage rate rises there will be an increase in the demand for money, for the several reasons we have already discussed. The problem that now confronts the economy can be put succinctly in the following terms. When the wage rate rises, and when higher prices are induced in accordance with the given wage-cost markup factor and the underlying productivity conditions, will the money supply increase by the extent that is necessary to enable the economy to support the previously existing level of real output and employment at the new higher level of prices? If the money supply does not increase by the requisite amount, then the relative tightness of monetary conditions that results will tend to cause a reduction in the real output and employment levels. In such a case we then have the outcome of simultaneous inflation and unemployment. This brings into focus again the fact that changes in the money supply are to a large extent endogenously determined in response to changes in the demand for money. It raises the question, also, of the extent to which the Federal Reserve Board might take exogenous action to permit the money supply to increase under the new demand pressures, or even to increase it by open market security purchases.

THE MONEY INCOME MULTIPLIER

In Chapter 18 we developed a simple real income multiplier, based on assumptions that real expenditures were related to real income. It was seen that the multiplier could be described as the reciprocal of the marginal propensity to save or, in more-sophisticated versions, as the reciprocal of the propensity for leakages to occur from the stream of income-generating expenditure. The so-called equilibrium level of real income was then equal to the total of the autonomous components in the income-generating expenditure stream multiplied by the multiplier. With the rather different analysis in this chapter it is similarly possible to develop an income multiplier. But in this case, because we are dealing with actual money flows and money incomes and expenditures and not real incomes, the multiplier will be referred to as a money income multiplier. Let us develop it in the following manner, and note briefly some of the features of it that could not be highlighted in the earlier real income case.

At the economy's effective demand point, such as A or B in Figures 19-5 or 19-6, the total expected proceeds and the total monetary demand will be equal. Expectations are realized, and the following relation holds:

(4) $$Z = D = Py$$

We know from previous analysis that the total national income, here described as Py, will be divided between the wage share and the profit share in such a way that

(5) $$Z = Py = kWN$$

The national income will be a multiple of the wage bill, WN. The relationship was examined in Chapter 16, in reference to the determinants of the value of money.

For use in what follows we note that the total wage income is equal to WN, and the profit income is equal to $(k - 1)WN$. The latter statement follows from the fact that profit income is equal to the total proceeds minus wage income, or Z minus WN. But given that the total proceeds, Z, are equal to the wage bill times a markup factor, or kWN in previous notation, the profit income appears as $Z - WN$, or $kWN - WN$, which provides the statement of profit income as $(k - 1)WN$.

Moreover, if we recognize that the wage-cost markup factor, k, is equal to the reciprocal of the wage share in the total proceeds, and refer to the wage share as α, the wage earners' income can be written as $WN = \alpha Z$, and the profit income as $(1 - \alpha)Z$.

We assume now that the economy has been brought, in the manner analyzed in the earlier sections of this chapter, to an effective demand point or a short-run or temporary equilibrium condition. To investigate the relations between employment and expenditure flows that exist at that point, let us assume initially that we are dealing with a purely private sector economy in which there is neither government expenditure nor taxation. In that case the total money expenditure flows can be broken into their consumption and investment components and described as

(6) $$Z = CW + CP + I$$

where the first two terms on the right-hand side of Equation (6) refer to wage earners' and profit earners' consumption expenditures, respectively.

The final term refers as before to the level of investment expenditure in money terms.

Making use of the construction of the consumption functions developed in Chapter 18, we can write the wage earners' consumption function as

(7) $$CW = a + C_w WN$$

where C_w now refers to the marginal propensity to consume out of wage income. Similarly, the profit earners' consumption function appears as

(8) $$CP = b + C_p(k - 1)WN$$

where C_p describes the marginal propensity to consume out of profit income.

From the relations developed immediately above in this section, and referring to total consumption in money terms as C, it follows that aggregate consumption expenditure can be written as

(9) $$C = a + b + \alpha C_w Z + (1 - \alpha)C_p Z$$

Substituting Equation (9) into Equation (6) yields the equilibrium condition at the effective demand point,

(10) $$Z = a + b + I + \alpha C_w Z + (1 - \alpha)C_p Z$$

Letting the symbol A refer to the sum of the autonomous or exogenous components of the spending stream, $a + b + I$, the short-run equilibrium relation can be stated as

(11) $$Z = A + \alpha C_w Z + (1 - \alpha)C_p Z$$

By transposition and the simplification of Equation (11) it follows that the equilibrium monetary expenditure level can be described as

(12) $$Z^* = A \frac{1}{1 - \alpha C_w - (1 - \alpha)C_p}$$

Equation (12) is the money income multiplier for which we have been seeking. It is again shown to be, in the same way as in the previous cases, equal to the reciprocal of the propensity for leakages to occur from the stream of income-generating expenditure. In this case, emphasizing the relevance of the distribution of income that we have all along shown to be implicit in the aggregate supply function, the leakages now equal

the total money income generated minus the sum of both the wage earners' and the profit earners' consumption expenditures.

Alternatively, we may write the wage earners' marginal propensity
to save out of wage income as $S_w = 1 - C_w$, and the profit earners'
comparable savings propensity as $S_p = 1 - C_p$. Then making these
substitutions in the multiplier expression in Equation (12) yields the
corresponding expression:

(13)
$$Z^* = A \frac{1}{\alpha S_w + (1 - \alpha)S_p}$$

Again the multiplier is defined as the reciprocal of the marginal propensity for leakages to occur from the income-generating expenditure
stream. More explicitly, that total leakage is shown to be the weighted
sum of the marginal propensities to save of the wage earners and the
profit earners, where those savings propensities are weighted by the relative shares of each income class in the total income.

Having reached this result, we can now take account quite simply
of the government sector's participation in the economy. First, we introduce an additional term, G, to describe government expenditure on goods
and services, on the right-hand side of Equation (6). At the same time,
the consumption propensities C_w and C_p are redefined to refer to the
marginal propensities to consume out of disposable income, which is referred to in the case of wage earners as $WN(1 - t)$, and in the case of
profit earners as $(k - 1)WN(1 - t)$. In these latter expressions the parameter t refers to the proportional tax rate. Making these necessary
amendments to the analysis and following a development similar to the
foregoing, we can incorporate the tax-adjusted multiplier into the expression for the equilibrium level of monetary expenditure:

(14)
$$Z^* = A \frac{1}{[\alpha S_w + (1 - \alpha)S_p](1 - t) + t}$$

Again the weighted sum of the different income classes' savings propensities, or in the alternative formulation their consumption propensities,
enters the multiplier expression.

THE MARGINAL INCOME AND
EMPLOYMENT MULTIPLIERS

The income multiplier we have developed in the preceding section is
similar in form to the multipliers developed in Chapter 18. An explicit
difference, of course, is that in the present case we have highlighted the

importance of the ways in which the distribution of income affects the magnitude of the multiplier. We can import this result into our earlier analysis and recall that as the economy moves up along its nonlinear aggregate supply curve, the profit share will tend to increase. The size of the multiplier will then increase or decrease, depending on the sizes of the relative marginal propensities to consume and save. If the saving propensity of the profit earners is greater than that of the wage earners, then as employment and the profit share increase, the denominator of the money income multiplier will increase, and the size of the multiplier will become smaller.

Considerations such as these focus our attention on the possible magnitudes of marginal or incremental multipliers, following a change in one of the exogenous components of the expenditure stream. In view of the incorporation into our analysis of the supply side effects implicit in the determinants of the form of the aggregate supply curve, the complete specification of the marginal multiplier is a complex task. The analytical issues involved can be illustrated by some indications of possible outcomes.

First, we know from the short-term dynamics we analyzed at the beginning of this chapter that when expenditures increase, as reflected for example in a movement upward of the aggregate demand curve, the initial excess demand will tend to call forth a higher level of employment and output. This will occur as producers revise their short-term expectations and raise their expected demand curves. But we also know, from the pressure of diminishing marginal productivity that determines the nonlinearity of the aggregate supply curve, that as employment and output rise the price level is also likely to rise. Account must therefore be taken of the ways in which the consumption expenditures of the different income classes may change as their real incomes change from the threefold influences of (1) higher employment levels, (2) higher commodity prices, and (3) an altered relative distribution of income.

Let us consider briefly the way in which the marginal multipliers will appear if some restrictive assumptions are introduced into the aggregate supply curve. These are illustrated in Figure 19-7.

In Figure 19-7 the assumption is made initially that the wage rate is given and that the wage bill, WN, is described by a linear ray from the origin. Additionally, we make the assumption that as employment and production increase the ratio of the marginal to the average product of labor remains constant, providing, as we examined in Chapter 17, a linear aggregate supply curve. Alternatively, we may state the assumption at this point that at the same time as the wage rate is constant, the wage-cost markup factor, k, is also constant, and that this accordingly implies the linear total proceeds function or the aggregate supply curve shown in the figure. It will be recalled from the supply curve analysis in

Figure   19-7.

Expenditure increases and linear supply conditions

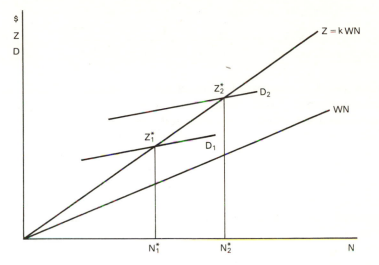

Chapter 17 that these assumptions imply that as employment increases the wage and profit shares remain constant.

With these assumptions in hand, let us return to the basic money income multiplier of Equation (14), reproduced here in expanded form:

$$(15) \qquad Z^* = (a + b + I + G) \frac{1}{[\alpha S_w + (1 - \alpha)S_p](1 - t) + t}$$

We can imagine, then, that an increase occurs in one of the autonomous components of the spending stream, here shown in the multiplicand term on the right-hand side of Equation (15). For purposes of illustration assume an incremental increase in investment expenditure, ΔI, which, in Figure 19-7, has the effect of raising the aggregate demand curve from its initial position of D_1 to D_2.

The new equilibrium employment shown in Figure 19-7 as N_2^* will have associated with it a new effective demand or total proceeds of Z_2^*. This expenditure magnitude is describable in terms of the total money income multiplier of Equation (15) as equal to the new aggregate autonomous expenditure $(a + b + I + \Delta I + G)$ multiplied by the now familiar multiplier:

$$(16) \qquad Z_2^* = (a + b + I + \Delta I + G) \frac{1}{[\alpha S_w + (1 - \alpha)S_p](1 - t) + t}$$

Subtracting Equation (15), taking this now as describing the initial equilibrium income at Z_1^*, from Equation (16), it follows that the incremental
multiplier can be stated as

(17)
$$\Delta Z^* = \Delta I \frac{1}{[\alpha S_w + (1 - \alpha)S_p](1 - t) + t}$$

This result has occurred because, as we assumed, the investment
function moved to the right in the investment–interest rate plane, owing
to some underlying cause that increased the marginal efficiency of investment. If, similarly, a change in consumption habits and propensities
should occur, reflected for example in an increase in the a or the b parameters in the wage earners' and profit earners' consumption functions,
the corresponding consumption functions would rise in the income–
consumption plane, and an incremental multiplicand would have been
introduced to the spending stream. In that case the multiplier described
in Equation (17) would have come into play in the same way as in the
case examined.

A further advance over the simple real income multiplier of Chapter
18 is also possible. We recall for this purpose that $Z = kWN$, and we
divide Equation (15) throughout by kW. The following employment multiplier can then be derived:

(18)
$$N = (a + b + I + G) \frac{1}{kW\{[\alpha S_w + (1 - \alpha)S_p](1 - t) + t\}}$$

The incremental employment multiplier also follows in terms analogous
to those contained in Equation (17):

(19)
$$\Delta N = \Delta I \frac{1}{kW\{[\alpha S_w + (1 - \alpha)S_p](1 - t) + t\}}$$

By way of further explanation of the employment multiplier, we
note that when the total proceeds of the sale of output increase, the wage
share will rise by $1/k$ times that increase. For this reason, Equation (19)
is in effect derived from Equation (17) by dividing the latter by k. But
that, in effect, provides the wage share multiplier. We have to take account also of the fact that each additional unit of labor employed will
attract a wage rate of W. We must then divide Equation (17) by W as
well as by k, in order to reduce it to a measure of the actual number of
units of labor employed. The final result is as shown in Equation (19).

COMPLEXITIES IN THE INCREMENTAL
EMPLOYMENT MULTIPLIER

The results we have just stated, focusing on the incremental employment that occurs after the introduction to the spending stream of an incremental multiplicand, follow from the rather special assumptions we made in the preceding section and summarized in Figure 19-7. It was possible to divide Equation (15) by kW to obtain the employment multiplier in Equation (18) because of the assumptions that the values of both k and W were given and fixed. In the general case, however, there is no reason to believe this will be true. We saw in Chapter 17 that certain possible forms of the technological production function (for example, the Cobb-Douglas form as referred to in footnote 10 of Chapter 17) will provide a ratio of the marginal product to the average product that remains constant as employment and output increase. Such a production function maintains a constant relative wage and profit share of total proceeds or income, and therefore a constant wage-cost markup factor, k, as assumed in Figure 19-7. But as we have seen from the extensive development of the determinants of the form of the aggregate supply curve, this will not in general be true.

The situation more likely to be encountered is that in which the markup factor, k, is itself functionally dependent on the level of employment. Generally, k will depend positively on employment and thereby impart, as we have seen, a nonlinearity and convexity to the aggregate supply curve. Moreover, it is quite possible that as employment increases the money wage rate will also increase. The effect of that, we noted previously in this chapter, will be to turn the aggregate supply curve to the left and, in accordance with the general pricing formula, raise the level of prices.

We can begin to take some of these complexities into account by noting carefully that in the case we considered on the basis of Figure 19-7, the assumed constancy of the wage rate and the markup factor do not imply a constancy of the price level. Prices can still be expected to rise in this case, depending on the form of the underlying production possibility relation. In other words, in the Cobb-Douglas case we cited as an example of a production relation that preserved a constant ratio of the marginal to the average product, the marginal product will diminish as employment increases (see again footnote 10 of Chapter 17). With the marginal and average products declining, therefore, or with producing firms' marginal costs rising, higher selling prices are to be expected even though the wage-cost markup factor remains constant. Consider, for example, the relations summarized in Figure 19-8.

Figure 19-8 preserves all the assumptions of Figure 19-7 and depicts again the effects on the equilibrium level of the expenditure stream, Z^*,

Figure   19-8.

Aggregate demand and price level variations

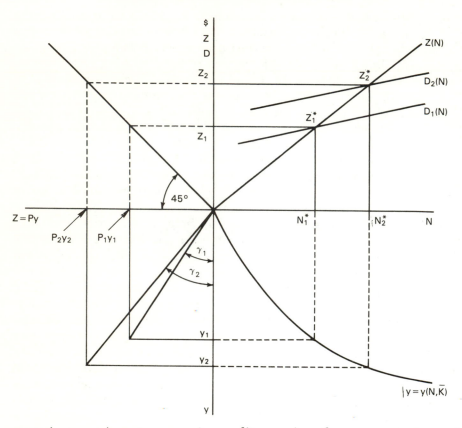

as an increase in autonomous expenditure raises the aggregate demand curve from $D_1(N)$ to $D_2(N)$. The lower (southeast) section of Figure 19-8, however, introduces the production possibility relation and exhibits the diminishing marginal and average productivity implicit in it. At the same time, Figure 19-8, which reproduces the analysis summarized in Figure 19-6, traces out the price increase effects of the assumed increase in monetary expenditure. This is depicted, as in the earlier analysis, by the increase in the magnitude of the angle γ in the southwest quadrant of the figure.

This price increase effect must be understood, of course, to have the same implications as previously for possible variations in consumption and investment expenditures as real incomes are varied as a result, and as the real values of investment expenditure budgets are reduced. In short, we observe from Figure 19-8 that even in the case of assumedly constant wage rates and a constant markup factor, some of the increased monetary expenditure will be dissipated in rising prices, and a less than proportionate increase in real output will occur.

THE EMPLOYMENT EFFECTS OF A VARIABLE MARKUP FACTOR

We now relax the assumption that the wage-cost markup factor is fixed or that, in other words, the wage earners' share in total proceeds remains constant as employment increases. The markup factor may need to be interpreted as functionally dependent on the level of employment, particularly if, as we recognize in the general case in Chapter 17, the pressures of diminishing marginal productivity impart a nonlinearity and convexity to the aggregate supply curve. In that case we can write $k = k(N)$.

Let us return, then, to Equation (14) and reconsider the expenditure equilibrium condition. We reproduce this in Equation (20) by writing Z in equivalent form as kWN, and by expressing the multiplier denominator in Equation (14) as s:

$$(20) \qquad\qquad kWN = A/s$$

Acknowledging the dependence of k on N, we rewrite Equation (20) as

$$(21) \qquad\qquad k(N)WN = A/s$$

If we now envisage an incremental increase in investment expenditure as in the preceding case, we can derive an incremental employment multiplier by differentiating Equation (21) with respect to I, recalling that the existing total of investment expenditure, I, is a component of the autonomous variable A on the right-hand side of Equation (21). Rewriting the resulting differential in terms of finite differences, it can be shown that[6]

$$(22) \qquad\qquad \Delta N = \Delta I \frac{1}{[k(N) + Nk'(N)]Ws}$$

For purposes of comparison the incremental employment multiplier in Equation (19) is reproduced in corresponding form in Equation (23):

$$(23) \qquad\qquad \Delta N = \Delta I \frac{1}{kWs}$$

[6] Equation (22) is derived by first differentiating the left-hand side of Equation (21) with respect to N, using the chain rule to differentiate with respect to I, and transposing the results to isolate the change in employment, dN, on the left-hand side of Equation (22).

It will be clear, from a comparison of Equations (22) and (23), that the denominator of the multiplier expression in Equation (22) is larger, given the positive sign on $k'(N)$, or given, that is, the tendency for the value of k, the wage-cost markup factor, to increase as employment increases. This, we have seen, is a reflection of the nonlinearity of the aggregate supply curve. For this reason, the incremental employment multiplier in Equation (22) will be smaller when the markup factor is variable in the manner indicated.

The implication is that when the level of expenditure increases, a larger proportion of it will be dissipated in higher commodity prices, implying, further, that a smaller net effect will be felt on increased employment and output. This reduction in the employment multiplier leaves out of account, moreover, the possible effects on the weighted average propensity to save, and hence on the magnitude of s, resulting from any redistribution of income as the value of k changes.

THE EMPLOYMENT EFFECTS
OF A VARIABLE WAGE RATE

In the same way as in the preceding section, it would be possible to investigate the effects on the incremental employment multiplier of an increase in the money wage rate as employment increased. In that case we could substitute the relation $W(N)$, showing the wage rate depending on the employment level, for the symbol W in Equation (20). The corresponding equilibrium expenditure relation, analogous to Equation (21), would then appear as

(24) $$kW(N)N = A/s$$

with the remaining symbols being used in the same sense as in the preceding section.

In that case the development of the incremental employment multiplier could proceed as before, and the following relation derived:

(25) $$\Delta N = \Delta I \frac{1}{k[W(N) + NW'(N)]s}$$

Again this result can be compared with Equation (23), from which the same conclusion will be observed. The tendency for the money wage rate to rise as employment increases, giving again a positive sign on $W'(N)$, increases the denominator of the incremental employment multiplier, and therefore decreases the magnitude of the multiplier. Again the implication is that when the expenditure level increases as assumed, part of that increase will be dissipated in increased wages and prices, implying a smaller increase in employment and real output than would otherwise occur.

The effects on incremental employment, output, and incomes of an increase in expenditure can therefore be summarized by saying that they depend on (1) the possible variation in money wage rates as conditions in the labor market tighten as employment increases; (2) the possible increase in the wage-cost markup factor if, as output and employment rise, industrialists raise the markup factor to take account of what they imagine to be increased market or monopoly power; (3) the possible change in the relative importance of diminishing marginal productivity, thereby taking us back to the original forces that contributed to the nonlinearity of the aggregate supply curve in the first place; and (4) the redistribution of income, with resulting effects on the weighted sum of the savings propensities in the multiplier formula, that occurs as the employment and activity levels increase.

THE RELEVANCE OF MONETARY CONDITIONS AND THE RATE OF INTEREST

Finally in connection with this development of the money income and employment multipliers, we must bear in mind that the analysis is not complete until we have taken the monetary sector and possible interest rate effects into account. We have commented on that earlier in this chapter. In the present exercise, the assumption is that once again the increased requirements of money can be assumed to be provided as the economy moves up along its aggregate supply curve, or up through the multiplier process that is lifting it to higher employment and output levels.

Another way of stating that requirement is to say that as the economy moves to higher activity levels, the investment component of the spending stream, or the location of the investment expenditure function, should not be altered as a result of any monetary stringency or increases in the rate of interest. If the latter should happen, an induced reduction in investment spending would occur, tending to offset the initial increase in investment that instigated the multiplier process.

THE SITUATIONAL VARIABLES

We have referred in earlier contexts to six important situational variables that, taken together, describe the condition of the macroeconomy at any time. These are M^s, the money supply; y, the real income or output; P, the price level; N, the level of employment; r, the rate of interest; and e, the international exchange rate. We can now combine the results of Chapters 15 through 18 and the present chapter to indicate the principal forces that determine these variables. In so doing, we are suggesting the principal determinative forces involved. We are not proceeding, in the manner of the neoclassical macroequilibrium theory, to state that a uniquely definable, mutually determined, equilibrium posture can actually be specified. We emphasize again that we have examined the principal determinative relations on the assumption that the state of expectations, on the part of both the producers and the consumers in the economy, is given. We referred earlier in this chapter to a *ceteris paribus* dynamics internal to the short-run situation. But there is no reason to believe that in actual fact all other things will remain equal for very long. We are much more impressed by what Shackle has called the possibility of kaleidic changes in economic states of affairs.[7]

The interaction of aggregate supply and aggregate demand, in the manner of the present chapter, determines the level of effective demand. This, then, enables us to specify the level of employment at which that demand will in fact be effective. The level of employment enables us to describe the level of real output, given the short-run production possibility relation in the economy. This is described, for example, in the southeast quadrant of Figure 19-6. Having determined real output and the employment level, y and N, the price level is deducible from the determinative variables in the general definitional equation of the price level, k, W, N, and A, as described in Chapter 16. The average product is derivable from the preceding determination of the real output, y, and the employment level, N. The money wage rate is understood to be exogenously given, in the manner described in Chapter 16. The wage-cost markup factor, k, is also empirically observable on a trend basis. Its possible short-run variations are derivable from productivity considerations and from possible changes in the degree of market power enjoyed by producers.

Having thus determined y, P, and N, the levels of monetary expenditure consistent with them are deducible in the manner exhibited in the derivation of the money expenditure flow functions in Chapter 18. The implicit level of monetary expenditure, which is again, of course, defined by the effective demand point determined by the aggregate supply and demand cross, then determines what we saw in Chapter 15 as the transactions demand for money. Taking this transactions demand for money in conjunction with the asset demand also developed in Chapter

---

[7] See G.L.S. Shackle, *Epistemics and Economics* (Cambridge: Cambridge University Press, 1972); and *Keynesian Kaleidics* (Edinburgh: Edinburgh University Press, 1974). See also Douglas Vickers, "Uncertainty, Choice, and the Marginal Efficiencies," *Journal of Post Keynesian Economics*, Winter 1979–80.

15 and the creation of money by the banking system, we can envisage the supply and demand functions for money in the money-interest rate plane. The rate of interest then emerges as the equilibrating variable that determines the market-clearing price of money in the market for money. At the same time, that market-clearing outcome determines the actual amount of the money supply that the banks and other depository institutions find it profitable to bring into existence.

We have so far left unexamined the supply and demand forces in the international foreign exchange markets that determine the international exchange rate, e. We have referred to these at some length in our discussion of the gold standard in Chapter 4 and we shall return to them in Part VIII.

SUMMARY

This chapter has brought together the aggregate supply relation developed in Chapter 17 and the aggregate demand relation of Chapter 18 to construct a postclassical short-run model of the macroeconomy. The *ceteris paribus* dynamics internal to the short-run situation were examined to describe the effective demand point. This took account, on the demand side, of the important distinction between the aggregate demand curve, reflecting the actual monetary expenditures by decision makers on the demand side of the commodity markets, and the producers' expected demand curves which reflect the state of producers' market expectations. The significance of an exogenously given money wage rate was emphasized, and the implications of changes in money wage rates, for both the supply side and the demand side of the model, were discussed.

The short-run internal dynamics were shown to imply both a money income multiplier and an employment multiplier. These were derived and comparisons were made between them and the simple real income multiplier described in Chapter 18. Emphasis was placed on the incremental income and employment multipliers, and attention was drawn to a number of complexities involved in the specification of their possible magnitudes.

A highly significant aspect of the money income and employment multipliers was that they took account of the distribution of income at different possible points on the economy's aggregate supply curve. Tracing the variations in income distribution as employment levels change permits corresponding estimates of the strength of the multipliers in the system. It also permits varying estimates of the strength of wage earners' and profit earners' money expenditure functions.

It was acknowledged, also, that the strength and the likelihood of a smooth operation of the implicit multipliers in the system depend on the extent to which accommodative developments occur in the monetary sector. A reluctance on the part of the banking system or the monetary authorities to permit the money supply to increase as rapidly as the demand for it, in the light of the employment and real output expansion, could inhibit the expansionary process itself.

A summary of the principal determinative forces contained in the preceding chapters permitted a statement to be made regarding the determination of the situational variables M^s, y, P, N, r, and e. These will again be subject to further discussion in the following chapters, and their possible relation to economic policies will be observed.

IMPORTANT CONCEPTS

Causes of inflation

Aggregate supply and demand curves

Producers' expected demand curve

Effective demand point

State of expectations

Distribution of income

Ceteris paribus dynamics

Efficiency wage

Short-run production possibility relation

Money income and employment multipliers

Propensity to consume out of wage and profit incomes

QUESTIONS FOR DISCUSSION AND REVIEW

1. List as fully as possible, and examine critically, the factors that contribute to the nonlinearity of the economy's aggregate supply curve.

2. Do you agree that, in general, the points lying on the aggregate supply curve reflect profit maximization production points for the individual producers in the economy? Explain why or why not.

3. What determines, and what is determined by, the distribution of income in the economy?

4. Why is it necessary to distinguish between (1) the aggregate demand curve and (2) the producers' expected demand curve, and what is meant by "the different determining forces underlying the respective curves"?

5. Why did Keynes introduce the concept of "shifting equilibrium"?

6. In what ways can the short-run model of the macroeconomy take account of changes in both (1) the money wage rate and (2) the wage-cost markup factor? Explain fully.

7. Can you explain "stagflation"?

8. What special difficulties exist in the specification of the incremental employment multiplier?

9. Trace the development of the forces you would expect to come into play in the United States economy if, in the existing structure and institutional arrangements, the marginal efficiency of investment were to improve.

10. Are the money supply and money market conditions relevant to the determination of the short-run effects of an increase in autonomous expenditure? How and why?

20

THE NEOCLASSICAL– KEYNESIAN SYNTHESIS

STUDY OBJECTIVES:

• To understand the structure of the neoclassical model as a branch of equilibrium theorizing, and to examine its view of mutually determined equilibrium market outcomes
• To gain a clear view of the meaning and importance of equilibrium conditions in
    1. The goods market
    2. The money market
    3. The labor market
• To derive the *IS* and *LM* potential equilibrium loci, and to note the use of them to derive systemwide equilibrium results
• To use the neoclassical system to generate aggregate supply and aggregate demand curves, and to observe their usefulness and results
• To consider the policy implications of the model, observing some differences between the monetarist and the Keynesian viewpoints within the neoclassical system of thought
• To take account of some logical and methodological difficulties with the neoclassical analysis of the macroeconomic system

The analytical distinctions we have drawn throughout this book have been those that differentiate the postclassical from the neoclassical conceptions of the macroeconomy. We have focused consistently—on the level of theory construction, in the discussion of the structure and functioning of economic institutions, and in the brief remarks we have made so far on monetary and other economic policies—on the significance of monetary flows. Our model of the macroeconomy structured its aggregate supply and demand curves on the foundations of the money flows implicit in the cost-revenue-income-expenditure relationships inherent in it. Throughout, however, we have referred to alternative ways of looking at things, and in this chapter we shall summarize more systematically the main propositions of the neoclassical theory. Three preliminary comments will orient our approach to it.

First, the system of thought that we shall summarize in this chapter describes what has become known as the neoclassical–Keynesian synthesis. We have referred in the preceding chapters to differences between the analytical approaches of the monetarists on the one hand and the neo–Keynesians on the other. We shall see more fully in the following chapters on monetary policy that they also hold different views of the transmission mechanism in monetary theory and policy. Other differences will also be examined, such as their diverging assumptions regarding the ease and certainty with which the automatic self-equilibrating forces in the market system can be relied upon to return the economy to full employment if, for any reason, it is dislodged from it. But a deeper underlying unity between the neoclassical and the neo–Keynesian viewpoints can be discerned. In fact, many economists understand the debates on matters of analytical substance and method to have been almost completely submerged by this time, establishing a unified and common theoretical structure and leaving only differences of emphasis to be discussed. That common analytical structure has attracted the name of the neoclassical–Keynesian synthesis.

Second, this unified theoretical system has become possible because both schools of thought, the earlier neoclassical and the earlier Keynesian, quickly capitulated almost completely to a revival in macroeconomics of equilibrium theoretic analysis. That stemmed, in particular, from the Walrasian general equilibrium theory that has preoccupied economists in most areas of analysis since its revival in the 1930s. In the very year following the publication of Keynes' *General Theory of Employment, Interest, and Money* in 1936, John Hicks restated what he thought was the message of the work in general equilibrium theoretic terms in his famous "Mr. Keynes and the 'Classics.'" Neoclassicism and the earlier Keynesianism have come together in the contemporary equilibrium theory and have asked, in one way or another, what relations exist between the important macroeconomic variables in the system when full general equilibrium conditions are satisfied. The analysis proceeds in a search for the conditions that can be expected to exist when, after any disturbing storm in the economy, the sea is calm and the ocean is flat again.

It is significant to note, however, in anticipation of the equilibrium theoretic *ISLM* argument in this chapter, that Sir John Hicks has recently commented as follows on his earlier work that instigated the movement in this direction: "The IS–LM diagram, which is widely, but not universally, accepted as a convenient synopsis of Keynesian theory, is a thing

for which I cannot deny that I have some responsibility . . . I have, however, not concealed that as time has gone on I have myself become dis-
satisfied with it . . .[1] The 'Keynesian revolution' went off at half-cock.
The [general] equilibrists did not know that they were beaten . . . they
thought that what Keynes had said could be absorbed into their equilibrium systems; all that was needed was that the scope of their equilibrium
systems should be extended. As we know, there has been a lot of extension,
a vast amount of extension; what I am saying is that it never quite got
to the point . . . I must say that that [ISLM] diagram is now much less
popular with me than I think it still is with many other people. It reduces
the *General Theory* to equilibrium economics; it is not really *in* time.
That, of course, is why it has done so well."[2] Hicks has seen that time,
expectations, and uncertainty, and the structure of actual money flows
in the context of them, need to become the real subjects of analysis.

Third, it follows from this preoccupation with the conditions of equilibrium that the theory emphasizes the ways in which these conditions
are expressed in a number of separate markets in the economy. The
economy is described for analytical and policy purposes by a small number
of aggregated markets. These usually include (1) a goods market, (2) the
labor market, (3) the money market, (4) the nonmonetary asset market,
and (5) the foreign exchange market. The analytical problem, then, is
that of describing the relations between the forces that determine equilibrium in these different markets, the possible levels of interdependence
and interaction between them, and the equilibrium relations between
their separate outcome variables.

We recall from our earlier discussion of the money and the securities
markets that the rate of interest can be looked upon from two different
but closely related aspects. In its stock aspect, the rate of interest is the
market-clearing price of money. It is the variable that brings into a
market-clearing relation the separately specified supply of money and
the demand for money. In its flow aspect, the rate of interest is the variable
that establishes, for a given level of income, the flow of the supply of,
and the demand for, investable money capital funds. There is no logical
problem or contradiction in these dual aspects or functions of the rate of
interest. For the rate of interest at which individuals satisfy their desire
to hold money and securities on the one hand is precisely what is described

[1] John Hicks, "IS–LM: An Explanation," *Journal of Post Keynesian Economics*, Winter 1980–81, p. 139. See also J. R. Hicks, "Mr. Keynes and the 'Classics,' " *Econometrica*,
1937.

[2] Sir John R. Hicks, "Some Questions of Time in Economics," in Anthony M. Tang,
Fred M. Westfield, and James S. Worley, eds., *Evolution, Welfare, and Time in Economics:
Essays in Honor of Nicholas Georgescu-Roegen* (Lexington: Lexington Books, 1976), pp.
140–41, italics in original. See also John Hicks, *Causality in Economics* (New York: Basic
Books, 1979).

by the market yield on securities, which varies inversely with the market prices of securities, on the other.

This being given, there is no analytical need to examine both the market for money and the market for nonmonetary income-earning assets. When one is in equilibrium the other will be in equilibrium also. In the apparatus of the neoclassical–Keynesian synthesis, therefore, assuming initially that we confine our attention to a closed economy and leave aside the foreign exchange market, it will suffice to focus on the three markets for goods, money, and labor.

The neoclassical labor market was discussed in Chapter 17, in order to compare the derivation of its aggregate supply curve with the aggregate supply analysis in the postclassical system of thought. The principal result is summarized in Figures 17-7, 17-8, and 17-9 of that chapter. Essentially, the argument assumes that the money wage rate is determined as the equilibrating variable that brings together the demand for labor, as that is dependent on the marginal productivity of labor, and the supply of labor, as that is determined by individuals' preferences for income as against leisure. The supply and demand curves in the labor market having been specified, the market price of labor, or the money wage rate, is determined as what we called an endogenous variable.

The neoclassical labor market analysis leads to the derivation of an aggregate supply curve. But this is very differently specified from the aggregate supply curve we have incorporated into the preceding model of the macroeconomy. This difference, which is, in a sense, a principal end result of the contrasting analytical standpoints adopted, should be kept in mind as we proceed. The neoclassical supply curve is described in a price-output space. It was depicted in Figure 17-8 of Chapter 17 and will be incorporated into our discussion again below. It describes the attainable level of real income or output, y, as a function of, or as dependent upon, the price level, P. It is described by the equation $y = y(P)$.

The neoclassical analysis also derives an aggregate demand curve that is definable in the same space as its aggregate supply curve. Again we shall have a supply and demand cross. This relation between the aggregate demand, or $y^d = y^d(P)$, where the superscript d refers to demand, and the aggregate supply, or $y^s = y^s(P)$, determines the system's equilibrium price and real output results.[3]

EQUILIBRIUM IN THE GOODS MARKET

The analysis at this stage will proceed in the same terms as in the initial sections of Chapter 18, where the basic consumption and expenditure functions were derived. Much of the discussion at that earlier point forms

[3] For an excellent presentation of the neoclassical–Keynesian synthesis, to which parts of this chapter are heavily indebted, see William H. Branson, *Macroeconomic Theory and Policy*, 2nd ed. (New York: Harper & Row, 1979).

an essential part of what has developed as the neoclassical–Keynesian synthesis, and it must now be integrated with the following more-advanced argument. The variables in the analysis are real variables, using the lower-case c, for example, to refer to real consumption as distinct from consumption in current money values. The other variables, also in lower case, will be the same as those employed in Chapter 18 and will be self-explanatory in the following argument.

The level of real output, suppressing for the present the problem of the price variable in the same manner as is usually done in the neoclassical argument, depends on the total stream of real income-generating expenditures. Confining the analysis for the present to that of a closed economy, the expenditure stream comprises consumption expenditure, c; investment expenditure, i, which will again be assumed to depend on the rate of interest, r; and government expenditure on goods and services, g. The basic real income equation, or the goods market equilibrium condition, can be stated as follows:

(1) $$y = a + b(y - ty) + i(r) + g$$

Here the first two terms on the right-hand side of the equation describe the consumption expenditure as a function of the level of disposable income. The latter is equal to the actual level of real income, y, minus the tax revenue collected by the government. This tax revenue is assumed here, for convenience of exposition but without loss of generality, to be a proportion of real income, where the proportionality factor, t, is the tax rate. The first term on the right-hand side of Equation (1), a, is the constant term in the consumption function, representing as before the autonomous component of consumption expenditure. Investment expenditure is shown here as functionally dependent on the rate of interest, and the government expenditure is again assumed to be autonomous.

Equation (1) is referred to as the goods market equilibrium condition when the left-hand side is interpreted as the supply of real ouput and the right-hand side is understood as the total demand for it. In the usual fashion in all the equilibrium analysis that follows, the equality of supply and demand in the market, or more properly the market-clearing condition, is understood as the equilibrium condition. The analysis of the market system as a whole thereby structures a system of comparative static equilibrium theory.

We recall now the simple real income multiplier analysis of Chapter 18. On the basis of it, Equation (1) determines implicitly an equilibrium level of income describable as

(2) $$y^* = [a + i(r) + g] \frac{1}{1 - b(1 - t)}$$

So far as the income analysis is concerned, the autonomous consumption and government expenditures, to which is added the investment expenditure that is introduced to the income-generating expenditure stream after its magnitude is determined by the rate of interest, are multiplied up by the real income multiplier described in Equation (2). This multiplier, as before, is the reciprocal of the marginal propensity for leakages to occur from the circular flow of income-generating expenditure.

Equation (1) can be looked upon also, as we have said, as describing the equilibrium condition in the goods market. Let us note a significant chain of causal relations inherent in the equation. First, the level of investment expenditure is determined by the rate of interest, r. Then second, this is introduced into the implicit income multiplier condition described in Equation (2) to determine the equilibrium level of income. Recalling the incremental multiplier from Chapter 18, we can describe the manner in which an incremental change in income depends on an incremental change in investment expenditure, which depends, in turn, on a change in the rate of interest. This chain of causation is captured in Equation (3):

(3)
$$\Delta y = \Delta i(\Delta r) \frac{1}{1 - b(1 - t)}$$

In this equation the incremental multiplicand describes the change in investment expenditure dependent on the change in the rate of interest.

This chain of relationships is summarized in the familiar investment and income equilibrium diagrams depicted in Figures 20-1 and 20-2. At interest rate r_1 the level of investment expenditure will be equal to i_1 in

Figure   20-1.

Investment expenditure

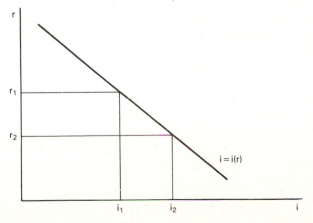

Figure   20-2.

Equilibrium income

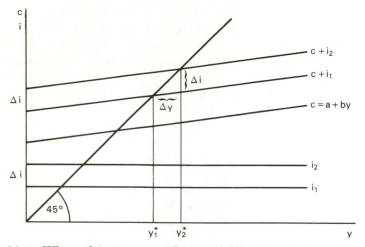

Figure 20-1. When this (measured on a different scale) is added to the consumption function in Figure 20-2, the total expenditure function, $c + i_1$, will generate the equilibrium level of income y_1, or the income level that is equilibrium in the sense in which we explained that term in Chapter 18. (Here, for purposes of simplifying the exposition, we are ignoring the government sector, and consumption is therefore shown as depending on the level of income without adjustment for taxes.) If, however, the rate of interest should fall to r_2 in Figure 20-1, investment expenditure would rise to i_2. When this is added to the consumption function in Figure 20-2, the new total expenditure function of $c + i_2$ will generate the higher equilibrium income level of y_2. An incremental multiplier is clearly at work, for the incremental change in equilibrium income in Figure 20-2, shown there as Δy, is greater than the incremental investment expenditure, or the multiplicand, shown as Δi.

We have, then, the successive relations: Investment depends on the interest rate, or $i = i(r)$, and income depends on the level of investment expenditure, or $y = y(i)$. In short, the final equilibrium level of income depends on a variable that itself depends on the rate of interest. Indirectly, therefore, the level of income depends on the rate of interest. Using the symbol y^* to represent this equilibrium income, the relation we have just deduced can be written as

(4) $y^* = y^*[i(r)],$

or more directly,

(5) $y^* = y^*(r)$

This relation, which shows that the equilibrium income level depends on the rate of interest, is depicted in Figure 20-3.

Let us underline precisely what is involved in this relation. On the vertical axis of Figure 20-3 we measure the rate of interest, and on the horizontal axis we describe the equilibrium level of income that is consistent with a given or specified rate of interest, or the level of income that will exist when the multiplier process has worked out its effects. Note that the arrow in the diagram indicates the direction of causation involved in the relation. The causation runs from the rate of interest to the level of income. The implied functional relation has been given a special designation in the neoclassical–Keynesian theory. It is referred to as the *IS* function, and the curve in Figure 20-3 is known as the *IS* curve. This is so for the following reason.

We recall that (dealing here with a private sector economy for purposes of exposition) at any equilibrium level of income the leakages from the income-generating expenditure stream, in this case savings, will be precisely offset by injections into that spending stream, in this case investment expenditure. In short, at the equilibrium income level investment equals saving, or $i = s$. The curve in Figure 20-3 indicates the income levels at which, for given or specified interest rates, this equality between savings and investment will be satisfied. It is therefore in effect what we can call a potential equilibrium locus. It describes what would be the equilibrium levels of income consistent with different specified rates of interest. Any point on the locus is a potential economywide equilibrium income point. Of course, we still need further information to be able to conclude which point, of all the possible equilibrium points on the *IS* curve, is the one at which the economy will come to rest.

Figure   20-3.

The *IS* curve

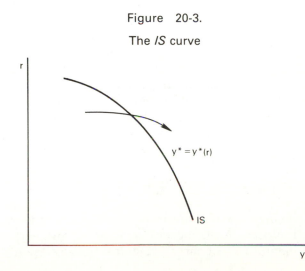

But first, one final point might be made about the *IS* curve. This is that the slope of the curve, or the sensitivity of the change in equilibrium income to the change in the rate of interest, depends on the sensitivity of the investment expenditure to the change in the interest rate and on the magnitude of the multiplier, which depends, in turn, on the marginal propensity to consume. This follows, of course, from Equation (3) above. For the mathematically inclined reader it can also be shown very simply in the following manner.

We rewrite Equation (1) in the form

(6) $y = a + b(1 - t)y + i(r) + g$

Then focusing on simultaneous changes in the interest rate and the income level, Δr and Δy, and ignoring the autonomous elements of expenditure, a and g, which, by the assumption that they are autonomous, do not change, we have the following statement of incremental differences:

(7) $\Delta y = b(1 - t)\Delta y + i'\Delta r$

In Equation (7) the expression i' refers to the change in the investment expenditure induced by the change in the rate of interest. Dividing Equation (7) throughout by Δr, transposing, and collecting terms, it follows that

(8) $\Delta y/\Delta r = \dfrac{i'}{1 - b(1 - t)}$

The left-hand side of Equation (8) describes the rate of change in y for a given change in r. It describes, that is to say, the slope of the *IS* curve in Figure 20-3. The slope of the curve is equal to the rate of change in the underlying investment expenditure function (as dependent on the rate of interest) multiplied by our now familiar multiplier. Again it is seen that the change in investment expenditure is being multiplied up to the resulting change in equilibrium income.

To complete the neoclassical argument we need to marry to this goods market result the implications of the simultaneous equilibrium in the markets for money and labor. We turn to the money market in the next section.

EQUILIBRIUM IN THE MONEY MARKET

The demand for money was shown in Chapter 15 to depend on the level of real income, the price level, the rate of interest, and expectations of changes in the magnitudes of those variables. Setting aside the expectational variables for the time being, the demand-for-money function can be expressed as

(9) $$M^d = M^d(y,P,r)$$

Focusing now on the relation between the real variables in the system, we can speak, in standard neoclassical language, of the demand for real money. Expressing this as M^d/P, we can conceive of the corresponding demand function:

(10) $$\frac{M^d}{P} = f(y,r)$$

If, for the present, we set aside the possibility of variations in the price level, and if we assume with the neoclassical theory that the money supply as determined by the central bank is also fixed, we can state the equilibrium condition in the market for money. We shall assume, for purposes of exposition, that the transactions demand for money is dependent principally on the level of income, and that the asset demand depends on the rate of interest. The money market equilibrium condition then appears as follows:

(11) $$m = k(y) + l(r)$$

Here the symbol m refers to the given supply of real money, or the actual nominal money supply, which is fixed by the central bank, divided by the given price level. The first term on the right-hand side of Equation (11) describes the transactions demand for money as depending on the level of income, and the second term describes the familiar asset demand, depending on the rate of interest.

This money market equilibrium condition performs a number of functions in the neoclassical scheme. We shall see that the construction of the economy's aggregate demand curve is actually embedded in it. But first, let us observe the manner in which, as shown in Figure 20-4, the equilibrium position is reached.

The demand for money is described in Figure 20-4 by a family of demand curves. Each curve describes the way in which the demand for real money, here referred to as m^d, depends on the rate of interest, on the assumption that the level of income is specified. For higher levels of income the demand-for-money curve will lie farther from the origin, to reflect the fact that the higher income will also be absorbing a larger amount of money for transactions purposes. At interest rate r_2, for example, the total demand for money would be OB if income level y_1 obtained, but it would be larger, or OA, if the income level were y_2. This is

Figure   20-4.

Money market equilibrium

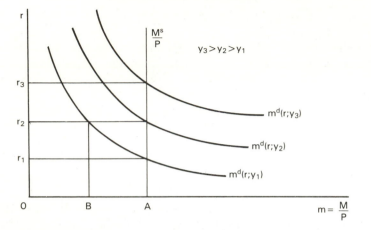

similar to the relationships described in Figure 15-7 of Chapter 15, where the demand for nominal or actual money balances was discussed in the context of our money flow analysis.

The money supply curve in Figure 20-4, labeled M^s/P to describe the supply of real money, is drawn as a vertical line to reflect the assumption that the money supply is fixed. The supply-and-demand cross in the money market then determines the equilibrium rate of interest, or the market-clearing price of money. At income level y_1, for example, the rate of interest that equilibrates the money market will be r_1. At a higher income, say y_2, the equilibrium rate of interest will be r_2.

These successive equilibrium conditions in the money market imply that a positive relation exists between the postulated level of income and the rate of interest that will equilibrate the money market consistent with that level of income. The higher the income, the higher will be the equilibrium rate of interest in the money market. Using the symbol r^* to describe this equilibrium rate of interest, we have the relation

(12) $$r^* = r^*(y)$$

This relation has also been given a special designation in the neoclassical theory. It is usually referred to as the *LM* relation, and the curve describing it in Figure 20-5 is known as the *LM* curve. This *LM* curve describes the rates of interest at which, for successively higher levels of income, the money market will be in equilibrium. The designation *LM* comes from the fact that many economists have employed the symbol L to describe the demand for money (L standing for liquidity) and M to refer to the supply of money. When the money market is in equilibrium

Figure 20-5.

The *LM* curve

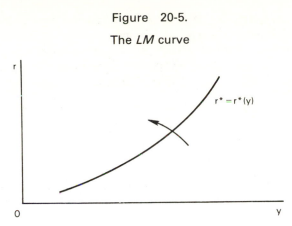

the demand for money equals the supply of money, and $L = M$. The positive slope of the *LM* function in Figure 20-5 reflects the fact that if higher levels of income are assumed, the equilibrium rate of interest will be higher.

This analysis enables us to describe the *LM* curve as a locus of potential equilibrium points. We do not yet know, of course, which of all the possible money market equilibrium points on the *LM* curve will actually describe the point at which the economy will come to rest at any particular time. That will depend on the way in which, as we shall see in a moment, the equilibrium conditions in the goods market interact with those we have just derived for the money market.

But first, a good deal of significance attaches to the actual form or slope of the *LM* curve. This reflects the sensitivity of the interest rate to a change in the level of income. But this, in turn, depends on the sensitivity of the demand for money to the change in income, and the sensitivity of the interest rate to the change in the demand for money. As in the case of the *IS* curve and its relation to equilibrium conditions in the goods market, we have here a chain of causal relationships. First, the demand for money depends on the level of income. Second, given the supply of money the rate of interest depends on the demand for money. The rate of interest is therefore dependent on a variable that depends on the level of income. Again we have a chain relationship

(13) $$r^* = r^*[m^d(y)]$$

or more directly, $r^* = r^*(y)$ as in Equation (12). In Figure 20-5 we have also shown by the arrow the direction of causation involved. The causation runs from the postulated level of income to the rate of interest.

The slope of the *LM* curve can be deduced quite readily from the summary description of the money market equilibrium condition in Equation (11). Let us again envisage, as we did in deriving the slope of the *IS* curve, a simultaneous change in income and the rate of interest. The assumption of a given money supply will mean that when this occurs, the variable m on the left-hand side of Equation (11) will not change. The incremental variations in the equilibrium relations in Equation (11) can then be written as

(14) $$0 = k'\Delta y + l'\Delta r$$

Here the zero change in the money supply will be equal to the sum of the simultaneous changes in the transactions and the asset demands for money. If income and the interest rate both increase, for example, the increase in the transactions demand, resulting from the higher income, will have to be precisely offset by the reduction in the asset demand, resulting from the higher interest rate. The former is referred to in Equation (14) by k', and the latter by l'. It follows by transposition from Equation (14) that for such a simultaneous increase in both income and the interest rate

(15) $$\Delta r/\Delta y = -k'/l'$$

The slope of the *LM* curve is the negative of the ratio of the sensitivity of the transactions demand for money to the change in income, to the sensitivity of the asset demand to the change in the interest rate. The former, as we know, will in general be positive and the latter will be negative. The negative of their ratio therefore establishes the positive slope of the *LM* curve.

INCOME AND INTEREST RATE EQUILIBRIUM

We have in Figure 20-3 an *IS* curve describing a locus of potential equilibrium interest rate and income combinations. These depend on equilibrium conditions in the goods market. In Figure 20-5 we have an *LM* locus that again describes potential equilibrium points depending on conditions in the money market. We bring these relationships together in Figure 20-6. It follows that if every point on the *IS* locus is a potential equilibrium point, showing what the equilibrium income level will be for different specified rates of interest, and every point on the *LM* locus is also a potential equilibrium point, showing what the equilibrium interest rate will be for different specified levels of income, there must be one unique point in the income-interest rate space shown in Figure 20-6 at which the money market and the goods market are in mutually determined and

Figure   20-6.

The *ISLM* relation

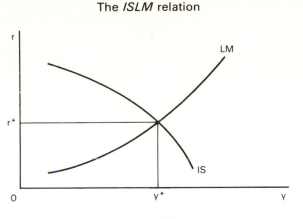

Figure   20-7.

ISLM interest rate and income equilibration

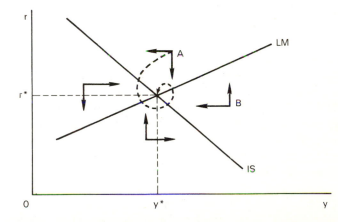

consistent equilibrium. This then determines the final r^* and y^* equilibrium levels as shown in the figure.

In Figure 20-6 we have, consistent with the neoclassical way of looking at things, a relationship between sets of equilibrium conditions. It is possible to grasp intuitively something of the dynamic processes that are understood to operate behind the scene. These bring the economy to the mutually determined equilibrium if, for any reason, it should temporarily be in a disequilibrium posture. Imagine, for example, that the economy is at an interest rate and income point indicated by A in Figure 20-7. Such a point cannot describe a permanently maintainable equilibrium, and forces will be set in motion to bring the economy to the *ISLM* intersection point.

Perpendiculars to the axis (not shown in the figure) will indicate the interest rate and real income or production levels described by point A. Consider first the income level. At that income level the rate of interest that would be consistent with it, in the sense that it would equilibrate the money market, would be lower than the interest rate at A. It would be the interest rate that lies on the LM curve immediately below A. Forces will therefore be set up to pull the system downward toward the LM curve, in the direction of the vertical arrow from A. The interest rate at A being higher than the money market equilibrium rate, individuals in the financial markets will find it profitable to buy securities, thereby driving up their prices and reducing their yields, until a rate of interest nearer the equilibrium has been established.

Similarly, consider the interest rate at point A and its inconsistency with the equilibrium real expenditure functions in the system. If the interest rate were to be maintained at A, the level of income consistent with it would lie on the IS curve horizontally to the left of A. At point A the interest rate is too high to generate sufficient investment to absorb the savings leakages, and a tendency will develop for the level of expenditure and income to fall. Similar arguments could be constructed to describe the forces that would be set in motion at any corresponding point off the IS and LM curves in any other of the four quadrants shown in the diagram. We remember that so far as the IS relation is concerned, the direction of causation is from the rate of interest to the income level. The rate of interest is the independent variable, and the income level is the dependent variable. At whatever nonequilibrium point the economy stands, therefore, a force will tend to draw it in a horizontal direction toward the IS curve. The movement is to the left from positions on the right of the IS curve, because in such positions conditions of excess leakages will be set up. The opposite holds for positions to the left of the IS curve.

In the case of the LM curve, on the contrary, the income is the independent variable in the relation, and the rate of interest is the dependent variable. In nonequilibrium positions, forces will be set in motion to move the economy in a vertical direction toward the LM curve. At point B, for example, the interest rate is too low for the posited income level. At that income level there will be excess demand for money in the money market, and the rate of interest will rise. From points to the right of, or below, the LM curve, the economy will be pulled up toward the LM curve, with contrary directions of movement being generated from points to the left of, or above, the LM curve.

The movement from point A, then, reflects a decline in expenditures, a fall in the demand for money, and a resultant movement in a direction somewhere between the horizontal and vertical arrows. Such a possible movement is indicated by the dashed curve in the diagram. Continuing the analysis, the neoclassical theory argues that the resultant forces would continue to operate until a mutually consistent equilibrium had been established. This, as before, is described by the r^*, y^* point in the diagram.

MOVEMENTS OF THE *IS* AND *LM* FUNCTIONS

The *slope* of the *IS* curve, as we have seen, is determined by the interest sensitivity of the investment expenditure function and the propensity to consume. The *level* of the *IS* curve is determined by the level of the investment function in relation to the interest rate and the autonomous components of the spending streams. Indeed, any change in the autonomous expenditures in the system—anything, that is, that we have previously seen could act as a multiplicand, such as the autonomous component of consumption expenditure—will change the location, as distinct from the slope, of the *IS* curve. If there were a technological advance somewhere in the economy, for example, that moved the marginal efficiency of investment function to the right, that would make a higher level of investment expenditure profitable at any given rate of interest, and it would have the effect of moving the *IS* curve to the right. This would reflect the fact that because of the higher level of investment, a higher level of equilibrium income is associated with any given rate of interest.

We can note also that the overall increase in equilibrium income that results from a change in the rate of interest will depend on the strength of the incremental multiplier at work in the system. This, as we have seen before, depends on the magnitude of the marginal propensity to consume. This latter magnitude is reflected, in turn, in the slope of the consumption function. Anything, therefore, that causes a change in the marginal propensity to consume will, by changing the magnitude of the multiplier, also change the overall responsiveness of the equilibrium income level to the rate of interest.

Similarly, the *slope* of the *LM* curve is determined by the interest rate sensitivity of the demand for money. The *level* of the curve is dependent on the level of the demand for money, or liquidity preference, in relation to the rate of interest, and on the availability of money to satisfy that demand. The underlying causes of change in the location of the *LM* curve are summarized in Figure 20-8.

The initial money demand and supply conditions are described by m_1^d and m_1^s, respectively, in the figure. We assume, for purposes of the point in hand, that the level of income is given. Suppose, then, that an increase in liquidity preference causes the demand-for-money curve to move to the right. This may result from an increased degree of uncertainty

Figure   20-8.

Changes in money market conditions

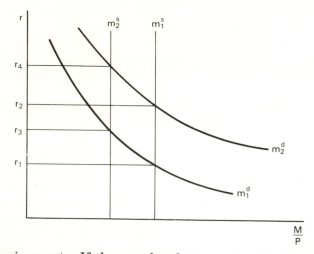

as to economic events. If the supply of money remained unchanged at m_1^s, the rate of interest that would equilibrate the money market under the new assumed demand conditions would rise from r_1 to r_2. This means that the given level of income we have posited now has associated with it a higher equilibrium rate of interest. But this is saying, in the light of our preceding development, that the *LM* curve has moved upward or to the left.

If, on the other hand, we were to assume that the demand for money continued to be described by the m_1^d curve in the figure, but that the money supply was reduced to m_2^s, the equilibrium rate of interest would rise to r_3. If the money supply were to be decreased at the same time as the demand increased, the interest rate might rise to r_4. In all such cases, arguments similar to the preceding could be adduced to show that the *LM* curve will move to the left. In the contrary cases, such as an increase in the money supply or a reduction in liquidity preference, the interest rate consistent with any posited level of income will be lower. The *LM* curve in that case moves to the right.

THE STRUCTURE AND LIMITATIONS
OF THE COMPLETE DEMAND SIDE MODEL

The *ISLM* apparatus as we have developed it so far in this chapter comprises what has generally been called the demand side model of the economy. It is sometimes referred to as the complete demand side model because it takes account not only of the demand conditions in the market for goods but also of the interdependent demand conditions in the market for money. We have seen the ways in which, taking a full specification of the supply and demand conditions in both these markets, a mutually determinate equilibrium posture in both the goods and the money markets can be envisaged.

This model, which is summarized most succinctly in Figures 20-6 and 20-7, was for a long time generally accepted as the essential Keynesian model of the economy. We have already noted its parentage in the famous paper by John Hicks titled "Mr. Keynes and the 'Classics.' " But it contains the obvious limitation that it says nothing, in the form in which it appears to this point, about the supply conditions in the economy. Considerable progress had undoubtedly been made by it in modeling macroeconomic forces, in that it took account of the interest rate effects on equilibrium outcomes. But what gained currency as the elementary Keynesian model needed a still further infusion, from the perspective we are now considering, from the neoclassical analysis of supply.

The analytical problem can be put more completely in the following terms. The need exists to develop an analysis that will simultaneously determine the level of real income or output, the rate of interest, the level of employment, and the commodity price level in the economy. If we put the problem in terms of what we referred to previously as the situational variables, the task of analysis is to determine the equilibrium solution values of y, P, N, and r. Now in the marriage of the IS and LM curves we have, in effect, two equations in the three unknowns, y, r, and P. Consider why this so. Equations (1) and (11) form a two-equation system that generates Equations (5) and (12), to provide solution values of y and r. But this can be done, as a moment's reflection will confirm, only if the third variable, P, is taken as given. The $ISLM$ analysis can potentially solve for the equilibrium income and interest rate levels consistent with a specified price level. Clearly, a large element of indeterminancy still exists in the scheme of things.

To fill the gap, the neoclassical–Keynesian system introduces two further equations. We shall see more fully below (as was anticipated in the discussion of the neoclassical aggregate supply curve in Chapter 17) that these describe (1) the labor market equilibrium condition and (2) the economy's aggregate production function.

While we acknowledge that the neoclassical–Keynesian system is not complete without the labor market and the supply side contribution, it is nevertheless true that economists have frequently concentrated attention for policy purposes on what we have termed the complete demand side model. The arguments that emerge have frequently been taken to describe the difference between the monetarist and the Keynesian wings of the neoclassical–Keynesian synthesis. Let us look at them briefly in the following terms.

SOME POLICY IMPLICATIONS

The results of the foregoing have immediate policy implications from the neoclassical–Keynesian point of view. Consider, for example, the *IS* and *LM* relations shown in Figure 20-9. Here we have drawn the *LM* curve with a somewhat pronounced horizontal segment at low levels of income. This could result from a highly elastic demand for money at low interest rates. When income levels are low and the economy is depressed, the money demand curve as shown in Figure 20-4 may be quite elastic. If, in that situation, the Federal Reserve were to increase the money supply, it might have negligible effects on the rate of interest because the new money supplies would be absorbed in idle balances. The interest rate is presumably already so low that the public does not expect it to go lower. Any attempt on the part of the monetary authorities to reduce it by purchasing securities would only lead to a larger monetization of debt without any effect on the interest rate. It would only lead to sales of securities by the public and increasing supplies of money (hence the term *monetization of the debt*) without significant effects on the rate of interest. Because such elastic demand-for-money conditions are generally associ-

Figure   20-9.

IS and *LM* variations

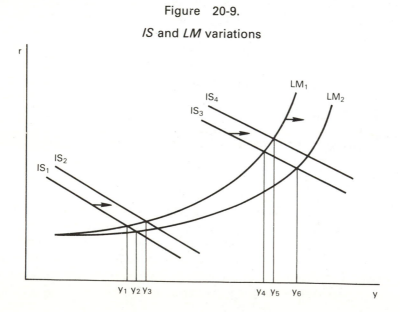

ated with depressed economic conditions, and because Keynes, when he was writing during the Depression of the 1930s, first drew attention to the possibilities we have just mentioned, this somewhat horizontal range of the *LM* curve has frequently been dubbed by the neoclassicists as the Keynesian range.

At the other extreme, as the economy nears full employment, the demand-for-money curve is likely to become quite inelastic, or nearly vertical. This is because, as we saw in Chapter 15, at higher interest rates the public are more ready to expect interest rates to fall rather than to rise further. This induces them to hold a relatively larger proportion of their assets in securities rather than money. The demand for money, as we have seen, is less sensitive to interest rate changes when the interest rate is high, but it is likely to become more sensitive as the interest rate falls.

In Figure 20-9 we have shown the possibility of both a movement to the right of the *LM* curve, resulting perhaps from an increase in the money supply, and a movement to the right of the *IS* curve. The various combinations of results are shown in both the low-employment, or so-called Keynesian range, and the high-employment, or classical, range.

Let us suppose that the economy is at income level y_1, given by the intersection of IS_1 and LM_1. In that case an attempt may be made to raise the level of output and income by monetary policy. The money supply may be increased, thereby moving the *LM* curve to the right to LM_2. But the effect on income, it is seen, is minimal. Income would rise only to y_2. As the diagram indicates, a larger effect on income could be achieved if other policies, fiscal policy for example, were used to move the *IS* curve to the right to IS_2. For example, higher government outlays could be made, or a corporate tax reduction might stimulate investment expenditure, thus introducing a new multiplicand and raising the level of income. In Figure 20-9 income would rise from y_1 to y_3. In that case fiscal policy appears to take precedence over monetary policy as effective antirecession policy.

Consider now the opposite extreme, or the classical or near full-employment range of income levels. If income is now at y_4, as determined by the intersection of IS_3 and the initially given *LM* curve, LM_1, a further rise in autonomous expenditures that moved the *IS* curve to IS_4 would not have as much effect. It would raise income only to y_5. This is because the demand-for-money function is here quite inelastic, and the main effect of the increased investment expenditure that moved the *IS* curve would be dissipated in a higher interest rate. If, in that situation, room exists for expansion in the economy without the danger of undue price disturbances, a larger effect could be achieved by moving the *LM* curve to LM_2. This is a case where monetary policy, such as increasing the money supply to move the *LM* curve, dominates fiscal policy in effectiveness. The monetary policy could raise income to y_6, rather than to the y_5 level that fiscal policy could achieve.

This entire analysis, of course, has been conducted in real terms. We have real income on the income axis. The price level has been suppressed. But it is quite likely that when incomes are high, further attempts to increase output will encounter more severe price barriers. The price level needs to be taken very much into account. But before that is considered, the possible cleavages between monetary and fiscal policy can be put in somewhat different form, to highlight what has sometimes been said to differentiate the monetarist from the Keynesian view of policy possibilities.

Monetarism has generally assumed that the elasticity of demand for money is low. In general, therefore, the *LM* curve, according to this view, is fairly steeply sloped. At the same time, it has generally been thought that the expenditure streams in the economy are fairly elastic, giving a much shallower slope to the *IS* curve. The relationships are described in Figure 20-10.

Suppose that the economy is at income level y_1. Given the slopes and elasticities of the *IS* and *LM* functions in Figure 20-10, a fairly large lateral movement of the *IS* curve (by means, for example, of a change in fiscal policy) would not accomplish much if the money supply were held fixed and the *LM* curve remained at LM_1. The income level would rise only to y_2. If, however, monetary policy were used, an increase in the money supply that shifted the *LM* curve to LM_2 would move it across the given *IS* curve to raise the income level to y_3. The assumed elasticities in the macroeconomic system make monetary policy potentially more effective.

Figure   20-10.

Monetarist view of *ISLM* relations

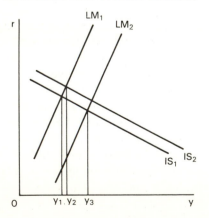

Figure   20-11.

Keynesian view of *ISLM* relations

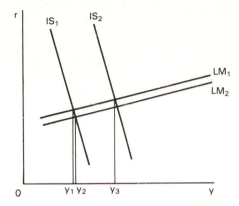

The contrary case, which is frequently dubbed the Keynesian view, sees the elasticities of the *IS* and *LM* curves as shown in Figure 20-11. If the economy is again assumed to be at income level y_1, monetary policy, by causing a fairly large lateral move in the *LM* curve, will raise the income level only to y_2 if the *IS* curve remains unchanged. If, however, fiscal policy is used to move the *IS* curve to IS_2, income can be increased to y_3 even if no monetary change is introduced and the *LM* curve remains at LM_1.

Policy preferences, therefore, depend on one's view of the actual quantitative nature of the relationships in the system, even though a common format of theoretical analysis might be employed. For this reason there is still room within the orbit of the neoclassical–Keynesian synthesis for debate among economists of goodwill as to the preferred kind of policies.

THE AGGREGATE DEMAND CURVE

We now have in hand the equipment we need to establish the aggregate demand curve in the price-output space as it is conceived by the neoclassical theory. We need to work again through the effects in the market for money.

For this purpose let us refer again to the basic money market equilibrium condition as summarized, for example, in Figure 20-8. We assume here that the income level is specified, and that m_1^d describes the demand curve for money and m_1^s the corresponding supply curve. Now we introduce the effect of an increase in the price level. Up to this point the price dimension has been completely suppressed. We suppose now that the

general commodity price level increases, but that no action is taken by
the monetary authorities to increase the nominal money supply. In that
case the real money supply will decrease. Suppose that in Figure 20-8 it
decreases to m_2^s. As we saw before, the equilibrium rate of interest in the
money market will rise to r_3 in the figure. Again as before, this implies
that a higher rate of interest is now associated with the posited level of
income, and that the *LM* curve therefore has risen, or has moved to the
left. Assuming for the present that no changes have occurred in the
underlying spending propensities and that the *IS* curve therefore has not
shifted, the results of the decreased real money supply on the *ISLM*
relation are traced in Figure 20-12.

The effect of the price increase, working via the induced reduction
in the real money supply, or M^s/P, is to move the *LM* curve in Figure 20-
12 to the left across the given *IS* curve. The effects of further price increases are also illustrated in the diagram. The three *LM* curves shown
are each derived in the presence of a postulated price level, with $P_3 > P_2$
$> P_1$.

The implications of this relation follow quite clearly. As the price
level is assumed to be higher, the equilibrium income determined from
the *ISLM* cross is lower. Higher prices are associated with lower real
output levels. This relation is depicted in Figure 20-13. The form of the
relation is $y = y(P)$. It is called the aggregate demand function.

The aggregate demand curve, which, the derivation establishes, is
downward sloping in the price-output space, may be thought to be analogous to the downward-sloping market demand curve we encountered in

Figure   20-12.

The effect of a price increase on the *ISLM* relation

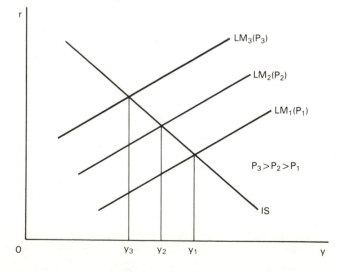

Figure   20-13.

The neoclassical aggregate demand curve

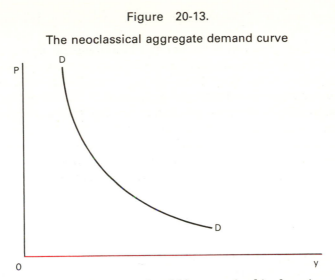

microeconomic theory. But care should be exercised in drawing such analogies. For the demand curve we have just drawn is not a behavioral
relation. It is a locus of equilibrium points. It says that if a certain price
level is assumed, then after all the interdependent markets in the system
have been brought to simultaneous equilibrium the level of real output
and income will be as indicated.

THE AGGREGATE SUPPLY CURVE

The derivation of the neoclassical aggregate supply curve need not be
developed at length at this point. That has been done in Chapter 17, in
the context of Figures 17-6 through 17-9, and the analysis there might
be reviewed in anticipation of the following discussion. The essence of
the argument, it will be recalled, is as follows.

When the price level rises, the demand curve for labor will move to
the right, as the marginal revenue products of labor are now higher. But
because the suppliers of labor do not adjust their price expectations as
rapidly as the actual price level changes (or, in another view, because
there is an element of money illusion on the supply side of the labor
market), the supply curve of labor will not move to the left as a result of
the price increase as far as the demand curve moves to the right. An
increase in the market-clearing volume of labor employed will therefore
result. This increase in employment makes possible an increase in the
level of real output, given the production possibility function in the economy. Thus an increased level of real income is associated with an increased price level. This association is taken to describe the aggregate

supply curve which is therefore positively inclined in the price-output space.

If, of course, there were no money illusion on the supply side of the labor market, or if, as we saw in Chapter 17 may be the case, the suppliers of labor adjusted their price expectations immediately and proportionately to any change in existing prices, then any movement to the right of the demand-for-labor curve resulting from the price increase would be accompanied by a corresponding move to the left of the supply-of-labor curve. The money wage rate will in that case increase proportionately with the increase in the price level. This means that the real wage rate will remain unchanged and the level of employment will remain the same as before the price rise. In that case there will be no induced change in the level of real output, and the aggregate supply curve will be vertical at the previously established real output level. This indicates that a high degree of importance is attached to the nature of the expectations in the system. This will reenter our analysis again, especially when some policy implications are considered, under the heading of what has become known as rational expectations.

The neoclassical aggregate supply and demand curves are brought together in Figure 20-14. By this means the final equilibrium real income and the effective commodity price level in the macrosystem are obtained. Again, however, we should bear in mind that in the aggregate supply curve, as in the aggregate demand curve, we have a locus of potential equilibrium points, rather than a direct behavioral relation.

THE NEOCLASSICAL EQUILIBRIUM VARIABLES

We have used the words "equilibrium variables" in the heading of this section because we have demonstrated that the neoclassical analysis is

Figure   20-14.

Neoclassical aggregate supply and demand

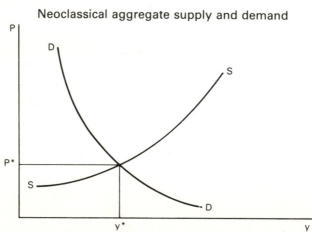

concerned with the determination of mutually consistent equilibrium values of certain macroeconomic variables, working through the interdependent markets in the system. We refer to the variables of M^s, the money supply; y, the real income; N, the level of employment; P, the price level; r, the rate of interest; and W, the money wage rate.

The neoclassical system introduces the nominal money supply, M, as substantially an exogenous variable. The relations shown in Figure 20-14 determine the equilibrium solution values of y and P. Given the value of P, the IS and LM cross in Figure 20-12 provides the solution value of r. The derived value of y enables us to work through the production function relation $y = y(N)$, to determine through its inverse the solution value of N. Alternatively, the introduction of the price level, P, to the supply and demand determinants in the labor market enables us to determine the solution value of N in that market. In this manner the money wage rate, W, is determined as an endogenous variable in the labor market. The real wage is immediately derived by dividing the money wage by the known price level.

POLICY RECOMMENDATIONS

The policy implications of the neoclassical analysis will be referred to more extensively in Chapter 23, where the place of money in economic policy is examined. At that point also further comments will be made on the important question of the significance of expectations. The following preliminary remarks highlight some immediate implications of what has been said to this point. We now want to envisage how different economic and monetary policies are thought to be capable of changing the equilibrium outcomes in the system we have described, and how, by altering the level of income and employment, they might achieve new levels of general well-being in the economy.

Any action that is designed to shift the IS curve to the right, such as a rise in autonomous investment, will also move the aggregate demand curve in the same direction. Similarly, if the monetary authorities should increase the money supply and thus move the LM curve to the right, this will lead to a lower rate of interest and an increased level of investment expenditure. This can also be interpreted in our present context as a move to the right of the aggregate demand curve. In that case a higher price level will result as the new expenditure creates a temporary excess demand. The rise in prices will move the economy up along its aggregate supply curve, as shown in Figure 20-14.

Policies to improve the marginal productivity of labor, by improved efficiencies, will move the labor demand curve to the right and shift the aggregate supply curve in the same direction. A tightening of the money supply will shift the LM curve to the left and may move both the aggregate supply and demand curves to the left. The demand curve will move to the left if the monetary restraint causes a reduction in investment expenditure. The supply curve may move to the left also if the declining rate of investment expenditure reduces the effective capital stock-to-labor force ratio in the economy, or if the monetary restraint causes laborers to leave the labor force in discouragement. But these last-mentioned possibilities really take the argument out of the short-run context in which we have argued so far.

Perhaps the most important comment to be made on the level of policy implications, however, is that addressed to the situation in which the United States found itself in the late 1970s and early 1980s. The basic problem was one of wringing the persistent tendencies to inflation out of the system and reviving the level of activity. The neoclassical theory, appearing frequently in its peculiarly monetarist guise, argued principally for a policy of tight money. In terms of the model we have just established, this has the effect of moving the *LM* curve to the left, raising the interest rate, reducing expenditures, moving the aggregate demand curve to the left, and thereby reducing the level of output. If such proposals work as suggested by the model, the price level problem will be alleviated but the recession will be worsened. It is difficult to contemplate the full effects on the aggregate supply and demand curves because, as we have indicated before, the neoclassical theory is an equilibrium theory that finds it difficult to conceive logically of unemployment at all. Employment will automatically be full employment at the level at which the labor market equilibrates. If unemployment does actually exist, then it has to be said by the neoclassical theory that the economy is temporally "off its supply curve," or "off its labor demand curve."

Nevertheless, the following can be said in relation to the tight money policy to which we have just referred. The reduction in demand induced by the monetary restraint will generate excess supplies in the commodity markets, and this will tend to cause prices to fall. The fall in prices will mean that the demand-for-labor curve in the labor market, as analyzed more fully in Chapter 17, will move to the left, tending to reduce the equilibrium amount of employment. This will move the economy back along its aggregate supply curve to a lower level of income and output, tending to bring supply closer to the underemployment level of demand. The economy, in that situation, has worsened its recession in order to arrest the price increase. Action would then be needed to move the demand curve to the right and restore higher activity levels in such a way as not to put upward pressure on prices again. Conceivably this might be done by increasing investment and raising the capital stock in order to improve productivity. But that extends the analysis again into longer-run possibilities. In the short run, moreover, such a rise in investment expenditures, directed ostensibly to productivity improvements, would tend to be inflationary.

If attention is focused primarily on the employment problem, it might be thought that the price rise can be left to take its course. A rise in prices might have the effect in the labor market of reducing the real wage of labor and thereby allowing the economy to move to higher employment levels. Higher employment would conceivably then be profitable to industrialists, as the assumedly lower real wage made it possible to raise employment until the falling marginal product of labor equaled the lower real wage. But this, of course, may be thwarted by pressure on the part of the suppliers of labor for increased money wages as price levels rise. If such pressures can be contained, the economy will then be moving up along its aggregate supply curve as the demand curve rises under the impetus of the inflationary pressure. Conceivably also, the rise in prices may improve the prospective marginal efficiency of investment, and the increased capital formation that results may move the aggregate supply curve to the right. But this again is taking the argument outside the purely short-run analysis. In the short run, if the price rise stimulated investment it will simply shift the aggregate demand curve out farther to the right and worsen the underlying inflationary pressure. In these cases, whatever beneficial effect is realized on the level of employment will be at the cost of worsened inflation.

The neoclassical policy dilemma is that it is not equipped to fight inflation and unemployment simultaneously. The problem is that the price formation forces that are actually bearing on the economy, and therefore the real genesis of the inflation, have not been completely perceived. To the extent, as we have seen, that the explanation of inflation requires some attention to the wage-cost-productivity relations in the producing sectors of the economy as well as to the pressures on the demand side, the remedy for inflation lies partly in the establishment of a rational and sustainable relation between the rate of change of incomes on the one hand and the periodic rate of change in productivity on the other.

DIFFICULTIES IN THE NEOCLASSICAL SYSTEM

A number of difficulties inhere in any scheme of analysis that describes the macroeconomic system by a set of multimarket equilibrium relations. We leave aside such fundamental questions as the endogeneity or exogeneity of the money wage, and the appropriateness of holding to the consistently causal effects of changes in the money supply. We leave aside the question of the difference of perspective that emerges if money is regarded as an effect rather than a cause. In the following comments we shall note three levels on which the deeper methodological thrust of the neoclassical theorizing can be called in question.

First, in the form in which it is generally presented the neoclassical theory purports to describe the interdependent relations between a set of well-defined behavioral and equilibrium relations in the various markets. But in the actual world those functions and relations are conceivably not stable in the sense envisaged by the analysis. That is precisely the problem with all equilibrium theoretic analysis. The world is subject, as Shackle has put it, to kaleidic change. We can never be sure of what tomorrow's outcome will be. Too many determining forces bear on the fundamental behavior relations to enable us to rely on their stability. Keynes has observed, for example, that "if . . . our knowledge of the future was calculable and not subject to sudden changes it might be justifiable to assume that the liquidity preference curve was stable."[4] But that would be the opposite of the conditions in the real world that his theory set out to describe. The same had to be said, he observed in other places, about the prospective instability of the investment function also. Putting this in the enlarged form in which it affects the neoclassical scheme we have discussed in this chapter, the problem is that the *IS* curve and the *LM* curve cannot be relied upon to be, or assumed to remain, stable while we are working out the probable effects of our policy recommendations with relation to them.[5]

Second, the *IS* and *LM* curves are not only unstable. They are also interdependent. In more ways than we can pause to analyze at this stage, the aggregate supply and demand curves are not independent. They are interdependent. To take a simple example, let us return to the determinants of outcomes in the market for money and observe their effects on the *IS* and *LM* relations. Imagine a situation in which a reduction in the rate of interest, due perhaps to an easing of their loan policies by the banks, causes an increase in investment expenditure. The economy is moving down along its investment function and *IS* curve. This increased expenditure, however, will give rise to an induced increase in the demand for money, emanating from what we called in Chapter 15 the finance demand, as distinct from the transactions and asset demands. The total demand-for-money curve will move to the right. This will put a new upward pressure on the rate of interest and, in accordance with the system of relations in this chapter, will cause the *LM* curve to move to the left.

    [4] John Maynard Keynes, "The General Theory of Employment," *Quarterly Journal of Economics*, 1937, pp. 218–19.
    [5] On the question of the stability of the determinant relations in the macroeconomy, see Brian J. Loasby, *Choice, Complexity, and Ignorance* (Cambridge: Cambridge University Press, 1976); G.L.S. Shackle, *Keynesian Kaleidics* (Edinburgh: Edinburgh University Press, 1974); Hyman P. Minsky, *John Maynard Keynes* (New York: Columbia University Press, 1975); and Douglas Vickers, "Uncertainty, Choice, and the Marginal Efficiencies," *Journal of Post Keynesian Economics*, Winter 1979–80. See also the important paper by Franco Modigliani, "The Monetarist Controversy or, Should We Forsake Stabilization Policies?" *American Economic Review*, March 1977, where he analyzes the significance of the fact that "obviously the economy has been and will continue to be exposed to many significant shocks," the sources of which are discussed.

We have, then, a situation in which a movement *along* the *IS* curve has induced a movement *of* the *LM* curve. The *IS* and *LM* curves are not stable and independent. They are unstable and interdependent.

Third, it should be kept in mind that the model of the macroeconomy that we developed in earlier chapters was explicitly based on the assumption that the state of long-run as well as short-run expectations was given. This question of the state of expectations is, of course, related to that of the underlying uncertainties that abound in the real world, and of which economic theory, especially in its macroform, needs to be aware. In the orderedness of interacting equilibrium relations, however, the neoclassical scheme has no way of taking uncertainty into account. This problem is, in a sense, related to the first point we raised above regarding the instability of the behavioral and determinant functions in the system. But a difference is also in view. For we acknowledge now that not only may the facts and outcomes of economic conditions be different from what might have been anticipated. The state of the subjective expectations, hopes, and imagined conclusions based on them may also change. We have already seen that certain institutions exist in the real world to help us overcome the burden of uncertainty and the formation of expectations. One of them is money. Money serves one of its most important functions in providing a refuge from uncertainty when we cannot be clear as to the course of action we should pursue. Liquidity is often a substitute for knowledge. It enables us to behave as rational economic beings in the presence of ignorance.

It might be added, finally, that the neoclassical system we have outlined in this chapter is subject to the same fundamental objection as applies to equilibrium theorizing in other areas of economic analysis. Logically, by virtue of its immersion in the notion of mutually consistent equilibrium outcomes, the theory is competent only to describe the situation that can be shown to exist when full generalized equilibrium conditions are satisfied. In that sense it is static. It is timeless. But the really interesting and important questions and problems in the real world have to do with the actual flows of events and the manner in which they interact to work out their final objectives. We have spoken consistently in this book of "money on the wing." We have been interested consistently in money flows. It is this conception, the changing kaleidics of actual time, that lends excitement as well as credibility to economic thought and argument.

SUMMARY

This chapter has provided a summary view of the principal results of the neoclassical model of the macroeconomy, incorporating those Keynesian elements that have made a common theoretical model possible. The analysis is essentially an application on the macroeconomic level of the general equilibrium theorizing that has filled the horizons of economists during the years since Keynes' *General Theory*. The analysis accordingly derives certain results that describe the mutually consistent relations between market-clearing and equilibrium conditions in the goods, labor, money, and nonmonetary asset markets. Methodological distinctions between such equilibrium theorizing and the model of the macroeconomy we constructed in earlier chapters were noted.

A study of the equilibrium conditions in the goods market led to the derivation of the *IS* curve. Similarly, the implications of equilibrium conditions in the money market established the *LM* curve. The relations between the *IS* and *LM* curves as potential equilibrium loci were noted, and they led to the neoclassical specification of the equilibrium income and interest rate outcomes.

Some potential policy implications of the *IS* and *LM* analysis were discussed, and some differences of viewpoint within the neoclassical camp, such as those between the monetarists and the Keynesians, were noted.

The equilibrium money market theory was used to derive the neoclassical aggregate demand curve. This was employed in conjunction with the neoclassical aggregate supply curve that had been developed in an earlier chapter to provide a solution to the equilibrium price and real income levels. A distinction was drawn between the aggregate supply and demand analysis in the neoclassical system and that in our preceding model of the macroeconomy. It was shown how the neoclassical system determined, in accordance with its own presuppositions, the equilibrium values of what we referred to as the important situational variables in the macroeconomy.

The chapter concluded with a note on some logical and methodological difficulties in the neoclassical approach to macroeconomic theorizing.

IMPORTANT CONCEPTS

Equilibrium in the goods, labor, money, and nonmonetary asset markets

Neoclassical aggregate supply and demand curves in the price-output space

Difficulties in the neoclassical system, associated with uncertainty, expectations, instabilities, and interdependence between determinant functions

The neoclassical labor market and the endogenous money wage rate

The *IS* and *LM* curves

The *IS* and *LM* cross

Movements of the *IS* and *LM* curves

Neoclassical equilibrium values of M^s, y, N, P, r, W

QUESTIONS FOR DISCUSSION AND REVIEW

1. Within the framework and assumptions of the neoclassical–Keynesian synthesis, write a system of four equations describing (1) the economy's aggregate production function and (2) the equilibrium conditions in the goods market, the money market, and the labor market. Then explain how the relations in this four-equation model determine the equilibrium solution values of y, P, N, and r, the levels of real output, prices, employment, and the rate of interest.

2. Is it useful analytically to distinguish between (1) equilibrium and (2) market-clearing conditions? Why?

3. How, on the basis of the neoclassical–Keynesian synthesis, would you expect a rise in the price level to affect the equilibrium level of real output?

4. What factors determine the neoclassical aggregate supply curve, and how, if at all, are the conditions on the supply side of the labor market relevant?

5. Distinguish carefully between the determinants of (1) the neoclassical aggregate supply and demand curves in P–y (price–output) space and (2) the postclassical aggregate supply and demand curves in Z–N (expected proceeds–employment) space.

6. What factors determine, respectively, the slopes of the IS and LM curves? Is the multiplier relevant?

7. Within the framework of the neoclassical–Keynesian synthesis, how would you expect an increase in the money supply to affect the mutually determined solution values of output, employment, and the price level?

8. Under what conditions is antirecession monetary policy likely to be effective?

9. How does the monetarist view of the $ISLM$ relation differ from the neo–Keynesian view? Are the relative elasticities of the separate functions relevant? Why?

10. Discuss the logical difficulties, if any, that you perceive in the neoclassical system of thought.

21

THE ECONOMIC POLICY PROBLEM: INFLATION AND UNEMPLOYMENT

STUDY OBJECTIVES

• To observe some implications for economic policy of the preceding models of the macroeconomy
• To highlight the short-run economic policy problem of simultaneous inflation and unemployment
• To note the possible sources of inflationary disequilibrium and relevant corrective policies
• To note the relations between monetary, fiscal, and incomes policy options

The view that is taken of the need for economic policy depends on an analytical vision of the structure and functioning of the macroeconomy. The effectiveness of policy measures depends on the manner in which the forces that determine economic outcomes are related. The models of the macroeconomy developed in the preceding chapters make it possible to bring certain policy options into fuller perspective, and in this and the following chapters some aspects of monetary, fiscal, and incomes policies will be considered in closer relation with each other. We shall examine the implications of the aggregate supply and demand model of Chapter 19, in particular the determinants of its supply and demand cross and the effective monetary demand point.

THE ECONOMIC POLICY AUTHORITIES: MONETARY, FISCAL, AND INCOMES POLICIES

The question of who administers economic policy, or where policy-making responsibility lies, can be recalled briefly. *Monetary policy*, we have said by way of definition, refers to those actions of the monetary authorities, in our case the Federal Reserve Board, designed to influence the cost and availability of money. In taking the actions available to it the Federal Reserve Board will, of course, keep an eye on the larger objectives of economic organization and policy, of the kind we outlined in our introduction in Chapter 2. Such objectives as a high and stable level of employment, stable commodity prices, sustainable economic growth, and stability on the international balance of payments are accorded appropriate weights. Problems arise, of course, in deciding what relative importance should be accorded to each of these legitimate policy objectives. Difficulties ensue when, for one reason or another, it becomes clear that the objectives might not all be mutually compatible under all possible economic conditions. Conflicts may arise between them, and some trade-off of one against the other may become necessary or be thought desirable.

An easy money and low interest rate policy, for example, may stimulate economic activity and development to an extent that puts unacceptable pressure on prices to rise. The low interest rates that might be desirable to increase domestic spending and employment might destabilize the balance of payments and weaken the exchange rate, by causing an outflow of money capital to take advantage of relatively higher interest rates in overseas capital markets. Tight money and high interest rates designed to cool off an inflationary trend may have seriously disruptive effects in some sectors of the economy, at the same time as they reduce the levels of employment and activity. The housing and construction industry, for example, and other industries such as the automobile industry that rely on the ready availability of consumer credit, may be disproportionally affected. The housing industry has frequently been affected in the past by the fact that a high interest rate policy caused money capital funds to flow to institutions that could offer a higher rate of return than those, such as the savings banks and the savings and loan associations, that traditionally channel funds to the housing and construction sector.

Fiscal policy, which we defined succinctly as the government's activities in taxing and spending and borrowing and lending, will be formulated by the government budget makers and implemented substantially by the Treasury. We saw, in our discussion in Chapter 5 of the financial institutional framework and the flow of investable funds, that government borrowing could become, from time to time, a highly significant force in the money capital market. We need to be aware not only of the impact of government borrowing to finance whatever budget deficits may occur in a particular year but also of the capital market impact of what we described as refinancing operations when outstanding securities mature. Interest rate effects and the possibility of the crowding out of private sector borrowing and investment activity can become significant at such times.

Fiscal policy becomes highly relevant to our overall policy discussion because of the impact and structure of annual expenditure and tax-raising devices. The structure of the federal government budget will affect the economy differently, depending on the relative importance in it, for example, of defense expenditures versus social welfare payments, or public works construction versus space exploration. Any number of such possible comparisons could be made. But they would all have a similar implication. The structure of government expenditure, or the directions in which government outlays are channeled, will affect the structure of resource use in the economy and the competition for resources between the public sector and the private sector. Different taxation policies, individual versus corporate taxes for example, will also affect the economy in different ways.

Incomes policies we have defined briefly as those arrangements that are introduced into the market system in order to maintain a reasonable balance between changes in wages, productivity, and prices. It is difficult to state precisely where, in the case of incomes policies, the policy-making responsibility and authority lies. For much depends on the kind of incomes policy contemplated. If one were to favor the introduction of a strict set of wage and price controls, such as were introduced in the United States economy in the early 1970s, the authority for the design and implementation of them lies with the federal government and the relevant congressional mandate.

But if it were thought desirable to establish a system of guidelines within the influence of which the market system can operate, the design and implementation authority would need the cooperation of both the corporate sector and the suppliers of labor. The guidelines, of course, need not be voluntary in the full sense. For a system of penalty taxation could be imposed on those business firms, or possibly on those individuals, whose rates of change in annual income payments or receipts did not remain within the guidelines made viable by the productivity changes in the economy. Such schemes bring into focus an interconnection between incomes policies and some aspects of fiscal policy.

THE SUPPLY AND DEMAND CROSS
IN THE MODEL OF THE MACROECONOMY

As an example of the reasons why economic policies are needed, and of the possible ways in which they may be relevant, let us consider the supply and demand determinants of the effective monetary demand point in the postclassical model of the macroeconomy.

PRODUCTIVITY AND INVESTMENT

In the course of developing the supply side of the model we observed that an upward pressure on prices may develop for a number of reasons. First, the expansion of employment as the economy moves up along its nonlinear supply curve will tend to cause an increase in prices to the extent that diminishing productivity sets in. On the policy level, the actions that might be taken in the light of this would have to do mainly with measures designed to raise, as consistently as possible, the general productivity potential of the economy. Monetary and fiscal policies are both potentially relevant in this connection.

On the monetary side it would be desirable to maintain as low a long-term rate of interest as possible in the light of other economic requirements and objectives. At this point the overall mix of economic policies becomes crucially relevant. For if, for example, the federal administration's economic policy forces the economy to rely on a relatively tight money policy as virtually the sole anti-inflation measure, then investment in the private productive sector is likely to be seriously choked off rather than facilitated. In that case the ratio of gross domestic capital formation to the gross national product will be lower than is desirable for the maintenance of steady improvements in productivity.

Fiscal measures directed to the productivity question also take up wider socioeconomic questions, such as the provision of education, training, retraining, and industrial and worker relocation programs, and the provision of employment exchanges and job information. But highly relevant also are the rates of corporate taxation and the possible degree of progression in the corporate tax rate, and the use of fiscal policy to affect the corporate tax base as well as the tax rate.

By *tax base* we mean the size of a corporation's taxable income, relative to the gross income it actually earns. The tax base relative to any earned income level can be altered by varying the allowable tax deductions. In the case of business firms this has to do largely with the rates at which real capital assets are allowed to be depreciated for tax purposes. The larger the amount of the investment written off for tax purposes in a given year, or the more rapidly the value of the assets can be depreciated, the smaller will be the tax liability of producing firms. This will increase the net incomes available for either dividend distribution or reinvestment. To the extent that such higher net incomes are paid out in the form of dividends, the level of consumption expenditures may be raised more rapidly than investment. The benefit of potential capital formation would then come indirectly, through the motivation provided by the prospect of more favorable markets for final outputs in the future. Even in the case of higher dividend distribution, however, direct capital formation may well benefit to the extent that a part of the dividend income is channeled back to the money capital market in the form of individuals' portfolio investment.

INFLATION AND UNEMPLOYMENT

In the short run, the issues calling for analysis relate primarily to what it is that permits stability in employment, price, and output levels. To put the matter negatively, we are interested in the underlying causes of price instability or inflation on the one hand, and unemployment and its accompanying economic distress on the other. If the neoclassical way of looking at things had complete cogency, we should have to agree that unemployment could not permanently, or even for a very significant time, exist. For the labor market would automatically clear at a full-employment level; at least it would clear at a level at which all those willing to work for the going market-clearing wage rate would find employment. Whatever residual unemployment existed would be voluntary unemployment. The full-employment problem would be solved by defining it away.

As to inflation, the neoclassical model, particularly in its monetarist guise, accords priority of emphasis to the rate of money creation as the cause of instability, and it argues that if the money supply can be made to increase no more rapidly than the rate of increase in real national output, the price problem will be solved. For some economists inflation is primarily a monetary phenomenon. Nonmonetarists, or those within the neoclassical–Keynesian synthesis who come to the common theoretical system from the neo–Keynesian side, have in the past placed heavy weight on excessive demand or monetary expenditures as the principal cause of inflation. Some attention has been given to so-called cost-push inflation, and to the degree of monopolistic or oligopolistic market power and the control of prices, in the explanation of inflation. And since the incorporation into the neoclassical–Keynesian model of the supply side features that we examined in the preceding chapter, significant influences have been seen to stem from the various possible forms of the economy's aggregate supply function.

The important short-run problem that calls for attention, then, is that of the simultaneous occurrence in the economy of inflation and unemployment. In the heyday of Keynesianism, it was confidently imagined that the economy could be fine tuned to eliminate both of these worrying problems. If the level of unemployment were to rise, as a result, presumably, of a deficiency of aggregate demand for goods and services, the government could step in to bolster the spending streams and raise the employment and output levels. It could do this by using fiscal policy to raise the government's own expenditure, or to reduce corporate and individual taxes as a means of stimulating and motivating higher private sector expenditures. Or it could use monetary policy to loosen the general monetary situation, to increase money supplies and lower the rate of interest, and once again motivate higher expenditure levels. If, on the other hand, too brisk a state of affairs developed and the economy needed to be cooled off somewhat, fiscal and monetary policy could, it was thought, be made to work in the opposite direction. The economic administration could work as a balancing mechanism. Fortunately, it was imagined, inflation and unemployment would not occur together, and all that was needed was a skillful mixture of policies, a little fiscal and a little monetary policy, a trade-off of one against the other, and the economy could be kept on an even keel.

The argument worked with apparent success for quite some time. The seeds of underlying and structural disequilibrium were hardly noticed in the heady growth and relatively stable decade of the 1960s. But in due course harsher realities broke through. With the troubles of the 1970s, with cost-push problems from oil price increases, poor international commodity harvests in some years, and, predominantly, pressures to income increases that could not possibly be matched by increases in productivity, the nicely adjusted and adjustable system collapsed. Now, as the instabilities of the 1970s gave way to increased uncertainties and to policy indecisions in the 1980s, inflation and unemployment occurred together. A trade-off between them that offered any degree of comfort was no longer possible. Both economic policy and economic theory now needed to address the simultaneous price and employment problem.

We can observe the nature of the problem in Tables 21-1 and 21-2. In Table 21-1 the first two data columns indicate the annual percentage rate of increase in prices and the simultaneous level of unemployment between 1960 and 1982. Data are shown at five-year intervals for the earlier part of the period to reveal the relative calmness that prevailed at that time. No attempt is made to analyze all the cyclical fluctuations that occurred in the economy during those years. In 1960, for example, at the beginning of a fairly strong and stable growth trend, the price level, measured by the GNP deflator, was rising at only 1.6 percent per annum. More extensive data show that during the first half of the 1960s the average annual rate of increase in the GNP deflator was only 1.5 percent. During the same period the unemployment rate averaged 5.7 percent of the labor force, a level that was to be improved upon as the 1960s unfolded.

During the second half of that decade the unemployment rate was held down to the relatively low annual average level of 3.8 percent while the rate of price increase edged upward to an annual average of 3.6 percent. But in the rather more troubled 1970s the economy encountered a steady deterioration on both fronts. For the two halves of that decade

Table   21-1

Inflation and unemployment in the United States economy, 1960–1982

Year	GNP deflator (percent change from preceding period at annual rates; quarterly data seasonally adjusted)	Unemployment (as percent of civilian labor force; annual or monthly data)	Percentage point excess of increase in compensation per hour, over increase in output per hour in the business sector
1960	1.6	5.5	2.7
1965	2.2	4.5	0.4
1970	5.4	4.9	6.5
1975	9.3	8.5	7.4
1980	9.3	7.1	11.1
1981	9.4	7.6	7.8
1982	6.0	9.7	6.9
1981 March	10.9	7.3	6.1
June	6.8	7.4	7.5
September	9.0	7.6	7.9
December	8.8	8.6	10.3
1982 March	4.3	9.0	8.3
June	4.6	9.5	5.4
September	5.0	10.2	2.5
December	4.3	10.8	1.9

Source: *Economic Report of the President,* February 1983, pp. 167, 199, 209; and Table 16-2 in Chapter 16 above.

the rate of price increase climbed to an annual average of 5.8 percent and then to 7.3 percent. At that time, however, the price increase was not accompanied by generally lower unemployment. As prices rose, so did unemployment, almost precisely reflecting the price data, with average annual levels during the two halves of the 1970s of 5.4 and 7.0 percent.

These more-detailed data are reflected in summary form in Table 21-1. Price increases in the region of 9 and 10 percent per annum in the later years were accompanied by quite high unemployment, which reached an average level of just under 10 percent in 1982, having risen, as the lower section of the table indicates, to almost 11 percent by the end of that year. While the price rise had been sustained through 1981, it was moderated in 1982 as the recession caused by a tight money policy generated high unemployment and reduced the price momentum.

Something structural had clearly happened to the economy. Economic power was increasingly being exercised in a way that maintained an upward pressure on prices, even though slack, measured by the un-employment data, had also emerged. The final column of Table 21-1 highlights an important contributing factor. It is one that we have already referred to in different contexts and specifically analyzed at some length in our discussion of the theory of prices and the value of money in Chapter 16. The table shows the extent to which, in each of the time periods referred to, the percentage increase in compensation per hour in the business sector exceeded the simultaneous percentage increase in output per hour of all persons employed in that sector.

Again this important datum performed relatively satisfactorily in the early 1960s. But in the years that followed, the extent to which increases in compensation exceeded those in productivity widened, and this, as is to be expected from our earlier analysis of the price-forming forces in the economy, was accompanied by higher price rises. The point is made in another manner in Table 21-2, where the average annual percentage rates of change are noted for each of the five-year periods between 1960 and 1980.

In the four five-year periods in Table 21-2, the rate of increase in compensation increased consistently from a low of 4.3 percent to 8.8 per-cent. At the same time the rate of increase in output diminished consis-tently, from a high of 3.3 percent at the beginning of the two decades to a low of only 1.5 percent in the final five years. As is to be expected from this simultaneous occurrence of increasing compensation rates and de-clining productivity rates, prices rose consistently during the twenty years from a 1.1 percent rate to a high of 7.3 percent. The more-detailed data for the last three years in the lower section of the table indicate again that poor productivity performances, accompanied by continuing high compensation increases, pointed to further price increases.

Table   21-2

Average annual percentage rates of increase in prices (implicit price deflator), compensation per hour, and output per hour of all persons, in the United States business sector, 1960–1982

Period	Prices	Compensation	Output
1960–64	1.1	4.3	3.3
1965–69	3.3	6.2	2.5
1970–74	5.5	7.6	1.6
1975–80	7.3	8.8	1.5
1980	9.4	10.4	−0.7
1981	9.5	9.6	1.8
1982	5.5	7.3	0.4

Source: *Economic Report of the President,* February 1983, p. 209.

The challenge these data provide is that of constructing an analytical model to explain them on the one hand, and of designing a set of economic policies to correct and control them on the other. We have looked at the former in our earlier chapters on macroeconomic models in Part V. On the level of policy, it is necessary to consider again what we earlier termed the critical wage-price-productivity nexus. We turn to that immediately in what follows. But we shall take account also of the manner in which money and monetary policy play a necessary and significant role in the larger scheme of things. We shall find here again that money is not simply or primarily a cause of what happens in the economy. It is, in important respects, very much an effect. From another perspective, money cannot be considered exclusively, or even primarily, an exogenous phenomenon. It is to a large and influential degree endogenous.

MONEY WAGE CHANGES AND THE
INFLATION RATE

Our basic model in Chapter 19 has made it clear that an upward pressure on prices will occur when the supply curve turns to the left, and the aggregate money wage rate increases more rapidly than the average productivity in the economy. At this point the design of incomes policies to maintain a viable relation between wage rates and productivity is relevant. The need for such a set of arrangements was established in our discussion in Chapter 16 of the price-forming forces in the wage-productivity relation. A number of suggestions have been made as to how policy might proceed on this level.

Several such proposals have been introduced under the general heading of TIP, referring to tax-based incomes policies. In effect, such proposals incorporate provisions for a penalty tax to be levied on those business firms that, in any given year, pay average wage and salary increases in excess of the increase in the average productivity in the economy. Such tax rates can properly be regarded as penalty rates that, it is hoped, will not have to be paid. They are conceived in the same way as penalty fines incurred for driving one's automobile at a speed in excess of the posted allowable maximum. It is highly desirable, in the interests of social stability, that such speeding fines should not have to be paid. They are not designed to be revenue-raising devices. So, it is argued, the penalty rates of taxation for the violation of nationally agreed wage rate guidelines in the manner suggested would not be primarily revenue-raising devices. They would be similarly designed in the interest of economic and social stability.

Such incomes policy suggestions contain much that is highly desirable, and a number of imaginative variations on this important theme can be inspected in the work of Sidney Weintraub, an articulate and prominent advocate.[1] It is cogently argued that such arrangements need not be regarded as predatory on the interests of labor, or directed particularly to the benefit of industrial corporations. For it is only too clear that containing unnecessary inflationary pressures is of benefit to the suppliers of labor as well as the users. The latter benefit from the slower advance in money wages. Both the employers and the employed benefit from the stability in prices that, it is hoped, will thereby be induced. With more stable prices, industrial planning could go ahead with more confidence and less uncertainty, a smaller part of the nation's resources would need to be devoted to protecting decision makers against inflation, and further benefits would ensue from the change in policy mix that could then be adopted.

A stabilization of the price-forming forces by an incomes policy, designed to keep wage changes and productivity improvements more closely in line, would liberate monetary policy from the impossibly heavy burden it has too often been required to carry. For so long as the money wage rate is allowed to increase more rapidly than productivity, as has been the case in the United States economy in recent years, a heavier responsibility for policies to contain inflation is thrown onto the monetary managers. This is made more difficult, and brings the entire system so much closer to complete disruption, when a loose fiscal policy, such as has also been tolerated in recent years, leaves monetary policy as the only mechanism left to fight the inflation. That this had been happening in the United States was the reason in the early 1980s for the killingly high interest rates, the decline in employment, and the rise in bankruptcies and unemployment to higher levels than had existed since the Great Depression of the 1930s.

The adoption of a rationally designed incomes policy would in no sense mean that there would be no part for monetary and fiscal policy to play. On the contrary, if incomes policies can be used to bring about a better price performance, then the traditional instruments of monetary and fiscal policy can be used more effectively for purposes of short-run economic stabilization in the face of business fluctuations, and for purposes of encouraging and facilitating economic growth. Incomes policies need not cripple monetary policy or the scope or potential of it. They can liberate monetary policy to function effectively for the purposes for which it is useful and competent. An incomes policy of the penalty tax kind, moreover, is designed to allow the normal forces of the markets in the

---

[1] See Sidney Weintraub, *Capitalism's Inflation and Unemployment Crisis* (Reading, Mass.: Addison-Wesley, 1978), and the same author's "TIPs against Inflation," in Michael P. Claudon and Richard R. Cornwall, eds., *An Incomes Policy for the United States: New Approaches* (Boston: Martinus Nijoff Publishing, 1981). See also, for a more complete evaluation, Claudon and Cornwall, *An Incomes Policy for the United States: New Approaches.*

economy to function freely. Unlike a system of strict wage and price controls, the TIP proposals are designed simply to provide a framework within which the normal allocative function of the price level can operate more freely.

Incomes policies of this kind are basically addressed to an inflationary problem that emanates from a disagreement in the productive system over the distributive shares of output. The attempt to push up wage rates more rapidly than the increase in productivity permits is an attempt to raise the share of total output and income going to the suppliers of labor. The structural characteristics of the system are such, however, that the result has been a rise in the price level, to the consequent disadvantage of the workers as well as everybody else (except, perhaps, those who have the power and resources to protect themselves against the inflation). The same kind of thing happens when producers attempt to raise the established wage-cost markup factor. We have referred to this previously as profit rate inflation, or the inflationary pressure that arises from an attempt to exploit perceived degrees of monopoly or market power. Attempted increases in the markup factor, in the same way as increases in efficiency wage rates, have the effect in our model of turning the aggregate supply curve upward and to the left. From the model's point of view, these attempts to change the distributive shares of output by raising the markup factor or efficiency wages induce a leftward movement *of* the aggregate supply curve, while an increase in employment at an existing wage rate induces a movement *along* the supply curve. We have seen that an upward pressure on prices may result from both these different kinds of movement.

MONEY WAGE RATES, PROFIT INCOMES, AND CONSUMPTION EXPENDITURE

The postclassical analysis perceives the two-sided importance of the money wage rate. It is an element of production costs and thereby a determinant of commodity prices. But it would be wrong to imagine that we can therefore embrace simply what has been called a cost-push theory of inflation. For we have already emphasized at every relevant point the fact that wage incomes have a dual significance in the monetary market system. Not only are they elements of costs in the manner we have observed. They are also the most important source of consumption expenditures.

On the one hand, therefore, money wages can give a cutting edge to the supply side causes of inflation. On the other hand they also give a cutting edge to the demand side. This will be clear from reflection on the manner in which, in Chapter 18, we developed the consumption function. The analysis is summarized in Figure 18-11, depicting the wage earners' money income and consumption expenditure functions. Anything, then, that exerts an upward pressure on the level of the consumption function will, by raising the aggregate demand curve in the model, also tend to increase the effective price level. We argued at some length in Chapter 19 that a rise in money wages would lift the aggregate demand curve at the same time as it would also tend to raise the aggregate supply curve. We must take careful note of the dual aspects of wage incomes that are clearly at work.

We acknowledge also that other forces may similarly tend to raise the consumption function. A change in the corporate tax rate or in allowable corporate tax deductions may lead to increased dividend payments and higher consumption expenditures by profit earners. Taking these income-consumption relations as given, we can observe the ways in which economic policies might be brought to bear upon them. We can again look briefly at both monetary and fiscal policy effects.

If, for any reason, it was thought that a principal contributor to inflation was an excessively rapid buildup of consumption expenditure, an increase in the interest rate might have a corrective effect. Higher interest rates can have a powerful effect, as was demonstrated again in the United States in the early 1980s, in reducing some forms of durable goods consumption. A tightening of consumer credit and an increase in the price of it can fairly quickly cut back such consumer durable purchases as automobiles and heavy household items. A generally higher interest rate may also cut back purchases associated with housing construction, as the traditional suppliers of funds to that sector are less able to compete for funds in the money capital market. But we should bear in mind that the interest rate, emanating from a generally tighter monetary policy, is a blunt instrument to use against an imagined consumer-led inflation. For it is capable of significantly restraining investment expenditure also, to the detriment of potentially growth-inducing, as well as productivity-increasing, capital formation.

Policy effects on the consumption function may also come from changes in fiscal policy. If, for example, the individual tax rate is increased, this will automatically decrease the disposable income component of total incomes at each level of employment. The potential significance of the personal tax rate was observed in the discussion of Equations (28) through (30) in Chapter 18. If it is desired to change the level of consumption expenditures through fiscal policy, this may be accomplished by a change in the tax base as well as by a change in the tax rate. The tax base in this case is analogous to the same concept that applied to corporate taxation. In the present case the allowable tax deductions that may be changed as a means of changing the level of disposable income, and thereby changing consumption, would be personal exemption allowances, deduction of mortgage interest payments, and such items. If it were desired to increase disposable incomes in order to induce higher consumption expenditures as an antirecession move, the level of personal exemption allowances could be increased.

In any such fiscal policy move, however, the outcome would depend very much on whose taxes were being cut or increased. To illustrate the possible points at issue we might consider a tax cut designed to increase expenditures. The reduction in tax revenue collections could be accomplished in various ways. First, there could be an across-the-board tax cut, in which all income receivers' tax liabilities were reduced by a common percentage. In that case the high-income earners would receive a larger absolute benefit. If, then, the marginal propensity to consume of the high-income earners was lower than that of the low-income earners (as we imagined in Chapter 18 might be the case when we drew the aggregate consumption function concave), the reduction of taxes would not give as relatively large a boost to consumption expenditures as it would if all income earners had received more nearly equal absolute benefits. The high-income earners in this case are likely to save a larger proportion of their increased disposable income. This was the design and intention behind the large across-the-board tax reduction effected by the Reagan administration in 1981. These tax reductions, however, were made at the same time as increased tax payments were being collected from a sharp rise in the social security tax. Their effect was therefore blunted.

This matter of potentially differential tax effects can be put in terms of our aggregate supply and demand model by observing that the tax policy will alter the distribution of total disposable income between wage earners and profit earners. This distribution is an important factor determining the strength of the money income and the employment multipliers in the system. Any policy development that increases the relative share of the profit earners, who may well have a lower propensity to consume and a higher propensity to save, may introduce a lower multiplier into the analysis. It will conceivably have an effect on the size of the multiplicand also, or on the initial boost in spending that the tax reduction was designed to accomplish. In so far as that spending effect comes about from higher consumption expenditure at any given level of employment, we can interpret this by saying that the exogenous term in the consumption function has increased and the level of the consumption function is higher. This initial boost in spending which tends to instigate a multiplier process is referred to as the multiplicand.

If, to continue with the case in hand, a tax reduction were to provide more absolute benefit to the high-income earners, the multiplicand effect from any increase in consumption would be smaller. But if higher savings were to flow through and induce lower interest rates in the money capital markets, there would be some possibility that an increase in investment outlays would occur, thereby introducing a further multiplicand effect

from a lift in the investment expenditure function. The size of the multiplicand effect, then, would be ambiguous, depending on both an investment effect and a consumption effect. But the size of the multiplier
would be smaller, for the reasons we examined above.

For purposes of anti-inflationary policy, fiscal measures might be
used to impact on consumption expenditure and reduce it or moderate its
rate of increase, by raising taxes and reducing exemption allowances.
The detailed possibilities and potential effects would depend on the same
kinds of relationships that we have already discussed.

INVESTMENT AND GOVERNMENT EXPENDITURES

Any policy-induced effects on the investment function can be analyzed
in terms similar to the foregoing. We have seen that both monetary and
fiscal policies can work in various ways to introduce an investment multiplicand. Similarly, a fiscal policy that focused on the expenditure side
of the government budget rather than the revenue side could be analyzed
in comparable terms in the context of our basic model. An increase in
government expenditure would raise the G component of the spending
stream, as discussed in Chapter 18. This would in turn raise the aggregate
demand curve and would operate in the same way to raise the effective
demand point. The implications of this for employment, output, and price
levels, and the possibilities of a reverse policy for anti-inflation purposes,
can then be analyzed in the same way as we have considered similar
possibilities previously.

INFLATION AND THE QUESTION
OF INDUSTRIAL STRUCTURE

Our brief discussion of the economic policy problem in this chapter has
been confined to a general view of some of the more immediate implications of the model of the macroeconomy we developed in the preceding
chapters. We have highlighted the meaning of what we anticipated at an
earlier point as (1) diminishing returns inflation, resulting from a movement up along the economy's nonlinear aggregate supply curve; (2) wage-
cost inflation, resulting from a movement to the left of the aggregate
supply curve; and (3) profit rate, or markup, inflation, which also turns
the supply curve to the left. Additionally, we have looked at the demand
side as well as the supply side implications and have traced the possibility
of a demand inflation emanating from whatever forces tend to cause the
aggregate demand curve to rise.

The foregoing has not, however, given an exhaustive discussion of the inflationary problem or of its possible solution. Nor has it touched on the large number of other questions that have to be considered in the full context of economic policy. Many of those are properly outside our immediate province in a book on money, banking, and monetary economics.

In particular, we have said nothing about the significance of changes in the industrial structure that may cause certain industries, or certain geographical areas, or certain types of skills and economic endowments to become relatively depressed or obsolete. In recent years the United States heavy manufacturing industries, steel and automobiles for example, have found it increasinging difficult to compete against foreign producers. Advances in freight technology have shrunk the world and increased the proximity of markets. Miniaturization, the introduction of new and lightweight materials, and changes in technology have drastically changed the face, as well as the competitive ability, of a number of industries. Expanding defense industries in the United States have been located outside of the older Northeast and Midwest industrial areas, and shifts of population as well as industries to the Sunbelt have occurred. Revolutions in office procedures, information transmission, and communications techniques have raised other problems of structural and technological unemployment. Not all of these questions, and not all of the policy possibilities that might be relevant in the light of them, fall clearly within the limited compass we have set ourselves in this book. But as we noted at some length in Chapter 2 where we asked "What are the questions?," we need to be continually aware that the problems themselves raise questions that impinge on the issues we have discussed in more detail.

THE WAGE IMPACT ON CONSUMPTION DEMAND

To underline the dual aspects, or the interdependent supply and demand side significance of wage and salary income as we referred to it in the preceding discussion, Table 21-3 presents some relevant data. The table confirms the importance of wage and salary incomes on the supply side, where they account for somewhat more than 60 percent of total personal incomes, and on the demand side, where they amount to about 80 percent of total personal consumption expenditures. A fuller analysis of the factors underlying the trends in the data is not intended at this time. The figures shown have been taken at five-year intervals simply as a means of indicating the orders of magnitude involved and to illustrate the two-sided aspects of wage and salary payments incorporated into the model of the macroeconomy.

Table   21-3

Personal income, wage and salary payments, and personal consumption
expenditure for selected years (Data are in billions of dollars)

Year	Personal income	Wage and salary payments	Wages and salaries as percent of personal income	Personal consumption expenditure	Wages and salaries as percent of personal consumption
1970	811.1	548.7	67.6	621.7	88.3
1975	1,265.0	806.4	63.7	976.4	82.6
1980	2,160.4	1,356.1	62.8	1,667.2	81.3
1981	2,415.8	1,493.9	61.8	1,843.2	81.0
1982	2,569.7	1,560.1	60.7	1,972.0	79.1

Source: *Economic Report of the President,* February 1983, pp. 188, 190.

In the following two chapters we shall turn explicitly to the place
of money in the larger context of economic policies.

SUMMARY

This chapter has summarized some of the more direct economic policy
questions relevant to the model of the macroeconomy we constructed in
the preceding chapters. Following an indication of the principal authorities responsible for monetary, fiscal, and income policies, a definition of
each of the general policy areas was given. Particular attention was given
to the policy challenge presented by the simultaneous occurrence of inflation and unemployment.

The possible scope for economic policies was discussed against the
aggregate supply and demand determinants incorporated into the postclassical model of the macroeconomy. Productivity considerations, wage
rate and profit rate changes, including variations in the wage-cost markup
factor, were reexamined to illustrate the sources from which an inflationary rise in the price level may emanate. Monetary, fiscal, and incomes
policies were shown to have potential effects on both the aggregate supply
curve and the aggregate demand curve. Comments were made on the
applicability of the argument to recent trends in the United States
economy.

The chapter concluded with an indication from recent United States
data of the importance of wage and salary incomes for both income payments or costs on the supply side, and consumption expenditures on the
demand side, of the model.

IMPORTANT CONCEPTS

Definitions of monetary, fiscal, and   *TIP, tax-based incomes policy*
  incomes policies   *Economic policy mix*
Policy incompatibilities   *Distributive shares*
Sectoral policy effects   *Dual significance of wage incomes*
Causes of inflation

QUESTIONS FOR DISCUSSION AND REVIEW

1. What changes in the structure of the American economy have been responsible for the simultaneous problems of inflation and unemployment?

2. Are monetary, fiscal, and incomes policies complementary? How? Why?

3. Using the literature referred to in this chapter, examine possible forms of TIP (tax-based incomes policy) proposals.

4. "The explanation of inflation cannot be monocausal. The principal determining forces operate on both the supply and demand sides." Discuss critically.

5. How, if at all, are questions of investment and productivity relevant to the causes and explanation of inflation?

6. "A severe restriction of the money supply can always arrest inflation, but it demands a high price in unemployment, depression, and bankruptcies." Discuss critically.

7. What is meant by, and what is the significance of, the wage-price-productivity nexus?

8. Is income distribution relevant to the presence or control of inflation?

9. Do any considerations of economic policy argue for or against the traditional independence of the monetary authorities (the Federal Reserve Board) from the government of the day?

10. Evaluate the argument that rather than arresting inflation it would be entirely adequate to invent ways, such as indexation, to make it more comfortable to live with. In the course of your answer consider the economic and social costs of inflation.

22

INSTRUMENTS OF MONETARY POLICY

STUDY OBJECTIVES:

- To review the relation of the instruments of monetary policy to the three-fold aspects of our study: (1) monetary analysis, (2) monetary institutions, and (3) monetary policy
- To establish a perspective for the discussion in this and the following chapter by observing the relation between (1) the objectives, (2) the targets, (3) the indicators, and (4) the instruments of monetary policy
- To extend our understanding of the nature, the method of use, and the potential effectiveness of the Federal Reserve Board's general instruments of credit control: (1) open market operations, (2) the discount rate mechanism, and (3) reserve requirement regulations
- To observe recent developments in the use of monetary policy instruments
- To note the possible use and effectiveness of selective measures of credit control
- To establish a connection between the instruments and implementation of monetary policy and the place of monetary theory in the analysis of the macroeconomy

The concept that has recurred most frequently and has, in many ways, coordinated our view of the macroeconomy is that of the flow of money. We have been looking at "money on the wing." The discussion in Part V, "Money Flows and the Macroeconomy," developed a theory that focused on the determinants and effects of the flows of money payments. Income receivers are also income spenders. Money flows that the producing sectors of the economy take into account as costs of production are income receipts from the point of view of the providers of factors of production. In the matter of price formation and inflation we found that it was not possible to be satisfied with a single or simplified explanation such as a demand-pull or a cost-push theory. Inflation, as we have seen, is a problem of dynamic disequilibrium between the rate of flow of monetary expenditure and the rate of flow of the production of goods and services, or the willingness of producers to supply a previously existing level of goods and services at previously existing prices. This disjunction between rates of flow came into focus in our analysis under the heading of the wage-price-productivity nexus.

This analysis was supplemented by a discussion of what determined the demand for money and the market-clearing price of money or the rate of interest. An extensive analysis was given of the determination of the supply of money. The actual amount of money in existence at any time is, of course, a stock variable. But we have consistently examined its relation to the specification of the money flows to which it gives rise. Similarly, our discussion of the institutional structure of the macroeconomy made extensive use of the balance sheet or stock variables that were relevant. But the focus was consistently on the causes and effects of changes in those stock variables. We saw, for example, how changes in the public's asset portfolio habits may cause changes in the balance sheets of the depository institutions. Changes in the institutions' lending and asset-holding decisions were also reflected in the balance sheets we employed. Again the focus of our analysis was the effect of such changes on the level and variability of the money flows in the system.

The chapters in Part III on the structure and operations of the commercial banks and other financial institutions, along with the discussion in Part IV of central banking and the functions of the Federal Reserve, complemented the chapters that provided our monetary theoretic models. One's view of the importance and significance of the financial institutions is determined by an understanding of the manner in which the macroeconomy functions. Institutions give pragmatic expression to the relationships that the theory of the macroeconomy envisages. Reciprocally, one's theory of the macroeconomy must be determined by the realities of the institutional structure of the economy.

Similarly, an understanding of the scope and potential of economic policy depends on a grasp of the relations between theory and institutional realities. The need for certain kinds of economic policy, and the understanding of their potential benefits, will be determined by the theoretical viewpoint in terms of which the macroeconomy is interpreted. It will be dependent, likewise, on the ability of the institutional framework of the system to implement policies that may lead to desired ends. Analysis, institutions, and policy are highly interdependent.

MONETARISTS AND KEYNESIANS

This interdependence has come to expression in interesting ways in the history of monetary theory and the management of the macroeconomy. In most recent times, for example, debates have developed between the monetarists and the Keynesians regarding the importance of money and monetary policy. The literature on money and banking has not been considered complete unless it contained a treatment of the difference between these competing ways of looking at things. For ourselves, as the analytical parts of our study have made clear, we have preferred to bring both the monetarist and the neo–Keynesian visions under the more embracive category of neoclassical macroeconomics, or the neoclassical–Keynesian synthesis. But there are nevertheless differences between them.

The monetarists have generally held the view that the economy contains what we have called automatic equilibrating systems and processes. The optimum outcome and maximum economic benefits will be realized, it has been thought, if the automatically equilibrating free-market system is left to take its course. This is particularly true of the manner in which the theory has come to expression in the new classical macroeconomics. The neoclassical faith is eloquently expressed by Professors Merton Miller and Charles Upton in their *Macroeconomics, a Neoclassical Introduction.* "We believe," they say, "that a market economy left to its own devices will settle into a full employment equilibrium. External shocks, of a variety of kinds, will dislodge it from equilibrium from time to time, but the economy's internal defenses will speedily [sic] return it to equilibrium barring new shocks or actively destabilizing policies by the government."[1] The neoclassical faith seems to have been almost completely belied by the simultaneous existence during the late 1970s and early 1980s of inflation and unemployment.

The neoclassical theoretical vision determines, in turn, neoclassical policy. In economic policy in general the monetarist wing of the neoclassical synthesis calls for a minimum of regulatory interference and a maximum reliance on the unimpeded market system. In the area of monetary policy it calls for the adherence to a set of rules, rather than discretionary monetary management. Some economists argue that the discretionary monetary policy operations of the Federal Reserve should be replaced by a basic rule that would allow the money supply to expand at a constant annual rate. The latter, it is usually said, would be determined by the potential rate of growth of the output of goods and services in the economy.

A deeper understanding of our earlier chapters on central banking and the potential control of the money supply, together with those of Part III that explained the operation of the commercial banking system, throws considerable doubt, however, on the central bank's ability to engineer a steady growth in the money supply. It is not even possible to know definitely at all times how much money actually exists. Much depends on the importance one attaches to the alternative definitions of the money supply we have already examined. Relevant also are the factors that

---

[1] Merton H. Miller and Charles W. Upton, *Macroeconomics, a Neoclassical Introduction* (Homewood, Ill.: Richard D. Irwin, 1974), p. vii.

influence the money supply but are subject to wealth portfolio decisions by the public, rather than under the direct control of the Fed.

The Keynesian wing of the neoclassical synthesis has less faith in inherent equilibrating forces in the macroeconomic system. It is much more impressed by the fact that the system is shot through with forces tending to disequilibrium and disruption. It has turned its back more completely on the earlier classical theorem that insisted on automatic harmonies in economic affairs. Say's Law, the Keynesians insist, is simply wrong and irrelevant. Savings do not necessarily and automatically flow into investment. There may be reasons why a more or less permanent diminution of the expenditure flows in the economy may emerge. Some kind of offsetting regulatory action may be necessary to raise the expenditure streams sufficiently to bring the economy back towards a full-employment level of operation.[2] But the Keynesian escape from the strictures of the classical analysis was not complete. As Axel Leijonhufvud put it in the title of his important book, an unfortunate distinction emerged between "Keynesian economics" and "the economics of Keynes."[3] The earlier vision of John Maynard Keynes' General Theory was quickly submerged into the static thought forms of the neo–Walrasian equilibrium theory that gained ascendency in professional minds.

There can be no doubt, however, that in all systems, with differing emphases and different degrees of relevance, money matters. An earlier and extreme monetarist dictum that only money matters has moderated and formed an alliance with the Keynesian view. This claims that, in unique ways, money matters, but that behavior and developments in a number of real markets in the economy need to be taken carefully into account. The analytical perspective we established in Part V was described there as a postclassical view. In that view, money is again of central importance.

Against this background of the interdependence of analysis, institutions, and policy, we shall clarify in this chapter the nature, scope, and potential effectiveness of the monetary policy instruments that exist. We shall introduce that discussion by commenting briefly on (1) the objectives, (2) the targets, (3) the indicators, and (4) the instruments of monetary policy.

THE OBJECTIVES OF MONETARY POLICY

Monetary policy plays its part in the attempt to realize the objectives of economic policy we discussed in Chapter 2. It is most directly relevant to the achievement of (1) a high and stable level of employment; (2) a

---

[2] See Franco Modigliani, "The Monetarist Controversy or, Should We Forsake Stabilization Policies?" American Economic Review, March 1977.

[3] Axel Leijonhufvud, On Keynesian Economics and the Economics of Keynes: A Study in Monetary Theory (New York: Oxford University Press, 1968).

stable price level, or stability in the domestic purchasing power of money; (3) a sustainable rate of economic growth; and (4) stability in the international exchange rate, or in the external purchasing power of the nation's money supply. These are the kinds of objectives to which the Federal Reserve Board gives primary attention in its formulation of policy, as illustrated in the directive of the Federal Open Market Committee that we reproduced in Chapter 12.

In the analysis of the policies directed to these ends it is necessary to examine what has become known as the transmission effects or the transmission channels of monetary policy, that is, the channels through which a change in the supply of money, an increase for example, transmits its effects to the several financial markets and the real sectors of the economy. Analytically, we need to have a view of precisely how monetary policies and changes in the money supply actually work out their effects on the level of employment, real output, prices, and incomes, as well as the rate of interest, security prices and yields, and other financial variables.

In the present chapter we shall explain the nature and potential usefulness of the monetary policy instruments by emphasizing the ways in which the use of them causes changes in the reserve base of the depository institutions. Specifically, and to make use of the commercial banks as examples of the depository institutions in general, we shall trace the ways in which monetary policies work out their effects by changing bank reserves. More generally, we shall be interested in the ways in which, as a result, monetary policy developments cause changes in bank reserves, the money supply, and security market prices and yields.

THE TARGETS OF MONETARY POLICY

Given the larger economic objectives to which monetary policy contributes, the monetary authorities must direct their policies to achieving a smaller number of well-defined monetary targets. Once again, the definition of the appropriate monetary policy target will depend on the view that is held of the manner in which the monetary and economic system operates.

Monetarism, for example, has assumed that the important objective of policy is to control the money supply. The target variable in that case is the money supply as defined, for example, as M1, or as M2 or some broader variable if account is taken of a wider measure of liquidity in the financial system. The Federal Reserve Board operated on principles such as these following its dramatic change of posture and policy thinking in October 1979. The directive of the Federal Open Market Committee reproduced in Chapter 12 indicates the target ranges for the growth of the money supply during the months following the February 1983 meeting at which the directive was prepared. In conjunction with the money supply target, some attention was given also to the range within which, it was hoped, the growth rate of the total domestic nonfinancial debt would lie.

Other schools of economic thought, the neo–Keynesians for example, argue that monetary policy should focus, not on the money supply as the target variable, but on what are referred to as money market conditions. This means that some appropriate interest rate, such as the long-term rate of interest (the long-term government securities yield or the corporate bond rate), should be taken as the target. The reason for this, presumably, is that such a rate of interest most directly affects or determines the level of spending in the economy and, therefore, most vitally captures the probable overall effects of monetary policy.

In defining the appropriate targets of monetary policy, however, the options are by no means exhausted by the earlier monetarist emphasis on the money supply or the early Keynesian emphasis on money market conditions and the level of interest rates. Ideally, it is necessary to target some variable or variables that are closely related to, or correlated with, the movements in the ultimate objective variable it is desired to influence. If, for example, the task of monetary policy was to contribute to stability or to a certain rate of growth in GNP, it would be ideally desirable to adopt as the monetary policy target a variable that was closely correlated with GNP. It would need to be one that the monetary authorities were effectively able to influence, and one that, when changes in it were observed, pointed to subsequent induced changes in GNP. Some economists have argued that other variables, such as the total domestic nonfinancial debt or credit outstanding (for example, the total of the loans and investments of commercial banks) may be more effectively used as the target variable, and monetary policy should be changed from time to time, to effect easier or tighter monetary conditions, as variations in such targets warranted.[4]

Recalling our earlier discussions of the changes that have occurred not only in the definitions of the money supply but also in the structure and functions of financial institutions and the availability of new forms of near-money and monetary substitutes, serious doubt exists as to the

[4] See Frank E. Morris, "Monetarism without Money," *New England Economic Review*, March/April 1983; and the same author's "Do the Monetary Aggregates Have a Future as Targets of Federal Reserve Policy," *New England Economic Review*, March/April 1982. See also Richard W. Kopcke, "Must the Ideal 'Money Stock' be Controllable," *New England Economic Review*, March/April 1983; Edward J. Kane, "Selecting Monetary Targets in a Changing Financial Environment," and Benjamin M. Friedman, "Using a Credit Aggregate Target to Implement Monetary Policy in the Financial Environment of the Future." Both of the last-mentioned papers appeared in *Monetary Policy Issues in the 1980s, A Symposium Sponsored by the Federal Reserve Bank of Kansas City*, 1982.

wisdom or effectiveness of targeting a simple monetary aggregate such as M1 or M2. Associated with the availability of new forms of money and money substitutes, more or less rapid changes have occurred in the relative demand for money as variously defined, implying that less reliance can now be placed on the stability in the velocity of circulation of money. In the early 1980s, for example, variations in the velocity of circulation rendered it particularly difficult for the Federal Reserve Board to be sure to what extent it should adhere to its announced target for the range of increase in M1 or M2. The Fed could not be sure whether variations in velocity should be regarded as a temporary or a more permanent trend phenomenon.

Differences of view regarding the appropriateness of monetary targets imply, in turn, differences in the understanding of the actual transmission effects of monetary policy. Those economists who emphasize the money supply as the target variable generally imagine that the principal determinant of money expenditure flows is the money supply. This is based on an ingenious theoretical argument. An increase in the money supply, it is thought, will mean that people in general will be holding more money than they desire at existing price levels and interest rates. Differently stated, the marginal utility realized from holding money will be lower, relative to the marginal utilities available from holding wealth in alternative asset forms. Wealth holders will therefore, the argument goes, wish to spend some of their new holdings of money in order to acquire other portfolio assets that are substitutes for money. In some formulations of the argument, real commodities, including durable consumer goods and industrial capital goods, are asset substitutes for money in this sense. When the money supply increases, the expenditures on these commodities will therefore also increase. This line of argument traces out the transmission effects of monetary policy via such asset portfolio substitution effects. The validity or otherwise of these substitution effects, or of the so-called gross substitution theorem on which the argument depends, is an important question at the heart of modern monetary theory.

Those economists, on the other hand, who argue that the appropriate long-term rate of interest should be taken as the monetary policy target hold a somewhat different view of the transmission effect. From their viewpoint monetary policy works by changing the relative price of money or the rate of interest. By doing so, it changes the worthwhileness of real capital investment and other durable goods expenditures. We recall from our discussion in Chapter 6 that the level of investment expenditure can be thought to depend, as a first approximation, on the relation between the rate of interest, or the cost of money capital, and the marginal efficiency of investment. The relationship was expressed in the investment expenditure function $i = i(r)$, where i and r refer to the investment expenditure and the interest rate, respectively.

These differences of view reflect recurring debates in the history of monetary theory. The first-mentioned view, or the perspective generally embraced by the monetarists, reflects one of the implications of the neo-classical quantity theory of money. It was against the assumed explanatory competence of this line of thought that John Maynard Keynes argued in his *General Theory* in 1936.

INDICATORS OF MONETARY POLICY

By the term *indicators* in the context of monetary policy, we refer to those variables whose magnitudes at any time indicate to the monetary authorities the need for a change in monetary policy action. The definition of the indicator variables will depend on what is taken to be the important target variable of monetary policy.

Those economists who argue that the money supply, or one of the definitional variants of the money supply, is the target variable will generally argue that the indicator variable to which attention should be paid is the monetary base. We defined and analyzed the monetary base at some length in Chapter 13. It is imagined, from this point of view, that by adapting monetary policy to variations in the monetary base the Federal Reserve can in effect exercise a reasonable degree of control over the money supply, the ultimate target variable. We have already seen a number of reasons for being cautious about taking a firm stand on this argument. For as the analysis in Chapter 13 revealed, the control that the Federal Reserve is able to exercise over the monetary base is itself quite uncertain and ambiguous. But apart from that basic fact, even a fairly tight degree of influence over the monetary base would not necessarily imply a close control over the money supply. The latter will depend on the magnitude at any time, or over any period of time, of the particular money multiplier that was thought to be important. Moreover, a number of factors entering into the money supply multipliers are under the control of the public as a result of its asset portfolio decisions, or the depository institutions as a result of their desired excess reserve positions, and not under the control of the Federal Reserve at all.

Those economists who, on the other hand, take the long-term cost of money capital, or the rate of interest, to be the important target variable will generally argue that the appropriate indicator variable is some measure of short-term money market conditions. They will usually place more weight on the short-term money market interest rates. If monetary policy, they say, is adapted to keeping the money market stable, as indicated by the short-term rate of interest, this will feed through to achieve desired results on the long-term rates and thereby on the level of money expenditure. A desired change in the long-term rate should be achieved by an intervention in the money market that moves the short-term rates in the required direction.

This question of what is taken as the proper target variable, and what, accordingly, is regarded as the appropriate indicator variable, is extremely important for monetary theory and policy. Suppose, for example, that the Federal Reserve Board decides that it should take whatever action is necessary to maintain the short-term interest rate at some specified level. If, then, there should be an increased demand for money, due to either an increased level of trade or an increase in the economy's liquidity preference (a movement to the right of the demand-for-money schedule described in Chapter 15), this will cause the interest rate to rise. This may be expressed as a decline in the market prices of securities as the public endeavors to sell securities with a view to increasing their holdings of money. In that case it will be necessary for the Federal Reserve Bank, if it wants to implement its policy of maintaining the interest rate, to purchase whatever securities are offered to it in the market. The more elastic the demand-for-money schedule, the greater will be the volume of securities the Fed will have to purchase in order to maintain the interest rate within any narrowly defined range. This implies that a rigid policy of preserving the interest rate at a specified level may mean that the central bank effectively surrenders control over the money supply.

Alternatively, if the policy stance calls for the Federal Reserve Bank to control the monetary base and the money supply, the achievement of this objective may have precisely the opposite effects. By maintaining the money supply in the face of tendencies for it to fluctuate, it may be necessary to allow the market rate of interest to become more unstable than it would otherwise be. In the complex reality of simultaneous variations in the demand for money and the monetary base, it may be extremely difficult for the Federal Reserve to stabilize both the money supply and the interest rate.

Examples of these very different policy stances can be seen in the history of the Federal Reserve. In the years following World War II, prior to the famous "accord" between the Federal Reserve Bank and the Treasury in 1951, the Federal Reserve intervened continuously in the securities market to maintain the interest rate at a so-called peg. The purpose of keeping the interest rate low was to minimize the Treasury's burden of financing the national debt and was a holdover from the wartime conditions. The policy meant, however, that the money supply increased rapidly. In effect, the Federal Reserve stood ready to monetize whatever amount of the federal debt the economy wished.

At the opposite end of the policy possibilities, the stance of the Federal Reserve following October 1979 was directed toward controlling the monetary base and the money supply. It endeavored to accomplish this by controlling the total level of the banking system's nonborrowed reserves.[5] An inspection of the market data shows that since that time there have been rather larger fluctuations than previously in the market rates of interest.

THE INSTRUMENTS OF MONETARY POLICY

We have referred to the objectives, the targets, and the indicators of monetary policy. We come now to the examination of the instruments by which, given the need for a particular kind of monetary policy as stimulated by the behavior of the indicator variables, the targets might eventually be realized.

Experience in thinking about the instruments of monetary policy will have been obtained from a study of the preceding chapters. We are concerned initially with the three so-called general instruments of credit control: (1) the open market operations conducted by the Federal Open Market Committee and described at some length in Chapter 12; (2) the Federal Reserve discount rate, described in Chapter 12 also, in the context of the discussion of the Federal Reserve Bank's management of the member banks' reserve accounts; and (3) reserve requirement regulations, which were discussed in the context of commercial bank operations and in describing the structure of the Federal Reserve System. The following sections will assume that the reader is generally familiar with the manner in which the use of these instruments of credit control impact on the member banks' reserve positions. We shall refer to the member banks as a principal example of the depository institutions in general, to all of which, of course, the analysis applies.

OPEN MARKET OPERATIONS

Open market purchases and sales of securities are conducted by the Federal Reserve Bank of New York as the market agent of the FOMC. Purchases of securities will increase the reserves of the banks. Sales of securities will reduce them. At the same time, open market purchases will tend to lever security prices upward, and to press their yields, or the general market rate of interest, downward. Open market purchases would generally be made when either of two conditions exist.

First, it may be thought as a matter of fundamental Federal Reserve policy that tendencies to recession in the economy make it desirable to

[5] See the valuable survey of Federal Reserve policy operations in Paul Meek, *U.S. Monetary Policy and Financial Markets* (New York: Federal Reserve Bank of New York, 1982).

stimulate a higher level of monetary expenditure. Open market purchases then serve as traditional antirecession monetary policy. By using such purchases to increase the reserves of the banks, and therefore their excess reserves, a higher level of bank lending might be induced. This, taken in conjunction with the multiple expansion of loans and deposits that potentially follows from an increase of excess reserves, will lead to a larger-scale easing of monetary conditions than is immediately indicated by the size of the Federal Reserve Board's security purchases. The security purchases add to the monetary base, to use the language of earlier chapters. But the potential effect on the money supply depends not only on the change in the monetary base but also on the size of the money supply multiplier.

The open market purchases will also tend to press interest rates downward, and this will make investment expenditures more attractive. Thus the lowering of interest rates can be expected to motivate higher money expenditures, and the increased money supply made available by the multiple loan expansion of the banks will facilitate that expenditure. This is traditional antirecession monetary policy at work. Higher monetary expenditures are both motivated and facilitated by the monetary policy action.

At the same time, open market purchases may be made by the Federal Reserve Bank purely as a part of normal day-to-day defensive operations. The security purchases will then be intended merely to offset what would otherwise be an unwanted reduction in the banks' reserve positions. Similarly, open market sales may be made to offset undesired increases in the banks' reserves. The latter may follow, for example, from a return of currency to the banks, such as normally occurs at the first of the year, or from an increase in Federal Reserve float. These are examples of the distinction we drew previously between defensive and dynamic monetary policy actions.

We have spoken of the manner in which the open market operations will have an effect on the market rates of interest. The point in the market at which the impact is felt will depend on the kinds of securities being bought or sold. Most of the operations summarized in Table 22-1 occurred in the market for Treasury bills, which are the shortest-term government securities outstanding. They generally mature in ninety-one days. The Federal Reserve does, however, operate in the medium- and long-term sections of the market also. It can generally be expected that any change in interest rates in one sector of the market will be fed through, principally as a result of private arbitrage, to other sectors. A movement in short-term rates will in general be reflected in a corresponding change in the long-term rates. Of course, there is no automatic and rigid relationship between such rates. The degree of movement effected in the different sectors of the market will differ at different times and under different

Table   22-1

Open market transactions of the Federal Reserve System, 1981 and 1982
(Amounts are in millions of dollars)

Type of transaction	1981	1982
U.S. government securities		
Outright transactions		
Gross purchases	16,690	19,870
Gross sales	6,769	8,369
Redemptions	1,816	3,000
Matched sale-purchase transactions		
Gross sales	589,312	543,804
Gross purchases	589,647	543,173
Repurchase agreements		
Gross purchases	79,920	130,774
Gross sales	78,733	130,286
Net change in U.S. government securities	9,626	8,358
Federal agency obligations		
Outright transactions		
Gross purchases	494	0
Gross sales	0	0
Redemptions	108	189
Repurchase agreements		
Gross purchases	13,320	18,957
Gross sales	13,576	18,638
Net change in Federal agency obligations	130	130
Bankers' acceptances		
Outright transactions (net)	0	0
Repurchase agreements (net)	− 582	1,285
Net change in bankers' acceptances	− 582	1,285
Total net change in the Federal Reserve System		
open market account	9,175	9,773

Source: *Federal Reserve Annual Reports,* 1981, pp. 222– 23; and 1982, pp. 214– 15.

economic conditions. In this connection the reader might refer again to the discussion in Chapter 6 of the term structure of interest rates, and the reasons why yield curves of different possible shapes might emerge.

Part of the difficulty in anticipating this feed-through effect of changes in security yields or interest rates lies in the fact that the monetary policy move may itself set up expectations effects in the economy. Open market purchases, for example, which tend to lower the general level of interest rates, may be interpreted as a sign that the monetary authorities foresee recessionary trends in the economy. This may induce business firms to curtail their expenditure plans, to reduce their borrowing, and to fail to take advantage of the increased supply of money that is now available.

Or again, the open market purchases, by raising security prices, may lead investors to expect that further policy moves in the same direction may follow. They may therefore increase their security purchases. Security prices will increase and their yield will decrease still further.

Table 22-1 summarizes the open market operations of the Federal Reserve System for the years 1981 and 1982. Some aspects of the data can be noted briefly. First, by far the largest part of the transactions during each of the years consisted of what are described as "matched sale-purchase transactions" and "repurchase agreements." We encountered these terms previously in the context of commercial bank operations. We saw there that a commercial bank may engage in a repurchase agreement (or so-called Repo) with its depositors. The bank then sells a security to the depositor under an agreement to repurchase it from him on a specified date, often the following day. The difference between the agreed purchase price and the selling price of the security provides a rate of return to the depositor who has temporarily bought it.

The repurchase agreements referred to in Table 22-1 result from essentially the same kind of transaction. The Federal Reserve Bank purchases securities from the market under an agreement that the seller will repurchase them from the Federal Reserve at a specified time. The matched sale-purchase transactions referred to in Table 22-1 result from essentially the opposite kind of transaction. In that case the Federal Reserve sells securities under an agreement to repurchase them.

Most of the securities transactions in Table 22-1 refer to government securities. Treasury bills account for the largest share. But transactions occur also in the securities of federal government agencies, most of these being repurchase agreements. Bankers' acceptances, or bills of exchange accepted by commercial banks, were described in Chapter 13, and the Federal Reserve has at times conducted a small amount of market operations in these also. Early in 1984 the Fed announced that it was discontinuing market operations in bankers' acceptances.

It is noteworthy that the total annual turnover of these open market operations is quite large compared with the actual holding of securities at any one time. The magnitude of the transactions recorded in Table 22-1 can be compared with the fact that at the end of 1982 the combined Federal Reserve Banks' balance sheet showed holdings of U.S. government and federal agency securities of some $148,836 million. The data in Table 13-1 in Chapter 13 showed a comparable total at March 31, 1983, of $145,566 million. Clearly, operations of the magnitude described in Table 22-1, as compared with balance sheet positions, are purely defensive in character. They afford a highly informative view of the extent of the need, during the course of a given year, for the Federal Reserve to use defensive operations to iron out what would otherwise be undesired changes in the banks' reserve positions.

In the early years following the Treasury–Federal Reserve Accord of 1951 the Federal Reserve avoided monetary policy changes during the period immediately before and after major new Treasury financing. The objective was to allow the Treasury to price its new security issues at a fair market price such that they could be absorbed in the private market and distributed to investors. The Federal Reserve was then said to be keeping the market on an even keel. But this implied that for that period of time the Federal Reserve had virtually surrendered its freedom and ability to conduct monetary policy operations. In the 1970s, however, this policy was abandoned, and in order to enable new Treasury issues to be made without inhibiting in this way the Fed's monetary policy operations, the Treasury increased the frequency of its new offerings and reduced them each to manageable size.

A number of other points can be noted more briefly in connection with open market operations. First, in comparison with the other two general instruments of credit control—the discount rate mechanism and reserve requirement regulations—open market operations are capable of the finest degree of control. Purchases and sales of securities may be made for any amount the Federal Reserve judges to be necessary in the light of existing monetary conditions. The impact on the banks' reserve situation will not be as blunt as, for example, a change in the reserve requirements. Moreover, in view of the large volume of defensive open market operations, a change in the volume for dynamic policy purposes can easily and quickly be accomplished by varying the extent to which the Federal Reserve is in the market on any particular day or week. For short-run variations in monetary policy control, therefore, open market operations are the most powerful and flexible instrument available to the monetary authorities.

Second, by making use of open market operations to affect the banks' reserve positions, the Federal Reserve is maintaining the initiative as to how the monetary situation is affected. In the case of changes in the discount rate, the initiative that leads to a change in the banks' reserve positions lies not with the Federal Reserve but with the banks themselves.

Third, there are, however, a number of problems associated with the use of open market operations as a monetary policy instrument. The complexity of managing defensive as well as dynamic changes in the level of operations opens the way to miscalculations and unintended effects on the financial markets. Overadjustments to an inflow of currency to the banks may occur, and erroneous signals may be given to the markets and the public. These possibilities may make it difficult for the market to interpret correctly the significance of the Federal Reserve's operations. We have already referred to the induced expectations effects that may follow from the Federal Reserve's security transactions. An increase in the money supply may be interpreted as a sign that recession is ahead, with adverse rather than beneficial effects.

Finally, difficulties of interpretation arise from the fact that the Federal Reserve will from time to time use its open market operations instrument in conjunction with either discount rate changes or changes in reserve requirements or both. A change in reserve requirements is a very blunt instrument. If, for example, the banks are subject to a 5 percent reserve requirement, a change in the reserve requirement ratio of only one-fourth of a percentage point will mean an actual reduction of required reserves by 5 percent. We saw in Chapter 13 that at March 31, 1983, the depository institutions held deposits at the Federal Reserve Bank of some $23,419 million. Taking account of their cash holdings, their total reserves were approximately $45 billion. A 5 percent reduction in required reserves could, under these circumstances, increase excess reserves by some $2 billion. That could then form the basis for a multiple expansion of bank loans and deposits.

In this sense the reserve requirement is extremely powerful, but it is not capable of achieving very fine degrees of adjustment to the monetary situation. If, therefore, the Federal Reserve were to lower reserve requirements as part of an anti-recession policy, it might at the same time engage in open market sales in order to mop up some of what might otherwise be the excessive effects of the change in reserve requirements. We would then have a traditionally expansive reserve requirement change working simultaneously with traditionally contractionary open market operations.

Other combinations of monetary policy operations may be envisaged. As part of a general anti-inflationary monetary policy the Federal Reserve Board may raise its discount rate. The objective would be to discourage borrowing by the member banks, to increase the overall cost of money, and to dampen the expenditure streams in the economy. If it was thought that the more direct initiative provided to the Federal Reserve by the open market instrument should also be used, open market sales might be made. The two credit control instruments would then be working in concert. At the same time, day-to-day developments in the financial markets may make it necessary for the Federal Reserve to engage in open market purchases for defensive reasons. In that case the open market operations would appear to be working against the discount rate change, and the difficulties of interpretation would be enhanced.

THE FEDERAL RESERVE DISCOUNT RATE

The Federal Reserve *discount rate* was defined in Chapter 12 as the rate of interest at which the Federal Reserve will sell or lend reserves to the commercial banks and other depository institutions. Again in discussing this instrument we are interested primarily in its impact on the banks' reserve positions. The balance sheet reflections of the actual effect on bank reserves have been discussed in Chapter 12.

The depository institutions in general enjoy, as it is said, the *privilege* of borrowing at the Federal Reserve discount window. They do not possess the *right* to borrow. While that privilege is now granted to all depository institutions under the Depository Institutions Deregulation and Monetary Control Act of 1980, as a matter of operating policy the Federal Reserve has announced that it will accommodate requests for funds from the nonbank institutions only after they have exhausted their traditional sources of funds. For the savings and loan associations, for example, that would refer to the borrowing facilities made available to them by the Federal Home Loan Bank Board.

The Federal Reserve is normally prepared to lend to the banks for only short periods, generally for less than two weeks. The intention of the borrowing privilege is to enable banks to meet their reserve requirements during periods of fluctuating loan demands and temporary credit strains. The short-term nature of the loan accommodation will generally be relaxed, according to Federal Reserve procedures, only "under unusual and exceptional circumstances."

In the use of open market operations, the initiative as to when and to what extent the banks' reserves will be affected lies with the Federal Reserve. In the case of discount rate changes, however, the initiative is with the member banks, in the sense that the level of reserves will not be affected following a change in the discount rate until the banks actually respond in their operating decisions to the new level of the rate. The intention of a reduction in the discount rate would be to make it easier for the banks to acquire temporary accommodation and to increase their lending activities. This may occur at times when it was thought by the Federal Reserve that somewhat higher levels of expenditure would be beneficial to the economy. For that reason the discount rate will not generally be changed in what we have called a defensive sense, as in the case of open market operations. A change in the rate will be part of a dynamic policy move by the Federal Reserve. It will in general be a signal that somewhat easier monetary conditions are in order and lie ahead. The announcement effect of the change could, however, have conflicting repercussions. For it might well be thought that a reduction of the rate after a period of relative prosperity and high activity in the economy was a signal that recession and more difficult times lay ahead. In that case business firms might be induced to slacken, rather than increase, their investment expenditures.

In the course of their normal liability management, moreover, the banks will make use of the borrowing privilege at the Federal Reserve only when it is the cheapest method of raising the funds they need. Traditionally, there has been a reluctance on the part of the banks to borrow from the Federal Reserve, aside from the need to make very temporary adjustments to their sources of funds. The borrowing has mainly been by the larger banks. The smaller country banks have traditionally maintained excess reserves which they have held on deposit with their correspondent banks. In situations of need they have been able to call on these funds.

Before a bank will borrow from the Federal Reserve, however, it will compare the cost of funds from other liability sources. These include the federal funds market, certificate of deposit funds, Eurodollar loans, commercial paper floated by bank holding companies, and repurchase agreements. What we should be interested in for purposes of considering member bank borrowing from the Federal Reserve, then, is not simply the discount rate itself, but the differential between the discount rate and the cost of other sources of funds.

The significance of this differential alerts us to one of the reasons why the discount rate might not work as smoothly in a contracyclical fashion as we might at first suppose. This follows from the fact that the largest amount of bank borrowing from the Federal Reserve may well occur in periods of high, rather than low, interest rates. In its explanatory publication, *The Federal Reserve System: Purposes and Functions* (1974), the Board of Governors has stated that "the Federal Reserve adjusts the discount rate from time to time to relate it more closely to other money market rates." This is saying that in general it is the Federal Reserve policy to follow the market with its discount rate rather than try to lead the market. Presumably, any attempt to lead the market and induce changes in market rates of interest can be better accomplished by the open market instrument.

This implies that in times of high interest rates the discount rate may be below the open market short-term rates. If that is so, it will be profitable for the banks to expand their assets in order to obtain the relatively high income yields available on them, and to cover their liquidity needs to a larger extent than usual by borrowing from the Federal Reserve. It has been popular with some monetary economists to look, at certain phases of the business cycle, not merely at the banks' excess reserve positions but at what has been called their net free reserve position. *Net free reserves* are defined as excess reserves minus borrowed reserves. In the kind of instance we have just referred to, borrowed reserves can be expected to be positively related to the differential between the market rate of interest and the discount rate. Using the symbol B for borrowed reserves, and the notations r and r_d to refer to the market rate of interest and the discount rate, respectively, it follows that we have the relation $B = B(r - r_d)$. When the rate of interest rises and the discount rate lags behind it, the value of B rises. Borrowing increases and net free reserves decline. But this means that the overall reserves available are being used more intensively, and bank expansion of loans and deposits can occur on the basis of them. The overall implication of these possible developments is that the discount rate effects on the economy may not be contracyclical as we might initially suppose, but procyclical.

In addition to its traditional short-term accommodation of the banks, the Federal Reserve does lend to banks and other financial institutions that face emergency situations or find themselves in particular financial distress. In 1970, for example, when the Penn Central Railroad declared bankruptcy, it defaulted on a large amount of commercial paper it had outstanding. This had understandably adverse effects on the commercial paper market in general, and some firms that had previously raised funds by this means found it difficult to reissue their commercial paper when it matured. Under these circumstances the Federal Reserve permitted the banks that were involved in the resulting difficulties to borrow at the discount window to a larger extent than would otherwise have been the case. A similar situation occurred in 1974 when the Franklin National Bank was in acute financial difficulties. It was allowed to borrow funds for a longer period than usual while a plan for selling the bank was being worked out.

Early in 1980, in a situation in which it was desired to restrict credit, the Federal Reserve took an unusual step. It not only raised its discount rate to 13 percent but also added a surcharge of a further 3 percent for certain kinds of borrowers. The surcharge applied only to the 270 large banks with deposits of $500 million or more, and it came into effect only when one of those banks borrowed for more than one week consecutively or for more than four weeks in a calendar quarter. The surcharge, along with other measures of direct credit control, was withdrawn in the middle of 1980. By that time it had become clear that recessionary conditions had developed in the economy, and such restrictive monetary policies were no longer in order.

The tradition under which the Federal Reserve generally makes funds available to the banks at the discount rate for temporary purposes only can be seen in the light of its bank examination responsibilities. If a bank is tending to make excessive requests for funds the Federal Reserve will study the bank's situation carefully, and if the bank appears to be borrowing for improper reasons the Federal Reserve will recommend that it sell securities, reduce its loans, or otherwise adjust its asset and liability portfolios. Recalling that the banks' access to the discount window is a privilege and not a right, the Federal Reserve may, if it thinks such an action appropriate, suspend a bank's borrowing privilege entirely.

RESERVE REQUIREMENT REGULATIONS

Changes in reserve requirements as an instrument of monetary policy differ in a number of respects from the open market operations and the discount rate mechanism. The impact effects of the latter are seen in the magnitude of the banks' reserves. While the initiative is with the Federal Reserve in the case of open market operations, and with the member banks in the case of the discount rate, the monetary situation, and, it is hoped, the expenditure streams in the economy, will be affected to the extent that the total reserves available to the banks are affected. When reserve requirements are changed, however, there is no such impact effect. The total reserves remain the same. But there is, of course, a change in the proportion of those reserves that can now be counted as excess reserves. Raising the reserve requirement ratios will reduce the excess reserves. Such a move might therefore be thought to be useful anti-inflationary monetary policy. Similarly, a reduction of the reserve requirements will increase the lending ability of the banks and might be thought to be effective anti-recession policy. In actual fact, however, matters are not that straightforward.

The direction of impact is as we have just described it. But a variation in the requirement ratios, of only one-fourth of one percentage point for example, can release a large amount of excess reserves in the case of a reduction, or impound a large amount of reserves in the case of an increase. For that reason, the reserve requirement instrument has not been used frequently by the Federal Reserve. When the Federal Reserve System was established in 1913 reserve requirements were quite rigid. The Federal Reserve Act preserved the classification of banks that had been employed under the preceding National Banking System. Banks located in New York and Chicago were classified as *central reserve city banks*, those in some sixty other large cities were known as *reserve city banks*, and the remainder were referred to as *country banks*. The minimum reserve requirements at that time were set at 13 percent for central reserve city banks, 10 percent for reserve city banks, and 7 percent for country banks.

By the Banking Act of 1935 the Board of Governors of the Federal Reserve System was empowered to vary the reserve requirements of all or any class of member banks. In fact, one of the historically most significant instances of the use of this flexibility occurred in the latter years of the 1930s. At that time, in the context of very disturbed conditions associated with the deep international Depression, a very large inflow of gold came into the United States. It was thought at the time (mistakenly, it now appears with the benefit of hindsight) that the consequent increase in the banks' reserves contained dangerous inflationary potential. The Federal Reserve, therefore, desired to neutralize the effects of the gold inflow. To do so by using open market sales of securities to mop up excess reserves would have been an impossibly large task. The more direct and effective way was to raise the reserve requirements.

When the Banking Act of 1935 gave the Federal Reserve authority to vary the reserve requirements in this way, it set maximum limits above which the ratios could not be raised. These were set at twice the levels that had previously existed. At the same time, the reserve requirement against time deposits, which had previously been set at 3 percent, could now be varied also up to 6 percent.

In the 1960s the system of reserve requirements was changed further. Initially, the banks were allowed to count as required reserves only those funds held on deposit with a Federal Reserve Bank. In November 1960 the regulations were changed to permit banks to include their vault cash in legal reserves, and therefore as potentially a part of required reserves. Two years later the central reserve city and the reserve city classifications of banks were merged into a single class, to which the reserve requirements of the reserve city classification were to apply. It was specified also that the magnitude of those requirements should be changed to permit variations between 10 and 22 percent. In 1966 a further change permitted the reserve requirement against time deposits to vary between 3 and 10 percent.

This tinkering with the regulations did not, however, meet what the Board of Governors thought to be desirable in the changing banking structure of the 1960s. In 1972 a further change occurred. Now the classification of banks by geographical location was abolished. Instead, reserve requirements were set depending on the bank's size. The complexity to which this scheme of arrangements gave rise is indicated in Table 22-2. The requirements that became effective on December 30, 1976, are indicated in the table, as this represents the position that existed up to the introduction of the Depository Institutions Deregulation and Monetary Control Act of 1980.

A fuller examination of the source mentioned in Table 22-2 reveals that between 1972, when the classification of banks by size was adopted, and 1980, changes in the reserve requirement ratios, which were made only infrequently, were generally about one-half of a percentage point. The final change adopted in 1976 varied some classes by only one-quarter of a percentage point.

In general, the Federal Reserve has been reluctant to use the reserve requirement instrument as a means of influencing the monetary situation in recent times. It is, as has been said, a blunt instrument. Its effects are felt immediately and universally throughout the banking system. As a result of an increase in the requirements, all banks in the system would be required to curtail their loans, or to refrain from renewing them as they matured, or to sell securities or otherwise reduce their asset portfolios. This would tend to depress security prices in the same way as does the use of other monetary policy instruments, and to lever upward the general level of the rate of interest. An increase in the reserve requirements that placed banks in reserve deficiency positions might give rise to increased activity in the federal funds market, in repurchase agreements, and in other attempts to bolster reserve positions by managing liabilities. It would be likely to raise the average cost of funds to the

Table   22-2

Member bank reserve requirements, December 30, 1976, as percent of
deposits (Deposit intervals are in millions of dollars)

Reserve requirements against net demand deposits	%
0–2 million dollars	7
2–10	9.5
10–100	11.75
100–400	12.75
Over 400	16.25
Reserve requirements against time deposits	%
0–5, classified by term to maturity	
30–179 days	3
180 days to 4 years	2.5
4 years or more	1
Over 5, classified by term to maturity	
30–179 days	6
180 days to 4 years	2.5
4 years or more	1
Reserve requirements against savings deposits	3

Source: *Federal Reserve Annual Report*, 1980, p. 268.

Note: The average of reserves on savings and other time deposits had to be at least 3 percent, the legal minimum at the time.

banks as they thereby tapped more expensive sources. This, in turn, could lead them to restructure their portfolios away from lower-yielding to higher-yielding investments. It might thereby increase the average level of risk in the banks' portfolios.

The system of reserve requirements was drastically simplified by the provisions of the 1980 legislation. Henceforth the deposits of all depository institutions were to be subject to the reserve requirements specified by the Federal Reserve. Required reserves can be held in the form of deposits at a Federal Reserve Bank or in vault cash. A nonmember bank may hold reserves on deposit with a member bank, provided the latter passes them on, dollar for dollar, to a Federal Reserve Bank.

The reserve requirements that became effective in November 1980 are described in Table 22-3. The transaction accounts referred to in the table include "all deposits on which the account holder is permitted to make withdrawals by negotiable or transferable instruments, payment orders of withdrawal, telephone and preauthorized transfers (in excess of three per month), for the purpose of making payments to third persons or others." For nonmember banks and thrift institutions a phase-in period was provided for, ending on September 3, 1987. For member banks there was a phase-in period of about three years, depending on whether their

Table   22-3

Depository institution reserve requirements, beginning November 13, 1980

Type of deposit, and deposit interval	Reserve requirement after implementation of the Monetary Control Act
	%
Net transaction accounts	
$0–25 million*	3
Over 25 million	12
Non-personal time deposits	
By original maturity	
Less than 4 years†	3
4 years or more	0
Eurocurrency liabilities	
All types	3

Source: *Federal Reserve Annual Report*, 1980, p. 268.
* This breakpoint of $25 million is increased each year by 80 percent of the percentage increase during the preceding year in the total transaction accounts of the depository institutions.
† This 4-year breakpoint is subject to annual reductions until 1986, when a common reserve requirement will be imposed against all reservable time deposits.

new reserve requirements were larger or smaller than the old requirements. All new institutions were to have a two-year phase-in beginning with the date on which they open for business. Fuller details, including some amendments introduced by the Garn–St. Germain Depository Institutions Act of 1982, were discussed in Chapter 7.

RESERVE REQUIREMENTS AGAINST MANAGED (OR NONDEPOSIT) LIABILITIES

An element of flexibility was introduced into the administration of the reserve requirement regulations by requiring the banks, at certain times in the past, to hold reserves against managed liabilities. Several changes occurred in this connection subsequent to the banks' more active use of nondeposit sources of funds after the mid-1960s. In October 1979, for example, the Federal Reserve introduced a marginal reserve requirement of 8 percent of all managed liabilities above a base amount. These liabilities included large time deposits (in excess of $100,000), federal funds borrowed from nonmember banks, Eurodollars, and repurchase agreements. The Federal Reserve stated at the time that "this action is directed toward sources of funds that have been actively used by banks in recent months to finance the expansion of bank credit." In March 1980 this marginal reserve requirement was increased to 10 percent, in an effort to restrict the growth in bank credit further. Flexibility can be expected in this connection if the Federal Reserve believes that it is warranted in the future.

THE GENERAL INSTRUMENTS OF CREDIT CONTROL IN PROSPERITY AND RECESSION

The analysis to this point can be summarized, in somewhat oversimplified terms, by saying that antirecession monetary policy would be expected to include (1) open market purchases of securities, (2) lowering the Federal Reserve discount rate, and (3) lowering the reserve requirements. The potential effects of these actions on the availability of reserves, on the basis of which the depository institutions can advance credit, have been analyzed. In the opposite direction, anti-inflationary monetary policy would envisage (1) open market sales, (2) a higher discount rate, and (3) higher reserve requirements. In actual fact, however, there will generally be an interaction between the use of the different instruments. At times they will be used in a complementary manner. At other times it may be necessary to use one of them, such as the sale of securities, to offset what might be an excessive effect of another, say a reduction in the reserve requirements. We have illustrated a number of such possible interrelations earlier in this chapter.

Moreover, the actual operation of policy may be complicated by a number of technical considerations. Following the accord between the Treasury and the Federal Reserve in 1951, as a result of which the Federal Reserve withdrew its peg from the government securities market and ceased to maintain a low interest rate in concession to the Treasury's financing requirements, the Federal Reserve operated for quite some time only in the short-term sector of the securities market. It bought and sold only short-term Treasury bills. It was said thereby to be operating a "bills only" policy. Its purchases and sales in this sector of the market were designed, in the ways we have examined, to affect the reserve positions of the banks and to influence the monetary situation. In the late 1950s and early 1960s, however, a situation developed in which the Federal Reserve thought it necessary to depart from this bills only policy.

At that time a deficit had emerged in the United States balance of international payments. As a result, foreigners began to convert their dollar balances into gold, rather than continue to build up deposit balances in the United States. At that time also the concentration by the Federal Reserve on purchases of securities in the bills market led to relatively low short term rates of interest. This, unfortunately, worsened the balance-of-payments difficulties, as short-term money market interest rates in the United States were now lower than comparable rates in some overseas markets and short-term capital flowed out of the United States to take advantage of the higher interest yields available elsewhere. Foreign claims against dollars and gold rose accordingly.

To offset this it would have been necessary for the monetary authorities to tighten credit in such a way as to raise domestic interest rates. But at the same time it was desired to maintain as low a long-term interest rate as possible in order not to restrict the level of investment expenditure in the economy. What was needed, it seemed, was (1) a higher short-term interest rate to dampen the short-term money capital outflow and (2) a lower long-term rate in the interest of domestic economic activity.

To accomplish this twofold objective the Federal Reserve abandoned its bills only policy and engaged in what became known as operation twist. This policy was designed to twist the yield curve, such as we discussed in Chapter 6. The operation involved the sale of Treasury bills to raise the short-term interest rate, and the purchase of long-term securities to lower the long-term rate. This was the objective of the operation. In actual fact, the structure of interest rates was not markedly altered. For while the Federal Reserve was aggressively buying medium-term and long-term securities, the Treasury was selling them. Their actions largely offset each other. There was, moreover, a rise in the short-term rates at that time, but this was due to a recovery in the economy that led to increased demand for bank credit. At the present time the Federal Reserve does operate in all sections of the market, as we have illustrated in the discussion of Table 22-1.

The order in which the instruments of monetary policy are used, and the magnitude of the changes effected in them, will depend on the apparent extent and seriousness of the change in economic conditions. If, for example, tendencies to recession exist in only a modest degree, it may be sufficient to increase the magnitude of open market purchases. This would amount to a dynamic change in policy superimposed on the day-to-day defensive open market operations. If, on the other hand, recessionary conditions had been allowed to develop more seriously, it might be necessary to supplement the open market operations with a downward change in the discount rate. Reserve requirement changes might also become advisable under conditions that threatened a more-prolonged depression. But a flexible use of the open market operations and the discount rate instruments will, it is hoped, maintain monetary conditions in a sufficiently stable posture and make the heavy-handed use of the reserve requirement regulations generally unnecessary. Such policy operations, however, may all be complicated by a further consideration. This has to do with the simultaneous occurrence of inflationary price changes on the one hand, and recession, as reflected in rising unemploy-

ment, on the other. Monetary policy in the presence of such a stagfla-
tionary situation raises more difficult questions.

We shall confront these questions again in the next chapter when
we consider the place of money in economic policy in general. It will
suffice to say at this point, first, that this is precisely the situation that
existed during the late 1970s and early 1980s. At that time the Federal
Reserve Board followed a policy of tight money and high interest rates.
Second, we shall explain in the next chapter that a tight money policy
cannot generally be expected to have any *impact* effect on the price inflationary problem. The *impact* effects of tight money are always on the
level of economic activity and employment. As happened during the early
1980s, monetary policy succeeded only in worsening the recession as
astronomically high interest rates dampened investment expenditures,
consumer durable purchases, and the housing and construction industry.
As a result, the seriously dampened economic conditions did in turn cause
inflationary pressures in the economy to moderate. The high interest rates
in this situation were due also to the unprecedented government budget
deficits, the financing of which increased the demand for funds in the
money capital markets.

In general, however, there is a definite order in which the monetary
policy instruments will be used. Because of the fine degrees of effect that
can potentially be achieved by using it, the open market operations instrument can be expected to come into play first in general contracyclical
policy. Second, this will generally be followed by discount rate changes,
with the reserve requirement instrument being used as the third leg of
policy.

It is possible, in the present structure of Federal Reserve operations,
to achieve a high degree of coordination in the use of the policy instruments. Technically, the discount rate is set by each of the Federal Reserve
Banks individually. But the rates set are subject to approval by the Board
of Governors. The twelve separate Federal Reserve Banks also operate
their discount windows in such a way as to give them discretion over the
accommodation they provide to the banks. But again, they operate their
lending policy in accordance with guidelines laid down by the Board of
Governors. In the case of reserve requirement changes, full discretion
lies with the Board of Governors. When it comes to the important question
of open market operations, this, we have seen, is under the control of the
Federal Open Market Committee. The seven members of the Board of
Governors make up the majority of the twelve-member FOMC, with representatives of the other Federal Reserve Banks being present for monetary policy discussions, even though they vote only when they are full
members of the committee. In these several ways, a high degree of co-
ordinating power and authority rests with the Board of Governors. The

chairman of the Board, who is also chairman of the FOMC, enjoys considerable influence in the conduct of policy.

SELECTIVE CREDIT CONTROLS

The general instruments of credit control are designed to influence the total amount of credit extended by the depository institutions. This they do either by affecting the monetary base or by varying the amount of excess reserves included in that base. From time to time the Federal Reserve has also employed a number of so-called selective measures of credit control. These have been designed not to influence the total amount of credit available but to affect the direction of its use. They have included measures to control real estate credit, consumer credit, and margin requirements in connection with loans to finance the purchase of capital market securities.

Real estate credit controls, for example, can be used to regulate the rate of interest that may be charged for mortgage loans, the minimum down payment that must be made for housing purchases, and the maximum time allowed for the repayment of the loan. Controls of this type were introduced during the Korean War in the early 1950s. A fairly large amount of building activity was taking place at that time as a result of the backlog that had accumulated during World War II, and the controls were not very effective. They were abandoned in 1953.

Consumer credit controls have had a more-varied history. They were introduced during World War II, in 1948 and 1949 when higher consumer expenditures were putting inflationary pressures on the economy, and during the Korean War. Again, the terms of loans for the financing of consumer durables, such as refrigerators, washing machines, and automobiles, can be varied to discourage or encourage spending, depending on the phase of the business cycle in which they are introduced. Generally, they have been used as anti-inflationary measures in periods of high economic activity.

It would seem, based on the experience of the early 1980s, that consumers are sensitive to the interest rates on loans for consumer goods purchases, as instanced in particular by the sagging fortunes of the automobile industry. But this was also due, it has to be acknowledged, to the approximately 10 percent unemployment that existed along with the recessionary conditions in general. Apart from this recent period of inordinately high interest rates, there was reason to believe that consumers were more influenced by the terms of loans such as down payments and maturity terms than they were by the interest rate. In early 1980, however, whatever theories existed in these respects were put to a further test. The Federal Reserve Board, acting under the powers given to it by the Credit Control Act of 1969, introduced a special credit constraint program that applied to all banks and finance companies. The objective was to curtail consumer spending. The rate of inflation was high, and it was thought that consumer restraint was needed. The Federal Reserve Board set deposit requirements for increases in the volume of loans outstanding at commercial banks, retailers, and finance companies.

These measures were part of a more comprehensive attempt to curtail credit in the inflationary situation that existed. The banks were asked voluntarily to restrict the growth of overall bank credit to a range of 6 to 9 percent per annum. The program imposed a reserve requirement of 15 percent on marginal increases of certain kinds of consumer lending. This, it should be noted, was a novel application of the reserve requirement principle. For hitherto depository institutions were required to hold reserves only against certain designated liabilities. Now, in the consumer credit control program, they were for the first time required to hold reserves against certain forms of assets also.

It was at this time also that the banks were required to hold 10 percent reserves against certain kinds of managed liabilities. Further, a 15 percent marginal reserve requirement was imposed on increases in the assets of money market mutual funds, above the level at which they stood on a specified date (March 14, 1980). At the same time a three percentage point surcharge was added to the existing Federal Reserve discount rate, which was then 13 percent, for borrowings by some of the large banks. By the middle of 1980, however, it had become clear that recessionary tendencies had developed, and the Federal Reserve removed the package of controls. A number of the provisions of this credit control program had been authorized under the terms of the Credit Control Act of 1969. Failing action by Congress to extend it, the provisions of this act were to expire in June 1982.

The provisions of the Truth-in-Lending Act of 1968, as amended and as subject to further refinements in a section of the Depository Institutions Deregulation and Monetary Control Act of 1980, required the Federal Reserve Board to issue regulations to promote the informed use of credit. The Federal Reserve has done this by the issue and amendment from time to time of Regulation Z. Its annual reports to the Congress, as required by the act, are referred to in the successive annual reports of the Federal Reserve Board.

MARGIN REQUIREMENTS

Margin requirements as a form of credit control came into existence in 1934, when Congress gave the Federal Reserve Board of Governors power to regulate the volume of credit advanced to finance the purchasing or holding of capital market securities. The regulations applied to security brokers and dealers (under Federal Reserve Regulation T), to banks (under Regulation U), to other persons (under Regulation G), and to borrowers (under Regulation X). The margin requirements were introduced as a reaction to the excessive speculation in securities that preceded the stock market crash of 1929 and the debacle of the 1930s.

The margin requirements effectively specified the maximum proportion of the value of securities that could be advanced as a loan for which they were the collateral. Government securities and certain others were exempted from the regulations. For example, if the margin requirement were set at 60 percent, this would mean that no loan against the collateral of securities could amount to more than 40 percent of their market value. The so-called margin referred to the maximum allowable difference between the market value of the security and the amount of the loan. It represented, in effect, the down payment on the purchase of stock. In January 1946 the margin requirement was actually raised to 100 percent. It has fluctuated considerably since then, depending on stock market conditions and the need for credit restraint in the economy. Since 1974 it has stood at its present level of 50 percent.

It is unclear to what extent the margin requirement regulations have been effective. They have conceivably moderated the market activity of those individuals who have had no other means of obtaining credit. But many borrowers could purchase securities out of funds raised for ostensibly other purposes. Credit can be raised on the collateral, for example, of houses, businesses, and securities exempt from the regulations. Moreover, to the extent that credit for the purpose of stock market activity is restrained by this means, a larger amount of credit may be available for other economic purposes. The regulation, then, like selective credit controls in general, does not so much moderate the total amount of credit made available by the financial sector as it does redistribute the amount among competing uses.

While there has been no change in the general margin requirements on security loans since 1974, a 30 percent margin requirement on the writing of stock options was introduced in 1977. This form of investment market activity, or more probably a form of speculation, had recently developed to a greater extent than previously. The Federal Reserve Board's action in extending Regulation T to cover option purchases is an indication of its continuing concern for this particular aspect of its legally mandated responsibilities. The margin requirement against the writing of stock options (which are essentially contracts giving the holder an option to purchase a specified security at a specified price by a specified date) is understood to be a percentage of the market value of the stock underlying the option.

The margin requirements work in an interesting way to curb speculative market activity. Imagine, for example, that a margin requirement of 60 percent made it possible for an individual to obtain a loan for 40 percent of the market value of a security when its market price was $100. If, then, the market value were to decline to $80, the loan against it would then amount to 50 percent of its market value. In that event the borrower (the holder of the security) would be required to make a payment to the lender sufficient to reduce the amount of the loan outstanding to no more than 40 percent of the new market value of $80. The maximum loan that could then be outstanding and still meet the margin requirement regulations would be 40 percent of $80, or $32. The borrower would therefore be required to reduce his loan from the original $40 to $32. He must repay $8. In the face of a very extensive stock market decline this might well imply hardship, and it could lead to the selling of securities in an attempt to cover the margined positions if the margin requirements had not been high enough in the first place. As a result, security prices could sag still further. It was to prevent this kind of cumulative downward spiral in the securities market, resulting from previously excessive speculation on very low margined positions, that the margin requirements were introduced.

Economists have not in general taken a very kind view of selective measures of credit control. These measures have been thought to interfere unduly with the natural competitive processes of credit allocation. They are difficult to enforce, as individuals may very well borrow for one purpose and use the borrowed funds for quite a different purpose. Even if loans are used for the purpose for which they are acquired, they may thereby release other funds for use in the very kind of stock market speculation that the margin requirements were designed to inhibit.

RECENT MONETARY POLICY DEVELOPMENTS

Our survey of the instruments of monetary policy leads to a consideration of the actual performance of monetary policy in recent times. A few minimal comments will be made on this question in anticipation of the discussion in the next chapter of the place of money in economic policy.

First, the Federal Reserve Board has allowed open market operations to dominate monetary policy in recent years. This is consistent with the order and emphasis of exposition we have adopted in this chapter. The literature of monetary economics has concentrated not so much on the possible use and effectiveness of the other instruments of monetary policy as on issues such as those we raised at the beginning of this chapter. These include questions, for example, of the appropriate targets and indicators of monetary policy. We have seen that a significant cleavage of opinion exists between the monetarist and the Keynesian approaches to the relevant arguments.

We can note also that for many years the Federal Reserve appeared to operate in such a way as to maintain orderly money market conditions. Following its escape, by the terms of the accord of 1951, from the policy of pegging interest rates, and subsequent to its retreat from the bills only policy in the early 1960s, the Federal Reserve has generally adopted a monetary policy that would ease the interest rates in times of recession and lever them upward in periods of prosperity. It generally endeavored to engineer a contracyclical interest rate policy. The policy of controlling interest rates was generally implemented by using the open market operations instrument. Net free reserves in the banking system were frequently taken as the appropriate indicator of policy. If net free reserves (excess reserves minus borrowed reserves) were high, this was a sign that generally easy money market conditions existed. The Federal Reserve would in that case have no need to ease the situation further. It could, if anything, tighten up somewhat.

But there were problems with this procedure. The Federal Reserve may find it difficult or impossible to restrain the monetary situation adequately in an inflationary situation by concentrating only on the net free reserves target. Suppose that it engaged in open market security sales or reduced its security purchases sufficiently, as it thought, to force the banks to a targeted level of free reserves. It might imagine that by doing so it would cause the interest rate to rise to a level that would sufficiently restrain expenditures and control the inflation. But if, in this situation, the banks were to respond to the higher interest rates by being prepared to reduce their free reserves even further than the Federal Reserve imagined they would wish to, then the banks would continue to borrow from the Federal Reserve and increase their lending. Or the banks might even be prepared to hold negative free reserves (that is, an overall net borrowed reserve position) to a larger extent than the Federal Reserve had bargained for. In cases such as these, if the Federal Reserve adhered to its targeted net free reserves figure, it would continue to pump funds into the banking system via the discount window. This would follow from the divergence of view between the banks and the Federal Reserve as to what the target size of net free reserves should be.

So long as the Federal Reserve continued to give primary emphasis in its policy thinking to preserving a targeted set of money market conditions, it paid attention to such measures as the federal funds rate of interest. It proceeded to control this by open market operations. But it became clear that it was difficult to maintain both a control over the federal funds rate and a control of the money supply. In the outcome, a greater degree of stability or orderliness was maintained in the interest rate than in the money supply prior to the change in thinking and policy in October 1979.

In the light of its new policy announcements in 1979,[6] the Federal Reserve Board effectively adopted at that date a decidedly monetarist stance. It was stated that henceforth the principal objective would be a firmer control over the money supply aggregates. The Federal Reserve set out to influence the size of the monetary base, in the hope that by doing so it would be able to control the actual money supply. The targets in this connection are spelled out in such FOMC directives as the one we reproduced in Chapter 12. The data since 1979, however, continue to indicate sizable fluctuations in the money supply. Criticisms of the Federal Reserve's performance continue to come from many economists.

The Fed, however, was not able to maintain its promonetarist stance indefinitely. The high interest rate structure it engineered after October 1979 generated the deep recession that led in 1981 and 1982 to heavy unemployment, bankruptcies, and declines in industrial activity. Unfortunately, the complex of economic policies at that time, given the fiscal policies of the recently elected Reagan administration, with heavy increases in defense expenditures accompanied by what seemed to be unsustainable income tax reductions, meant that virtually all of the burden of controlling the existing price inflation was imposed on monetary policy. A severely tight monetary situation was the nation's only anti-inflation mechanism.

In these conditions it became apparent by the middle of 1982 that with the financial system in danger of serious disarray, with savings and loan associations failing and even some of the larger banks encountering difficulty, a lower interest rate structure was needed in the interests of general economic recovery. At that time, therefore, the Fed announced that it would be prepared for the foreseeable future to relax its target for the rate of increase in the money supply. In any event, the emergence of new kinds of interest-bearing checkable deposit accounts, together with other developments in the competitive ability of financial institutions, was making it increasingly difficult to interpret the meaning of the money supply data. Added to this was the particular difficulty of interpreting the need for, and the meaning of, tighter or looser control of the money supply because of changes that were occurring in the velocity of circulation of money. If conditions should develop that make it impossible to rely on stability in the velocity of circulation of money, that would amount to a deathblow to monetarist theory and policy effectiveness, with its reliance on the control of the money stock.

These developments meant that from the middle of 1982 the Federal Reserve appeared to have departed significantly from its earlier, some-

---

[6] See the discussion in Chapter 7 in the context of commercial bank regulation.

what doctrinaire, monetarist stance. Interest rates declined at that time and a recovery in the economy began. But the policy announcements of the Federal Reserve continued to indicate that a close control of the monetary situation would continue to be followed in the interests of guarding against a reemergence of inflation. A period of what has been called pragmatic monetarism began. The Fed faced the acutely difficult task of loosening the monetary situation sufficiently to promote the seriously needed economic recovery, but at the same time appearing determined to maintain a sufficiently tight monetary situation to prevent the recovery from setting off a new inflationary spiral.

We shall argue in the following chapter that a radically new perspective on the objectives of monetary policy, and on its potential complementarity with a wider range of other economic policies, is necessary.

SUMMARY

The initial sections of this chapter laid the foundations for the discussion of the scope, functioning, and importance of monetary policy. A brief review was given of the concept of money flows that has coordinated our argument throughout the theoretical and institutional parts of our work. The mutual relevance and interdependence of monetary analysis, institutions, and policy were recognized. Though the developments in the banking system that arise from policy actions were explained in terms of stock or balance sheet concepts, emphasis was consistently placed on the notion of changes in such balance sheet variables and on the implied dynamic changes and flows that they reflect.

The objectives of monetary policy were considered in relation to the larger objectives of economic policy that were examined in Chapter 2, "What Are the Questions?" Monetary targets, indicators, and instruments were also shown to be interdependent. Principal emphasis was placed on the Federal Reserve Board's three general instruments of credit control: (1) open market operations, (2) the discount rate mechanism, and (3) reserve requirement regulations. The methods of operation and the relative efficiencies of each were examined. The discussion proceeded mainly in terms of the policy effects on the commercial banks' reserve situations, the banks being taken for purposes of this exposition as representative of the depository institutions in general. The actual relations between the banks and the nonbank depository institutions have been discussed at length in preceding chapters.

Briefer consideration was given to some measures of selective credit control. The objective of these policy instruments is to influence not so much the total amount of credit available in the financial system as the direction of its allocation and use. Real estate credit, consumer credit, and the margin requirements imposed on loans for the purchase and holding of securities were discussed.

The chapter concluded with a brief discussion of the principal thrusts of monetary policy in recent years, in anticipation of the discussion in the next chapter of the place of money in economic policy.

IMPORTANT CONCEPTS

Money on the wing

Stock versus flow variables

Monetarism

Keynesianism

Monetary rules

Discretionary monetary management

Objectives, targets, indicators, and instruments of monetary policy

Transmission effects

FOMC policy directive

Money market conditions

Margin requirements

Monetary base

Money supply multiplier

The Accord of 1951

Open market operations

Expectation effects

Monetary policy mix

Federal Reserve discount rate

Reserve requirement regulations

Reserves against managed liabilities

Bills only policy

Operation twist

Selective credit controls

Portfolio substitution effects

QUESTIONS FOR DISCUSSION AND REVIEW

1. Discuss the potential complementarity between the Federal Reserve Board's three general instruments of credit control.

2. What recent developments in financial institutional structures and operations make a money aggregate a less significant target of monetary policy?

3. Examine the relative merits, as viable targets of monetary policy, of (1) the money stock, (2) the volume of credit outstanding, (3) the size of domestic nonfinancial debt, and (4) the level of such real economic indicators as the GNP and the real rate of interest.

4. Distinguish between the monetarist and the Keynesian views of the relation between targets and indicators of monetary policy.

5. Making use of relevant balance sheet entries, trace the manner in which Federal Reserve open market operations may affect the money supply.

6. Can a tight monetary policy control inflationary pressure? How? At what cost?

7. Distinguish between the form, objectives, timing, and significance of Federal Reserve dynamic and defensive monetary policies.

8. Do you consider that selective credit controls have a significant part to play in contracyclical monetary policy? Explain fully.

9. "The task of monetary policy is to regulate the amount of credit available, not to influence the direction of its use." Discuss critically.

10. What do you consider would be the effects of requiring depository institutions to maintain required reserves against certain specified assets as well as, or instead of, deposit liabilities?

23

THE PLACE OF MONEY IN ECONOMIC POLICY

STUDY OBJECTIVES:

• To consolidate our understanding of the ways in which the supply and use of money are interrelated with developments in the real markets in the economy
• To trace the relations of monetary policy to (1) the theory of the macroeconomy and (2) the larger range of economic policies
• To gain an understanding of the transmission mechanism in monetary theory and policy
• To note some of the divergences between alternative approaches to monetary theory and policy
• To take account of the possibility that the nature of expectations formation in the macroeconomy, particularly the presence of so-called rational expectations, may render short-run monetary and other stabilization policies ineffective
• To consider the appropriate locus of authority for monetary policy in relation to the overall objectives of economic organization and welfare

This final chapter on monetary policy brings together many of the implications of our theory of the macroeconomy. In doing so, it expands the discussion in the preceding chapter of the relation between the targets, indicators, and instruments of monetary policy.

We need to consider how the money supply, the creation of it, and the changes in the amount that exists are related to developments in the real sectors of the economy. This will require us to look again at the determination of the situational variables we have referred to, the level of real output, employment, prices, and the rate of interest. It will be necessary also to take note of some of the principal differences of view that have gained currency in these matters. Within the orbit of neoclassicism, for example, or within the scope of the neoclassical–Keynesian synthesis, differences of view exist between the monetarists on the one hand and some traditional neo–Keynesians on the other.

Throughout our discussion three questions will repeatedly arise. First, where do changes in the money supply come from and why do they occur? Second, what are the channels of mutual causation—or the transmission channels—through which developments in the real markets affect the money supply, and through which variations in the money supply affect outcomes in the rest of the system? Third, how are the answers to these questions dependent on, and related to, the phenomena of money flows that are central to the understanding of the macroeconomy?

These questions are interdependent. The second question regarding the transmission channels has been put in its present form for an important reason. The question of the transmission mechanism has been prominent in discussions of monetary theory and policy. The monetarists and the Keynesians have occupied us with their differences of view. But we need to examine not only the traditional arguments regarding the ways in which effects are transmitted from the monetary to the real sectors, the more usual province of the debate. We need to understand also the interdependent transmission of effects from the real to the monetary sectors.

The third of the questions we have just raised takes us to the heart of our understanding of the macrosystem. Our theory of the macroeconomy is a monetary flow theory. Money flows give expression to production costs and determine the aggregate supply function on the one side, and they form the basis of expenditure streams and determine the form of the aggregate demand function on the other.

To conclude our analysis we shall take brief account of an important question that can never be far below the surface in serious economic policy discussion, namely, What is the appropriate locus of authority for monetary policy? The question turns on whether the historic and legal independence of the Federal Reserve is in the best interests of overall economic policy, and whether it best meets the objectives of economic organization and welfare which, presumably, we want to achieve.

The National Banking System, it will be recalled, did not function with a high degree of efficiency as the spread of demand deposit banking continued during the latter part of the nineteenth century. It did not provide the economy with an efficient form of banking reserves or a lender of last resort. It did not protect the system against recurring financial panics and liquidity strains. It did not provide an adequate system for the clearing of checks and the intranational mobility of funds. And it did not provide an adequately elastic supply of the circulating medium. The Federal Reserve System as it was established in 1913 was designed to overcome these defects. But the needed reforms did not all come at once. The Federal Reserve System was not initially designed to cope with the financial problems that soon emerged. Further evolution necessarily occurred.

On the level of policy, the Federal Reserve had to wait until the economically disturbed conditions of the 1930s to acquire (1) a Board of Governors that was able to exercise a higher degree of centralized control, (2) flexible reserve requirements that gave the Federal Reserve a new instrument of monetary policy, (3) the recognition of the usefulness of open market operations as a flexible instrument of contracyclical policy, (4) the severing of the tie between the currency and gold, and (5) the benefit of a sister institution, the Federal Deposit Insurance Corporation, which added a new degree of confidence and stability to demand deposit banking. The post—World War II years brought their own new sets of financial developments, and further significant changes in the system—the most comprehensive since the Banking Act of 1935—came with the legislation of the early 1980s.

But debate continues. A fundamental question arises as to whether there should be any scope for discretionary monetary policy at all. It is argued by some economists, generally as part of a wider set of monetarist prescriptions, that certain monetary rules—for example, a rule that the money supply should increase consistently at a constant weekly, monthly, or annual rate—should replace the Federal Reserve Board's discretionary management policies. The problem with this, of course, is that it leaves open the question as to what discretion is to be exercised in setting the rules, and what discretion is open to whom to change the rules. Arguments regarding the supposed ineffectiveness of activist monetary policy are also advanced by those economists who rely on the theory of rational expectations that we shall refer to below.

THE SITUATIONAL VARIABLES AGAIN

Our model of the macroeconomy threw light on the determination of the variables that together describe the condition of the economy at a given time. These include the level of real national output or income, y; the level of employment, N; the commodity price level, P; and the rate of interest, r. In addition, the determination of the money supply, M^s, and the international exchange rate, e, are interdependent with the other variables. It will be useful to remind ourselves briefly of that theoretical discussion as a background to the propositions on monetary policy that follow from it.

The theoretical model is oriented on the ways in which the employment of labor, at a specified money wage rate and in the context of specified production possibilities, determines the form of the aggregate supply curve in the economy. This was embedded in the relation between the productivity money wage, or the so-called efficiency wage of labor, and the profit markup expectations of the employing and producing firms.

Given the money wage rate, which was imported into the analysis as an exogenous variable, and given the average productivity of labor and the wage-cost markup factor, two important conclusions were derived. First, the producer's expected proceeds function gave rise to the concept of the macroanalytic analogue, the economy-wide expected proceeds function or the aggregate supply curve. This important relation described the proceeds of the sale of output that employers must be able to expect in order to make the employment of certain designated amounts of labor economically worthwhile. Second, it was inherent in the analysis that every point on this economywide supply curve had embedded in it an implicit commodity price level and an implicit distribution of income.

These relations provided us with the concept of the money flows implicit in assumed employment and output levels. The incomes generated form the basis of consumption expenditures. Adding the investment and government expenditure functions provided the economy's aggregate demand curve. The aggregate demand curve and the aggregate supply curve, each embedded in its own way in money flows, together gave us a point of effective monetary demand.

This level of effective demand was uniquely determined as a supply and demand cross, as a macroeconomic analogue of the Marshallian microeconomic market conception. The supply and demand cross provided a solution to two of our situational variables—the level of employment and the level of real output. The latter it provided by specifying first the level of aggregate monetary expenditure or nominal money national income. Given the implicit specification of the price level contained in the aggregate supply curve (as clarified further, for example, in Figure 19-6 of Chapter 19), the level of real output followed from the division of the money national income by the price level, or $y = Y/P$. Alternatively (as also indicated in Figure 19-6), the real output was directly defined by the short-run production possibility relation, once the effective level of employment was given.

Our macromodel thus determined the $y, P, N,$ and Y variables. The rate of interest, r, and the specification of the demand for money, M^d, and the money supply, M^s, followed from the examination of relations in the market for money. The connections between the rate of interest and the expenditure flows in the system were also clearly exposed. The rate of interest functioned in its stock aspect as the market-clearing price of money, and in its flow aspect it related the demand for loanable money capital funds to the supply of loanable funds.

THE ORIGIN OF THE DEMAND FOR MONEY

Let us focus initially on the function of money as a medium of exchange. We shall trace the way in which the demand for money is embedded in the wage-price-productivity-expected-proceeds relations we have specified. The geometry of the argument will be recalled again from the discussion of Chapter 19.

Let it be supposed that an increase occurs in the exogenously determined money wage rate. If, then, the proportional increase in the money wage rate exceeds the proportional increase during the same period in the average productivity per unit of labor, the shift upwards and to the left of the aggregate supply curve will be accompanied by an implicit increase in the efficiency wage rate. At the same time the increased money wage incomes, accompanied by the higher money profit incomes that arise because of a given profit markup factor, will cause the aggregate demand curve to rise. The conjunction of the new higher aggregate supply curve and the new higher aggregate demand curve will generate a new, mutually determined, employment, income, and price level.

We must now consider the needs for money implicit in these developments. First, the higher money wage rate, under the productivity and efficiency conditions assumed in the example, induces a higher commodity price level. Second, it then becomes necessary to ask what level of the money supply will be required in order to enable the economy to maintain the previously existing level of production and employment at the new higher level of prices. This leads to the question as to whether the reaction of the monetary system is, or is able to be, such that the new higher requirements for money can be satisfied.

Schematically, the causation can be described in the following manner:

$$\Delta W \longrightarrow \Delta P \longrightarrow \Delta M^d$$

The causation runs from the increase in the wage rate to the induced increase in the price level, and to the consequent increase in the demand for money. We can add to this the money supply variable, with an interrogation mark over the implication sign to indicate that much depends on the way in which the suppliers of money react to the increased demand for money:

$$\Delta W \longrightarrow \Delta P \longrightarrow \Delta M^d \overset{?}{\longrightarrow} \Delta M^s$$

An important difference exists between the relations we now have in view and those embraced, on comparable levels, by the neoclassical theory. We have said, in effect, that the money wage rate is exogenous and the money supply is largely endogenous. For the neoclassical argument the relationships are reversed. The money supply is generally seen as essentially exogenous for purposes of analysis, and the money wage rate is endogenous.

This being the case, the direction of causation of the wage, price, money supply relation appears in the neoclassical view as follows:

$$\Delta M^s \longrightarrow \Delta P \longrightarrow \Delta N^d \longrightarrow \Delta W$$

The increased supply of money induces a higher price level, which in turn moves the demand curve for labor to the right in the labor market and raises the money wage rate. We can bring the two very different views of causation together and summarize them as follows:

1. Postclassical view: $\Delta W \longrightarrow \Delta M$
2. Neoclassical view: $\Delta M \longrightarrow \Delta W$

This crystallizes one of the most important differences of perspective that underlie the following monetary policy analysis.

THE SUPPLY OF MONEY

At this point the question of monetary policy enters. The demand for money has increased, we have assumed, because of the higher expected expenditure streams implicit in the wish to maintain the previous level of real transactions at the new higher price level. We are therefore interested in whether the increase in the money supply does, or can, keep pace with the increased demand. The relation can be expressed as follows, where the interrogation mark indicates the uncertainty as to the outcome that exists at this point:

$$\Delta M^s \overset{?}{\gtreqless} \Delta M^d$$

If, of course, the increase in the money supply is less than the increase in the demand for money, it will not be possible to sustain the previously existing output at the new higher price level. We have, then, a new degree of monetary tightness. In the nature of the case, this must be reflected in a decline in the level of output and employment unless the tighter monetary conditions are offset by (1) improved efficiency in the industrial management of money balances, which amounts to an increase in the effective velocity of circulation of money, or (2) the invention of money substitutes and changes in the structure of payments habits in the economy. If, however, general conditions of monetary tightness are allowed to develop, perhaps because of the Federal Reserve Board's view that it is necessary to control the inflationary price rise that has developed, then the result will be a general recession of real activity and employment.

It is in this way that monetary tightness as a policy move expresses itself. Tight money can never have a *direct* or *impact* effect on the price level. The price level, as we have seen, is embedded in the conjunction of real determining forces. The *impact* of monetary tightness will necessarily be not on the price level but on the level of economic activity.

The increased demand for money may express itself in a number of ways. Industrialists may endeavor to bolster their liquidity positions by selling securities. This will depress the market value of securities and put a general upward pressure on the interest rate or security yields. Immediately, the Federal Reserve will be confronted with the question of whether it will intervene in the securities market by open market purchases to preserve the rate of interest. By doing so, it would increase the reserve positions of the depository institutions and make it possible for them to increase the money supply.

Alternatively, industrialists may adopt other methods of bolstering their liquidity. They may endeavor to delay payments to current liability creditors, though there is, of course, a limit to which this can be done if credit ratings are to be maintained. Even if such payments were delayed, however, sooner or later business firms would have to take further action to improve the liquidity of the system as a whole by going to the banks and increasing their requests for loans. The question then becomes one of whether the banks will, or will be able to, accommodate the increased loan requests.

To meet the increased demand for funds, the banks will have to engage in asset portfolio reorganizations and perhaps move out of securities into loans if, at the time of the increased demands, they are fully lent. Such action will again put pressure on security prices and yields, and again the Federal Reserve will be faced with the need to take supportive action by some monetary policy means. In this situation the Federal Reserve could use any of the monetary policy instruments we have already discussed. As we have seen, it would be most likely to vary its open market operations activity.

THE BANKING SYSTEM'S BALANCE SHEET EFFECTS

The relations we have just discussed can be reflected on a consolidated balance sheet of the banks in the following manner:

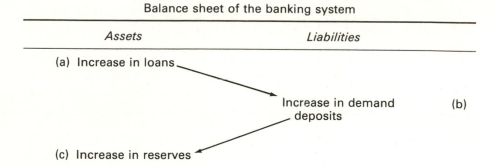

Balance sheet of the banking system

Note the directions of the arrows in the balance sheet. They are designed to indicate the direction and order of causation. As we have argued above, the increased commodity price level makes it necessary for producers and others to increase their demands for bank loans. As these are granted, they give rise to increased demand deposits and a larger money supply. But in that case the banks' reserve positions will be put in jeopardy if, prior to the increased demand, they were, or were close to being, fully lent. If, then, the monetary authorities wish to validate the price increase by making a permanent increase in the money supply possible, they will in one way or another have to take action to create bank reserves.

The viewpoint taken by the quantity theory of money approach, on the other hand, sees the relations developing in a different order:

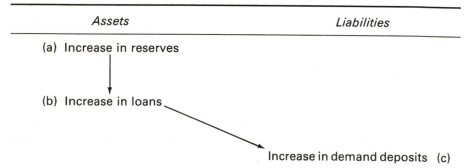

Balance sheet of the banking system

Again the arrows indicate the order and direction of causation. In this case the Federal Reserve authorities are assumed to judge the need for either the defensive or the dynamic monetary policy action that will increase the banks' reserves. If, then, the banks find themselves in possession of new excess reserves, they will be motivated to increase the level of lending and deposit creation. The resulting increase in the amount of money in circulation can be expected to lead to a higher price level in the way this has been envisaged by the quantity theory of money.

These contrasting views of the price formation and the money-creating processes can also be summarized in a different way. Consider the basic quantity theory of money expression for the price level:

$$P = MV/y$$

The price level equals the money supply times its velocity of circulation divided by the volume of real output. The direction of causation in the price level equation runs, according to the quantity theory, from the right to the left. Given, that is, the velocity of circulation of money, and given also the volume of real output during a specified period (usually imagined under the quantity theory analysis to be approximated by full-employment output), a change in the money supply will lead to a change in the price level. In terms of incremental increases we have

$$\Delta M \longrightarrow \Delta P$$

Recall now the fundamental explanatory equation of the price level developed in Chapter 16:

$$P = kW/A$$

The commodity price level is, in this way of looking at things, equal to the efficiency wage, W/A, multiplied by the wage-cost markup factor, k. Given the average productivity per unit of labor, A, and given also the wage-cost markup factor, the following relation between incremental changes emerges:

$$\Delta W \longrightarrow \Delta P$$

Now the price level follows from the behavior of the money wage rate.

These considerations lead to a number of questions regarding the use and potential of monetary policy.

MONETARY POLICY ACTION IN INFLATION AND DEPRESSION

The causes and origin of inflation were previously discussed in the context of the postclassical model of the macroeconomy. The explanation of inflation was neither a simple demand-pull theory nor a cost-push theory. Forces from the cost or production side and forces from the demand side were both seen to be involved. Income earners are income spenders. The aggregate demand curve plays its part and the aggregate supply curve plays its part. Our discussion now raises a further question that has to do with the possibility of accommodative variations in the supply of money.

The quantity theory approach, which provides the logical underpinning for the monetarist analysis, sees the price phenomenon as depending principally and directly on the amount of money in circulation. This it does because of its implicit assumption that the economy tends consistently to full employment. In such a condition, an increase in the money supply will lead to an increase in prices. In order to restrain the price increases, therefore, close control must be kept over the money supply.

Even though we have seen that commodity price formation follows from other and more fundamental real economic forces, we can stay with the neoclassical argument for a moment and ask whether a restraint on the increase of the money supply, or conceivably a reduction of the money supply, would be able to restrain the price increase. In short, can we control inflation by monetary policy action? We have said above that the *impact* effect of monetary policy is always on the level of output and employment, and not on the price level. But we can still ask whether a policy of monetary tightness can arrest the inflation.

The answer, it is important to note, is that it can. Policies of monetary restraint can arrest an inflationary trend. But in doing so, a very high price in economic distress may have to be paid. If, for one reason or another, the monetary authorities choose not to validate the price increase that emerges from the wage-cost-productivity relations, and if they refrain from accommodating the increased requirements for money, the level of economic activity will not be able to be maintained. Recession will ensue. In that situation some wage contracts may be rewritten to require the suppliers of labor to surrender previous monetary gains. Sagging economic conditions may take the pressure off the demand for industrial materials sufficiently to cause their prices to fall. The inflationary trend may be stopped. The tighter the monetary restraint that is applied, the more serious the economic recession will become, and the greater the likelihood that price declines, or shallower rates of increase, will occur. But in such developments as these the cost of arresting the price increases is a potentially serious decline in employment and output. That is precisely what happened in the United States economy during the late 1970s and early 1980s.

Restrictive monetary policy, then, can be effective against an inflation. But the price that it exacts from the economy may be high. In the contrary case, we can ask whether monetary policy will be effective against a recession. We want to know whether a general easing of monetary conditions can stimulate the economy to higher levels of production and employment. The answer, in short, is that the monetary instruments may not be as effective against a recession as they can potentially be against an inflation. This is so for a number of reasons.

First, to recall a technical matter of commercial bank policy, the banks may not, in a general recessionary situation, always be in a fully lent position. They may maintain higher excess reserves than would normally be the case. Or they may have restructured their asset portfolios to carry a larger proportion of government securities, rather than higher-yielding commercial and industrial loans. In the Great Depression of the 1930s, for example, the banks held large amounts of excess reserves. In such conditions a Federal Reserve policy of further general monetary ease may not have any impact on the activity levels. The demand for loans may simply not exist. The banks may not be able to make profitable expansions of their loan portfolios.

Second, in conditions of recession the interest rate may already be low, and the demand for money (the public's liquidity preference) may be high and quite elastic. If that is so, then any attempt on the part of the monetary authorities to depress the interest rate further by increasing the money supply may be unsuccessful. Open market purchases may lead to a large-scale monetization of the federal debt, without having any appreciable effects on the interest rate or the level of expenditures.

Third, it should be kept in mind that expenditure on investment goods is determined not simply by the price of money or the cost of money capital. Important also are the prospects for increased commodity sales in the future, as expressed in the estimation of the prospective marginal efficiency of investment. In the conditions of recession that we have supposed, this marginal efficiency may be too low to enable reductions in the price of money to have significant effects on the expenditure streams.

This raises, of course, the question of the part that monetary policy can and should effectively play in the overall economic policy mix. Monetary policy remains important. Money does matter. But it must be seen in relation to other arms and instruments of economic policy.

THE MONETARY, FISCAL, AND INCOMES POLICY MIX

In recessionary conditions such as we referred to in the preceding section, it might not be possible for monetary policy alone to revive the economy. In that situation a direct stimulus to the expenditure streams might need to be introduced by fiscal policy. It might be desirable to increase government expenditures on goods and services, with a view to raising the aggregate demand curve in such a way as to lead to higher employment. The impact of such expenditures on the economy would depend on the structure of the government outlays. But by introducing a multiplicand in the form of higher government outlays, an employment and income multiplier process may be instigated.

On the other hand, if the recession has not been allowed to become very deep, a fiscal stimulus may be introduced by reducing government revenues rather than raising government expenditures. In that case room for debate and differences of view exists as to whose tax liabilities should be reduced. The public will be concerned not only with the quantitative effects of different fiscal policy packages but also with the ideological or philosophic issues that always surround government participation in the economy. Those on the ideological left would conceivably prefer fiscal stimulus to take the form of increased government outlays. Others might prefer that government revenues be reduced in order to leave the public freer to make their own decisions as to the direction of expenditures and the structure of economic activity that results.

If fiscal policy is used, however, a question that engaged us previously will again arise. How should the proposed government expenditure, or the budget deficit that may result from revenue reduction, be financed? If the necessary borrowing takes place by the sale of new government securities to the public, this will not imply an immediate increase in the money supply. What was previously idle money may be transformed into active money. In other words, the overall velocity of circulation of money may increase. Beneficial effects on the economy may result. But if a larger degree of stimulation is desired, it may be advisable to finance the deficit in such a way as to cause the money supply to increase simultaneously.

This can be accomplished by borrowing from the depository institutions if the Federal Reserve takes supportive action in the securities market and increases the depository institutions' reserves to enable them to accommodate the government's demand for funds. Depending on the severity of the recession in which the fiscal stimulus is being introduced, it would be necessary to be careful that the government borrowing did not compete with, or crowd out, private sector demand for funds that might be needed to support a revival in investment activity.

In this way, the possibility of combinations of monetary and fiscal policy action exists. In more-advanced economic analysis care is frequently taken to separate the monetary policy or monetary accommodation effects from the fiscal effects. Some analysts, who generally adopt a monetarist way of looking at things, go so far as to argue that in general a pure fiscal policy cannot have enduring beneficial effects on the economy. An increase in government expenditure that was not accompanied by an increase in the money supply would, it is argued, crowd out private investment demand and have no net beneficial effects at all. That must depend, of course, on the state of the general economic conditions in which the fiscal policy is introduced. A total crowd-out of private sector financing will not necessarily occur. But the point does alert us to the importance of considering from another perspective the ever-present need for the money supply to accommodate to the needs of the economy. It must do this in order to facilitate the actual expenditure streams that the economy wishes and plans to maintain. From another view, an increase in the money supply is necessary in order to prevent the interest rate or the price of money from rising and choking off whatever revival of expenditures might otherwise be provoked.

John Maynard Keynes, who clearly saw the savings-investment relation in aggregate economic analysis, also saw the importance of the point that has just been made. He also confronted the question, in connection with the real multiplier processes, of where the money supply and changes in the money supply come from. He observed that

> If there is no change in the liquidity position, the public can save ex-ante and ex-post and ex-anything else until they are blue in the face, without alleviating the problem in the least—unless, indeed, the result of their efforts is to lower the scale of activity to what it was before . . . the banks hold the key position in the transition from a lower to a higher scale of activity. If they refuse to relax, the growing congestion of the short-term loan market or the new issue market, as the case may be, will inhibit the improvement, no matter how thrifty the public purpose to be out of their future income . . . The investment market can become congested through shortage of cash. It can never become congested through shortage of savings. This is the most fundamental of my conclusions within this field.[1]

To say, therefore, that the principal task and objective of monetary policy is not that of influencing the price level directly, and that a policy of monetary restraint as the sole or principal anti-inflationary policy is misdirected, in no sense implies that no role exists for monetary policy. On the contrary, the task of monetary policy is essentially that of keeping the financial markets on an even keel and making sure that the legitimate needs of the real sector for financial accommodation are met. It will thereby contribute to steady conditions and stable economic growth. If the fundamental price level problem is handled by measures directed precisely to the origins of the price-forming forces, monetary and fiscal policies will be released to perform their legitimate tasks of stabilizing the short-term fluctuations in the economy and facilitating and fostering a secular economic advance.

At this point a clear understanding of the scope and possible forms of an incomes policy is necessary. We have already referred to this, and only a brief further comment is called for at this stage. It is in no sense necessary to argue for a system of wage and price controls. Incomes policies may mean something quite different. A system of wage rate adjustments and income remunerations can be invented that preserves a

---

[1] John Maynard Keynes, "The General Theory of the Rate of Interest," *Economic Journal*, 1937.

sustainable relation between the annual rates of change in contractual incomes and the annual rates of change in the economy's ability to pay increased incomes. The latter, of course, is determined by the rate of increase in the average level of productivity in the economy.

Ordinary arithmetic as well as economic logic makes it clear that only disruption and disequilibrium can ensue in the economy if income payments are increased at a greater rate than the productivity of the income earners. If the value of money is continually permitted to decline by 10 percent per annum because incomes are raised by 12 percent while productivity increases by 2 percent, further distortions are likely to be imparted to the problem of distributive shares. It is in the interests of the suppliers of labor as well as the users of labor to stabilize the value of money. Economic calculation requires it. The moral dilemma of the distress otherwise imposed on those who cannot protect themselves against inflation demands it. Of course, distributional problems exist and are important. They need to be continually addressed. Fiscal arrangements can be directed to that end. But a rational anti-inflation incomes policy should not have to wait forever until all other issues of social and economic equity have been settled.

The details of incomes policies that might be considered have also been mentioned previously. They have to do basically with the use of fiscal instruments. Penalty taxes might be imposed on those employers who pay, or those employees who receive, increases in incomes at a greater rate than the norm established by the average rate of increase of productivity in the economy. Incomes policies need not impose a heavy bureaucratic policing system on the economy. A set of workable arrangements may be designed that, with minimal additions to income tax returns for example, can keep the wage rate changes in line with productivity norms. Producing corporations could provide the necessary annual cost, productivity, and income payment records with minimal calculation. The details need not detain us at this time. But one final point can be noted.[2]

If it were possible in this way to establish a rational relation between changes in productivity and changes in contractual incomes, unusually large changes might occur at certain times in noncontractual incomes, such as residual corporate profits. If the incomes-productivity relation is firmly established, this could be expected to lead to commodity price stability. But the flux and dynamic change in the system of market demands could quite well cause unusually large profits to appear in sectors that were benefiting from increased demand for their products. Other sectors would at the same time conceivably experience reduced profits or

[2] See Sidney Weintraub, *Capitalism's Inflation and Unemployment Crisis* (Reading, Mass.: Addison-Wesley, 1978); and Michael P. Claudon and Richard R. Cornwall, eds., *An Incomes Policy for the United States: New Approaches* (Boston: Martinus Nijhoff Publishing, 1981).

even losses. There is no reason why the normal allocative and reallocative processes of the market system should not be allowed to operate in the manner this would imply. But in the interests of equity and stability an excess profits tax could be applied in instances where the incomes restraint called for by the basic incomes policy was enhancing residual profits unduly. There need not be any net damage, as a result, to the economy's incentive structures and allocative processes. After-tax rates of return on invested capital would still be allowed to be high enough, consistent with the risks being undertaken, to permit the flow of capital to its economically most desirable line of employment.

THE TRANSMISSION MECHANISM

We have been speaking already of an important transmission mechanism. We have discussed the transmission of implications and effects from the real sector of the economy to the monetary sector and the price dimension. Generally, however, the concept of the transmission mechanism in monetary economics has been taken to refer to the ways in which, following a change in the money supply, the effects of that change are transmitted to the real sector and other parts of the financial sector. We want to know, in general terms, how an increase in the money supply will lead to changes in the level of real output, employment, prices, and the interest rate. Different conceptions of this transmission mechanism have been held by the monetarist and the neo–Keynesian economists, respectively.

The monetarist view of the transmission mechanism has already been considered. It places heavy emphasis on the concept of the asset portfolios held by the public in general. Such wealth portfolios, it is understood, contain what are referred to as several different "temporary abodes of purchasing power." The demand for money is seen as an instance of a more general demand for wealth assets. Money, as a highly liquid abode of purchasing power, is only one of the forms in which wealth might be held. Other asset forms compete with money for positions in the portfolio. The optimum portfolio will be that which combines the various wealth forms in such a way that the marginal net benefit derived from each asset form is equal.

This conception at the base of the monetarist analysis has also been taken over to a large degree by the portfolio theorists in the neo–Keynesian camp. Much is made in contemporary monetary economics of such portfolio theorizing. At the heart of the theory is the assumption that a high degree of substitutability exists between the different asset forms. When the money supply increases, the public's wealth portfolios will in general contain a larger amount of money in proportion to nonmonetary assets than is consistent with the equimarginal portfolio optimization principle. The marginal net benefit of the holding of money is now lower than the marginal net benefit derived from a dollar's worth of other assets. Individuals will therefore wish to substitute other assets for money.

This substitution effect implies that part of the new money created by the financial system and temporarily held by the public will be spent. Commodities will replace money in general wealth portfolios. The demand for goods increases and the total level of national expenditure and income will rise. The question as to how this increase in monetary expenditure will be reflected in either an increase in real production or an increase in the price level or both has not been clearly stated in the monetarist theory. So far as the older quantity theory of money is implicit in it, and so far as the usual neoclassical assumption is held that the economic system tends naturally to full employment, or what has more recently been envisaged as a natural rate of unemployment, the increased money supply and expenditure can be expected to give rise to an increase in the price level. Under the older quantity theory such an increase in prices would continue until the level of total market expenditure was such that the public was prepared to hold the new higher money supply. It would then be consistent with their proportionate money requirements. The present-day monetarists, or the new quantity theorists, have taken the argument to the point of saying that the new higher money supplies will lead to generally higher levels of money national income. But the separation of the effects into a price dimension and an output dimension has not been clearly explained.

The neo–Keynesian view of the transmission mechanism places principal emphasis on the interest rate effect in the market for money. Under the monetarist scheme also, of course, the demands for non-monetary assets, such as securities that may be substituted for money in wealth portfolios, would generate an interest rate effect. Increased security demands and prices would imply reduced security yields and interest rates. The same lines of causation exist also in the neo–Keynesian case. But here a more explicit relation is envisaged between the rate of interest as the price of money capital and induced expenditure streams.

Let it be imagined, for example, that the Federal Reserve Board takes action to increase the money supply by open market purchases. The interest rate will tend to be reduced and this will tend to raise investment expenditure, given the existing marginal efficiency of investment and assuming no adverse expectations effects are generated by the expansionary monetary policy. Making use of previous terminology, this introduction of a multiplicand will instigate a multiplier process and lead to higher levels of employment and output.

Consumption expenditure may also be stimulated by the reduction in interest rates. The price of consumer loans will now be lower and increased expenditure may occur in durable goods, automobiles, and the

housing and construction areas. Moreover, even if reductions in the rate
of interest on consumer loans do not appear immediately, the more ready
availability of funds in the intermediary institutions may mean that
consumers who could not previously obtain loans, by reason of a backlog
of borrowers, may now be accommodated. Finally, the reduction of interest
rates in general will imply an increase in the market values of income-
earning asset portfolios. A positive financial wealth effect will therefore
follow, and this may also stimulate a higher level of consumer expenditures. As stock and security prices rise, individual investors feel more
wealthy. They may be prepared to consume a larger proportion of any
given level of income, and the consumption function may therefore rise,
introducing another multiplicand element into the expansionary process.

   If the expansion of the money supply were effected by a change in
the reserve requirements or a reduction of the discount rate, the effects
would follow from the impacts on the banks' reserve positions we considered in the preceding chapter. In one way or another, the neo–Keynesian
view focuses on the implied change, or the potentialities for change, in
the spending streams in the economy. The probable lines of causation
may be summarized as follows:

$$\Delta M^s \to -\Delta r \quad \begin{matrix} \Delta A \to \Delta C \\ \nearrow \qquad\qquad \searrow \\ \\ \searrow \qquad\qquad \nearrow \\ (\Delta I \text{ and } \Delta C) \end{matrix} \quad \Delta Y(= \Delta(Py)) \quad \begin{matrix} \Delta P \\ \nearrow \quad \searrow \\ \\ \searrow \\ \Delta y \end{matrix} \quad \Delta W \to \Delta P \to \Delta M^d \to \Delta r$$

   In this summary, the variables refer to the money supply, M^s; total
asset wealth, A; investment, I; consumption, C; nominal national income,
Y; real output, y; the price level, P; the money wage rate, W; and the rate
of interest, r. We have supposed that the initial increase in the money
supply occurred as an element of a dynamic policy change instituted by
the Federal Reserve Board as a general expansionary or reflationary
policy. Reading the diagram from left to right, the increased money supply
will initially reduce the rate of interest, leading to increased investment
and consumption expenditures via the price-of-money effect as shown in
the lower channel in the diagram, and increased consumption via the
wealth effect as suggested in the upper channel. This produces a higher
level of money or nominal income, which will be divided between a price
dimension effect on the one hand and an output effect on the other.
Visualizing our model of the macroeconomy, this division into a price
level effect and a real output effect will depend on the form of the economy's aggregate supply curve. The rise in prices can be expected to be
reflected, in due course, in the money wage contracts struck in the labor
market, leading to further price increases, higher demand for money, and

induced increases in the rate of interest. Each of the steps in the process has already been discussed in some detail in the preceding analysis.

TARGET AND INDICATOR VARIABLES

At the beginning of the preceding chapter we discussed different possible views of the targets and indicators of monetary policy. The debates that have occurred on this level have centered mainly on the question of whether the Federal Reserve should endeavor to exercise a control and influence over (1) the money supply or (2) money market conditions as indicated by some appropriate rate of interest. The monetarists have in general argued for the former. The neo–Keynesians have preferred a policy that attempted to stabilize money market conditions.

In October 1979, as we have seen, the Federal Reserve Board announced that henceforth it would pay more attention to the money supply data, focusing on the monetary base as a short-run indicator, and would give less attention to interest rate stability. In the outcome, interest rates have fluctuated more widely since that time, though mainly at unusually high levels in view of the policy of monetary restraint. Significant stability in the money supply or in the rate of increase in the money supply, however, was not achieved. The changing structure of the financial institutions and of the nonbank depository institutions in particular has made it increasingly difficult to measure the money supply. New forms of money substitutes have appeared, and debate still occurs as to what precisely ought to be included in the M1 or the M2 measures.

It is possible, however, to make a few rather general statements as to the conditions under which the Federal Reserve might be advised to aim at either interest rate or money supply stability. Much depends on the existing state of expectations regarding the prospective stability of (1) the level and determinants of the expenditure streams and (2) the demand for money.

The monetarists have generally argued that the demand for money can be described as a stable function of a well-defined set of variables including wealth, income, the rate of interest, and price expectations. This is not saying that the demand for money is constant in magnitude. It is saying that the demand for money is described by a stable function, in the sense that if the determinant variables in the function take on certain magnitudes the demand for money can be estimated in a reliable way from the defined functional relation. In actual fact, empirical work has cast some doubt on the stability of the functional forms that the monetarists have envisaged. But if the proposition that the money demand function is stable is granted for the moment, it would follow that it would make sense for the monetary authorities to adopt a policy that aimed to keep the money supply stable also.

Let us expand this question of the relative stabilities in the system, and the relation to them of different possible kinds of monetary policies, in the following way. Consider the traditional *ISLM* relation generated by the neoclassical–Keynesian synthesis as shown in Figure 23-1. Here we may assume that an interest rate and real income equilibrium exist at the coordinates r_1^* and y_1^*, as given by the intersection of the *LM* curve and the *IS* curve IS_1. We now suppose that a greater degree of instability exists in the prospective expenditure streams than in the demand for money. This is depicted in the figure by the movements to the curves IS_2 and IS_3, traversing a stable *LM* curve.

If, in that case, the money supply is held stable, the variations in expenditure demands will cause the interest rate to rise or fall along the *LM* curve, at the same time as the equilibrium level of real income fluctuates between y_2 and y_3. These new output levels are given by the intersection of the *LM* curve and the new *IS* curves. This, then, defines the range of income fluctuation achievable by adopting a policy that holds the money supply stable. If, on the other hand, monetary policy were aimed at maintaining the interest rate at its previous level of r_1^*, it would be necessary for the monetary authorities to reduce the money supply when expenditures fell and increase it when they rose. In that case, as Figure 23-1 indicates, the fluctuations in real income would be larger, moving between y_4 and y_5. By maintaining the money supply and allowing the interest rate to move, what would otherwise be wider fluctuations in expenditure are to some extent counteracted, and the fluctuations in real activity are minimized.

Figure   23-1.

Relative expenditure instability

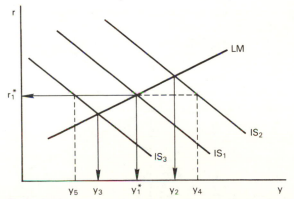

Suppose, on the contrary, that the demand for money is expected to be more unstable than the expenditure streams. The possible relations are exhibited in Figure 23-2, where the *LM* curve is assumed to move across a given *IS* curve. In this case a policy of holding the money supply stable would be reflected in variations in the real income level between y_2 and y_3 as the interest rate fluctuated in response to the variations in the demand for money.

If, in this case, a policy of maintaining the interest rate stable at r_1^* were adopted, and if, in order to accomplish this, the money supply were allowed to fluctuate in response to the demand for money, then there would be no fluctuations in real income. The expenditure streams, and therefore the *IS* curve, being assumed to be stable, a policy of maintaining the interest rate at r_1^* will also maintain real income at y_1^*.

The outcome of this analysis is that if the greater relative degree of instability appears to lie in the expenditure streams, fluctuations in real income, and therefore in employment, will be minimized by a policy of holding the money supply relatively stable. But if, on the contrary, the greater relative degree of instability appears to lie in the demand for money, variations in real income will be minimized by allowing the money supply to vary and holding the interest rate relatively stable.

The policy options facing the Federal Reserve Board are never very clear-cut. Monetary management remains very much an art, depending on the day-to-day "feel of the market" as much as on any narrow set of economic prescriptions. Perhaps the clearest lesson we can derive from the discussion in this chapter is that it is certainly a mistake to imagine, as has been done in recent times in the United States, that monetary policy can be relied upon as virtually the sole instrument with which to fight tendencies to inflation. Monetary policy plays its part. But broader

Figure   23-2.

Instability in the demand for money

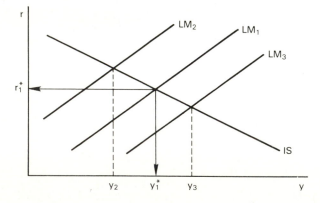

issues of economic policy, and a broader range of economic policy instruments, need to be brought into focus.

RATIONAL EXPECTATIONS AND THE EFFECTIVENESS OF STABILIZATION POLICIES

The analysis to this point has assumed that activist economic policies, of either a monetary or a fiscal variety, could be effective in stabilizing, or contributing to the relative stability of, the macroeconomic system. In the minds of some economists, however, this can in no sense be taken for granted or assumed to be the case. For much depends, it is claimed, on the nature of the formation of expectations that determine individuals' reactions to economic situations and events. In particular, the theory of so-called rational expectations claims that what might be thought to be advisable contracyclical policy action might in fact have no stabilizing effects at all or might even be destabilizing.

If we held the assumption that the macroeconomy is inherently stable (which we noted in an earlier chapter is frequently espoused by exponents of the neoclassical–Keynesian synthesis, notably by those who come from the monetarist wing of that synthesis), there would, of course, be no need to engage in positively contracyclical policy. Moreover, if we held, as do some monetarist economists, to the proposition that rather long and variable lags in the effects of activist policies render their ultimate results quite uncertain, and raise the danger that those results might be the opposite of what was initially intended, we should again avoid deliberate contracyclical policy on the grounds that it might well worsen, rather than improve, the instabilities in the system.

Beyond these arguments against the need for stabilization policies, the rational expectations theory adds a further dimension of thought that points in the same direction. By *rational expectations* is meant simply that economic decision makers, in their forecasts of future economic developments and trends, take into account in a rational way all the information available to them, or all the information they can acquire at a cost they are prepared to incur. Economic sophistication, it is claimed, is fairly widespread, at least among the significant leaders of economic action and among economic opinion makers. Moreover, the information on which action is based is assumed to include not only the fact situations as they emerge but also the nature of the policy actions the economic authorities are likely to take in response to those facts. A couple of brief examples will indicate the nature of the claim at this point.

Let it be supposed that the monetary authorities attempted to reduce unemployment below what, as conceived by the neoclassical theory, was thought to be the natural long-run equilibrium level. The easing of the monetary situation, resulting from an increase in the money supply, would at first tend to raise the level of output and employment. But if, in accordance with the postulate of rational expectations, everyone knows that when such an increase in the money supply occurs the price level will in due course rise, then workers will quickly take this expectation into account and demand higher wage payments to compensate them for the expected price rise they foresee. As a result, a simultaneous rise in both prices and wages will tend to occur, and no motivation will exist for employers to increase the level of employment. The increased money supply will then bring about a short burst of inflation and a quick return to the previously existing level of unemployment.

Or suppose that monetary policy attempts to reduce the rate of interest below its equilibrium long-run level by increasing the money supply, perhaps by purchasing securities. Again the rational expectations theory concludes that decision makers will take into account the inevitable effects that the increased money supply will have on the price level and the prospect of worsened inflation in the period ahead. In that event, the financial markets will quickly add an increased inflation premium to the nominal interest rate, and the effective cost of money capital will be raised as a result. Any potential beneficial effects that might have been exerted on the expenditure streams by a lower interest rate will therefore be destroyed.

These arguments assume, of course, that market prices are in general highly flexible. Not only is the interest rate or the market price of money flexible but commodity prices and, in particular, wage rates are also assumed to be flexible. It is because of the assumedly high degree of flexibility in the wage rate that the suppliers of labor cannot be induced to work for a given money wage when, as in the example we noted above, they foresee higher commodity price levels ahead. To revert to a proposition we noted in Chapter 17 in connection with the neoclassical analysis of the labor market, the rational expectations theory assumes that there is in fact no money illusion on the supply side of the labor market. What we might call high price-adjustment velocities exist in all markets.

The implications of these arguments are that there is no point in the monetary and fiscal authorities' endeavoring to implement what they might regard as contracyclical policies, because the possible effects of such policies are rendered nugatory by the fact that the public quickly takes into account the possible results of them. If, as a final example, the public knows that the Federal Reserve Board will always react to an increase in the money supply by tightening money again to prevent inflationary pressures from developing, market operators will quickly adjust the interest rates in a way that takes account, not of the immediate increase in the availability of money, but of the anticipated tightening of the money supply. In that event, the emergence of increased money supplies, rather than leading to lower interest rates as we might expect, will actually give rise to higher interest rates.

If, however, all prices and wages were as highly flexible as the rational expectations theory assumes, then there is one situation in which beneficial effects could be achieved. If, for example, the authorities wanted to eliminate inflation from the economy without, in accordance with the usual neoclassical implication, suffering prolonged unemployment, they could simply announce that they intended to take as strong a restrictive policy action as was necessary to kill the inflation in the shortest possible time. Then if rational expectations existed universally, the suppliers of labor would immediately take into account the lower price level that would come into effect, and they would immediately reduce their money wage demands proportionately also. As the contemplated reduction of prices will not therefore cause any increase in the real wage rate and will not, as a result, impose any burden on industrialists' costs of production, there will be no reason for output and employment to fall. The inflation could be cured simply by an announcement by the authorities that they fully intended to do what was necessary to cure it.

The rational expectations theory has led to the development of what has been called a new classical macroeconomics, based on the twofold notions of rational expectations and the rapid clearing or equilibration of markets. It might be thought, however, that a number of reasons exist why the rational expectations theory does not have the empirical significance that has been claimed, and why, therefore, stabilization policies, of a monetary and fiscal kind, continue to have relevance. In the first place, the theory appears to require people to know more about the economy, and the likely behavior of the policy authorities in different possible economic situations, than is realistically possible. Moreover, a full knowledge or even a high degree of accuracy in the knowledge of the structure of the economy is irrelevant if, as many economists claim, the economy and its structure are subject to many kinds of completely unforeseeable and unpredictable shocks. In actual fact, the gathering of information is costly, trading takes place in widely dispersed and differentiated markets, and there does not exist as high a degree of price flexibility, or mobility of labor and other factors of production, as would be necessary if the rapid adjustments implicit in the rational expectations view of things were to obtain.

Most important, much of the activity in the economy takes place under well-established contracts, such as contracts for the employment and remuneration of labor, as well as for the supply of other factor inputs and the purchase of commodity outputs. In actual fact, the existence of legally enforceable contracts lends an orderedness to economic affairs, at the same time as it acts as a means of diminishing, or redistributing, the uncertainties that inhere in economic events.

It would therefore be difficult to accept the claim of the rational expectations theory that activist stabilization policy could be effective only if the policy action were able to take the public by surprise, or if the policy authorities were actually to possess information that the public did not. It seems safer to question the assumption of an automatically and rapidly adjusting economic system and to expect that, as has happened repeatedly during the post–World War II years, a suitably adapted and sensibly designed economic policy mix is likely to be not only necessary but also reasonably effective in ironing out what might otherwise be more serious fluctuations in economic activity and welfare.

THE LOCUS OF MONETARY POLICY AUTHORITY

The goals of monetary policy are generally taken to be those compatible with the larger objectives of economic policy as set out, for example, in the Employment Act of 1946. This act stated that "it is the continuing policy and responsibility of the Federal Government to use all practicable means . . . to promote maximum employment, production, and purchasing power." This in itself, of course, is a somewhat vague set of economic objectives, and no clear guidance is given as to the division of responsibilities between the monetary and the fiscal authorities.

A further attempt to get agreement on economic policy goals was made in the Full Employment and Balanced Growth Act of 1978. This was the so-called Humphrey–Hawkins Bill. The act made mention of a large number of economic goals, including full employment, price stability, a balanced federal budget, increased capital formation, reduced government spending, and freer international trade. Moreover, it required the administration to announce specific and quantified goals in a number of these areas for five years ahead. The Federal Reserve was required to report to Congress twice a year on its plans and objectives for monetary policy, and to give Congress its evaluation of the government's announced economic plans. The act actually specified the unemployment rate and the rate of price inflation that should be achieved by 1983. The president has been permitted, however, to change the timetable of achievement of these goals subject to his explaining his adjusted timetable in his annual economic report.

It is clear that a robust and operational body of monetary theory is necessary, along with whatever specification of goals we might like to make, to keep the economy on an even keel. But beyond this there is also a need for the closest possible collaboration and coordination of policies in the principal areas we have mentioned—monetary, fiscal, and incomes policies. The Federal Reserve is technically and legally an independent institution. It is owned by the member banks, and not by the government. The president of the United States and the Congress do have a large degree of residual control over the Federal Reserve, by reason of the fact that the president appoints the seven-member Board of Governors, subject to confirmation by the Senate. The Board of Governors, in turn, exercises a high degree of operating control over the monetary policy actions of the Federal Reserve. But many economists have raised the question as to whether the technical independence of the Federal Reserve is wise or necessary in this age of complex economies and economic policy problems.

In practice, the Federal Reserve is quite free to follow monetary policies that may complement or conflict with the economic policies of the government of the day. A number of arguments favor this independence. First, it may be a protection against an inflationary bias in general government policy, such as that inherent in the gaping budget deficits of the Reagan years in the early 1980s. It is quite remarkable that whereas the total federal debt outstanding, representing the entire accumulation of previous deficits, passed the $1,000 billion mark at that time, the budgets of the four Reagan years increased that debt by approximately a further 50 percent. In other words, one-half of what it took the nation two hundred years to accomplish has been accomplished in as little as four or five years. In this kind of situation many economists have argued that the independence of the Federal Reserve can operate as a defense against undue pressures to inflation.

In addition, the old and deeply rooted fear of undue political interference with the nation's monetary management (such as we encountered in the attempts to establish central banking arrangements in the nineteenth century) also argue in favor of the Federal Reserve's independence. It is thought, moreover, that an independent body will get the cooperation of the private banks and the other financial institutions more readily.

On the other hand, consistency of policy is clearly desirable, and the highest degree of coordination between the various arms of policy should be achieved. It has been argued also that monetary policy, given its preeminent importance for the general outcome of economic affairs, is too important to be left in private hands and should be brought under the control of a body that is accountable to the electorate.

In actual fact, there is a high degree of consultation between the Federal Reserve and the government. Regular meetings occur between the chairman of the Board of Governors, the secretary of the Treasury, and the chairman of the President's Council of Economic Advisers. In addition, the chairman of the Board of Governors makes frequent appearances to testify before committees of Congress. But consultation does not, of course, necessarily imply coordination of policies. In many countries, notably the United Kingdom, the central bank is owned by the government and is charged with a high degree of responsibility for integrating monetary policy into the larger orbit of overall economic management.

SUMMARY

This chapter has drawn out the monetary policy implications of the model of the macroeconomy we established earlier in this book. At several points distinctions were made between the policy requirements that this model recommended and the corresponding implications of the neoclassical and the neo–Keynesian points of view.

The origin of the demand for money was traced to developments in the real sector of the economy. It was necessary to take note of a transmission mechanism working from the real to the monetary sector, as well as that traditionally understood to work in the opposite direction. The impact of a change in the demand for money was traced, in the light of the operating reactions of the banking system and the monetary policy reactions of the Federal Reserve.

The question of the appropriate mix of monetary, fiscal, and incomes policies was discussed, and attention was given to the different relative efficiencies of the policy arms in anti-recession and anti-inflationary situations. The conventional monetary transmission mechanism was examined and distinctions were drawn between the monetarist and the neo–Keynesian views. A more-extended comment was made on the view of the transmission mechanism implicit in the postclassical model.

In the light of a new and influential theory of rational expectations, comments were made on the need for, and the reasons for the potential effectiveness of, contracyclical stabilization policies. Arguments were adduced against the claims of the so-called new classical macroeconomics.

The operational difficulties confronting the Federal Reserve, in its choice, for example, between the interest rate and the money supply as the appropriate target and indicator variables, were discussed. A concluding comment was made on some arguments for and against the traditional and legal independence of the Federal Reserve. It was emphasized that whatever legal and technical structure of monetary authority exists, the maximum possible degree of consultation and coordination of policies is necessary between all of the policy-making arms.

IMPORTANT CONCEPTS

The origin of the demand for money

Endogeneity and exogeneity of the money supply

Endogeneity and exogeneity of the money wage rate

Monetary policy reaction to the increased demand for money

The monetary, fiscal, and incomes policy mix

Rational expectations

The new classical macroeconomics

Transmission mechanism

Monetarism versus neo–Keynesianism

Portfolio substitution effect

Supply responses to the increased demand for money

Interest rate effect

Validation of price increases

Interest rate versus money supply targets

Crowding out

Federal Reserve independence

QUESTIONS FOR DISCUSSION AND REVIEW

1. In the light of the full analysis now completed in this book, explain what determines the demand for money.

2. Trace the transmission mechanism that operates (1) from the real to the monetary sector and (2) from the monetary to the real sector.

3. Compare the relative wisdom and efficiencies of rules versus discretion in the management of monetary policy.

4. Do you believe that an increase in bank reserves leads to an increase in the money supply, or that an increase in the money supply leads to an increase in bank reserves?

5. Discuss fully the alternative macroeconomic theories that underlie the alternative views referred to in Question 4.

6. It has been suggested that the neoclassical theory inverts the postclassical view of endogenous and exogenous variables. In one the money wage rate is endogenous and the money supply is exogenous, while in the other the descriptions are reversed. Explain and evaluate this statement as fully as possible.

7. How are the financial asset market and related portfolio decisions relevant to the monetary transmission mechanism in the monetarist view, the Keynesian view, and the postclassical view?

8. Would the introduction of an incomes policy eliminate the need for contracyclical monetary and fiscal policy? Why or why not? What functions, if any, would each perform?

9. Do you think the Federal Reserve should aim to stabilize the money supply or the level of interest rates? Discuss as fully as possible.

10. In what sense is the money wage rate the linchpin of the monetary economy?

24

THE TRADE AND PAYMENTS BASIS OF INTERNATIONAL MONEY FLOWS

STUDY OBJECTIVES:

• To review the theory of international comparative advantage, as a basis for understanding export and import flows
• To specify the export and import expenditure functions, and to develop from them the basic foreign trade multiplier
• To gain an understanding of the actual balance-of-trade and payments data and their significance in the United States economy
• To observe the methods of financing balance-of-payments surpluses and deficits
• To trace the influence of the trade and payments flows on the foreign exchange rate or the international value of a country's currency
• To derive a basic balance-of-payments equation and the balance-of-payments function implicit in it

Our analysis to this point has dealt almost exclusively with money flows, income and employment generation, and monetary policy in a closed economy. We have set aside for most of our discussions the fact and significance of international monetary relations. We did observe in Chapter 4 that it was necessary to pay attention to the income effects, the price level effects, and the interest rate effects of money flows between countries. Under the international gold standard it was possible to conceive of a self-balancing monetary mechanism that would bring the exchange rate between currencies into line with their mint parities if the rules of the gold standard were adhered to. Though we do not live under a gold standard in that sense at the present time, the same income, price, and interest rate effects must be taken into account in explaining international money flows and the exchange rates that result.

In our previous discussions of monetary policy we observed also the impact of international interest rate differentials. If interest rates in the New York money market are lower than the corresponding rates in the London money market, there will be a tendency for short-term money capital to flow from New York to London. This will increase the outflow of funds relative to the inflow on the balance-of-payments accounts and will increase the demand for British currency in the foreign exchange market. Given the supply of British pounds in that market, this will mean that the United States dollar price of the pound will tend to rise, implying an effective devaluation of the dollar. This will have further effects on export and import demands.

In the following analysis of these and related questions we shall focus on the money flows implicit in the various relations involved. As a preliminary to that, however, we must confront the basic question as to why international trade takes place at all. It turns, as we shall see, on the prospect of increasing, by international specialization of production and trade, the total economic welfare that the global allocation of resources provides.

THE THEORY OF COMPARATIVE ADVANTAGE

We begin this new stage of analysis with a highly abstract and simple example. It contains, however, essentially all the analytical foundations we need. In Figure 24-1 we have described what we shall call a comparative production possibility matrix. The production possibilities in the United States are indicated in the first row of the matrix, and those in the rest of the world, here referred to as Australia, are described in the second row. The hypothetical numbers in the rows of the matrix indicate the number of units of economic resources that must be devoted, in the countries indicated, to produce one unit of the specified commodity output. At the present level of abstraction we may envisage a unit of economic resources as a unit of homogeneous labor. Thus it takes one unit of resources to produce one unit of machinery in the United States, and two units of resources to produce one unit of food. In Australia it takes four units of resources to produce one unit of machinery, and three units of resources to produce one unit of food.

On the basis of these production possibility data, the United States is more efficient in both lines of production. It can produce machinery by using only one-fourth of the resources that have to be used for the same purpose in Australia, and in producing food the United States needs to use only two-thirds of the resources needed for food production in Australia. It might seem on the surface of things, therefore, that nothing would be gained by international trade. This, however, is not so. Paradoxically, both countries can benefit from specialization and trade. A grasp of the reason why this is so unlocks the puzzle of international trade theory.

The United States has an absolute advantage in both lines of production. But it has a greater comparative advantage in the production of machines. Australia, on the other hand, has an absolute disadvantage in both lines of production, but it has a comparative advantage in the production of food. In other words, Australia's absolute disadvantage in the production of food is not as serious as it is in the production of machinery. To produce machinery Australia has to use four times as much resources as does the United States. But to produce food it needs to use only one and one-half times as much. We shall show, then, that even though the United States enjoys absolute superiority in the production of both commodities, it will be advantageous for it to specialize in the production of machinery, and for Australia to specialize in the production of food. The proposition we shall adduce is referred to as the principle of comparative advantage. It states that each country should specialize in the production of that commodity in which it enjoys the greatest comparative advantage, or, in other words, the least absolute disadvantage.

Figure   24-1.

The comparative production possibility matrix

	Machinery	Food
United States	1	2
Australia	4	3

Let us examine production and trading possibilities in the following order. If the United States devotes one unit of resources to the production of machinery, it will produce one machine. Suppose that unit of machinery is then shipped to Australia. In Australia one unit of machinery has command over four units of resources. Acquiring those resources, then, by the sale of a unit of machinery in Australia enables those resources to be allocated there to the production of food. As indicated in Figure 24-1, those four units of resources in Australia will produce one and one-third units of food. The one and one-third units of food can then be shipped by the United States exporter of machinery back to the United States.

By engaging in such indirect production and trade, one unit of United States resources produces one and one-third units food. If, on the other hand, United States resources had been devoted to direct production of food, each unit of resources would have produced only one-half a unit of food. This follows from the stated meaning of the number 2 in the production possibility matrix. Specialization and trade, therefore, definitely increase the United States potential food consumption.

Similarly, by producing machines directly, a unit of Australian resources produces one-fourth of a unit of machinery. By indirect production and trade, by producing and exporting food in exchange for machinery, that unit of Australian resources can produce two-thirds of a unit of machinery.

This example assumes that both the United States and Australia enjoy constant unit production costs as the output of the respective commodities changes. Their internal production possibility frontiers are assumed to be linear, as indicated in Figures 24-2 and 24-3. The figures show the combinations of output that could be produced in the respective countries if each had a total endowment of 100 units of resources. In actual fact, production is not likely to be subject to such constant returns. The principle of decreasing marginal productivity implies that as successive increments of resources are devoted to a particular line of pro-

Figure   24-2.

Internal production possibility frontier: United States

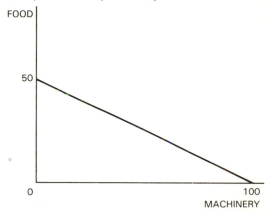

Figure   24-3.

Internal production possibility frontier: Australia

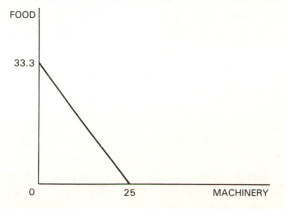

Figure   24-4.

Diminishing marginal returns production possibility frontier

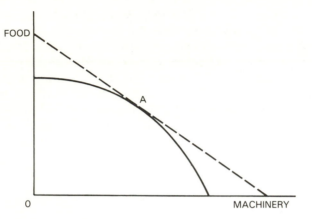

duction, the incremental addition to output will diminish. In that case the production possibility frontiers will not be linear but will be concave, as shown by way of example in Figure 24-4. Each country, then, might be assumed to suffer from diminishing marginal returns and have a frontier of this nonlinear kind.

The broken line in Figure 24-4 has considerable importance for the theory of international trade. It is a relative commodity price line that shows the real rate of exchange at which one commodity can be exchanged for another in the international market. Measuring as it does the price of food relative to the price of machinery, its slope will depend on the relative strengths of the market demands for food and machinery, respectively. If the demand for food is relatively strong, the price of food will be high relative to the price of machinery. In that case the slope of the price line in Figure 24-4 will be shallower, or will cut the vertical axis nearer the origin. The actual slope of the line is derived from the working of three important analytical propositions.

First, if both countries had precisely the same comparative advantage in the production of the respective commodities, no trade would take place. If, for example, the United States could produce both machinery and food by using one-half the resource inputs that Australia needed to produce each of the commodities, there would be no potential benefit in trade.

Second, the data in Figure 24-1 indicate that the ratio of internal production costs in the United States is such that 1 unit of machinery = ½ units of food. In Australia the corresponding ratio is 1 unit of machinery = 1⅓ units of food. In order for trade to be profitable, therefore, the rate of exchange between machinery and food in the open market (that is, the relative price ratio) must be between ½ and 1⅓ units of food per unit of machinery. If the United States received less than ½ unit of food in exchange for a unit of machinery, it would be more economically worthwhile for it to produce food directly rather than to obtain it indirectly by trading. Similarly, if Australia had to surrender more than 1⅓ units of food for a unit of machinery, it would be more beneficial for it to produce machinery directly. The levels of ½ and 1⅓ units of food per unit of machinery therefore set the limits within which the actual real price ratio of exchange between the two commodities must be found in the market. The ratios of ½ to 1, and 1⅓ to 1, describe the respective internal terms of trade between the commodities. The ratio at which the market exchange ratio actually settles between these two different internal terms of trade ratios is referred to as the external terms of trade.

Third, the actual market ratio of exchange between food and machinery will be determined by the relative strengths of the demands for the commodities. Such a market price ratio is described by the slope of the broken line in Figure 24-4. The tangency condition illustrated in that figure leads to our final proposition regarding the foundation of international trade. At the tangency point A, the slope of the price line, or the ratio of market prices, equals the slope of the internal production possibility frontier, or the marginal rate of technical transformation between machinery and food. This equality, it is shown in more detail in the microeconomics literature, describes the optimization condition for the allocation of resources between the respective lines of production.

It follows that if the ratio of prices equals the marginal rate of technical transformation in production in the United States, it must also do so in Australia. One common market price ratio will be etablished by the demand forces that exist. It further follows, therefore, that when both countries are allocating their resources between machinery and food production in an optimal manner, their respective marginal rates of technical substitution will be equal. This is illustrated in Figure 24-5.

In Figure 24-5 the internal production possibility frontiers of Australia and the United States have been married to each other. The origin of the United States production possibility set is at the southwest corner of the figure. That for Australia is at the northeast corner. Australia's production of machinery is read to the left along the top horizontal axis, and its production of food is read downward along the right-hand vertical axis. The United States productions are read in the more familiar manner, horizontally to the right for machinery production and vertically on the left for food production.

At point M in Figure 24-5 the common slopes of the production possibility frontiers are tangential to the indicated price ratio line. This establishes that the United States will allocate its resources in such a way as to produce OA machinery and OB food. Australia will produce $O'C$ food and $O'D$ machinery. This degree of international specialization of production, and the trading exchanges implicit in it at the indicated

Figure   24-5.

Production and trade optimization

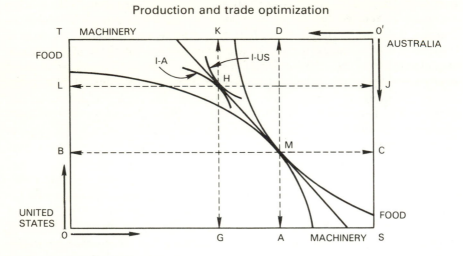

price ratio, determine the optimum outcome achievable, given the underlying production and market demand data. The total production of machinery is OS, divided between the United States and Australia in the proportions of OA and AS (= $O'D$), respectively. Food production is divided between the United States and Australia in the proportions of OB and BT(= $O'C$).

We have not yet established, however, how much of each country's production of each commodity will be traded and how much will be consumed at home. This result is represented in Figure 24-5 by the hypothetical point H. We know that the United States economy, for example, will enjoy both production and consumption optima when the marginal rate of substitution between machinery and food in consumption also equals the established market price ratio. Having produced at point M, therefore, the economy will move back along the market price opportunity line from M to H. This implies that machinery output equal to AG will be traded in the market for food equal to BL. This exchange takes place, it is clear, at the market price ratio. Similarly, Australia will move from M to H by trading CJ (= BL) food for DK (= AG) machinery. In the outcome, the United States is specializing on machinery production and trading some of its output for food. Australia is specializing on food production and trading it for machinery.

At the consumption optimum point H in Figure 24-5, or, in other words, at the optimum trading exchange point, the United States economy is on a consumption indifference curve, labeled I—US, that is in the region outside of, and to the northeast of, its internal production opportunity set. The latter is bounded by the concave production possibility frontier. The United States final consumption combination of machinery and food provides it with a larger benefit than could have been realized by internal production alone. Similarly, at the trading point H the Australian economy is on a consumption indifference curve, $I—A$, that is outside its internal production opportunity set. Once again, the Australian economy is able to realize a higher benefit from specialization of production and trade than could be obtained from internal production alone. This possibility that both countries can be better off as a result of engaging in trade lies at the heart of international trade and payments theory.

THE FOREIGN TRADE MULTIPLIER

Two questions lie ahead. First, we need to show the connections between the trade flows we have just considered and the determination of the level of income and employment in the macroeconomy. Second, we need to look beneath the commodity flows to the money flows implicit in them, and to examine the determination of the exchange rate between different countries' currencies. The latter, the international exchange rate or the international value of the currency, we have already referred to by the symbol e. This is one of the so-called situational variables that need to be explained by the monetary analysis and macroeconomic model we set out to construct.

In what follows we shall use the symbol x to refer to real exports, and m to refer to real imports. Initially we shall discuss the incorporation of the foreign trade flows, exports and imports, into the macromodel in real terms. The argument initially will parallel the early sections of Chapter 18, where the simple real income multiplier was derived.

The volume of a country's exports will depend essentially on three factors: first, the level of national incomes being generated abroad, which determines the ability of foreign countries to purchase imports; second, the domestic price level in the exporting country; and third, the rate of exchange. We can express the real export function as

(1) $$x = x(P,e)$$

suppressing for the present the level of incomes abroad.

An increase in the domestic price level is likely to diminish exports, as export commodities will then be more expensive relative to goods available in the importing countries. Similarly, a rise in the exchange rate, e, will also tend to diminish exports. The *exchange rate*, it will be recalled, was defined as the number of units of foreign currency that must be given in exchange for one unit of the domestic currency. A rise in the exchange rate implies that exports will then cost more in the importing countries, in terms of their own currency units, and this effective increase in the relative prices of exports will tend to reduce the export volume.

A country's imports will depend on three factors: first, the level of income, which determines the need to import raw materials and other industrial items to sustain the production process, as well as influencing the expenditure by income earners on imported consumption goods; second, the domestic price level; and third, the exchange rate. The real import function can be expressed as

(2) $$m = m(y,P,e)$$

An increase in the domestic price level will be likely to increase the volume of imports. Import prices will now be relatively lower compared with the prices of import substitute commodities produced at home. Similarly, an increase in the exchange rate will tend to make the price of imported goods lower in terms of the domestic currency, and again import volumes can be expected to rise. Finally, a rise in domestic incomes will similarly tend to have a positive effect on import volumes.

Let us recall the real income analysis presented in Chapter 18. The demand for real exports will now constitute an element of the total real income generating expenditure stream. The total real demand for goods and services will now be equal to the sum of the consumption, investment, and government expenditures as before, plus the demand by foreigners for domestically produced goods and services. At the same time a part of the income generated in the economy will be spent, not on purchasing domestically produced goods, but on purchasing imports. To obtain the actual level of incomes generated by domestically employed factors of production, therefore, we must deduct from the total demand for goods and services the amount of real expenditure that goes abroad to acquire foreign goods and services.

We can put this in another way. In Chapter 18 we drew attention to the total of the leakages from the circular flow of income-generating expenditure and the injections into that flow. Now we have a new form of injection, namely export demand, and we have a new form of leakages, the expenditure on imports. We can bring these new leakages and injections into the picture by restating the previous real income equilibrium condition. Replacing the term GNP by the symbol y to indicate real national income, the so-called goods market equilibrium condition can be stated as

(3) $$y = c(y - ty) + i(r) + g + x(P,e) - m(y,P,e)$$

The first term on the right-hand side of Equation (3) refers to consumption expenditures, dependent as before on the level of disposable income. The investment expenditure is again assumed to be a function of the rate of interest in the now familiar way. Government expenditure is again assumed to be exogenous. The real exports and real imports are introduced as an injection and a leakage, respectively.

Let us assume for the present that the level of domestic prices and the exchange rate are given and fixed. We can then investigate the effects on the level of real income of an autonomous increase in the export volume, taking account also of the induced effects on the level of imports. Taking the incremental differences involved, we can write

$$(4) \qquad \Delta y = c'(1 - t)\Delta y + \Delta x - m'\Delta y$$

In this expression we assume that the other exogenous components of the spending stream, such as the exogenous component of consumption expenditure, and investment and government expenditure, also remain unchanged.

As before, the symbol c' indicates the rate of change in consumption expenditure in relation to an incremental change in disposable income. It is more fully represented by $\Delta c/\Delta y(1 - t)$. We similarly introduce now the symbol m' to refer to the rate of change in imports in relation to a change in income. Again it is more fully expressed as $\Delta m/\Delta y$ and is referred to as the marginal propensity to import, analogous to the previous marginal propensity to consume. By collecting terms, transposing, and rearranging the results in the same way as in Chapter 18, we can derive a corresponding expression for the change in equilibrium income under our new assumptions that incorporate the foreign trade effects. It follows that

$$(5) \qquad \Delta y = \Delta x \frac{1}{1 - c'(1 - t) + m'}$$

Equation (5) describes what is known as the foreign trade multiplier. It can be compared with the simple real income multiplier of Chapter 18.

At that earlier stage we interpreted the real income multiplier as being equal to the reciprocal of the marginal propensity for leakages to occur from the circular flow of income-generating expenditure. Recalling previous expositions, we need only add now that we have in the present case a new term in the denominator of the multiplier, namely m', or the marginal propensity to import. This is, in other words, a new marginal leakage from the expenditure streams. Its incorporation into the simple multiplier formula is therefore consistent with the generalized description of the multiplier we have given.

A FIRST APPROXIMATION TO
THE MONEY FLOW EFFECTS

We shall now use the capital letter X to refer to the money expenditure flow generated by the demand for exports, and the symbol M to refer to the money flow out of the economy to pay for imports. As in the model of the macroeconomy in Chapter 19, we take the symbol Z to refer to total expenditures on home-produced goods and services. The total expenditure relationship is then as follows:

$$\text{(6)} \qquad\qquad Z = C + I + G + X - M$$

The terms on the right-hand side of Equation (6) refer, respectively, to the money flows on consumption, investment, government, export, and import expenditures. In the same manner as in Chapter 19 we recognize that at the effective monetary demand point,

$$\text{(7)} \qquad\qquad Z = kWN$$

We can then write the effective demand condition as

$$\text{(8)} \qquad kWN = A + \alpha C_w Z + (1 - \alpha)C_p Z - m'kWN$$

analogous to Equation (11) of Chapter 19. All the terms in Equation (8) above are defined in the same manner as previously, with the exception of the new term, $m'kWN$. This is a measure of the cash flow on the purchase of imports. It is equal to the money incomes earned, kWN, multiplied by the marginal propensity to import, m'. The expenditure on exports, as reflected again in Equation (9) below, is included here in the autonomous expenditure, A.

It can be shown then, again by the same derivation as was explained fully in Chapter 19, that the effective monetary demand point can be described as

$$\text{(9)} \qquad Z^* = (a + b + I + G + X)\frac{1}{[\alpha S_w + (1 - \alpha)S_p](1 - t) + t + m'}$$

Here we have a formulation of the foreign trade multiplier, incorporating into the denominator, as in the case of the simple real income multiplier, the marginal propensity to import. The further exposition of the multiplier follows precisely that given in Chapter 19 for the closed economy case and is left as an exercise for the reader.

To focus on the significance of this result for incremental changes in the spending streams, we can write the multiplier expression as

(10)
$$\Delta Z = \Delta X \frac{1}{[\alpha S_w + (1 - \alpha)S_p](1 - t) + t + m'}$$

In Chapter 19 we also derived the implicit employment multiplier. Analogous to that result we can now write also

(11)
$$\Delta N = \Delta X \frac{1}{kW\{[\alpha S_w + (1 - \alpha)S_p](1 - t) + t + m'\}}$$

Again the multipliers are seen to be dependent on the weighted average of the income earners' savings propensities (where the proportionate income shares are used as the weights), with the marginal propensity to import again entering the denominator of the multiplier in the same manner as in the simpler cases.

The analysis to this point provides a foundation for the examination of the actual money flows involved in exports and imports. We shall now bring these flows together in an explicit manner. In doing so, we are interested in two kinds of economic outcomes. First, the total inflow of money funds from abroad and the total outflow of funds together determine what is referred to as the overall balance of payments. Second, the money flows summarized in the balance-of-payments accounts will, under varying possible assumptions, determine the level of the international exchange rate.

THE BALANCE OF PAYMENTS

International money flows can be conveniently classified under five headings. Those transactions that give rise under the following headings to an inflow of funds from abroad are referred to as positive items in the balance of payments, and those giving rise to money outflows are referred to as negative items. The net difference between the inflows and the outflows is referred to as the balance of payments.

Inflows of money funds from abroad result from (1) the receipt of payments for merchandise exports; (2) the receipt of payments for the export of services, or so-called intangible items in the current account (such as insurance and freight services); (3) gifts and transfers received from foreigners; (4) the import of capital, or the inflow of money capital funds for short-term or long-term investment in the United States; and (5) the net change in international reserve assets held by the government. Similarly, outflows of money funds are caused by (1) imports of commodities, (2) invisible imports, (3) gifts and transfers abroad, (4) capital exports, and (5) net change in the government's reserve assets. Each of these items is illustrated in the summary of the United States international transactions in Table 24-1.

On a net basis the magnitude of the international transactions for the United States is quite small compared with the total gross national product. The total merchandise exports for 1982, shown in Table 24-1 as $211 billion, was only 6.9 percent of the gross national product in current money terms for that year. The total merchandise imports amounted to 8.1 percent of the GNP, so that the balance-of-trade deficit shown in the table, $36.3 billion, was a little more than 1 percent of GNP. The net deficit on current account in 1982, $8.1 billion, was about 0.26 percent of the gross national product. The sum of merchandise exports and imports as a percentage of gross national product is often taken as an indicator

Table   24-1

United States international transactions, 1981 and 1982
Amounts are in billions of dollars (+ = inflow, − = outflow)

Item	1981	1982
Merchandise exports	236.3	211.0
Merchandise imports	− 264.1	− 247.3
Balance of trade	− 27.9	− 36.3
Other current account items:		
Investment income	33.0	28.7
Other service transactions	7.5	6.7
Military transactions	− 1.5	− 0.6
Remittances, pensions, and other transfers	− 2.1	− 2.5
U.S. government grants (non-military)	− 4.5	− 5.4
Balance on current account	4.5	− 8.1
Changes in capital account:		
Increase in U.S. private assets held abroad	− 99.0	− 107.5
Increase in foreign private assets held in the U.S.	73.1	81.5
Increase in foreign official assets held in the U.S.	4.8	3.0
Statistical discrepancy	25.8	41.9
Balance on current and capital account (including statistical discrepancy)	9.2	10.8
Balance accounted for by:		
i. Increase in U.S. government assets (other than official reserve assets)	− 5.1	− 5.8
ii. Increase in U.S. government official reserve assets	− 5.2	− 5.0
iii. Allocation of SDRs to the U.S. Treasury	+ 1.1	0.0
Total financing of Balance of Payments	− 9.2	− 10.8

Source: *Federal Reserve Bulletin*, April 1983, p. A54. Amounts may not add to totals because of rounding.

of a country's foreign trade dependence. In the United States in 1982 this foreign trade dependence measure was about 15 percent of GNP. For particular industries, of course, the impact of foreign trade is much heavier. Some industries feel the adverse effects of imports very heavily, and the United States' ability to compete has been seriously diminished as inflation has taken its toll. The automobile and steel industries are only prominent examples of a wider set of industries facing strenuous import competition.

Table 24-1 summarizes the balance-of-payments accounts for the years 1981 and 1982. The general similarity of the outcomes for the two years will be noted, though some important differences occurred, particularly in the deterioration of the merchandise trade discount. The table has been arranged to exhibit the three conceptual measures that need to be kept clearly in mind. These are first, the balance of trade; second, the balance of payments on current account; and third, the balance of payments on current and capital account. (The rather large statistical discrepancy, which will be commented on again below, has been included in the last-mentioned item.) A number of factors bearing on the outcomes reported in Table 24-1 for 1982 will illustrate the principal issues involved in the balance of payments.

In 1982 the deficit on the merchandise balance of trade worsened compared with the preceding year. In the years immediately following World War II when the European countries and Japan were undergoing their industrial reconstruction, United States exports were consistently higher than imports. The resulting balance-of-trade surplus gave rise to a dollar shortage, which was offset to a large extent by United States economic aid, such as that provided under the Marshall Plan. Such government grants enabled other countries to finance their balance-of-payments deficits and to continue to purchase goods and services in the United States. Later, however, as the other industrial countries recovered their productive capacities and competitive abilities, United States imports expanded. This occurred at a time when the United States government was expanding its expenditures abroad for military purposes. This meant that in the 1960s and early 1970s a deficit on the balance of trade developed, together with an outflow of funds on government purchases abroad. During this period also an increase occurred in private capital outflow, to take advantage of higher interest rates and investment returns available in overseas countries. By 1971 the merchandise trade balance had become negative, and a condition of dollar surplus abroad replaced what had previously been a dollar shortage.

A persistent deficit on the balance of payments implies the possibility of a depreciation of the exchange rate. A deficit on the balance of payments means that the total inflow of money funds from abroad is less than the total outflow of funds. The number of United States dollars being offered in the international foreign exchange markets in exchange for other currencies therefore increases, and this tends to raise the dollar price of foreign currencies. In terms of the notation adopted previously, where the exchange rate, e, referred to the number of units of foreign currency that are exchangeable for one unit of the domestic currency, this balance-of-payments deficit and the excess outflow of dollars means that the value of e was declining. The United States dollar was worth less in the foreign exchange markets. That is the meaning of an exchange rate depreciation.

The balance-of-payments deficits of the early 1970s led to the expectation that the dollar would have to be devalued, and this set up a fairly heavy pressure of speculation against the dollar. As a result, the dollar was devalued in 1972 and again in 1973. The dollar was at that time allowed to float in value in the foreign exchange markets, with only varying degrees of official United States intervention to support its value. At the present time, particularly since a Treasury announcement to that effect in April 1981, the United States is minimizing its official intervention in the foreign exchange markets, intervening "only when necessary to counter conditions of severe disorder."

Taking account of fluctuations in the foreign exchange value of the dollar, the net effect was that in 1981 and 1982 the dollar appreciated somewhat in the foreign exchange markets. This was due principally to the fact that the Federal Reserve Board was adopting a policy of monetary restraint which raised interest rates in the New York money markets. At the same time, better progress had been made in reducing inflation in the United States than in other major industrial countries, and the demand for dollars increased as dollar assets were regarded as a "safe haven" for internationally mobile funds. The higher exchange value of the dollar, moreover, contributed to the reduction in the United States inflation rate by lowering the prices of imported goods. But at the same time, it reduced the international competitiveness of United States exports, increased the demand for imports, and contributed to the decline in the real GNP in 1982.[1]

The balance of merchandise trade shown in Table 24-1 worsened in 1982 compared with the preceding year. Another factor in the trade account was the relative weakness of economic activity in a number of foreign industrial countries, instancing again the income effect to which we referred earlier. During 1982 also, a number of developing countries reduced their demands for imports in order to help them meet large payments due on external debts. A decline in automobile imports into the United States moderated the increase in import expenditure, as did

---

[1] See the detailed analysis of the balance-of-payments accounts in Thomas C. Glaessner, "U.S. International Transactions in 1982," *Federal Reserve Bulletin*, April 1983.

a reduction in the import of steel. This was due largely to recession conditions and lower economic activity in the United States. Further, an agreement with Japan limits the annual number of passenger cars exported to the United States, though such imports account for approximately 23 percent of annual new-car sales in the United States.

The negative effect on the balance of trade of the exchange rate appreciation was partly offset by a reduction in the value of oil imports. The price of oil had peaked in April 1981 and had fallen by about 14 percent by the end of 1982. The decline in oil imports was again due partly to the United States recession, though energy conservation and the substitution of other energy sources were also contributing factors.

In Table 24-1 the balance of payments on current account is derived from the balance of merchandise trade by adding the investment income earned abroad and the income from other service transactions, and deducting the transfer items and government grants indicated there. In 1982 the net portfolio income from foreign investments rose slightly, but this was offset to some extent by lower returns on direct investments abroad. In the outcome, the overall current account deficit of $8 billion in 1982 was the first such deficit recorded since 1979.

The next section of Table 24-1 records the inflow and outflow of funds on private investment account. In 1982 United States private assets held abroad increased by $107.5 billion, giving rise to an outflow of money funds to that extent (which accounts for the minus sign against that amount in Table 24-1). Foreign private assets held in the United States increased in 1982 by the lesser amount of $81.5 billion. The resulting net outflow of funds on private capital investment account during the year of some $26 billion was approximately the same as it had been in the preceding year.

Unfortunately, it is necessary to include the very large statistical discrepancy item in this section of the table. This represents, so far as the official statisticians are able to conclude, mostly unrecorded private capital flows. These result from the fact that a number of innovations in international financial markets have caused funds to flow outside the normal banking system channels where adequate reporting systems have not been in effect.

The final item in the capital account section of the balance of payments summarized in Table 24-1 refers to foreign official assets in the United States. An increase in this item gave rise to an inflow of funds. The $3 billion increase in 1982 was lower than it had been in previous years, having stood at approximately $15 billion in 1980. Reserve inflows from members of OPEC declined sharply, however, as the OPEC countries had a combined current account deficit in 1982 of some $10 billion.

Tracing these items through the balance-of-payments accounts leads to a net positive balance of payments of some $10.8 billion in 1982, compared with $9.2 billion in 1981. The main item that increased as a result of this net favorable balance was the government's official reserve assets. The $5 billion increase in these assets was made up by increases in (1) the official reserve position in the International Monetary Fund, $2.6 billion; (2) Special Drawing Rights, $1.3 billion; and (3) holdings of foreign currencies, $1.1 billion. The last-mentioned item was due in large part to the acquisition of foreign currencies in connection with official credits extended to Brazil and Mexico, through the Treasury's Exchange Equalization Fund and the Federal Reserve's swap arrangement with Mexico. The net increase in United States government assets held abroad (other than official reserve assets) amounted to some $5.8 billion. This amount represents principally government loans to foreign governments, net of repayments. The increases in United States government assets held abroad, including both reserve and nonreserve assets, absorbed the overall balance-of-payments surplus of $10.8 billion.

THE BALANCE-OF-PAYMENTS EQUATION

The preceding analysis provides the background we need for the final step in explaining the money flows on international payments account. In this section we shall summarize these money flows in a balance-of-payments equation.[2] For that purpose, the capital account items in the balance of payments are aggregated in what we shall call a net capital outflow function. Using the symbol F, we express this as a function of the domestic rate of interest as follows:

(12) $$F = F(r)$$

The net capital outflow will be a negative function of the rate of interest. Increases in the domestic rate of interest diminish the international interest rate differential and reduce the net capital outflow. In the balance-of-payments equation, real exports will again be expressed as a function of both the domestic price level and the exchange rate. Real imports will be taken to be a function of the level of real income, the price level, and the exchange rate. Increases in the domestic price level and in the exchange rate will tend to increase imports and decrease exports. A rise in domestic incomes will raise imports, working through what we defined as the marginal propensity to import.

It is necessary now to transform all flow magnitudes in the balance-of-payments equation from real to money terms. The net capital outflow variable, of course, is already expressed in money terms. To obtain the

[2] This section is heavily dependent on the analysis in William H. Branson, *Macroeconomic Theory and Policy*, 2nd ed. (New York: Harper & Row, 1979), Chap. 15.

monetary flow from export earnings, we must multiply real exports by the domestic price level. Using X, as before, for the money flow from exports, we have

$$(13) \qquad\qquad X = P \cdot x(P, e)$$

The cash outflow to pay for imports is slightly more complicated. First, we take account of the foreign price level at which imports are purchased. We shall refer to this by the symbol Pf. Money expenditures on imports, measured at foreign price levels, will then be equal to $Pf \cdot m(y, P, e)$. To convert this money flow to equivalent domestic values, we must divide this import expenditure in foreign money values by the exchange rate. We therefore have

$$(14) \qquad\qquad M = \frac{Pf}{e} \, m(y, P, e)$$

At this point the elasticity of demand for exports and imports becomes relevant. Let it be supposed that the domestic price level has risen. This will decrease the level of real exports if all other determinants remain unchanged. If the elasticity of demand for exports is, at the previously existing price level, less than unity, the increase in price will give rise to an increase in the actual cash flow from export sales. If export demand is elastic, on the other hand, the rise in prices will cause a more than proportionate reduction in the volume of exports being sold, and export revenues will fall.

Similarly, if the demand for imports is elastic with respect to domestic prices, when the domestic price level rises there will be a more than proportionate increase in demand for imports in money terms, and money outflows on this account will increase to a relatively large extent. If import volumes do not react significantly to increased domestic prices, the price increase will lead only to a lesser increase in the outflow of funds for import purchases.

Similar considerations apply in the case of a change in the exchange rate. An increase in the exchange rate, e, will reduce real exports, and therefore reduce the money flow, X, for any given domestic price level. The increase in the exchange rate, by reducing the domestic currency price of imports and increasing the level of real imports, may or may not increase the actual dollar money flow for the purchase of imports. If the import demand is price-elastic with respect to United States domestic prices of imports, the increase in import volumes will be proportionately greater than the reduction in their effective price (in domestic dollar terms) and the money outflow to purchase imports will increase. We may then have the money flow from export sales decreasing, and the money outflow on imports increasing, thereby confirming that the net export income in money terms $(X - M)$ will decrease.

We bring these factors together in a balance-of-payments equation, using the symbol B to refer to the net balance of overall payments transactions:

$$(15) \qquad B = X - M - F = Px(P,e) - \frac{Pf}{e}\, m(y,P,e) - F(r)$$

If it were desired to maintain the net balance of payments at a level of zero, or to have $B = 0$ in Equation (15), this would imply that the net capital outflow, the final term on the right-hand side of the equation, would have to equal the net export income, the algebraic sum of the first two terms. In that case there would not be any change in official net reserve assets. From this proposition we can develop some important results.

First, let us consider the possible effects of a rise in the domestic income level. If we concentrate on the effects of this change and leave aside for the present any possible change in the price level, the income effect will induce a rise in imports. This will mean that the net export income will decline. If, then, the net balance of payments, or B in Equation (15), is to continue to be zero, the decline in net export income must be offset by a simultaneous decline in the net capital outflow. But this will happen, our analysis suggests, only if the domestic rate of interest rises sufficiently to reduce the capital outflow or increase the capital inflow. To maintain balance on the overall international account, that is, the rise in incomes must be accompanied by a rise in the interest rate.

This relation may be expressed in a balance-of-payments function, as shown in Figure 24-6. The BP curve in the figure is the locus of income and interest rate combinations that will make $B = 0$ in Equation (15).

Figure   24-6.

The balance-of-payments function

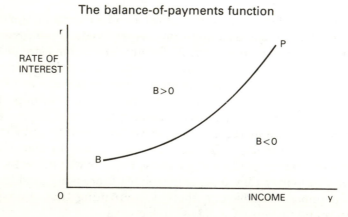

For income and interest rate combinations lying to the northwest of the *BP* curve, the interest rate is higher than it needs to be in order to ensure balance in the international payments accounts. This can be expected to induce a higher than necessary inflow of capital funds, and the balance of payments will therefore be in surplus. On the other hand, the balance of payments will be in deficit for income and interest rate combinations to the southeast of the *BP* curve, where the interest rate is lower than the level necessary to preserve balance. Money capital funds will therefore tend to flow out in search of higher interest earnings abroad.

Second, Equation (15) can be used to enable us to determine the rate of exchange that will preserve a zero balance in the overall payments accounts. If, as we shall see in the next chapter, a policy of flexible exchange rates were adopted, with the government authorities intervening only minimally in the foreign exchange market and leaving the exchange rate to find its own market-clearing level, the rate can be expected to vary until the condition of $B = 0$ is satisfied.

Third, if the exchange rate is fixed, Equation (15) tells us the extent to which, as a result of the determining forces we have examined, the government's holdings of official reserve assets will have to change to offset the net positive or negative balance on the payments accounts. We saw in the preceding discussion that notwithstanding its substantially nonintervention policy, some change occurred in such government official reserve assets in the United States in 1981 and 1982.

Finally, let us suppose that a surplus occurs in the international payments accounts. This implies that when the banks that receive the net inflow of funds sell them to the Federal Reserve Bank, an increase will occur in the domestic monetary base. We recall that such an increase in the monetary base will potentially lead to a multiple expansion of the banking system's assets and the money supply. The money supply multipliers may come into play. If, then, the Federal Reserve did not wish this to happen, it would have to take some action to neutralize the net money inflow. It could do this by engaging in an appropriate amount of open market security sales to mop up the banking system's new excess reserves, and thereby cut short the potential monetary expansion. At the same time, however, the general level of domestic interest rates might be edged upward as the security sales depress their prices and raise their yields. The rise in interest rates will again tend to attract foreign investment funds. Clearly, the Federal Reserve may find itself in a tricky monetary management position when it takes account not only of this possible effect but also of the possibility that any induced rise in interest rates may have adverse effects on domestic economic activity. We shall return to some aspects of these monetary policy problems in the next chapter.

SUMMARY

The economic forces underlying the international money flows that determine the balance of payments were highlighted in this chapter in terms of the theory of comparative advantages. Commodity flows between countries depend on differences in resource endowments, skills, and production possibilities. A country's consumption opportunities can be increased beyond what would be made possible by its own internal production possibility frontier. Such commodity flows give rise to money flows, which are increased by international movements of money capital and other transfers. Taken together, such money flows determine the net balance of payments on a country's overall international transactions account.

If the exchange rate between the domestic currency and foreign currencies is fixed, the net balance of payments must be financed by changes in the government's holdings of official reserve assets. These include gold, the reserve position with the International Monetary Fund, IMF Special Drawing Rights, and holdings of foreign currencies. If the exchange rate is free to fluctuate in the foreign exchange markets, then movements in the rate, depending on the net balance of supply and demand conditions, will tend to bring the net balance of payments to zero and eliminate the need for changes in official reserve assets as a balancing item.

A linkage was established in this chapter between the international real and monetary expenditure flows by developing income and employment multipliers analogous to those derived in Chapters 18 and 19.

The United States balance-of-payments accounts for the years 1981 and 1982 were summarized, and a brief discussion of the principal forces at work in international trade and payments relations in 1982 exemplified aspects of the analysis. It was emphasized that exports depended on such determining factors as the domestic price level and the exchange rate. Imports depended on the same factors and the domestic income level. The translation of real commodity flows to the implicit money flows depended also on the elasticity of demand for exports and imports.

Such money flows were summarized in the final section of the chapter in a balance-of-payments equation. A balance-of-payments function, drawn in the interest rate and income space, highlighted the manner in which simultaneous variations in those variables may be necessary to maintain the balance-of-payments equilibrium.

If, at a given income level, too high an interest rate exists, the resultant inflow of money capital will tend to establish a balance-of-payments surplus. Too low an interest rate would lead to a deficit, as a result of the opposite kind of capital flows. It was noted, however, that the monetary authorities may confront a number of difficulties in maintaining an interest rate policy that will meet such international payments requirements, at the same time as the needs of domestic economic stability and growth are also satisfied. Further comments on monetary policy objectives will be made in the following chapter.

IMPORTANT CONCEPTS

Price level, interest rate, and income effects of international money flows

Interest rate differentials

Principle of comparative advantage

Internal production possibility frontier

Internal and external terms of trade

The exchange rate, e

The foreign trade multiplier

Real export and import functions

Marginal propensity to import

Neutralization of money inflows

Positive and negative items in the balance of payments

Merchandise balance of trade

Balance of payments on current account

Official reserve assets

The balance-of-payments equation

Net capital outflow function

Elasticity of demand for exports and imports

Balance-of-payments function in the interest rate and income space

Effect of balance-of-payments surplus on the monetary base

QUESTIONS FOR DISCUSSION AND REVIEW

1. What connections can you trace between monetary policy actions in the United States, the balance of payments, and the exchange rate?

2. How, if at all, can balance-of-payments trends and developments constrain the scope for domestic monetary policy action?

3. Why, if at all, are international interest rate differentials significant?

4. Making use of official statistical sources, trace the developments in the United States balance of payments during the last five years. What explanations can you give of the pattern that emerges?

5. What features of international trade relations make it possible for a country to live outside of its domestic production possibility frontier?

6. What determines the magnitude of the foreign trade multiplier? Be careful to consider all possible secondary-induced effects, including capital market effects, of any changes in economic magnitudes you might posit.

7. What are the several analytical purposes for which the balance-of-payments function may be used?

8. What determines net foreign investment? Why?

9. Are export and import demand elasticities relevant to balance-of-payments equilibrium? Why?

10. How are balance-of-payments deficits or surpluses financed?

25

INTERNATIONAL MONETARY POLICIES

STUDY OBJECTIVES:

• To clarify the potential conflicts between economic policies directed to domestic economic conditions and the requirements of international balance of payments and exchange rate stability
• To trace the possible adjustment mechanisms to deal with balance-of-payments disequilibrium
• To examine the nature and implications of alternative exchange rate policies, including
    1. Freely floating exchange rates
    2. Flexible exchange rates, with some degree of official intervention in the foreign exchange markets
    3. Fixed exchange rates
• To note the principal forms of international monetary cooperation and the resulting methods of providing adequate international liquidity
• To note some forms of international banking activities engaged in by the United States banks, including the establishment of IBFs (International Banking Facilities) under Regulation D of the Federal Reserve Board

In this final chapter we shall consider a number of remaining questions that bear on the relations between domestic and international monetary problems and policies. First, what are the ways in which international economic developments, such as inflationary or deflationary trends, can give rise to disequilibrium on the international balance of trade and payments; and what might be the resulting constraints imposed on policies directed to domestic economic stability? Second, what alternative exchange rate policies might be adopted by the government authorities; and what significance might they have for both international payments and domestic stability? Third, what forms of international monetary co-operation might be adopted to guarantee adequate international liquidity; and how might such cooperation affect the domestic monetary authority's policy actions? Finally, how, in the course of normal operations, does the United States banking system actually participate in international monetary transactions?

The exchange rate is the important variable in almost all the questions that arise on these levels. If the exchange rate is flexible, we need to know how fluctuations in it are induced by underlying supply and demand forces and the economic developments that give rise to them; and we need to know how variations in the exchange rate may redefine the external monetary problems with which the monetary authorities have to deal. If, on the other hand, the exchange rate is fixed, we need to know how disequilibria in the international payments accounts must then be addressed by a different array of economic policies; and we need to know what repercussions they might have on trends and activity levels in the domestic economy.

We begin our discussion by assuming that in the presence of a fixed exchange rate a balance-of-trade and payments deficit emerges. We shall observe the policy actions to which this might give rise and then trace out briefly the difficulties that might be involved in it.

A HYPOTHETICAL INTERNATIONAL ADJUSTMENT PROCEDURE

In Figure 25-1 we have depicted the foreign exchange market for United States dollars, under the assumption that market-clearing conditions are initially established by supply and demand curves SS and DD, respectively. We assume that in this initial situation the market clears at the exchange rate, designated by e^*, at which the monetary authorities have announced they will "peg" the rate. This means that the authorities will take whatever action is necessary, by exchange market intervention or by more fundamental economic and monetary policies, to maintain the exchange rate at e^*. The underlying forces that determine the levels of the SS and DD curves have already been noted in the preceding chapter. They have to do with the causes of money outflows (determining the supply of dollars) and money inflows (determining the demand for dollars) that enter into the balance-of-payments.

Let it be supposed now that a balance-of-payments deficit occurs, due to either an excess of merchandise imports over merchandise exports or an outflow of money capital for investment abroad or both. In that case a larger supply of dollars in the foreign exchange market will emerge and be searching for foreign currencies. The supply curve in Figure 25-1 can be assumed to move to the right to $S'S'$.

Figure   25-1.

The foreign exchange market for U.S. dollars

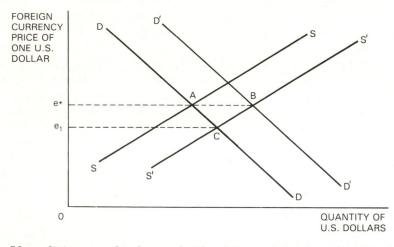

FOREIGN
CURRENCY
PRICE OF
ONE U.S.
DOLLAR

QUANTITY OF
U.S. DOLLARS

If conditions on the demand side of the exchange market for dollars are unchanged and the demand curve DD remains in its initial position, the increased supply of dollars will tend to push the exchange rate down from its previous equilibrium level of e^* to e_1. The monetary authorities, however, are obligated, in accordance with their announced policy, to take action to preserve the rate at e^*. In the immediate situation they could do this by entering the demand side of the market and purchasing dollars. But in exchange for the dollars they would have to give up some of their holdings of foreign currencies or, that is, a part of their official reserve assets. If the United States monetary authorities should not have sufficient holdings of foreign currencies to intervene in the exchange market for dollars in this manner, they could acquire the necessary currencies by surrendering some part of their holdings of other official reserve assets. Or they may acquire foreign currencies by entering into swap arrangements with other central banks.

But on more fundamental levels of economic and monetary policy, further reactions are possible. When the SS curve in Figure 25-1 moves to its new $S'S'$ position, policies may be adopted that, it was thought, would reestablish a market-clearing exchange rate at e^* as before. This would involve either a movement of the supply curve back to its initial SS position or a movement of the demand curve to the right. If the demand curve could be moved to $D'D'$ it would reestablish a market-clearing price of dollars at point B, which would meet the exchange rate requirements. Our concern now is with the policy developments that might effect such fundamental changes in the SS and DD curves. We consider the demand side of the market first.

The demand for dollars would be increased if foreign countries were to cause their price and income levels to rise. The reason for the initial exchange market disturbance may be that the United States has recently experienced a higher rate of inflation than other countries, or foreign countries may have been deflating and lowered their price and income levels. In such cases a rise in prices and incomes abroad would tend to revive the demand for United States exports and increase the demand for dollars. That would move the DD curve to the right. At the same time, of course, the rise in foreign prices may choke off some of the United States import demand, thereby reducing the supply of dollars and moving the SS curve back to the left again. The effect, then, of the movement of the demand curve to the right and the supply curve to the left will be to arrest the tendency for the exchange rate to move toward e_1 and bring it back toward e^*.

Under a fixed exchange rate regime, such as we noted previously in connection with the "rules of the game" of the international gold standard, a country experiencing a persistent surplus on its balance of payments would normally be expected to take action to raise its activity level and prices, and a balance-of-payments deficit would call for a policy of economic contraction.

The DD curve in Figure 25-1 would again move to the right if foreign countries were to take action to lower their interest rates. In that case money capital funds would tend to move from the money markets in those countries to the New York money market in search of what would then be relatively higher rates of return. At the same time, the reduction or elimination of the interest rate differential between the New York and overseas money markets would tend to reduce the outflow of dollars on capital account. The SS curve in Figure 25-1 would therefore move back to the left somewhat. This would again tend to hold the exchange rate closer to its desired e^* level.

But the possible developments we have considered so far have to do mainly with actions in foreign countries that might eliminate the problem we started with. The problem was that the United States dollar had fallen in value, or, to use the technical term, had depreciated in the foreign exchange markets. Let us ask now what policy action the United States authorities might take to remedy the situation. Conceivably, some fundamental policy maneuvers are necessary, for if the market conditions continue to be described by the old demand curve, DD, and the new supply curve, $S'S'$, the monetary authorities will have to continue to support the rate by paying out the amount of AB from official reserve assets. The longer this is allowed to continue, the lower the total reserve asset position will fall. It will then become more difficult to maintain the exchange rate at e^* as desired.

We consider, therefore, possible action in the United States to move the supply curve in Figure 25-1 back from $S'S'$ toward its initial position at SS. First, action might be taken to reduce the domestic price level. This implies a general anti-inflation policy of tighter money and possibly reduced fiscal outlays by the government, or increased taxation. The objective would be to reduce the levels of the expenditure streams in order to moderate demand pressures in the commodity markets, which presumably have been causing domestic prices to increase more rapidly than foreign prices. If this were so, the reduction in domestic demand would affect the level of the SS curve in several possible ways. First, the lower domestic price level would reduce the level of imports, as domestically produced import substitutes would be more competitive in price. The supply of dollars in the foreign exchange market would therefore be reduced. The supply curve would move back to the left, tending to bring the exchange rate nearer to the desired level of e^* again.

The foregoing assumes, however, that domestic prices are flexible. In the neoclassical theory that is generally taken to be the case. But if prices were sticky, the reduction in monetary expenditures produced by the general policy of contraction would have a larger effect in reducing output volumes and employment. This again, of course, would tend to reduce the demand for imports as the need for imported materials and industrial supplies diminished. Income earners would reduce their demand for imported consumer goods, as determined by the marginal propensity to import. Again the exchange rate would tend to be preserved nearer the desired e^* level.

Such policy developments as these, however, raise problems for internal economic stability. In order to maintain the international exchange rate, such a policy of deflation deliberately sets out to lower the level of domestic economic activity and employment. A conflict arises between the requirements of international exchange rate stability on the one hand and internal economic stability on the other.

It may be true, of course, that the price inflation problem in the United States could be addressed by rather different means than monetary and fiscal restriction. As our model of the macroeconomy suggests, the price problem may have arisen because wages and other forms of compensation have been allowed to increase at a greater rate than productivity. If, in response to that, a policy could be adopted that would preserve a more rational relation between changes in income remunerations and productivity, the price inflationary pressure would be relieved. Such an incomes policy would reestablish a relation between domestic and foreign prices that would affect the SS and DD curves in Figure 25-1. The moderation of the domestic price inflation would improve United States producers' ability to compete in the international markets and tend to raise the demand for exports, thereby moving the demand for dollars, as reflected in the DD curve in Figure 25-1, to the right. At the same time, import expenditure would decline as home produced commodities were again relatively cheaper, and the SS curve in the figure would thereby be moved to the left.

It is necessary to consider the extent to which, and the ways in which, minimum disruption can be imposed on the domestic economy if, as a matter of policy objective, it is wished to maintain a fixed international exchange rate. Not many countries at the present time find it politically possible to use the measures of domestic restriction we have just discussed. Full employment and high activity levels, it has generally been agreed, are national economic goals. It is not easy to sacrifice the political desire for continuing economic growth on the sole ground of protecting the international value of the currency. One possible outcome, then, would be to take note of the fundamental forces that bear on the determination of the exchange rate and allow it to fall to a new market-clearing level. We shall return to that possibilty.

But if, in the meantime, it were desired to maintain the rate of exchange, interest rates in New York might be raised with a view to diminishing the net capital outflow and again moving the supply curve in Figure 25-1 to the left. At the same time, money capital funds would tend to flow in from abroad in order to take advantage of the new higher interest rates. But here again a potential conflict arises between such policy maneuvers and the requirements of internal economic stability and growth. For an increase in domestic interest rates may well reduce the level of investment and other expenditures and lead to a reduction of activity and employment.

The recognition of this dilemma caused the Federal Reserve Board in the 1960s to adopt a policy of simultaneously selling securities in the short-term market and purchasing securities in the long-term market. The object of this so-called operation twist was to lever the short-term rate of interest upward somewhat in order to prevent a money capital outflow from worsening the balance of payments, and to keep the long-term rate low in order not to cause an undesirable reduction in domestic investment expenditures.

Additionally, the Federal Reserve may use the discount rate instrument for international balance-of-payments purposes. If interest rates in London rise and open up a differential that attracts an unduly large amount of short-term money capital from the United States, the Federal Reserve may respond by raising its own discount rate. In recent years the Federal Reserve has maintained a tight money policy as part of its general anti-inflation stance, and this has led to very high interest rates. The United States has therefore continued to attract foreign money capital funds and to improve, rather than diminish, the international value of the dollar. In terms of Figure 25-1, the demand-for-dollars curve has been moving to the right, and the foreign currency value of the dollar has risen. The European countries, in fact, have complained that this United States high interest rate policy has interfered with their own domestic money flows and contributed to worsening recession there.

In 1964, at a time when the United States was experiencing balance-of-payments difficulties, a very different kind of step was taken to shift the *SS* curve to the left. At that time a so-called Interest Equalization Tax was introduced. The tax applied to all new or outstanding securities purchased abroad by United States citizens and was imposed on the differential between the rates of interest on United States and foreign securities, hoping thereby to reduce the flow of dollars to the foreign exchange markets. The tax was renewed several times by Congress, and in 1973 it amounted to 0.75 percent of the interest paid to a holder of bonds and 11.25 percent of the purchase price of a foreign stock. The Interest Equalization Tax was reduced to zero in 1974.

ALTERNATIVE EXCHANGE RATE REGIMES

The preceding section serves two main purposes. First, it highlights the difficulties of maintaining a fixed international exchange rate when that calls for policy measures in conflict with those required by domestic economic conditions. Second, it raises the question as to whether it is necessary or desirable that fixed exchange rates should actually be preserved. Couldn't the entire system of international monetary and economic relations function perfectly efficiently if exchange rates were left to find their own levels, as determined by whatever underlying forces generated the supply and demand curves in Figure 25-1? Many economists have argued for precisely such arrangements. Let us consider also, therefore, different possible degrees of exchange rate flexibility.

FLEXIBLE EXCHANGE RATES

The principal advantage of flexible exchange rates, it is frequently argued, is that they permit domestic economic policy to be insulated from foreign exchange market considerations. But it would be going too far to say that they permit domestic policy to be freed completely from taking international monetary and economic relations into account. For as we have seen, a deficit on the balance of payments may develop for any number of fundamental reasons that demand policy attention in their own right. An excessive inflation generated, for example, by allowing an unsustainable gap to develop between annual income increases and annual productivity increases, or by permitting unmanageably large government budget deficits, will tend to reduce exports, increase imports, and lead to trade deficits. It may thereby generate unemployment in export industries and in those industries producing import substitutes. As a result, a worsening unemployment situation may be encountered at the same time as the price inflation continues.

In such circumstances it may be necessary to adopt a domestic policy mix composed of an incomes policy to get at the root cause of the inflation, a monetary policy to keep interest rates sufficiently low to maintain investment expenditures and housing and durable goods purchases, and a sufficiently tight rein on the government's fiscal position not to crowd out private sector activity and the chances of revival there. The latter could happen if heavy government deficits brought government borrowers into the money capital market to an extent that put upward pressure on the interest rate.

It is nevertheless clear that economic policy in general, and monetary policy in particular, have more freedom to maneuver and are subject to fewer constraints if a flexible exchange rate policy leaves the foreign exchange market to find its own equilibrium level. Monetary and fiscal policy can be focused more directly on the internal objectives of high employment, economic growth, and price stability. For a number of reasons, however, business practitioners and economists have frequently raised objections to a flexible exchange rate policy.

First, it has been argued that uncertainty as to what the exchange rate will be at any particular time is likely to impede the flow of international trade, as exporters and importers could not be sure what proceeds they would obtain in their own domestic currencies from such trade operations. Of course there are ways of overcoming that uncertainty to some extent. Simultaneous transactions may be undertaken in both the spot and the forward exchange markets, as explained in the following simplified terms.

When foreign currencies bought and sold in international exchange markets are delivered on the day of the transaction, a "spot" transaction is said to have occurred. The purchases and sales are said to have taken place in the "spot market." It is possible also to purchase foreign currencies on what are known as "forward markets." A "forward transaction" is one in which, for example, United States dollars may be purchased "three months forward," meaning by this that the dollars are purchased today but delivery is not taken, or the purchase price actually paid, until a specified date three months in the future. The price or the rate of exchange at which the actual delivery of the dollars will take place in three months' time is agreed upon today, at the time the forward purchase is made.

The following are examples of forward transactions. A United States exporter may sell commodities to a British importer at a price in British pounds agreed upon today, with the understanding that delivery will take place in three months' time when the goods have been manufactured and are ready for export. The United States exporter therefore knows that in three months time he will come into the possession of a certain number of British pounds. But he has no way of knowing today how many United States dollars he will get for those pounds when, three months from now, he wants to sell them on the foreign exchange market for dollars. The exchange rate between dollars and pounds may change significantly in the meantime. He can protect himself against such a so-called exchange rate risk by immediately purchasing United States dollars forward, or selling British pounds forward, for delivery in three months' time. In that case he knows now precisely what the dollar sales value of his export to Britain will be.

The forward price of dollars will, of course, differ from the spot price, depending on expectations held in the market as to the most likely change in the exchange rate during the interval covered by the forward transaction. Indeed, changing expectations can themselves generate purchases and sales in the forward markets for purely speculative purposes. An exporter who is simply setting out to cover what would otherwise be his risk on a commercial transaction is said to be making a covered hedge. Such operations are sometimes expensive, depending not only on transactions costs but also on the existing differential, or the so-called spread, between the spot and the forward exchange rates.

Transactions of this kind also come into play in connection with the international movement of capital. We have said that if interest rates are higher in the London money market than they are in New York, there will be a tendency for short-term money capital to flow from New York to London. But we also have to take into account the exchange rate risk that accompanies such a transaction. Suppose a United States investor were to transfer $1 million to London for placement in a 90-day certificate of deposit with a financial institution. He could immediately sell British pounds forward, or, equivalently, purchase United States dollars forward for delivery in 90 days, or for delivery at the same time as his certificate of deposit in British pounds becomes repayable. To calculate the effective rate of return he would receive on his 90-day investment in London, he would have to deduct from the interest rate on the 90-day certificate of deposit the cost of making the covering forward purchase of dollars. The net rate of return is then the nominal 90-day interest rate in London minus the cost of the exchange rate hedge. It is then this narrower interest rate differential that must be taken into account in deciding the advisability of moving funds to the London market.

But the facilities of the forward exchange markets cannot take all the uncertainty and risk out of normal trade transactions between countries. Not only may these facilities be inadequate to handle the amount of transactions desired at the time they are required, but costs are involved, and speculation can change the forward rates as well as flexible spot rates. Moreover, the forward market facilities are not available to cover long-term investment transactions.

A second argument against freely flexible rates of exchange is that disturbances in the rate due to temporary variations in financial flows may have adverse effects on the domestic economy. The exchange rate may change, for example, due to an unusual increase in short-term capital movements. If funds are moving from the United States to England the supply curve in Figure 25-1 will be moving to the right, the British pounds price of dollars will decrease, and changes will thereby be effected in the relative profitability of exports and imports of commodities. With the exchange rate moving down (with the dollar declining in value in the international markets), United States exports will be more attractive abroad and export incomes may increase. Similarly, imports to the United States will now cost more in terms of United States dollars, and import expenditures might be reduced. In this way a movement in a flexible exchange rate for reasons that are not associated directly with underlying trade considerations may destabilize export and import relations.

A further argument against flexible exchange rates is that speculation may destabilize, rather than stabilize, the rate of exchange. There are arguments on both sides of this question. But it is by no means true that speculators would always have a stabilizing influence. They may purchase a currency that was declining in value with a view to making a profit when it returned to its normal level, or sell a currency that was rising in value for the opposite reasons. As happens in any speculative market, individuals could sell a currency whose value was declining, simply because they imagined that its value would fall still further. Speculation could then amplify, rather than moderate, the day-to-day fluctuations in the market-clearing prices of international currencies. Speculative sales can thus have the effect of reinforcing the trend that brings the speculators into the market in the first place.

Expectations of exchange rate movements must be considered, together with the more fundamental forces of export and import demands and investment capital flows, as a determinant of the actual rates in a flexible exchange rate regime. Expectations and induced speculation can set up movements in the exchange rate even when the monetary authorities are committed to maintain an exchange rate "peg." This has often happened. In the early 1970s the deterioration of the United States balance of merchandise trade gave rise to speculation against the dollar. Speculators sold dollars in increasingly large amounts. This meant that so long as the United States was determined to maintain the "peg," it was necessary to part with increasing amounts of reserve assets to meet the demand for foreign currencies as the supplies of dollars in the exchange market increased. In the outcome, the previous peg could not be maintained and the United States devalued the dollar in 1972 and again in 1973.

A MANAGED FLOAT IN THE EXCHANGE RATE

In the context of balance-of-payments difficulties in the late 1960s, the United States announced in August 1971 that it would no longer intervene in the exchange markets to maintain the dollar exchange rate against other currencies. Nor would the United States after that date redeem dollars in gold if they were offered by foreign holders. From August 15, 1971, the United States dollar was allowed to float. But it was widely thought among the industrial nations that a more permanent solution to the United States balance-of-payments difficulties should involve a return to more stable exchange rate conditions.

A final attempt to maintain fixed exchange rates was made when the major industrial nations met in conference at the Smithsonian Institution in Washington, D.C., in December 1971. The Smithsonian agreement effectively devalued the United States dollar by raising the price of gold by approximately 8½ percent, from $35 to $38. After a number of other countries had revalued their currencies (that is, altered the market peg), the United States dollar was effectively devalued by about 12 percent. At this level a system of international pegged exchange rates was reestablished. At the same time the United States again agreed to exchange gold for dollars presented to it by foreign central banks. This realignment of currencies should have made United States exports cheaper in terms of foreign currencies and thereby increased United States export incomes. The opposite effect could have been expected on United States import expenditures.

The Smithsonian arrangements, however, did not work with the smoothness and efficiency that had been hoped. The United States trade balance continued to worsen, and with the fear of further inflation in the United States the Smithsonian agreement collapsed. Anticipating that the United States would find it difficult to maintain the exchange rate at a level consistent with the $38 price of gold, fairly heavy selling of dollars in various foreign exchange markets, largely in exchange for German marks and Japanese yen, set in. Again in 1973 the United States was forced to move the exchange rate "peg," this time changing the dollar price of gold by a further 11 percent, from the $38 level to $42.22. But this did not suffice. Pressure against the dollar continued and a return was made to a system of floating rates.

The exchange rate system that emerged, however, did not function with the complete flexibility that we supposed for purposes of discussion at the beginning of this chapter. It is referred to as a "managed system of floating exchange rates." The United States does not now intervene in the foreign exchange markets to maintain a specific peg. The rate floats fairly freely, subject only to minimal intervention from time to time "when necessary to counter conditions of severe disorder." Some other countries, however, do endeavor to maintain a stable relation between their own currencies, even though, as a bloc, they may fluctuate in value against the dollar. The countries in the European Monetary System, for example, including West Germany, France, Holland, Belgium, Luxembourg, Denmark, the United Kingdom, Ireland, and Italy, maintain relatively stable exchange rates among themselves. The exchange rates between the members of the European Monetary System are not rigidly fixed, of course, and it has occasionally been necessary, since the system was established in its present form in 1979, to realign their currencies.

For purposes of classification of international exchange rate systems we can visualize, then, four main types:

1. *Fixed exchange rates.* Under these arrangements the central bank intervenes in the market to maintain a rigidly established peg. The principal disadvantage of this system is that it can sacrifice the stability of the internal economy to the vagaries of exchange rate fluctuations and the necessary policies to deal with them.
2. *Quasi-fixed exchange rates, incorporating a variable peg.* The issues that arise under this heading do not differ substantially from those that have already been mentioned. The monetary authorities who set the peg, however, or who change it from one level to another from time to time, may not be able to assess the strength and influence of the underlying determinant forces any more efficiently than market operators in general. The possibility of speculation against a currency that shows signs of weakness will continue to exist. As in the case of the United States dollar in the late 1960s, this speculation can be self-fulfilling. Speculation is in that case destabilizing, rather than stabilizing.
3. *Managed floating rates.* The only difference between this system and that of freely fluctuating rates is that in this case varying degrees of central bank intervention may be undertaken to stabilize any one or a number of rates at a desired level.
4. *Freely flexible rates.* The arguments for and against freely flexible rates were noted briefly in the preceding section of this chapter.

INTERNATIONAL MONETARY COOPERATION, AND THE QUESTION OF LIQUIDITY

Under a system of perfectly flexible exchange rates the supply and demand forces in the foreign exchange market will determine the market-clearing exchange rate from day to day, under the influence of the fundamental determinants in the balance-of-payments accounts. This, theoretically, will maintain in balance the overall total of the trade and capital account items in the balance of payments, and there will therefore be no need for significant changes in the government's holdings of official reserve assets. Theoretically, there is no reason why reserve assets need be held. There is no particular need for a residual source of liquidity in the system.

Under any other system, however, the need for such a source of residual liquidity exists. Given the general preference among governments for some kind of quasi-fixity in the exchange rates, most of the discussions regarding international monetary cooperation since World War II have centered on the question of how, and by whom, adequate liquidity reserves should be provided. The question continues to be important.

The first post–World War II attempt at international monetary cooperation led to the establishment of the International Monetary Fund in 1946, as an outcome of the Bretton Woods conference held in New Hampshire in 1944. A principal purpose of the IMF was to eliminate as quickly as possible the multiple and complex systems of foreign exchange restrictions that had been developed by various countries during the 1930s. It was generally thought that a system of free multilateral trade should be established to take maximum advantage of the international distribution of resources. A system of exchange parities was established between the currencies of all members of the IMF, stating the par value, or the effective gold value, of each of them. It was agreed that each country would subscribe a so-called quota to the IMF, that quota to be paid in gold and its own currency. They would then be allowed to borrow from the fund at subsequent times to provide them with liquidity to settle international payments in conditions of emergency.

Initially, the rules of the IMF stated that members must intervene in the foreign exchange markets to the extent necessary to prevent their exchange rates from moving outside of a band set at 1 percent above and below the fixed par rate. This, however, meant that the central banks of the respective countries needed to have access to sufficient international reserve assets to enable them to support the exchange rates in this way. The IMF agreement provided that a change in the par value of currencies, or the level around which the rate was to be allowed to fluctuate, could be made only "to correct a fundamental disequilibrium" in a country's balance of payments. Not very clear guidance was given as to the meaning of fundamental disequilibrium, but it was intended to mean a situation in which international imbalances could not be corrected by the otherwise established processes of exchange market support, without excessive cost to the country's reserve asset position.

Under the IMF rules, a country experiencing balance-of-payments difficulties can obtain foreign exchange by drawing it from the IMF, in exchange for its own currency. The drawing must be repaid to the fund within five years. It was presumed that by limiting the time period of this accommodation to five years, the borrowing country would in the meantime take more fundamental corrective action to eliminate the causes of its balance-of-payments problem. If its difficulties obviously stemmed from the toleration of too high a level of inflation in its domestic economy, the IMF members expected that anti-inflationary policies would be introduced to correct the situation.

Because of the high volume of international trade and the need for larger international reserves to meet the pressures of temporary payments imbalances, the need was felt some years ago to increase the source of international liquidity beyond that provided by the initial quotas of the IMF member countries. In 1970, therefore, the "Group of Ten" industrial countries—Belgium, Canada, France, West Germany, Italy, Japan, the Netherlands, Sweden, the United Kingdom, and the United States—together devised a scheme to provide supplementary international reserves through the IMF. A special facility known as SDRs (Special Drawing Rights) was introduced. These are made available to the member nations in proportion to their original quotas. When a country now has a larger deficit than it is able to handle through other normal channels, it can draw foreign currencies from the IMF against both its quotas and its SDR allocation. The SDRs have become known as "paper gold."

The International Monetary Fund does not now fulfill its originally intended function completely, because the international trading community has moved away from the concept of fixed exchange rates on which the arrangements of the fund were initially posited. But there continue to be, as we have seen, relative degrees of fixity. In many cases exchange rate floats, and managed floats, or, as they are referred to, "dirty floats," are widely used forms of exchange rate policy. Some form of international liquidity will no doubt continue to be necessary as a contribution to overall stability in international monetary relations, and such schemes as that introduced by the SDRs of the IMF appear to be the kind of thing that will increasingly be needed in the future.

In the early 1980s, when a number of developing countries experienced difficulty in meeting the interest and capital repayment obligations on their loans, the liquidity resources of the IMF were bolstered by an increase of $8.4 billion in the U.S. quota contributed to the fund. This action, which was made possible by an act of Congress in November 1983, was of considerable indirect assistance to some U.S. commercial banks that had made large loans, at rather high interest rates, to developing countries, notably Brazil. Again in March 1984 the governments of Mexico, Brazil, Venezuela, Colombia, and the United States cooperated in a $500 million loan package to rescue Argentina from default on international loan interest payments. It was agreed at that time that the United States would lend Argentina $300 million to enable it to repay loans to the other four countries mentioned when Argentina had negotiated a new understanding with the International Monetary Fund.

Apart from the International Monetary Fund as the principal form of monetary cooperation, a number of other devices were invented at different times following World War II. They need not detain us at length, as they are not all now operative. First, as a result of the United States balance-of-payments deficits that became quite serious in the late 1960s, the country's holdings of gold had declined sharply from some $22.9 billion at the end of 1957 to only $10.9 billion at the end of 1968. The awareness of this, and the expectation that the United States would not be able to continue to redeem internationally held dollars in gold, led to the speculation against the dollar that we noted previously. At that time a group of leading central banks joined together to form a so-called gold pool with the objective of defending the price of gold at its then official price of $35 per ounce. But the effort was not successful. The market price of gold rose on the London market to $40 an ounce, but defensive gold sales by the gold pool were not able to stabilize the market at the desired level. Further speculation in 1968 proved to be heavier than the gold pool could deal with, and the market price rose to approximately $45 an ounce. The gold pool had failed in its objective, and the United States shortly after was forced to take the other actions we have already discussed. It devalued the dollar in a series of steps during the early years of the 1970s and finally moved to a fairly free float of the dollar in the exchange markets.

The pressures that marked the speculative developments of 1968 led to the establishment at that time also of a two-tier gold price system. This scheme drew sharper distinctions than previously between monetary gold and gold held and used for nonmonetary purposes. It was agreed that while gold would still be sold between central banks at the official parity price, the market price of gold was free to fluctuate. It has since reached the region of $600 an ounce, and in December 1983 the market price was approximately $400 an ounce. The importance of this development was that it effectively brought to an end the long history of the monetization of gold.

Another cooperative method of providing international liquidity was the establishment of a so-called Swap network. Under these arrangements a central bank will agree to supply its country's currency for that of another country up to a specified amount for a limited period of time. Such an arrangment enables countries to withstand temporary balance-of-payments deficits and the consequent outflow of reserve assets, as well as the speculative pressures that might develop against their currencies. But such arrangements as this are, of course, only temporary expedients for dealing with international monetary difficulties, and the continuing need for fundamental adjustments and policies of the kind we have discussed in this chapter is apparent.

INTERNATIONAL BANKING IN THE UNITED STATES

We looked at the complex banking structure and regulation in the United States in Chapter 7, where it was seen that interstate banking is effectively prohibited by the McFadden Act. This has led to some interesting developments. In 1974 the Franklin National Bank, which was at that time in considerable financial difficulty, was declared insolvent and was acquired by the European Bank and Trust. The latter was a bank, chartered in New York State, that was owned by an association of European banks. Thus it transpired, in effect, that the Franklin National Bank was purchased by a consortium of foreign banks because the domestic banks that might have been ready and able to acquire it were prohibited by the banking laws from operating in the state of New York.

The operation of foreign banks in the United States is subject to the International Banking Act of 1978. This act provides for the licensing and supervision of foreign banks by the federal authorities, thereby putting them all on the same regulatory level. They are permitted to engage in branch banking according to the regulations of the state they select to regard as their home state. They must then restrict their deposits to offices in that state. They also enjoy FDIC privileges and are required to insure with the Federal Deposit Insurance Corporation all deposits under $100,000.

In order to allow domestically chartered commercial banks to compete with international banks in certain kinds of transactions, the domestic banks have been given permission to establish subsidiary corporations under the provisions of the Edge Act. These Edge Act Corporations are permitted to hold equity interests in other business firms that are not primarily engaged in United States production for United States consumption. They may also hold interests in foreign financial institutions located outside the United States. They are permitted to accept deposits in the United States, even in states other than that of the parent corporation, provided those deposits are related to international transactions. They may finance the production of goods in the United States, provided those goods are primarily intended for export. These provisions considerably improve the competitive ability of United States domestic banks in relation to their foreign bank competitors in international transactions.

Recent changes in the regulations permit Edge Corporations to be owned by foreign banks, thus expanding further the potential range of operations of the foreign banks in the United States. In 1981, 130 foreign banks had chosen home states, as required by the regulations permitting their activities, as follows: 95 in New York, 29 in California, 2 in Illinois, 2 in Florida, and 1 in each of the District of Columbia and Massachusetts.

A further important regulation affecting international banking in the United States was issued by the Federal Reserve Board under Regulation D, to become effective on December 3, 1981. This provided for the establishment of so-called IBFs, or International Banking Facilities. Subject to conditions specified by the Federal Reserve Board, IBFs may be established by United States depository institutions and by Edge Corporations. They may also be set up by United States branches and agencies of foreign banks. An IBF is essentially "a set of asset and liability accounts that is segregated from other accounts of the establishing office. In general, deposits from and credit extended to foreign residents or other IBFs can be booked at these facilities free from domestic reserve requirements and interest rate limitations."[1] This provision that reserve requirements are not imposed on the liabilities of the IBF gives it maximum flexibility in the conduct of international transactions. By the end of 1981, or less than one month after the enabling regulation was introduced, IBF facilities had been established by 270 offices, and one year later this total had risen to 430.

In December 1981 also, the Federal Deposit Insurance Act was amended to exclude from federal deposit insurance coverage all IBF deposits, as defined by the Federal Reserve Board. Certain other proposals for amendment of the International Banking Act have been made to Congress by the Federal Reserve Board. It has been proposed that the act be amended to authorize Edge Corporations to have access to the Federal Reserve discount window without requiring them to become members of the Federal Reserve System. It has also proposed that the Board be authorized to impose reserve requirements on all foreign banking institutions in the United States, including commercial lending companies and agencies of foreign banks with consolidated worldwide assets of less than $1 billion. As the law stands at present, the Federal Reserve is permitted to impose reserve requirements on the deposits of foreign banks only when their worldwide operations have assets of more than $1 billion.

Special arrangments such as these are designed to enhance the competitive ability of domestically chartered banks in international transactions by bringing domestic banks (through their Edge Corporation subsidiaries and the IBF facilities) more cloesly into line with foreign banks operating in the United States. Apart from transactions coming under the control of such corporations and facilities, the banks do, of course,

---

[1] Board of Governors of the Federal Reserve System, *69th Annual Report, 1982* (Washington, D.C., 1983), p. 180.

engage in a large amount of international transactions in connection with their normal banking operations. Most banks throughout the United States maintain correspondent relations with a bank in New York, or with another large bank that in turn maintains correspondent relations with a New York bank. By this means, the payment or collection of funds in overseas centers is facilitated by the use of the overseas banks with which the New York banks in turn maintain relations.

The large United States banks, moreover, such as Chase Manhattan, First National City Bank, Bank of America, Continental Illinois Trust, and Morgan Guaranty Trust, operate foreign branches, in just the same way as certain foreign banks operate branches in the United States. These foreign branch and correspondent bank relations make it possible for the domestic commercial banks to provide a very wide range of services to United States exporters, importers, and investors.

The Federal Reserve Board, under Regulation K, may approve the establishment of foreign branches by member banks, and 43 such branches were approved in 1982. At the end of that year, 163 member banks were operating 877 branches in foreign countries and overseas areas of the United States. Of these, 129 were national banks and the remaining 34 were state member banks.

The United States domestic banks also perform a highly important function related to international trade and finance in their lending to developing countries. During the three years up to 1982 net bank loans to foreign borrowers increased from $30 billion to $40 billion per annum. Much of this was made available to third world and smaller industrial nations, thus accounting for a large share of the total international bank lending to such borrowers. As some of the developing countries have experienced the effects of worldwide recession and lower export earnings, they have encountered difficulty in servicing the interest and repayment obligations on the very large debts they have incurred. The provision to them of additional loan facilities, and the improved availability of such liquidity arrangements as those provided by the International Monetary Fund, are questions for urgent discussion on an international scale. Under the provisions of the act of November 1983 authorizing an increase of $8.4 billion in the U.S. quota in the IMF, U.S. banks making loans to countries that regulators decide have a protracted history of nonpayment, such as Zaire, the Sudan, Poland, Romania, and Nicaragua, are required to establish special reserves against such loans.

In 1982 the United States banks were able to increase such international lending as a result of some of the domestic financial developments we have discussed in earlier chapters. The introduction of the new money market deposit accounts and interest-bearing Super-NOW accounts brought substantial new funds into the banks, and these funds were partially lent abroad because of relatively weak demand for credit

in the domestic economy. These new sources of funds to a large extent
made it possible for the banks to rely less heavily on borrowings in the
London C.D. market and other Eurodollar centers.

But the banks are, of course, private-enterprise, profit-making institutions, and full attention must be given to the risk—return trade-off
involved in incorporating foreign assets into their overall portfolios. The
total debt that the developing countries owe to all lenders is probably
now around $1,000 billion, much of which is short-term debt that needs
to be refinanced from time to time. It is understandable that the banks
should show caution in lending, for example, to some developing countries
outside OPEC (Organization of Petroleum Exporting Countries), such as
Mexico and Brazil.

SUMMARY

The important variable in most questions concerned with international
monetary problems and policies is the foreign exchange rate, or the international value of the domestic currency. The *exchange rate* has been
defined throughout this book as the number of units of a foreign currency
that must be given in exchange for one unit of the domestic currency. It
has been referred to by the symbol e.

In the initial sections of this chapter a simple supply and demand
model of the foreign exchange market was constructed. Consideration
was then given to the various ways in which monetary and economic
policies might be designed to maintain the established par value of the
currency, or the parity exchange rate, under the conditions of a fixed
exchange rate regime. It was seen that policies directed to the preser-
vation of the exchange rate might well have adverse effects on the domestic level of economic activity and employment. Different possible levels of such interaction were observed.

The principal advantage of a flexible exchange rate system, it has
been claimed, is that it allows the monetary authorities a greater degree
of freedom in the conduct of policies directed to the stabilization and
growth of the domestic economy. The flexible variations in the exchange
rate will normally bring the net current account and capital account items
in the overall balance-of-payments transactions into equality with each
other. By that means the flexibility in the exchange rate effectively in-
sulates the domestic from the international policy problems. Reasons were
given, however, why care should be exercised in this direction, and why
a high degree of interdependence between countries and their respective
internal economic policies continues to exist. Some arguments against
flexible exchange rates were noted. It was pointed out that the risks and
uncertainties to which they may give rise could be moderated to some

extent by the use of forward, as well as spot, foreign exchange markets. Some examples of operations in forward exchange markets were given.

Comments were made on recent United States experience in foreign exchange market developments and in the international value of the dollar. Particular attention was given to questions of international monetary cooperation and the provision of adequate liquidity or international reserve assets. The main functions of the International Monetary Fund were explained, and it was noted that the IMF has not only adjusted to the emergence of fairly widespread flexible exchange rate systems but has invented a new form of ultimate reserve asset, the Special Drawing Rights, for use in those instances where temporary needs for increased liquidity exist. Other forms of international monetary cooperation were the gold pool, the Smithsonian agreement, and the use of certain currency swap agreements.

The operation of foreign banks in the United States was noted, together with the special facilities made available to domestically chartered banks to enable them to compete effectively in international transactions with the foreign banks. In this connection the regulations regarding the establishment of Edge Corporations and IBFs (International Banking Facilities) were described. It was noted that the Federal Reserve Board has proposed still further amendments to the International Banking Act of 1978. It was observed that domestically chartered commercial banks maintain foreign branches, through which, together with a network of correspondent relations with foreign banks, a wide range of international trading facilities is made available to United States citizens.

IMPORTANT CONCEPTS

Exchange rate regimes

Determinants of supply and demand for currencies in the foreign exchange market

Income, price, and interest rate effects in international adjustment processes

Advantages and disadvantages of flexible exchange rates

IBFs (International Banking Facilities)

Managed float

International Monetary Fund (IMF) quotas

SDRs (Special Drawing Rights)

Edge Act Corporations

Conflicts between internal and international monetary policies

Forward exchange markets

QUESTIONS FOR DISCUSSION AND REVIEW

1. Examine the nature of the problems that a country is likely to encounter in the administration of economic and monetary policy if it wishes to maintain a fixed international exchange rate.

2. Explain the price effect, the income effect, and the interest rate effect of international movements of funds.

3. Set out the arguments for and against the different kinds of exchange rate regimes. Which do you consider the most preferred? Why?

4. "The international balance-of-payments problem can be solved automatically by a system of freely flexible exchange rates." Do you agree? Why or why not?

5. Why is international liquidity important?

6. Do you think the monetization of gold is important, and in what form, if any, would you recommend that a gold standard be reintroduced?

7. Explain and discuss the usefulness of operations in forward foreign exchange markets.

8. "International interest rate differentials need to be modified by the cost of covered exchange rate hedges before the profitability of international money flows can be evaluated." Discuss.

9. Do you agree with the proposition that floating exchange rates insulate the domestic economy and monetary policies from international disturbances? Why or why not?

Index